Heath Grammar and Composition

The program that **PRACTICES** what you teach and teaches what you need!

Students *practice* traditional grammar concepts and *apply* them to writing.

✓ **Diagnostic Tests** offer an early practice or pretest opportunity for evaluation.

✓ **Traditional grammar concepts are clearly presented.**

✓ **Exercises provide abundant practice.**

---

3 Phrases

DIAGNOSTIC TEST

Number your paper 1 to 10. Write the phrases in the following sentences. Then label each one *prepositional, appositive, participial, gerund,* or *infinitive.*

EXAMPLE The last speech, given by Pam, was excellent.
ANSWER given by Pam—participial

1. Pauline, a wonderful actress, is the star of this year's school play.
2. Mother doesn't approve of my telephoning long distance before five o'clock.
3. The dog may have been the first animal domesticated by humans.
4. The temperature, rising since morning, is now 98 degrees.
5. To see *Hamlet* on the stage is a wonderful experience.
6. In 1820, Missouri bachelors were required to pay a special tax of one dollar.
7. Flying a kite isn't always easy.
8. They found the deed in a box under the bed.
9. A horse chestnut, a beautiful tree, stands in our front yard.
10. You need a special permit to use the local beaches.

52

Participles

VERBALS AND VERBAL PHRASES 3e

You are constantly reading sentences with verbals in them. For example, just pick up the sports section of your newspaper. It is full of verbals: a player's *batting* average, the *designated* hitter, and the team's *fighting* spirit—to name a few.

A *verbal* is a verb form that is used as another part of speech. A verbal often has the action and the movement of a verb and can create vitality and interest in your writing. There are three kinds of verbals: *participles, gerunds,* and *infinitives.*

Participles and Participial Phrases

The examples of baseball terms above contain participles.

3e A **participle** is a verb form that is used as an adjective.

Like an adjective, a participle modifies a noun or a pronoun. The participles in the following examples are in heavy type. An arrow points to the word each participle modifies.

From the **raging** fire soared **billowing** clouds of smoke.
His **worried** expression indicated an **unresolved** problem.

There are two kinds of participles: a present participle and a past participle. A *present participle* ends in *-ing,* while a *past participle* has a regular ending of *-ed* or an irregular ending of *-n, -t,* or *-en.*

PRESENT PARTICIPLES acting, flying, reading, trotting
PAST PARTICIPLES discarded, torn, lost, written

NOTE: Do not confuse a participle with the main verb of a sentence. A participle will have one or more helping verbs if it

---

Participial Phrases 3f

EXERCISE 6 Finding Participial Phrases
Number your paper 1 to 10. Write the participial phrase in each sentence. Then beside each one, write the word or words it modifies.

1. We saw the hawk soaring effortlessly above us.
2. The Sahara, covering more than three million square miles, is the largest desert in the world.
3. The catcher's mitt found on the field belongs to Patrick.
4. This is the first patchwork quilt sewn by my great-aunt.
5. Having served his country, Thomas Jefferson retired in 1809 to his Virginia home.
6. The woman wearing the red dress is a famous actress.
7. We bought an old bookcase made of oak.
8. In 1793, the United States Mint, established in Philadelphia, issued the first coins for general circulation.
9. Looking for her ring, Jody retraced her steps.
10. The wheat stalks, waving slightly in the breeze, stretched as far as the eye could see.

EXERCISE 7 Identifying and Punctuating Participial Phrases
Write the following sentences and underline each participial phrase. Then add a comma or commas where needed.

The Eagle
1. The Romans thinking of the eagle as a symbol of strength and bravery made it their chief military emblem.
2. Replacing the lion the eagle became the favorite design on the shields of medieval knights and noblemen.
3. The American bald eagle pictured on the great seal of the United States is the national bird.
4. Benjamin Franklin objecting to the eagle on the national emblem suggested the wild turkey instead.
5. Viewed from a distance the snow-white head of the American eagle looks bald.
6. Being a solitary bird the eagle keeps the same mate for life.
7. Its nest built in a tree or on a cliff is a lifelong home.
8. The eagle collecting sticks and leaves enlarges its nest.
9. One eagle's nest found in Ohio measured 12 feet deep and weighed 2 tons.
10. Having once been put on the endangered-species list the eagle is making a slow comeback.

61

T2

Heath Grammar and Composition

✓ **Writing Sentences** gives students practice in applying new knowledge.

✓ **High-interest exercises relate grammatical rules to practical communication.**

✓ **Application to Writing** gives students an understanding of how grammar relates to composition.

Subject and Verb Agreement

12. It (doesn't, don't) seem like a good day for a picnic.
13. *Leaves of Grass* (was, were) one of Walt Whitman's greatest efforts.
14. This month's bills (hasn't, haven't) been paid yet.
15. (Isn't, Aren't) the duplicating machine working today?
16. The potholes in the road (is, are) a nuisance.
17. My brother (isn't, aren't) taking chemistry this year.
18. *Fruit Bowl, Glass, and Apples* (is, are) the name of a famous painting by Cézanne.
19. (Hasn't, Haven't) anyone started dinner?
20. Telephones (is, are) available in many styles.

EXERCISE 11 Oral Practice
Read aloud the following items, adding *is* or *are* after each one. Then repeat the exercise, using *doesn't/don't* and *wasn't/weren't*.

1. the flock of sheep
2. everyone in the room
3. *The Last of the Mohicans*
4. some of the roses
5. a number of people
6. mumps
7. the number of coins
8. one third of the test
9. the United States
10. most of the apples

EXERCISE 12 Writing Sentences
Write a sentence for each of the items in Exercise 11, using only present-tense verbs. Make sure each verb agrees with its subject.

EXERCISE 13 Time-out for Review
Number your paper 1 to 20. Find and write the verbs that do not agree with their subjects. Then write them correctly. If a sentence is correct, write *C* after the number.

1. The first manufactured item ever exported by American merchants were tar.
2. Two presidents of the United States, George Washington and James Monroe, was unopposed in their elections.
3. One of the largest tomatoes from the garden weighs two pounds.
4. Two hundred and sixty dollars were the cost of a Ford in 1925.
5. A favorite fruit in the United States are bananas.

182

Editing for Agreement

6. There are two word processors in the school library.
7. Both Missouri and Tennessee touches on eight other states.
8. John Steinbeck's novel *Of Mice and Men* have been made into several movies.
9. Each year the United States loses billions of tons of soil through erosion.
10. At graduation there was 2,000 people in the audience.
11. One fourth of all the energy in the United States are used to heat and cool homes and other buildings.
12. The life expectancy of Americans in 1876 was about 40.
13. Orville Wright, who with his brother Wilbur invented the airplane, was badly injured in an airplane crash.
14. In 1910, a football team were penalized 15 yards for an incompleted forward pass.
15. There was no public library in the United States in 1800.
16. In 1805, half of the Harvard students was suspended after protesting against the terrible dormitory food.
17. In 1915, the average family income in the United States were about $650 a year.
18. Is there any documented proof that Betsy Ross designed the American flag?
19. The practice of identifying baseball players by number was begun by the Cleveland Indians in 1916.
20. Two thirds of the orchestra members plays two or more instruments.

Application to Writing

When you finish writing a report, an essay, or even a friendly letter, always reread it to check just for subject and verb agreement.

EXERCISE 14 Editing for Subject and Verb Agreement
Find and write the verbs that do not agree with their subjects in the following paragraphs. Then write them correctly.

Outer Space Litter

In addition to approximately 1,200 satellites now in orbit around the earth, there is nearly 3,500 pieces of orbiting space debris. These include spent rockets, fragments of wrecked satellites, and miscellaneous nuts, bolts, and ceramic tiles. The

183

T3

Step-by-step *practice* ensures success in all types of *writing.*

Expository Paragraphs

Paragraphs that explain are called expository paragraphs. In school you write expository paragraphs on essay tests and in reports. On the job you will write expository paragraphs to convey information. Whenever your purpose is to explain, you will be writing exposition.

 An **expository paragraph** explains, gives a set of directions, or informs.

Paragraph Development. There are many different ways to develop an expository paragraph. The topic sentence and the questions it raises usually hold the key to the best method of explaining. Study the following examples of expository topic sentences.

1. Symphony orchestras are part of the backbone of cultural life in cities around the world.
   - QUESTIONS RAISED: How are they part of the backbone? In what cities?
   - WAY TO EXPLAIN: facts and examples
2. Rehearsing an orchestra is a painstaking process.
   - QUESTION RAISED: What is this process?
   - WAY TO EXPLAIN: steps in a process
3. Young people can often try out for a symphonic training orchestra.
   - QUESTION RAISED: How does a person go about trying out?
   - WAY TO EXPLAIN: set of directions
4. I began to appreciate how hard musicians work when I attended a rehearsal of the Seattle Symphony Orchestra.
   - QUESTION RAISED: What happened to make you appreciate musicians?
   - WAY TO EXPLAIN: incident
5. Most orchestral music from the seventeenth century is contrapuntal.
   - QUESTION RAISED: What does *contrapuntal* mean?
   - WAY TO EXPLAIN: definition

✓ The **purpose** and **audience** of writing are always defined.

2.

Astronomers call exploding large stars supernovas. The ancients, who observed and described such events, believed they were witnessing the appearance of a new star, or nova. Today we recognize that what the ancients actually saw with their unaided eyes were not new stars being born but large, old stars dying. The term *super* refers to something great, or large, and so the name *supernova*. Supernovas shine with a brilliance many billions of times brighter than our sun. Therefore, were a supernova to appear in a neighboring part of our galaxy, it would be clearly visible even in daytime.

3.

At least three appearances of supernovas have been recorded in history. The most recent, in 1604, was observed and described by the German astronomer Johannes Kepler and the Italian Galileo Galilei. Before that, the Danish astronomer Tycho Brahe witnessed one in 1572. Still earlier, Chinese astronomers noted the occurrence of a similar event in the constellation Taurus, the Bull, in the summer of the year A.D. 1054. Today, more than 900 years later, evidence of the supernova described by the Chinese is still visible.

4.

The vast distances of space may be easier to understand if we reduce their scale. Think of the sun as an orange; then the earth would be a mere grain of sand, circling at a distance of 30 feet. Pluto, the farthest planet in our solar system, would be another grain of sand, orbiting the sun ten city blocks away. The sun's nearest neighbor, Alpha Centauri, would be another orange, 1,300 miles distant. On this scale the whole Milky Way becomes a bundle of 200 billion oranges that are about 2,000 miles apart.

5.

If we could soar out into the Cosmos in an intergalactic spaceship, we would see hordes of galaxies, and they would have different shapes. Most of them, including the Milky Way and Andromeda, would appear to be great spirals whirling in space. Edwin Hubble studied hundreds of galaxies and classified them by form. He divided galaxies into four main types; elliptical, spiral, barred spiral, and irregular.

—PARAGRAPHS FROM FRANCINE JACOBS, *COSMIC COUNTDOWN*

✓ High-interest models appear throughout each chapter.

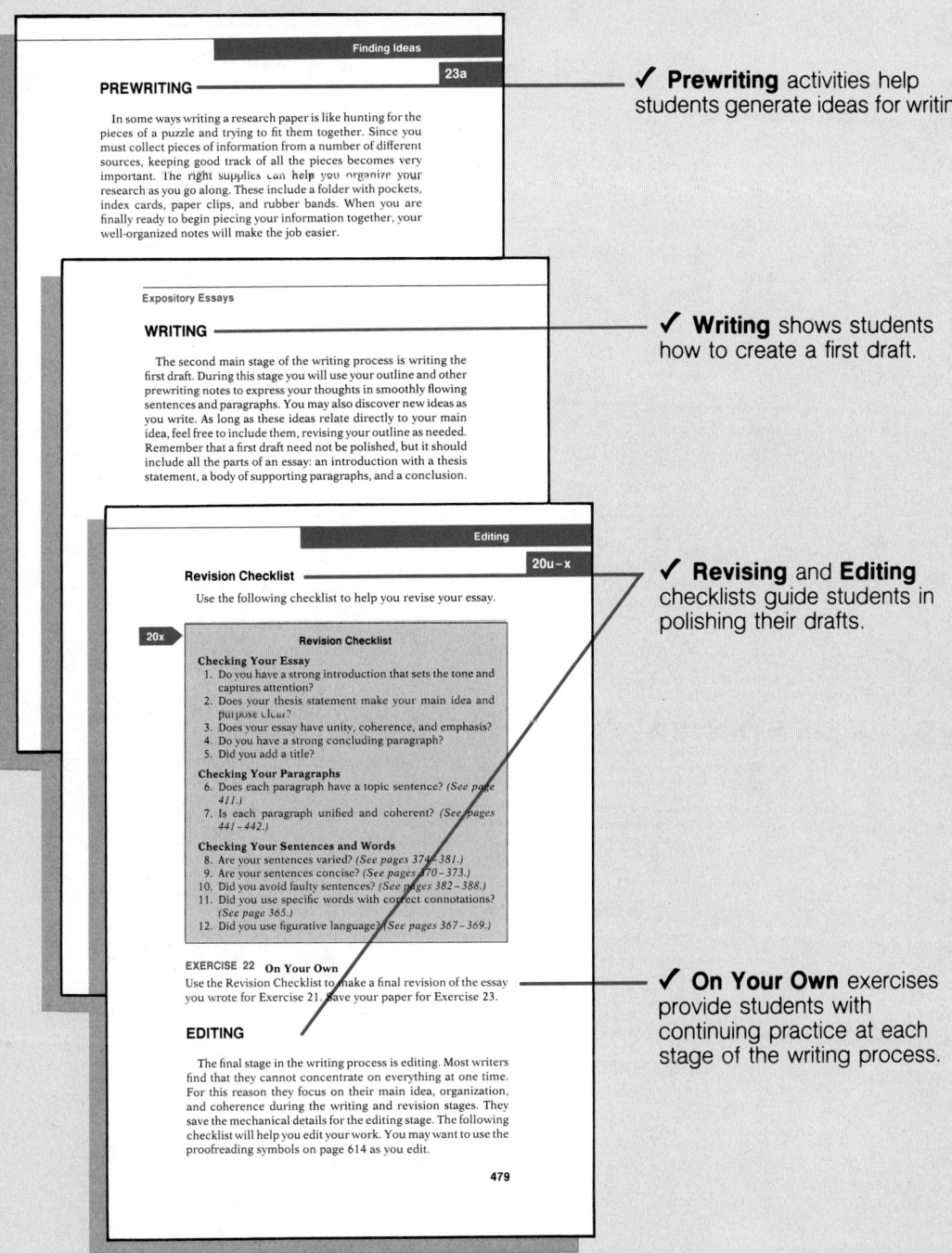

Practice promotes *understanding* of grammar and composition.

✓ Students move from identification to application of a grammatical concept.

✓ **Time-out for Review** provides cumulative practice to reinforce learning.

✓ High-interest exercises keep students involved with the material.

Mood

EXERCISE 22 Writing Sentences
Write sentences that follow the directions below.

1. Include a verb in the indicative mood.
2. Include a verb in the imperative mood.
3. Include a verb in the subjunctive mood that is used to express an idea contrary to fact.
4. Include a verb in the subjunctive mood that is used to express a wish.

EXERCISE 23 Time-out for Review
Write the correct form of the verb in parentheses.

1. Sue suddenly realized that she (promised, had promised) to meet Phil at the mall.
2. I reached the station just as the train (is, was) leaving for North Carolina.
3. I wish that I (was, were) more self-confident about trying out for the lead in the play.
4. The polar bear dived into the water and in a few minutes (appears, appeared) on the other side of the ice.
5. On the voyage to America in 1620, the *Mayflower* (broke, has broken) a mast.
6. Just then Carlotta's uncle came along, and we (ask, asked) him for a ride.
7. If I (was, were) on the committee for a cleaner environment, I would vote for the water conservation bill.
8. For the past two years, Joel (sang, has sung) tenor in the chorus.
9. The elephant filled its trunk with water and (give, gave) itself a cool shower.
10. I wish I (was, were) in the glee club.

Application to Writing

Since verbs account for so many errors in students' writing, you should carefully edit your work for mistakes in the use of verbs. Check for the correct use of tenses and any shifts in tense. Look for weak passive verbs.

137

Using Verbs

EXERCISE 24 Editing for Verb Errors
Write any incorrect verb form. Then write it correctly. If a sentence is incorrectly written in the passive voice, write the sentence in the active voice.

Mark Twain (1835–1910)

Mark Twain was born Samuel Langhorne Clemens in Florida, Missouri. He grew up in the Mississippi River town of Hannibal, the main setting for his famous novels *The Adventures of Huckleberry Finn* and *The Adventures of Tom Sawyer*. He leaved school to become a printer, but his first job is as a reporter for his brother's newspaper. Then he abandoned his plans to seek his fortune in South America and choose a career as a steamboat pilot instead. After he had left the river at the outbreak of the Civil War, he begun to write.

Two great contributions to American literature were made by Clemens: clever use of local language and humor. Rather than use the stiff, formal language of English writers, he writes as people speaked. Then he use that very language to create humor. Without a doubt, Clemens was one of the great humorists of all times. He was loved by millions of readers around the world.

CHAPTER REVIEW

A. Write the correct form of the verb in parentheses.

1. For our parents' anniversary, we made dinner, cleaned up, and (promise, promised) to do the dishes for a week.
2. When Mr. Butler inspected his orchard, he found that the hurricane (destroyed, had destroyed) several trees.
3. Study for that test as if it (was, were) the final exam.
4. The fire fighters left the station and (arrive, arrived) at the burning house five minutes later.
5. Mrs. Steel (is, has been) a member of the local school board for the past three years.
6. Last summer Evelyn (taught, has taught) horseback riding for the Park Department.
7. No one (saw, has seen) the boat again after it left the wharf at Provincetown.
8. Many covered bridges in New England (stood, have stood) for the past 100 years.

138

✓ **Application to Writing** shows how an understanding of grammar is relevant to improving written communication.

T6

Heath Grammar and Composition

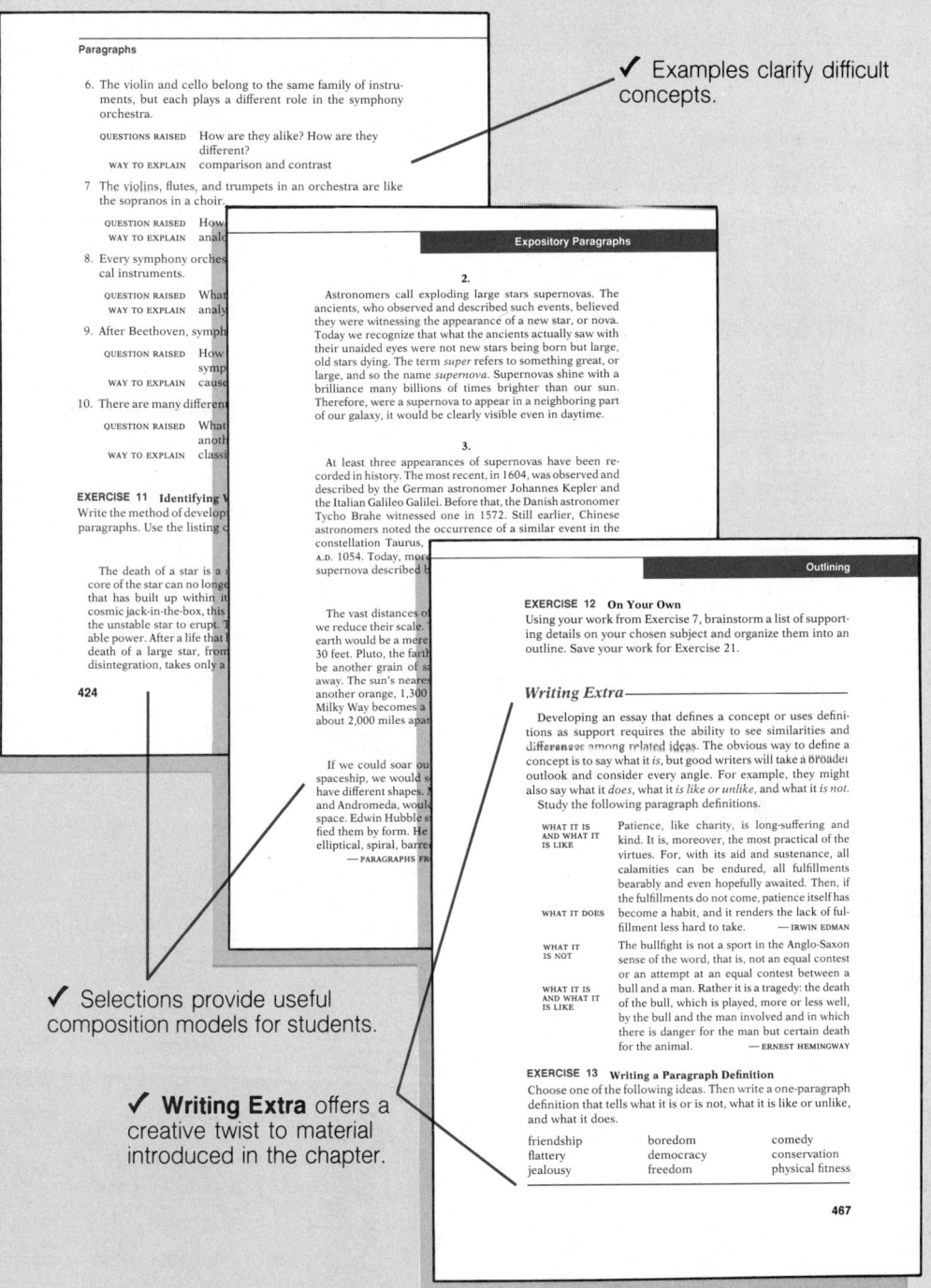

✓ Examples clarify difficult concepts.

✓ Selections provide useful composition models for students.

✓ **Writing Extra** offers a creative twist to material introduced in the chapter.

T7

Practice with *testing* leads to mastery in *Heath Grammar and Composition.*

✓ **Diagnostic Test** begins every chapter to assess student knowledge.

✓ **Chapter Review** reinforces chapter instruction.

✓ **Mastery Test** ends every chapter to measure student comprehension.

1

The Parts of Speech

DIAGNOSTIC TEST

Number your paper 1 to 10. Write the underlined words in each sentence. Then beside each word, write its part of speech: *noun, pronoun, verb, adjective, adverb, preposition, conjunction,* or *interjection.*

EXAMPLE We saw a gray rabbit near the garden.
ANSWER gray — adjective   garden — noun

1. I want to make bran muffins, but I have lost the recipe.
2. Many Canadian citizens have relatives in France.

Chapter Review

15. Which is the largest city south of the equator, Buenos Aires or Rio de Janeiro?
16. The banana has been called the most ancientest fruit.
17. Dan can swim 300 yards easy.
18. Flora earns better grades than anyone in biology class.
19. Of all the planets, Jupiter has the shortest day.
20. We can't hardly wait to see the Whalers play again.
21. At 282 feet below sea level, California's Death Valley has a lower elevation than any place in the United States.
22. I haven't been feeling well for a week now.
23. The animal with the most longest life span is generally conceded to be the Galápagos Islands tortoise.
24. My salary is smaller than Tim, but I enjoy my job more.
25. Which instrument is more popular in the music department — the violin, the guitar, or the piano?

MASTERY TEST

Number your paper 1 to 10. Then write the correct form of the modifier in parentheses.

1. After the storm the ocean became (calm, calmly).
2. Which magazine has the (greater, greatest) circulation, *Reader's Digest* or *TV Guide?*
3. I think ice hockey is more exciting to watch than (any, any other) sport.
4. Covering a square block, the world's (largest, most largest) log cabin stands in Portland, Oregon.
5. Where would you like to live (more, most), in Maryland, Nebraska, or Oregon?
6. Which color do you like (better, best), blue or yellow?
7. Beefalo meat contains (less, least) fat and cholesterol than beef.
8. If you (haven't never, haven't ever) tasted bread pudding, you're in for a treat.
9. Of these four artists, whose paintings do you like (more, most)?
10. I hope one day to play the piano (good, well).

199

STANDARDIZED TEST

USAGE

Directions: Each sentence may contain an underlined part that is unacceptable. On your answer sheet, fill in the circle containing the letter of the unacceptable part. If there is no underlined part requiring change, fill in *E.*

SAMPLE   Ed and I have chosen foods with less calories. No error
              A   B   C   D   E

ANSWER Ⓐ Ⓑ Ⓒ ● Ⓔ

1. None of the contestants appear calmer than she. No error
       A   B   C   D   E
2. Are there a whole herd of goats inside that fence? No error
     A   B   C   D
3. Whom do Ellen and he like more, Tamara or Leslie? No error
       A   B   C   D   E
4. There is Carl and he lying on the beach beside Joe. No error
              A   B   C   D   E
5. Kathleen fell over the cat because hardly no sun or light was
                      A   B   C
   coming into the attic. No error
              D   E
6. "He who hesitates is lost," Cora said to Ben and I. No error
      A   B   C   D   E
7. By noon I had already sold a large amount of books. No error
                 A   B   C   D
8. Everyone whose answer is correct know his facts well.
                        A   B   C   D
   No error
   E
9. If Ramona or I were president, who do you think would
                         A   B   C
   advise us? No error
      D   E
10. I took the skate with the loose blade to Mr. Liu to be fixed, and
        A   B
    he brings it back looking like a new skate. No error
          C   D   E

227

✓ **Standardized Tests** give students practice with familiar test formats.

Teacher's Resource Book *offers a complete test package providing prebook, chapter, postbook, and standardized tests.*

T8

Teacher's Editions provide plenty of *teaching support* before every chapter.

Teacher's Editions include fully annotated student text pages.

Chapter 10 Capital Letters

OBJECTIVES
- To capitalize the first word of a sentence and the first word of a line of poetry.
- To capitalize the words *I* and *O*.
- To capitalize all proper nouns and most proper adjectives.
- To capitalize certain titles of people and all works of art.
- To capitalize the salutations and closings of letters.
- Application: To learn and apply the rules of capitalization in all writing in and out of school.

MOTIVATIONAL ACTIVITY

Write the following sentences on the board. Then ask your students if the sentences make sense.

The father is very tall. The baby is a little Taller.

The capital letter on "Taller," turns sense to sense. The baby's last name is Taller! This is just one example of the role that capital letters play in making written words easier to understand.

TEACHING SUGGESTIONS

One reason for drill in the mechanics of writing is to help students achieve an automatically correct application of the rules in all their writing. On a literature test or in a history report, students sometimes cannot understand why deductions from their grades are made for errors in capitalization, punctuation, or spelling. That is why it is so important that you stress that there are no separate languages called *literature* or *history*. Students write English, and they should write it correctly at all times.

To encourage your students to submit their best efforts, make editing a part of every writing assignment. Call time five minutes before the end of a class-writing or test period, and tell your students to check what they have already written. Occasionally return compositions

Chapter 10 a

Capital Letters

citizens during the French Revolution. [proper nouns and proper adjectives]

The movie *Around the World in Eighty Days* won the Academy Award in 1956. [title and proper noun]

ACTIVITIES FOR DIFFERENT ABILITIES

Basic Students

ACTIVITY 1 Capital Letter Review
For additional practice duplicate the following sentences. Then have your students write each word that should begin with a capital letter.

Facts and Figures

1. "murder in the rue morgue" and "the gold bug" are two stories by edgar allan poe.
2. on august 1, 1876, colorado was admitted as the 38th state to join the united states.
3. in the midwest sudden and violent storms are a constant threat at harvest time.
4. the pentateuch is another name for the first five books of the old testament.
5. the great symbol of american independence, the liberty bell, cracked on july 8, 1835.
6. c. w. ceram, a german archeologist, has written several books about the discovery of ancient civilizations.
7. the superstition of groundhog day is an old one.
8. any scandinavian trip should include a stop in odense, denmark, the birthplace of hans christian andersen.
9. according to "know your money," a booklet put out by the united states secret service, counterfeit money is easily distinguishable from real money.
10. lewis and clark, explorers of the northwest, started their famous expedition in 1804 and returned to st. louis on september 23, 1806.

Capital Letters

11. the first place on which the famous dutch explorer henry hudson set foot when he arrived in new york

last minute and asked to return to the Ship, but the Captain refused and left him on the uninhabited Island.

Selkirk took little with him besides his clothing and bedding, a few weapons, a bible, and a kettle. The Author of *Robinson Crusoe* gave his fictional Hero a faithful friend named Friday, but the real-life Hero had no human companionship at all.

During his four years on the Island, he saw two boats anchor there for wood and water, but he was afraid to approach them because they were spanish. His Country and Spain were then at War, and he didn't want to be captured and sent to South America as a prisoner.

Fortunately, the weather on Juan Fernandez Island was never severe. There was some frost in june and july, when it is Winter in the Southern hemisphere; but partly because of Ocean currents, it never was really cold there during the Winter or hot in the Summer.

Large numbers of goats lived on the Island, and Selkirk trained himself to run fast enough to catch them. He made his clothes and lined his house with goatskins. He also became skilled in capturing the giant turtles on the Beach. His food tasted terrible at first because he had no salt, but he soon learned to use the fruit of the Pimento Tree for flavoring.

Selkirk lived on the Island until he was found in January of the Year 1709 by captain Woodes Rogers of the british navy. Selkirk returned to england after his rescue but soon began sailing the Seas again. He died in 1721 while serving as a Mate aboard the ship *weymouth*.

ACTIVITY 2 Capital Letters and Library Skills

Give your students the following broad topics. Then have them go to the library and find a fact that pertains to each topic.

Capital Letters

Each fact should include a proper noun, a proper adjective, or a title.

1. basketball
2. literature
3. the planet Earth
4. firsts
5. winter
6. religion
7. languages
8. holidays
9. automobiles
10. a state

ACTIVITY 3 Writing Sentences

Have your students choose one of the facts they researched for Activity 2 and expand it by writing 10 to 15 sentences about that topic. Once they have finished, have them edit their sentences for the correct use of capital letters.

ADDITIONAL PRACTICE

Basic Students
Teacher's Resource Book: pages 159–160
Workbook: pages 117–122

Average Students
Teacher's Resource Book: pages 161–162
Workbook: pages 117–122

Advanced Students
Teacher's Resource Book: pages 163–164

REVIEW EXERCISES AND TESTS

Student Text
Diagnostic Test: page 230
Chapter Review: pages 245–246
Mastery Test: page 247

Teacher's Resource Book
Chapter 10 Test: pages 29–30
(Also available as spirit duplicating masters.)

Chapter 10 d

Teaching material appears immediately before each chapter on blue-tinted paper for handy reference. This teaching support for each chapter includes

✓ OBJECTIVES
✓ MOTIVATIONAL ACTIVITY
✓ TEACHING SUGGESTIONS
✓ ACTIVITIES FOR DIFFERENT ABILITY LEVELS
✓ ADDITIONAL PRACTICE
✓ REVIEW EXERCISES AND TESTS
✓ ADDITIONAL ANSWERS

Heath Grammar and Composition
has all the support you need.

WORKBOOK — a consumable practice book for each level

- Additional activities in Grammar, Usage, Mechanics, Vocabulary, Composition.
- Teacher's Annotated Edition also available.

TEACHER'S RESOURCE BOOK — a softbound booklet of copymasters

- Complete testing program of prebook, chapter, postbook, and standardized tests.*
- Practice Worksheets keyed to all chapters; exercises in Grammar, Usage, and Mechanics designed to meet the individual needs of basic, average, and advanced students.
- Composition Evaluation Forms for self-, peer-, and teacher evaluation.
- Answer Keys for all tests and practice worksheets.
- Answer Sheet for standardized tests.

* TESTS are also available separately as duplicating masters.

WRITING FOLDER — colorful three-pocketed folder for written work

- Leads students through the stages of writing: prewriting, writing, revising, and editing.
- Provides a convenient storage place for papers during each stage.

TEACHER'S RESOURCE BINDER — one for each level

- Convenient 3-ring binder.
- Contains the TEACHER'S RESOURCE BOOK copymasters and the Teacher's Edition of the WORKBOOK.

Teacher's Edition

Heath Grammar and Composition

Fifth Course

Carol Ann Bergman
J. A. Senn

D.C. Heath and Company
Lexington, Massachusetts   Toronto

Series Titles

Heath Grammar and Composition: Third Course
Heath Grammar and Composition: Fourth Course
Heath Grammar and Composition: Fifth Course
Heath Grammar and Composition: Complete Course

Supplementary Materials (for each course)

Annotated Teacher's Edition
Teacher's Resource Book
Workbook
Tests

Contributing Authors

Florence Harris
Gerald Tomlinson

Editorial Barbara Brien (Project Editor), Carol Clay, Lynn Duffy, Peg McNary, Mary Ellen Walters; *Freelance Assistance:* Karen Gabler, Anne Jones, Judy Keith, William Ray, Ellen Whalen
Editorial Services Marianna Frew Palmer (Manager), K. Kirschbaum Harvie
Design Sally Thompson Steele
Cover Design Dawn Ostrer Emerson
Production Ilene Harsip

Acknowledgments: page 654

Copyright © 1986 by D.C. Heath and Company

All rights reserved. No part of this publication may be reproduced or transmitted in any form or by any means, electronic or mechanical, including photocopy, recording, or any information storage or retrieval system, without permission in writing from the publisher.

Printed in the United States of America.

International Standard Book Number: 0-669-06584-6 /0-669-06591-9

Heath
Grammar and Composition
Fifth Course

Series Consultants

Henry I. Christ
Former Chairman of the English Department
Andrew Jackson High School
St. Albans, New York

Richard Marius, Ph.D.
Director of the Expository Writing Program
Harvard University
Cambridge, Massachusetts

Reviewers

Alabama
Fran West
Red Bay High School
Red Bay, Alabama

California
Dorothy Gillmann
Portola Junior High School
Tarzana, California

Florida
Sonya M. Crown
Ely High School
Pompano Beach, Florida

Elynore Schott
South Broward High School
Hollywood, Florida

Illinois
Margaret J. Blaufuss
Glenbard East High School
Lombard, Illinois

Marion P. Johnson
Andrew High School
Tinley Park, Illinois

Virginia Riedel
Willowbrook High School
Villa Park, Illinois

Sister Julia Ann Rogers
Driscoll Catholic High School
Addison, Illinois

Maine
Michael S. Weatherwax
Camden-Rockport High School
Camden, Maine

Massachusetts
Lorraine A. Plasse, Ph.D.
Springfield Public Schools
Springfield, Massachusetts

David C. Reid
Minuteman Vocational Technical High School
Lexington, Massachusetts

Shirley M. Westrate
Hamilton-Wenham Regional High School
South Hamilton, Massachusetts

Michigan
Marilyn Bright
Andover High School
Bloomfield Hills, Michigan

New York
Joseph F. Cammarano
Patchogue-Medford High School
Medford, New York

Joseph R. Teta
Baldwin High School
Baldwin, New York

Oregon
Deborah L. Sommer
Cedar Park School
Portland, Oregon

Paul Williamson
Cedar Park School
Portland, Oregon

Pennsylvania
Sandra M. Couch
Solanco High School
Quarryville, Pennsylvania

Bernadette Fenning
Cardinal O'Hara High School
Springfield, Pennsylvania

South Carolina
Francie C. Brown
Dreher High School
Columbia, South Carolina

Idris B. McElveen, Ph.D.
Spring Valley High School
Columbia, South Carolina

Zelder N. Pressley
Keenan High School
Columbia, South Carolina

Texas
Karen Hibbs
Richland Senior High School
Fort Worth, Texas

Frankye Taylor
Euless Junior High School
Euless, Texas

Virginia
Cindy K. Driskill
Clover Hill High School
Midlothian, Virginia

Washington
Cindy Mar
Liberty High School
Issaquah, Washington

Contents

UNIT 1 GRAMMAR

Chapter 1 **The Parts of Speech** — 2

DIAGNOSTIC TEST — 2
Nouns and Pronouns — 3
  Nouns — 3
  Pronouns — 5
Verbs — 8
  Action Verbs — 8
  Linking Verbs — 9
  Verb Phrases — 11
Adjectives and Adverbs — 14
  Adjectives — 14
  Adverbs — 16
Other Parts of Speech — 18
  Prepositions — 18
  Conjunctions — 20
  Interjections — 21
Parts of Speech Review — 23
Application to Writing: Substituting Specific
  Nouns, Verbs, and Adjectives — 25
CHAPTER REVIEW — 26
MASTERY TEST — 27

Contents

Chapter 2	**The Sentence Base**		28
	DIAGNOSTIC TEST		28
	The Sentence		29
	Subjects and Predicates		29
	Simple Subjects and Predicates		30
	Position of Subjects		32
	Compound Subjects and Verbs		33
	Application to Writing: Combining Sentences		35
	Complements		36
	Direct Objects		36
	Indirect Objects		38
	Objective Complements		39
	Subject Complements		40
	Diagraming the Sentence Base		43
	Subjects and Verbs		43
	Adjectives and Adverbs		44
	Complements		45
	Application to Writing: Using Sentence Patterns		48
	CHAPTER REVIEW		50
	MASTERY TEST		51
Chapter 3	**Phrases**		52
	DIAGNOSTIC TEST		52
	Prepositional Phrases		53
	Adjective Phrases		53
	Adverb Phrases		54
	Appositives and Appositive Phrases		56
	Verbals and Verbal Phrases		59
	Participles and Participial Phrases		59
	Gerunds and Gerund Phrases		62
	Infinitives and Infinitive Phrases		64
	Misplaced and Dangling Modifiers		67
	Diagraming Phrases		69
	Application to Writing: Combining Sentences		72
	CHAPTER REVIEW		74
	MASTERY TEST		75
Chapter 4	**Clauses**		76
	DIAGNOSTIC TEST		76
	Independent and Subordinate Clauses		77
	Uses of Subordinate Clauses		79
	Adverb Clauses		79

Contents

Adjective Clauses	82
Misplaced Modifiers	86
Noun Clauses	87
Kinds of Sentence Structure	89
Diagraming Sentences	91
Application to Writing: Combining Sentences	93
CHAPTER REVIEW	95
MASTERY TEST	97

Chapter 5 Sound Sentences 98

DIAGNOSTIC TEST	98
Sentence Fragments and Run-on Sentences	99
Sentence Fragments	99
Ways to Correct Sentence Fragments	101
Run-on Sentences	102
Application to Writing: Editing for Sentence Errors	104
CHAPTER REVIEW	105
MASTERY TEST	106
Standardized Test: Grammar	107

UNIT 2 USAGE

Chapter 6 Using Verbs 110

DIAGNOSTIC TEST	110
Principal Parts	111
Regular Verbs	111
Irregular Verbs	112
Verb Tense	123
Conjugation of a Verb	123
Uses of the Tenses	128
Shifts in Tense	131
Active and Passive Voice	133
Use of Voice	134
Mood	135
Application to Writing: Editing for Verb Errors	137
CHAPTER REVIEW	138
MASTERY TEST	139

vii

Contents

Chapter 7 Using Pronouns   140

   DIAGNOSTIC TEST   140
   The Cases of Personal Pronouns   141
      The Nominative Case   142
      The Objective Case   145
      The Possessive Case   150
   Pronoun Problems   153
      Who and *Whom*   153
      Elliptical Clauses   156
   Pronouns and Their Antecedents   158
      Indefinite Pronouns as Antecedents   160
   Application to Writing: Eliminating Pronoun Errors   162
   CHAPTER REVIEW   164
   MASTERY TEST   165

Chapter 8 Subject and Verb Agreement   166

   DIAGNOSTIC TEST   166
   Agreement of Subjects and Verbs   167
      Interrupting Words   169
      Compound Subjects   171
      Special Agreement Problems   174
   Application to Writing: Editing for Subject and Verb Agreement   183
   CHAPTER REVIEW   184
   MASTERY TEST   185

Chapter 9 Using Adjectives and Adverbs   186

   DIAGNOSTIC TEST   186
   Comparison of Adjectives and Adverbs   187
      Regular and Irregular Comparison   188
      Problems with Modifiers   191
   Application to Writing: Editing for the Correct Use of Modifiers   197
   CHAPTER REVIEW   198
   MASTERY TEST   199

Glossary of Usage   200

   Levels of Language   200
      Standard English   200
      Nonstandard English   202

Contents

Glossary of Usage	202
GLOSSARY REVIEW	225
Standardized Test: Usage	227

UNIT 3 MECHANICS

Chapter 10 Capital Letters — 230

DIAGNOSTIC TEST	230
Rules for Capital Letters	231
First Words	231
I and *O*	231
Proper Nouns	232
Proper Adjectives	238
Titles	240
Letters	242
Application to Writing: Editing for Capital Letters	244
CHAPTER REVIEW	245
MASTERY TEST	247

Chapter 11 End Marks and Commas — 248

DIAGNOSTIC TEST	248
Kinds of Sentences and End Marks	249
Periods with Abbreviations	251
Commas	252
Commas That Separate	252
Commas That Enclose	260
Application to Writing: Editing for Commas	266
CHAPTER REVIEW	267
MASTERY TEST	269

Chapter 12 Other Punctuation — 270

DIAGNOSTIC TEST	270
Apostrophes	271
Apostrophes to Show Possession	271
Other Uses of Apostrophes	274
Semicolons and Colons	276
Semicolons	276
Colons	280

Contents

Underlining	282
Quotation Marks	284
Quotation Marks with Titles	284
Quotation Marks with Direct Quotations	285
Other Uses of Quotation Marks	291
Other Marks of Punctuation	293
Hyphens	293
Dashes, Parentheses, and Brackets	296
Application to Writing: Editing for Punctuation Marks	298
CHAPTER REVIEW	299
MASTERY TEST	300
Standardized Test: Mechanics	301

UNIT 4 VOCABULARY AND SPELLING

Chapter 13 Vocabulary — 304

Word Meaning	304
Context Clues	305
Prefixes, Suffixes, and Roots	308
Synonyms and Antonyms	317
Word Etymology	318
Tracing Word Histories	318
Words with Unusual Origins	319
Increasing Your Vocabulary	321
Vocabulary List	322
CHAPTER REVIEW	322

Chapter 14 Spelling — 324

Spelling Rules	324
Spelling Patterns	324
Plurals	325
Prefixes and Suffixes	328
Commonly Misspelled Words	331
CHAPTER REVIEW	331
Standardized Test: Vocabulary and Spelling	333

Contents

UNIT 5   REFERENCE SKILLS

Chapter 15   The Dictionary — 336

   Kinds of Dictionaries — 336
   Information in a Dictionary — 338
      Special Sections — 338
      Information in an Entry — 339
   CHAPTER REVIEW — 346

Chapter 16   The Library — 348

   Library Arrangement — 348
      The Dewey Decimal Classification System — 348
      The Library of Congress System of
         Classification — 352
      The Card Catalog — 352
   Reference Materials — 356
      Encyclopedias — 356
      Specialized References — 356
      Reference Materials about Language and
         Literature — 360
   CHAPTER REVIEW — 362

UNIT 6   COMPOSITION

Chapter 17   Words and Sentences — 364

   Word Choice — 364
      Specific Words — 365
      Figurative Language — 367
   Concise Sentences — 370
      Redundancy — 370
      Empty Expressions — 371
      Wordiness — 372
   Sentence Variety — 374
      Sentence Combining — 374
      Varying Sentence Structure — 379
      Varying Sentence Beginnings — 380

Contents

	Faulty Sentences	382
	Faulty Coordination and Faulty Subordination	382
	Rambling Sentences	384
	Faulty Parallelism	386
	Passive Voice	388
	CHAPTER REVIEW	389
	CHAPTER SUMMARY	391
Chapter 18	**Clear Thinking**	392
	Facts and Opinions	392
	Generalizations	395
	Hasty Generalizations	395
	Platitudes	398
	Fallacies	400
	Attacking the Person Instead of the Issue	400
	The Fallacy of Either-Or	401
	The Fallacy of Non Sequitur	402
	Confusing Chronology with Cause and Effect	403
	False Analogies	405
	Begging the Question	406
	CHAPTER REVIEW	408
	CHAPTER SUMMARY	409
Chapter 19	**Paragraphs**	410
	Paragraph Structure	410
	Topic Sentence	411
	Supporting Sentences	413
	Concluding Sentence	414
	Kinds of Paragraphs	415
	Narrative Paragraphs	415
	Descriptive Paragraphs	419
	Expository Paragraphs	423
	Persuasive Paragraphs	429
	The Process of Writing Paragraphs	433
	Prewriting	433
	Writing	438
	Revising	441
	Editing	443
	CHAPTER REVIEW	444
	STEPS FOR WRITING PARAGRAPHS	446
	CHECKLISTS FOR REVISING PARAGRAPHS	447

Contents

Chapter 20 Expository Essays — 448

- Essay Structure — 448
  - Introduction — 449
  - The Body of an Essay — 453
  - Conclusion — 455
- Prewriting — 456
  - Finding Ideas — 457
  - Choosing and Limiting a Subject — 458
  - Listing Supporting Details — 460
  - Outlining — 462
- Writing — 468
  - Writing the Thesis Statement — 468
  - Writing the Introduction — 469
  - Writing the Body — 472
  - Writing the Conclusion — 475
- Revising — 477
  - Checking for Unity, Coherence, and Emphasis — 477
  - Revision Checklist — 479
- Editing — 479
- CHAPTER REVIEW — 480
- STEPS FOR WRITING EXPOSITORY ESSAYS — 483

Chapter 21 Other Kinds of Essays — 484

- Descriptive Essays — 484
  - Essay Structure — 485
  - Selecting and Organizing Descriptive Details — 488
- Persuasive Essays — 490
  - Essay Structure — 491
  - Developing and Organizing Strong Arguments — 496
- Literary Essays — 500
  - Essay Structure — 501
  - Developing and Organizing a Critical Essay — 504
- CHAPTER REVIEW — 509
- STEPS FOR WRITING ESSAYS — 510
- CHECKLISTS FOR REVISING ESSAYS — 511

Chapter 22 The Summary — 512

- The Features of a Summary — 512
- Prewriting — 517
  - Understanding Vocabulary — 517
  - Recognizing the Main Idea — 518

Contents

	Writing	521
	Condensing	521
	Using Your Own Words	524
	Revising	526
	Editing	527
	CHAPTER REVIEW	527
	STEPS FOR WRITING SUMMARIES	529
Chapter 23	**Research Papers**	530
	Prewriting	531
	Finding Ideas	531
	Choosing and Limiting a Subject	532
	Gathering Information	534
	Evaluating Sources	535
	Taking Notes and Summarizing	538
	Organizing Your Notes	541
	Outlining	542
	Writing	546
	Writing the Thesis Statement	546
	Structuring the Research Paper	548
	Using and Citing Sources	554
	Revising	560
	Editing	561
	CHAPTER REVIEW	562
	STEPS FOR WRITING RESEARCH PAPERS	563
Chapter 24	**Business Letters**	564
	Using the Correct Form	564
	Types of Business Letters	566
	Letters of Request	567
	Order Letters	568
	Letters of Complaint	569
	Application Letters	571
	CHAPTER REVIEW	573
	STEPS FOR WRITING BUSINESS LETTERS	574
	Standardized Test: Composition	575

UNIT 7 TEST TAKING

Chapter 25 **Standardized Tests** — 578

    Vocabulary Tests — 579
        Synonyms and Antonyms — 579
        Analogies — 582
        Sentence Completion — 586
    Reading Comprehension Tests — 591
    Tests of Writing Ability — 594
        Tests of Standard Written English — 594
        The 20-Minute Essay — 602
    CHAPTER REVIEW — 604

APPENDIX

Study Skills
    Taking Notes — 608
    Studying for a Test — 610
    Using Standard Manuscript Form — 611
    Using Proofreading Symbols — 614
    Using Correct Footnote Form — 615

Communication Skills
    Speaking to an Audience — 618
    Participating in Group Discussions — 622
    Listening for Information — 624
    Glossary of Computer Terms — 625

Career Skills
    Writing a Résumé — 626
    Writing Letters about Employment — 628
    Writing Letters to Schools and Colleges — 630
    Interviewing for a Job — 632

INDEX — 635

TAB INDEX — 649

To the Student

This book is about communication—the act of expressing your thoughts and ideas effectively to someone else. Think of how much of your day is spent speaking with members of your family, friends, and many others in your school and community. Speaking, however, is only one means of communication. Writing is another, and writing clearly and concisely is an essential skill. In this electronics age, more and more businesses are using computers to communicate information. The written word—whether displayed on a computer screen or printed in books—is the backbone of communication.

Although this book is divided into different units, it has one unified goal: to help you speak and write clearly and effectively. The first unit, on grammar, shows you how the structure of the English language gives you choices to improve your speaking and writing. The next unit, on usage, explains ways to speak and write with clarity and exactness of meaning. Mechanics, the third unit, emphasizes the importance of capitalization and punctuation in precisely transmitting your written message. The fourth unit, on vocabulary and spelling, points out the power of individual words within your total message. The fifth and sixth units show you how to find, organize, and communicate information, including your own ideas and insights. The last unit, on test taking, helps you communicate what you know in a test situation.

The composition unit in this book is unique. Each chapter includes all the help and information you need to understand and write a different type of composition—from a single paragraph to an essay or a report. Within chapters, you are taken step by step through the four stages in the writing process. In the *prewriting* stage, you learn how to choose and limit a subject and how to find and organize your thoughts or information. In the *writing* stage, you learn how to write a topic sentence or a thesis statement; how to write the body of a paragraph, an essay, or a report; and how to write a conclusion. In the *revising* stage, you learn how to pull your writing together—how to give it unity and coherence. Finally, in the *editing* stage, you learn how to polish your work by applying the information in the first three units.

Going through these writing stages is like having someone sit beside you as you learn to drive a car for the first time. If you are unsure of yourself, there is an abundance of help in the form of practice, models, and checklists to show you exactly what to do, how to do it, and when to do it. Following these stages in the writing process will ensure success and build your confidence in your ability to write well.

To the Student

As you go through each unit in this book, remember its underlying purpose: to help you speak and write clearly and effectively. Each chapter has been written with this goal in mind, because speaking and writing are essential skills for success in today's world.

Special Helps

Your teacher will probably go through some of the chapters in this book with you. All of the chapters, however, have been written and organized so that you can refer to them and use them on your own throughout the year. You may find some of the following features of the book particularly helpful.

Keyed Rules All the rules are clearly marked with keyed blue arrows. An index at the back of the book tells you where to find each rule.

Tinted Boxes Throughout the text, important lists, summaries, and writing steps are highlighted in tinted boxes for easy reference.

Application to Writing These sections in the first three units of the book clearly show you how you can use the various grammatical concepts you have learned to improve your writing.

Diagnostic and Mastery Tests You can use the diagnostic and mastery tests to measure your progress. The diagnostic test at the beginning of a chapter will show you what you need to learn; the mastery test at the end will show you how well you learned it.

High-Interest Exercises Many of the exercises throughout the book are based on interesting topics. You will not only practice learning a particular skill, but you will also find the material in these exercises informative and interesting.

Composition Models Clearly marked models in the composition chapters provide interesting examples by professional writers.

Composition Checklists Almost all the composition chapters end with a checklist that you can follow—step by step—when you are writing a paragraph, an essay, or a report.

Standardized Tests Standardized tests, which follow five of the units, give you practice and build your confidence in taking tests.

Appendix In a clear, concise format, the appendix at the end of the book provides assistance with various study skills, communication skills, and career skills. For example, you will find helpful information about taking notes, using proofreading symbols, speaking to an audience, and writing a résumé.

Unit 1

Grammar

1 The Parts of Speech
2 The Sentence Base
3 Phrases
4 Clauses
5 Sound Sentences

Chapter 1 The Parts of Speech

OBJECTIVES

- To identify common, proper, concrete, abstract, compound, and collective nouns.
- To identify the antecedent of a personal pronoun.
- To identify personal, reflexive, intensive, indefinite, demonstrative, and interrogative pronouns.
- To distinguish between action and linking verbs.
- To distinguish between transitive and intransitive verbs.
- To identify a verb phrase, consisting of a main verb and helping verbs.
- To identify common, proper, and compound adjectives as modifiers of nouns and pronouns.
- To identify adverbs as modifiers of verbs, adjectives, and other adverbs.
- To identify prepositions and prepositional phrases.
- To identify coordinating and correlative conjunctions and to use them correctly in sentences.
- To identify interjections.
- To review the eight parts of speech and identify the dual role of some words.
- Application: To make writing more colorful by substituting specific nouns, verbs, and adjectives for general ones.

MOTIVATIONAL ACTIVITY

Have your students write several sentences in which they use the word close as different parts of speech. This reminder that one word can be used as different parts of speech is a good introduction to this chapter.

Sample Board Sentences
The close of the century was marked with great celebrations. [noun]
Did you close the back door? [verb]
That was a close call! [adjective]
Stand close to her on the stage. [adverb]

TEACHING SUGGESTIONS

When you begin this chapter, you may want to remind your students that the object of this chapter is *not* to label sentence elements but to learn how to use them to build clear, concise, interesting sentences.

This chapter should be a review for most of your students. If you find that your students have mastered the parts of speech, you may want to move on to the next chapter. (The results of the Diagnostic Test should give you some indication of your students' abilities.)

If your basic students are still unfamiliar with the nomenclature in this chapter, you may want to spend most of your time on the practical applications to writing—without using the terminology.

Parts of Speech Review *(pages 23–25)*

Be sure to emphasize that a word's part of speech depends on its use in a sentence. For example, you may want to ask your students what part of speech *from* is in the following sentence.

In the dictionary *from* is listed as a preposition.

Application to Writing *(page 25)*

You may want to point out that ordinarily students should use specific, colorful words rather than general or weak words. For instance, *miser* is preferable to *greedy person; scamper* to *run hastily*. Also point out that concise writing works better than wordiness. *Speedily* is usually preferable to *with great speed*. Write the following sentences on the board and have students make them more vigorous and concise.

1. The puppy with the brown fur walked unsteadily along the hall.
2. During our vacation in Arizona, we enjoyed skies of blue and days with sun.
3. Maynard was not a cowardly person, but he was very much afraid of injections.

Chapter 1 a

The Parts of Speech

4. In Holland the shoes of wood protect against the fields of mud.
5. Modern, very tall buildings often look like peaks of glass.

ACTIVITIES FOR DIFFERENT ABILITIES

Basic Students

ACTIVITY 1 Parts of Speech Review
For additional practice, duplicate the following sentences. Have your students identify the part of speech of each italicized word. Then have them identify whether each verb is action or linking.

Dolley Madison
1. The wife of *our* fourth president *is* one of history's many interesting women.
2. The *first* name of this unusual lady is *often* misspelled.
3. The official name on her *birth certificate* is spelled *with* an *e*.
4. *Many* historians of the period *incorrectly* wrote her name.
5. *Dolley Madison* was the foremost woman in the nation's capital in the opening *years* of the 1800s.
6. Thomas Jefferson *chose* James Madison as *his* secretary of state.
7. The dynamic wife *of* James Madison became unofficial First Lady *during* Jefferson's eight years as president.
8. This charming *and* talented woman became the official First Lady during *her* husband's eight years in office.
9. Most historians *give* Dolley Madison credit for the style and tone of the nation's capital in *those* years.
10. Dolley Madison's attractive face *later* appeared on a *United States* stamp.

ACTIVITY 2 Parts of Speech Review
For additional practice, duplicate the following sentences. Have your students identify the part of speech of each italicized word. Then have them identify whether each verb is action or linking.

Lassen Volcanic National Park
1. Last July *my* family *and* I visited Lassen Volcanic National Park.
2. We entered the *park* territory *from* the south.
3. *Our* first stop *inside* the park was the Sulphur Works.
4. The overpowering *smell* of sulphur *gave* an eerie quality to the bubbling hot springs.
5. *Along* Lassen Peak Highway we drove by *snowdrifts* ten feet high.
6. From the summit we *had* an excellent view of *Mount Lassen*.
7. Not many years ago, the cone of Mount Lassen sent *forth* smoke, lava, and *volcanic* ash.
8. The area of destruction is *still* visible farther to the *north*.
9. From the *high* point on the highway, we *carefully* drove down to Kings Creek Meadows.
10. After a night in camp, *we* took a *hike* to Kings Creek Falls.

ACTIVITY 3 Using Specific Nouns
Write the following sentences on the board or duplicate them. Then have your students substitute specific nouns for each italicized expression.
1. After school I ate *fruit*.
2. In the drawer I found *four things*.
3. At the florist Dad bought some *flowers*.
4. My brother has *two unusual pets*.
5. During gym one squad played *one game;* the second squad played *another*.

ACTIVITY 4 Using Specific Verbs
Write the following sentences on the board or duplicate them. Then have your students write the verb that expresses vividly or exactly the action of each sentence.
1. Dirk can be boring whenever he ____ on and on about his new car.
whispers   jabbers   talks
2. The path to the barn was ____ with snowdrifts.
blocked   covered   hidden
3. In the winter, turtles and frogs ____ under the mud at the bottom of

Chapter 1 b

The Parts of Speech

streams and ponds.
hide go burrow
4. Dozens of bats ____ out of the entrance to the cave.
flew fluttered poured
5. Ms. Jacobs grabbed her briefcase and ____ papers into it.
stuffed put slipped

Advanced Students

ACTIVITY 1 Parts of Speech Review
For additional practice, duplicate the following sentences. Then have your students identify the part of speech of each italicized word.

Unseen Eyes
1. On a *leisurely* stroll through a *summer* woodland, you may seem like a lonely visitor.
2. You cannot see *any* living creatures *except* an occasional bird.
3. Many keen eyes are *upon* you, however, during that casual *walk*.
4. The timid *creatures* of the forest *are* quiet spectators.
5. *They* hide in silence, fearful of you, a strange intruder *into* their lives.
6. *You* see many things *but* recognize only a few.
7. Many creatures are *actually* in plain *sight*.
8. You pass *them* by with a vague glance and miss them *because of* their camouflage.
9. Many forest animals *have unusually* sharp eyesight.
10. Some eyes are *especially* effective at dusk *or* during the hours of total darkness.

ACTIVITY 2 Parts of Speech Review
For additional practice, write the following sentences on the board or duplicate them. Then have your students identify the part of speech of each italicized word.
1. *Many* candidates filed petitions.
2. Cactus plants store *water*.
3. *Both* girls made the swimming team.
4. Several helicopters flew *above* during the parade.
5. Will you *try* again?
6. How *many* were at the meeting?
7. Did you *water* the lawn?
8. That was a good *try*.
9. Have you looked *above* the sink?
10. Do you want *both*?

ACTIVITY 3 Parts of Speech Review
Have your students write sentences in which they use each of the following words as the different parts of speech listed after the word. Have your students use the dictionary if they need help.
1. *flower*—noun, verb, adjective
2. *beyond*—adverb, preposition
3. *neither*—pronoun, adjective, conjunction
4. *those*—pronoun, adjective
5. *light*—noun, verb, adjective

ACTIVITY 4 Using Specific Verbs
Write the following sentences on the board or duplicate them. Then have your students substitute a specific, vigorous verb for each italicized verb.
1. Onto the playing field *went* the Mason High Band.
2. Florida State *defeated* Memphis State by a lopsided score.
3. When I'm on a hike, I always *want* a tall glass of ice water.
4. A large sailboat *moved* under the Golden Gate Bridge.
5. Led by a white stallion, a band of wild horses *ran* across the valley.

ACTIVITY 5 Writing Sentences
Have your students write ten to fifteen sentences in which they put themselves inside an object—such as a chair, a telephone booth, or a frying pan. They should give the object a personality. Then they should imagine and describe how the object sees things around it. Remind your students to use as many specific nouns, verbs, and adjectives as possible.

Chapter 1 c

The Parts of Speech

ADDITIONAL PRACTICE
Basic Students
　Teacher's Resource Book:
　pages 81–83
　Workbook: pages 1–14
Average Students
　Teacher's Resource Book:
　pages 84–86
　Workbook: pages 1–14
Advanced Students
　Teacher's Resource Book:
　pages 87–89

REVIEW EXERCISES AND TESTS
Student Text
　Diagnostic Test: page 2
　Chapter Review: pages 26–27
　Mastery Test: page 27
Teacher's Resource Book
　Prebook Test: pages 1–8
　Chapter 1 Test: pages 9–10
　(Also available as spirit duplicating masters.)

ADDITIONAL ANSWERS

EXERCISE 8　Writing Sentences *(page 14)*
Sample answers:
1. I feel fine.
   I feel the key in the bottom of the basket.
2. The jogger looked weary.
   We looked everywhere for my wallet.
3. The chili tastes unusually spicy.
   John tasted the chili and added more seasoning.
4. Lalia appeared calm throughout the rehearsal.
   Martin finally appeared for dinner.
5. Sarah grew bored with the TV program.
   My mother grows her own herbs.

EXERCISE 10　Writing Sentences *(page 16)*
Sample answers:
1. The candlestick was made of brass.
   The brass trophy stood on the shelf.
2. Those are the magazines I want.
   Those poems of yours are excellent.
3. Glass is less expensive than crystal.
   The display featured glass figurines.
4. I'll take several of those games.
   I have several ideas.
5. Rock is a type of music with a heavy bass beat.
   A rock wall surrounded the house.
   The waves rocked the sailboats at their moorings.

EXERCISE 16　Writing Sentences *(page 22)*
Sample answers:
1. Neither Mike nor Karen is working tonight.
2. I left at eight but returned later.
3. Anne is both athletic and musical.
4. The horse trotted rapidly and steadily.
5. Stay here, for I'll be back very soon.

Chapter 1 d

1 The Parts of Speech

For additional practice for this chapter, see the Teacher's Resource Book and the Workbook.

DIAGNOSTIC TEST

Number your paper 1 to 10. Write the underlined words in each sentence. Then beside each word, write its part of speech: *noun* (n.), *pronoun* (pron.), *verb* (v.), *adjective* (adj.), *adverb* (adv.), *preposition* (prep.), *conjunction* (conj.), or *interjection* (interj.).

EXAMPLE We saw a <u>gray</u> rabbit near the <u>garden</u>.
ANSWER   gray—adjective   garden—noun

1. I want to make bran muffins, <u>but</u> (conj.) I have lost the <u>recipe</u> (n.).
2. Many <u>Canadian</u> (adj.) citizens have relatives in <u>France</u> (n.).
3. <u>Which</u> (pron.) of the West Indies was <u>first</u> (adv.) discovered by Columbus?
4. <u>Many</u> (pron.) of the tourists found the food in the new restaurant <u>too</u> (adv.) spicy for them.
5. The members of the <u>track</u> (adj.) team voted <u>for</u> (prep.) Diane.
6. The severe snowstorm <u>stranded</u> (v.) a <u>herd</u> (n.) of cattle in the north pasture.
7. Has <u>anyone</u> (pron.) seen my <u>recipe</u> (adj.) book?
8. <u>Wow</u> (interj.)! Mavis <u>was</u> (v.) the first player to hit four home runs in one game.
9. Hurry home, <u>for</u> (conj.) dinner will be ready <u>at</u> (prep.) six o'clock.
10. How <u>many</u> (adj.) times can you run around the <u>track</u> (n.)?

Each word in the dictionary is labeled according to its *part of speech*. There are eight parts of speech: *noun, pronoun, verb, adjective, adverb, preposition, conjunction,* and *interjection*. Keep in mind that a word's part of speech is determined by its use in a sentence. As a result, the same word may be labeled as two, three, or four different parts of speech in the dictionary.

As you review the eight parts of speech in this chapter and the various other grammatical elements in this first unit, do not look at them as an end in themselves. Rather, review each one as a means to an end—that "end" being a better writing style. If, for example, you understand the construction and the use of the participial phrase, you will be able to include participial phrases in your writing. The addition of participial phrases will add variety to your sentence structure and maturity to your writing style.

NOUNS AND PRONOUNS

Nouns are the words in a sentence that name people, places, things, and ideas. Pronouns are words that can be substituted for nouns.

Nouns

A *noun* is a name that may consist of one or more words.

1a A **noun** is the name of a person, place, thing, or idea.

My **dog Penny** always displays great **affection** for all the **people** who come into our **house**.

Nouns can be classified in several ways.

Common and Proper Nouns. A *common noun* names any person, place, or thing, but a *proper noun* names a particular person, place, or thing.

COMMON NOUNS worker, state, document
PROPER NOUNS Rob Warner, Michigan, Bill of Rights

The Parts of Speech

NOTE: Some proper nouns, such as *Bill of Rights,* include more than one word. They are still considered one noun. *Bill of Rights,* for example, is the name of *one* document.

Concrete and Abstract Nouns. A *concrete noun* names an object that you can actually see, touch, taste, hear, or smell. An *abstract noun* cannot be perceived through your senses. An abstract noun names a quality, a condition, or an idea.

CONCRETE NOUNS   hat, fur, children, bell, flowers, peppers
ABSTRACT NOUNS   love, anger, liberty, success, hope, ambition

Compound and Collective Nouns. A *compound noun* is made up of more than one word. As the following examples show, compound nouns can be written in three different ways. Since you may not know which form a particular compound noun takes, check the dictionary. A *collective noun* names a group of people or things.

COMPOUND NOUNS   viewpoint, stagecoach, airstrip [one word]
double-talk, brother-in-law [hyphenated]
living room, missing link [two words]
COLLECTIVE NOUNS   committee, council, flock, group, family

EXERCISE 1   Finding Nouns

Number your paper 1 to 40. Then write the nouns in the following paragraphs. (A date should be considered a noun.)

Beyond the Solar System

Somewhere in interstellar space, where Earth is a mere pinpoint of light, *Pioneer 10* cruises on and on. Launched in 1972, the tiny spacecraft was expected to have only a 21-month life span. It withstood radiation from Jupiter and bombardments of micrometeoroids. Eleven years later, while still sending back faint messages, it left most of the known planets behind.

With its deep-space antennae and scientific instruments still functioning, *Pioneer 10* continues to send back information from its eight-watt transmitter. Communication may continue until 1991 — out to a distance of five billion miles. About every million years, the craft could come close to another star system. It might then be found by other intelligent beings. With that idea in mind, scientists attached a plaque with pictures of a <u>man</u> and a <u>woman</u>, the <u>location</u> of <u>Earth</u>, and some <u>points</u> of basic <u>science</u>. This could be its most important <u>message</u>.

Pronouns

By taking the place of a noun, a *pronoun* can eliminate unnecessary repetition and awkwardness in your writing.

> **1b** A **pronoun** is a word that takes the place of one or more nouns.

The word that the pronoun replaces or refers to is called its *antecedent*. In the following examples, an arrow has been drawn from the pronoun to its antecedent or antecedents.

Dan, did **you** really make this chair?

"Did Alex say **he** would meet **us**?" Seth asked Earl.

Notice that the antecedents *Seth* and *Earl* follow *us*.

Personal Pronouns. The most common kind of pronoun is the *personal pronoun*. Personal pronouns can be divided into the following three groups.

Personal Pronouns	
FIRST PERSON	(The person speaking)
SINGULAR	I, me, my, mine
PLURAL	we, us, our, ours
SECOND PERSON	(The person spoken to)
SINGULAR	you, your, yours
PLURAL	you, your, yours
THIRD PERSON	(The person or thing spoken about)
SINGULAR	he, him, his, she, her, hers, it, its
PLURAL	they, them, their, theirs

FIRST PERSON   I can't wait to see **my** costume.
SECOND PERSON   Why aren't **you** taking **your** coat with **you**?
THIRD PERSON   **They** asked **her** to wait for **him** at the library.

The Parts of Speech

EXERCISE 2 Finding Personal Pronouns and Their Antecedents

Number your paper 1 to 10. Write the personal pronouns in each sentence. Then beside each one, write its antecedent.

1. Jessica, where have you put your umbrella?
2. "I hope we can find jobs this weekend," Ann said to Bob.
3. Alice and Fred will sing their duet at the concert.
4. Mr. and Mrs. Chin said that they had just moved here from Hong Kong.
5. "That suit is lovely, but I think its sleeves are a little short," the clerk told Irene.
6. "Our parents will be celebrating their 20th anniversary next Friday," Nancy told Charles.
7. "If these books are yours, Audrey, why did you leave them here?" Ms. Davis asked.
8. "Someone found my bicycle and left it in your garage," Daniel told Pepe.
9. Charlotte asked Linda if she had seen their brother.
10. Rosa earned her letter in track last year, and her brother earned his this year.

Reflexive and Intensive Pronouns. A reflexive or an intensive pronoun is formed by adding *-self* or *-selves* to a personal pronoun.

Reflexive and Intensive Pronouns

SINGULAR myself, yourself, himself, herself, itself
PLURAL ourselves, yourselves, themselves

A *reflexive pronoun* refers back to a noun or another pronoun. It is needed to make the meaning of the sentence clear. An *intensive pronoun*, on the other hand, is not a necessary part of a sentence. It is included only to add emphasis—or intensity—to a noun or another pronoun in the sentence.

REFLEXIVE PRONOUN Did Matthew make **himself** breakfast? [*Himself* cannot be dropped from the sentence without changing its meaning.]

Pronouns

INTENSIVE PRONOUN   The queen **herself** will be present. [*Herself* can be dropped from the sentence. The queen will be present.]

Indefinite Pronouns. *Indefinite pronouns* often refer to unnamed people or things. They usually do not have specific antecedents as personal pronouns do.

Common Indefinite Pronouns

SINGULAR	another, anybody, anyone, anything, each, either, everybody, everyone, everything, much, neither, nobody, no one, one, somebody, someone, something
PLURAL	both, few, many, others, several
SINGULAR/PLURAL	all, any, most, none, some

We have **many** left over because **everyone** brought **some**. **Both** of the reporters may speak with **anyone** on the team.

Demonstrative and Interrogative Pronouns. A *demonstrative pronoun* is used to point out a specific person, place, or object. An *interrogative pronoun* is used to ask a question.

Demonstrative Pronouns

this, that, these, those

Interrogative Pronouns

what, which, who, whom, whose

DEMONSTRATIVE PRONOUNS   **This** is the book I need.
Do you really want to buy **those?**

INTERROGATIVE PRONOUNS   **Which** is the quickest route?
Who is going to answer the phone?

NOTE: *Relative pronouns* introduce adjective clauses. *(See pages 83–84.)*

7

The Parts of Speech

EXERCISE 3 Finding Pronouns

Number your paper 1 to 10. Then write each <u>pronoun</u>.

1. Take <u>these</u> and give <u>them</u> to <u>someone</u> in the office.
2. <u>Who</u> can drive <u>both</u> of <u>us</u> to the concert?
3. <u>This</u> must belong to <u>somebody</u>.
4. The tickets <u>themselves</u> cost over twenty dollars.
5. <u>I</u> haven't noticed <u>anyone</u> volunteering for the project.
6. <u>Those</u> are the sneakers <u>everyone</u> should buy.
7. Robin made <u>herself</u> a timetable to follow.
8. <u>Which</u> is the <u>one</u> <u>he</u> wants to take?
9. <u>Neither</u> of <u>my</u> friends has seen <u>that</u> yet.
10. <u>No one</u> would buy <u>anything</u> like <u>that</u>!

VERBS

A *verb* is an essential part of a sentence. A group of words without a verb is a fragment, not a sentence.

Action Verbs

Action verbs are used most frequently when you write or speak.

1c An **action verb** tells what action a subject is performing.

An action verb can show physical action, mental action, or ownership.

PHYSICAL ACTION	run, pull, stir, dive, shout, yawn, bounce
MENTAL ACTION	think, wish, believe, understand, imagine
OWNERSHIP	have, possess, keep, own, control

Transitive and Intransitive Verbs. All action verbs fall within two general classes. An action verb that has an object is *transitive*. You can find an object by asking the question *What?* or *Whom?* after the verb. (See pages 36–37 for more information about objects.) An action verb that has no object is *intransitive*.

TRANSITIVE   I **forgot** the key to my locker today. [*Forgot* what? *Key* is the object.]

Verbs

1c–d

INTRANSITIVE   Frank **studied** in the library last night.
[*Studied* what? *Studied* has no object.]

Some action verbs can be transitive in one sentence and intransitive in another sentence.

TRANSITIVE   April **played** the piano at the party. [*Played* what? *Piano* is the object.]

INTRANSITIVE   The band **played** during halftime. [*Played* what? *Played* has no object.]

EXERCISE 4 Identifying Transitive and Intransitive Verbs
Write the action verb in each sentence. Then label it *transitive* or *intransitive*.

Facts about Sports

1. Ice hockey started in Canada.
2. Before 1859, baseball umpires sat in a padded rocking chair behind the catcher.
3. Wilma Rudolph won the 100-meter dash in the Olympic Games in 1960.
4. Modern gymnastics originated in Germany in the early nineteenth century.
5. At home games the Denver Broncos play in Mile High Stadium.
6. In baseball, home plate has five sides.
7. The ancient Egyptians bowled on alleys with stone balls and stone pins.
8. Johnny Vander Meer pitched two straight no-hitters in 1938.
9. The game of soccer probably first occurred in England in A.D. 217.
10. In 1979, ice skater Beth Heiden captured four gold medals in the women's World Championships.

Linking Verbs

A verb that links or joins the subject with another word in the sentence is called a *linking verb*.

1d   A **linking verb** links the subject with another word in the sentence. The other word either renames or describes the subject.

9

The Parts of Speech

Norman **was** a judge at the art show. [*Was* links *judge* with the subject *Norman*. *Judge* renames the subject.]

That chili **is** too hot for me. [*Is* links *hot* with the subject *chili*. *Hot* describes the subject.]

The most common linking verbs are the various forms of *be*.

Common Forms of *Be*

be	shall be	have been
being	will be	has been
is	can be	had been
am	could be	could have been
are	should be	should have been
was	would be	would have been
were	may be	might have been
		must have been

NOTE: The forms of the verb *be* are not always linking verbs. To be a linking verb, a verb must link the subject with another word in the sentence that renames or describes that subject. In the following examples, the verbs simply make a statement.

They **were** here earlier.
Ida **is** in the cafeteria.

In addition to the forms of the verb *be*, the following verbs can also be used as linking verbs.

Additional Linking Verbs

appear	grow	seem	stay
become	look	smell	taste
feel	remain	sound	turn

Luisa **became** the leader of the discussion group.
[*Leader* renames the subject.]

Kenneth **seems** unusually quiet today.
[*Quiet* describes the subject.]

10

Most of the additional linking verbs listed in the preceding box can also be used as action verbs.

LINKING VERB   Ryan **looked** handsome in his tuxedo.
ACTION VERB   Jed **looked** cautiously into the old trunk.

EXERCISE 5   Finding Linking Verbs

Number your paper 1 to 20. Then write the linking verb in each sentence. If a sentence does not have a linking verb, write *none* after the number.

1. Length, breadth, depth, and time <u>are</u> the four dimensions.
2. I smell smoke in the kitchen.   *(none)*
3. Pat <u>has been</u> the editor for two years.
4. Four ghosts appeared to Ebenezer Scrooge.   *(none)*
5. George Eliot's real name <u>was</u> Mary Ann Evans.
6. Milk often <u>turns</u> sour at warm temperatures.
7. The room <u>seemed</u> hot and stuffy.
8. Miguel <u>grows</u> taller every year.
9. Houston <u>is</u> one of the warmest cities in the United States.
10. That table <u>looks</u> old but valuable.
11. Mr. Wilson <u>became</u> the principal this week.
12. Next year <u>will be</u> my last year of high school.
13. Steven <u>appeared</u> nervous during his solo.
14. The barbecued spareribs <u>tasted</u> delicious.
15. My older brother grows many different vegetables on his farm.   *(none)*
16. Frank always turns the pages for any guest pianist.   *(none)*
17. Mary Cassatt's favorite subjects for her paintings <u>were</u> mothers and their children.
18. These roses <u>smell</u> so fragrant.
19. Saturday <u>must have been</u> Karen's birthday.
20. Every day he looks in the newspaper for a job.   *(none)*

Verb Phrases

The main verb of a sentence is often more than one word. *Helping verbs,* or auxiliary verbs, can be added to the main verb to form a *verb phrase.*

11

The Parts of Speech

1e   A **verb phrase** is a main verb plus one or more helping verbs.

Common Helping Verbs	
be	am, is, are, was, were, be, being, been
have	has, have, had
do	do, does, did
others	may, might, must, can, could, shall, should, will, would

In the following examples, the helping verbs are in heavy type.

Breakfast **is being** prepared for everyone.
      ⎡— verb phrase —⎤

The dog **should have** eaten its dinner before now.
      ⎡— verb phrase —⎤

Often a verb phrase is interrupted by other words.

> Pauline **has** already **notified** the police.
> He **should** never **have answered** so quickly.
> She **did**n't **notice** the note on the refrigerator door.

NOTE: Throughout the rest of this book, the term *verb* will refer to the whole verb phrase.

EXERCISE 6   Finding Verb Phrases

Write the verb in each sentence. Include all helping verbs.

1. Most small bears can climb trees.
2. My grandparents will be visiting us for two weeks.
3. He might have ridden with someone else.
4. The first seven presidents of the United States were not born United States citizens.
5. Manuel will work with you on that project.
6. I should never have taken a part-time job.
7. Charles Lindbergh did not carry a radio receiver or a transmitter with him on the *Spirit of St. Louis*.
8. Someone must have taken your coat by mistake.
9. You should always edit your own compositions.
10. Virginia hasn't found her contact lens yet.

Verb Phrases

1e

EXERCISE 7 Time-out for Review

Number your paper 1 to 20. Write the verbs in the following sentences. Then label each one *action* or *linking*.

Hope for Survival

L 1. The story of the fate of the passenger pigeon is alarming.
L 2. Passenger pigeons were once one of the most populous of all birds.
A 3. Before 1840, for example, between five and nine billion passenger pigeons existed.
A 4. The birds usually roosted in large flocks.
L 5. As a result they were easy prey for hunters.
L 6. By 1914, the passenger pigeon was extinct.
A 7. Now no one will ever see another passenger pigeon again.
A 8. Since the year 1600, about 200 different kinds of animals have disappeared forever.
L 9. Besides the passenger pigeon, the California grizzly bear and the Labrador duck are some other extinct species.
L 10. During the past 60 years, approximately one vertebrate species has become extinct each year.
A 11. Many factors have contributed to the extinction of various species.
A 12. Natural changes in the environment have endangered some wildlife.
A 13. Bulldozers have sometimes destroyed species' natural habitats.
A 14. Developers have cleared forests and grasslands for new roads, farms, and cities.
A 15. The use of poisonous chemicals has harmed other wildlife populations.
L 16. The future of some endangered species appears somewhat brighter today.
A 17. State and federal governments have established wildlife refuges and state and national parks for some threatened species.
A 18. In addition, stricter hunting and fishing laws are protecting wild animals.
A 19. Scientists are also developing safer methods for weed control.
A 20. With new laws, species such as the California condor now have a better chance of survival.

13

The Parts of Speech

EXERCISE 8 Writing Sentences
Write two sentences for each of the following verbs. First use the verb as a linking verb. Then use it as an action verb.
Sample answers precede this chapter.
1. feel   2. look   3. taste   4. appear   5. grow

ADJECTIVES AND ADVERBS

Adjectives and *adverbs* are modifiers. They modify, or describe, other parts of speech. Adjectives and adverbs bring clarity to sentences by adding vividness and exactness to them.

Adjectives

An *adjective* makes the meaning of a noun or a pronoun more precise.

1f   An **adjective** is a word that modifies a noun or a pronoun.

An adjective answers one of the following questions: *What kind? Which one(s)? How many? How much?*

WHAT KIND?	**wet** towels	**portable** typewriter
WHICH ONE(S)?	**this** one	**blue** dress
HOW MANY?	**two** bananas	**many** steps
HOW MUCH?	**infinite** wisdom	**more** money

Proper and Compound Adjectives. There are two special kinds of adjectives. A *proper adjective* is formed from a proper noun and begins with a capital letter. A *compound adjective* is made up of more than one word.

PROPER ADJECTIVES	**French** people	**Atlantic** coastline
COMPOUND ADJECTIVES	**downhill** skiing	**all-star** team

Adjectives most often come before the noun or the pronoun they modify. Sometimes, however, they follow the noun or the pronoun. They may also follow a linking verb.

BEFORE A NOUN   The **large friendly** crowd cheered the speaker.

14

Adjectives

1f

AFTER A NOUN The crowd, **large** and **friendly,** cheered the speaker.

AFTER A LINKING VERB The crowd was **large** and **friendly.**

NOTE: The words *a, an*, and *the* form a special group of adjectives called *articles. A* comes before a word that begins with a consonant sound, and *an* comes before a word that begins with a vowel sound. You will not be asked to list articles in the exercises in this book.

Other Parts of Speech Used as Adjectives. A word's part of speech is determined by how it is used in a sentence. As a result, a word can be a noun in one sentence and an adjective in another sentence.

NOUNS gold, cereal, telephone
ADJECTIVES **gold** coins, **cereal** boxes, **telephone** wires

The same word can be a pronoun in one sentence and an adjective in another sentence. The following words are adjectives when they come in front of a noun or a pronoun and modify that noun or pronoun. They are pronouns when they stand alone.

Words Used as Pronouns or Adjectives

Demonstrative	Interrogative	Indefinite	
that	what	all	many
these	which	another	more
this	whose	any	most
those		both	neither
		each	other
		either	several
		few	some

ADJECTIVE **This** scarf is mine.
PRONOUN **This** is mine.

ADJECTIVE **Many** people will be needed to help.
PRONOUN **Many** will be needed to help.

15

The Parts of Speech

NOTE: The possessive pronouns *my, your, his, her, its, our,* and *their* are sometimes called *pronominal adjectives* because they answer the adjective question *Which one(s)?* Throughout this book, however, these words will be considered pronouns.

EXERCISE 9 **Finding Adjectives**
Number your paper 1 to 25. Write the adjectives in the following paragraphs. Beside each one, write the word it modifies.

A Distant Image

For many years science-fiction writers have created new and strange worlds. In the book *Mission of Gravity,* Hal Clement created Mesklin. It was a giant world that spun so fast that an entire day occupied just nine minutes of Earth time. The atmosphere was cold and bitter. It was composed entirely of hydrogen. The immense continents, smooth and featureless, were extensive plains. These vast stretches of land were covered by a tangle of vine trees.

Mesklin had an intelligent population of foot-long caterpillars, which were able to withstand the enormous gravitational forces that governed life on this distant planet. The civilization of these creatures was similar to that of Earth in the 1700s and 1800s.

EXERCISE 10 **Writing Sentences**
Number your paper 1 to 5, skipping a line between each number. Then write sentences that follow the directions below.
Sample answers precede this chapter.
1. Use *brass* as a noun and an adjective.
2. Use *those* as a pronoun and an adjective.
3. Use *glass* as a noun and an adjective.
4. Use *several* as a pronoun and an adjective.
5. Use *rock* as a noun, an adjective, and a verb.

Adverbs

An adverb makes the meaning of a verb, an adjective, or another adverb more precise.

1g ▶ An **adverb** is a word that modifies a verb, an adjective, or another adverb.

16

Adverbs

1g

An adverb answers one of the following questions: *Where? When? How?* or *To what extent?*

MODIFYING A VERB	stopped **here** [Where?]
	speak **now** [When?]
	softly sang [How?]
MODIFYING AN ADJECTIVE	**so** happy [To what extent?]
MODIFYING AN ADVERB	**very** quickly [To what extent?]

NOTE: Adverbs that describe verbs modify the whole verb phrase.

Recently his mail has been sent **there**.

Although many adverbs end in *-ly*, a few adjectives also end in *-ly*.

ADVERB   He works **nightly** from six to eleven.

ADJECTIVE   Do you watch the **nightly** news?

Many common adverbs such as *always, never, not (n't), often, perhaps, rather, then, too,* and *very* do not end in *-ly*. The adverb questions *when, where,* and *how* are also adverbs.

Nouns Used as Adverbs. The same word can be used as a noun in one sentence and an adverb in another sentence.

NOUN   **Yesterday** was very hectic.

ADVERB   I had an appointment **yesterday**. [When?]

NOUN   The Gregsons just moved into their new **home**.

ADVERB   Go **home** after the game. [Where?]

EXERCISE 11   Finding Adverbs

Number your paper 1 to 10. Write each adverb. Then beside each one, write the word or words it modifies.

1. The hawk suddenly swooped down.
2. Our choir sings quite professionally.
3. They did not try very hard.

17

The Parts of Speech

4. Are you still waiting for the bus?
5. The comedian spoke too rapidly.
6. Where is that extremely easy bread recipe?
7. The audience laughed uproariously.
8. I talked briefly with her today.
9. Far away the high goalpost gleamed brightly.
10. An unusually hot sun was shining directly overhead.

EXERCISE 12   Finding Adjectives and Adverbs
Number your paper 1 to 25. Write each adjective and adverb in the paragraphs. Then label each one *adjective* or *adverb*.

No Relief

In 1816, there was no summer. Across northern Europe and the eastern United States, the daytime temperatures rarely reached 50°F. In June an extremely severe blizzard actually dumped many inches of snow on parts of New England. What caused these unusual weather conditions? A volcano that had erupted violently on the other side of the world on April 5, 1815, may have been the cause.

As a result of the eruption, a massive cloud of volcanic dust slowly worked its way around the world. By 1816, the cloud became temporarily suspended over the Northern Hemisphere, deflecting the radiation of the sun. During the night the mercury often registered temperatures below 32°F. On July 4, the high temperature in normally hot Georgia was in the forties. It was one summer when the living was hardly easy.

EXERCISE 13   Writing Sentences
Briefly describe your activities on your favorite holiday. Include and label at least five adjectives and five adverbs.
Answers will vary.

OTHER PARTS OF SPEECH

The three remaining parts of speech are *prepositions, conjunctions,* and *interjections.*

Prepositions

A preposition shows relationships between words. *On, under,* and *behind,* for example, change the relationship between the dog and the couch in the following example.

18

Prepositions

1h

The dog { **on** / **under** / **behind** } the couch is Betsy's.

> **1h** A **preposition** is a word that shows the relationship between a noun or a pronoun and another word in the sentence.

Following is a list of common prepositions. Prepositions of two or more words are called *compound prepositions*.

Common Prepositions

about	below	in front of	outside
above	beneath	in place of	over
according to	beside	inside	past
across	besides	in spite of	prior to
after	between	instead of	through
against	beyond	into	throughout
ahead of	by	in view of	to
along	despite	like	toward
among	down	near	under
apart from	during	next to	underneath
around	except	of	until
aside from	for	off	up
at	from	on	upon
because of	in	on account of	with
before	in addition to	opposite	within
behind	in back of	out	without

A preposition is always part of a group of words called a *prepositional phrase*. A prepositional phrase begins with a preposition and ends with a noun or a pronoun called the *object of a preposition*. One or more modifiers may come between the preposition and its object. The prepositional phrases in the following examples are in heavy type.

By the fifth race, many **of the runners** were exhausted.
In place of Hank, Philip will go **with you.**
Maria walked **to the store and the library.**
[The words *store* and *library* form a compound object of the preposition *to*.]

19

The Parts of Speech

Preposition or Adverb? A word can be a preposition in one sentence and an adverb in another sentence. A word is a preposition if it is part of a prepositional phrase. The same word is an adverb if it stands alone.

PREPOSITION   Did you look *inside* the box?
    ADVERB   Did you look *inside*?

PREPOSITION   Walk carefully *down* the icy steps.
    ADVERB   Turn that music *down*!

EXERCISE 14 Finding Prepositional Phrases

Number your paper 1 to 10. Then write the prepositional phrases in the following sentences. There are 20 phrases.

Striking Facts about Lightning

1. Throughout the world nearly 100 lightning flashes occur each second.
2. Despite popular opinion lightning can strike twice in the same place.
3. The average lightning bolt strikes with millions of volts behind it.
4. According to scientific investigations, lightning bolts do not move at the speed of light.
5. Photographs of lightning can be obtained by radar.
6. Benjamin Franklin discovered the connection between electricity and lightning.
7. In 1752, Franklin built the first lightning rod.
8. This device protected homes and other buildings from damage by lightning.
9. If lightning is striking near you, stay away from any tall objects.
10. In spite of contrary advice, get inside a car but don't touch any of the metal parts.

Conjunctions

A *conjunction* connects two or more words or groups of words. *Coordinating conjunctions* are single connecting words. Pairs of connecting words are called *correlative conjunctions.*

> **1i** A **conjunction** connects words or groups of words.

Conjunctions and Interjections

1i–j

Conjunctions			
Coordinating		**Correlative**	
and nor yet		both/and	not only/but also
but or		either/or	whether/or
for so		neither/nor	

Did you feed the *dog* **and** the *cat*? [connects nouns]

Either *type* **or** *write* your reports. [connect verbs]

The flowers were **both** *colorful* **and** *fragrant*. [connect adjectives]

The sun was shining, **yet** the forecast was for rain. [connects sentences]

NOTE: *Subordinating conjunctions* are used to introduce adverb clauses. *(See page 80.)*

Interjections

An *interjection* is a word that expresses an emotion, but it has no grammatical connection with the rest of the sentence. An interjection is separated from the rest of the sentence by an exclamation point or a comma.

1j An **interjection** is a word that expresses strong feeling or emotion.

Wow! I can't believe that I won.
Oh, you dropped your wallet!

EXERCISE 15 Finding Conjunctions and Interjections
Number your paper 1 to 10. Then write each conjunction and interjection in the following sentences.

1. All food-preservation techniques are designed to kill *or* [conj.] to limit the growth of bacterial life.
2. The coat was *both* [conj.] warm *and* [conj.] practical.
3. Salamanders have bulging eyes, long bodies, *and* [conj.] short legs.

21

The Parts of Speech

4. *interj.* Yes! Julio *conj.* not only won the contest *conj.* but also received one hundred dollars in prize money.
5. *conj.* Either the picture of the horse *conj.* or the forest scene would look nice in your room.
6. We should do that now, *conj.* for tomorrow we won't have time.
7. *interj.* Incredible! The graduation exercises had *conj.* neither music *conj.* nor guest speakers.
8. They invited me, *conj.* but I have to work that evening.
9. *interj.* Well, I have heard every explanation *conj.* and excuse now!
10. The Grand Canal in China is 20 times longer than the Panama Canal, *conj.* yet it was completed around A.D. 1300.

EXERCISE 16 Writing Sentences
Write five sentences that follow the directions below.
Sample answers precede this chapter.
1. Use *neither/nor* to connect two nouns.
2. Use *but* to connect two verbs.
3. Use *both/and* to connect two adjectives.
4. Use *and* to connect two adverbs.
5. Use *for* to connect two sentences. (Place a comma before the conjunction *for*.)

EXERCISE 17 Time-out for Review
Number your paper 1 to 10. Write the underlined words in each sentence. Then beside each one, write its part of speech: *noun*, *pronoun*, *verb*, *adjective*, *adverb*, *preposition*, *conjunction*, or *interjection*.

Birds on the Move

1. The mystery of *adj.* bird migration has *adv.* never been satisfactorily explained.
2. In their flight south, birds *adv.* supposedly are seeking a greater *adj.* food supply.
3. Some birds, *prep.* like the blue jay, do not migrate, *conj.* yet they still find food throughout the winter months.
4. How do birds find their way *prep.* from their *adj.* winter home to their summer home?
5. *interj.* Alas! Many theories have been offered, *conj.* but no one knows for sure.
6. Certain *n.* information, nevertheless, has been gathered from *n.* years of close observation.
7. Some birds *v.* travel *prep.* along well-established flyways.

22

8. Most small birds usually [adv.] fly at night, guiding themselves [pron.] by the stars.
9. The champion globe-trotter [n.], the arctic tern, nests in the Arctic and winters [v.] in the Antarctic.
10. This [pron.] is a trip of over 12,000 miles in each [adj.] direction.

PARTS OF SPEECH REVIEW

Language is very much like music. Various words—like notes—are extremely versatile. *Inside,* for example, can be used as four different parts of speech. Its use in a particular sentence determines its part of speech.

NOUN	The **inside** of the box was lined with velvet.
ADJECTIVE	We just received some **inside** information.
ADVERB	Let's go **inside**.
PREPOSITION	Lights were on **inside** the house.

Following is a summary of the eight parts of speech that will help you determine how a word is used in a sentence.

NOUN   Is the word naming a person, a place, a thing, or an idea?

After careful **thought Janet** moved to **New York** and found a **job** in a **matter** of **days**.

PRONOUN   Is the word taking the place of a noun?

Anything you say to **him** will certainly be helpful to **us**.

VERB   Is the word showing action? Does the word link the subject with another word in the sentence?

They **are** attractive, but they **cost** too much.

ADJECTIVE   Is the word modifying a noun or a pronoun? Does it answer the question *What kind? Which one(s)? How many?* or *How much?*

The **full yellow** moon was very **bright**.

23

The Parts of Speech

ADVERB
: Is the word modifying a verb, an adjective, or another adverb? Does it answer the question *How? When? Where?* or *To what extent?*

  The cars and the trucks crawled **very slowly** through the **extremely** busy intersection.

PREPOSITION
: Is the word showing a relationship between a noun or a pronoun and another word in the sentence? Is it part of a phrase?

  According to the forecast, a storm is approaching **from** the ocean.

CONJUNCTION
: Is the word connecting words or groups of words?

  Neither Kim **nor** Lee can go with us, **for** they have to work tonight.

INTERJECTION
: Is the word expressing strong feeling?

  Ouch! A bee just stung me.

EXERCISE 18 Determining Parts of Speech

Write the underlined word in each sentence. Then beside each one, write its part of speech: *noun, pronoun, verb, adjective, adverb, preposition, conjunction,* or *interjection.*

1. Were you <u>outside</u>? — adv.
2. I'll take <u>those</u>. — pron.
3. He sings quite <u>well</u>. — adv.
4. Birds eat <u>insects</u>. — n.
5. <u>Those</u> books are mine. — adj.
6. We walked <u>across</u>. — adv.
7. Those are <u>for</u> us. — prep.
8. <u>That</u> was made for me! — pron.
9. The lawnmower uses <u>oil</u>. — n.
10. <u>Either</u> pen will do. — adj.
11. You should <u>oil</u> your skates. — v.
12. These <u>insect</u> bites itch. — adj.
13. I'll take <u>that</u> piece. — adj.
14. Please <u>wallpaper</u> the hall. — v.
15. Let's leave, <u>for</u> I'm tired. — conj.
16. Ted is <u>outside</u> the door. — prep.
17. I don't want <u>either</u>. — pron.
18. <u>Well</u>! I don't believe it. — interj.
19. He's <u>across</u> the street. — prep.
20. I like that <u>wallpaper</u>. — n.

EXERCISE 19 Labeling Parts of Speech

Copy the following sentences, skipping a line between each one. Then above each word, label its part of speech, using the following abbreviations. Remember that the articles *a*, *an*, and *the* are adjectives.

Parts of Speech Review

noun = *n.* adjective = *adj.* conjunction = *conj.*
pronoun = *pron.* adverb = *adv.* interjection = *interj.*
verb = *v.* preposition = *prep.*

EXAMPLE The enthusiastic audience applauded the actors.

ANSWER The enthusiastic audience applauded the actors.
         adj.   adj.   n.   v.   adj.   n.

1. A herd of shaggy buffalo was thundering across the grassy plain.
2. The weather was unusually cloudy for the first week in August.
3. We went to the mountains and stayed for two weeks.
4. You should have written the directions yourself.
5. Vikings may have landed in the Western Hemisphere before Columbus.
6. The apple trees in the park have been blooming for three weeks now.
7. Oh! Our reports for English class are due tomorrow.
8. The hikers struggled toward the mountaintop through the deep snow.
9. Someone told me something about a trip on Saturday and Sunday through the mountains.
10. Under the direction of Mr. Sanchez, the band will perform in the parade on Memorial Day.

Application to Writing

In certain situations some nouns are more effective than others. This is also true of some verbs and adjectives. When you write, choose your words with care. Books such as a thesaurus can help you use specific words that will make your writing clearer and more interesting to your readers.

	GENERAL	MORE SPECIFIC
NOUN	baby	newborn, infant, toddler, tot
VERB	eat	nibble, devour, gobble, consume
ADJECTIVE	beautiful	exquisite, stunning, elegant

NOTE: Substituting a proper noun for a common noun whenever possible will also add vividness to your writing.

He raced down the **street**.   He raced down **Elm Street**.

25

The Parts of Speech

EXERCISE 20 Substituting Specific Nouns, Verbs, and Adjectives

Write at least two specific words for each of the following general words. Then write sentences that use two of the specific words from each column. Use a dictionary or a thesaurus if necessary.

Sample answers:

NOUNS	VERBS	ADJECTIVES
1. sport hockey, bowling	6. fall sprawl, tumble	11. funny comic, hilarious
2. officer captain, general	7. won gained, achieved	12. old ancient, antique
3. car hardtop, Mustang	8. move shift, transfer	13. little tiny, minute
4. song melody, ballad	9. run jog, sprint	14. fast brisk, speedy
5. food pizza, carrots	10. said declared, snapped	15. plain modest, simple

Sample sentence: Hockey is one sport in which I have succeeded.

EXERCISE 21 Writing Sentences

Choose an object, such as a piece of sports equipment, an item of clothing, or a household appliance. Then write a five- to ten-sentence advertisement for it. Include as many specific nouns, verbs, and adjectives as possible.
Answers will vary.

CHAPTER REVIEW

Number your paper 1 to 50. Write the numbered, underlined words. Then beside each one, write its part of speech: *noun,* *pronoun, verb, adjective, adverb, preposition,* or *conjunction.*

Edgar Allan Poe (1809–1849)

   Edgar Allan Poe is known (1)<u>around</u> the world as the (2)<u>master</u> of the (3)<u>Gothic</u> tale of gloom and (4)<u>terror</u>. (5)<u>Poe</u> (6)<u>said</u> that he had (7)<u>little</u> use for the "dull realities of (8)<u>science</u>." His poems and stories (9)<u>take</u> readers (10)<u>to</u> the world of dreams and nightmares. (11)<u>It</u> (12)<u>is</u> a grim world of ancient (13)<u>vaults</u> dimly lit by flickering torches, of (14)<u>heavy</u> doors grating on (15)<u>their</u> (16)<u>hinges</u>, and of shadowy phantoms. In (17)<u>this</u> nightmare world, readers (18)<u>often</u> see (19)<u>half-mad</u> characters act out fiendish (20)<u>schemes</u> of revenge. His fictional world is (21)<u>also</u> occupied (22)<u>by</u> bereaved people crazed (23)<u>with</u> grief, yearning for (24)<u>things</u> that cannot be.
   Poe (25)<u>himself</u> did (26)<u>not</u> have a (27)<u>happy</u> life. Born in (28)<u>Boston</u> in 1809, he lost (29)<u>both</u> parents (30)<u>early</u> in his

Chapter Review

life. (31)He[pron.] was later raised by a wealthy New England (32)couple[n.], (33)but[conj.] he often (34)quarreled[v.] with his foster father. (35)After[prep.] several (36)false[adj.] starts, Poe (37)became[v.] (38)both[conj.] a writer of stories (39)and[conj.] a reviewer for several (40)magazines[n.]—but only (41)for[prep.] a short period of (42)time[n.]. (43)At[prep.] the (44)young[adj.] age of 40, Poe (45)died[v.] in misery and (46)poverty[n.]. His (47)influence[n.], nevertheless, is (48)still[adv.] felt throughout the (49)literary[adj.] world (50)today[adv.].

MASTERY TEST

Number your paper 1 to 10. Write the underlined words in each sentence. Then beside each word, write its part of speech: *noun*[n.], *pronoun*[pron.], *verb*[v.], *adjective*[adj.], *adverb*[adv.], *preposition*[prep.], *conjunction*[conj.], or *interjection*[interj.].

1. The eager[adj.] players suddenly[adv.] appeared on the field.
2. Some[adj.] gardeners plant the crab apple because of[prep.] its attractive flowers and delicious fruit.
3. In winter[n.] the howl of the wind sounds[v.] eerie.
4. Hurray[interj.]! The baseball team[n.] won the championship.
5. What[pron.] can you tell me about[prep.] the accident?
6. Something[pron.] is wrong[adj.] with the telephone.
7. Watch the soup or[conj.] it will boil over[adv.].
8. The winter[adj.] winds howl with eerie sounds[n.].
9. Some[pron.] of the beans and[conj.] a few of the tomatoes are ripe.
10. The extremely[adv.] large bear invaded their campsite[n.].

27

Chapter 2   The Sentence Base

OBJECTIVES
- To identify a group of words as a sentence.
- To identify subjects in an inverted sentence.
- To identify compound subjects and verbs.
- Application: To create sentence variety by combining two sentences into one with a compound subject or a compound verb.
- To identify direct and indirect objects.
- To identify objective complements.
- To identify predicate nominatives and predicate adjectives.
- Application: To identify and be able to use the six basic sentence patterns to create a variety of sentences.

MOTIVATIONAL ACTIVITY
Have your students fill in each blank in the following sentences.
1. The large orange _____ _____ above the rooftops.
2. The dark, mysterious _____ _____ by the streetlight.

Point out that neither group of words makes any sense without the missing words, which are the subjects and the verbs.

TEACHING SUGGESTIONS
Subjects and Predicates *(pages 29–36)*
After you give the Diagnostic Test on page 28, you should be able to determine how much time you should spend on this section.

Before your students take the Diagnostic Test, however, you may want to remind them that a subject is never part of a prepositional phrase *(pages 18–20)* and that a sentence in inverted order should be turned around to its natural order.

Sample Board Sentences
Identical <u>twins</u> always <u>have</u> the same eye color. [subject and verb]
Both <u>honeybees</u> and <u>bumblebees</u> <u>gather</u> pollen and <u>live</u> in colonies. [compound subjects and verbs]

Complements *(pages 36–43)*
Being able to identify complements is essential before your students learn the nominative and objective cases of pronouns *(Chapter 7)*. Because this section is so important, you may want to review action verbs and linking verbs *(pages 8–11)* before you begin.

If you cover this section with your basic students, you may want to disregard formal identification of the patterns. Some basic students cannot expand sentences without running into serious structural difficulties. For these students, concentration upon simple, direct expression should be the goal.

Sample Board Sentences
A grapefruit tree can bear 1,500 <u>pounds</u> of fruit each year. [direct object]
Sesame Street teaches young children <u>letters</u> and <u>numbers.</u> [indirect objects]
The Siberian tiger is the largest *member* of the cat family. [predicate nominative]
Pure sea water is <u>colorless.</u> [predicate adjective]

ACTIVITIES FOR DIFFERENT ABILITIES
Basic Students
ACTIVITY 1 Subjects and Verbs
To provide additional practice, duplicate the following sentences. Then have your students draw one line under each subject and two lines under each verb.

Mount Rainier National Park
1. Not far from Tacoma and Seattle towers Mount Rainier.
2. In the continental United States, there are only four taller peaks.
3. The top of the mountain was reached for the first time in 1870.
4. Mount Rainier National Park was established in 1899.

Chapter 2 a

The Sentence

5. This magnificent mountain is part of the beautiful Cascade Range.
6. The entire Cascade Range is a series of dormant volcanoes.
7. The cone of Mount Rainier was built by successive volcanic eruptions.
8. On the higher slopes are many glaciers.
9. Forests of hemlocks and other evergreens cover the lower slopes.
10. Captain George Vancouver of the British Navy named Mount Rainier after a friend.

ACTIVITY 2 Compound Subjects and Verbs

To provide additional practice, duplicate the following sentences. Then have your students draw one line under each subject and two lines under each verb.

United States Coins

1. Before the adoption of the Constitution, no central system or plan for uniform coinage existed.
2. In 1792, the United States Mint began the issuance of coins and stabilized the currency.
3. Because of the public distrust of paper money, the Mint issued no paper money for 70 years but concentrated on coins.
4. Gold and silver were the most popular metals for coins.
5. The gold coins had greater value and were issued regularly until 1933.
6. In the United States, nickel, copper, tin, zinc, and even steel have been used in coins.
7. Throughout the years certain coins were tried but were finally dropped.
8. A half-cent piece and a twenty-cent piece were once minted but are no longer in circulation.
9. The famous Indian head penny lasted from 1859 to 1909 and was very popular.
10. The Liberty head nickel, the "Mercury" dime, and the Liberty quarter still circulate along with more recent coins.

ACTIVITY 3 Complements

To provide additional practice, duplicate the following sentences. Then have your students underline each complement and label each one, using the following abbreviations: *d.o.* = direct object; *i.o.* = indirect object; *p.n.* = predicate nominative; *p.a.* = predicate adjective.

The Wizard of Oz

1. After failures in several fields, L. Frank Baum wrote *The Wizard of Oz*.
2. It was immediately successful.
3. Baum gave the reading public the first great American fairy tale.
4. The colorful characters of Oz have become favorites because of the movie version.
5. The success of *The Wizard of Oz* astonished Baum.
6. He did not originally plan a series of books about Oz.
7. He wrote many other books for children.
8. None captured the hearts and the imaginations of his audience in the same way.
9. Children were enthusiastic about the Oz characters.
10. After Baum's death in 1919, other authors continued the series for many years.

Advanced Students

ACTIVITY 1 Subjects and Verbs

To provide additional practice, duplicate the following sentences. Then have your students draw one line under each subject and two lines under each verb.

Air Plants

1. Air plants do not have roots in the ground or in the water. (*Air plants* is a compound noun.)
2. They attach themselves to other living things or grow on stones and buildings.
3. Dust, fog, rain, and dew furnish air plants with food and moisture.
4. Most air plants gather moisture through their leaves.
5. Certain ferns and tree-dwelling orchids of the tropics dangle their roots in the moist air and extract water from it.

Chapter 2 b

The Sentence

6. In their dwelling place on the surface of trees and other vegetation, air plants make their own food, provide their own self-protection, and live their own lives.
7. In the cold and temperate climates are found many small air plants, like lichens, liverworts, and mosses.
8. In the moist, shady forests along the equator live the largest and most beautiful types of air plants.
9. There are large quantities of low-hanging Spanish moss on many cypress trees in the southern part of the United States.
10. From the stems of this air plant comes the stuffing material for some upholstery.

ACTIVITY 2 Complements
To provide additional practice, duplicate the following sentences. Then have your students underline each complement. (Have them use the abbreviations on page 50 to label each complement.)

Presidents
1. Beverly lent me an article giving curious facts about presidents.
2. The writer of the article considers our presidents fascinating human beings.
3. George Washington had a set of ivory false teeth.
4. Of all our presidents to date, James Madison was the shortest.
5. James Buchanan was our only bachelor president.
6. Woodrow Wilson gave sheep the White House lawn for grazing.
7. William Henry Harrison was president for only 31 days.
8. During his speech at Gettysburg, Lincoln was sick with a mild case of smallpox.
9. John Quincy Adams was a Harvard graduate.
10. The people of the United States elected John F. Kennedy president at the age of 44.

ACTIVITY 3 Writing Sentences
Have your students write ten to fifteen sentences that explain what would happen or what they would do if they suddenly became invisible. To reinforce the grammar taught in this section, you also may want to have your students underline each subject once and each verb twice.

ADDITIONAL PRACTICE
Basic Students
   Teacher's Resource Book:
   pages 90–92
   Workbook: pages 15–28
Average Students
   Teacher's Resource Book:
   pages 93–95
   Workbook: pages 15–28
Advanced Students
   Teacher's Resource Book:
   pages 96–98

REVIEW EXERCISES AND TESTS
Student Text
   Diagnostic Test: page 28
   Chapter Review: page 50
   Mastery Test: page 51
Teacher's Resource Book
   Chapter 2 Test: pages 11–12
   (Also available as spirit duplicating masters.)

ADDITIONAL ANSWERS
EXERCISE 11 Writing Sentences *(page 43)*
Sample answers:
1. White pines have five-needle <u>clusters</u>. (d.o.)
2. Our guidance counselor gave <u>us</u> some <u>booklets</u>. (i.o., d.o.)
3. Ms. Keene calls my <u>poetry</u> <u>lyrical</u>. (d.o., o.c.)
4. My beautiful Persian kitten was a <u>stray</u>. (p.n.)
5. The weather stayed <u>cold</u> and <u>gusty</u> all week. (p.a., p.a.)

The Sentence

EXERCISE 2 Diagraming Sentences *(pages 47–48)*

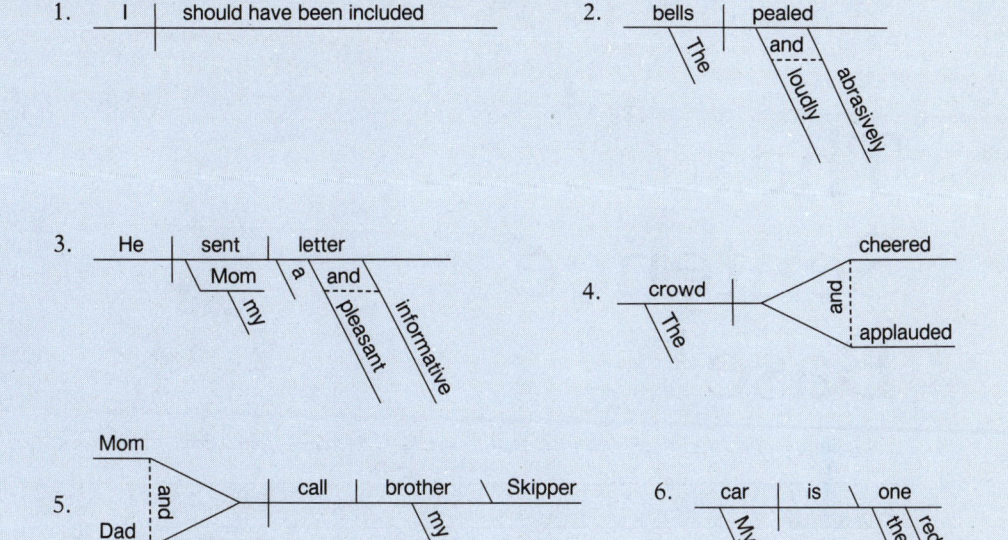

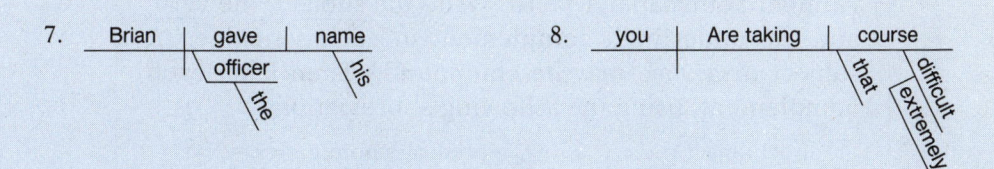

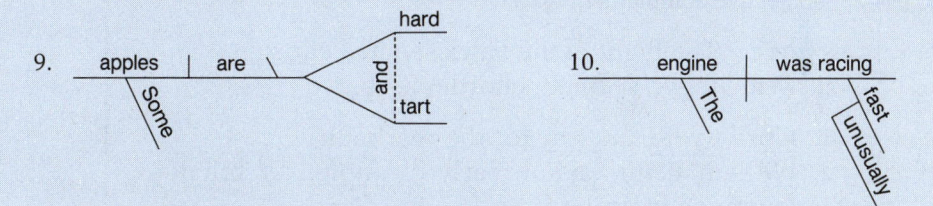

1. I | should have been included

2. The bells | pealed (and) loudly, abrasively

3. He | sent | letter — Mom (a, and) — my, pleasant, informative

4. The crowd | cheered and applauded

5. Mom and Dad | call | brother — Skipper — my

6. My car | is \ one — the, red

7. Brian | gave | name — officer (the), his

8. you | Are taking | course — that, extremely difficult

9. Some apples | are \ hard and tart

10. The engine | was racing — unusually fast

EXERCISE 14 Writing Sentences *(page 49)*

Sample answers:
1. The four girls walked to school together in the morning. (S-V)
2. My aunt in New York finally bought a new house. (S-V-O)
3. The president of the company sent my mother an explanation of the bill. (S-V-I-O)
4. My brother became captain of the hockey team. (S-V-N)
5. The flowers in the garden are especially fragrant. (S-V-A)
6. The invitation to the party made me happy. (S-V-O-C)

Chapter 2 d

2 The Sentence Base

For additional practice for this chapter, see the Teacher's Resource Book and the Workbook.

DIAGNOSTIC TEST

Number your paper 1 to 10. Write the subject, the verb, and the underlined complement in each sentence. (A subject or a verb may be compound.) Then label each complement, using the following abbreviations.

direct object = *d.o.* predicate nominative = *p.n.*
indirect object = *i.o.* predicate adjective = *p.a.*
objective complement = *o.c.*

EXAMPLE The flight of the hawk seemed effortless.
ANSWER flight, seemed, effortless — *p.a.*

1. Flora wrote an essay [d.o.] for the yearbook.
2. William Penn was an early champion [p.n.] of religious tolerance in America.
3. Tchaikovsky and Beethoven wrote music [d.o.] for both the violin and the piano.
4. He wrapped the package yesterday and mailed it [d.o.] this morning.
5. Four runners in the marathon are physicians [p.n.].
6. The guide showed us [i.o.] the Paul Revere House.
7. There were many seats still empty [p.a.].
8. Is she the one [p.n.] in the tweed suit?
9. The jury's verdict has made everyone happy [o.c.].
10. Daniel and I have built the wrens [i.o.] a birdhouse.

28 *Note: Kinds of sentences are taught on pages 89–90.*

Subjects and Predicates

Have you ever stopped and watched the workers at a construction site? If you have, you probably noticed someone mixing cement, sand, stones, and water. Together these elements form concrete. From the concrete many things can be made—everything from a sidewalk to a skyscraper.

A sentence is very similar to concrete. It is formed by combining two essential elements: a subject and a verb. Sometimes a third element is also needed—a complement. Once you know what these elements are and how to put them together, your results will be limitless. You can create everything from simple sentences to compound-complex sentences.

THE SENTENCE

Sometimes in conversation, individual words or only parts of a sentence are expressed. Still they can be understood. The context, or setting, of these incomplete expressions gives them meaning. The result is not always the same, however, when individual words or parts of a sentence are written. These incomplete expressions, called *fragments*, often leave a reader bewildered and in need of more information to understand what was intended. Each group of words you write that begins with a capital letter and ends with an end mark must express a complete thought. *(See pages 99–101 for more information about fragments.)*

2a A **sentence** is a group of words that expresses a complete thought.

FRAGMENT	SENTENCE
One of my friends.	One of my friends is Bart Holmes.
Turned the corner.	He turned the corner too fast.
After the game.	I went home after the game.
To play soccer.	We wanted to play soccer.

SUBJECTS AND PREDICATES

To express a complete thought, a sentence must have a subject and a predicate. The subject tells the reader who or what the sentence is about. The predicate completes the thought by telling something about the subject.

The Sentence Base

2b A sentence has two main parts: a **subject** and a **predicate**. A *subject* names the person, place, thing, or idea the sentence is about. A *predicate* tells something about the subject.

COMPLETE SUBJECT	COMPLETE PREDICATE
My cousin Pedro	is driving us to the airport.
The tree in our backyard	extends above the roof.
The cars on the turnpike	moved slowly during the storm.
Daffodils	flourished in the empty lot.

Simple Subjects and Predicates

Within each complete subject is a simple subject; and within each complete predicate is a simple predicate, or *verb*.

2c A **simple subject** is the main word in the complete subject.

2d A **simple predicate,** or **verb,** is the main word or phrase in the complete predicate.

In the following examples, the simple subjects and the verbs are in heavy type.

⎯⎯ complete subject ⎯⎯ ⎯⎯ complete predicate ⎯⎯
A **windmill** on Nantucket **grinds** cornmeal to this day.

⎯⎯ complete subject ⎯⎯ ⎯⎯ complete predicate ⎯⎯
Our **camp** in the woods **was** a welcome sight after the hike.

⎯⎯ complete subject ⎯⎯ ⎯⎯ complete predicate ⎯⎯
The **City Bank** on Elm Street **is offering** high interest rates.

In the last example, *City Bank* is a single proper noun; therefore, both words are the simple subject. Notice also that the verb phrase *is offering* is considered the verb of the sentence. *(See pages 11-12 for more information about verb phrases.)*

NOTE: Throughout the rest of this book, the term *subject* will refer to a simple subject. The term *verb* will refer to a simple predicate, which may be a single verb or a verb phrase.

Finding Subjects and Verbs. To find the subject, first find the action verb or the linking verb in the sentence. *(See page 10 for lists of linking verbs.)* If the verb is an action verb, ask yourself *Who?* or *What?* before the verb. The answer to either question

Subjects and Predicates

2b–d

will be the subject. In the following examples, each subject is underlined once, and each verb is underlined twice.

Grandfather has made some delicious banana bread. [The action verb is *has made*. Who has made? *Grandfather* is the subject.]

The light was shining in my eyes. [The action verb is *was shining*. What was shining? *Light* is the subject.]

If the verb is a linking verb, ask yourself, *About whom or what is some statement being made?* The answer to that question will be the subject.

Craig will become the editor of the yearbook. [The linking verb is *will become*. About whom is some statement being made? *Craig* is the subject.]

The purple and red sunset was spectacular. [The linking verb is *was*. About what is some statement being made? *Sunset* is the subject.]

NOTE: When you look for a subject and a verb, it is sometimes helpful if you first eliminate all modifiers and prepositional phrases from the sentence. *A subject is never part of a prepositional phrase.*

The students at Haywood High worked together in the cleanup drive. [*Students* is the subject; *worked* is the verb.]

EXERCISE 1   Finding Subjects and Verbs
Number your paper 1 to 10. Then write the subject and the verb in each sentence.

Four Faces

1. A huge carving is located on the side of a mountain in South Dakota.
2. This magnificent sculpture honors Washington, Lincoln, Jefferson, and Theodore Roosevelt.
3. The carved faces of the presidents average 60 feet, from the top of the head to the chin.
4. This is proportionate to men 456 feet tall.
5. The ambitious creator of these colossal figures was Gutzon Borglum.
6. In 1927, he began his work.

31

The Sentence Base

7. Fourteen years later his <u>work</u> <u>came</u> to an end with his death.
8. His <u>son</u>, however, <u>continued</u> the project.
9. Within a year the <u>project</u> <u>was completed</u>.
10. Today the <u>sculptures</u> <u>comprise</u> the Mount Rushmore National Memorial.

Position of Subjects

Normally a subject will precede a verb in a sentence. Sometimes, however, a sentence will appear in *inverted order*—the verb or part of a verb phrase will come before the subject. In the following examples, each subject is underlined once, and each verb is underlined twice.

Questions. A question sometimes results in an inverted sentence. To find the subject and the verb in a question, turn the question around to make a statement.

QUESTION   <u>Have</u> <u>you</u> <u>finished</u> your report?
STATEMENT <u>You</u> <u>have finished</u> your report.

***There* and *Here*.** A sentence beginning with *there* or *here* is in inverted order. To find the subject and the verb, turn the sentence around to its natural order.

INVERTED ORDER   Here <u>are</u> two <u>messages</u>.
NATURAL ORDER   Two <u>messages</u> <u>are</u> here.

INVERTED ORDER   There <u>is</u> no <u>electricity</u> in the old house.
NATURAL ORDER   No <u>electricity</u> <u>is</u> in the old house.
[Sometimes *there* or *here* must be dropped before the sentence can be placed in its natural order.]

Emphasis or Variety. Sometimes a sentence might be written in inverted order for emphasis or variety. To find the subject and the verb, put the sentence into its natural order.

INVERTED ORDER   Over the roof of the house <u>scampered</u> the <u>squirrel</u>.
NATURAL ORDER   The <u>squirrel</u> <u>scampered</u> over the roof of the house.

32

> Subjects and Predicates

> 2e

Understood You. In all the preceding examples, the subjects appeared in the sentences—even though they were not in their normal position. In a command or a request, the subject *you* will not actually appear in the sentence, but it is understood to be there. In the following examples, *you* is the understood subject of each sentence.

> Make a dessert for the party. [*You* is the understood subject; *make* is the verb.]
>
> Ben, take your sister with you. [*You* is the understood subject—even though the person receiving the command is named. *Take* is the verb.]

> **EXERCISE 2** Finding Subjects and Verbs in Inverted Sentences

Number your paper 1 to 10. Then write the subject and the verb in each sentence. If the subject is an understood *you*, write it in parentheses.

(you)
1. Be home in time for dinner.
2. Where does the Missouri River join the Mississippi?
3. There were no permanent English settlers in New England before the Pilgrims.
4. Was the concert on Saturday a success?
5. Here in the newspaper are the rules of the contest.
6. In the heart of the beautiful bluegrass region of Kentucky lies the city of Lexington.
7. Have you ever attended a performance of *Aïda*?
8. There are several kinds of delicate wild flowers in these woods.

(you)
9. Read the next chapter in your history text.
10. Along the Hudson River can be found reminders of our Dutch heritage.

Compound Subjects and Verbs

A sentence can have more than one subject and more than one verb.

> 2e ▶ A **compound subject** is two or more subjects in one sentence that have the same verb and are joined by a conjunction.

33

The Sentence Base

In the following examples, each subject is underlined once, and each verb is underlined twice.

Cattle and sheep are grazing in the far field.
My sister and her friend are taking ballet lessons.

2f A **compound verb** is two or more verbs that have the same subject and are joined by a conjunction.

Bill bought new earphones but gave them to Patsy.
The snow on the slopes of the Rockies melts and waters the surrounding lowlands.

A sentence can have both a compound subject and a compound verb.

The balloons and streamers decorated the backyard and added to the festive spirit.

EXERCISE 3 Finding Compound Subjects and Verbs

Number your paper 1 to 10. Then write the subjects and the verbs in the following sentences.

1. We rode the subway into the city and walked to the Museum of Science.
2. Pictures and statues are cleverly arranged in my aunt's antique shop.
3. Tree squirrels either find a hollow tree for a home or build a nest on a branch.
4. The handsome actor seems very confident but often misses his cues.
5. William Henry Harrison caught pneumonia during his inauguration and died a month later.
6. Both Flora and I went to the same theater but saw different movies.
7. The root system of a plant anchors the plant and absorbs water.
8. We drove to the river and fished for trout.
9. Both my aunt and my grandmother are living with my family.
10. The blood type of a person is inherited and remains the same throughout his or her life.

Sentence Combining

2f

EXERCISE 4 Time-out for Review

Number your paper 1 to 10. Then write the <u>subjects</u> and the <u>verbs</u> in the following sentences. If the subject is an understood *you*, write it in parentheses.

1. The <u>trip</u> from New York to Philadelphia <u>took</u> a day and a half by stagecoach.
2. <u>Did</u> the lacrosse <u>team</u> <u>practice</u> on Tuesday?
3. The first <u>bridge</u> across the Mississippi River <u>was built</u> by the Rock Island Railroad in 1855.
4. <u>I</u> <u>swept</u>, <u>washed</u>, and <u>waxed</u> the kitchen floor.
5. There <u>are</u> some extra <u>hangers</u> in the hall closet.
6. From the airplane <u>jumped</u> the <u>sky divers</u>.
7. <u>Waxed paper</u>, the dictating <u>machine</u>, and the <u>mimeograph</u> <u>were</u> some of Thomas Edison's inventions.
8. (you) <u>Plant</u> your daffodils before the first frost.
9. <u>Do</u> <u>you</u> <u>know</u> O. Henry's real name?
10. The <u>people</u> on the committee and the <u>mayor</u> <u>met</u> and <u>discussed</u> plans for the new library.

Application to Writing

You can avoid repetition in your writing by using a compound subject or a compound verb to combine sentences.

TWO SENTENCES	Philadelphia <u>is</u> rich in historical attractions. <u>Boston</u> and <u>Charleston</u> <u>are</u> also rich in historical attractions.
ONE SENTENCE WITH A COMPOUND SUBJECT	<u>Philadelphia</u>, <u>Boston</u>, and <u>Charleston</u> <u>are</u> rich in historical attractions.
TWO SENTENCES	<u>Lola</u> <u>went</u> to the mall. <u>She</u> <u>bought</u> a new tape.
ONE SENTENCE WITH A COMPOUND VERB	<u>Lola</u> <u>went</u> to the mall and <u>bought</u> a new tape.

EXERCISE 5 Combining Sentences

Combine each pair of sentences into one sentence, using a compound subject or a compound verb. *Sample answers:*

1. Squirrels~and chipmunks~ don't sleep right through the winter. ~~Chipmunks don't sleep through the winter either~~.

35

The Sentence Base

2. Bears﹐hibernate﹐Other animals, like skunks and bats, also hibernate. [edits: *and* inserted, *O* lowercased, *also* deleted]
3. After hibernation animals are weak﹐ They soon regain their strength with food. [edit: *but* replaces *They*]
4. The *Lakeview Chronicle* is published once a month﹐ It is distributed to everyone in town. [edit: *and* replaces *It is*]
5. The ghost of Jacob Marley rattled its chains﹐ It warned Scrooge of other ghostly visitors. [edit: *and* replaces *It*]
6. The colors﹐of Persian rugs have made them famous. Their patterns have also made them famous. [edits: *and patterns* inserted, second sentence deleted]
7. Marcy﹐and Chris﹐are trying out for the field-hockey team. My sisters are also trying out. [edits: *and my sisters* inserted, second sentence deleted]
8. We finally dragged ourselves over the jutting ledge﹐ We saw the summit only a few hundred feet away. [edit: *and* replaces *We*]
9. Members of the search party threw a line to the stranded climber﹐ They carefully raised him above the ledge. [edit: *and* replaces *They*]
10. The Franklins﹐are on vacation. The Andersons are also on vacation. [edits: *and the Andersons* inserted, second sentence deleted]

COMPLEMENTS

Sometimes only a subject and a verb are needed to express a complete thought. At other times a third element, called a *complement,* is needed. As its name suggests, a complement completes the meaning of a sentence. Neither of the following sentences would be complete without the complements *flashlight* and *confident.*

Keith held the **flashlight.** Jason seems **confident.**

There are five kinds of complements. *Direct objects, indirect objects,* and *objective complements* complete the meaning of action verbs. The other two kinds of complements, called *subject complements,* are *predicate nominatives* and *predicate adjectives.* Subject complements complete the meaning of linking verbs.

Direct Objects

A direct object follows an action verb and completes the meaning of the sentence by naming the receiver of the action.

Complements

Only a sentence with an action verb will have a direct object.

2g > A **direct object** is a noun or a pronoun that receives the action of the verb.

To find a direct object, ask *What?* or *Whom?* after an action verb. Notice in the third example that a direct object can be compound.

                   d.o.
David dried the **dishes** after dinner. [David dried what? *Dishes* is the direct object.]

                d.o.
Did you see **Gretchen** at the dance? [You did see whom? *Gretchen* is the direct object.]

                              d.o.   d.o.
At the market Ingrid bought **corn** and **tomatoes**. [Ingrid bought what? *Corn* and *tomatoes* are the compound direct object.]

A complement is never part of a prepositional phrase. *(See page 19 for more information about prepositional phrases.)*

Roscoe rode with us to the game. [Since *us* and *game* are objects of prepositions, they cannot be direct objects.]

EXERCISE 6 Finding Direct Objects

Number your paper 1 to 10. Then write each direct object. If a sentence does not have a direct object, write *none* after the number.

1. At the last minute, we changed our plans.
2. Call Lucinda before six o'clock.
3. Gold prospectors of the 1890s often carried food and supplies on dogsleds to their camps.
4. The documentary lasted for three and a half hours. *(none)*
5. Which costume should I wear to the party?
6. Termites had invaded the massive timbers of the historical building.
7. The auditorium was filled with hundreds of concerned citizens. *(none)*
8. Our weekend plans include a game of tennis, a swim at the lake, and a hike around the reservoir.

37

The Sentence Base

9. The drum major led the <u>parade</u> down Center Street.
none 10. In 1790, only 5 percent of the American population lived in cities.

Indirect Objects

If a sentence has a direct object, it also can have another complement called an *indirect object.*

2h ▶ An **indirect object** answers the questions *To or for whom?* or *To or for what?* after an action verb.

To find an indirect object, first find the direct object. Then ask yourself, *To or for whom?* or *To or for what?* after the direct object. An indirect object always comes before a direct object in a sentence. Notice in the third example that an indirect object can be compound.

             i.o.   d.o.
Mr. Gorman loaned **them** two **bicycles** for the weekend. [*Bicycles* is the direct object. Mr. Gorman loaned bicycles to whom? *Them* is the indirect object.]

          i.o.   d.o.
I gave the **fence** a new **coat** of paint. [*Coat* is the direct object. (*Paint* is the object of the preposition *of*.) I gave a coat of paint to what? *Fence* is the indirect object.]

        i.o.   i.o.   d.o.
Brad told **Paul** and **Scott** the **details** of his plan. [*Details* is the direct object. Brad told the details to whom? *Paul* and *Scott* are the compound indirect object.]

Like a direct object, an indirect object cannot be part of a prepositional phrase.

         i.o.   d.o.
My aunt sent **me** some **shells** from California. [*Me* is the indirect object. It comes before the direct object *shells* and is not part of a prepositional phrase.]

              d.o.
My aunt sent some **shells** to me from California. [*Me* is not the indirect object because it follows the direct object *shells* and is the object of the preposition *to*.]

Complements

2h–i

EXERCISE 7 Finding Indirect Objects and Direct Objects

Number your paper 1 to 10. Write each indirect object and each direct object. Then label each one *indirect object* (i.o.) or *direct object* (d.o.).

1. The principal told Jerry (i.o.) the news (d.o.) about the scholarship.
2. The coach offered each team member (i.o.) extra help (d.o.).
3. Mom gave the newspaper (i.o.) a quick glance (d.o.).
4. Leroy sold balloons (d.o.) to the children at the fair.
5. Did you sell Cathy (i.o.) and Carlos (i.o.) the tickets (d.o.)?
6. Pay your dues (d.o.) to the club's treasurer.
7. Mr. Green rented us (i.o.) his cottage (d.o.) for two weeks.
8. Please send me (i.o.) your new address (d.o.) and telephone number (d.o.) as soon as possible.
9. I gave my room (i.o.) a thorough search (d.o.).
10. Did you buy Mom (i.o.) and Dad (i.o.) a card (d.o.) for their anniversary?

Objective Complements

If a sentence has a direct object, it can also have another object called an *objective complement*.

2i An **objective complement** is a noun or an adjective that renames or describes the direct object.

To find an objective complement, first find the direct object. Then ask the question *What?* after the direct object. An objective complement will always follow the direct object. Notice in the third example that an objective complement can be compound.

The juniors chose Jessie class **president.** [*Jessie* is the direct object. The juniors chose Jessie what? *President* is the objective complement. It follows the direct object and renames it.]

We consider Paula the best **applicant** for the job. [*Paula* is the direct object. We consider Paula what? *Applicant* is the objective complement. It follows the direct object and renames it.]

39

The Sentence Base

Patrick painted his room **blue** and **green**. [*Room* is the direct object. Patrick painted his room what? *Blue* and *green* are the compound objective complement. These words follow the direct object and describe it.]

EXERCISE 8 Finding Complements

Number your paper 1 to 10. Write each complement in the following sentences. Then label each one *direct object*, *indirect object*, or *objective complement*.

1. The sudden noise made me afraid.
2. Mr. LaMar called us a cab.
3. The American people elected Franklin D. Roosevelt president four times.
4. Many people consider the dogwood the most beautiful tree.
5. Aunt Helen gave Will an album for his birthday.
6. Amanda considers Rico her best friend.
7. Many poets have called the oak majestic.
8. The jury found the defendant guilty.
9. Unusual circumstances can make ordinary people heroes.
10. Heavy insulation will make our house warm and cozy.

Subject Complements

Two kinds of complements, called *subject complements*, follow linking verbs: *predicate nominatives* and *predicate adjectives*. (See page 10 for lists of linking verbs.)

> **2j** A **predicate nominative** is a noun or a pronoun that follows a linking verb and identifies, renames, or explains the subject.

To find a predicate nominative, first find the subject and the linking verb. Then find the noun or the pronoun that follows the verb and identifies, renames, or explains the subject. Notice in the second example that a predicate nominative can be compound.

The flower for February is the **violet**. [violet = flower]

Victor is both the **secretary** and the **treasurer** of the computer club. [secretary and treasurer = Victor]

Complements

2j–k

A predicate nominative is never part of a prepositional phrase.

Mindy is only **one** of my friends. [*One* is the predicate nominative. *Friends* is the object of a preposition.]

2k A **predicate adjective** is an adjective that follows a linking verb and modifies the subject.

To find a predicate adjective, first find the subject and the linking verb. Then find an adjective that follows the verb and describes the subject. Notice in the second example that a predicate adjective can be compound.

That woman is **famous**. [*Famous* describes the subject.]

The down quilt was **light** but extremely **warm**. [*Light* and *warm* both describe the subject.]

NOTE: Do not confuse a regular adjective with a predicate adjective. Remember that a predicate adjective follows a linking verb and describes the *subject*.

REGULAR ADJECTIVE   The buffalo is a very **large** animal.

PREDICATE ADJECTIVE   The buffalo is very **large**.

EXERCISE 9 Finding Subject Complements

Number your paper 1 to 10. Write each subject complement in the following sentences. Then label each one *predicate nominative* (p.n.) or *predicate adjective* (p.a.).

1. Four of our first five presidents were Virginians. [p.n.]
2. The rooms in their new apartment are spacious. [p.a.]
3. The fox terrier is small [p.a.] but energetic. [p.a.]
4. Upon the death of George VI, Elizabeth became queen. [p.n.]
5. All snow crystals are hexagonal. [p.a.]
6. The chickadee is one [p.n.] of America's friendliest birds.
7. During the rehearsal the director remained calm [p.a.] and courteous. [p.a.]
8. Clarissa Harlow Barton was the founder [p.n.] of the American Red Cross.

41

The Sentence Base

9. The blood of some insects is colorless. (p.a.)
10. The quilters of Appalachia are skillful artists. (p.n.)

EXERCISE 10 Time-out for Review

Number your paper 1 to 20. Write each complement. Then label each one, using the following abbreviations.

direct object = d.o.   predicate nominative = p.n.
indirect object = i.o.   predicate adjective = p.a.
objective complement = o.c.

Eva Jessye

1. The life of Eva Jessye is one (p.n.) of the nation's many success stories.
2. Her family in Coffeyville, Kansas, was very poor. (p.a.)
3. In spite of personal hardship, her parents gave Eva (i.o.) a college education. (d.o.)
4. As a young woman, Eva chose New York (d.o.) for her home.
5. There she formed the Original Dixie Jubilee Singers. (d.o.)
6. In 1929, the director, King Vidor, gave her (i.o.) an unusual opportunity. (d.o.)
7. She became the choir director (p.n.) for a Hollywood film.
8. In addition to all her other responsibilities, she wrote music (d.o.) of her own.
9. In 1931, radio station WNBC broadcast one (d.o.) of her pieces.
10. The late composer George Gershwin considered Eva (d.o.) a major musical talent. (o.c.)
11. She directed the choir (d.o.) for Gershwin's *Porgy and Bess*.
12. During all these busy years, she was friendly (p.a.) with people from all walks of life.
13. Some of her good friends were Bill Robinson (p.n.), Paul Robeson (p.n.), and Louis Armstrong (p.n.).
14. She even knew members (d.o.) of presidential families.
15. Her many experiences gave her (i.o.) a strong personal philosophy (d.o.) about life.
16. Injustice of any kind made her (d.o.) angry (o.c.).
17. Her disposition, however, remained pleasant (p.a.) and easy-going (p.a.) throughout her life.
18. Pittsburg State University in Kansas gave Eva (i.o.) an office (d.o.) on its campus.
19. It also created a special museum (d.o.) for her 8,500 pounds of mementos and documents.
20. Her native state of Kansas also proclaimed October 1 Eva (d.o.) Jessye Day (o.c.).

Diagraming

EXERCISE 11 Writing Sentences
Write five sentences. Use each of the five kinds of complements at least once. Then label each complement.
Sample answers precede this chapter.

DIAGRAMING THE SENTENCE BASE

A diagram is a picture or a blueprint of a sentence. By arranging a sentence in diagram form, you can often see the relationship between the parts of a sentence more easily.

Subjects and Verbs

The subject and the verb of a sentence go on a baseline and are separated by a vertical line. Capital letters are included in diagrams, but not punctuation. Notice in the second and third examples that compound subjects and verbs are placed on parallel lines. The conjunction is placed on a broken line between them.

Everyone has arrived.

| Everyone | has arrived |

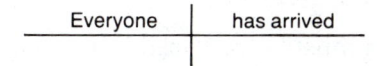

Robert, Harry, and Tim are leaving.

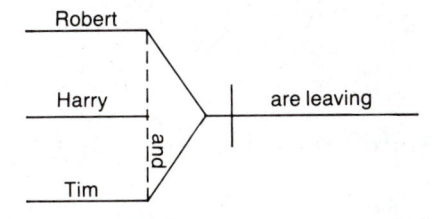

Beth both sang and danced.

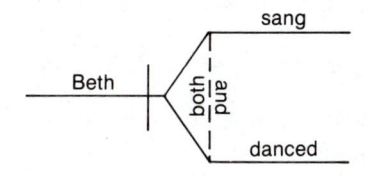

43

The Sentence Base

Inverted Order. A sentence in inverted order is diagramed like a sentence in natural order.

Are you finished?

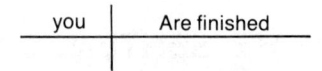

```
    you    |  Are finished
```

Understood Subjects. When the subject of a sentence is an understood *you*, put parentheses around *you* in the subject position.

Wait!

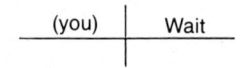

```
   (you)   |  Wait
```

Adjectives and Adverbs

Adjectives and adverbs are diagramed on a slanted line below the words they modify. Notice in the second example that a conjunction joining two modifiers is placed on a broken line between them.

Our front steps must be repaired immediately.

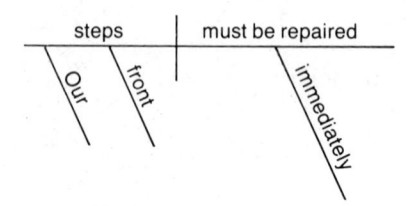

```
    steps         |  must be repaired
   \Our \front                   \immediately
```

The small but sturdy truck rides smoothly and efficiently.

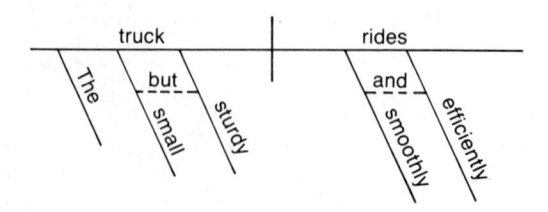

```
    truck         |      rides
  \The \but                \and
    \small \sturdy      \smoothly \efficiently
```

NOTE: Possessive pronouns, such as *our* in the first example, are diagramed like adjectives.

An Adverb That Modifies an Adjective or Another Adverb. This kind of adverb is connected to the word it modifies. It is written on a line parallel to the word it modifies.

The unusually eager runner started too quickly.

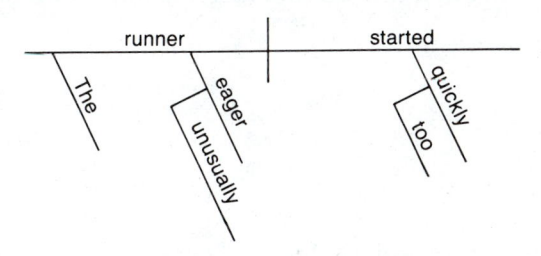

Complements

Since a complement is part of the sentence base, all complements, except an indirect object, are diagramed on the baseline.

Direct Objects. A direct object is separated from the verb by a vertical line that stops at the baseline. Notice in the second example that the parts of a compound direct object are placed on parallel lines. The conjunction is placed on a broken line between the direct objects.

We hid her presents.

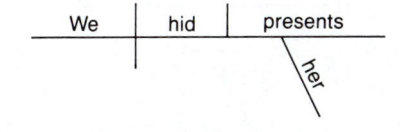

I need a black pen and a red pencil.

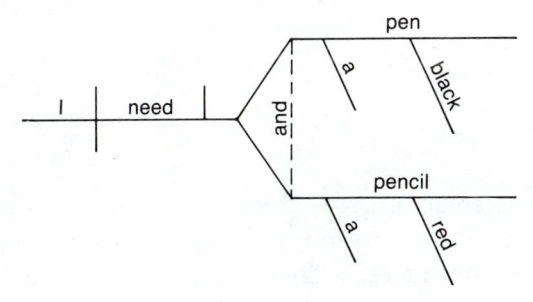

45

The Sentence Base

Indirect Objects. An indirect object is diagramed on a horizontal line that is connected to the verb. Notice in the second example that the parts of a compound indirect object are diagramed on separate parallel lines. The conjunction is placed on a broken line connecting the indirect objects.

Give me an answer.

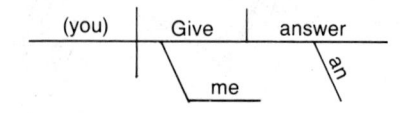

```
(you) | Give  | answer
          \         \ an
           \ me
```

He loaned Patty and me his new tape recorder.

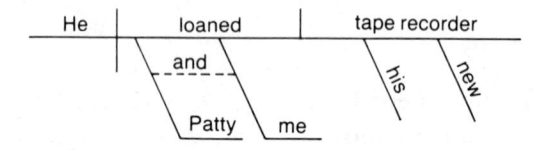

```
He | loaned   | tape recorder
      \ and \        \ his  \ new
   Patty  me
```

Objective Complements. An objective complement is placed to the right of the direct object. The two complements are separated by a slanted line that points back toward the direct object. Notice in the second example that a compound objective complement is diagramed on parallel lines.

The team elected Betsy captain.

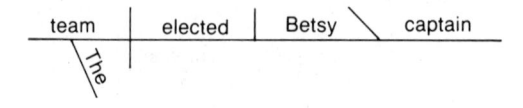

```
team | elected | Betsy \ captain
  \ The
```

We consider her capable and dependable.

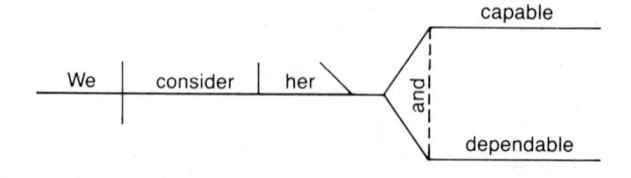

```
                          capable
                         /
We | consider | her \  / and
                         \
                          dependable
```

Subject Complements. A predicate nominative and a predicate adjective are diagramed in the same way. They are placed on the baseline after the verb. They are separated from the verb by

46

a slanted line that points back toward the subject. Notice in the third example that a compound subject complement is diagramed on parallel lines.

Lamb is my favorite meat.

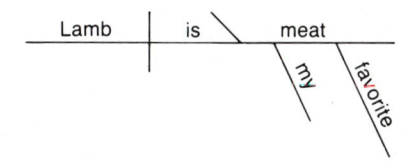

That movie was very scary.

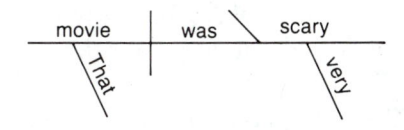

The prizes will be a radio and a camera.

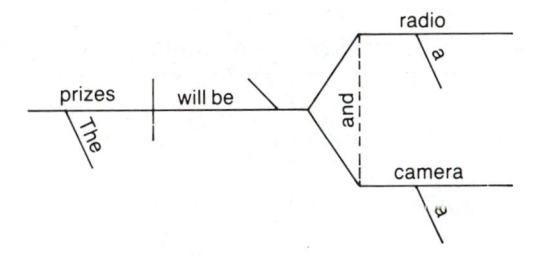

EXERCISE 12 Diagraming Sentences

Diagram the following sentences or copy them. If you copy them, draw one line under each subject and two lines under each verb. Then label each complement, using the following abbreviations. *Diagrams precede this chapter.*

direct object = *d.o.*
indirect object = *i.o.*
objective complement = *o.c.*
predicate nominative = *p.n.*
predicate adjective = *p.a.*

1. I should have been included.
2. The bells pealed loudly and abrasively.
3. He sent my mom a pleasant and informative letter.
4. The crowd cheered and applauded.
5. Mom and Dad call my brother Skipper.
6. My car is the red one.

47

The Sentence Base

7. Brian gave the officer his name. [i.o. over officer, d.o. over name]
8. Are you taking that extremely difficult course? [d.o. over course]
9. Some apples are hard and tart. [p.a. over hard, p.a. over tart]
10. The engine was racing unusually fast.

Application to Writing

From the three primary colors of red, blue, and yellow, every conceivable color can be made. From the six basic sentence patterns, nearly every conceivable sentence can be written. Once you know these sentence patterns, you can create an endless number of fresh, original sentences by simply adding prepositional phrases and other modifiers.

PATTERN 1: S-V (subject-verb)

S V
Rain fell.

S V
The light rain fell continuously throughout the day.

PATTERN 2: S-V-O (subject-verb-direct object)

S V O
Grandmother knits sweaters.

S V O
My grandmother in Toledo expertly knits warm ski sweaters.

PATTERN 3: S-V-I-O (subject-verb-indirect object-direct object)

S V I O
Signs gave hikers directions.

S V I
The signs at the fork in the road gave the two weary hikers
O
adequate directions.

PATTERN 4: S-V-N (subject-verb-predicate nominative)

S V N
Graduates become engineers.

Sentence Patterns

```
    S              V         N
College graduates sometimes become engineers for large
computer companies.
```

PATTERN 5: S-V-A (subject-verb-predicate adjective)

```
  S    V      A
Flowers are beautiful.
```

```
    S                         V             A
The flowers in the centerpiece are exceptionally beautiful.
```

PATTERN 6: S-V-O-C (subject-verb-direct object-objective complement)

```
 S     V    O    C
Most elected Paul captain.
```

```
  S                              V       O     C
Most of the players enthusiastically elected Paul captain of
the football team.
```

EXERCISE 13   Determining Sentence Patterns

Write the sentence pattern that each sentence follows.

Women Were There Too!

1. The great patriots of the Revolutionary period are famous.   S-V-A
2. We often hear about the founding fathers but not about the founding mothers.   S-V
3. Many Colonial women made great contributions to our country's freedom.   S-V-O
4. Historic events made Mercy Otis Warren a playwright.   S-V-O-C
5. Her plays gave other patriots courage for the struggle.   S-V-I-O
6. Molly Pitcher was at her husband's side in battle.   S-V
7. Deborah Sampson was one of the bravest heroines of the Revolution.   S-V-N
8. This fearless soldier received two nearly fatal wounds.   S-V-O
9. The Army finally gave her an honorable discharge.   S-V-I-O
10. These truly courageous women played an important role in the formation of this country.   S-V-O

EXERCISE 14   Writing Sentences

Write two sentences that follow each sentence pattern. Add prepositional phrases and other modifiers. Then after each sentence, identify the pattern.

Sample answers precede this chapter.

49

The Sentence Base

CHAPTER REVIEW

A. Number your paper 1 to 10. Write the subjects and the verbs in the following sentences. If the subject is an understood *you*, write it in parentheses.

1. My car has not been running properly for a month.
2. Both volleyball and basketball were created by Americans.
3. There are four eggs in that robin's nest.
4. Did the history test seem hard to you?
5. In the music room stood an antique harp.
6. Bulls and boars cannot tell one color from another.
7. (you) Try this homemade jam with your toast.
8. How many percussion instruments does our orchestra contain?
9. My sister was put on the committee and ran the next meeting.
10. Lee and I found a stray tiger cat, fed it, and located a home for it.

B. Number your paper 1 to 10. Write the complements in the following sentences. Then label each one, using the following abbreviations.

direct object = *d.o.*   predicate nominative = *p.n.*
indirect object = *i.o.*   predicate adjective = *p.a.*
objective complement = *o.c.*

1. Switzerland has four official languages. (d.o.)
2. That slice of watermelon tasted cool (p.a.) and refreshing (p.a.).
3. The shortstop threw the ball (d.o.) to the catcher.
4. The ant family contains 15,000 different species. (d.o.)
5. The reporters found the astronauts (d.o.) healthy (o.c.) and cheerful (o.c.).
6. The huge bear's trail through the brush was obvious (p.a.) and distinct (p.a.).
7. The directors unanimously elected Victor (d.o.) president (o.c.) of the hardware company.
8. The most famous geyser in Yellowstone National Park is Old Faithful. (p.n.)
9. Don't give Chris (i.o.) the combination (d.o.) to my locker.
10. George Washington planned one (d.o.) of the first American canals.

Chapter Review

MASTERY TEST

Number your paper 1 to 10. Write the <u>subject</u>, the <u>verb</u>, and the underlined complement in each sentence. (A subject or a verb may be compound.) Then label each complement, using the following abbreviations.

direct object = *d.o.*   predicate nominative = *p.n.*
indirect object = *i.o.*   predicate adjective = *p.a.*
objective complement = *o.c.*

1. <u>I</u> will never <u>forget</u> <u>that</u>. *(d.o.)*
2. <u>Cowboys</u>, <u>lumberjacks</u>, and railroad <u>workers</u> <u>have been</u> the <u>subject</u> of many ballads. *(p.n.)*
3. The <u>MacArthurs</u> <u>sent</u> <u>Sal</u> a bushel of oranges from Florida. *(i.o.)*
4. Destructive volcanic <u>eruptions</u> and <u>earthquakes</u> <u>are</u> comparatively <u>rare</u>. *(p.a.)*
5. <u>Will</u> <u>Cara</u> <u>be</u> the store <u>manager</u> soon? *(p.n.)*
6. <u>We</u> <u>painted</u> the living room a light <u>green</u>. *(o.c.)*
7. <u>Norman</u> <u>gave</u> <u>us</u> good directions to the civic center. *(i.o.)*
8. There <u>are</u> <u>tickets</u> still <u>available</u>. *(p.a.)*
9. <u>Windmills</u> <u>were</u> once a very common <u>sight</u> along the Massachusetts coast. *(p.n.)*
10. The <u>quarterback</u> <u>ran</u> to the right and <u>threw</u> the <u>ball</u> into the end zone. *(d.o.)*

Chapter 3   Phrases

OBJECTIVES

- To identify a prepositional phrase used as an adjective or as an adverb.
- To punctuate adverb phrases correctly.
- To identify appositives and appositive phrases.
- To punctuate appositives and appositive phrases correctly.
- To identify participles and participial phrases and to explain their function in a sentence.
- To punctuate participial phrases correctly.
- To identify gerunds and gerund phrases.
- To identify infinitives and infinitive phrases and to explain their function in a sentence.
- To identify and to correct misplaced and dangling modifiers.
- Application: To eliminate short, choppy sentences by using phrases to combine sentences.

MOTIVATIONAL ACTIVITY

Write the following group of words on the board and then ask your students if the group of words is a complete sentence.

The flag flying at half mast.

They should easily recognize this group of words as a fragment. Then ask them if they can correct the fragment in two different ways.

The flag was flying at half mast. [adding a helping verb]

We saw the flag flying at half mast. [adding a subject and a verb and keeping the participial phrase]

If they are able to correct the fragment by keeping the participial phrase, they will understand one of the main concepts of this chapter.

TEACHING SUGGESTIONS

Depending upon the level of your basic students, you may choose to teach only prepositional phrases, appositive phrases, and participial phrases.

Average and advanced students, however, should find the study of this entire chapter helpful for creating sentence variety, clarifying thoughts, showing relationships, expanding ideas, and making sentences more mature.

Prepositional Phrases *(pages 53–56)*

Before you begin this section, you may want to review the list of prepositions on page 19 and possibly do Exercise 14 on page 20. Since it is important that your students understand that a prepositional phrase can function as an adjective or an adverb, you also may want to write the following additional examples on the board.

SINGLE ADJECTIVE The <u>front</u> steps must be repaired.
ADJECTIVE PHRASE The steps <u>in the front</u> must be repaired.

The single adjective and the adjective phrase both answer the question *Which ones?* and modify the noun *steps*.

SINGLE ADVERB You must call Marvin <u>soon</u> because he's leaving.
ADVERB PHRASE You must call Marvin <u>in the next ten minutes</u> because he's leaving.

The single adverb and the adverb phrase both answer the question *When?* and modify the verb *must call*.

Participles and Participial Phrases *(pages 59–62)*

To help your students avoid confusing a participle with the main verb in a verb phrase, you may want to point out that a verb form ending in *-ing* can only be the verb if it has a helping verb. A participle will *never* have a helping verb. When students incorrectly use a participle for the main verb, a fragment results.

FRAGMENT The horse *running* across the plain.
VERB The horse *was running* across the plain.

Chapter 3 a

PARTICIPLE The horse *running across the plain* was a magnificent creature.

NOTE: Many of the *-ing* forms in this chapter have evolved from participles and are now listed in the dictionary as adjectives. For simplicity in teaching, however, these words are called *participles* in this text.

Gerunds and Gerund Phrases *(pages 62–64)*

With more advanced classes, you may want to emphasize the use of the possessive form of a noun or a pronoun before a gerund phrase. In spoken English it is common to hear people use the objective form.

NONSTANDARD All of us agreed to *him* driving us to the airport.
STANDARD All of us agreed to *his* driving us to the airport.

At this point you may want to cover the use of an apostrophe to form the possessive of nouns on pages 271–273.

Infinitives and Infinitive Phrases *(pages 64–67)*

With your advanced students, you may want to explain that sometimes an infinitive has a subject. After verbs of believing, commanding, expecting, knowing, letting, making, telling, thinking, wishing, and the like, the infinitive may have a subject. If the subject of an infinitive is a pronoun, it is in the objective case.

Thomas Jefferson urged *everyone* to take an active part in government. [*Everyone* is the subject of the infinitive phrase *to take an active part in government.*]

Some Americans wanted *George Washington* to become king. [*George Washington* is the subject of the infinitive phrase *to become king.*]

Sample Board Sentences

One of the oldest games, <u>played since prehistoric time,</u> is marbles. [participial phrase]

Kingfishers build nests by <u>tunneling into the sides of riverbanks.</u> [gerund phrase]

Joseph Lister was the first doctor <u>to use antiseptic methods during surgery.</u> [infinitive phrase]

ACTIVITIES FOR DIFFERENT ABILITIES

<u>Basic Students</u>

ACTIVITY 1 Prepositional Phrases

To provide additional practice, duplicate the following sentences. Then have your students underline each prepositional phrase and label it *adj.* or *adv.* The number in parentheses at the end of a sentence indicates the number of phrases in that sentence.

The Great Ice Age

1. During a number of periods in the earth's history, great sheets of ice formed over large portions of the earth's surface. (6)
2. These glaciers were a mile high in some areas. (1)
3. One glacier in New York covered the tops of the Catskill Mountains. (2)
4. The glaciers acted as rivers of ice and ground everything in the paths before them. (4)
5. States with extensive glacial erosion include New York, Ohio, and Iowa. (1)
6. A section of Wisconsin, oddly enough, was surrounded by a glacier, but not covered. (2)
7. At one time or other, all the New England states were under ice. (2)
8. Minnesota and Wisconsin have many lakes because of the glacial melt. (1)
9. During the Ice Age, mastodons and saber-toothed tigers lived in North America. (2)
10. After the retreat of the ice, some animals remained and survived under harsh conditions. (3)

ACTIVITY 2 Appositive Phrases

Have your students write sentences that include the following expressions as appositive phrases. Remind your students to punctuate the appositives correctly *(page 57)*. Give them the following example before they begin.

Phrases

EXAMPLE our next-door neighbors
POSSIBLE ANSWER The Evans, our next door neighbors, are moving soon.

1. my best friend
2. an outstanding athlete
3. a famous singer
4. the tallest building on Main Street
5. the best show on television

ACTIVITY 3 Verbals

If you teach verbals to basic students, the emphasis should be more on the recognition and use of verbals, rather than on the labeling of them. Seven of the following ten items include sentence fragments in which a verbal is used instead of a verb. Have your students find the fragments and change the verbal to a verb. Give your students the following example before they begin.

EXAMPLE The ducks landing and skidding on the frozen pond.
CHANGED TO VERB The ducks *were* landing and skidding on the frozen ice.

1. Buster Keaton's *The General* made in the 1920s.
2. The Academy Awards given for outstanding performances and contributions to the American movies.
3. Motorboats were pulling waterskiers across the lake.
4. That beautiful piece of Navaho jewelry carved out of silver and turquoise.
5. Butter made for at least 4000 years and sometimes used as a food by primitive people.
6. The audience at the football game was standing during the national anthem.
7. A new plastic developed by a toy company and never before offered to the public.
8. The coach juggling the lineup to find the winning combination.
9. The turkey was introduced from America into Europe.
10. The Taj Mahal considered by some the most beautiful building in the world.

Advanced Students

ACTIVITY 1 Appositive Phrases

Have your students combine each of the following pairs of sentences by substituting an appositive phrase for one of the sentences. Remind your students to punctuate the appositives correctly *(page 57).*

Women with Interesting Occupations

1. Anne Worsham Richardson has been called the Bird Lady of Charleston. She paints her subjects from life.
2. She has a federal permit to keep birds in a wildlife sanctuary. This is a natural refuge near her home city of Charleston, South Carolina.
3. She is like a doctor with many patients. These are injured birds from nearby areas.
4. Richardson is also a fine painter. She paints the birds during their recovery period.
5. Angelina Martinez is a famous Santa Fe tinsmith. She began learning her craft when she was 14.
6. Martinez has fashioned many tin objects. These are artistic creations of great beauty.
7. Modern machinery does not appeal to Martinez. She is a follower of the old craft.
8. Another interesting woman is Cherie Appleton. She is a dog-psychology instructor.
9. Unstable dogs are pets with serious behavior problems. These dogs usually reflect difficulties in the environment of their owners.
10. In fact, for Appleton, an important part of training a pet is training the owner. The owner is often the cause of the difficulty.

ACTIVITY 2 Punctuating Participial Phrases

To provide additional practice, duplicate the following sentences. After your students have underlined each participial phrase, tell them to punctuate each one as needed *(page 60).*

Oases in the Sahara

1. The Sahara covering approximately 3,500,000 square miles is the largest desert in the world.
2. Extinct volcanoes crossing the

Phrases

Sahara from west to east form a chain of mountains.
3. Narrow strips of fertile land scattered along the base of the Atlas Mountains break up the vast stretch of desert.
4. These fertile areas called oases are resting places for weary travelers.
5. Some oases linked to the outside world by landing fields have grown into towns or villages.
6. An oasis moistened by springs produces tropical fruits and grain.
7. The dates grown in an oasis are among the world's finest.
8. Discovered south of the Atlas Mountains by geologists vast oil deposits add greatly to the wealth of the Sahara.
9. Today buses and trucks carrying passengers and freight cross the Sahara in all directions.
10. Following ancient trails made by caravans modern vehicles wind their way from oases to oases.

ACTIVITY 3 Gerund Phrases
To provide additional practice, duplicate the following sentences. Then have your students underline each gerund phrase and write how it is used in the sentence.

Valuable Assistants
1. Through the ages people have found unusual ways of setting animals to work.
2. After domesticating the larger animals, farmers sought ways of working with other animals.
3. Human cleverness has even discovered ways of benefiting from the activities of insects.
4. Using spiders' nets benefits fishermen.
5. These nets are capable of holding a three-pound fish.
6. Another clever scheme was capturing fireflies for their light.
7. By bottling these beetles, one explorer devised a flashlight.
8. Long ago some doctors used leeches for sucking blood from patients.
9. Some people have even enjoyed making necklaces of colorful insects.

10. Eating honey from a beehive has provided nourishment for lost hikers.

ACTIVITY 4 Participles and Gerunds
To emphasize the importance of using the possessive before a gerund, have your students discuss the difference between the following sentences.
1. I could visualize him winning the speech contest. [*Him* is the direct object of *could visualize*. The participle *winning* describes *him*.]
2. I understand his wanting a job. [The gerund *wanting* is the direct object of *understand*. The possessive *his* must precede the gerund.]

Then have your students choose the correct alternative in parentheses in the following sentences.
1. We came upon (Ellen, Ellen's) shaking her head and frowning.
2. I like Alan, but I disliked (him, his) forgetting my birthday.
3. I saw (you, your) walking along the river at sunset.
4. Mother doesn't like (me, my) working so late.
5. It wasn't (them, their) winning that bothered Dean.

ACTIVITY 5 Infinitive Phrases
To provide additional practice, duplicate the following sentences. Then have your students underline each infinitive phrase and write how each phrase is used in the sentence.

Chimpanzees
1. To learn about animal behavior, scientists have tested chimpanzees.
2. Chimpanzees have been taught to operate all kinds of machines.
3. In a famous experiment at Yale University, Chimpanzees learned to operate a "Chimp-O-Mate."
4. To earn chips, the chimpanzees performed certain kinds of work.
5. Then they took the chips to the machine to buy food.
6. Some chimpanzees were willing to put off their purchases to the next day.
7. Others refused to work without immediate payment.

Chapter 3 d

Phrases

8. Sometimes the chimpanzees would give way to impatience and try to shake the machine for oranges or bananas.
9. The chimpanzees, however, quickly learned to use the right method.
10. Scientists study animal behavior to learn more about human actions.

ACTIVITY 6 Verbals
Have your students shorten or combine the following sentences by using participles, gerunds, or infinitives. Give them the following example.
EXAMPLE Paul and I traveled to Sebastian Inlet in order that we might watch the surfing contest.
ANSWER Paul and I traveled to Sebastian Inlet *to watch* the surfing contest.

1. Jan prepared for the cross-country season. She jogged half an hour each morning before school.
2. Amanda climbed to the top of the fire tower. She could see the other climbers still on the ridge below her.
3. Please check your backpacking equipment so that you will be ready for the weekend hike to Bald Mountain.
4. We had a great time at the Twin Lake campsite. We swam. We relaxed.
5. I especially enjoy one activity. I take pictures of historic buildings.
6. Mr. Ronney told us that we should wipe down our bikes after a long trip.
7. At Passover Jewish families have an interesting custom. They hide a half piece of matzo somewhere in the house.
8. The children look for the matzo in order that they might receive a reward.
9. This quest begins the Passover celebration. It sets a happy tone for the eight-day celebration.
10. Passover occurs in March or April. It is a spring festival.

ACTIVITY 7 Writing Sentences
Have your students write ten to fifteen sentences that describe a character from a song. Their sentences should include at least one participial phrase, one gerund phrase, and one infinitive phrase. Have your students underline the phrases and label them. Remind them to check their sentences for proper punctuation.

ADDITIONAL PRACTICE
Basic Students
  Teacher's Resource Book: pages 99–101
  Workbook: pages 29–44
Average Students
  Teacher's Resource Book: pages 102–104
  Workbook: pages 29–44
Advanced Students
  Teacher's Resource Book: pages 105–107

REVIEW EXERCISES AND TESTS
Student Text
  Diagnostic Test: page 52
  Chapter Review: pages 74–75
  Mastery Test: page 75
Teacher's Resource Book
  Chapter 3 Test: pages 13–14
  (Also available as spirit duplicating masters.)

ADDITIONAL ANSWERS
EXERCISE 14 Writing Sentences *(page 67)*
Sample answers:
1. To find a cure for cancer is the doctor's main ambition.
2. I want to take the dog with us on vacation.
3. My plan is to remain here for six months.
4. I don't know which coat to wear to the game.
5. It is too late to call her now.

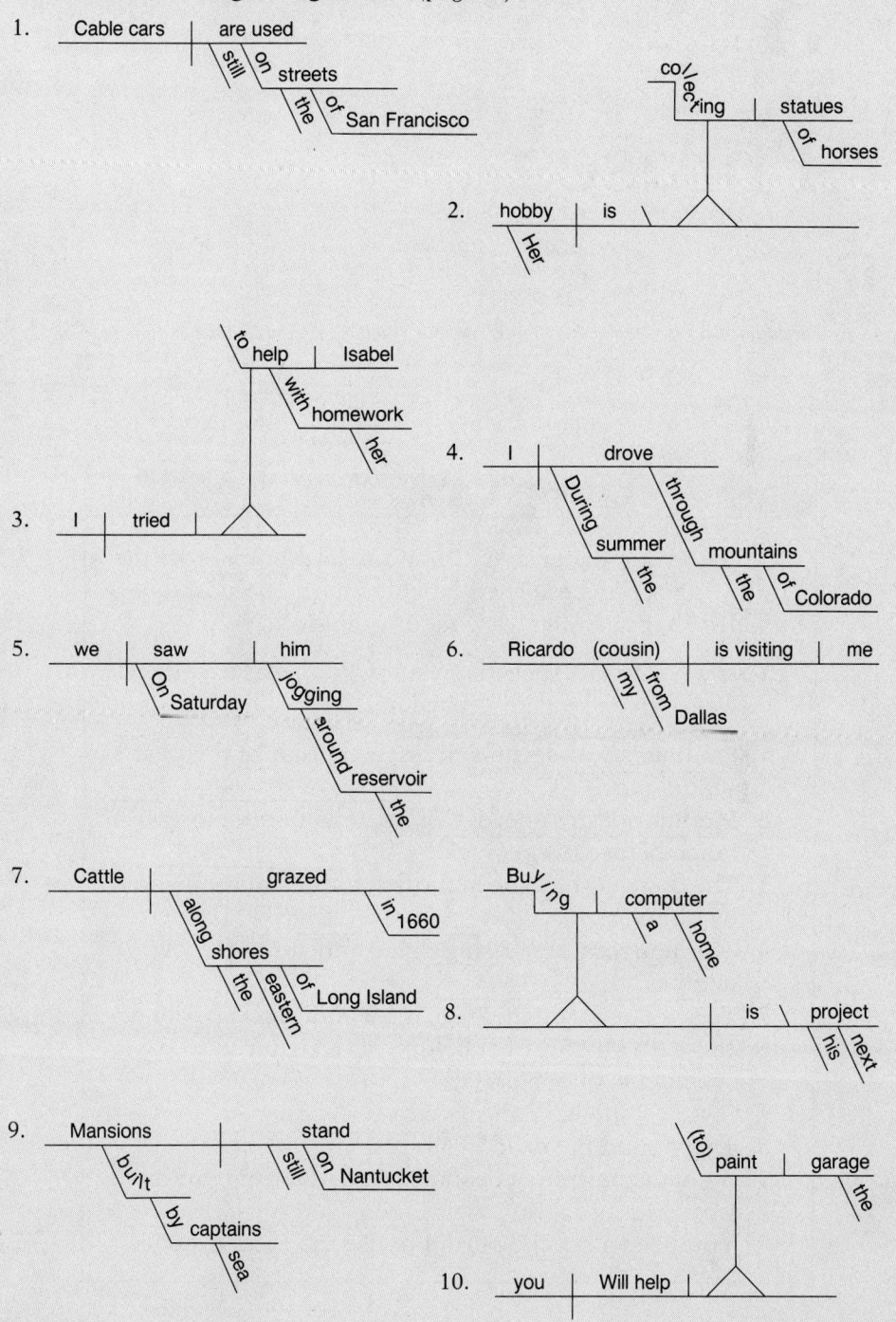

Phrases

EXERCISE 17　Diagraming Phrases *(page 72)*

3
Phrases

For additional practice for this chapter, see the Teacher's Resource Book and the Workbook.

DIAGNOSTIC TEST

Number your paper 1 to 10. Write the phrases in the following sentences. Then label each one *prepositional, appositive, participial, gerund,* or *infinitive.*

EXAMPLE   The last speech, given by Pam, was excellent.
ANSWER   given by Pam — participial

1. Pauline, a wonderful actress, is the star of this year's school play.
2. Mother doesn't approve of my telephoning long distance before five o'clock.
3. The dog may have been the first animal domesticated by humans.
4. The temperature, rising since morning, is now 98 degrees.
5. To see *Hamlet* on the stage is a wonderful experience.
6. In 1820, Missouri bachelors were required to pay a special tax of one dollar.
7. Flying a kite isn't always easy.
8. They found the deed in a box under the bed.
9. A horse chestnut, a beautiful tree, stands in our front yard.
10. You need a special permit to use the local beaches.

52 *Note:* Students need not identify prepositional phrases that occur within verbal phrases.

Adjective Phrases

3a–b

Why should you know about phrases? If you can recognize the different kinds of phrases, you can incorporate them into your writing. By using phrases you can add variety, interest, and maturity to your writing style.

3a > A **phrase** is a group of related words that function as a single part of speech. A phrase does not have a subject and a verb.

In this chapter you will review *prepositional phrases* and *appositive phrases,* as well as the three kinds of verbal phrases: *participial, gerund,* and *infinitive.* All these kinds of phrases share two things in common. First, the words in a phrase work together as a single part of speech. Second, the words in a phrase do not include a subject and a verb.

PREPOSITIONAL PHRASES

A prepositional phrase begins with a preposition and ends with a noun or a pronoun called the *object of a preposition.* (See page 19 for a list of common prepositions.) The prepositional phrases in the following examples are in heavy type.

The outside **of the trunk** was splashed **with paint.**
Instead of that coat, wear the one **in the closet.**

Prepositional phrases are used as adjectives and adverbs.

Adjective Phrases

An *adjective phrase* is a prepositional phrase that is used like a single adjective.

3b > An **adjective phrase** is a prepositional phrase that is used to modify a noun or a pronoun.

A single adjective and an adjective phrase answer the same questions: *Which one(s)?* and *What kind?*

WHICH ONE(S)?   Hand me the bowl **on the counter.**
WHAT KIND?   That is an opportunity **of a lifetime.**

53

Phrases

An adjective phrase usually modifies the noun or the pronoun directly in front of it. That word could be the object of a preposition of another prepositional phrase.

The woman **on the stage** is the mother **of my best friend.**

The light *from* **the lamp** *on* **your desk** is not bright enough.

Once in a while, two adjective phrases will modify the same noun or pronoun.

The carton *of* **milk** *in* **the refrigerator** has turned sour.

Adverb Phrases

An *adverb phrase* is a prepositional phrase that is used like a single adverb.

3c ▸ An **adverb phrase** is a prepositional phrase that is used to modify a verb, an adjective, or an adverb.

A single adverb and an adverb phrase answer the same questions: *Where? When? How? To what extent?* and *To what degree?* Occasionally an adverb phrase will also answer the question *Why?*

WHERE? Park **inside the garage.**

WHEN? The play begins **in ten minutes.**

HOW? Jim will accept the award **without me.**

WHY? No one attended the meeting **on account of the storm.**

As you can see from the preceding examples, an adverb phrase does not always come next to the word it modifies. Notice in the third example that an adverb phrase modifies the whole verb phrase. Also, two or more adverb phrases sometimes modify one verb.

The flour is stored *in* **the cupboard** *on* **the top shelf.**

Before class I will talk **with my guidance counselor.**

54

Adverb Phrases

3c

Although most adverb phrases modify a verb, some modify adjectives or adverbs.

MODIFYING AN ADJECTIVE   Ella was nervous **about the change.**

MODIFYING AN ADVERB   Her birthday occurs early **in the month.**

Punctuation with Adverb Phrases

Do not place a comma after a short introductory adverb phrase—unless it is needed for clarity. You should, however, place a comma after an adverb phrase of four or more words or after several introductory phrases.

NO COMMA   **At three o'clock** we will adjourn.

COMMA   **From the top of the mountain,** we could see two countries.

EXERCISE 1   Identifying Prepositional Phrases

Number your paper 1 to 10. Write the prepositional phrases in the following sentences. Then beside each phrase, write the word or words it modifies.

Sharks

1. The shark swims faster than any other fish in the ocean.
2. The skin of the shark contains many sharp scales like little thumbtacks.
3. The shark's mouth is on the underside of its body.
4. The mouth contains several rows of sharp, triangular teeth.
5. A shark's teeth are hard like steel.
6. Mysterious antibodies in a shark's system eliminate many types of illness.
7. Shark meat is high in nutrition and is eaten in some parts of the world.
8. The liver oil of some sharks contains large amounts of vitamin A.
9. Sharks are found in most seas but are most abundant in warm waters.
10. Despite their reputation sharks rarely attack humans.

55

Phrases

EXERCISE 2 Identifying Uses of Prepositional Phrases

Number your paper 1 to 10. Write the prepositional phrases in the following sentences. Then beside each phrase, label it *adjective* or *adverb*.

1. Gary was the only one from Central High in the race.
2. Before 1929, United States paper money was larger in size.
3. You should find the dictionary next to the atlas on the top shelf of the bookcase.
4. The United States would fit into the continent of Africa approximately three times.
5. The first federal income tax in American history was imposed by Congress in 1862.
6. Because of Malcolm's absence, Roberta will serve refreshments during the play's intermission.
7. The gifts for his birthday were hidden in a corner of Mom's closet.
8. Something outside the house was hitting against the window.
9. Upon the arrival of the team, the crowd gave a roar of welcome.
10. At the end of the concert, we went backstage for some autographs.

EXERCISE 3 Writing Sentences

Write five to ten sentences that describe what you think it would be like inside a space shuttle during takeoff. Then underline each prepositional phrase.

On each face was a look of concentration.

APPOSITIVES AND APPOSITIVE PHRASES

Sometimes you need to identify a noun or a pronoun in a sentence so your reader knows specifically who or what you are talking about. This identifying word is called an *appositive*.

3d An **appositive** is a noun or a pronoun that identifies or explains another noun or pronoun in the sentence.

An appositive usually follows the word it identifies or explains.

My cousin **Susan** will be with me.

Appositives

3d

She is partial to one color, **purple**.

Usually an appositive is used with modifiers to form an *appositive phrase*. Notice in the last sentence in the following examples that one or more prepositional phrases can be part of an appositive phrase.

We avoided Lambert Square, **a dangerous intersection**.

Bart Ramsey, **my sister's boyfriend**, is attending Florida State University in Tallahassee.

We bought her a nice present, **a brown leather purse with a zipper across the top**.

Punctuation with Appositives and Appositive Phrases

If an appositive contains information essential to the meaning of a sentence, no punctuation is needed. Information is essential if it identifies a person, place, or thing. If an appositive or an appositive phrase contains nonessential information, a comma or commas should be used to separate it from the rest of the sentence. Information is nonessential if it can be removed without changing the basic meaning of the sentence. An appositive that follows a proper noun is usually nonessential.

ESSENTIAL   The United States president **Zachary Taylor** was born in 1784. [No commas are used because *Zachary Taylor* is needed to identify which president.]

NONESSENTIAL   Zachary Taylor, **the 12th president of the United States**, was born in 1784. [Commas are used because the appositive could be removed from the sentence.]

EXERCISE 4 Finding Appositives and Appositive Phrases

Write the following sentences and underline each appositive or appositive phrase. Then add a comma or commas where needed.

1. Madoc a Welsh prince was believed by his countrymen to have discovered America 300 years before Columbus.

Phrases

2. Wyandotte Cave, a curious cavern in Indiana, has 35 miles of underground passageways.
3. My sister Kim is a singer in a rock group.
4. Together we bought Coach Braun a nice present, a brown leather wallet.
5. Mount McKinley, the highest summit in North America, is usually wrapped in snow.
6. The thigh bone, the longest bone in the body, is like a hollow tube.
7. Carol is taking lessons from Shirley Adams, a local weaver.
8. Our bulldog Trixie is nearly 13 years old.
9. The wonder drug penicillin was discovered by Sir Alexander Fleming.
10. Those cirrus clouds, the thin feathery ones, are the highest in the sky.

EXERCISE 5 Time-out for Review

Number your paper 1 to 10. Write the prepositional phrases and the appositive phrases in the following sentences. Then label each one *adjective*, *adverb*, or *appositive*.

First Ladies

1. In a letter to her husband, Abigail Adams demanded representation for women in the new government.
2. Eleanor Roosevelt, a future delegate to the United Nations, wrote a regular column for a newspaper.
3. Louisa Adams, wife of John Quincy Adams, read the *Dialogues of Plato* to her sons in the original Greek.
4. A library was installed in the White House at the insistence of Abigail Fillmore.
5. Jacqueline Kennedy once worked for a newspaper and covered Capitol Hill.
6. Bess Truman, the star athlete of her class in finishing school, was the wife of this country's 33rd president.
7. Prior to her husband's term of office, Dolley Madison was the official White House hostess for Thomas Jefferson.
8. Helen Taft was partly responsible for the gift from Japan of 3,000 cherry trees to Washington, D.C.
9. Sarah Knox Polk, the First Lady from 1845 to 1849, opened the Executive Mansion to the public.
10. In the 1800s, Martha Washington was pictured on the one-dollar bill.

Note: Students need not identify prepositional phrases that occur within appositive phrases.

Participles

VERBALS AND VERBAL PHRASES

You are constantly reading sentences with verbals in them. For example, just pick up the sports section of your newspaper. It is full of verbals: a player's *batting* average, the *designated* hitter, and the team's *fighting* spirit—to name a few.

A *verbal* is a verb form that is used as another part of speech. A verbal often has the action and the movement of a verb and can create vitality and interest in your writing. There are three kinds of verbals: *participles, gerunds,* and *infinitives.*

Participles and Participial Phrases

The examples of baseball terms above contain participles.

3e A **participle** is a verb form that is used as an adjective.

Like an adjective, a participle modifies a noun or a pronoun. The participles in the following examples are in heavy type. An arrow points to the word each participle modifies.

From the **raging** fire soared **billowing** clouds of smoke.

His **worried** expression indicated an **unresolved** problem.

There are two kinds of participles: a present participle and a past participle. A *present participle* ends in *-ing,* while a *past participle* has a regular ending of *-ed* or an irregular ending of *-n, -t,* or *-en.*

PRESENT PARTICIPLES   acting, flying, reading, trotting
PAST PARTICIPLES   discarded, torn, lost, written

NOTE: Do not confuse a participle with the main verb of a sentence. A participle will have one or more helping verbs if it is used as a verb.

PARTICIPLE   The **rising** sun awoke me.
VERB   The sun **is rising** earlier these days.

Participial Phrases. Since a participle is a verb form, it can have modifiers and complements. Together these words form a *participial phrase.*

59

Phrases

3f   A **participial phrase** is a participle with its modifiers and complements—all working together as an adjective.

The examples show three variations of the participial phrase.

PARTICIPLE WITH   The fire station **located nearby**
AN ADVERB   promptly responded to the alarm.

PARTICIPLE WITH A   After sunset we saw Venus, **shining**
PREPOSITIONAL PHRASE **in the western sky.**

PARTICIPLE WITH   **Forgetting the directions,** we got
A COMPLEMENT   lost.

NOTE: The present participle *having* is sometimes followed by a past participle.

Having read the book, I was disappointed with the movie.

Punctuation with Participial Phrases

Always place a comma after an introductory participial phrase.

Having spent her last dollar, Jill had to walk home.

Participial phrases, however, that come in the middle or at the end of a sentence may or may not need commas. If the information in a phrase is essential to identify the noun or the pronoun it describes, no commas are needed. If the information is nonessential, commas are needed to separate it from the rest of the sentence. A phrase is nonessential if it contains information that can be removed without changing the basic meaning of the sentence. A participial phrase that follows a proper noun is usually nonessential.

ESSENTIAL   The waterfall **thundering into the canyon below us** is Yellowstone Falls. [No commas are used because the participial phrase is needed to identify which waterfall.]

NONESSENTIAL   Yellowstone Falls, **thundering into the canyon below us,** really consists of two separate waterfalls. [Commas are used because the participial phrase can be removed.]

Participial Phrases

3f

EXERCISE 6 Finding Participial Phrases

Number your paper 1 to 10. Write the participial phrase in each sentence. Then beside each one, write the word or words it modifies.

1. We saw the hawk soaring effortlessly above us.
2. The Sahara, covering more than three million square miles, is the largest desert in the world.
3. The catcher's mitt found on the field belongs to Patrick.
4. This is the first patchwork quilt sewn by my great-aunt.
5. Having served his country, Thomas Jefferson retired in 1809 to his Virginia home.
6. The woman wearing the red dress is a famous actress.
7. We bought an old bookcase made of oak.
8. In 1793, the United States Mint, established in Philadelphia, issued the first coins for general circulation.
9. Looking for her ring, Jody retraced her steps.
10. The wheat stalks, waving slightly in the breeze, stretched as far as the eye could see.

EXERCISE 7 Identifying and Punctuating Participial Phrases

Write the following sentences and underline each participial phrase. Then add a comma or commas where needed.

The Eagle

1. The Romans thinking of the eagle as a symbol of strength and bravery made it their chief military emblem.
2. Replacing the lion the eagle became the favorite design on the shields of medieval knights and noblemen.
3. The American bald eagle pictured on the great seal of the United States is the national bird.
4. Benjamin Franklin objecting to the eagle on the national emblem suggested the wild turkey instead.
5. Viewed from a distance the snow-white head of the American eagle looks bald.
6. Being a solitary bird the eagle keeps the same mate for life.
7. Its nest built in a tree or on a cliff is a lifelong home.
8. The eagle collecting sticks and leaves enlarges its nest.
9. One eagle's nest found in Ohio measured 12 feet deep and weighed 2 tons.
10. Having once been put on the endangered-species list the eagle is making a slow comeback.

61

Phrases

EXERCISE 8 Distinguishing between Verbs and Participles
Write two sentences for each of the following words. The first sentence should use the word as a verb. The second sentence should use the word as a participle in a participial phrase. Use punctuation where needed.

> EXAMPLE purchased
> POSSIBLE ANSWER I purchased a red coat a year ago.
> My red coat, purchased only a year ago, is already worn out.

1. written
2. blazing
3. known
4. amazed
5. winding
6. hidden
7. cracked
8. annoyed
9. hiding
10. cheering

Sample sentences: Sam has written a letter to his father.
Kim is revising poems written several years ago.

Gerunds and Gerund Phrases

A *gerund*, another kind of verbal, looks like a present participle because it ends in *-ing*. A gerund, however, is used as a noun.

> **3g** A **gerund** is a verb form that is used as a noun.

The gerunds in the following examples are in heavy type. Notice that although each gerund ends in *-ing*, each one is used as a noun.

> **Traveling** can be very educational. [subject]
> I have studied **acting**. [direct object]

Gerund Phrases. Gerunds, like participles, can be combined with modifiers and complements to form a *gerund phrase*.

> **3h** A **gerund phrase** is a gerund with its modifiers and complements—all working together as a noun.

A gerund or a gerund phrase can be used in all the ways a noun can be used.

> SUBJECT **Talking loudly** always attracts attention.

Gerunds

3g–h

DIRECT OBJECT	Everyone in my house enjoys **watching the World Series.**
INDIRECT OBJECT	He gave **voting for class president** careful thought.
OBJECT OF A PREPOSITION	She worked eight hours without **taking a break.**
PREDICATE NOMINATIVE	A great thrill for her was **winning the state tennis tournament.**
APPOSITIVE	Dad's hobby, **carving wooden soldiers,** has taught him much about history.

As you see from the previous examples, a gerund in a gerund phrase can be followed by a modifier, a complement, or a prepositional phrase.

NOTE: The possessive form of a noun or a pronoun is used before a gerund and is considered part of the gerund phrase.

Mrs. Lambert insists on ***our* typing our compositions.**

EXERCISE 9   Finding Gerund Phrases

Number your paper 1 to 10. Write the gerund phrases in the following sentences. Then underline each gerund.

1. By eating many tons of insects a year, birds greatly help American farmers.
2. Mrs. Emerson encourages our using several research sources.
3. Penguins often travel great distances by tobogganing on their bellies over the ice.
4. Pepe's family objects to his practicing the trumpet after 10:00 P.M.
5. A dictionary can often be used for determining the origin of a word.
6. Fun in the winter often includes skiing down slopes and skating on the lake.
7. Powdered graphite is excellent for lubricating locks.
8. Noah Webster's important project, writing his dictionary, took 18 years.
9. She tried swimming very fast.
10. My parents had counted on John's finding a part-time job.

Phrases

EXERCISE 10 Determining the Uses of Gerund Phrases

Number your paper 1 to 10. Write each <u>gerund phrase</u>. Then label the use of each one, using the following abbreviations.

subject = *subj.*   object of a preposition = *o.p.*
direct object = *d.o.*   predicate nominative = *p.n.*
indirect object = *i.o.* appositive = *appos.*

o.p. 1. A horse focuses its eyes by <u>changing the angle of its head</u>.
p.n. 2. Kim's favorite rainy-day pastime is <u>writing poetry</u>.
subj. 3. <u>Collecting stamps</u> is one of the most popular hobbies in the world.
i.o. 4. The award gave <u>my practicing the piano</u> real meaning.
o.p. 5. Mom and Dad approve of <u>your handling of the problem</u>.
d.o. 6. Do you enjoy <u>swimming in the ocean</u>?
subj. 7. <u>Leaping up waterfalls</u> is not difficult for salmon.
appos. 8. Roberto thoroughly enjoys his new interest, <u>building remote-control airplanes</u>.
d.o. 9. Mr. Fitzgerald suggested <u>editing our term papers</u> on a computer.
o.p. 10. You can check the arrival time of their bus by <u>calling the terminal</u>.

EXERCISE 11 Distinguishing between Gerunds and Participles

Write two sentences for each of the following words. The first sentence should use the word as a gerund. The second sentence should use the word as a participle. Use punctuation where needed.

EXAMPLE   trusting
POSSIBLE ANSWER Trusting each other should be the basis of your relationship.
                Trusting her guidance counselor's advice, Margo elected bookkeeping.

1. walking   2. working   3. leaving   4. running   5. giving

Sample sentences: I enjoy walking to school.
Walking cautiously, we crossed the icy street.

Infinitives and Infinitive Phrases

The *infinitive*, a third kind of verbal, looks entirely different from a participle or a gerund. An infinitive usually begins with the word *to*.

Infinitives

3i An **infinitive** is a verb form that usually begins with *to*. It is used as a noun, an adjective, or an adverb.

An infinitive can take several forms; for example, the infinitives of *plan* are *to plan, to have planned, to be planned*, and *to have been planned*. The infinitives in the following examples are in heavy type.

He is the presidential candidate **to watch.** [adjective]
In the future I always plan **to be prepared.** [noun]

NOTE: Do not confuse an infinitive with a prepositional phrase that begins with *to*. An infinitive ends with a verb form, but a prepositional phrase ends with a noun or a pronoun.

INFINITIVE   It's my turn **to speak.**
PREPOSITIONAL PHRASE   Give that **to him.**

Infinitive Phrases. Like the other verbals, an infinitive can be combined with modifiers and complements to form an *infinitive phrase*.

3j An **infinitive phrase** is an infinitive with its modifiers and complements—all working together as a noun, an adjective, or an adverb.

An infinitive or an infinitive phrase can be used as a noun, an adjective, or an adverb. Notice the variations of an infinitive phrase. An infinitive, for example, can be followed by a complement, a modifier, or a prepositional phrase.

NOUN   **To discuss your differences** is very important. [subject]
I hope **to visit soon.** [direct object]
ADJECTIVE   That is the agency **to contact for more information.**
ADVERB   Eddie was happy **to help us.**

NOTE: *To* is sometimes omitted when an infinitive follows such verbs as *dare, feel, hear, help, let, make, need, see,* or *watch*. It is, nevertheless, understood to be there.

Did you help **paint** the posters? [to paint]

65

Phrases

EXERCISE 12 Finding Infinitive Phrases
Number your paper 1 to 10. Write the infinitive phrases in the following sentences. Then underline each infinitive.

1. In Paris Benjamin Franklin tried to enlist French aid for the American Revolution.
2. The place to go for help with your schedule is the guidance department.
3. One purpose of the Lewis and Clark expedition was to find a land route to the Pacific Ocean.
4. To write the first paragraph of my composition was the hardest part.
5. In a boat off the shore of Fort McHenry, Francis Scott Key was inspired to write the national anthem.
6. Greg is the only person to have completed the chemistry experiment.
7. Before the curtain rose, we all tried to appear calm.
8. No one over six feet tall can qualify to become an astronaut in the United States space program.
9. She is the first teacher to be honored with a banquet.
10. Our mayor refused to run for a third term.

EXERCISE 13 Determining the Uses of Infinitive Phrases
Number your paper 1 to 10. Write the infinitive phrase in each sentence. Then label how each one is used—*noun*, *adjective*, or *adverb*.

adj. 1. In 1847, Maria Mitchell was the first American astronomer to discover a new comet.
adv. 2. We have come to help the yearbook committee.
adv. 3. It's too late to practice your speech.
adj. 4. Joseph Lister was the first person to use antiseptic methods during surgery.
adv. 5. A mulch is placed over flower beds to conserve moisture.
n. 6. The committee plans to restore the old train station.
n. 7. To fly a glider must be an exciting experience.
n. 8. Do you dare try again?
adj. 9. Tenzing Norgay and Sir Edmund Hillary were the first persons to stand on the summit of Mount Everest.
adv. 10. The tongue of the chameleon is used to catch insects 12 inches away.

Misplaced Modifiers

EXERCISE 14 Writing Sentences
Write sentences that follow the directions below.
Sample answers precede this chapter.
1. Use an infinitive phrase as a subject.
2. Use an infinitive phrase as a direct object.
3. Use an infinitive phrase as a predicate nominative.
4. Use an infinitive phrase as an adjective.
5. Use an infinitive phrase as an adverb.

EXERCISE 15 Time-out for Review
Number your paper 1 to 10. Write each verbal phrase in the following paragraphs. Then label each one *participial*, *gerund*, or *infinitive*.

Edith Wharton (1862–1937)

Born in New York City, Edith Newbold Jones came from a wealthy family. Educated by private tutors and governesses at home, she started to write poetry at the age of 16. Then she decided to marry Edward Wharton, a wealthy Boston banker. It wasn't until after several years of a rather aimless marriage, however, that she began to write in earnest. She began by contributing poems and stories to magazines. Her first novel, *The Valley of Decision*, appeared in 1902. After many years of success in the United States, Wharton chose to spend the latter part of her life in France.

Many of Wharton's early books deal with the class structure existing in society and people's resistance to social change. Wharton disregarded this theme, however, in her famous novelette *Ethan Frome*. This story is about simple New England people who are doomed to live within the narrow confines of convention. After writing *The Age of Innocence* nine years later, she won a Pulitzer Prize. In all, Wharton published more than 50 books, one of which was an autobiography, *A Backward Glance*.

MISPLACED AND DANGLING MODIFIERS

All phrases except gerund and appositive phrases can be used as modifiers. As a modifier, each phrase should be placed as close as possible to the word it modifies. Often when a phrase is placed too far away from the word it modifies, it becomes a *misplaced modifier*.

Phrases

MISPLACED   We saw a moose **paddling our canoe on the lake.**

CORRECT   **Paddling our canoe on the lake,** we saw a moose.

MISPLACED   I read about my neighbor who ran the marathon **in the newspaper.**

CORRECT   I read **in the newspaper** about my neighbor who ran in the marathon.

Another problem arises when a phrase that is being used as a modifier lacks a word to modify. This kind of phrase is called a *dangling modifier.*

DANGLING   **Reading the chapter a second time,** the plot became clear. [The plot did not read the chapter.]

CORRECT   **Reading the chapter a second time,** I finally understood the plot.

DANGLING   **Running down the beach,** the kites were beautiful. [The kites were not running.]

CORRECT   **Running down the beach,** I admired the beautiful kites.

EXERCISE 16 Correcting Misplaced and Dangling Modifiers

Write the following sentences, correcting the error in each one. To do this, follow one of two steps: (1) Place a phrase closer to the word it modifies, or (2) Add words and change the sentence around so that the phrase has a noun or a pronoun to modify. Use punctuation where needed. *Sample answers:*

1. ~~Eating the sunflower seeds from the bird feeder,~~ Charlene took a picture of a squirrel ~~Charlene took a picture of a squirrel.~~ Eating the sunflower seeds from the bird feeder,
2. ~~In the top drawer of my dresser~~ I looked for my gloves. ~~I looked for my gloves.~~ In the top drawer of my dresser,
3. ~~Trotting up the sidewalk with a bone in his mouth,~~ Roger greeted his dog ~~Roger greeted his dog.~~ Trotting up the sidewalk with a bone in his mouth,
4. Having been on the honor roll for two years, Yoko received a personal letter from the principal. ~~the principal sent Yoko a personal letter.~~
5. Making the dessert, baking powder ~~baking powder was~~ accidentally substituted for baking soda.
6. ~~Covered with creamy Italian dressing,~~ Freddie served the salad, covered with creamy Italian dressing.
7. ~~I could see Paul fishing~~ Through my window, I could see Paul fishing.

68

8. Little white boxes of wedding cake~~,~~ , tied with white satin ribbon, were given to all the guests. ~~tied with white satin ribbon.~~
9. Having bitten the mail carrier twice, ~~Dad sold the dog~~. the dog was sold by Dad.
10. The names of the winners, ~~were announced by the principal~~ sitting in the audience~~.~~, were announced by the principal.

DIAGRAMING PHRASES

A phrase is diagramed according to the kind of phrase it is and its use in a sentence.

Prepositional Phrases. An adjective or an adverb phrase is always connected to the word it modifies. The preposition is placed on a connecting slanted line. The object of a preposition is placed on a horizontal line that is attached to the slanted line. The following example includes two adjective phrases and one adverb phrase. Notice that an adjective phrase can modify the object of the preposition of another phrase.

The tickets to the theater on James Street were ordered through the mail.

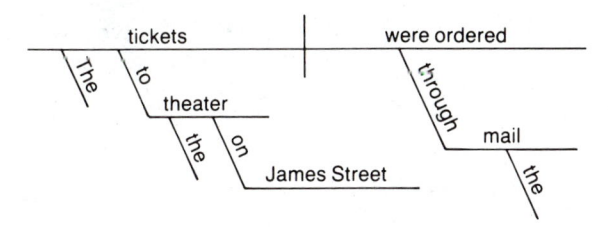

An adverb phrase that modifies an adjective or an adverb needs an additional line.

We were seated across from each other.

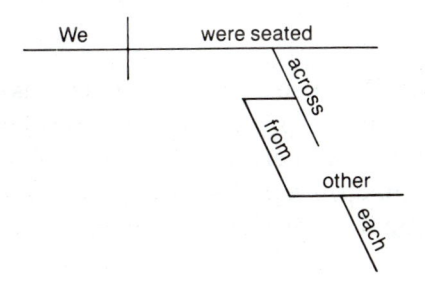

Phrases

Appositives and Appositive Phrases. An appositive is diagramed in parentheses next to the word it identifies or explains. Words that modify the appositive are placed directly underneath it.

The hyacinth, a member of the lily family, is grown in many parts of the world.

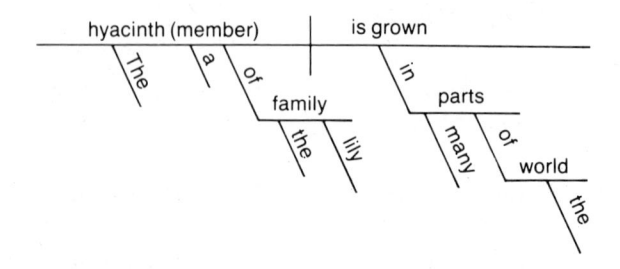

Participial Phrases. Because a participial phrase is always used as an adjective, it is diagramed under the word it modifies. The participle, however, is written in a curve. Notice in the following example that an adverb and a prepositional phrase are part of the participial phrase.

Sprinting first across the finish line, Davis won the race.

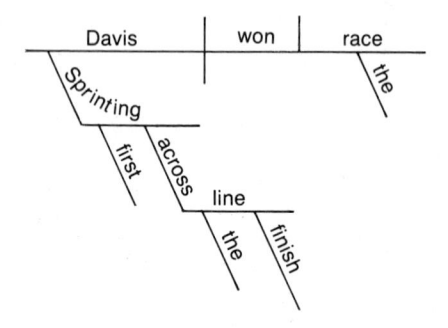

Gerund Phrases. Because a gerund phrase is used as a noun, it can be diagramed in any place a noun can be diagramed. In the following example, the gerund phrase that is used as a direct object is diagramed on a pedestal. Notice that a complement and a prepositional phrase are part of the gerund phrase.

DIAGRAMING

On Sunday I began studying my notes for the history test.

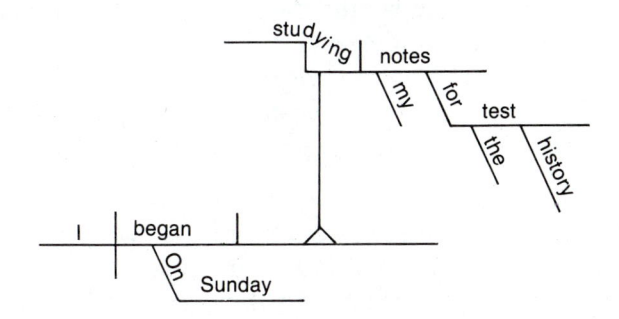

Infinitive Phrases. Because an infinitive phrase may be used as a noun, an adjective, or an adverb, it is diagramed in several ways. The following example shows how an infinitive phrase used as a subject and an infinitive phrase used as a predicate nominative are diagramed. Notice that a complement is part of the second infinitive phrase.

To procrastinate is to delay action.

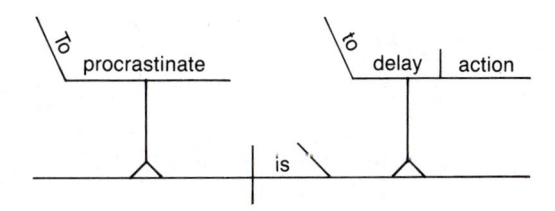

If the *to* of an infinitive is omitted from the sentence, it is diagramed in parentheses. In the following example, the infinitive phrase is used as a direct object.

No one dared go without his permission.

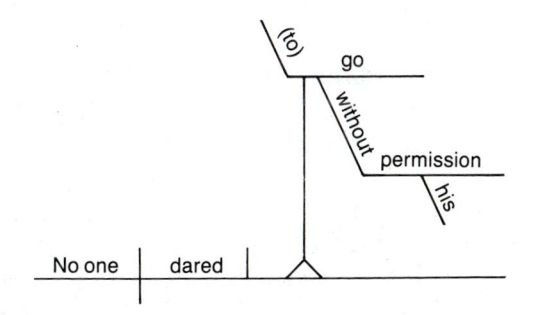

71

Phrases

EXERCISE 17 Diagraming Phrases

Diagram the following sentences or copy them. If you copy them, draw one line under each subject and two lines under each verb. Put parentheses around each phrase. Then label each phrase *prepositional, appositive, participial, gerund,* or *infinitive*. *Diagrams precede this chapter.*

1. Cable cars are still used (on the streets)(of San Francisco) [prep./prep.]
2. Her hobby is (collecting statues of horses) [ger.]
3. I tried (to help Isabel with her homework) [inf.]
4. (During the summer) I drove (through the mountains)(of Colorado) [prep./prep./prep.]
5. On Saturday we saw him (jogging around the reservoir) [part.]
6. Ricardo, (my cousin from Dallas) is visiting me. [appos.]
7. Cattle grazed (along the eastern shores)(of Long Island)(in 1660) [prep./prep./prep.]
8. (Buying a home computer) is his next project. [ger.]
9. Mansions (built by sea captains) still stand (on Nantucket) [part./prep.]
10. Will you help (paint the garage)? [inf.]

Note: Students need not identify prepositional phrases that occur within verbal and appositive phrases.

Application to Writing

Deliberately using phrases—particularly verbal phrases—will improve your writing. One way to incorporate phrases into your writing is to use them to combine two sentences.

TWO SENTENCES	The hikers' first landmark was a tree. It had an S-shaped trunk.
ONE SENTENCE	The hikers' first landmark was a tree **with an S-shaped trunk.** [prepositional phrase]
TWO SENTENCES	The atmosphere is a protective blanket around the earth. It actually eliminates harmful rays of the sun.
ONE SENTENCE	The atmosphere, **a protective blanket around the earth,** actually eliminates harmful rays of the sun. [appositive phrase]
TWO SENTENCES	For an hour we strolled along the beach. We watched the tide come in.
ONE SENTENCE	**Strolling along the beach for an hour,** we watched the tide come in. [participial phrase]

Sentence Combining

TWO SENTENCES	Many deer nibble the lichen beneath the snow. This is how they can survive the barren winters.
ONE SENTENCE	By **nibbling the lichen beneath the snow,** many deer can survive the barren winters. [gerund phrase]

TWO SENTENCES	From a distance some zebras' stripes blend together. Thus they create a gray effect.
ONE SENTENCE	From a distance some zebras' stripes blend together **to create a gray effect.** [infinitive phrase]

EXERCISE 18 Combining Sentences with Phrases

Combine each pair of sentences by using phrases. Use punctuation where needed. *Sample answers:*

1. The ukulele ~~is~~, a traditional Hawaiian instrument, ~~It~~ was introduced to Hawaii by Portuguese sailors.
2. Take Route 4, ~~It will take you~~ to the mall.
3. After watching ~~For a half hour we watched~~ Niagara Falls from above, for a half hour, ~~Then~~ we took an elevator down to the foot of the falls.
4. The wheel ~~is~~ considered one of the greatest inventions of all time, ~~It~~ has made our industrial civilization possible.
5. Quartz ~~is~~, a common mineral, ~~It~~ is sometimes used in rings and pins.
6. Parasol ants often carry large sections of leaves, to ~~With the sections they~~ fertilize their food.
7. The gravity of the moon affects the earth, by causing ~~It causes~~ tides in the ocean.
8. The cat could be hiding behind the couch, or ~~It also could be~~ under the bed.
9. Airlines maintain special schools, to ~~In these schools they~~ train their flight attendants.
10. The language of Taki-Taki ~~is~~ spoken in parts of French Guiana, ~~This language~~ contains many Dutch words.
11. As ~~When he was~~ prime minister, the Duke of Wellington lost popularity, by opposing ~~He opposed~~ parliamentary reforms.
12. Laura Ingalls Wilder, ~~is~~ the author of *Little House on the Prairie*, ~~She~~ began writing at age 65.
13. My mother was born on Maui, ~~It is~~ one of the Hawaiian Islands.

73

Phrases

14. The eruption of Krakatoa in 1883 produced a loud sound, ~~It could be~~ heard hundreds of miles away.
15. Study more frequently and for shorter periods of time, ~~In this way you can~~ to avoid examination panic.
16. Jennifer attended the concert, ~~It was~~ held at the civic center.
17. The Gutenberg Bible, ~~was~~ the first book printed with movable type, ~~It~~ was a masterpiece.
18. A mackerel sky is covered with rows of cirrocumulus clouds, ~~These resemble~~ resembling the patterns on a mackerel's back.
19. The French quadrille contributed to American music, ~~It~~ by providing ~~provided~~ the rhythm for some of jazz.
20. The annual fireworks display, ~~was~~ planned originally for July 4, ~~It~~ was postponed to July 5 because of rain.

CHAPTER REVIEW

Number your paper 1 to 20. Write the phrases in the following sentences. Then label each one *prepositional*, *appositive*, *participial*, *gerund*, or *infinitive*.

1. The forepaws of the raccoon look very much like small human hands.
2. Watching the sunrise from Mount Washington is a breathtaking experience.
3. The bassoon is sometimes used in a musical work to create a humorous effect.
4. Jacques Cousteau, the great underwater explorer, helped invent the Aqua-lung.
5. The batter looked up and saw the ball soaring out of the ball park.
6. Having been elected president, Thomas Jefferson encouraged westward expansion.
7. This week I plan to take the bus to school.
8. The figure of King Kong seen in the original movie version was actually a model 18 inches high.
9. You can find some information about your topic by consulting the encyclopedia.
10. When you sneeze, it is hard to keep your eyes open.
11. Julie, my oldest sister, is an accountant.

74   *Note: Students need not identify prepositional phrases that occur within verbal phrases.*

Chapter Review

12. At a very early age, Mozart began writing music.
13. Having become totally deaf by 1819, Beethoven never heard some of his finest music.
14. Mr. Kelly told the newspaper staff to arrive early.
15. Reaching into his hat, the magician dramatically produced two parakeets.
16. Barnie told me of your entering the marathon.
17. We found the dog sleeping in a bedroom closet.
18. The Homestake, this country's largest gold mine, is located in Lead, South Dakota.
19. We finally succeeded in finding the car keys.
20. One fourth of the 206 bones in the human body are located in the feet.

MASTERY TEST

Number your paper 1 to 10. Write the phrases in the following sentences. Then label each one *prepositional, appositive, participial, gerund,* or *infinitive.*

1. Sometimes the age of a fish can be told by counting the rings on its scales.
2. Tomorrow we plan to ride the Ferris wheel three times.
3. The school newspaper is looking for a way to increase circulation.
4. A daddy longlegs looks like a spider with long legs.
5. A neighbor across the street told us of his finding a ten-dollar bill on the sidewalk.
6. Having taken the math final, I began to study for my history exam.
7. Bryan Mallory, Channel 5's weather forecaster, predicts rain for today.
8. The parade route, covering two miles, begins at City Hall.
9. A starfish cut in two will become two starfish.
10. Martin Van Buren, the eighth president, was the first president to be born a citizen of the United States.

Note: Students need not identify the prepositional phrases that occur within verbal phrases.

75

Chapter 4 Clauses

OBJECTIVES

- To distinguish between independent and subordinate clauses.
- To identify adverb clauses and to exlain their function in a sentence.
- To punctuate adverb clauses correctly.
- To identify adjective clauses and to explain their function in a sentence.
- To explain the function of a relative pronoun within an adjective clause.
- To punctuate adjective clauses correctly.
- To identify and correct misplaced modifiers.
- To identify noun clauses and to explain their function in a sentence.
- To identify the different kinds of sentence structure.
- Application: To develop a mature writing style by using a variety of sentence structures.

MOTIVATIONAL ACTIVITY

Take a paragraph from a short story in an anthology and break it down into all simple sentences. After your students have read your "revised" version, have them read the original paragraph. Then have a class discussion on the merits of the original. What is the difference between the two versions? Which one sounds better? Why? Your students should then see the importance that sentence variety has in producing interesting, mature-sounding writing.

TEACHING SUGGESTIONS

By eleventh grade many of your students are probably including subordinate clauses in their writing, but they may only be using them in certain stereotyped ways. An adverb clause, for example, will usually follow the verb it modifies but will rarely open a sentence. A noun clause will usually be the object of the verb but rarely will be the subject of a sentence. The goal of this chapter, therefore, should be to have your average and advanced students use different clauses in a variety of ways in sentences.

The emphasis of this chapter with your basic students will probably be slightly different. When these students write, you should caution them against the overuse of the simple sentence and the compound sentence connected by *and* or *so*. A goal would be to have them write or say, "I have a cousin who lives on a farm" instead of "I have a cousin, and he lives on a farm." Encourage your basic students to combine two statements into one clear sentence by using an adjective or an adverb clause.

Adverb Causes *(pages 79 – 82)*

By grouping the subordinating conjunctions, you may be able to show your students more clearly the kinds of clauses the various conjunctions introduce.

PLACE where, wherever
TIME after, before, until, when, whenever, while
MANNER as, as if, as though
CAUSE OR REASON as, because, for, since, so that
CONDITION if, unless
CONCESSION although, even though, though
COMPARISON as, than

Help your students think through their sentences so that *and* is not used to connect parts of the sentence when the relationship is casual, conditioned, or related through time or place.

NOTE: You may want to refer to pages 378 – 379 in the composition section, which explain proper subordination of clauses.

Adjective Clauses *(pages 82 – 87)*

If you intend to cover the case of relative pronouns *(pages 153 – 156)*, your students will need to learn in this chapter the function of a relative pronoun. You may choose, nevertheless, to omit this section with basic students. Exercises 6 and 7 on pages 85 – 86 have been set up so that classes that do not cover the func-

Clauses

tion of a relative pronoun can still use Exercise 6 for identification.

NOTE: For further examples and practice in punctuating essential and nonessential clauses, refer your students to pages 262–265 in Chapter 11.

Noun Clauses *(pages 87–89)*

Since a noun clause can begin with *who*, *whom*, *which*, or *that*, students sometimes confuse a noun clause with an adjective clause. To help your students avoid this confusion, you may want to explain to them that the word *that* in an adjective clause can usually be replaced by *who* or *which*. The same substitution does not work in a noun clause. You may want to write the following examples on the board.

ADJECTIVE CLAUSE I like the jacket *that* she wore yesterday.
I like the jacket *which* she wore yesterday. [*Which* can be substituted for *that* in an adjective clause.]
NOUN CLAUSE I know *that* the jacket was expensive.
I know *which* the jacket was expensive. [*Which* cannot be substituted for *that* in a noun clause.]

Sample Board Sentences
The Battle of New Orleans was fought after the peace treaty had been signed. [adverb clause]
The impala, which can easily leap 30 feet, is one of the most graceful antelopes. [adjective clause]
Some botanists believe that the cabbage is the most ancient vegetable still grown today. [noun clause]

Kinds of Sentence Structure *(pages 89–91)*

You may want to emphasize that a compound sentence is used to tie together related ideas of equal importance. The coordinating conjunctions that usually join compound sentences, however, have distinct uses. *And* should be used like a plus sign, *but* should be used like a minus sign, and *or* should be used to indicate an alternative. You may want to give the following examples to illustrate the differences in meaning.

PLUS I invited John to my party, *and* he accepted.
MINUS I invited John to my party, *but* he can't come.
ALTERNATIVE Should I ask John, *or* will you ask him?

NOTE: You may want to refer your students to the mechanics section for the punctuation of compound sentences. Pages 255–256 cover using a comma with a compound sentence, and pages 276–282 cover using a semicolon with a compound sentence.

Sample Board Sentences
The great Gold Rush in the United States occurred in the late 1800s. [simple]
In 1870, Colorado had a population of almost 40,000, but by 1880, the population had jumped to 119,565. [compound]
During this time Americans realized that a canal across Panama would be helpful. [complex]
As early as 1850, the United States and Britain had agreed that they would work together and build a canal, but they never got around to it. [compound-complex]

ACTIVITIES FOR DIFFERENT ABILITIES

Basic Students

ACTIVITY 1 Subordinate Clauses
If your students are able to recognize a subordinate clause—even if they cannot label what kind it is—they will be able to eliminate many sentence fragments in their writing. To practice your students' recognition skills, write the following clauses on the board or duplicate them. Then have your students identify which are independent and which are subordinate.

1. because a coyote is almost the same color as the desert
2. where he bought a German shepherd
3. the guinea pig is not a pig

Chapter 4 b

Clauses

4. since the movie on TV ran beyond eleven o'clock
5. catacombs existed in ancient Rome
6. which became her favorite toy
7. that she enjoys roller coasters
8. rattlesnakes can use their poison fangs from birth
9. whoever is chosen president of the junior class
10. if you take the subway to Fifty-third Street

ACTIVITY 2 Writing Sentences
Have your students use each subordinate clause in Activity 1 in a complete sentence.

ACTIVITY 3 Turning Compound Sentences into Complex Sentences
Duplicate the following sentences. Then have your students change each compound sentence into a complex sentence by turning one independent clause into an adverb clause. Remind your students to use commas where needed *(page 80)*.

A Bold Experiment
1. Paul Boyton demonstrated a remarkable rubber suit in 1874, and the world acclaimed him.
2. In that year Boyton climbed out of a lifeboat of the steamer *Queen*, and the captain couldn't believe his eyes.
3. Boyton announced his intention of swimming to shore, and the crew didn't believe him.
4. The ship was 250 miles from shore, but Boyton persisted.
5. Boyton was determined to demonstrate the effectiveness of the rubber suit for lifesaving, and the captain finally listened.
6. Boyton spoke convincingly, and the captain finally allowed him to leave the ship 30 miles from shore.
7. The night was cold and stormy, but Boyton dropped from the ship and swam toward shore.
8. He had designed the suit with watertight compartments, and it floated like a kayak and could be paddled.
9. Boyton arrived on shore safely, and newspaper reporters were there to greet him.
10. Boyton's suit was never generally adopted, but his exploits helped arouse interest in water sports.

ACTIVITY 4 Combining Sentences with Noun Clauses
To provide additional practice, duplicate the following sentences. Then have your students combine each pair of sentences by making one sentence a noun clause.

1. My history book states an interesting fact. In 1790, only five percent of the American population lived in cities.
2. A square inch of skin on the human hand contains about 72 feet of nerve fiber. I was surprised to learn this.
3. Hurricane control may be a reality soon. The science film made this point.
4. Georgia Knapp will run for president of the junior class. I was happy to learn this.
5. Certain plants flower in freezing temperatures. This was news to me.
6. The maximum speed of a 20-horsepower car is very different from the maximum speed of a coach drawn by a 20-horse team. A moment's thought will show why.
7. Billions of meteors strike the earth daily. I was amazed to learn this.
8. A registered trademark is the exclusive property of its owner and may not be used by others without permission. The federal patent law states this definitely.
9. About one tenth of the earth's surface is covered with ice. Ms. Wakes told us this.
10. Snails have been in existence for many thousands of years. This has been proved by fossil remains.

Advanced Students

ACTIVITY 1 Identifying and Punctuating Adjective Clauses
To provide additional practice, duplicate the following sentences. Then after your students have underlined each adjective

Clauses

clause, have them add commas where needed *(page 85)*.

The Columbian Exposition
1. The Columbian Exposition which was built on 600 acres of Chicago swampland astonished the world in 1893.
2. The wonders science was developing were demonstrated at the fair.
3. Electricity about which visitors were curious was extensively used.
4. The art that was on display introduced new American artists to the public.
5. The Palace of Fine Arts where the art was displayed is the only surviving structure.
6. The building which is now the Museum of Science and Industry is one of Chicago's best-known institutions.
7. Seventy-seven countries prepared the exhibits that drew twenty-seven million visitors.
8. The gigantic Manufacturers' Building which used 17,000,000 feet of lumber could easily have enclosed a 10-story building.
9. The fair featured the original Ferris wheel whose 36 cars soared 264 feet above the ground.
10. This giant wheel whose dimensions challenge the imagination even today carried 2,160 people at one time.

ACTIVITY 2 Combining Sentences with Subordinate Clauses

To provide additional practice, duplicate the following sentences. Then have your students combine each pair of sentences by making one sentence an adjective clause, an adverb clause, or a noun clause. Remind your students to use commas where needed.

Incredible Structures
1. James Meyers's *Incredible Structures* describes 50 marvels from the ancient and the modern world. This book gave me new insights into the ingenuity of architects.
2. Here are a few examples. You may find these interesting.
3. The famous architect Frank Lloyd Wright designed the house "Fallingwater." It was actually built directly over a waterfall.
4. The gateway to the Fortress of Purandhar in India was constructed on marshy ground. The Rajah ordered that the foundation be built on solid gold bricks.
5. The highways of the Incas resemble modern superhighways in length and in engineering skill. They often climbed heights of over 10,000 feet or tunneled through mountain cliffs.
6. The Leaning Tower of Pisa is now 14 feet off perpendicular. It needs some kind of support to prevent its collapse.
7. The Gateway Arch in St. Louis is one of the world's tallest monuments. The book points this out.
8. The Pentagon contains 17½ miles of corridors. No two offices are more than 1,800 feet apart.
9. The Winchester mansion near San Jose, California, contained over 2,000 doors and 10,000 windows. It sprawled over 6 acres and had 160 rooms.
10. Other buildings may be higher. The Vertical Assembly Building at Cape Canaveral, Florida, encloses the greatest amount of space.

ACTIVITY 3 Reducing Clauses to Single Words

You may want to point out that no subordinate clause should be used unless it adds discrimination, color, or additional details that could not be expressed by a single word or phrase. The following examples may be helpful.

WORDY We left the party *when it was late*. [adverb clause]
CONCISE We left the party late.
WORDY The Cadillac, *which was long and black*, turned into the Smiths' driveway. [adjective clause]
CONCISE The long, black Cadillac turned into the Smiths' driveway.
WORDY I don't understand *what your point is*. [noun clause]
CONCISE I don't understand your point.

Chapter 4 d

Clauses

To practice this skill of writing concisely, duplicate the following sentences. Then have your students rewrite each sentence by changing each complex sentence into a simple sentence.

1. We looked on the beach for shells that were perfect.
2. Tell me what your suggestion is.
3. What John's reasons are will soon become apparent.
4. We could not get back to camp while there was still daylight.
5. Knives that are sharp should be handled with care.
6. Animals that are nocturnal are quiet during the day.
7. In the last chapter, the detective pointed out who the thief was.
8. Meals that are rich can impede digestion.
9. What your purpose is is not clear.
10. From a distance we could see the Teton peaks that are lofty.

ACTIVITY 4 Classifying Sentences

To provide additional practice, duplicate the following sentences. Then have your students label each sentence *simple*, *compound*, *complex*, or *compound-complex*.

Quotations

1. Happy is the house that shelters a friend. —*Ralph Waldo Emerson*
2. A person is not idle because he is involved in thought. —*Victor Hugo*
3. Independence is good, but isolation is too high a price to pay for it. —*Benjamin R. Tucker*
4. The law puts the safety of all above the safety of one. —*Cicero*
5. It looks impossible until you do it, and then you find it is possible. —*Evelyn Underhill*
6. It may be that all games are silly, but, then, so are human beings. —*Robert Lynd*
7. The chief obstacle to the progress of the human race is the human race. —*Don Marquis*
8. Bragging may not bring happiness, but no one who catches a large fish goes home through an alley. —*Anonymous*
9. Nothing is so exhausting as indecision, and nothing is so futile. —*Bertrand Russell*
10. We are all more average than we think. —*Gorham Munson*

ACTIVITY 5 Writing Sentences

Have your students write ten to fifteen sentences that describe what they imagine life might be on another planet. These sentences should include at least one simple sentence, one compound sentence, and one complex sentence. Remind your students to include commas where needed.

ADDITIONAL PRACTICE

Basic Students
 Teacher's Resource Book: pages 108–110
 Workbook: pages 45–60
Average Students
 Teacher's Resource Book: pages 111–113
 Workbook: pages 45–60
Advanced Students
 Teacher's Resource Book: pages 114–116

REVIEW EXERCISES AND TESTS

Student Text
 Diagnostic Test: page 76
 Chapter Review: pages 95–96
 Mastery Test: page 97
Teacher's Resource Book
 Chapter 4 Test: pages 15–16
 (Also available as spirit duplicating masters.)

ADDITIONAL ANSWERS

EXERCISE 13 Writing Sentences *(page 91)*

Sample answers:

Element and *isotope* are terms often used in inorganic chemistry. (simple)

Janet grows plants from seeds, but Kevin would rather buy flats of seedlings. (compound)
You ought to see a doctor about your ankle since it is still swollen. (complex)
Steven can't carry a tune, but he is such a good drummer that he is an important player in the school band. (compound-complex)

EXERCISE 14 Diagraming Sentences *(page 93)*

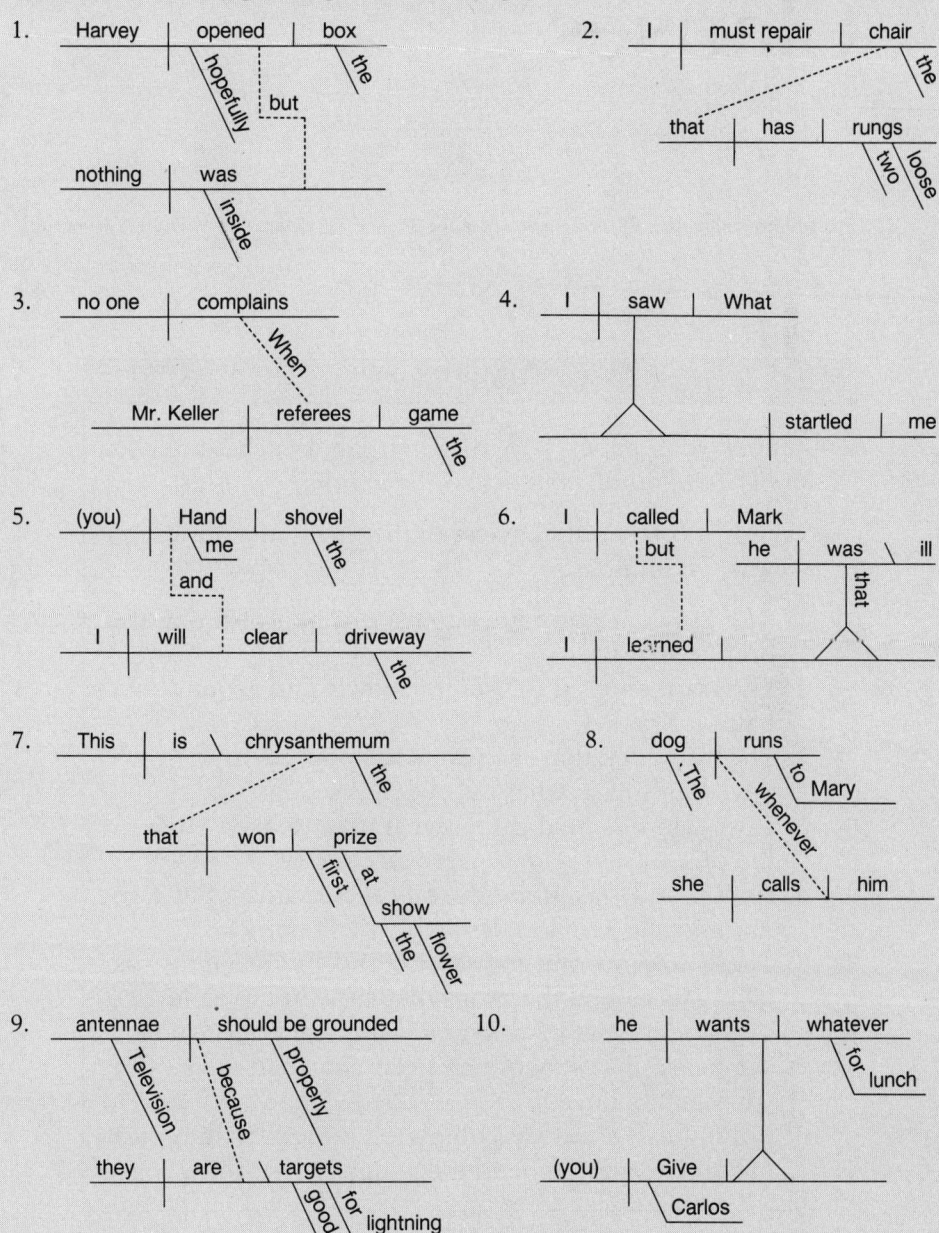

4 Clauses

For additional practice for this chapter, see the Teacher's Resource Book and the Workbook.

DIAGNOSTIC TEST

Number your paper 1 to 10. Then label each sentence *simple,* **S** *compound,* **Cd** *complex,* **Cx** or *compound-complex.* **CC**

EXAMPLE You should have seen the one that got away!
ANSWER   complex

Cd 1. Our gray cat had four kittens, but two of them are orange-striped.
S 2. The train entered the station slowly and ground to a halt on Track 3.
Cx 3. The notebook that she wants has pockets in it.
Cx 4. Pay attention to what the coach is saying.
Cx 5. If we win this final game, we'll play Meaken High in the play-offs.
Cd 6. *Detroit* and *Des Moines* are French names, but *San Antonio* and *Los Angeles* are Spanish names.
CC 7. There was no rain for weeks, and the drought was taking its toll on the crops that grew in the valley.
S 8. The students sat in class and waited for their teacher.
CC 9. We heard that school had been canceled today, but we didn't believe it.
Cx 10. Columbus's crew was completely amazed as the coast of San Salvador appeared through the morning fog.

A paragraph consisting of short simple sentences can be rather dull. The relationship of ideas may also be unclear, since each idea is expressed in a separate sentence. In the example below, notice how the short, choppy sentences make the paragraph uninteresting and difficult to understand fully.

> In the early years of this nation, Americans were moving westward. New lands were gained. New settlements sprang up. First there was Louisiana. It was bought from France. People settled in areas surrounding the Mississippi. Then they went west to explore the land.

Combining sentences will add variety to your sentence structure. In this chapter you will learn how to combine ideas by using clauses to form compound and complex sentences.

4a A **clause** is a group of words that has a subject and a verb.

In the following paragraph, ideas have been combined using clauses. Compare this paragraph to the one above.

> In the early years of this nation, Americans were moving westward. As new lands were gained, new settlements sprang up. First there was Louisiana, which was bought from France. After people settled in the areas surrounding the Mississippi, they went west to explore the land.

In this chapter you will review the two kinds of clauses, how they are used, and how they are combined to form different kinds of sentence structure. If you apply the information in this chapter to your writing, your style will become more mature and more interesting to read.

INDEPENDENT AND SUBORDINATE CLAUSES

The two kinds of clauses are *independent clauses* and *subordinate clauses.*

4b An **independent (or main) clause** can stand alone as a sentence because it expresses a complete thought.

Clauses

An independent clause is called a *sentence* when it stands alone, but it is called a *clause* when it appears in a sentence with another clause. In the following examples, each subject is underlined once, and each verb is underlined twice. Notice that each independent clause can stand alone as a separate sentence.

⌜——independent clause——⌝ ⌜——independent clause——⌝
Today was a very hot day, but tomorrow will be even hotter.

⌜———sentence———⌝ ⌜———sentence———⌝
Today was a very hot day. Tomorrow will be even hotter.

4c A **subordinate (or dependent) clause** cannot stand alone as a sentence because it does not express a complete thought.

Even though a subordinate clause has a subject and a verb, it does not express a complete thought. As a result, it cannot stand alone. A subordinate clause is dependent upon an independent clause to complete its meaning.

⌜——independent clause——⌝ ⌜—subordinate clause—⌝
I will meet you in the library after I go to my locker.

⌜—independent clause—⌝ ⌜——subordinate clause——⌝
I was born in Austin, which is the capital of Texas.

EXERCISE 1 Distinguishing between Independent and Subordinate Clauses

Label each underlined clause *independent* or *subordinate*.

George's Early Years

I 1. As a younger son in a land-poor family, <u>George Washington worked hard for acceptance as a Virginia gentleman</u>.
S 2. <u>When Washington was 11</u>, his father died.
I 3. <u>Washington wanted to run away to sea</u>, but his mother stopped him.
S 4. Washington did not attend college <u>as the next five presidents did</u>.
S 5. Washington, however, was a good student <u>who excelled in mathematics and surveying</u>.
S 6. A dominant figure in his early life was his brother Lawrence, <u>who married into the wealthy Fairfax family</u>.

Adverb Clauses

4c–d

7. <u>After Washington turned 17</u>, Lawrence got him a job as a surveyor for the Fairfaxes.
8. <u>For a few dollars a day</u>, Washington endured severe hardships while he mapped out new lands on the frontier.
9. The governor of Virginia then asked him to serve as a special messenger <u>so that an ultimatum could be delivered to the French outposts far to the west</u>.
10. Washington was commissioned a lieutenant colonel of the militia in 1754, and <u>35 years later he became president</u>.

USES OF SUBORDINATE CLAUSES

A subordinate clause, as well as a phrase, can be used as an adverb, an adjective, or a noun in a sentence. Just remember that a clause has a subject and a verb, but a phrase does not have a subject and a verb.

Adverb Clauses

An *adverb clause* can be used just like a single adverb or an adverb phrase. The single adverb, the adverb phrase, and the adverb clause in the following examples all modify *ran*.

SINGLE ADVERB	Jerry ran **swiftly.**
ADVERB PHRASE	Jerry ran **at top speed.**
ADVERB CLAUSE	Jerry ran **as though his life depended on it.**

4d An **adverb clause** is a subordinate clause that is used like an adverb to modify a verb, an adjective, or an adverb.

An adverb clause answers the same questions a single adverb answers: *How? When? Where? How much?* and *To what extent?* An adverb clause also answers *Under what condition?* and *Why?* Although most adverb clauses modify verbs, some modify adjectives and adverbs.

MODIFYING A VERB	I finished my report **before it was due.** [answers *When?*]
	Because his car was being fixed, Peter asked for a ride. [answers *Why?*]

79

Clauses

MODIFYING AN ADJECTIVE   Mike is taller **than I am.** [answers *To what extent?*]

MODIFYING AN ADVERB   Jan finished sooner **than I did.** [answers *How much?*]

Subordinating Conjunctions. Each adverb clause begins with a word called a *subordinating conjunction*. Some subordinating conjunctions, such as *after, before, since,* and *until,* can also be used as prepositions to introduce prepositional phrases.

Common Subordinating Conjunctions

after	as soon as	in order that	until
although	as though	since	when
as	because	so that	whenever
as far as	before	than	where
as if	even though	though	wherever
as long as	if	unless	while

Notice in the following examples that an adverb clause that modifies a verb modifies the whole verb phrase.

Chris will play his guitar **as long as anyone is listening.**

Whenever you vote, you are practicing good citizenship.

The jar, **when it toppled,** was sitting on the ledge.

Punctuation with Adverb Clauses

Place a comma after an introductory adverb clause.

While you wait for the doctor, you could read a magazine.

If an adverb clause interrupts an independent clause, place a comma before and after it.

The students, **after all the campaign speeches had been given,** voted in their homerooms.

Adverb Clauses

EXERCISE 2 **Finding Adverb Clauses**

Number your paper 1 to 10. Write each adverb clause. Then write the word or words each clause modifies.

1. Unfortunately, some people drive away from a green light as though they were going to a fire.
2. Marcia read her notes while she waited for the test to begin.
3. If time permits, we should meet at my house first.
4. Some wild animals can't tell a person from a tree if the person is standing still.
5. The score was closer than we expected.
6. As far as I know, the post office will be closed tomorrow.
7. Before John Knowles wrote *A Separate Peace*, he was a reporter for a Connecticut newspaper.
8. When the temperature of a star rises to a certain level, iron and other heavy elements are formed.
9. Ricardo works harder than anyone else does.
10. Maria listened attentively as Pat read the poem.

EXERCISE 3 **Identifying and Punctuating Adverb Clauses**

Write the following sentences and underline each adverb clause. Then add a comma or commas if needed.

1. Do not leave until you have finished your chores.
2. When the radio is playing, some students cannot concentrate on their homework.
3. Nickel, because it has exceptional ductility, can be stretched into a fine wire.
4. After the governor finished his speech, he answered questions from the audience.
5. Although Samuel Tilden had a majority of popular votes, he lost the presidency to Rutherford B. Hayes.
6. Join us as soon as you can.
7. As long as the dog is confined, the mail carrier will deliver the mail.
8. Thomas Jefferson was 33 years old when he drafted the Declaration of Independence.
9. Copy these directions so that you won't get lost.
10. Since the mayor is out of town, you should speak to Mrs. Patterson.

Clauses

Elliptical Clauses. A shortcut in the writing of an adverb clause is sometimes taken. Words are omitted, but they are understood to be there by both the writer and the reader. An adverb clause in which words are missing is called an *elliptical clause.* Notice in the following examples that an elliptical clause begins with *than* or *as. (See page 156 for information about pronouns in elliptical clauses.)*

> Lee is a better swimmer **than I.** [The completed elliptical clause reads "than I *am.*"]
>
> A ton of feathers weighs as much **as a ton of lead.** [The completed elliptical clause reads "as a ton of lead *weighs.*"]

EXERCISE 4   Recognizing Elliptical Clauses
Write the completed version of each elliptical clause.

1. Today there are some metals more costly than gold / is costly.
2. Pat dances better than Lamar / dances.
3. Toads have shorter hind legs than frogs / have.
4. Four ounces of cheese contains about as much calcium as a quart of milk / contains.
5. Roy is as athletic as Clarence / is.
6. The South American condor probably flies to higher altitudes than any other bird / flies.
7. Michael is as tall as his younger brother / is tall.
8. Some rubies are more valuable than diamonds of the same size and quality / are.
9. Sandy spends more time at the computer than I / spend.
10. In the marathon Flora ran faster than Amy / ran.

Adjective Clauses

An *adjective clause* can be used like a single adjective. The single adjective, the adjective phrase, and the adjective clause in the following examples all modify *clown.*

SINGLE ADJECTIVE	The crowd roared at the **comical** clown.
ADJECTIVE PHRASE	The crowd roared at the clown **with the oversized trousers and tiny hat.**
ADJECTIVE CLAUSE	The crowd roared at the clown **who rode backward on a horse.**

Adjective Clauses

4e > An **adjective clause** is a subordinate clause that is used like an adjective to modify a noun or a pronoun.

An adjective clause and a single adjective answer the same questions: *Which one(s)?* and *What kind?*

WHICH ONE(S)?   Sam is the player **who just made a home run.**

WHAT KIND?   She wants a wallet **that has room for her pictures.**

Relative Pronouns. A *relative pronoun* usually begins an adjective clause. A relative pronoun relates an adjective clause to its antecedent—the noun or pronoun the clause modifies. Sometimes words such as *where* and *when* are also used to introduce an adjective clause.

Relative Pronouns				
who	whom	whose	which	that

Thanksgiving, **which always falls on the fourth Thursday in November,** is a national holiday.

This is the place **where you should stand.**

NOTE: Occasionally the relative pronoun *that* will be omitted from an adjective clause. It is still understood to be there.

Is this the jacket **you want?** [The complete adjective clause is *(that) you want.*]

EXERCISE 5 Finding Adjective Clauses

Number your paper 1 to 10. Write the adjective clause in each sentence. Then beside each one, write the word it modifies.

The Red Badge of Courage

1. The hero of *The Red Badge of Courage* is young Henry Fleming, who is afraid of battle.
2. His ideas of war were formed from books that he had read during his childhood.

83

Clauses

3. The books described invincible heroes whose lives were a series of glorious combats.
4. Henry gets a less glamorous idea of war after arriving at the Army camp, where he hears many gruesome stories.
5. Henry, who had imagined himself a hero, now begins to doubt his own courage.
6. Most of the book is a minute-by-minute description of Henry's first battle, where he finds out for himself about war and about courage.
7. This first encounter, from which he runs in panic, prepares him for later battles.
8. Courage, which deserts him in the first battle, stays with him in the second battle and brings him to awareness and maturity.
9. Stephen Crane's war novel was one of the first books that told not only of many acts of heroism but also of the horrors of war.
10. At the time, both Union and Confederate soldiers, whose own feelings were accurately presented, praised the book.

Function of a Relative Pronoun. Within the adjective clause itself, the relative pronoun can function as a subject, a direct object, or an object of a preposition. It can show possession as well.

SUBJECT	Lobsters **that are found along the North Atlantic coast** are very tasty. [*That* is the subject of *are found.*]
DIRECT OBJECT	Bowling is one sport **Americans can enjoy throughout the year.** [The understood relative pronoun *that* is the direct object of *can enjoy.*]
OBJECT OF A PREPOSITION	The play **in which she starred** was a huge success. [*Which* is the object of the preposition *in.* Notice that *in* is part of the clause.]
POSSESSION	The person **whose glasses were found in the auditorium** should claim them at the office. [*Whose* shows possession of *glasses.*]

84

Adjective Clauses

> **Punctuation with Adjective Clauses**
>
> No punctuation is used with an adjective clause that contains information that is essential to identify a person, place, or thing in the sentence. The relative pronoun *that* always begins an essential clause. A comma or commas, however, should set off an adjective clause that is nonessential. A clause is nonessential if it can be removed without changing the basic meaning of the sentence. An adjective clause that follows a proper noun is usually nonessential.
>
> ESSENTIAL   The player **who made the decisive touchdown** is the captain of the team. [No commas are used because the clause is needed to identify which player.]
>
> NONESSENTIAL   Ben Deering, **who made the decisive touchdown,** is the captain of the team. [Commas are used because the clause can be removed from the sentence.]

Answers to Exercise 7 also appear below.

EXERCISE 6   Identifying and Punctuating Adjective Clauses
Write the following sentences and underline each <u>adjective clause</u>. Then add a comma or commas where needed.

1. The giant squid, <u>which can reach a length of more than 15 feet</u>, has a 15-inch eye. [subj.]
2. Wendy gave me a vase <u>that she had made on a potter's wheel</u>. [d.o.]
3. Lillian Todd, <u>whose airplane designs attracted the attention of many people in aviation</u>, never learned to fly. [poss.]
4. Ponce de León never found the fountain of youth <u>that he was seeking</u>. [d.o.]
5. The person <u>from whom Leroy bought the bicycle</u> is moving to Idaho. [o.p.]
6. Golda Meir, <u>who was prime minister of Israel</u>, once taught in Milwaukee. [subj.]
7. These are the same glasses <u>I have worn</u> for the past two years. [understood d.o.]
8. Diamonds, <u>which have been cherished since ancient times</u>, may be colorless, white, yellow, green, or even blue. [subj.]

85

Clauses

9. The manager, <u>whom (d.o.) you will meet shortly</u>, will show you around the store. *Commas may be omitted in sentence 9.*
10. The boiling point of a liquid is the temperature <u>at which (o.p.) it becomes vapor</u>.

EXERCISE 7 Determining the Function of a Relative Pronoun

Number your paper 1 to 10. Then label the use of each relative pronoun in Exercise 6, using the following abbreviations. If an adjective clause begins with an understood *that*, write *understood* after the number and then write how *that* is used.
See Exercise 6 for the answers.

subject = *subj.*   object of a preposition = *o.p.*
direct object = *d.o.*   possession = *poss.*

Misplaced Modifiers

Because an adjective clause works as a modifier, it should be placed as near as possible to the word it describes. A clause placed too far away from the word it modifies is called a *misplaced modifier*.

MISPLACED We saw *Romeo and Juliet* on television **which has always fascinated theatergoers.**

CORRECT On television we saw *Romeo and Juliet,* **which has always fascinated theatergoers.**

EXERCISE 8 Correcting Misplaced Modifiers

Write the following sentences, correcting each misplaced modifier. Use a comma or commas where needed. *Sample answers:*

1. From the car, *that we had rented,* we watched the ducks ~~that we had rented~~.
2. Greg had to push his car, *which had broken down,* to the gas station ~~which had broken down~~.
3. *On Saturday morning,* We visited Salem, ~~on Saturday morning~~ where the House of Seven Gables is still preserved.
4. Mother has made reservations ~~for a room~~ at the Taft Hotel *for a room* that has a private bath.
5. *Over the weekend,* I read *Microbe Hunters,* ~~over the weekend~~ which describes the obstacles overcome by famous research scientists.
6. The young girl ~~watched the old horse that~~ *who* was wearing the polka-dot dress, *watched the old horse.*

86

7. Hamburgers ~~were served to all the guests~~ that were smothered in onions/ , were served to all the guests.
8. The hikers ~~saw three extremely loose boulders~~ that were climbing the path to Eagle Rock/ , saw three extremely loose boulders.
9. Luis placed the tennis racket ~~in the trunk of his car~~ with which he hoped to beat Kim/ , in the trunk of his car.
10. Lee won a prize ~~in the national writing contest~~ which included a trip to London/ , in the national writing contest.

Noun Clauses

A *noun clause* can be used in all the ways a single noun can be used.

4f   A **noun clause** is a subordinate clause that is used like a noun.

The following examples show some of the ways a noun clause is used like a noun within a sentence.

SUBJECT	**Whoever cooks dinner** doesn't have to do the dishes.
DIRECT OBJECT	Do you know **when the dance starts?**
INDIRECT OBJECT	Give **whoever calls** this message.
OBJECT OF A PREPOSITION	The hikers left firewood for **whoever might use the cabin next.**
PREDICATE NOMINATIVE	Speed, not distance, is **what counts in launching a satellite into space.**

Words in the following list often introduce a noun clause. *Who, whom, whose, which,* and *that* can also be used as relative pronouns to introduce adjective clauses. For this reason do not rely on the introductory words themselves to identify a clause. Instead, determine how a clause is used in a sentence.

Common Introductory Words for Noun Clauses				
how	what	where	who	whomever
if	whatever	whether	whoever	whose
that	when	which	whom	why

Clauses

EXERCISE 9 Finding Noun Clauses
Write the noun clause in each sentence.
Answers to Exercise 10 also appear below.

1. The Declaration of Independence states <u>that all men are created equal</u>. [d.o.]
2. An acceptance at secretarial school was <u>what some students wanted most</u>. [p.n.]
3. <u>That plants grow toward a source of light</u> can be easily demonstrated. [subj.]
4. Have you thought about <u>where you will look for a job</u>? [o.p.]
5. Mary remembered <u>that she had left her coat in the gym</u>. [d.o.]
6. Mr. Thompson will give extra credit to <u>whoever tutors other students</u>. [o.p.]
7. Give <u>whoever comes to the house</u> the newspapers in the garage. [i.o.]
8. That is <u>what I was told</u>. [p.n.]
9. Did you know <u>that a plastic container won't decompose for thousands of years</u>? [d.o.]
10. <u>What you do now</u> may affect the rest of your life. [subj.]

EXERCISE 10 Determining the Use of Noun Clauses
Label the use of each noun clause in Exercise 9, using the following abbreviations.
See Exercise 9 for the answers.

subject = *subj.*   object of a preposition = *o.p.*
direct object = *d.o.*   predicate nominative = *p.n.*
indirect object = *i.o.*

EXERCISE 11 Time-out for Review
Number your paper 1 to 10. Write the subordinate clauses in the following paragraphs. Then label the use of each one — adverb, adjective, or noun.

Three Eyes

The most unusual of all reptiles may be the tuatara, which lives on the offshore coastal islets of New Zealand. The tuatara is the sole survivor of a group of reptiles that are known to scientists today by their fossil remains. What is so unusual about the tuatara is that it has three eyes! On top of the tuatara's head is a small third eye, which is protected by a hard, transparent scale. Although the optic nerve is completely developed, the iris, which is the colored portion of the eye, is missing. How the tuatara uses its third eye is a mystery, but scientists are looking for an explanation.

Even though other lizards have a third eye, it is covered and is no longer useful. A long time ago, many creatures had three eyes. The tuatara, however, is the only living creature that has kept its third eye virtually intact.

KINDS OF SENTENCE STRUCTURE

All sentences are classified as *simple, compound, complex,* or *compound-complex.* These classifications are determined by the number and the kind of clauses within a sentence.

4g A **simple sentence** consists of one independent clause.

Next year I will graduate from high school.

A simple sentence can have a compound subject, a compound verb, or both.

A sailboat and a motorboat were damaged but not destroyed in the storm.

4h A **compound sentence** consists of two or more independent clauses.

Independent clauses should be combined in a compound sentence only if they are closely related.

The train was due at noon, but it will be an hour late.

The French discovered New York, the Dutch settled it, and the English conquered it.

NOTE: See pages 255 and 276 for the punctuation of a compound sentence.

4i A **complex sentence** consists of one independent clause and one or more subordinate clauses.

I need some new shoes that are good for hiking.

89

Clauses

┌─── independent clause ───┐ ┌─────── subordinate
West Point got its name because it is on the high west
clause ─────────────┐
bank of the Hudson River.

NOTE: See pages 262–263 for the punctuation of a complex sentence.

4j ▶ **A compound-complex sentence consists of two or more independent clauses and one or more subordinate clauses.**

┌─ independent clause ─┐ ┌───── independent clause ─────┐
Ostriches cannot fly, but their legs are so long and strong
┌────── subordinate clause ──────┐
that they can outrun almost any pursuer.

NOTE: The punctuation of compound-complex sentences should follow the rules for both compound and complex sentences.

EXERCISE 12 Classifying Sentences

Number your paper 1 to 10. Then label each sentence *simple*[S], *compound*[Cd], *complex*[Cx], or *compound-complex*[CC].

Herman Melville (1819–1891)

[S] 1. Herman Melville was born in New York to a prosperous family.
[Cx] 2. Melville's father, whose business eventually failed, died when Melville was only 12 years old.
[S] 3. Because of the family's financial difficulties, Melville had to get a job.
[Cd] 4. Melville seemed ashamed of his family's loss of stature, and the remainder of his life was spent seeking security.
[CC] 5. Melville halfheartedly tried being a clerk and a teacher, but he eventually signed onto a whaling boat that was headed for the South Seas.
[Cx] 6. When his ship reached the Marquesas Islands, Melville jumped ship and lived among the natives for a while.
[S] 7. Eventually he got homesick and headed back to New York.
[Cx] 8. Then he wrote several novels that were based on his sea experiences.
[Cx] 9. *Moby Dick*, one of the novels, was based on his own experience on a whaling voyage and an old sailor's yarn about a huge albino whale that was named Mocha Dick.
[Cd] 10. Melville could not sustain his early writing pace, but he still completed *Billy Budd* just before his death.

EXERCISE 13 Writing Sentences
Number your paper 1 to 8. Write two simple sentences, two compound sentences, two complex sentences, and two compound-complex sentences. Remember to use punctuation where needed. *Sample sentences precede this chapter.*

DIAGRAMING SENTENCES

Each clause in a sentence—whether it is independent or subordinate—is diagramed on a separate baseline.

Compound Sentences. Each independent clause is diagramed like a simple sentence. The clauses are joined at the verbs with a broken line on which the conjunction is placed.

That restaurant looks expensive, but prices are reasonable.

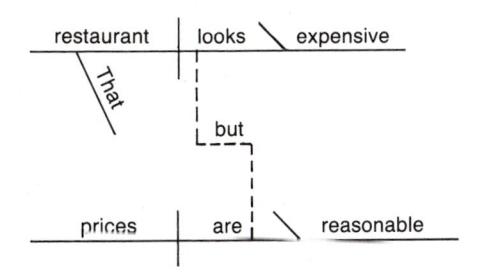

Complex Sentences. An adverb or an adjective clause in a complex sentence is diagramed beneath the independent clause it modifies. The following diagram contains an adverb clause. The subordinating conjunction goes on a broken line that connects the modified verb, adverb, or adjective in the independent clause to the verb in the adverb clause.

After you type a report, you should proofread it.

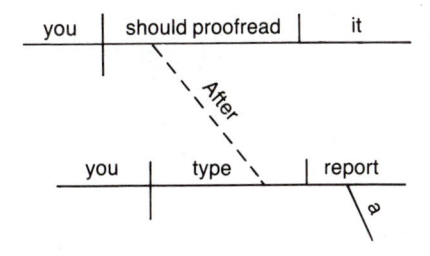

Clauses

The relative pronoun in an adjective clause is connected by a broken line to the noun or the pronoun the clause modifies.

Amy, whom I met in Texas, is visiting me.

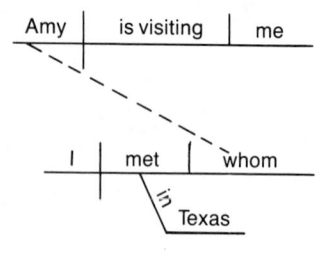

A noun clause is diagramed on a pedestal. Put the pedestal where a single noun with the same function would appear. In the following diagram, the noun clause is used as the subject.

What I do should not affect you.

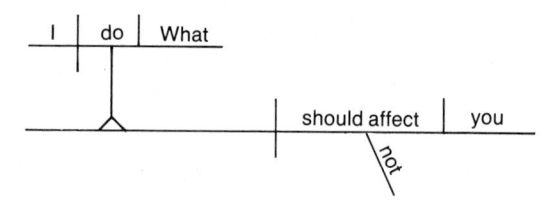

Compound-complex Sentences. To diagram this kind of sentence, apply what you just learned about diagraming compound and complex sentences. In the following diagram, the subordinate clause is a noun clause used as a direct object. If an introductory word in a noun clause has no function within the clause, it is written alongside the pedestal.

I lost my skates, but I think that I can borrow a pair.

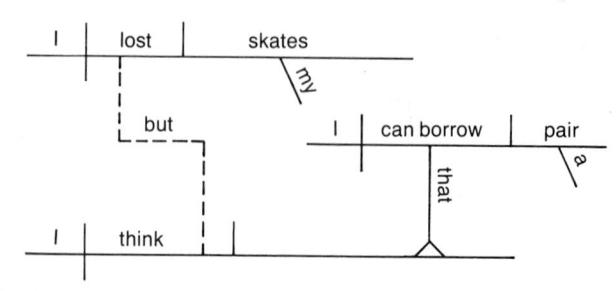

Sentence Combining

EXERCISE 14 Diagraming Sentences

Diagram the following sentences or copy them. If you copy them, draw one line under each subject and two lines under each verb. Then put parentheses around each subordinate clause and label each one *adverb*, *adjective*, or *noun*. *Diagrams precede this chapter.*

1. Harvey opened the box hopefully, but nothing was inside.
2. I must repair the chair (that has two loose rungs).
3. (When Mr. Keller referees the game), no one complains.
4. (What I saw) startled me.
5. (you) Hand me the shovel, and I will clear the driveway.
6. I called Mark, but I learned (that he was ill).
7. This is the chrysanthemum (that won first prize at the flower show).
8. The dog runs to Mary (whenever she calls him).
9. Television antennae should be properly grounded, (because they are good targets for lightning).
10. (you) Give Carlos (whatever he wants for lunch).

Application to Writing

By using a combination of different kinds of sentences, your writing will be more mature and definitely more interesting to read—whether you are writing a personal letter or a 15-page term paper.

After you have written your first draft, go back and analyze the sentences you have written. Are most of them simple sentences? If they are, combine some of them in compound or complex sentences.

TWO SIMPLE SENTENCES	Wrap the package. I will take it to the party for you.
A COMPOUND SENTENCE	Wrap the package, and I will take it to the party for you.
TWO SIMPLE SENTENCES	The light from the moon flooded the field. We had no trouble finding a big pumpkin.
A COMPLEX SENTENCE	**Since the light from the moon flooded the field,** we had no trouble finding a big pumpkin. [adverb clause]

93

Clauses

TWO SIMPLE SENTENCES	Washington's troops spent the bitter winter of 1777–1778 at Valley Forge. That place is now a national park.
A COMPLEX SENTENCE	Valley Forge, **where Washington's troops spent the bitter winter of 1777–1778,** is now a national park. [adjective clause]
TWO SIMPLE SENTENCES	Spiders can spin their webs in total darkness. An article in a magazine pointed this out.
A COMPLEX SENTENCE	An article in a magazine pointed out **that spiders can spin their webs in total darkness.** [noun clause]

EXERCISE 15 Combining Sentences

Combine the following pairs of sentences into compound sentences. Use punctuation where needed.
Sample answers:

1. Some pitchers base their success upon fastballs, but others rely on curveballs and a variety of pitches.
2. Earl went to basketball practice, but the coach was absent.
3. A hummingbird has offspring the size of a bumblebee, and its nest may be as small as a walnut.
4. For an hour the airplane remained on the runway, and the passengers grew uneasy.
5. Glaciers are now found on only a few parts of the earth's surface, but once they covered large areas of Europe, Asia, and North America.
6. A strong wind began to blow, and clouds darkened the sun.
7. The outboard motor suddenly stopped, and the boat began to drift aimlessly with the tide.
8. Mount Everest is the world's highest mountain, but some climbers consider Mount Godwin Austen more difficult to climb.
9. Our car stalled on the turnpike, but no one stopped to help.
10. The subway was delayed, and I decided to walk to work.

EXERCISE 16 Combining Sentences

Combine the following pairs of sentences into complex sentences. Use punctuation where needed.
Sample answers:

1. On Friday nights I usually go to the Plaza, because it always shows films from the 1940s and 1950s.

Chapter Review

2. ∧When The old house on Walden Street was torn down/. ~~T~~the workers found some valuable historical documents in the attic.
3. The Leaning Tower of Pisa∧, which is constructed of successive rows of marble pillars/. ~~It~~ is 177 feet high.
4. ∧The builder estimates that The new library will not be completed for another six months. ~~This is the estimate of the builder.~~
5. ∧Though Porpoises do not have the beaklike snout of a dolphin/. ~~T~~they are, nevertheless, mistaken for dolphins.
6. ∧That The tiny hummingbird can fly 55 miles per hour/. ~~This~~ is a surprising fact.
7. A violent thunderstorm ~~swept out of the mountains. It~~ that vanished as quickly as it had arrived/ swept out of the mountains.
8. ∧Everyone knows that Fruits and vegetables are good for your health. ~~Everyone knows this.~~
9. Leonardo da Vinci∧who won his greatest fame as a painter and sculptor/. ~~He~~ was also a musician and a scientist.
10. ∧After I lit the coals on the grill/. ~~Then~~ I started to make the salad.

CHAPTER REVIEW

A. Number your paper 1 to 20. Write the subordinate clause in each sentence. Then label the use of each one — *adverb*, *adjective*, or *noun*.

1. Did you know ⌐that fish are used⌐ to make glue? (n.)
2. ⌐When Gertrude Ederle swam the English Channel⌐, she was only 19 years old. (adv.)
3. Invertebrate animals ⌐that have six legs and segmented bodies⌐ are called insects. (adj.)
4. Ideas don't work ⌐unless you do⌐. (adv.)
5. Have you decided ⌐what you want for your birthday⌐? (n.)
6. I will listen patiently to ⌐whatever he says⌐. (n.)
7. He ⌐who hesitates⌐ is lost. (adj.)
8. ⌐What she accomplished on water skis⌐ was difficult. (n.)
9. Is the raccoon as clever with its hands ⌐as the monkey⌐? (adv.)
10. Lynn answered the letter ⌐that arrived this morning⌐. (adj.)
11. Some scientists believe ⌐that sunspots are storms in the lower atmosphere of the sun⌐. (n.)

95

Clauses

12. Anne Morrison worked harder than anyone else on the stage crew.
13. Justin, whose short stories are excellent, has just become the editor of our school's literary magazine.
14. Within seconds we could see that the third runner on our relay team would overtake the other runners.
15. The local newspaper will give an award to whoever writes the best essay on patriotism.
16. Stars are seen best when there is no moon.
17. The wonderful story that Ms. Gregory read to us was written by someone in our class.
18. That the future may learn from the past is the motto of colonial Williamsburg.
19. As a dolphin swims, it emits a steady clicking sound.
20. My English report, which is due on Friday, is about T. S. Eliot's poem "The Love Song of J. Alfred Prufrock."

B. Number your paper 1 to 10. Then label each sentence simple, compound, complex, or compound-complex.

S 1. The student drove through the school zone at a very slow speed during the middle of the afternoon.
Cd 2. Sundials are still popular in some areas of the world, but in the United States most people prefer clocks.
Cx 3. The dietician recommends that teenagers eat a nutritious breakfast every day.
Cx 4. When Tara heard from her cousin, she discovered that her relatives had moved to Florida.
S 5. The enormous Shire horse may measure more than 68 inches high and weigh over a ton.
Cx 6. "Moonlight" is an enchanting sonata that Ludwig van Beethoven wrote.
Cd 7. Many of my friends travel to school by bus, but a few walk over a mile each day.
CC 8. The gift that I bought for Daniel has been wrapped for a week, but his birthday is not until Friday.
Cx 9. Since my parents both work full time at the bank, our family shares many household tasks.
Cx 10. The Student Council will sponsor a hayride if the members vote for another student activity.

MASTERY TEST

Number your paper 1 to 10. Then label each sentence *simple, compound, complex,* or *compound-complex.* (S, Cd, Cx, CC)

- S 1. A car operates at maximum fuel economy at speeds from 25 to 35 miles per hour.
- Cd 2. We stopped by your house last night, but no one was there.
- Cx 3. Yesterday I bought the country-western album that you have.
- Cd 4. Most hailstones measure from a half inch to two inches in diameter, but some are significantly larger.
- Cx 5. If you could look inside a leaf, you would see that it is made of thin layers.
- Cx 6. I thought that everyone had forgotten my birthday.
- Cx 7. If a baby grew at the same rate as the larva of the monarch butterfly, it would weigh eight tons in two weeks.
- CC 8. The book that I need for my research paper has been checked out of the library, but it should be returned tomorrow.
- S 9. Frances Perkins fought for minimum wages and old-age pensions and was instrumental in the passage of the Social Security Act of 1935.
- Cx 10. Some goldfish can lose their color if they are kept in dim light.

Chapter 5   Sound Sentences

OBJECTIVES

- To identify and to correct sentence fragments.
- To identify and to correct run-on sentences.
- Application: To write in complete sentences.

MOTIVATIONAL ACTIVITY

Point out that some incomplete sentences occasionally may be acceptable in conversation. Following are some examples.

EXCLAMATIONS	What a beautiful sunset!
REQUESTS	Three tickets, please.
COMMANDS	Over here, Kate.
QUESTIONS AND ANSWERS	When? Tomorrow. Another helping? Yes.

Then discuss how the voice and the context of a conversation sometimes compensate for these incomplete sentences. Written expression, however, does not have these vocal or contextual clues. As a result, misunderstanding and confusion are often the result of incomplete sentences in written expression.

TEACHING SUGGESTIONS

The sentence fragment and the run-on sentence are primary writing problems. They may be attributed to (1) a lack of technical information, (2) carelessness, and (3) a groping for a more complex or scholarly sounding expression. Learning to recognize a subject and a verb is a partial solution to the first problem. Forming the habit of editing should solve the second problem, and analyzing sentence structure is one answer to the last problem.

Sentence Fragments *(pages 99–102)*

You can help your students recognize sentence fragments by having them read their written work aloud. When a student reads a fragment aloud, the rising inflection at the end indicates that the sentence is incomplete. Reading aloud, rather than emphasizing terminology, is particularly helpful with basic students.

Phrase Fragments *(pages 99–100)* Students often carelessly mistake a participle for a verb. Remind your students that a word ending in *-ing* must have a helping verb if it is the verb of the sentence.

FRAGMENT   The boys *playing* ball.
SENTENCE   The boys *are playing* ball.

Write the following fragments on the board or duplicate them. Then have your students correct each one. Average and advanced students should experiment with correcting the sentences in two ways: (1) by adding a helping verb to the *-ing* word and (2) by keeping the *-ing* word as a participle and then adding a main verb.

PARTICIPLE   The boys *playing ball* have formed a neighborhood team.

Before your students do the following exercise, remind them to use commas where needed with participial phrases. Refer them to the punctuation box on page 60 or to page 262 in Chapter 11.

1. The boat drifting in the storm.
2. The cars' headlights shining in my eyes.
3. The young child trying to roller skate.
4. The telephone ringing for 15 minutes.
5. The daffodils blooming early in the spring.

Other Fragments *(pages 100–101)* Since clause fragments are such common errors, you may want to have your students review the lists of subordinating conjunctions and relative pronouns on pages 80 and 83 respectively before they begin this section. Again, encourage your students to read their sentences aloud.

Run-on Sentences *(pages 102–103)*

Two sentences that are joined by a comma—without a conjunction—result in the most common type of run-on sentence. The best way to examine run-on sentences is to hand out examples of

Chapter 5 a

Sound Sentences

run-on sentences that students have written. Point out that each group of words has at least two sets of subjects and verbs, but no conjunction to connect them.

Stress to your average and advanced students that run-on sentences should be corrected in a variety of ways. Too often students tend to add an *and* between two independent clauses. Encourage your students to correct run-on sentences by changing them into complex sentences.

ACTIVITIES FOR DIFFERENT ABILITIES
Basic Students
ACTIVITY 1 Sentence Fragments
To provide additional practice, write the following groups of words on the board or duplicate them. Then have your students rewrite each fragment as a complete sentence by adding words or by joining the fragment to the complete sentence.

1. In 1823, Charles Macintosh, a Scotsman, made the first raincoat. Which he called a mackintosh.
2. Medusa had bronze claws and hair made out of serpents. According to mythology.
3. The bagpipe is most commonly used as a solo instrument or in small groups. But occasionally appears in large bands.
4. Southern Texas and the eastern coast of Florida are the homes of the indigo snake. The largest nonpoisonous snake in the United States.
5. Since in her day it was unusual for women to write novels. Mary Ann Evans, the author of *Silas Marner*, used the pen name George Eliot.
6. Flying in a perfect *V* formation. The flock of geese flew over the Missouri cornfield.
7. Kathy has originated an ingenious method. Of raising money for the new children's hospital.
8. Don Quixote was a Spanish knight. Who rode about the country challenging windmills.
9. Several door prizes will be given to audience members. A portable radio, an electric mixer, and gift certificates to local restaurants.
10. There had never been a woman cabinet member before President Franklin Roosevelt appointed Frances Perkins Secretary of Labor. A post she held for 12 years.

ACTIVITY 2 Run-on Sentences
To provide additional practice, duplicate the following run-on sentences. Then have your students correct each one by separating it into two sentences and using a capital letter and a period.

1. Timbuktu in the Republic of Mali has an average temperature of 84.7°F. at the other extreme is Ulan-Bator in Mongolia with an average temperature of 24.8°F.
2. In 1858, John Butterfield opened the overland mail route to California, he contracted to carry the mail between St. Louis and San Francisco in 25 days or less.
3. As a boy Peter Cooper had to help with the family laundry, he invented the washing machine to make his work easier.
4. On March 29, 1848, the waters of Niagara Falls stopped flowing, tons of ice had blocked the entrance to the tributary that feeds the falls.
5. Until 50 years ago, grizzlies were fairly common in many parts of the world, now they are found only in a few national parks and forests.
6. Keats made a mistake in one of his poems, the discoverer of the Pacific was Balboa, not Cortez.
7. For a thousand years, the athletic contests at Olympia brought together men from all over the ancient world the games were so important that the Greeks used them as the basis for their calendar.
8. Jane finished her letter, then Jeff mailed it on his way to work.
9. The first important engagement of the War between the States was the Battle of Bull Run, civilians from Washington came to watch the

Chapter 5 b

Sound Sentences

battle as though it were a football game.
10. Have you ever read *The Mystery of Edwin Drood*, it was written by Charles Dickens?

Advanced Students

ACTIVITY 1 Recognizing Sentence Errors

To provide additional practice, duplicate the following groups of words. Then have your students find and correct each sentence fragment and run-on sentence. Some fragments can be combined with the groups of words that either follows or precedes them. (Some groups of words are complete sentences.)

Monarch Butterflies

1. What do you know about the monarch butterfly?
2. With an wingspan of up to four inches, this butterfly is one of our largest and most interesting.
3. This magnificent butterfly is common throughout the United States it is usually seen in fields and along roadsides.
4. Even the pupa is unusual, it is pale green and is spotted with black and gold.
5. The monarchs are like the birds, each fall they migrate.
6. Vast numbers flying thousands of miles to their destination.
7. For a long time, a mystery associated with monarch migrations.
8. There was no problem about the migration of Western monarchs.
9. Which are not nearly so numerous as the Eastern monarchs.
10. Western monarchs make their way to the Monterey peninsula.
11. Each autumn these monarchs return to the same grove, they turn the trees orange with their brilliant colors.
12. Where the Eastern monarchs go during the winter was the mystery.
13. Fred A. Urquhart, a Toronto professor.
14. He began the search for the answer to this puzzle in 1937.
15. But had no success for 30 years.
16. As a check on the migration.
17. Urquhart and his assistants tagged thousands of monarchs with instructions to return the tags to Urquhart.
18. Tags eventually sent back to Urquhart.
19. Urquhart made dotted maps.
20. Showing where each tagged butterfly had been found.
21. The dots fell into lines that pointed to Mexico, then Urquhart assumed the destination was somewhere in Mexico.
22. Eventually he found them in a tiny, wooded, 20-acre region.
23. That was located at an altitude of 9,000 feet.
24. Because the air was chilly enough to inactivate the butterflies.
25. They were able to remain in one spot for long periods without having to eat.

ACTIVITY 2 Analyzing Literature

Occasionally when your advanced classes are reading short stories, analyze the style of the authors to see whether and why they use fragments. What effect was a particular author trying to achieve by using fragments? Then have your students turn the fragments into sentences. Could the author have achieved the same effect with sentences? Then discuss where in their own short stories fragments might be legitimately and effectively used. This type of analysis and discussion may help your students develop a keener feeling for effective writing.

ACTIVITY 3 Writing Sentences

Have your students choose a picture from a magazine or a photograph that could be used for the cover of a news magazine. Then have them write a news article of ten to fifteen sentences that relate to the cover. Remind them to use a variety of sentence structures. Then before your students hand in their articles, have them edit their sentences for sentence errors.

Chapter 5 c

Sound Sentences

ADDITIONAL PRACTICE

Basic Students
Teacher's Resource Book: pages 117–118
Workbook: pages 61–64

Average Students
Teacher's Resource Book: pages 119–120
Workbook: pages 61–64

Advanced Students
Teacher's Resource Book: pages 121–122

REVIEW EXERCISES AND TESTS

Student Text
Diagnostic Test: page 98
Chapter Review: pages 105–106
Mastery Test: page 106

Teacher's Resource Book
Chapter 5 Test: pages 17–18
(Also available as spirit duplicating masters.)

Workbook
Unit Review: pages 65–66

ADDITIONAL ANSWERS

EXERCISE 1   Finding Phrase Fragments *(page 100)*

Sample answers:
1. Life was rather uncomplicated in a small New England town in the early 1960s.
3. They planned to walk together around the reservoir.
4. Racing to the bus stop at the corner of Concord Street and Evergreen Avenue, Frank arrived just in time.
5. Mr. Emerson, the head of the English Department at Fitzgerald High School, is my neighbor.
7. By painting the room a bright yellow, we made it more cheerful.
8. A silver eagle, mounted to the hood of his car, shone in the sunlight.
10. I like that sweater, the one with the orange and purple stripes.

EXERCISE 2   Finding Sentence Fragments *(page 101)*

Sample answers:
1. Even though our reports aren't due until Friday, I have finished mine.
2. I was tired but couldn't sleep in strange surroundings.
3. We need poster board, some brushes and paint, and volunteers.
4. The noise that interrupted Theresa in the middle of her speech was a siren.
5. Unless you hear from us before the weekend, we will go with you.
7. The crowd applauded and waved to the soldiers in the parade.
9. Please buy a box of spaghetti, two cans of tomato sauce, and cheese.

Chapter 5 d

5
Sound Sentences

For additional practice for this chapter, see the Teacher's Resource Book and the Workbook.

DIAGNOSTIC TEST

Number your paper 1 to 10. Then label each group of words *sentence*, *fragment*, or *run-on*. (S, F, R)

EXAMPLE   Shipped from the farmlands of Arizona.
ANSWER   fragment

R 1. This morning we had sunshine and blue skies, now black clouds are closing in overhead.
F 2. Where the first volunteers were enlisted.
F 3. Remaining relatively unchanged for centuries.
S 4. In the summertime tourists enjoy the train trip from Fairbanks to Anchorage.
F 5. To help those less fortunate than we are.
F 6. When the referee tosses the ball into the air.
S 7. After repairing the old clock, Grandfather fixed the leaky faucet.
R 8. A knight saluted by raising the visor of his helmet, this gesture showed great trust and friendship.
F 9. According to a law passed in New England in 1647.
S 10. The Great Pyramid, one of the Seven Wonders of the World, is a solid mass of limestone blocks covering 13 acres.

Sentence Fragments

5a

When you revise the first draft of a composition, you may find some incomplete thoughts or two or more sentences that run together. These errors confuse your readers and prevent them from understanding what you have written. This chapter will help you recognize and correct these errors.

SENTENCE FRAGMENTS AND RUN-ON SENTENCES

The two most common sentence errors are sentence fragments and run-on sentences. A *sentence fragment* expresses an incomplete thought. A *run-on sentence* runs two or more sentences together as one sentence.

Sentence Fragments

A sentence fragment often leaves readers with unanswered questions.

5a   A **sentence fragment** is a group of words that does not express a complete thought.

There are many kinds of sentence fragments. Each one of them leaves out one or more elements needed to make a sentence.

Phrase Fragments. A phrase does not have a subject and a verb. As a result, a phrase never expresses a complete thought. Following are examples of different kinds of phrase fragments.

PREPOSITIONAL PHRASE	Warblers and tanagers fly south toward the equator. **In the late summer or early fall.**
PARTICIPIAL PHRASE	Woodpeckers have strong, pointed beaks. **Used to peck holes in trees.**
GERUND PHRASE	Cave dwellers finally learned to make a fire. **By rubbing two sticks together.**
INFINITIVE PHRASE	Everyone in the school worked hard. **To raise money for the new hospital.**
APPOSITIVE PHRASE	In 1880, prospectors for gold founded Juneau. **The capital of Alaska.**

99

Sound Sentences

EXERCISE 1 Finding Phrase Fragments

Label each group of words *sent^{S}ence* or *fra^{F}gment*. If a group of words is a fragment, add the words necessary to make it a sentence. Add capital letters and punctuation where needed.
Sample sentences for 1, 3, 4, 5, 7, 8, and 10 precede this chapter.

EXAMPLE   Leading the Red Sox at the end of the eighth inning.
ANSWER   fragment—Leading the Red Sox at the end of the eighth inning, the Yankees went on to win the game.

F 1. In a small New England town in the early 1960s.
S 2. A roaring fire swept through the nearby forest.
F 3. To walk together around the reservoir.
F 4. Racing to the bus stop at the corner of Concord Street and Evergreen Avenue.
F 5. The head of the English Department at Fitzgerald High School.
S 6. Members of the high school band were dressed as cartoon characters.
F 7. By painting the room a bright yellow.
F 8. Mounted to the hood of his car.
S 9. Making ends meet wasn't easy.
F 10. The one with the orange and purple stripes.

Other Fragments. A subordinate clause is a fragment if it stands alone; only an independent clause can function as a complete sentence. *(See pages 77–78.)* Following are examples of clause fragments and other common fragments.

ADVERB CLAUSES	A boat owner should know how to make emergency engine repairs. **Since there are no repair shops at sea.**
	Take your time. **Because no one is ready.**
ADJECTIVE CLAUSES	Earthquakes occur often in Japan. **Where there can be several a day.**
	I don't think I want to see the play. **That is at the Shubert.**
PART OF A COMPOUND VERB	Davis hit a long, high fly to left field. **And ran the bases for a home run.**
ITEMS IN A SERIES	We have everything we want. **A roof over our heads, food in our stomachs, and peace within our hearts.**

Sentence Fragments

EXERCISE 2   Finding Sentence Fragments

Label each group of words *sent*^S*ence* or *frag*^F*ment*. If a group of words is a fragment, add the words necessary to make it a sentence. Add capital letters and punctuation where needed.

Sample sentences for 1, 2, 3, 4, 5, 7, and 9 precede this chapter.

F 1. Even though our reports aren't due until Friday.
F 2. But couldn't sleep in strange surroundings.
F 3. Poster board, some brushes and paint, and volunteers.
F 4. That interrupted Theresa in the middle of her speech.
F 5. Unless you hear from us before the weekend.
S 6. Where did they go after school?
F 7. And waved to the soldiers in the parade.
S 8. The package was delivered to our house.
F 9. A box of spaghetti, two cans of tomato sauce, and cheese.
S 10. After practice had ended for the day, we went home.

Ways to Correct Sentence Fragments

When you find a sentence fragment, you can correct it in one of two ways. You can, as you have been doing in the two previous exercises, add words to make the fragment a complete sentence. You can also attach a fragment to a sentence that is next to it by adding or dropping words as necessary.

SENTENCE AND FRAGMENT	Otters are the free spirits of the animal world. Sliding down banks into streams, playing tag, and teasing other animals.
SEPARATE SENTENCES	Otters are the free spirits of the animal world. **They slide down banks into streams, play tag, and tease other animals.**
ATTACHED	**Sliding down banks into streams, playing tag, and teasing other animals,** otters are the free spirits of the animal world.

EXERCISE 3   Correcting Sentence Fragments

Write the following sentences, correcting each sentence fragment. Either make the fragment a complete sentence by adding any necessary words, or attach it to the other sentence. Add capital letters and punctuation where needed.

Sample answers:
1. Emily Dickinson wrote nearly 2,000 short poems. Only 7 of which were published during her lifetime.

101

Sound Sentences

2. Pewter is made by combining tin and one or more other metals; ˢSuch as lead or copper.
3. Crystal Falls is a wonderful place, ᵗTo see the rushing water churning over the rocks.
4. Sam caught the pass, ᵃAnd ran for a touchdown.
5. Swimming is one of the most healthful of all sports; ˢSince it uses muscles usually inactive in daily life.
6. Uncle Albert had one hope, ᵗTo get the wheat planted in time for an early crop.
7. Wyoming is the home of many wild animals. ₌Some of them are₌ The grizzly bear, the elk, and the mountain lion.
8. Standing in the kitchen, Lee entertained us with an amusing story.
9. After an hour at the fine-arts exhibit, I decided to try calligraphy.
10. The last runner on the relay team grabbed the stick. ˢʰᵉ ~~And~~ headed for the finish line.

Run-on Sentences

Run-on sentences bombard readers with too much information at one time. Usually adding to the confusion of several sentences running together is the lack of punctuation or the use of incorrect punctuation.

5b > A **run-on sentence** is two or more sentences that are written as one sentence and are separated by a comma or no mark of punctuation at all.

A run-on sentence is usually written in one of two ways.

WITH A COMMA	The national parks preserve the scenic wonders of our country, also they provide recreational facilities for visitors.
WITH NO PUNCTUATION	Swift-moving streams move boulders and cobblestones slow-moving streams carry mainly mud.

You can correct a run-on sentence in several ways. You can turn it into separate sentences or into a compound sentence or a complex sentence.

Run-on Sentences

5b

RUN-ON SENTENCE	A polished diamond has a brilliant luster, an unpolished diamond resembles frosted glass.
SEPARATE SENTENCES	A polished diamond has a brilliant luster. An unpolished diamond resembles frosted glass.
COMPOUND SENTENCE	A polished diamond has a brilliant luster, but an unpolished diamond resembles frosted glass. [A compound sentence can also be joined with a semicolon or a semicolon and a transitional word. *(See pages 276–277.)*]
COMPLEX SENTENCE	Although a polished diamond has a brilliant luster, an unpolished diamond resembles frosted glass.

EXERCISE 4   Correcting Run-on Sentences

Correct the following run-on sentences. Write them as separate sentences or as compound or complex sentences. Add capital letters and punctuation where needed.
Sample answers:

1. Otis hoped to make the swim team. He didn't succeed, though, and joined the basketball team instead.
2. The gangplanks were raised; then the huge ship slowly inched toward the open sea.
3. Mozart died at the age of 35. He composed more than 600 works during his brief life.
4. The Great Salt Lake in Utah is fed by freshwater streams and has no connection with the ocean. It is, however, at least four times as salty as the ocean.
5. My sister attends college at night. In the day she works as a nurse's aide.
6. Hearing the roar, I looked up into the sky. There I saw two silvery dots followed by long white vapor trails.
7. Stephen flipped the puck over Alvin's stick; then he whirled in a flash to corral the loose puck at center ice.
8. Tapioca pudding is very popular in the United States, but the plant from which it comes is found only in tropical areas.
9. There are about 100 minerals valued as gems. Many of the 100, however, are found in two or more colors.
10. The Grand Canyon, which is one of the most popular natural attractions in the United States, became a national park in 1919.

103

Sound Sentences

EXERCISE 5 Time-out for Review

Write the following sentences, correcting each sentence fragment or run-on sentence. Add capital letters and punctuation where needed.

Sample answers:

A Bit of Americana

1. Article 3 of the Constitution established the Supreme Court. This is The highest court of the United States.
2. Although James Fenimore Cooper had intended to become a farmer, he turned to writing instead.
3. Andrew Jackson was the only president ever to pay off the final installment of the national debt. He did this in 1835.
4. Belva Lockwood argued a case before the Supreme Court. She was nominated for president of the United States by a California women's convention in 1884.
5. The Erie Canal was completed in 1825. It linked the Hudson River with the Great Lakes.
6. President Franklin Pierce graduated from Bowdoin College in Maine. Schoolmates of his were Longfellow and Hawthorne.
7. The first regular airmail service began in 1918. It had runs between New York City, Philadelphia, and Washington, D.C.
8. The history of the Old West is filled with names of rough, tough towns. Three of them were Hangtown, Deadwood, and Tombstone.
9. Only one president was the father of another president. John Adams was John Quincy Adams's father.
10. By studying peanuts and other crops, George Washington Carver made many discoveries that helped farmers.

Application to Writing

Most sentence fragments and run-on sentences are a result of fast, careless writing. By reading your written work—preferably aloud—you will find most of your errors.

EXERCISE 6 Editing for Sentence Errors

Rewrite the following paragraphs, correcting all sentence fragments and run-on sentences. Make sure that you correct the errors in a variety of ways. Otherwise, you will have all short, choppy sentences. Add capital letters and punctuation where needed.

104

Chapter Review

Sample answers:

Robert Frost (1874–1963)

Robert Frost was born in San Francisco. Upon the death of his father when Frost was ten years old, he and his mother moved to New England, where his family had lived for nine generations. After briefly attending Dartmouth and Harvard, he worked as a shoemaker, schoolteacher, editor, and farmer during the last decade of the nineteenth century.

In 20 years Frost earned very little money selling poems. Determined to make his writing successful, Frost and his family moved to England for three years. There he published two volumes of poetry that were extremely popular, both in England and the United States.

Returning home, Frost continued to write. During the following years, he received four Pulitzer Prizes for his poetry. Frost also became the unofficial poet laureate of the United States. In 1961, he read his poem "The Gift Outright," at the inauguration of President John F. Kennedy. He was the first poet to be involved in the inauguration of a United States president.

CHAPTER REVIEW

Write the following sentences, correcting each sentence fragment or run-on sentence. Add capital letters and punctuation where needed. *Sample answers:*

1. Napoleon's handwriting was considered illegible. Some of his letters were mistaken for maps of battlefields.
2. A chameleon's hormones and nervous system control its color changes, which take place in the layers of cells beneath its transparent skin.
3. When you buy a food product, it is wise to read the label.
4. The fall is a busy time of year for us; we can tomatoes.
5. Crickets and other animals call to one another to warn other animals to stay out of their territory.
6. The tomato was unknown in Italy until the sixteenth century; now it is the mainstay of modern Italian cuisine.
7. I'll meet you in the music room, the last room at the end of the hall.
8. I looked all through the house and finally found my math homework lying under the newspaper.
9. No alphabetic language in existence today contains more than 72 letters. Most contain far fewer.

105

Sound Sentences

10. In buildings across the United States~~,~~ **P**eople are adding insulation to conserve energy.
11. On my way to school yesterday~~,~~ I noticed two deer.
12. Great Britain is sometimes known as the United Kingdom~~/~~ **B**ecause it is made up of four smaller parts.
13. ~~Hadley took a picture of the flock of geese.~~ Using color film and a manual camera~~,~~ , Hadley took a picture of a flock of geese.
14. Mozart produced *The Marriage of Figaro*~~,~~ **I**t is an opera.
15. Lee walked across the porch~~,~~ **A**nd knocked on the door.
16. Harbor seals sleep underwater, **but** they rise to the surface to breathe every 15 minutes or so without waking up.
17. Despite the popularity of television, radio is not dead. **R**adios still sell at a brisk rate.
18. A popular tourist attraction in Kentucky is Mammoth Cave~~,~~ **W**hich contains five levels of corridors and several lakes, rivers, and waterfalls.
19. From the shore we watched the sailboats~~,~~ **T**acking into a strong northwest wind out of the bay.
20. Asia**, which** is the largest of all continents, ~~it~~ touches three oceans.

MASTERY TEST

Number your paper 1 to 10. Then label each group of words *sentence*, *fragment*, or *run-on*.

S 1. Many accidents within the home are the result of carelessness.
F 2. One of the best-known artists in this country.
F 3. Throughout the pages of medieval history.
R 4. Rachael Carson was a marine biologist for 15 years then she wrote *Silent Spring*.
F 5. To fly around the world on a nonstop flight.
R 6. Young wheat plants are bright green, they turn golden brown in ripening.
S 7. The assembly is during fourth period.
S 8. Enclosed in the envelope is a résumé.
F 9. Because the guests came early for dinner.
R 10. In Italian *pizza* means "pie," *spaghetti* means "little cords."

STANDARDIZED TEST

GRAMMAR

Directions: Look carefully at the structure of each sentence. In the appropriate row on your answer sheet, fill in circle

A if the sentence is a simple sentence.
B if the sentence is a compound sentence.
C if the sentence is a complex sentence.
D if the sentence is a compound-complex sentence.

SAMPLE   We baked four dozen muffins for the class breakfast.

ANSWER   Ⓐ Ⓑ Ⓒ Ⓓ

A 1. At the barn door, four honking geese greeted us.
B 2. Sarah is a wonderful actress, but she can't sing a note.
A 3. The plane shuddered for a moment but then rose smoothly.
C 4. As you break the eggs, separate the whites from the yolks.
B 5. Before supper the cat goes out, and the dog comes in.
D 6. Ed was in the lead, and he was sure that he would stay there.
A 7. Isolating the virus was Dr. Gould's greatest accomplishment.
C 8. Baxter realized that this time there was no escape.
B 9. At noon the rain ended, but the damage had already been done.
C 10. If we don't hurry, the museum will close before we get there.
B 11. Did Oscar see the ball coming, or did the sun blind him?
D 12. I saw the shoes that I wanted, but they were too expensive.
C 13. My dog runs to the window and howls whenever he hears thunder.
D 14. We must leave as soon as Peg comes, or we'll miss the bus.
A 15. I don't have time to wait very long.
A 16. Awakened by a noise, Ella tiptoed to the door and listened.
D 17. Is it a rash that is making Pal itch, or does he have fleas?
B 18. On one side of Earth is Venus, and on the other is Mars.
C 19. When the applause began, the actors knew they had a hit.
D 20. What he saw was frightening, and what he did was courageous.

107

Directions: Decide which sentence best combines each pair of sentences. In the appropriate row on your answer sheet, fill in the circle containing the same letter as your answer.

SAMPLE   The cloud floated toward us. It was like a boat.
  A The cloud floated toward us and was like a boat.
  B The cloud floated toward us like a boat.
  C As it was like a boat, the cloud floated toward us.

ANSWER Ⓐ Ⓑ Ⓒ

c 21. The umbrella had red and orange stripes. It had been left on the school bus.
  A Having red and orange stripes, the umbrella had been left on the school bus.
  B The umbrella had been left on the school bus with red and orange stripes.
  C The umbrella with red and orange stripes had been left on the school bus.

A 22. The computer beeped. Then an error message appeared.
  A The computer beeped, and an error message appeared.
  B After an error message appeared, the computer beeped.
  C Beeping, an error message appeared on the computer.

c 23. The phone rings. Three people race to answer it every time.
  A The phone rings, but three people race to answer it.
  B Ringing, three people race to answer the phone.
  C Whenever the phone rings, three people race to answer it.

B 24. Anthony was biking down the path. He came upon a skunk.
  A Anthony came upon a skunk biking down the path.
  B Biking down the path, Anthony came upon a skunk.
  C Coming upon a skunk, Anthony biked down the path.

A 25. Accidents are the leading cause of death among young people in this country. They can often be avoided.
  A Accidents, which are the leading cause of death among young people in this country, can often be avoided.
  B Often being avoided, accidents are the leading cause of death among young people in this country.
  C Accidents are the leading cause of death among young people in this country and can often be avoided.

Unit 2

Usage

6 Using Verbs
7 Using Pronouns
8 Subject and Verb Agreement
9 Using Adjectives and Adverbs
   Glossary of Usage

Chapter 6 Using Verbs

OBJECTIVES

- To identify the principal parts of regular and irregular verbs.
- To identify the six tenses and the progressive forms of a verb, and to explain their uses.
- To avoid unnecessary shifts in tense.
- To distinguish between active and passive voice and explain the uses of each voice.
- To explain and be able to use the indicative, imperative, and subjunctive mood of a verb.
- Application: To convey meaning accurately by using the correct form of a verb.

MOTIVATIONAL ACTIVITY

Write the following sentences on the board. Then ask your students if they know how the sentences differ in meaning.

Ronald *played* the piano for three years.
Ronald *has played* the piano for three years.

In the first sentence, *played*, the past tense, describes an action completed in the past. Ronald played the piano for three years but no longer plays the piano. In the second sentence, *has played*, the present perfect tense, refers to an action begun in the past and still going on in the present. Ronald began to play the piano three years ago and is still playing the piano.

By giving these examples and their explanations, your students should see that the whole meaning of a sentence can change when the tense of a verb is changed. As a result using verbs correctly is a necessary part of clear communication.

TEACHING SUGGESTIONS

Since most students' usage errors involve verbs, you may want to do each, or some, of the exercises twice—once written and once orally. *Hearing* the correct principal part in a sentence is one of the best reinforcements possible.

NOTE: The verbs *lie/lay*, *rise/raise/*, and *sit/set* are covered and practiced in the Glossary of Usage.

Regular Verbs *(pages 111–112)*

Reminding or informing your students that most verbs are regular verbs is probably the most positive way you can begin this chapter. You may want to point out, however, that spelling changes occur when *d* or *ed* is added to some regular verbs, such as *trim* and *stop* in Exercise 1 on page 112.

Irregular Verbs *(pages 112–123)*

The irregular verbs in this chapter have been put into six groups, according to how they form their past and past participle. This grouping should be helpful when teaching or reviewing the irregular verbs. When the irregular verbs are broken down into small groups, students are not as easily overwhelmed by the task of learning them. These groupings also help students learn the irregular verbs more quickly because they are learning groups of verbs, rather than individual verbs.

Verb Tense *(pages 123–128)*

The following chart shows how the various tenses are formed from the principal parts of a verb. It may help your students learn to form the tenses more easily.

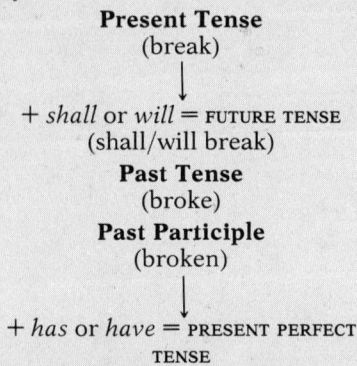

Present Tense
(break)
↓
+ *shall* or *will* = FUTURE TENSE
(shall/will break)
Past Tense
(broke)
Past Participle
(broken)
↓
+ *has* or *have* = PRESENT PERFECT TENSE

Chapter 6 a

Using Verbs

(has/have broken)
+ *had* = PAST PERFECT TENSE
(had broken)
+ *shall* or *will have* = FUTURE PERFECT TENSE
(shall/will have broken)

NOTE: You may want to point out that the conjugation of the *be* verb on pages 126–127 can be used as a reference throughout the year.

Uses of the Tenses *(pages 128–131)*

The uses of some tenses, more than others, tend to be a problem to many students. You may want to spend some extra time on the present perfect and the past perfect tenses.

Present Perfect Tense Students sometimes incorrectly use the past tense instead of the present perfect tense. You may want to point out that the past tense should be used for actions that occurred at a definite time in the past. Frequently a word, a phrase, or a clause in the sentence or in a preceding sentence places the action at a definite time. The present perfect tense, however, is used to express an action that occurred at an indefinite time in the past.

PAST The Hamiltons *found* their dog yesterday. [The finding occurred at a definite time in the past—yesterday.]

PRESENT PERFECT The Hamiltons *have found* their dog. [The speaker does not say exactly when the Hamiltons found their dog.]

The present perfect tense is also used to express a present situation resulting from an action that began or occurred in the past and is continuing in the present.

PRESENT PERFECT Uncle Louis *has worked* on a farm for two years. [He started to work on the farm two years ago and is still working there.]

Past Perfect Tense The past perfect tense is used to express the earlier of two past actions. In other words the past perfect tense is the "before-past" tense.

After we left Washington, we realized that we *had forgotten* to see the moon rocks at the Smithsonian Institution. [Although the leaving, the realizing, and the forgetting all took place in the past, the forgetting occurred before the leaving and the realizing.]

To practice the distinctions among these tenses, write the following sentences on the board or duplicate them. Then have your students indicate the correct tense of each verb in parentheses.

1. The Tigers (lose) only three games last season.
2. Sandra (be) the manager of that health spa for two years.
3. Phil stopped in at the camera shop to get the special film he (order).
4. When I got home, I found out that Mom (make) my favorite dinner.
5. Marty (work) as an usher at Cinema Plaza.

Active and Passive Voice *(pages 133–135)*

The point to emphasize throughout this section is that whenever possible, students should use the active voice because it makes writing more forceful and vivid to a reader. (You may want to omit this section with your basic students.)

ACTIVITIES FOR DIFFERENT ABILITIES

Basic Students

ACTIVITY 1 Irregular Verbs
After you have done the exercises for irregular verbs on pages 114–123, divide your class into two teams. In spelling-bee fashion, read the sentences in the exercises aloud and have your students take turns giving the past or the past participle of the irregular verbs. This activity will orally reinforce the principal parts of the irregular verbs.

ACTIVITY 2 Irregular Verbs and Dictionary Skills
Write the following irregular verbs on the board or duplicate them. Then have your students look up each one in the dictionary and write its principal parts. This exercise will show your students

Chapter 6 b

Using Verbs

that the principal parts of irregular verbs can be found in the dictionary.

1. bite
2. creep
3. wear
4. grind
5. split
6. build
7. fight
8. stride
9. seek
10. beat

ACTIVITY 3 Verb Tenses
Have your students write similar sentences that use the six tenses of different verbs. Provide the following example.

I *do* exercises every day.
I *did* some exercises yesterday.
I *will do* some exercises tomorrow.
I *have done* exercises for six months.
I *had* never *done* any exercises before that.
I *shall have done* many exercises by the end of this year.

Advanced Students
ACTIVITY 1 Chapter Review
To give your students additional practice, duplicate the following sentences. Then have them write the correct form of the verb in parentheses.

1. The farmer ran across the field to the place where the plane (land).
2. For several years Mrs. Mosley (sing) "The Star-Spangled Banner" at the Fourth of July concert in the park.
3. Only Captain Draper (know) what was in the old chest.
4. After the warning bell (ring), Terry ran into class.
5. My neighbor (write) several books about raising children.
6. Luther Burbank once (grow) plums on an almond tree.
7. The Clarks (live) in Arlington for only six months.
8. When we arrived at the ice-skating rink, I was glad that I (take) an extra sweater along.
9. Randy stood up in the boat and (throw) the weighted net out across the water.
10. Thomas (make) an appointment with the dentist.

ACTIVITY 2 Writing Sentences
Read your students the following limerick.

There was a young lady named Bright,
Whose speed was much faster than light.
  She set out one day
  In a relative way
And returned on the previous night.

Then have your students write 10 to 15 sentences that describe what their lives might be like if time suddenly started to run backward. When they have finished, have them edit their sentences for any verb errors.

ADDITIONAL PRACTICE
Basic Students
  Teacher's Resource Book:
  pages 123–124
  Workbook: pages 67–80
Average Students
  Teacher's Resource Book:
  pages 125–126
  Workbook: pages 67–80
Advanced Students
  Teacher's Resource Book:
  pages 127–128

REVIEW EXERCISES AND TESTS
Student Text
  Diagnostic Test: page 110
  Chapter Review: pages 138–139
  Mastery Test: page 139
Teacher's Resource Book
  Chapter 6 Test: pages 19–20
  (Also available as spirit duplicating masters.)

Using Verbs

ADDITIONAL ANSWERS

EXERCISE 1 Determining the Principal Parts of Regular Verbs *(page 112)*

PRESENT	PRESENT PARTICIPLE	PAST	PAST PARTICIPLE
1. ask	asking	asked	(have) asked
2. trim	trimming	trimmed	(have) trimmed
3. use	using	used	(have) used
4. play	playing	played	(have) played
5. stop	stopping	stopped	(have) stopped
6. end	ending	ended	(have) ended
7. mend	mending	mended	(have) mended
8. boil	boiling	boiled	(have) boiled
9. wait	waiting	waited	(have) waited
10. suppose	supposing	supposed	(have) supposed

EXERCISE 3 Determining the Principal Parts of Irregular Verbs *(page 115)*

PRESENT	PRESENT PARTICIPLE	PAST	PAST PARTICIPLE
1. let	letting	let	(have) let
2. sit	sitting	sat	(have) sat
3. buy	buying	bought	(have) bought
4. hurt	hurting	hurt	(have) hurt
5. say	saying	said	(have) said
6. lose	losing	lost	(have) lost
7. make	making	made	(have) made
8. lead	leading	led	(have) led
9. tell	telling	told	(have) told
10. lay	laying	laid	(have) laid

EXERCISE 14 Conjugating a Verb *(page 125)*

SINGULAR		PLURAL	
		Present	
I	do/begin	we	do/begin
you	do/begin	you	do/begin
he, she, it	does/begins	they	do/begin
		Past	
I	did/began	we	did/began
you	did/began	you	did/began
he, she, it	did/began	they	did/began
		Future	
I	shall/will do/begin	we	shall/will do/begin
you	will do/begin	you	will do/begin
he, she, it	will do/begin	they	will do/begin
		Present Perfect	
I	have done/begun	we	have done/begun
you	have done/begun	you	have done/begun
he, she, it	has done/begun	they	have done/begun
		Past Perfect	
I	had done/begun	we	had done/begun
you	had done/begun	you	had done/begun
he, she, it	had done/begun	they	had done/begun
		Future Perfect	
I	shall/will have done/begun	we	shall/will have done/begun
you	will have done/begun	you	will have done/begun
he, she, it	will have done/begun	they	will have done/begun

EXERCISE 22 Writing Sentences *(page 137)*

Sample answers:
1. The sun is shining brightly today.
2. Don't walk on the clean floor with your muddy boots!
3. If I were rich, I'd buy a new car.
4. I wish I were a movie star.

Chapter 6 d

6

Using Verbs

For additional practice for this chapter, see the Teacher's Resource Book and the Workbook

DIAGNOSTIC TEST

Number your paper 1 to 10. Then write the past or the past participle of each verb in parentheses.

EXAMPLE Many branches were (break) by the fierce wind.
ANSWER broken

1. Elsie (tear) [tore] open the special delivery letter from her brother.
2. Only Sherlock Holmes (know) [knew] who the thief was.
3. Robert Frost was (give) [given] honorary degrees by many colleges and universities.
4. Henry (see) [saw] his wallet stuck between the cushions of the couch.
5. Have you (choose) [chosen] the topic for your term paper yet?
6. The temperature has (rise) [risen] five degrees since this morning.
7. Have you (begin) [begun] your homework yet?
8. We (buy) [bought] some kitchen chairs at an auction.
9. The telephone hasn't (ring) [rung] all day.
10. After shoveling all that snow, I thought my hands and feet were (freeze) [frozen] solid.

Regular Verbs

This chapter begins a unit on usage. Throughout this unit you will discover how to *use* the elements of grammar that are covered in the first unit of this textbook. Since mistakes in the use of verbs account for approximately half of all students' errors in speech and writing, this first chapter will cover verbs. It will review the many forms of a verb and the uses of those forms.

PRINCIPAL PARTS

Each verb has four basic forms called its *principal parts*. It is important to know the principal parts of a verb because all the tenses of a verb are formed from them.

6a The **principal parts** of a verb are the *present*, the *present participle*, the *past*, and the *past participle*.

Notice in the following examples that helping verbs are needed with the present participle and the past participle when they are used as the main verb of a sentence.

PRESENT	I **cook** dinner once a week.
PRESENT PARTICIPLE	I am **cooking** dinner tonight.
PAST	I **cooked** dinner last week.
PAST PARTICIPLE	I have **cooked** dinner many times.

Regular Verbs

The majority of verbs form their past and past participle in the same way.

6b A **regular verb** forms its past and past participle by adding *-ed* or *-d* to the present.

PRESENT	I often **watch** sports.
PRESENT PARTICIPLE	Today I am **watching** soccer.
PAST	Once I **watched** a polo match.
PAST PARTICIPLE	I have even **watched** cricket.

Using Verbs

A spelling change sometimes occurs when certain endings are added to the present. Check a dictionary if you are unsure of a particular spelling.

NOTE: *Have* is not part of the past participle. It has been added, however, to help you remember that a past participle must have a helping verb when it is used as a verb.

PRESENT	PRESENT PARTICIPLE	PAST	PAST PARTICIPLE
hope	hoping	hoped	(have) hoped
share	sharing	shared	(have) shared
drop	dropping	dropped	(have) dropped
regret	regretting	regretted	(have) regretted

Be careful not to drop the *-ed* or *-d* ending from the past or the past participle of a verb when you write or speak. This commonly happens with such verbs as *asked, helped, looked, seemed, supposed, talked, used,* and *walked.*

INCORRECT   I **use** to work every weekend.
CORRECT   I **used** to work every weekend.

EXERCISE 1   Determining the Principal Parts of Regular Verbs

Make four columns on your paper. Label them *present, present participle, past,* and *past participle.* Then write the four principal parts of the following verbs.
Answers precede this chapter.

1. ask
2. trim
3. use
4. play
5. stop
6. end
7. mend
8. boil
9. wait
10. suppose

Irregular Verbs

Most verbs are regular verbs; however, there is a small group of verbs called *irregular verbs.* They form their past and past participle in a number of different ways.

6c > An **irregular verb** does not form its past and past participle by adding *-ed* or *-d* to the present.

The following irregular verbs have been divided into groups according to the way they form their past and past participle.

112   *Additional practice for* lie/lay, sit/set, *and* rise/raise *is in the Glossary of Usage.*

Irregular Verbs

Group 1

These irregular verbs have the same form for the present, the past, and the past participle.

PRESENT	PRESENT PARTICIPLE	PAST	PAST PARTICIPLE
burst	bursting	burst	(have) burst
cost	costing	cost	(have) cost
hit	hitting	hit	(have) hit
hurt	hurting	hurt	(have) hurt
let	letting	let	(have) let
put	putting	put	(have) put
set	setting	set	(have) set

Group 2

These irregular verbs have the same form for the past and the past participle.

PRESENT	PRESENT PARTICIPLE	PAST	PAST PARTICIPLE
bring	bringing	brought	(have) brought
buy	buying	bought	(have) bought
catch	catching	caught	(have) caught
feel	feeling	felt	(have) felt
find	finding	found	(have) found
get	getting	got	(have) got or gotten
hold	holding	held	(have) held
keep	keeping	kept	(have) kept
lay	laying	laid	(have) laid
lead	leading	led	(have) led
leave	leaving	left	(have) left
lose	losing	lost	(have) lost
make	making	made	(have) made
say	saying	said	(have) said
sell	selling	sold	(have) sold
send	sending	sent	(have) sent
sit	sitting	sat	(have) sat
teach	teaching	taught	(have) taught
tell	telling	told	(have) told
win	winning	won	(have) won

Using Verbs

EXERCISE 2 **Using the Correct Verb Form**

Write the past or the past participle of each verb in parentheses. Then read each sentence aloud to check your answer.

1. Because the pipe had not been buried deep enough, it (burst) *burst* when the temperature dropped below zero.
2. At the Army-Navy game, we (sit) *sat* on the 50-yard line.
3. In Vermont we (buy) *bought* some pure maple syrup.
4. Where have you (put) *put* tonight's newspaper?
5. That watch must have (cost) *cost* a month's salary!
6. You should have (make) *made* reservations last week.
7. Has Jennifer (leave) *left* for school yet?
8. Yesterday I (catch) *caught* a five-pound bass.
9. The instructor (teach) *taught* us how to parallel park today.
10. I have (keep) *kept* all my weekly tests in geometry.
11. How long have you (feel) *felt* weak and dizzy?
12. Tim (find) *found* the play most enjoyable.
13. Corinne (buy) *bought* five rolls of film to take with her.
14. Have you (send) *sent* Marsha a birthday card?
15. That is the third ball Pedro has (hit) *hit* out of the ball park today.
16. They (lay) *laid* the logs by the fireplace.
17. Anthony (say) *said* he would meet us at Jake's Garage.
18. I have never (win) *won* anything in my life.
19. The car was (sell) *sold* just before you called.
20. Have you ever (lead) *led* an orchestra?
21. Who (tell) *told* you that?
22. While we were shopping, I (lose) *lost* a glove.
23. Have you (set) *set* the table for dinner?
24. My brother (get) *got* a job at the First National Bank.
25. That candidate has never (hold) *held* public office before.
26. When the Robinson family visited us, they (bring) *brought* a delicious fruit salad.
27. My best friend and I laughed so hard at Brian's joke, our stomachs (hurt) *hurt*.
28. Since Elizabeth received her license, her parents have often (let) *let* her drive the family car.
29. The blue coat with the white collar was beautiful, but it (cost) *cost* too much.
30. Many times Tara has unexpectedly (find) *found* a valuable item at a flea market.

Irregular Verbs

EXERCISE 3 Determining the Principal Parts of Irregular Verbs

Make four columns on your paper. Label them *present, present participle, past,* and *past participle.* Then write the four principal parts of the following verbs.
Answers precede this chapter.

1. let
2. sit
3. buy
4. hurt
5. say
6. lose
7. make
8. lead
9. tell
10. lay

EXERCISE 4 Oral Practice

Say aloud the principal parts of any irregular verbs you missed in Exercises 2 and 3. The more you say them, the easier they will be to remember when you use them.

Group 3

These irregular verbs form the past participle by adding *-n* to the past.

PRESENT	PRESENT PARTICIPLE	PAST	PAST PARTICIPLE
break	breaking	broke	(have) broken
choose	choosing	chose	(have) chosen
freeze	freezing	froze	(have) frozen
speak	speaking	spoke	(have) spoken
steal	stealing	stole	(have) stolen

Group 4

These irregular verbs form the past participle by adding *-n* to the present.

PRESENT	PRESENT PARTICIPLE	PAST	PAST PARTICIPLE
blow	blowing	blew	(have) blown
draw	drawing	drew	(have) drawn
drive	driving	drove	(have) driven
give	giving	gave	(have) given
grow	growing	grew	(have) grown
know	knowing	knew	(have) known
rise	rising	rose	(have) risen
see	seeing	saw	(have) seen
take	taking	took	(have) taken
throw	throwing	threw	(have) thrown

Using Verbs

EXERCISE 5 Using the Correct Verb Form
Write the past or the past participle of each verb in parentheses. Then read each sentence aloud to check your answer.

1. Has the winning photograph been (choose) *chosen* yet?
2. Ben (steal) *stole* third base in the fourth inning.
3. Because you forgot the yeast, the bread hasn't (rise) *risen*.
4. Have you ever (drive) *driven* across the country?
5. I think I (see) *saw* you last night at the mall.
6. Who (draw) *drew* the cartoon in the school newspaper?
7. Lucia has (break) *broken* the school record for the high jump.
8. The principal (speak) *spoke* about student absenteeism.
9. Have you (take) *taken* your shoes to the repair shop yet?
10. The President (throw) *threw* out the first ball of the baseball season.
11. Lake Matoba has finally (freeze) *frozen* over.
12. I (give) *gave* my class dues to Melinda last week.
13. The wind has (blow) *blown* down our cherry tree.
14. Membership in the camera club has (grow) *grown* this past year.
15. The veterinarian (know) *knew* instantly what was wrong with Carrie's dog.
16. Lai Ling (choose) *chose* a difficult subject for her term paper.
17. I would have (give) *given* him a ride home, but I was late.
18. Has anyone (see) *seen* my notebook?
19. Who (drive) *drove* you to school?
20. Ellis (take) *took* his brother bowling with him.
21. This is the first still life I have ever (draw) *drawn*.
22. The sun (rise) *rose* yesterday at 5:15 A.M.
23. Have you (speak) *spoken* to him yet?
24. After we picked the green beans, we (freeze) *froze* them.
25. All the old magazines should be (throw) *thrown* out.
26. Ted (make) *made* an appointment at the orthodontist because he wanted his braces removed before graduation.
27. For the school dance, our committee (blow) *blew* up 100 colorful balloons.
28. At the age of 21, Michael's older brother (grow) *grew* a terrific mustache.
29. Melanie has (know) *known* her neighbor Stephanie for over seven years.
30. During the seventeenth century, the treasure on merchant ships was sometimes (steal) *stolen* by pirates.

Irregular Verbs

EXERCISE 6 **Finding Errors in Verb Forms**

Number your paper 1 to 30. Then write the correct form of each underlined verb. If the verb is correct, write *C* after the number. (This exercise includes verbs in the first four groups.)

1. Carl <u>throwed</u> the ball too high, but the catcher made a spectacular catch. [threw]
2. Have you <u>saw</u> the unusual display in the window of Kenmore's Department Store? [seen]
3. Be careful! You almost <u>broke</u> the window with the end of the broom. [C]
4. Mr. Miller <u>brang</u> several watermelons to the picnic. [brought]
5. Because the car window wouldn't shut, we were nearly <u>froze</u> by the time we got home. [frozen]
6. Of all the dogs in the pound, I would have <u>chosen</u> the German shepherd. [C]
7. The soap bubble floated lazily against the wall and <u>bursted</u>. [burst]
8. For three days the winds have <u>blew</u> steadily. [blown]
9. At one time I <u>knew</u> the names of all the constellations. [C]
10. I must have <u>drove</u> a thousand miles during my vacation. [driven]
11. Phyllis has <u>took</u> a part-time job. [taken]
12. Augustín has <u>lain</u> the sleeping bag on the cot. [laid]
13. The house <u>felt</u> cooler than the air-conditioned car. [C]
14. Has Charlene <u>growed</u> three inches in one year? [grown]
15. Yes, that is what I was <u>told</u>. [C]
16. I should have <u>send</u> the letter by overnight express. [sent]
17. He must have <u>gave</u> the tickets to Willie. [given]
18. Lenny had <u>spoke</u> only a few words at the meeting. [spoken]
19. I have <u>drawed</u> sketches of animals all my life. [drawn]
20. Melissa <u>teached</u> him everything he knows about jazz. [taught]
21. Terry <u>selled</u> his portable radio to Martin. [sold]
22. You shouldn't have <u>put</u> the fish on the counter where the cat could reach it. [C]
23. The temperature <u>rose</u> to an all-time high yesterday. [C]
24. How long have you <u>keeped</u> them waiting? [kept]
25. The lawyer proved that her client had not <u>stole</u> the checks. [stolen]
26. On a rainy day, Curtis <u>losed</u> his tan umbrella. [lost]
27. Rachel's interest in science has <u>lead</u> her to a career. [led]
28. Yesterday Amy <u>says</u> she will audition for the play. [said]
29. Ben has <u>sit</u> on the front steps for over an hour. [sat]
30. Our town has not <u>won</u> a baseball game this season. [C]

Using Verbs

EXERCISE 7 Oral Practice
Read aloud all the forms of the irregular verbs you missed in Exercises 5 and 6.

Group 5

These irregular verbs form the past and the past participle by changing a vowel.

PRESENT	PRESENT PARTICIPLE	PAST	PAST PARTICIPLE
begin	beginning	began	(have) begun
drink	drinking	drank	(have) drunk
ring	ringing	rang	(have) rung
shrink	shrinking	shrank	(have) shrunk
sing	singing	sang	(have) sung
sink	sinking	sank	(have) sunk
swim	swimming	swam	(have) swum

Group 6

These irregular verbs form the past and the past participle in other ways.

PRESENT	PRESENT PARTICIPLE	PAST	PAST PARTICIPLE
come	coming	came	(have) come
do	doing	did	(have) done
eat	eating	ate	(have) eaten
fall	falling	fell	(have) fallen
go	going	went	(have) gone
lie	lying	lay	(have) lain
ride	riding	rode	(have) ridden
run	running	ran	(have) run
tear	tearing	tore	(have) torn
wear	wearing	wore	(have) worn
write	writing	wrote	(have) written

EXERCISE 8 Using the Correct Verb Form
Write the past or the past participle of each verb in parentheses. Then read each sentence aloud to check your answer.

1. A gnarled chestnut tree had (fall) *fallen* across the road.
2. Have you ever (ride) *ridden* on the scrambler at the county fair?

Irregular Verbs

3. The Lincoln penny (begin) [began] to appear in 1909.
4. In the basketball game, Linda (do) [did] well, scoring 14 points.
5. Who (drink) [drank] my glass of carrot juice?
6. The dropped fishing rod promptly (sink) [sank] in the lake.
7. Did you have a good rest when you (lie) [lay] down?
8. Judy (write) [wrote] for a free software catalog.
9. Oh no! I just (tear) [tore] a hole in my new coat.
10. The chorus (sing) [sang] several songs from the musical *Camelot*.
11. David has (swim) [swum] on the team for two years.
12. This package (come) [came] for you in the morning mail.
13. I (eat) [ate] the corn muffin Dad had saved for me.
14. Hurry! The orchestra has (begin) [begun] to play the overture.
15. Before last summer I had never (run) [run] the lawn mower.
16. Their car skidded on the ice and (go) [went] off the road.
17. All the visitors (wear) [wore] name tags.
18. The shirt has (shrink) [shrunk] so much that it doesn't fit.
19. After Rico had (ring) [rung] the fire alarm, he ran back to help.
20. In recent years several ships that had (sink) [sunk] have been raised to the surface.
21. Lani has (do) [done] excellent research for her oral report.
22. Ted (run) [ran] really fast, but he still missed the bus.
23. We should have (sing) [sung] the song with the piano.
24. Cara has (go) [gone] to visit her aunt in Chicago for a week.
25. The cat had (lie) [lain] on the windowsill for 20 minutes.
26. Jeffrey has always (drink) [drunk] milk with his dinner.
27. The telephone (ring) [rang] just as we were leaving.
28. When the sweater (shrink) [shrank], I gave it to my sister.
29. Twice Joseph (swim) [swam] to the island and back.
30. Everyone in the English class has (write) [written] ten poems.

EXERCISE 9 Supplying the Correct Verb Form

Number your paper 1 to 10. Then complete each pair of sentences by supplying the correct form of the verb in parentheses at the beginning of the sentence.

EXAMPLE (ring) Has the bell ___ yet? It ___ already.
ANSWER rung—rang

1. (come) We [came] to the game in the bus with the team. You should have [come] with us.
2. (wear) Have you ever [worn] a down vest? I [wore] one last winter.

119

Using Verbs

3. (swim) Have the members of the swim team ever _swum_ out to the island? Yes, they _swam_ out there a week ago.
4. (begin) Have they _begun_ putting up the walls? They _began_ this morning.
5. (do) I _did_ ten laps across the pool this morning. I have _done_ that for two months now.
6. (eat) Who _ate_ the last piece of pizza? I have just _eaten_ the last bite.
7. (drink) Have you ever _drunk_ limeade? Yes, I _drank_ some when I was in Florida last year.
8. (go) Have you _gone_ to the doctor's yet? I _went_ last Monday.
9. (write) I _wrote_ for more information. Have you _written_ for more?
10. (run) Have you ever _run_ for office before? Last year I _ran_ for class treasurer.

EXERCISE 10 Finding Errors in Verb Forms

Number your paper 1 to 30. Then write the correct form of each underlined verb. If a verb is correct, write *C* after the number. (This exercise includes verbs from all six groups.)

c 1. Have you <u>torn</u> the coupons out of the newspaper?
   2. Don't you think we should have <u>went</u> with them? (gone)
   3. I have already <u>rode</u> in her new car. (ridden)
   4. No one in our school has <u>ran</u> the mile as fast as he did yesterday. (run)
   5. Felicia wished that she had <u>wore</u> a warmer sweater. (worn)
   6. We have <u>sang</u> all the old songs; let's try some new ones. (sung)
   7. After Jerry <u>throwed</u> the ball into the water, his dog retrieved it. (threw)
   8. The canoe had <u>sank</u> right before our eyes. (sunk)
   9. Yesterday I <u>seen</u> my first ice-hockey game. (saw)
   10. That plant sure has <u>growed</u> since you bought it. (grown)
c 11. The quarterback has been <u>hurt</u> in the leg.
   12. Kevin thought he had <u>losed</u> his literature book. (lost)
   13. The coach, followed by his players, <u>come</u> onto the field. (came)
c 14. I haven't <u>done</u> my biology project yet.
   15. Have you <u>ate</u> your dinner? (eaten)
   16. The baby <u>laid</u> in her crib, sleeping peacefully. (lay)
   17. I thought he would have <u>wrote</u> to you by now. (written)

Irregular Verbs

18. Has Mr. Gregson spoke [spoken] to you about working part-time?
19. Pat recently teached [taught] her brother to swim.
c 20. Has he been given an award for his bravery?
21. I drunk [drank] all the fresh orange juice I could.
22. The kitten has broke [broken] the glass on the counter.
c 23. Has the television special begun yet?
24. The player on third base catched [caught] the fly ball.
25. Why haven't you ever swam [swum] in Lake Mead?
26. The hiker has lay [lain] in the shade for almost an hour.
27. My sister shrinked [shrank] my favorite sweater in the dryer.
28. Was it you who drawn [drew] the charcoal sketch?
29. My grandmother has growed [grown] day lilies for many years.
c 30. We nearly froze on our way to school yesterday.

EXERCISE 11 Using the Correct Verb Form

Write the past or the past participle of each verb in parentheses. Then read each sentence aloud to check your answer. (This exercise includes verbs from all six groups.)

Fillmore to the Rescue

1. Millard Fillmore (win) [won] the presidency in 1850.
2. Before then, all White House cooking had been (do) [done] over open fireplaces.
3. Because Fillmore didn't like the White House food, he (buy) [bought] a cast-iron stove.
4. After it arrived, the cook discovered that no instructions had (come) with it.
5. Because Fillmore's cook had never (see) [seen] a stove before, he refused to use it.
6. Determined to solve the crisis, Fillmore (go) [went] to the U.S. Patent Office.
7. There he (find) [found] the model of his stove and studied it very carefully.
8. Returning to the White House, he (speak) [spoke] to his cook, who had (choose) [chosen] to ignore the stove.
9. Fillmore personally (teach) [taught] the cook how to use the stove.
10. From then on the quality of the food served at the White House (begin) [began] to improve.

EXERCISE 12 Oral Practice

Read aloud all the forms of the irregular verbs you missed in Exercises 8, 9, 10, and 11.

121

Using Verbs

EXERCISE 13 Time-out for Review

Write the past or the past participle of each verb in parentheses. Then read each sentence aloud to check your answer.

1. Esther Forbes has (write — *written*) a biography of Paul Revere.
2. Dad has (drive — *driven*) our car for nearly 100,000 miles.
3. Donald (throw — *threw*) the ball over the shortstop's head.
4. Patsy is the most unselfish person I have ever (know — *known*).
5. I don't think the wind has ever (blow — *blown*) harder than it did during last August's hurricane.
6. Have you (give — *given*) your speech yet?
7. Yesterday I (speak — *spoke*) to my guidance counselor.
8. Last week in archery, I (hit — *hit*) three bull's-eyes.
9. Has he (find — *found*) his lost notebook?
10. I (ride — *rode*) to school with Theresa all last week.
11. The kite (lie — *lay*) motionless in the treetop.
12. The birds (sing — *sang*) cheerfully from the maple tree.
13. Leroy has (begin — *begun*) to lift weights at the gym.
14. Who (send — *sent*) these flowers to you?
15. I haven't (sell — *sold*) my old stereo yet.
16. Amazingly, he (hold — *held*) on to the rope until help came.
17. I think you (leave — *left*) your scarf at my house.
18. Paul (say — *said*) he couldn't come to the party.
19. Have you (see — *seen*) the new exhibit at the art museum?
20. I haven't (choose — *chosen*) my courses for next year.
21. Nancy (tell — *told*) everyone her summer plans.
22. Have you ever (swim — *swum*) in the ocean?
23. He (drink — *drank*) the water too fast.
24. Rosa (make — *made*) the decorations all by herself.
25. I haven't (do — *done*) the final editing of my essay yet.
26. Yesterday we (go — *went*) cross-country skiing.
27. Finally their business (grow — *grew*) too large to manage.
28. Veronica has (teach — *taught*) me how make poached eggs.
29. By accident we (sit — *sat*) next to them at the movies.
30. Have you (came — *come*) to get Lola's books?
31. Who (win — *won*) the election?
32. We have (eat — *eaten*) chicken twice this week.
33. Has the baby's toy (fall — *fallen*) behind the couch?
34. Why haven't you (take — *taken*) the creative writing course?
35. He (rise — *rose*) before dawn to go fishing.
36. Ben (draw — *drew*) a funny caricature of Mr. Jacobson.

37. How long have you (keep) [kept] the steak in the freezer?
38. Yesterday Ossie (buy) [bought] a new cassette.
39. We (feel) [felt] sad when Ms. Harris retired.
40. Who (lay) [laid] the newspaper on the clean laundry?
41. I think I have (lose) [lost] the key to the house.
42. Has she (put) [put] her name on the petition?
43. Jacob (break) [broke] the door handle by accident.
44. He (get) [got] all *A's* on his report card.
45. The batter (run) [ran] to second base and stopped.
46. In celebration the church bells (ring) [rang] throughout the city.
47. Roy must have (bring) [brought] those flowers from his garden.
48. One of the bridesmaids (catch) [caught] the bouquet.
49. Mr. Foster (lead) [led] the concerned parents into the office.
50. You should have (freeze) [frozen] some of the blueberries.

VERB TENSE

If you know the principal parts of a verb, you can easily form the six tenses. Different verb forms express the *tense,* or time, of a verb. The six tenses are *present, past, future, present perfect, past perfect,* and *future perfect.* In the following examples, the six tenses of *fly* are used to express action at different times.

PRESENT	She often **flies** on business.
PAST	She **flew** to Wisconsin yesterday.
FUTURE	She **will fly** to Ohio next week.
PRESENT PERFECT	She **has flown** over 100,000 miles.
PAST PERFECT	She **had** not **flown** much before last year.
FUTURE PERFECT	By the end of the year, she **will have flown** over 200,000 miles.

Conjugation of a Verb

One way to learn the different tenses of a particular verb is to look at a conjugation of that verb. A *conjugation* is a list of all the singular and plural forms of a verb in its various tenses. Following is a conjugation of the irregular verb *see.*

NOTE: The present participle is used only to conjugate the progressive forms of a verb. They are covered on page 125.

Using Verbs

Conjugation of *See*
PRINCIPAL PARTS

PRESENT	PRESENT PARTICIPLE	PAST	PAST PARTICIPLE
see	seeing	saw	seen

Present

This tense expresses action that is going on now.

SINGULAR	PLURAL
I see	we see
you see	you see
he, she, it sees	they see

Past

This tense expresses action that took place in the past.

SINGULAR	PLURAL
I saw	we saw
you saw	you saw
he, she, it saw	they saw

Future

This tense expresses action that will take place in the future. It is formed by adding *shall* or *will* to the present.

SINGULAR	PLURAL
I shall/will see	we shall/will see
you will see	you will see
he, she, it will see	they will see

Present Perfect

This tense expresses action that was completed at some indefinite time in the past or action that started in the past and is still going on. It is formed by adding *has* or *have* to the past participle.

SINGULAR	PLURAL
I have seen	we have seen
you have seen	you have seen
he, she, it has seen	they have seen

Verb Tense

Past Perfect

This tense expresses action that took place before some other past action. It is formed by adding *had* to the past participle.

SINGULAR	PLURAL
I had seen	we had seen
you had seen	you had seen
he, she, it had seen	they had seen

Future Perfect

This tense expresses action that will be completed by some given time in the future. It is formed by adding *shall have* or *will have* to the past participle.

SINGULAR	PLURAL
I shall/will have seen	we shall/will have seen
you will have seen	you will have seen
he, she, it will have seen	they will have seen

EXERCISE 14 **Conjugating a Verb**

Using the conjugation of *see* as a model, write the conjugation of the following verbs.
Answers precede this chapter.
1. do, doing, did, done
2. begin, beginning, began, begun
Answers to Exercise 15 appear below.

Progressive Forms. Each tense has an additional form called the *progressive form*. It is used to express continuing action and is formed by adding a form of the verb *be* to the present participle. Following are the progressive forms of *see*.

PRESENT PROGRESSIVE	am, is, are seeing (beginning)
PAST PROGRESSIVE	was, were seeing (beginning)
FUTURE PROGRESSIVE	shall/will be seeing (beginning)
PRESENT PERFECT PROGRESSIVE	has, have been seeing (beginning)
PAST PERFECT PROGRESSIVE	had been seeing (beginning)
FUTURE PERFECT PROGRESSIVE	shall/will have been seeing (beginning)

Emphatic Forms. The present and past tenses have another form called the *emphatic form*. The emphatic form is used to show emphasis and is often used in questions and with *not*. It is

Using Verbs

formed by adding *do, does,* or *did* to the present. Following are the emphatic forms of *see*.

PRESENT EMPHATIC   do, does see *begin*
PAST EMPHATIC   did see *begin*

EXERCISE 15   **Forming the Progressive and the Emphatic** Using the two preceding models of *see*, write the progressive and emphatic forms of the verb *begin*. *Answers appear following Exercise 14, with the progressive and emphatic forms of see.*

Conjugation of the Irregular Verb Be. Since the principal parts of the verb *be* are highly irregular, the conjugation of that verb is very different from that of other irregular verbs.

Conjugation of *Be*
PRINCIPAL PARTS

PRESENT	PRESENT PARTICIPLE	PAST	PAST PARTICIPLE
am	being	was	been

Present

SINGULAR	PLURAL
I am	we are
you are	you are
he, she, it is	they are

Past

SINGULAR	PLURAL
I was	we were
you were	you were
he, she, it was	they were

Future

SINGULAR	PLURAL
I shall/will be	we shall/will be
you will be	you will be
he, she, it will be	they will be

Verb Tense

Present Perfect

SINGULAR	PLURAL
I have been	we have been
you have been	you have been
he, she, it has been	they have been

Past Perfect

SINGULAR	PLURAL
I had been	we had been
you had been	you had been
he, she, it had been	they had been

Future Perfect

SINGULAR	PLURAL
I shall/will have been	we shall/will have been
you will have been	you will have been
he, she, it will have been	they will have been

EXERCISE 16 **Identifying Verb Tenses**

Write the tense of each underlined verb.

EXAMPLE   He <u>will run</u> in the marathon next month.
ANSWER   future

1. *My Antonia* by Willa Cather <u>is</u> on the reading list. *present*
2. Stacy <u>has been working</u> in the library all semester. *present perfect progressive*
3. Every year the northern fur seal <u>will go</u> from the Bering Sea to northern Mexico and back—a distance of more than 5,000 miles. *future*
4. We <u>will be visiting</u> Nevada on our trip to the West Coast. *future progressive*
5. Before Scott Carpenter became an astronaut, he <u>had participated</u> in the Navy's Man-in-the-Sea program. *past perfect*
6. I <u>was noticing</u> your new watch. *past progressive*
7. English <u>has been</u> my favorite subject in high school. *present perfect*
8. I <u>introduced</u> Kevin to my neighbor. *past*
9. Everyone <u>was</u> ready on time. *past*
10. We <u>had been rehearsing</u> every night before opening night. *past perfect progressive*
11. Ernest Hemingway <u>wrote</u> *Old Man and the Sea.* *past*
12. <u>Did</u> you <u>lock</u> the doors? *past emphatic*

Using Verbs

13. If heated sufficiently, diamonds <u>will burn</u>. *future*
14. In case you <u>have forgotten</u>, Woodrow Wilson's picture is on the $100,000 bill. *present perfect*
15. The Battle of New Orleans was fought 15 days after the War of 1812 <u>had ended</u>. *past perfect*
16. By the time we get there, the ballet <u>will have started</u>. *future perfect*
17. Sandy <u>will have worked</u> 12 hours by the time she leaves. *future perfect*
18. The Constitution <u>does</u> not <u>provide</u> for political parties. *present emphatic*
19. Come August, we <u>will have been</u> friends for six years. *future perfect*
20. The painter Robert Rauschenberg's collages <u>became</u> popular in the 1970's. *past*

Uses of the Tenses

All the tenses and their various forms fall into three general time categories: present, past, and future. Each tense within those general categories has a particular use that is different from that of the others. Knowing the distinctions between tenses when you write is very important if you want to communicate your ideas clearly and effectively.

The Present Tense. This tense mainly expresses action (or state of being) that is taking place at the present time. The present tense is also used to express customary or habitual action and a general truth.

PRESENT ACTION	This homemade soup **tastes** delicious.
HABITUAL ACTION	He **sits** beside me in English class.
A GENERAL TRUTH	Patience **is** a virtue.

The present progressive form expresses a present, ongoing action, and the present emphatic form emphasizes a present action.

PRESENT PROGRESSIVE	We **are studying** for our finals.
PRESENT EMPHATIC	He **does know** the answer.

The present tense can also be used to express past action when you want to make certain events come alive in a narrative. This use of the present is called the *historical present*.

HISTORICAL PRESENT	John F. Kennedy **places** his left hand on the Bible, **raises** his right hand, and **repeats** the oath of office.

Verb Tense

The Past Tense. This tense expresses action (or state of being) that occurred at a definite time in the past. Words such as *last summer, a week ago,* or *yesterday* often indicate that the action took place at a definite time. The past progressive expresses a continuous action that was completed in the past, and the emphatic past emphasizes action that occurred in the past.

PAST	Yesterday I **auditioned** for the chorus.
PAST PROGRESSIVE	They **were accepting** donations.
PAST EMPHATIC	Yes, Jim **did deliver** the newspapers.

The Future Tense. This tense expresses action (or state of being) that will take place in the future. The future progressive expresses a continuous action that will take place in the future.

FUTURE	Lana **will notify** you of any changes.
FUTURE PROGRESSIVE	He **will be writing** his paper soon.

NOTE: Sometimes the present or the present progressive is used to express future action.

I **start** ballet lessons at the local dance studio next month.
I **am starting** ballet lessons at the local dance studio next month.

The Present Perfect Tense. This tense expresses action (or state of being) that was completed at some indefinite time in the past. It also expresses action that started in the past and is still going on. All the progressive forms of the perfect tenses show continuing action.

PRESENT PERFECT	She **has won** several writing awards for her short stories and poems. [She has won them over an indefinite time in the past.]
	John **has been** my friend for two years. [John became my friend two years ago and is still my friend.]
PRESENT PERFECT PROGRESSIVE	I **have been taking** a photography class on Saturdays.

129

Using Verbs

The Past Perfect Tense. This tense expresses action (or state of being) that took place before some other event in the past.

PAST PERFECT I **had** just **gone** out to the yard when the telephone rang. [The going out occurred before the telephone's ringing.]

Mom reminded me that I **had promised** to clean my room after school. [The promising occurred before the reminding.]

PAST PERFECT PROGRESSIVE Until recently the committee **had been working** on a set of bylaws for the club.

NOTE: Sometimes the past tense is used instead of the past perfect if it is not important to show that one action came before another.

After the light **changed,** two drivers blew their horns.

The Future Perfect Tense. This tense expresses action (or state of being) that will be completed at some future time before some other future event.

FUTURE PERFECT The movie **will have started** by the time we get there.

FUTURE PERFECT PROGRESSIVE On Friday Nathan **will have been working** part-time for two months.

EXERCISE 17 Choosing the Correct Tense

Write the correct form of the verb in parentheses. Be prepared to identify the tense you choose and to tell why that tense is correct.

1. Tammy told us that she (studied, had studied) very late the night before.
2. Yesterday in the assembly, two juniors (receive, received) awards for their essays.
3. For three years now, I (take, have been taking) gymnastic classes.
4. When Alexander Graham Bell was 15, he (become, became) a speech teacher in Scotland.

Shifts in Tense

5. Last Thursday I (begin, <u>began</u>) my new job at the market.
6. For weeks now she (works, <u>has been working</u>) on her biology project.
7. Last night I told Mom and Dad that I (decided, <u>had decided</u>) to become a chemical engineer.
8. Lance (<u>wants</u>, wanted) his turn at bat now.
9. By the time anyone noticed the fire, the whole top floor of the abandoned building (collapsed, <u>had collapsed</u>).
10. Last year Gary (win, <u>won</u>) two blue ribbons at the fair.
11. Ryan (<u>brought</u>, had brought) his tapes to the party.
12. So far this summer I (wore, <u>have worn</u>) out two pairs of sneakers.
13. On Friday I (type, <u>typed</u>) my research paper.
14. After he (took, <u>had taken</u>) the toaster apart, he tried to put it back together again.
15. When I was 14, I (learn, <u>learned</u>) to play the guitar.
16. Ms. Foster told me that she (entered, <u>had entered</u>) my painting in the art contest.
17. Before I knew what (happened, <u>had happened</u>), I was sliding helplessly down the icy hill.
18. Last night I (attend, <u>attended</u>) my aerobic dance class.
19. Dan suddenly realized that he (forgot, <u>had forgotten</u>) his dentist appointment.
20. Over the roar of the storm (come, <u>came</u>) the wail of a foghorn.

Shifts in Tense

A compound verb in a simple sentence and the verbs in a compound sentence should be written in the same tense. Avoid a shift between the present and the past tenses.

6d Avoid shifting tenses when relating a sequence of events that occur at the same time.

INCORRECT   The audience **cheered** [past] wildly, but the band **refuses** [present] to give an encore.

CORRECT   The audience **cheered** [past] wildly, but the band **refused** [past] to give an encore.

Using Verbs

In complex sentences some shifts in tense are correct and are made to convey a particular meaning. Following are some examples.

⌜past⌝ ⌜past perfect⌝
The doctor **said** that I **had strained** my eyes. [*Said* is in the past, and *had strained* is in the past perfect to show that the *straining* came before the *saying*.]

⌜past⌝
Since the afternoon temperature **rose** above 90 degrees, I
⌜present perfect⌝
have experienced dizziness and light-headedness. [*Rose* is in the past because that happened at a definite time, but *have experienced* is in the present perfect because the *experiencing* started in the past and is still going on.]

⌜present⌝ ⌜past⌝
I **believe** that she **attended** the meeting last night. [*Believe* is in the present because it describes action that is occurring now, but *attended* is in the past because it happened at a definite time in the past.]

EXERCISE 18   Correcting Shifts in Tense

Number your paper 1 to 10. If the second verb in a sentence incorrectly shifts in tense, write it correctly. If a sentence is correct, write *C* after the number.

1. Everything worked fine until the electric drill ~~blows~~ *blew* a fuse.
2. When Kenneth finally hooked a marlin, he ~~has~~ *had* a hard time reeling it in.
C 3. I think that the concert last night was excellent.
C 4. Yesterday when we opened the door, a stray cat unexpectedly marched in.
5. As Roger mowed the lawn, Alex ~~watches~~ *watched* him from the front porch.
C 6. Since I heard the news on television, I have called all my friends.
7. Al Brodie throws the ball, and the shortstop ~~caught~~ *catches* it.
8. The weather forecaster reported that the high humidity ~~has~~ *had* lasted ten days.
9. Michael dashed out of the barn and ~~races~~ *raced* across the field toward the back road.
C 10. The principal said that we had done the right thing.

Voice

ACTIVE AND PASSIVE VOICE

The *voice* of a verb indicates whether the subject is doing the action or the subject is receiving the action. Some verbs can be in the *active voice* or the *passive voice*.

6e The **active voice** indicates that the subject is performing the action.

6f The **passive voice** indicates that the action of the verb is being performed upon the subject.

Notice in the following examples that the verb in the active voice has a direct object, but the verb in the passive voice has no direct object.

                                                                      d.o.

ACTIVE VOICE   The tornado **leveled** three buildings. [The subject *tornado* is performing the action. *Buildings* is the direct object.]

PASSIVE VOICE   Three buildings **were leveled** by the tornado. [The action of the verb is being performed upon the subject *buildings*. *Were leveled* has no direct object.]

Most verbs in the active voice can also be used in the passive voice.

                                                  d.o.

ACTIVE VOICE   Keith **made** the winning touchdown.
PASSIVE VOICE   The winning touchdown **was made** by Keith. [no direct object]

                                      d.o.

ACTIVE VOICE   Rob **returned** my book to the library.
PASSIVE VOICE   The book **was returned** to the library by Rob. [no direct object]

Notice in the preceding examples that when an active verb is changed to the passive voice, the direct object becomes the subject. In the first set of examples, *touchdown* was the direct object when the verb was active. *Touchdown*, however, became the subject when the verb became passive. In the second set of examples, the direct object *book* became the subject. Notice also that both of the verbs in the passive voice consist of

Using Verbs

some form of the verb *be* plus a past participle. *Was made* is in the passive voice in the first set of examples, and *was returned* is in the passive voice in the second set of examples.

                                     d.o.
ACTIVE VOICE   Martin **cooks** breakfast every Sunday.

                            subj.
PASSIVE VOICE   Breakfast **is cooked** by Martin every Sunday.

EXERCISE 19   Recognizing Active and Passive Voice

Number your paper 1 to 10. Write the verb in each sentence. Then label each one *active* or *passive*.

White House Pets

P 1. George Washington's dogs <u>were treated</u> as members of the family.
A 2. Teddy Roosevelt's children <u>played</u> with a one-legged rooster.
P 3. The Roosevelts' pony <u>was given</u> rides in the White House elevator.
A 4. Woodrow Wilson's sheep <u>grazed</u> on the White House lawn.
A 5. William Howard Taft <u>owned</u> a cow named Pauline.
P 6. Warren Harding's dogs <u>were trained</u> to do tricks.
A 7. They often <u>performed</u> at cabinet meetings.
A 8. President Franklin Roosevelt never <u>went</u> anywhere without Fala, his black Scottish terrier.
P 9. The most famous photograph of Fala <u>was taken</u> of her sitting between Roosevelt and Prime Minister Winston Churchill.
P 10. Macaroni, Caroline Kennedy's pony, <u>was given</u> the run of the White House grounds.

Use of Voice

As a general rule, avoid using the passive voice. A sentence is clearer and more forceful when it is written in the active voice.

ACTIVE VOICE   Brad **slammed** the ball to left field, **circled** the bases, and **made** a home run.
PASSIVE VOICE   The ball **was slammed** to left field, the bases **were circled**, and a home run **was made** by Brad.

Use the passive, however, (1) when the doer of the action is unknown or unimportant, (2) when you want to emphasize the receiver of the action, or (3) when you want to emphasize the results.

Refreshments **were served** at the open house. [doer unknown or unimportant]

In 1944, Franklin D. Roosevelt **was elected** to his fourth term as president. [emphasis on the receiver]

Great numbers of American beech trees **were cut** down by the pioneers. [emphasis on the results]

EXERCISE 20 Using the Active Voice

Number your paper 1 to 10. Then write each sentence, changing the passive voice to the active voice if appropriate. If a sentence is better in the passive voice, write *C* after the number. *Answers may vary.*

1. Amazingly, our car climbed Mount Washington ~~was climbed by our car.~~
2. ~~Dinner tonight was prepared by~~ My sister Beth prepared dinner tonight.
3. Marianna found Two kittens ~~were found~~ in the barn ~~by Marianna.~~
c 4. Traffic lights were installed at the busy intersection.
c 5. The swallow is regarded as a weather prophet by some country people.
c 6. The poem "O Captain! My Captain!" was written by Walt Whitman in honor of Abraham Lincoln.
7. The guests ate Strawberries and melon ~~were eaten by the guests.~~
8. ~~A foreign language is studied by~~ Only a small percentage of the high school students in the United States study a foreign language.
c 9. The goal of one thousand dollars was reached by the students of Emerson High School.
10. Jerry found Ann's watch ~~was found~~ in the wastepaper basket ~~by Jerry.~~

MOOD

Mood is the way in which a verb expresses an idea. In English there are three moods: indicative, imperative, and subjunctive. The *indicative mood* is used most often because it is used to state a fact or to ask a question. The *imperative mood* is used to give a command or to make a request.

Using Verbs

INDICATIVE   Improved nutrition **has contributed** to the increased height of Americans.
IMPERATIVE   **Read** the next chapter in your history book.

The *subjunctive mood* has two main uses.

6g   The **subjunctive mood** is used to express (1) a condition contrary to fact that begins with words such as *if*, *as if*, or *as though* or (2) a wish.

CONTRARY TO FACT   If today **were** Saturday, I could sleep late. [Today is not Saturday.]

You're acting as if he **were** already the winner. [He is not the winner yet.]

A WISH   I wish I **were** as well prepared as you.
I wish he **were** my brother.

To form the subjunctive mood in conditions contrary to fact and in wishes, change *was,* the past indicative, to *were.*

If I ~~was~~ were you, I'd take French III next year.
I wish I ~~was~~ were going with you.

EXERCISE 21   Using the Subjunctive Mood

Number your paper 1 to 10. Write each <u>verb</u> that should be in the subjunctive mood. Then write it correctly.

EXAMPLE   I wish I was a famous movie star.
ANSWER   was — were

1. If I was (were) you, I would apply for the job.
2. I wish I was (were) on a sandy beach in Florida right now.
3. I feel as if I was (were) your relative.
4. You act as though Rico was (were) the only player on the field.
5. Kathy wishes she was (were) just like her older sister.
6. If he was (were) more ambitious, he could succeed in his job.
7. My younger brother talks as if he was (were) president of the freshman class.
8. If he was (were) more experienced, I would vote for him.
9. I wish I was (were) the captain of the basketball team.
10. The old house looked as though it was (were) haunted.

Mood

6g

EXERCISE 22 Writing Sentences

Write sentences that follow the directions below.
Sample sentences precede this chapter.
1. Include a verb in the indicative mood.
2. Include a verb in the imperative mood.
3. Include a verb in the subjunctive mood that is used to express an idea contrary to fact.
4. Include a verb in the subjunctive mood that is used to express a wish.

EXERCISE 23 Time-out for Review

Write the correct form of the verb in parentheses.

1. Sue suddenly realized that she (promised, <u>had promised</u>) to meet Phil at the mall.
2. I reached the station just as the train (is, <u>was</u>) leaving for North Carolina.
3. I wish that I (was, <u>were</u>) more self-confident about trying out for the lead in the play.
4. The polar bear dived into the water and in a few minutes (appears, <u>appeared</u>) on the other side of the ice.
5. On the voyage to America in 1620, the *Mayflower* (<u>broke</u>, has broken) a mast.
6. Just then Carlotta's uncle came along, and we (ask, <u>asked</u>) him for a ride.
7. If I (was, <u>were</u>) on the committee for a cleaner environment, I would vote for the water conservation bill.
8. For the past two years, Joel (sang, <u>has sung</u>) tenor in the chorus.
9. The elephant filled its trunk with water and (give, <u>gave</u>) itself a cool shower.
10. I wish I (was, <u>were</u>) in the glee club.

Application to Writing

Since verbs account for so many errors in students' writing, you should carefully edit your work for mistakes in the use of verbs. Check for the correct use of tenses and any shifts in tense. Look for weak passive verbs.

Using Verbs

EXERCISE 24 Editing for Verb Errors

Write any incorrect verb form. Then write it correctly. If a sentence is incorrectly written in the passive voice, write the sentence in the active voice.

Mark Twain (1835–1910)

Mark Twain was born Samuel Langhorne Clemens in Florida, Missouri. He ~~growed~~ [grew] up in the Mississippi River town of Hannibal, the main setting for his famous novels *The Adventures of Huckleberry Finn* and *The Adventures of Tom Sawyer*. He ~~leaved~~ [left] school to become a printer, but his first job ~~is~~ [was] as a reporter for his brother's newspaper. Then he abandoned his plans to seek his fortune in South America and ~~choose~~ [chose] a career as a steamboat pilot instead. After he had left the river at the outbreak of the Civil War, he ~~begun~~ [began] to write.

^[Clemens made] Two great contributions to American literature ~~were made by Clemens:~~ clever use of local language and humor. Rather than use the stiff, formal language of English writers, he ~~writes~~ [wrote] as people ~~speaked~~ [spoke]. Then he ~~use~~ [used] that very language to create humor. Without a doubt, Clemens was one of the great humorists of all times. He was loved by millions of readers around the world.

CHAPTER REVIEW

A. Write the correct form of the <u>verb</u> in parentheses.

1. For our parents' anniversary, we made dinner, cleaned up, and (promise, <u>promised</u>) to do the dishes for a week.
2. When Mr. Butler inspected his orchard, he found that the hurricane (destroyed, <u>had destroyed</u>) several trees.
3. Study for that test as if it (was, <u>were</u>) the final exam.
4. The fire fighters left the station and (arrive, <u>arrived</u>) at the burning house five minutes later.
5. Mrs. Steel (is, <u>has been</u>) a member of the local school board for the past three years.
6. Last summer Evelyn (<u>taught</u>, has taught) horseback riding for the Park Department.
7. No one (<u>saw</u>, has seen) the boat again after it left the wharf at Provincetown.
8. Many covered bridges in New England (stood, <u>have stood</u>) for the past 100 years.

Chapter Review

9. We (lived, <u>have lived</u>) in our present house for the past six years.
10. As we entered the cave, our eyes gradually (begin, <u>began</u>) to adjust to the dim light.

B. Number your paper 1 to 10. Label the verb in each sentence *active* or *passive*. Then rewrite any sentence in the passive voice that should be in the active voice.

P 1. The leading parts in the drama ~~were played by Elsie Foster and Kenneth James.~~ (A) *Elsie Foster and Kenneth James played*
A 2. The heat from the sun reaches the earth through radiation.
P 3. Missouri has been nicknamed the Show Me State.
A 4. The sun suddenly appeared on the horizon.
P 5. The photography contest ~~was won by Ann.~~ (A) *Ann won*
P 6. Thousands of acres of forest were destroyed by the fire.
P 7. A pleasant atmosphere ~~was created~~ in the office ~~by the recorded music.~~ (A) *The recorded music created*
A 8. The astronauts themselves named their capsules in the early days of the manned space program.
A 9. The dance troupe performed last night in Memorial Hall.
P 10. Some famous paintings have been reproduced for United States postage stamps.

MASTERY TEST

Number your paper 1 to 10. Then write the past or the past participle of each verb in parentheses.

1. He (send) the package to the wrong address. — *sent*
2. I have (do) my best. — *done*
3. Melinda (sing) a solo in the spring concert. — *sang*
4. Has he ever (drive) a stick shift before? — *driven*
5. I (choose) a color that matched the bedspread. — *chose*
6. Frieda hadn't (see) him for three years. — *seen*
7. Kate and I (run) in the Boston Marathon last year. — *ran*
8. Have you (begin) dinner without us? — *begun*
9. We (make) the trip to Seattle in only two hours. — *made*
10. Each day I have (go) to visit Betsy in the hospital. — *gone*

Chapter 7 Using Pronouns

OBJECTIVES

- To identify and use correctly personal pronouns in the nominative, objective, and possessive cases.
- To distinguish between possessive pronouns and contractions.
- To use correctly forms of the pronouns *who* and *whoever* in questions and in clauses.
- To use correctly personal pronouns in elliptical clauses.
- To make personal pronouns agree with their antecedents in person, number, and gender.
- To make personal pronouns agree with indefinite-pronoun antecedents.
- Application: To identify and be able to correct a pronoun shift and a vague, missing, or unclear antecedent.

MOTIVATIONAL ACTIVITY

At the beginning of this chapter, point out that a usage error often distracts the attention of the listeners from what a speaker is saying, just as mud on a windshield interferes with one's view or enjoyment of the scenery. Then read your students the following paragraph and ask them to see if they can hear any pronouns used incorrectly.

"My cousin Gene is the only one of my relatives whom I think knows anything about sailing," Tina said. "I asked Gene to give Beth and I some pointers on steering and turning, but he said us girls should take lessons from an experienced teacher. He suggested Mr. Brown, a neighbor, whom I'm afraid charges more than Beth and me can afford on our present budgets."

If your students can recognize some or all of the errors, point out that many others—peers, teachers, people in business—can recognize the errors as well. Then you may want to discuss situations in which usage errors could be detrimental to your students.

TEACHING SUGGESTIONS

Only a handful of pronouns—*I, me; he, him; she, her; we, us;* and *they, them*—have different forms for the nominative and objective cases. Unfortunately, however, these are the most commonly used pronouns, and they are responsible for the greatest number of pronoun errors. *Who* and *whom* could be added to the previous list, although informal English is more tolerant of *who* used for *whom* than of *he* used for *him*.

Compound subjects and objects present problems for most students. When you cover these constructions, however, watch for overcorrections, in which students assume that a formal-sounding expression like *between you and I* is correct. Remind them that the best way to detect such an error is to say each pronoun separately.

The Nominative Case *(pages 142–145)*

You may want to point out that pronouns used as predicate nominatives often sound awkward. When writing, your students can avoid this awkwardness by turning a sentence around—just as they did when checking a pronoun in a compound predicate nominative.

Sentences in which a pronoun is followed by a noun appositive may also sound stilted to many students. These sentences can be changed, as well, by simply dropping the pronoun or the appositive or by changing the sentence around.

We enthusiastic fans raised hundreds of dollars for the athletic fund.
We raised hundreds of dollars for the athletic fund.
The enthusiastic fans raised hundreds of dollars for the athletic fund.
Because we are such enthusiastic fans, we raised hundreds of dollars for the athletic fund.

These examples also show your students the flexibility and versatility of the English language.

Chapter 7 a

Using Pronouns

The Objective Case *(pages 145–150)*

Because oral practice is so important, you may want to do each exercise in this section twice—once in writing and once orally. The ideal would be for your students to *hear* the correct form of each pronoun to the point that each one "sounds" correct to them.

The Possessive Case *(pages 150–151)*

Since students commonly substitute a contraction for a possessive pronoun, it may be helpful if your students write sentences that use the following possessive pronouns and contractions.
1. its, it's
2. your, you're
3. their, they're

Pronoun Problems *(pages 153–158)*

You may wish to omit the study of this section with your basic students. With average or advanced students, you may want to review clauses quickly before beginning this section.

You may want to tell your students to use *who* when speaking if there is any doubt. *Who* is almost always appropriate in any informal situation.

Pronouns and Their Antecedents *(pages 158–162)*

Alternative solutions are given to the problem of the unknown gender of an antecedent. Since style requirements vary in colleges and businesses, it may be best to have your students avoid this problem by rewriting such sentences.

ACTIVITIES FOR DIFFERENT ABILITIES
Basic Students
ACTIVITY 1 Oral Drill
Write the following sentences and their possible answers on the board. Then have your students read the following sentences four times, quickly filling the blanks with (1) *he and I* or *him and me*, (2) *she and Chris* or *her and Chris*, (3) *Don and I* or *Don and me*, (4) *we students* or *us students*.

1. Are _____ too late?
2. The last to arrive were _____.
3. _____ are cousins.
4. Jeff looked for _____.
5. They chose _____.
6. Al met _____ at the door.
7. _____ were waiting for us.
8. The semifinalists were _____.
9. _____ were puzzled.
10. Were _____ frightened?

ACTIVITY 2 Pronoun Review
To provide additional practice, duplicate the following sentences. Then have your students find and correct each error. (Some sentences are correct.)

1. Another student and me worked the lights for the class play.
2. Uncle Mark took my sister and I to lunch at the Regis Restaurant.
3. We should send an invitation to Kelly and she.
4. Dad gave James and me a second-hand tape recorder.
5. His brother and him do small printing jobs at home.
6. It was her who pulled Randy out of the water.
7. Between you and I, Lana would make the best class president.
8. Us experts can hit the bull's-eye from 50 yards.
9. Were he and Dan going sailing today?
10. Only two juniors, Scott Judson and her, are on the tennis team this year.

ACTIVITY 3 Pronouns and Their Antecedents
To provide additional practice, duplicate the following sentences. Then have your students supply a pronoun for each blank.

1. Neither Lynn nor Mary brought _____ lunch today.
2. All of the women in the Framingham Garden Club are growing roses in _____ backyards.
3. After you exercise a horse or a pony, please see that _____ has a good rubdown.
4. Each of the men had earned _____ reputation in the field of law.

Chapter 7 b

Using Pronouns

5. Both Michael and Richard forgot _____ locker keys today.
6. If any boy wants to join the football team, _____ should report to the gym after school.
7. Many of the apples have lost _____ crunchiness.
8. Everyone in the men's choir needs to supply _____ own robe.
9. Neither Brenda nor Elaine sold all _____ tickets to the game.
10. Most of the book has colored illustrations in _____.

ACTIVITY 4 Writing Sentences
Write the following groups of words on the board. Then have your students write a sentence that uses each group.

1. you and I
2. him and me
3. Sheila and she
4. we players
5. Mark or me
6. you and she
7. Bryan or him
8. her and Cathy
9. us members
10. them and us

Advanced Students

ACTIVITY 1 *Who* or *Whom*
To provide additional practice, duplicate the following sentences. Then have your students choose the correct form of *who* or *whoever* in the following sentences.

1. Alice is one of those people (who, whom) never seems to get tired.
2. (Who, Whom) do you think will win the game on Saturday?
3. Give the package to (whoever, whomever) answers the door.
4. Peter is one person (who, whom) I'm sure will be successful in life.
5. There's plenty of food for (whoever, whomever) wants to stay for dinner.
6. Ted Michelson, (who, whom) graduated from college last year, is now working at the bank.
7. (Who, Whom) did you see at the fair?
8. The President will appoint as secretary of agriculture a person (who, whom) will give attention to the problems of the farmers.
9. Tryouts will be held at four for (whoever, whomever) wants to be in the junior class play.
10. Tommy Cannon is the senior (who, whom) I think won the scholarship.

ACTIVITY 2 Pronoun Review
To provide additional practice, duplicate the following sentences. Then have your students find and correct each error. (Some sentences are correct.)

The Curies
1. Marie Curie, whom many biographers say was the world's most renowned woman scientist, was the daughter of a college professor in Warsaw, Poland.
2. Her and her sisters grumbled at the rule forbidding women to study at the university.
3. The three girls, all of who were gifted students, envied their brother, a medical student.
4. They were devoted to him, however, and cherished hopes of him becoming a distinguished surgeon.
5. In 1894, three years after enrolling at the Sorbonne in Paris, Marie met Pierre Curie, the only man with whom she could have found happiness.
6. Pierre, whom his colleagues said was a genius, was a dedicated physicist.
7. For four poverty-filled years, Marie and him dedicated themselves to proving the existence of radium.
8. After Pierre's death in a street accident, Marie, who the university officials agreed deserved the honor, became the first woman to gain a full professorship at the Sorbonne.
9. On July 4, 1934, Marie, whom doctors said had been affected by overexposure to radiation, died of pernicious anemia.
10. Albert Einstein once said, "Marie Curie is, of all celebrated beings, the only one who fame has not corrupted."

ACTIVITY 3 Writing Sentences
Have your students research the hometown of a former president of the United States. Then have them write 10 to 15 sentences that describe that place. When they have finished, have them edit their sentences for the correct case of each pronoun and any vague, missing, or unclear antecedents.

Chapter 7 c

ADDITIONAL PRACTICE

Basic Students
Teacher's Resource Book:
pages 129–131
Workbook: pages 81–90

Average Students
Teacher's Resource Book:
pages 132–134
Workbook: pages 81–90

Advanced Students
Teacher's Resource Book:
pages 135–137

REVIEW EXERCISES AND TESTS

Student Text
Diagnostic Test: page 140
Chapter Review: pages 164–165
Mastery Test: page 165

Teacher's Resource Book
Chapter 7 Test: pages 21–22
(Also available as spirit duplicating masters.)

ADDITIONAL ANSWERS

EXERCISE 5 Writing Sentences *(page 145)*

Sample answers:
1. You and she should meet us at seven o'clock. (compound subject)
2. Two members of the swim team, Jeff and I, went to the district meet. (compound appositive)
3. The loudest fans were we and they. (compound predicate nominative)

EXERCISE 11 Writing Sentences *(page 150)*

Sample answers:
1. Take her and him to the mall.
2. Give Luis and me the tickets.
3. Have you spoken with Mary and her?
4. The principal invited two students, him and her, to attend the meeting.
5. We tried to tell the Jeffersons and them.

EXERCISE 16 Writing Sentences *(page 156)*

Sample answers:
1. Who was knocking at the door?
2. Whom did you see at the game?
3. Jennifer, who lives in Texas, is visiting us.
4. The person whom you met at our house yesterday is my cousin.
5. The secretary said that the teacher for whom I left a message would get it tomorrow.

7
Using Pronouns

For additional practice for this chapter, see the Teacher's Resource Book and the Workbook.

DIAGNOSTIC TEST

Number your paper 1 to 10. Then write the correct form of the pronoun in parentheses.

EXAMPLE Pat and (I, me) are taking the bus tomorrow.
ANSWER I

1. Is that (she, her) standing by the water fountain?
2. Are Bianca and (he, him) trying out for the swim team?
3. John runs faster than (I, me).
4. As we were arriving at the concert, Mr. Cook greeted Beverly and (I, me).
5. Most employers will hire the applicant (who, whom) is best qualified for the job.
6. Dad was surprised at (me, my) offering to mow the lawn.
7. Stephen, (who, whom) I introduced to the coach, is a fine athlete.
8. (We, Us) reporters were the first on the scene.
9. To (who, whom) did you address the envelope?
10. One of the women at the meeting misplaced (her, their) briefcase.

Cases of Pronouns

7a

The English language is filled with clues to help a reader understand exactly what a writer had in mind. The different forms of a pronoun are a good example of one type of clue. Most pronouns have different forms to show how they are being used in a sentence. The pronoun *I*, for example, is used as a subject or a predicate nominative. The pronoun *me* is used as an object, and *my* or *mine* is used to show possession.

Today nouns have only two forms. *Man*, for example, is used for a subject or an object, but *man* becomes *man's* to show possession or ownership. The changes in form for nouns and pronouns occur because all nouns and pronouns have *case*.

7a **Case** is the form of a noun or a pronoun that indicates its use in a sentence.

THE CASES OF PERSONAL PRONOUNS

English has three cases: the *nominative case*, the *objective case*, and the *possessive case*. Many pronouns change form for each of the cases.

Nominative Case
(Used for subjects and predicate nominatives)

SINGULAR I, you, he, she, it
PLURAL   we, you, they

Objective Case
(Used for direct objects, indirect objects, objects of prepositions, and objects of verbals)

SINGULAR me, you, him, her, it
PLURAL   us, you, them

Possessive Case
(Used to show ownership or possession)

SINGULAR my, mine, your, yours, his, her, hers, its
PLURAL   our, ours, your, yours, their, theirs

NOTE: *You* and *it* are the same in both the nominative and the objective cases.

141

Using Pronouns

EXERCISE 1 Determining Case

Number your paper 1 to 10. Write the personal pronouns in each sentence. Then write the case of each one: *nominative, objective,* or *possessive.*

1. They haven't finalized the plans for their trip yet.
2. I hope he finds his lost camera.
3. Does she know that we are meeting her at the barn?
4. This book belongs to either him or her.
5. My car is seven years older than hers.
6. Show me how to give the dog its pill.
7. Please join us for dinner at our home on Friday.
8. I suggested that we use theirs instead of mine.
9. Tell them to follow the signs to Route 17.
10. Did they see ours or yours?

The Nominative Case

The personal pronouns in the nominative case are *I, you, he, she, it, we,* and *they.*

7b The **nominative case** is used for subjects and predicate nominatives.

Pronouns as Subjects. A single pronoun used as the subject of an independent clause or a dependent clause is seldom a problem.

> **They** are moving to New Mexico.
> **She** answered the phone when **I** called.

Because it is harder to determine the pronoun or pronouns for a compound subject, always double-check to make sure they are in the nominative case. There is a test you can use to check them. Say each pronoun separately.

> Randy Jackson and (he, him) designed the scenery.
> **He** designed the scenery.
> **Him** designed the scenery.

The nominative case *he* is the correct form to use.

> Randy Jackson and **he** designed the scenery.

This test also works if both subjects are pronouns.

Nominative Case

7b

Pronouns as Predicate Nominatives. A predicate nominative follows a linking verb and identifies, renames, or explains the subject. *(See page 10 for lists of common linking verbs.)*

That is **he** in the front row.

The preceding example may sound wrong to you because it is common to hear *That's her* and *It's me.* As common as it is to use an objective-case pronoun as a predicate nominative in casual conversation, it should be avoided in written work.

That is **she**.   It is **I**.

Check each pronoun in a compound predicate nominative by turning the sentence around and making the predicate nominative the subject. Then say each pronoun separately.

The winners are Judy and (he, him).
He is the winner.   **Him** is the winner.

The nominative case *he* is the correct form to use.

The winners are Judy and **he**.

NOTE: Sometimes the wording of sentences becomes awkward when pronouns are used as predicate nominatives. This can be avoided by turning the sentence around.

AWKWARD   The coeditors are **he** and **she**.
TURNED AROUND   **He** and **she** are the coeditors.

Appositives with Nominative Case Pronouns. A pronoun in the nominative case will sometimes have a noun appositive. *(See pages 56–57.)* The appositive, however, will never affect the case of the pronoun. In fact, the best way to check to see if you have used the correct pronoun is to mentally drop the appositive from the sentence.

We *Student Council members* will be conducting a survey.
[*We* will be conducting a survey.]

Nominative Case Pronouns as Appositives. Occasionally a pronoun itself will be part of an appositive to a noun that is a subject or a predicate nominative. When it is, the pronoun should be in the nominative case.

143

Using Pronouns

The junior class presidential candidates, Stan Phillips and **she**, will give their speeches at the class meeting. [*Stan Phillips* and *she* are appositives to the subject *candidates*. Since a subject is in the nominative case, an appositive to the subject is also in the nominative case.]

EXERCISE 2 Using Pronouns in the Nominative Case
Number your paper 1 to 10. Then write the correct form of the pronoun in parentheses. Read each sentence aloud to check your answer.

1. Susan and (he, him) are planning a barbecue for the soccer team.
2. With help from Mrs. MacLean, (we, us) math students created our own programs on the computer.
3. The students selected to go to Washington, D.C., were Brenda and (she, her).
4. The winners of the essay contest, Mandy Oliver and (I, me), must give a speech at the assembly.
5. Neither (he, him) nor (I, me) have finished the posters.
6. Anna and (they, them) want to meet us at the stadium.
7. (We, Us) members of the chorus sang several songs by Paul McCartney during the concert.
8. (She, Her) and (I, me) didn't go to the dance after all.
9. The people in the convertible must have been (they, them).
10. Are you and (he, him) sure it was (she, her)?

EXERCISE 3 Supplying Pronouns in the Nominative Case
Number your paper 1 to 10. Complete each sentence by writing an appropriate pronoun in the nominative case. (Do not use *you* or *it*.) Then write how the pronoun is used—*subject*, *predicate nominative*, or *appositive*. Read each sentence aloud to check your answer.

Pronouns will vary, but all should be in the nominative case.

subj. 1. Nathan and __I__ just joined the wrestling team.
subj. 2. __We__ sailors were glad to get back home.
p.n. 3. The creators of that six-foot snowman were Jeff and __she__.
subj. 4. Are __they__ the relatives you met at the picnic?
subj./subj. 5. Because __he__ was late, __he__ missed the first act.
appos. 6. The halfbacks, Scott Garvey and __he__, are the only juniors on the varsity team this year.

Objective Case

7c

p.n./p.n. 7. The only ones to enter the contest were _she_ and _they_.
p.n. 8. The new Student Council officers are Leroy, Kathy, Lee, and _I_.
subj. 9. Mom and Dad told us that _they_ had volunteered to help.
subj./subj. 10. _She_ and _he_ joined us after the game.

EXERCISE 4 Finding Nominative Case Errors

Number your paper 1 to 10. If an underlined pronoun is in the wrong case, write it correctly. If it is in the correct case, write C after the number. Read each sentence aloud to check your answer.

1. Connie and <u>her</u> [she] are planning to take the SAT's in the spring.
C 2. Were you and <u>he</u> the ones making all that noise?
3. The club members to receive a medal from the mayor were <u>him</u> [he] and <u>me</u> [I].
C 4. The Murphys and <u>they</u> are going together.
5. Is that <u>her</u> [she] driving up the driveway?
6. Two *Clarion* reporters, Pam Turner and <u>me</u> [I], interviewed the governor.
7. Didn't the coach tell you that <u>us</u> [we] soccer players must attend every practice?
8. I'm sure it was <u>him</u> [he] at the refreshment stand.
9. The soloists at the concert were Glenda and <u>me</u> [I].
10. The fortunate ones were <u>us</u> [we] students.

EXERCISE 5 Writing Sentences

Write a sentence for each of the following groups of words. Use one group as a compound subject, one as a compound predicate nominative, and one as a compound appositive. Then label how each one is used.
Sample answers precede this chapter.

1. you and she   2. Jeff and I   3. we and they

The Objective Case

The personal pronouns in the objective case are *me, you, him, her, it, us,* and *them.*

7c **The objective case** is used for direct objects, indirect objects, objects of prepositions, and objects of verbals.

Using Pronouns

Pronouns as Direct and Indirect Objects. A pronoun used as a direct object will answer the question *Whom?* after an action verb. A pronoun used as an indirect object will answer the question *To whom?* or *For whom?* after a direct object.

> DIRECT OBJECTS   Mom asked **me** about the open house.
> Take **her** with you to the store.

> INDIRECT OBJECTS   Frankie gave **us** good directions. [*Directions* is the direct object.]
> Throw **him** the football. [*Football* is the direct object.]

Make sure that any pronoun used in a compound direct object or in a compound indirect object is in the objective case. You can do this by saying each pronoun separately.

> Carolyn introduced Joel and (he, him) to Mr. Hanley.
> Carolyn introduced **he** to Mr. Hanley.
> Carolyn introduced **him** to Mr. Hanley.

The objective case *him* is the correct form to use.

> Carolyn introduced Joel and **him** to Mr. Hanley.

This same test works with a compound indirect object.

> Mom gave Alex and (I, me) a lecture about promptness.
> Mom gave **I** a lecture about promptness.
> Mom gave **me** a lecture about promptness.

The objective case *me* is the correct form to use.

> Mom gave Alex and **me** a lecture about promptness.

EXERCISE 6 Using Pronouns as Direct and Indirect Objects
Number your paper 1 to 10. Write the correct form of the pronoun in parentheses. Then label each one — *direct object* or *indirect object*. Read each sentence aloud to check your answer.

1. Did you give Peg and (she, her) tickets to the concert?
2. We invited the Franklins and (they, them) to dinner.
3. Tonia sent Earl and (I, me) postcards from Iowa.
4. Mr. Wilson gave Maria and (we, us) a job.
5. Last week Dad took Daniel and (he, him) to the boat show.

146

Objective Case

i.o. 6. Have you given the Ryans and (they, **them**) a tour of your new apartment?
d.o. 7. No, I didn't see Jay or (she, **her**) in the gym.
d.o. 8. Coach Bentley switched Andrew and (I, **me**) to the infield.
d.o. 9. The coast guard rescued Angelo and (he, **him**) after their sailboat capsized.
i.o. 10. Amanda sent the Jacksons and (we, **us**) invitations to the school musical.

Pronouns as Objects of Prepositions. A prepositional phrase begins with a preposition and ends with a noun or a pronoun called the *object of a preposition*. A pronoun used as the object of a preposition is in the objective case. *(See page 19 for a list of common prepositions.)*

Will you have dinner with **us**? [*With us* is the prepositional phrase.]

Dad gave his old camera to **me**. [*To me* is the prepositional phrase.]

Check to see that any pronoun used in a compound object of a preposition is in the objective case. You can do this by saying each pronoun separately.

Mr. Hubbard was very proud of Matt and (she, her).
Mr. Hubbard was very proud of **she**.
Mr. Hubbard was very proud of **her**.

The objective case *her* is the correct form to use.

Mr. Hubbard was very proud of Matt and **her**.

EXERCISE 7 Using Pronouns as Objects of Prepositions
Write the correct form of the pronoun in parentheses. Read each sentence aloud to check your answer.

1. Do you want to go to the basketball game with Jeremy and (we, **us**)?
2. The referee called a double foul on Max and (he, **him**).
3. I sat with the Smiths and (they, **them**) during the concert.
4. The votes were divided evenly between Ginny and (I, **me**).
5. With help from Dennis and (she, **her**), Dad was able to repair the television set.
6. Shall I give this note to Mr. Richardson or (he, **him**)?

147

Using Pronouns

7. Mom and Dad are going with Kevin and (I, **me**).
8. Spot barked at the Lees and (they, **them**) as they arrived.
9. Do you have any messages for Charlene or (we, **us**)?
10. Between you and (I, **me**), he should coach the track team.

Pronouns as Objects of Verbals. Participles, gerunds, and infinitives are all verbals. *(See pages 59–65.)* Because verbals are verb forms, they can take objects. The object of a verbal is in the objective case.

PARTICIPIAL PHRASE	Seeing **him** on the corner, Steve pulled over to the curb. [The phrase is *seeing him on the corner. Him* is the object of the participle *seeing*.]
GERUND PHRASE	Asking **her** to the dance made Jordan anxious. [The phrase is *asking her to the dance. Her* is the object of the gerund *asking*.]
INFINITIVE PHRASE	Tell Ann to call **me** at home. [The phrase is *to call me at home. Me* is the object of the infinitive *to call*.]

When the object of a verbal is compound, say each pronoun separately.

Telling Jason and (they, them) wasn't easy.
Telling **they** wasn't easy.
Telling **them** wasn't easy.

The objective case *them* is the correct form to use.

Telling Jason and **them** wasn't easy.

Appositives with Objective Case Pronouns. Sometimes a pronoun in the objective case will have an appositive. Such an appositive will never affect the case of the pronoun it identifies or explains. Check to see if you have used the correct pronoun by dropping the appositive from the sentence.

Give **us** *reporters* our new assignments. [*Us* is used as an indirect object. Give us our new assignments.]

Objective Case Pronouns as Appositives. Occasionally a pronoun itself will be part of an appositive to a noun that is a direct or indirect object or an object of a preposition. When it is, the pronoun should be in the objective case.

Objective Case

Mr. Talbot sent two students, Marcia and **me**, to the office to get the supplies. [*Marcia* and *me* are appositives to the direct object *students*. Since a direct object is in the objective case, an appositive to a direct object is also in the objective case.]

EXERCISE 8 Using Pronouns in the Objective Case
Write the correct form of the pronoun in parentheses. Read each sentence aloud to check your answer.

1. I want to thank Terry and (they, <u>them</u>) personally.
2. Mr. Lansing gave (we, <u>us</u>) boys five dollars for shoveling his driveway.
3. Finding Angela and (he, <u>him</u>) at the mall was impossible.
4. Informing (they, <u>them</u>) of the accident, James spoke softly.
5. Give your dues to any class officer—Ray, Martha, Tim, or (she, <u>her</u>).
6. The audience gave (we, <u>us</u>) actors a standing ovation.
7. Uncle Tony enjoys telling (I, <u>me</u>) about his childhood in Italy.
8. The editor of the school paper welcomed the new staff members, Jerry and (he, <u>him</u>).
9. The race was first suggested by (we, <u>us</u>) members of the track team.
10. Mr. King plans to promote Stacy and (she, <u>her</u>) next month.

EXERCISE 9 Supplying Pronouns in the Objective Case
Number your paper 1 to 10. Complete each sentence by writing an appropriate pronoun in the objective case. (Do not use *you* or *it*.) Then use the following abbreviations to write how each pronoun is used. *Pronouns will vary, but all should be in the objective case.*

direct object = *d.o.*
indirect object = *i.o.*
object of a preposition = *o.p.*
object of a verbal = *o.v.*
appositive = *appos.*

i.o. 1. Tell <u>us</u> the latest news about the election results.
d.o. 2. The principal praised <u>him</u> for his accomplishments.
o.p. 3. There are no secrets between Nancy and <u>me</u>.
appos. 4. The quarterback sent two linemen, Henry Myers and <u>him</u>, to block the tackler.

149

Using Pronouns

i.o.   5. Mom offered Brad and <u>her</u> a snack after school.
d.o.   6. I forgot to tell <u>them</u> about my new job.
o.p.   7. Some of <u>us</u> students volunteered to collect for the paper drive.
o.v.   8. Taking <u>her</u> with <u>us</u> was a pleasure.
d.o.   9. Mr. Carlson's goat chased Gus and <u>him</u> across the back pasture.
o.v.   10. Answering <u>her</u> correctly, Lenore sighed with relief.

EXERCISE 10   **Finding Objective Case Errors**

Number your paper 1 to 10. If an underlined pronoun is in the wrong case, write it correctly. If it is in the correct case, write *C* after the number. Read each sentence aloud to check your answer.

1. Try to stall Oliver and <u>she</u> until six o'clock. [her]
2. Trophies were given to the most valuable players, Alvin Brooks and <u>he</u>. [him]
3. To Barry and <u>I</u>, the solution was simple. [me]
4. Draw Kevin and <u>he</u> a map to your house. [him]
5. My sister and brother always beat Diana and <u>I</u> at tennis. [me]
6. Why don't you ask three people—Marcia, Ronnie, and <u>he</u>—to work at the refreshment stand? [him]
7. The reduced school budget will affect <u>we</u> athletes. [us]
   C   8. Seeing <u>him</u> all alone, we invited him to join us.
9. Officer Morrison gave Wendy and <u>I</u> our driving tests. [me]
10. Will you take a picture of Randy and <u>I</u> as we cross the finish line? [me]

EXERCISE 11   **Writing Sentences**

Write five sentences that follow the directions below.
Sample answers precede this chapter.

1. Use *her* and *him* as a compound direct object.
2. Use *Luis* and *me* as a compound indirect object.
3. Use *Mary* and *her* as a compound object of a preposition.
4. Use *him* and *her* as a compound appositive.
5. Use *the Jeffersons* and *them* as an object of a verbal.

The Possessive Case

The personal pronouns in the possessive case are *my, mine, your, yours, his, her, hers, its, our, ours, their,* and *theirs.*

Possessive Case

7d The **possessive case** is used to show ownership or possession.

Possessive case pronouns can be used to show possession before a noun or before a gerund. Others can be used by themselves.

BEFORE A NOUN	**Her** attendance was perfect.
BEFORE A GERUND	There is a good chance of **his** winning the art contest. ["There is a good chance of *him* winning the art contest" is *not* correct.]
BY THEMSELVES	These gloves are **mine.**

NOTE: Do not confuse certain personal pronouns in the possessive case with contractions. A personal pronoun in the possessive case never includes an apostrophe. *Its, your, their,* and *theirs* are possessive pronouns. *It's, you're, they're,* and *there's* are contractions.

EXERCISE 12 Using Pronouns in the Possessive Case
Write the correct word in parentheses.

1. (Theirs, There's) is the apartment on the third floor.
2. Everyone was amazed at (my, me) finishing so quickly.
3. Who objected to (your, you're) taking piano lessons?
4. Dad advised against (them, their) buying the old car.
5. That couldn't be (ours, our's), could it?
6. Mr. Walters seemed pleased to hear of (my, me) choosing Eleanor Roosevelt as my report topic.
7. That should be (their, they're) tent next to the big spruce tree.
8. After reading the story, we will have a chance to talk to (its, it's) author.
9. Why haven't you registered (your, you're) car yet?
10. Did you know about (his, him) running in the New York Marathon?

EXERCISE 13 Supplying Pronouns in All Cases
Number your paper 1 to 10. Then complete each sentence by writing appropriate pronouns. (Do not use *you* or *it.*)
Sample answers:
1. _They_ met _us_ at the football game.
2. Rebecca showed _her_ and _me_ her new outfit.
3. _We_ left before _them_.
4. Peter told _us_ about _his_ riding down the rapids.

151

Using Pronouns

5. The contestants with the most points are __he__ and __I__.
6. __We__ members are giving __our__ support to Craig.
7. __My__ driving __her__ to school saves half an hour.
8. Is that __she__ with __them__?
9. The team captains, Ed and __he__, were invited to join __us__.
10. __I__ didn't recognize the car that __she__ was driving.

EXERCISE 14 Time-out for Review

Number your paper 1 to 20. Find and write each pronoun that is in the wrong case. Then write each one correctly. If a sentence is correct, write *C* after the number. Read each sentence aloud to check your answer.

1. With some help from Fred and I (*me*), the Baxters were able to put up their storm windows.
2. Shall I give the tapes to Stephen or he (*him*)?
3. During the intermission of the high school variety show, Linda, Lou, and me (*I*) sold over 100 bags of peanuts.
4. Haven't you heard about us (*our*) moving to Memphis?
c 5. The only witnesses to the accident were she and I.
6. Pleasing Robert and they (*them*) wasn't as hard as it first seemed.
7. The chairman of the cleanup committee will be Jan or him (*he*).
8. Manuel invited you and I (*me*) to his house after school.
9. Kimberly told me of you (*your*) entering the Superstars athletic competition.
c 10. He is going to Mohawk Island with Michael and me next Saturday.
11. It was a great day for we (*us*) fans when our team won the state finals.
12. We chose two representatives, Leroy and she (*her*), to speak to the principal for us.
13. Was it him (*he*) who broke the school's pole-vault record at yesterday's track meet?
14. Tell Barry to call Lee and I (*me*) at the Murphys' house.
15. Us (*We*) American history students must write a ten-page report.
16. Them (*They*) are the girls who were lifeguards at the pool last summer.
c 17. Are you sure it was he who called last night?
18. My sister and her (*she*) have been taking scuba-diving lessons.
c 19. Just between you and me, Brian was very disappointed.
c 20. Recognizing them, Hannah introduced herself.

PRONOUN PROBLEMS

Since you first learned to talk, certain speech patterns have become part of your conversation. Some of them are correct; some are not. After years of using these speech patterns, they all probably *sound* correct to you. For some constructions, therefore, you must learn to use the correct pronouns—even though they may *sound* incorrect. The more you use them, however, the more they will begin to *sound* correct.

Who and Whom

Who and *whoever* are pronouns that have different forms for each case—just as personal pronouns do.

NOMINATIVE CASE   who, whoever
OBJECTIVE CASE   whom, whomever
POSSESSIVE CASE   whose

Who and *whoever* and their related pronouns are used in questions and in subordinate clauses.

> **7e** The correct case of *who* is determined by how the pronoun is used in a question or a clause.

In Questions. *Who* or *whom* is often used in a question. The case of *who* that you should choose is determined by how the pronoun is used in a question.

NOMINATIVE CASE   **Who** saw the accident? [subject]

OBJECTIVE CASE   **Whom** did you see? [direct object]

    From **whom** did you get that book? [object of the preposition *from*]

NOTE: In casual conversation you might hear people say, *Who did you see?* This informal use of *who,* however, should be avoided in formal, written work.

In Clauses. *Who* or one of its forms is often the first word of an adjective clause or a noun clause. The form you use depends on how the pronoun is used within the clause—not by any

Using Pronouns

word outside the clause. The following examples show how forms of *who* are used in adjective clauses.

NOMINATIVE CASE — Mr. Roy is the architect **who designed this building.** [*Who* is the subject of *designed*.]

OBJECTIVE CASE — He is the electrician **whom we hired to do the rewiring in our house.** [*Whom* is the direct object of *hired*. We hired whom.]

Pat is the person **with whom I was just speaking.** [*Whom* is the object of the preposition *with*.]

The following examples show how forms of *who* and *whoever* are used in noun clauses.

NOMINATIVE CASE — Give **whoever calls** this message. [*Whoever* is the subject of *calls*.]

Do you know **who the winner is?** [*Who* is a predicate nominative. The winner is who.]

OBJECTIVE CASE — Interview **whomever you want.** [*Whomever* is the direct object of *want*. You want whomever.]

Brad generally likes **whomever he works with.** [*Whomever* is the object of the preposition *with*. He works with whomever.]

NOTE: Questions and clauses sometimes contain an interrupting expression such as *I believe, we know, do you suppose,* or *she hopes.* Before you decide the case of a pronoun, mentally drop this expression so that the choice will be easier to make.

Who do you think will be the new captain? [Who will be the new captain? *Who* is the subject of *will be*.]

I'm lending this book to Buddy, **who** I know likes spy thrillers. [I'm lending this book to Buddy, who likes spy thrillers. *Who* is the subject of *likes*.]

EXERCISE 15 Using *Who* and Its Related Pronouns

Number your paper 1 to 25. Write the correct form of the pronoun in parentheses. Then write how each pronoun is used in the question or the clause.

Who and Whom

subject = *subj.*   direct object = *d.o.*
predicate nominative = *p.n.*   object of a preposition = *o.p.*

EXAMPLE   Give (whoever, whomever) arrives first the best seats.
ANSWER   whoever — subj.

subj. 1. Janet, (who, whom) is a senior, is attending the University of Colorado.
d.o. 2. (Who, Whom) did you visit in California?
subj. 3. Rob and he were bragging about (who, whom) could catch the most fish.
d.o. 4. Bud Miller, (who, whom) I have always admired, made the winning touchdown.
subj. 5. I wonder (who, whom) the winner will be.
subj. 6. (Who, Whom) did you say will play the lead in the play?
o.p. 7. For (who, whom) did you buy this book?
p.n. 8. No one knew (who, whom) the driver of the car was.
d.o. 9. Bring (whoever, whomever) you like with you.
subj. 10. Carlos telephoned Maria, (who, whom) he thought had sent him the funny valentine.
p.n. 11. Andrew couldn't tell (who, whom) the person was behind the mask.
subj. 12. Michael, (who, whom) everyone thought had never ridden a horse, was the star of the local rodeo.
o.p. 13. To (who, whom) should we give this information?
o.p. 14. Ben is attentive to (whoever, whomever) he is with.
d.o. 15. Kate Symonds is the actress (who, whom) I've known since grammar school.
o.p. 16. From (who, whom) did you get the calculator?
subj. 17. Give the message to (whoever, whomever) is at the receptionist's desk.
d.o. 18. My grandparents, (who, whom) we weren't expecting until the weekend, arrived today.
subj. 19. (Who, Whom) is in charge of this committee?
subj. 20. Seth Baxter is a player (who, whom) everyone predicts will be chosen for the all-American team.
subj. 21. (Who, Whom) did Mom say was going with us to the lake?
p.n. 22. The mail carrier asked Jennifer (who, whom) our new neighbor was.
o.p. 23. Charles always liked (whoever, whomever) he worked with at the World Health Organization.

Using Pronouns

<small>d.o.</small> 24. Invite to dinner (whoever, <u>whomever</u>) Joan wants.
<small>subj.</small> 25. Benjamin Franklin, (<u>who</u>, whom) everyone knows was a versatile man, invented many things.

EXERCISE 16 **Writing Sentences**
Write five sentences that follow the directions below.
Sample answers precede this chapter.
1. Begin a question with *who*.
2. Begin a question with *whom*, used as a direct object.
3. Include *who* as the subject of a subordinate clause.
4. Include *whom* as the direct object in a subordinate clause.
5. Include *whom* as an object of a preposition in a subordinate clause.

Elliptical Clauses

An *elliptical clause* is an adverb clause that is only partially expressed. The missing words, nevertheless, are understood to be there by both the writer and the reader. Most elliptical clauses begin with *than* or *as*.

Dick admires Ellen more **than I.**
Dick admires Ellen more **than me.**

Both of the preceding examples are correct—depending upon what words are missing.

Dick admires Ellen more **than I admire Ellen.** [*I* is correct because it is the subject of *admire*.]

Dick admires Ellen more **than he admires me.** [Now *me* is correct because it is the direct object of the verb *admires*.]

7f In an **elliptical clause,** use the form of the pronoun you would use if the clause were completed.

You can decide the case of a pronoun in an elliptical clause by mentally completing the clause. Then choose the form of the pronoun that expresses the meaning you want. Some elliptical clauses, however, can express only one meaning.

Are you as tired as (I, me)?
Are you as tired **as I am?**

Elliptical Clauses

7f

EXERCISE 17 Using Pronouns in Elliptical Clauses

Write the sentence, completing the elliptical clause. Be sure to choose the pronoun that is correct for each clause. Then underline the pronoun you chose.
Note that 4, 7, 10, 14, 16, and 18 can use either pronoun. See below for alternative answers.
EXAMPLE They worked harder than (we, us).
ANSWER They worked harder than <u>we</u> worked.

1. Brian missed the school bus because he can't run as fast as (<u>I</u>, me)./ can run.
2. I think Tina's sister is more athletic than (<u>she</u>, her)./ is.
3. You did better on the history exam than (<u>I</u>, me)./ did.
4. Mr. Mallory spent more time training Chris than training (I, <u>me</u>).
5. Does Julie sing as well as (<u>she</u>, her)?/ sings?
6. I'm sure Burt is stronger than (<u>I</u>, me)./ am.
7. Art likes them as much as (<u>we</u>, us)./ like them.
8. Carl knows more about whales than (<u>he</u>, him)./ knows.
9. Do you think Betsy is taller than (<u>I</u>, me)?/ am?
10. Joseph seems closer to Jon than (<u>I</u>, me)./ seem.
11. Tony is better at the high jump than (<u>he</u>, him)./ is.
12. Rosa is much faster on skates than (<u>I</u>, me)./ am.
13. Do you think Ann is a better dancer than (<u>she</u>, her)?/ is?
14. Melinda scolded them more than (<u>we</u>, us)./ scolded them.
15. Yes, Terry can certainly dive as well as (<u>she</u>, her)./ can.
16. The instructor praised Kim more than he praised (I, <u>me</u>).
17. After the contest was over, Roy had to admit that Louis was as good an archer as (<u>he</u>, him)./ was.
18. Sometimes I think Patrick likes the dog more than he likes (I, <u>me</u>).
19. No one can do better imitations than (<u>she</u>, her)./ can.
20. Raymond could see that his friend was tiring faster than (<u>he</u>, him)./ was.

EXERCISE 18 Time-out for Review

Number your paper 1 to 10. Find and write each <u>pronoun</u> that is used incorrectly. Then write it correctly. If a sentence is correct, write *C* after the number.

c 1. For whom are you making that sweater?
2. Pauline has never been at practice for the school play earlier than me.
3. The men on board the ship frantically pulled in the diver whom they feared was seriously injured.

4. . . . than I spent.
7. . . . as he likes us.
10. . . . than to me.
14. . . . than she scolded us.
16. . . . than I praised him.
18. . . . than I like the dog.

Using Pronouns

    4. Ann is a person in who̅ (whom) I place a great deal of trust.
c 5. I get frustrated because Allison reads much faster than I.
    6. I always give advice to whomever (whoever) is interested.
c 7. The announcer called out the name of Mrs. Randle, who was holding the winning ticket.
    8. Can Ned win as many points in a row as him (he)?
    9. I could see that Lucy was swimming almost as fast as me (I).
c 10. Raymond, who I believe is running for class president, should have an excellent chance to win.

PRONOUNS AND THEIR ANTECEDENTS

Most pronouns have an *antecedent,* the word that a pronoun refers to, or replaces. Because the pronoun and its antecedent are both referring to the same person, place, or thing, they must agree in both number and gender.

Number is the term used to indicate whether a noun or a pronoun is singular or plural. *Singular* indicates one; *plural* indicates more than one. *Gender* is the term used to indicate whether a noun or a pronoun is *masculine, feminine,* or *neuter.*

Masculine	Feminine	Neuter
he, him, his	she, her, hers	it, its

7g **A pronoun must agree in number and gender with its antecedent.**

To make a pronoun agree with its antecedent, first find the antecedent. Then determine its number and gender. Agreement between a single antecedent and a pronoun usually presents no problem.

Maria carefully typed the final draft of **her** report.
[*Maria* is singular and feminine; therefore, *her* is correct because it also is singular and feminine.]

Members of the class warmed up before **they** began to exercise. [*Members* is plural; therefore, *they* is plural.]

158

You need to remember two rules, however, if the antecedent of a pronoun is more than one word.

7h ▶ If two or more singular antecedents are joined by *or, nor, either/or,* or *neither/nor,* use a singular pronoun to refer to them.

All the conjunctions listed in the previous rule indicate one *or* the other. In the following example, Lana *or* Emma will give her speech — not both of them. As a result, the pronoun must be singular.

Either Lana or Emma will give **her** speech tomorrow.

NOTE: When one antecedent is singular and the other is plural, the pronoun agrees with the closer antecedent.

Either Gerry or the Davis twins will bring **their** tapes.

7i ▶ If two or more singular antecedents are joined by *and* or *both/and,* use a plural pronoun to refer to them.

The conjunctions listed in the previous rule indicate more than one. In the following example, both Ted and Paulo — two people — cleaned their uniforms. As a result, the pronoun is plural.

Ted and Paulo cleaned **their** uniforms for Saturday's game.

Knowing the gender of the antecedents in the previous examples was no problem. *Lana* and *Emma* are feminine; *Ted* and *Paulo* are masculine. The gender of some antecedents, however, is not so obvious. Standard English solves this agreement problem by using *his* or *his or her* to refer to antecedents with unknown gender.

Each student must choose **his** topic by Friday.

Each student must choose **his or her** topic by Friday.

This awkward wording can be avoided entirely by rewriting such sentences, using the plural form.

All students must choose **their** topics by Friday.

Using Pronouns

EXERCISE 19 Making Pronouns and Antecedents Agree
Number your paper 1 to 20. Then write the pronoun that correctly completes each sentence.

1. If any boy wants to try out for soccer, _he_ should report to the gym at three o'clock.
2. All members of the band have been measured for _their_ new uniforms.
3. Both Elizabeth and Christopher won _their_ varsity basketball letters.
4. Will you ask Sarah or Lisa to stop by after school with _her_ history book?
5. Either David or his brothers will take you in _their_ old station wagon.
6. Neither Pearl nor Flora can get _her_ driver's license until next spring.
7. Each book in the library has _its_ proper place.
8. Mom and Dad prefer back roads to the highways because _they_ can see more.
9. Both Nancy and Pauline like _their_ new schedules.
10. Neither Ray nor his parents can find _their_ dog.
11. The members of the cast promised that _they_ would know _their_ lines by the next rehearsal.
12. Either Sandra or Susan will loan you _her_ dictionary.
13. During the holidays Dad collects old toys, repairs _them_, and gives _them_ to needy children.
14. Jack and Luke showed _their_ cousin around Springfield.
15. Neither Douglas nor Jonathan has had _his_ picture taken for the yearbook.
16. I have so many things to do and so little time to do _them_.
17. Either Pepe or Justin will take _his_ car to the dance.
18. Both Mary and Ellen have finished _their_ costumes for the party.
19. Neither Alma nor her sisters want to paint _their_ bedrooms.
20. I wrote a letter to Andrew last week, but _he_ hasn't answered _it_ yet.

Indefinite Pronouns as Antecedents

Based on their number, the common indefinite pronouns have been divided into the following three groups.

Pronoun Antecedents

> **Common Indefinite Pronouns**
>
> SINGULAR anybody, anyone, each, either, everybody, everyone, neither, nobody, no one, one, somebody, someone
> PLURAL both, few, many, several
> SINGULAR/PLURAL all, any, most, none, some

A personal pronoun must be singular if its antecedent is one of the singular indefinite pronouns in the first group.

One of the boys lost **his** tennis racket.

A personal pronoun must be plural if its antecedent is one of the plural indefinite pronouns in the second group.

Both of the women submitted **their** résumés.

If the antecedent of a personal pronoun is one of the indefinite pronouns in the third group, the personal pronoun must agree in number and gender with the object of the preposition following the indefinite pronoun.

Most of the cheese had mold on **it**. [singular]
Most of the books had lost **their** covers. [plural]

The gender of a singular indefinite pronoun sometimes is not indicated by other words in the sentence. Standard English solves this problem by using *his* or *his or her* or by rewriting the sentence, using the plural form.

Everyone must have **his** physical by next week.
Everyone must have **his or her** physical by next week.
All of the athletes must have **their** physicals by next week.

EXERCISE 20 Making Pronouns Agree

Write the pronoun that correctly completes each sentence.

1. Each of the men kept __his__ body fit by working out an hour each day.
2. None of the parents want __their__ children to work after school.

Using Pronouns

3. Neither of the girls finished __her__ test.
4. Both of the farmers planted __their__ wheat early this year.
5. Someone on the men's volleyball team hurt __his__ hand.
6. Some of our neighbors park __their__ cars on the street.
7. One of the boys gave __his__ name to the reporter.
8. Several of my friends ride __their__ bicycles to school.
9. Most of the lettuce had lost __its__ crispness.
10. Each of the girls works for __her__ father.

EXERCISE 21 Time-out for Review

Write the <u>pronoun</u> in parentheses that correctly completes each sentence.

1. Both Gary and Leon will give (his, <u>their</u>) reports at the beginning of the meeting.
2. Everyone on the girls' softball team will be excused from (<u>her</u>, their) homeroom on Friday.
3. Most of the coins could be identified from (its, <u>their</u>) markings.
4. Neither Anna nor Melinda had time to clean out (<u>her</u>, their) gym locker before lunch.
5. Some of the men on the committee are going to withhold (his, <u>their</u>) votes.
6. David and Willie asked (his, <u>their</u>) father to go swimming with them.
7. Both a letter and a package should be mailed with a return address on (it, <u>them</u>).
8. All of my brothers received *B*'s on (his, <u>their</u>) report cards.
9. Many of the girls in our gym class have completed (her, <u>their</u>) swimming requirements.
10. Somebody in the male quartet has forgotten (<u>his</u>, their) music.

Application to Writing

As you edit your written work, always check to see if the pronouns you have used are in the right case and if they agree with their antecedents in number and gender. Check also for four other common pronoun errors: pronoun shifts; vague antecedents; missing antecedents; and an unclear *it, you,* or *they.*

Pronoun Errors

PRONOUN SHIFT	I like living in the South because **you** can swim all year.
CORRECT	**I** like living in the South because **I** can swim all year.
VAGUE ANTECEDENT	If cans are left lying around by campers, bury **them.** [Is the antecedent of *them* the cans or the campers?]
CORRECT	Any cans left lying around by campers should be buried.
VAGUE ANTECEDENT	Mike told Kent that **he** should be captain of the baseball team.
CORRECT	Mike told Kent, "You should be captain of the baseball team."
MISSING ANTECEDENT	After you have skated for an hour, please lend **them** to me. [There is no antecedent for *them*.]
CORRECT	After you have skated for an hour, please lend me your **skates.**
UNCLEAR PRONOUN	In Quebec **they** have many narrow streets. [Who is "they"?]
CORRECT	Quebec has many narrow streets.

EXERCISE 22 Eliminating Pronoun Errors

Rewrite each sentence to make its meaning clear.
Sample answers:

1. If climbers in the Himalayas do not wear sun goggles, ~~it~~ *the sun* causes snow blindness.
2. ~~In~~ Brazil ~~they grow~~ *grows* cocoa for export.
3. Ida told Pearl ~~that she had~~ "*You have* won first prize in the writing contest."
4. I was nervous about giving my speech because ~~you're~~ *I'm* afraid of making mistakes in front of the class.
5. Michael had several mosquito bites on both arms, but ~~they~~ *the bites* have disappeared.
6. Athletes at our school keep their grades up because ~~you~~ *they* can't stay on a team unless ~~you~~ *they* have at least a C average.
7. ~~In~~ *T*he movie ~~they~~ showed how justice triumphs.
8. I saw your ad in the *Times* and would like to apply for ~~it~~. *the job*
9. May 11 would be a better day for our picnic than May 4 because ~~it~~ *May 11* is the day after our history exam.

163

Using Pronouns

10. Roy stood on the 10-yard line and kicked ~~it~~ *the ball* 60 yards down the field.
11. Remove the chicken from the roasting pan and soak ~~it~~ *the pan* in soapy water.
12. I'm still a little squeamish about hooking the worm, but I love ~~it~~ *fishing* just the same.
13. Occasionally, I like to watch TV after I finish my homework because ~~it~~ *TV watching* clears ~~your~~ *my* mind.
14. Mrs. Taylor told Aunt May ~~that her~~ *Your* dog knocks over the trash cans."
15. Last year ~~they added~~ computer programming ^*was added* to the school's curriculum.
16. Maria asked her mother, ~~where her sweater was.~~ *"Where is my sweater?"*
17. He ~~took the books out of~~ *waxed* the bookcases and waxed them. *after he took the books out.*
18. Most people like to read if ~~it~~ *the material* is interesting.
19. I like swimming as an exercise because ~~it~~ *swimming* uses all your muscles.
20. ~~If~~ *Freeze the strawberries* the guests don't eat ~~the strawberries, freeze~~ them.
21. With the vegetarian lunch, ~~they give~~ *there is* a choice of soup or juice.
22. Mr. Brennan pulled out a red bandana, mopped his face, and stuffed ~~it~~ *the bandana* into his pocket.
23. I like a story that keeps ~~you~~ *me* in suspense until the end.
24. I wrote to Tom last week, but he hasn't answered ~~it~~ *my letter* yet.
25. During the winter months, I seldom get to the movies, but I enjoy ~~them~~ *winter* nevertheless.

CHAPTER REVIEW

A. Write the correct form of the pronoun in parentheses.

1. Where did Juan and (he, him) go last night?
2. (Who, Whom) do you think is the best candidate?
3. Mr. Robb and (he, him) should run for office.
4. The principal was amazed at (us, our) selling so many ads for the school paper.
5. Are you and (she, her) going to the football game?
6. Mom promised a special treat to (whoever, whomever) raked the leaves.

164

Chapter Review

7. Ask Gail and (they, <u>them</u>) to dinner.
8. Senator Ruiz spoke with (we, <u>us</u>) honor society members.
9. We selected two students, Allison and (he, <u>him</u>), to plan the paper drive.
10. Did you notice whether it was Peter or (<u>he</u>, him) in the science lab?

B. Write the pronoun that correctly completes each sentence.

1. Neither of the boys had an identification card with <u>him</u>.
2. Did all of the teachers bring <u>their</u> students to the library?
3. Each of my aunts likes flowers on <u>her</u> kitchen table.
4. I have three reports to write and only a week in which to write <u>them</u>.
5. Neither Steve nor Henry has received <u>his</u> paycheck.
6. Both Carol and Lee entered <u>their</u> dogs in the pet show.
7. Some of the watermelon doesn't have any seeds in <u>it</u>.
8. Have you ever seen a bird build <u>its</u> nest?
9. Most of the senators cast <u>their</u> votes in favor of the bill.
10. Both of my parents signed <u>their</u> names on the petition.

MASTERY TEST

Number your paper 1 to 10. Then write the correct form of the pronoun in parentheses.

1. Come here and sit between Melba and (I, <u>me</u>).
2. Some of the boys couldn't find (his, <u>their</u>) helmets.
3. My uncle was surprised to hear of (me, <u>my</u>) building my own stereo.
4. Kathleen can memorize spelling words so much faster than (<u>I</u>, me).
5. Joshua and (<u>I</u>, me) are going to the basketball game.
6. (<u>Who</u>, Whom) did you say wanted to talk to me?
7. Are you sure it was Lee and (<u>she</u>, her) at the movies?
8. Will you take (I, <u>me</u>) with you?
9. (<u>We</u>, Us) joggers feel good and fit.
10. The person to (<u>whom</u>, who) you should speak is Mr. Macklin.

Chapter 8 Subject and Verb Agreement

OBJECTIVES
- To explain the number of a noun, a pronoun, and a verb.
- To make main verbs or helping verbs agree with their subjects.
- To make verbs agree with subjects that are interrupted by other words.
- To make verbs agree with compound subjects.
- To make verbs agree with subjects that are indefinite pronouns.
- To make verbs agree with subjects in inverted order.
- To make verbs agree with collective nouns, words expressing an amount, *the number of* and *a number of*, and singular words that have a plural form.
- To make *doesn't* and *don't* and other contractions agree with subjects.
- To make verbs agree with subjects, not predicate nominatives; and with titles.
- Application: To recognize and be able to correct any mistake in subject and verb agreement.

MOTIVATIONAL ACTIVITY
Write the following columns on the board. Then have your students match a subject in column A with a verb in column B.

A	B
1. A plane	a. grows.
2. Plants	b. fly.
3. A plant	c. grow.
4. Planes	d. flies.

Then point out that subjects change form, depending upon whether they are singular or plural. Also point out that a verb also changes form, depending upon whether it has a singular or a plural subject. These changes occur because verbs must agree with their subjects in number. Then tell your students that this chapter will explain how this process works.

TEACHING SUGGESTIONS
The usage errors in this chapter are perhaps more common in spoken English than in written English. Such errors often appear, however, in quick or careless writing that is not edited. One solution to this problem, then, is to remind and encourage your students to edit their written work for any errors in subject and verb agreement.

Interrupting Words *(pages 169–171)*

Since making a verb agree with the object of a preposition is such a common mistake, you may want to review the list of prepositions on page 19 before beginning this section. Then remind your students to drop mentally all prepositional phrases when checking for subject and verb agreement.

Compound Subjects *(pages 171–173)*

You may want to omit the two exceptions to rule 8g with your basic students. With your average and advanced classes, you may want to point out that only one article is used when a reference is being made to one person.

The coach and president of the athletic club was honored at the banquet. [This sentence refers to only one person because only one article *(the)* is used before the nouns *coach* and *president*. As a result, the verb is singular.]

The coach and *the* president of the athletic club were honored at the banquet. [This sentence refers to two people because two articles are used—one before each noun. As a result, the verb is plural.]

Special Agreement Problems *(pages 174–183)*

Except for "Indefinite Pronouns as Subjects" *(pages 174–175)* and "*Doesn't* and *Don't*" *(page 180)*, you may want to omit this section with your basic students. Your time may be better spent concentrating on the first part of this

Chapter 8 a

chapter, since it includes the areas in which students make most of their mistakes.

Subjects in Inverted Order *(pages 176–177)* In preparation for this section, your students may benefit from reviewing Exercise 2 on page 33. The instruction preceding this exercise will remind your students to change an inverted sentence to its natural order before looking for subject and verb agreement.

Words Expressing Amount *(pages 177–178)* You may want to tell your students that a singular verb is used when an amount answers the question *How much?* A plural verb is used when an amount answers the question *How many?*

Three fourths of the lake *has* already been searched. [How much of the lake?]

Three fourths of the juniors *are* taking the SATs in the spring. [How many juniors?]

Sample Board Sentences
The average <u>pulse</u> for adults <u>is</u> 70 or 80 beats per minute. [interrupting words]

<u>Iceland</u> and <u>Costa Rica</u> have no armed forces. [compound subject]

Neither <u>Mozart</u> nor <u>Schumann</u> was ever wealthy. [compound subject with neither/nor]

There <u>are</u> about 9,000 <u>stars</u> visible to the naked eye. [inverted order]

In the 1950s, <u>twenty-five cents was</u> the price of a gallon of gasoline. [amount]

<u>My Life and Hard Times tells</u> about amusing incidents in James Thurber's childhood. [title]

ACTIVITIES FOR DIFFERENT ABILITIES
Basic Students
ACTIVITY 1 Interrupting Words
To provide additional practice, duplicate the following sentences. Then have your students choose the correct form of the verb in parentheses.

1. Heat, as well as the time of year and other factors, (determines, determine) how long a camel can go without water.
2. In chess, the advantages of patience (is, are) obvious.
3. A Canada goose, surrounded by sea gulls, (was, were) flying high above the beach.
4. Two classrooms on the second floor (is, are) now being used for a library.
5. Many survivors of the disaster (was, were) present at the first showing of the movie *Titanic*.
6. The taste of orange juice, as well as its vitamins, (makes, make) it a favorite drink of mine.
7. The balloon, with four men and a dog aboard, (was, were) blown off course.
8. Windsor Castle, the most famous of the English royal residences, (has, have) sheltered British sovereigns for over 900 years.
9. The chief characters in the story "The Devil and Daniel Webster" (is, are) Jabez Stone, Daniel Webster, and Scratch.
10. A thick mist of smoke and fog often (hangs, hang) over our city.

ACTIVITY 2 *Doesn't* and *Don't*
Have your students make up questions that require a negative answer using either *doesn't* or *don't*. Give them the following examples before they begin.

Do the front lights go off by themselves?
No, the front lights don't go off by themselves.

If this exercise seems helpful, do it with other contractions.

ACTIVITY 3 Subject and Verb Agreement Review
To provide additional practice, duplicate the following paragraphs. Then have your students correct each error in agreement.

Not For Sale
Mr. Loomis and his wife (1)<u>enjoys</u> bargain hunting for antiques. One of their favorite shops (2)<u>are</u> Sam Miller's. Sam (3)<u>don't</u> charge too much, and all of the articles in his store (4)<u>is</u> genuine.

Subject and Verb Agreement

One day neither Mr. Loomis nor Mrs. Loomis (5)see anything of interest until they are about to leave. Then some soft noises from the other side of the room (6)catches their attention. On the floor near a pile of pictures (7)are a striped alley cat, lapping milk. Mr. Loomis and his wife (8)recognizes the cat's saucer as a valuable antique but (9)doesn't want Sam to see how eager they are to buy it.

"There (10)isn't many cats as handsome as that one," says Mr. Loomis casually. (11)"Was you thinking of selling her, Sam?"

"Well, each article in my two rooms (12)are for sale if you meet my price," replies Sam. "Belle is a good mouser and (13)don't cause me any trouble. She's worth five dollars."

Mr. and Mrs. Loomis (14)exchange looks happily. One of them (15)pay Sam; the other, filled with happy thoughts, (16)pet the cat. Then Mrs. Loomis, glancing carelessly at the precious saucer, says, "We'll just take the cat's saucer along. (17)Isn't cats supposed to become attached to certain dishes?"

"Sorry," says Sam, "that saucer (18)don't go with the cat."

"All right," Mrs. Loomis says quickly, "neither of us (19)want to cheat you. How much is the saucer?"

(20)Here's three other saucers for sale," remarks Sam stubbornly, "but that saucer (21)don't leave my shop."

"That's ridiculous, Sam," (22)says both of the customers. "You said all of the articles in your shop (23)was for sale. Why won't you sell that dish?"

"Because of that saucer," the owner of the antique shop (24)reply with a smile, "139 cats of every description (25)has been sold!"

Advanced Students

ACTIVITY 1 Special Agreement Problems
Have your students write sentences that follow the directions below.
1. Begin a sentence with *there*.
2. Write a question.
3. Include *don't* in a sentence.
4. Write a sentence in inverted order (the subject following the verb).
5. Begin a sentence with *here*.
6. Include *doesn't* in a sentence.
7. Include *committee* as the subject of a sentence.
8. Include *five miles* as the subject of a sentence.
9. Include *economics* as the subject of a sentence.
10. Include the title of a book as a subject. (The title should be underlined.)

ACTIVITY 2 Subject and Verb Agreement Review
To provide additional practice, duplicate the following sentences. Then have your students choose the correct form of the verb in parentheses.
1. The number of people hurt in traffic accidents over the recent holiday (was, were) slightly smaller than last year's.
2. Under the broken window (was, were) found several footprints.
3. Every bush and tree in our yard (is, are) budding.
4. Two thirds of Joseph's prize money (is, are) being put away for his college education.
5. *The Three Musketeers* (was, were) written by Alexandre Dumas.
6. Most of this milk (is, are) sour.
7. Fifteen minutes (is, are) too much time to spend looking for a parking space.
8. Neither Mr. Allen nor my dad (plays, play) golf.
9. All last winter waffles and maple syrup (was, were) our regular Sunday night supper.
10. There (has, have) not been many opportunities for us to go skating this winter.

ACTIVITY 3 Writing Sentences
Have each student bring a photograph to class. Then have each student write a 10- to 15-sentence description of his or her own photograph, using only present tense verbs. When they have finished, have them edit their sentences for correct subject-verb agreement. At another

Subject and Verb Agreement

time you could post the pictures where they are visible to the whole class and then have each student read a description. The class can then match each description with its photograph.

ADDITIONAL PRACTICE
Basic Students
   Teacher's Resource Book:
   pages 138–140
   Workbook: pages 91–100
Average Students
   Teacher's Resource Book:
   pages 141–143
   Workbook: pages 91–100

Advanced Students
   Teacher's Resource Book:
   pages 144–146

REVIEW EXERCISES AND TESTS
Student Text
   Diagnostic Test: page 166
   Chapter Review: pages 184–185
   Mastery Test: page 185
Teacher's Resource Book
   Chapter 8 Test: pages 23–24
   (Also available as spirit duplicating masters.)

ADDITIONAL ANSWERS
EXERCISE 5 Writing Sentences *(page 173)*

Sample answers:
1. You tell very funny jokes.
2. Carrie is my best friend.
3. They all walk to school together.
4. Jamie and Ken stay for baseball practice every day.
5. The lion paces impatiently in its cage.
6. Either Mom or Dad drives us to the movies every weekend.
7. The price of tickets is fairly reasonable.
8. Each horse and cow always has a clean stall in our barn.
9. His choice of words is very clever.
10. Neither the cats nor the dog eats leftovers.

EXERCISE 12 Writing Sentences *(page 182)*

Sample answers:
1. The flock of sheep graze in the back meadow.
2. Everyone in the room wants to attend the film.
3. *The Last of the Mohicans* is on the third shelf.
4. Some of the roses are wilted.
5. A number of people assemble in front of the school every morning.
6. Mumps is an uncomfortable illness.
7. The number of coins in my bank totals five dollars.
8. One third of the test contains essay questions.
9. The United States holds a presidential election every four years.
10. Most of the apples for sale here are Golden Delicious.

8 Subject and Verb Agreement

For additional practice for this chapter, see the Teacher's Resource Book and the Workbook.

DIAGNOSTIC TEST

Number your paper 1 to 10. Write the subject in each sentence. Then next to each one, write the form of the verb in parentheses that agrees with the subject.

EXAMPLE The house with the two barns (is, are) for sale.
ANSWER   house — is

1. Neither the pitcher nor the infielders (was, were) able to get to the ball in time to throw out the runner.
2. The roads to the summit of the mountain (was, were) impassable after the snowstorm.
3. When my grandfather was young, seventy-five cents (was, were) enough for a good dinner.
4. (Doesn't, Don't) that movie sound interesting?
5. There (is, are) two letters on the table for you.
6. One of my friends (has, have) already applied to nursing school.
7. The rides at Riverside Amusement Park (is, are) a major attraction.
8. (Hasn't, Haven't) Greg and Will arrived yet?
9. Spring and autumn (is, are) particularly beautiful seasons in New England.
10. Each of the ten-speed bicycles (is, are) on sale.

Agreement

In a special type of IQ test, children are told to put differently shaped wooden blocks into matching holes in a board. A square block, for example, fits only into the square hole, and a triangular block fits only into the triangular hole.

The subject and the verb of a sentence are like the blocks in the IQ test. Some subjects and verbs fit together; others do not. When they do fit together, they are said to have *agreement*. This chapter will review different types of subjects and verbs and show which ones fit together and which ones do not.

AGREEMENT OF SUBJECTS AND VERBS

The blocks and the holes in the IQ test have one matching feature—their shape. A subject and a verb have one matching feature as well—their number. *Number* is the term used to indicate whether a noun or a pronoun is singular or plural. *Singular* indicates one, and *plural* indicates more than one.

8a — A verb must agree with its subject in number.

The plural of most nouns is formed by adding *-s* or *-es* to the singular form. A few nouns, however, form their plurals irregularly; for example, *men* is the plural of *man*. Certain pronouns form their plural by changing form.

Nouns		Pronouns	
Singular	Plural	Singular	Plural
diamond	diamonds	I	we
bus	buses	he, she, it	they
child	children		

Present-tense verbs also have singular and plural forms. The third person singular ends in *-s* or *-es*. Most plural forms of verbs do *not* end in *-s* or *-es*.

THIRD PERSON SINGULAR   he, she, it **runs**
PLURAL   I, you, we, they **run**

NOTE: *I* and *you* agree with the plural form of *run*.

Subject and Verb Agreement

In the following box are the singular and plural forms of the irregular verbs *be, have,* and *do* in the present tense and *be* in the past tense. Notice that *be* has irregular forms for both the singular and plural in the past tense as well.

Present Tense

Singular	Plural
I **am, have, do**	we **are, have, do**
you **are, have, do**	you **are, have, do**
he, she, it **is, has, does**	they **are, have, do**

Past Tense

Singular	Plural
I **was**	we **were**
you **were**	you **were**
he, she, it **was**	they **were**

Since a subject and a verb both have number, they must agree in a sentence.

> **8b**   A singular subject takes a singular verb.

> **8c**   A plural subject takes a plural verb.

The **diamond sparkles.**   The **diamonds sparkle.**
The school **bus is** late.   All the school **buses are** late.
The **child was** here.   The **children were** here.
He has my books.   **They have** my books.

Be, have, and *do* are also often used as helping verbs. When they are, they must agree in number with the subject.

> **8d**   The helping verb must agree in number with its subject.

Rob is making a spaghetti dinner.
The **men have** been waiting.
Mary Ellen has finished her homework.
The **girls are** practicing their dance routines.

Interrupting Words

8b-e

EXERCISE 1   Making Subjects and Verbs Agree
Write the form of the verb in parentheses that agrees with each subject.

1. He (sings, sing).
2. Butterflies (flies, fly).
3. Wayne (is, are) speaking.
4. The cats (was, were) fed.
5. The apples (is, are) bad.
6. The phone (rings, ring).
7. They (does, do) notice.
8. The men (has, have) left.
9. The books (is, are) heavy.
10. The car (does, do) stall.
11. Mom (has, have) jogged.
12. She (has, have) mine.
13. He (sails, sail).
14. I (was, were) here.
15. The dog (barks, bark).
16. You (is, are) ready.
17. Henry (teaches, teach).
18. Students (votes, vote).
19. We (is, are) needed.
20. It (has, have) vanished.

Interrupting Words

Agreement between a subject and a verb is usually easy to recognize when the subject and the verb are side by side. Many times, however, a phrase or a clause will come between a subject and a verb. Then a mistake in agreement sometimes occurs. The tendency is to make the verb agree with a word that is closest to it—rather than with the subject.

8e ▶ The agreement of a verb with its subject is not changed by any interrupting words.

Notice that the subjects and verbs in the following examples agree in number—regardless of the words that come between them.

> The **books** on the second shelf **are** mine. [The plural verb *are* agrees with the plural subject *books,* even though *shelf* is closer to the verb.]
>
> The **planes** circling the airport **are** waiting to land. [*Are* agrees with *planes,* not *airport.*]
>
> The **students** who must attend the meeting **are** excused from third period. [*Are* agrees with *students,* not *meeting.*]

NOTE: Occasionally a parenthetical expression, beginning with a word (or words) such as *like, with, as well as,* or

169

Subject and Verb Agreement

including, will interrupt a subject and a verb. Do not make the verb agree with a word in the parenthetical expression.

Mr. Taylor, as well as some other teachers, **was** mentioned in the article. [*Was* agrees with *Mr. Taylor*, not *teachers*.]

EXERCISE 2 Making Interrupted Subjects and Verbs Agree
Number your paper 1 to 20. Write the subject in each sentence. Then next to each one, write the form of the verb in parentheses that agrees with the subject.

1. The rings around Saturn (is, are) composed of billions of pieces of ice.
2. Constant use by heavy trucks (causes, cause) damage to the old bridge.
3. The linemen, as well as the quarterback, (is, are) worth watching on this series of downs.
4. A clock carved entirely of pieces of wood (was, were) constructed in 1753 by Benjamin Banneker.
5. The people who are speaking with Senator Barker (is, are) a television crew from Channel 8.
6. The stars in the Big Dipper (is, are) slowly moving apart.
7. The starling, as well as the blue jay and the English sparrow, (does, do) not migrate south in the winter.
8. The packages wrapped with silver-and-red ribbon (is, are) from me.
9. Billions of barrels of oil (lies, lie) under the waters of the Gulf of Mexico.
10. Rich deposits of iron ore (was, were) helpful in the development of the steel industry in the United States.
11. The towels that were in the dryer (feels, feel) warm.
12. Training, as well as courage, (is, are) needed to make an expert skier.
13. Salt in our bodies (tends, tend) to draw water from body tissue.
14. All the cars parked in that lot (belongs, belong) to people who work in the Mason Building.
15. The words in the English language (totals, total) more than 800,000.
16. The holes in Swiss cheese (is, are) formed by air bubbles.
17. The largest clams living in the world today (weighs, weigh) close to 500 pounds.

18. Kevin, not one of his brothers, (**delivers**, deliver) our newspaper.
19. Only seven **poems** by Emily Dickinson (was, **were**) published during her lifetime.
20. The **pears** sold at that store (is, **are**) grown locally.

Compound Subjects

There are two rules you should remember when making a verb agree with two or more subjects.

8f When subjects are joined by *or, nor, either/or,* or *neither/nor,* the verb agrees with the closer subject.

Either Douglas or Rico **was** present at the meeting. [*Was* agrees with the closer subject *Rico*.]

Pancakes or eggs **are** served daily. [*Are* agrees with the closer subject *eggs*.]

This rule applies even when one subject is singular and the other subject is plural.

Neither the moon nor the stars **were** visible behind the clouds. [*Were* agrees with the closer subject *stars*—even though *moon* is singular.]

The second rule involving compound subjects is based on other conjunctions.

8g When subjects are joined by *and* or *both/and,* the verb is plural.

These conjunctions always suggest more than one. Since more than one is plural, the verb must be plural also—whether the individual subjects are singular, plural, or a combination of singular and plural.

The bread and the cheese **are** covered with mold. [Two things—the bread and the cheese—are covered with mold. The verb must be plural to agree with both of them.]

Three tapes and a record **were** left at my house. [Even though *record* is singular, the verb is still plural because the record and the tapes—together—were left.]

Subject and Verb Agreement

There are two exceptions to the second rule. Two subjects joined by *and* occasionally refer to only one person or one thing. In such a case, the verb must be singular.

Spaghetti and meatballs **is** the cafeteria special today.
[*Spaghetti and meatballs* is considered one item of food.]

The author and illustrator **was** given a special award.
[*Author* and *illustrator* refer to the same person.]

The words *every* and *each* are the basis of the second exception. If one of these words comes before a compound subject that is joined by *and*, each subject is being considered separately. As a result, the verb must be singular to agree with a singular subject.

Every father and mother **was** invited to the open house.
Each suitcase and trunk **was** packed.

EXERCISE 3 Making Verbs Agree with Compound Subjects
Write the correct form of the verb in parentheses.

1. Neither the hot dogs nor the hamburgers (is, <u>are</u>) ready.
2. Heat, humidity, and smoke in a room often (gives, <u>give</u>) people headaches.
3. A map or good directions (is, <u>are</u>) needed for the trip.
4. Nearly every brook and creek on Mr. Bradley's land (<u>has</u>, have) dried up during the drought.
5. Either a dictionary or a thesaurus (<u>is</u>, are) a good source of colorful verbs.
6. Ham and cheese (<u>is</u>, are) my favorite sandwich.
7. The size of the desk and the price (is, <u>are</u>) perfect.
8. Neither Kim nor the twins (is, <u>are</u>) on the swim team.
9. By morning the trees and the telephone wires (was, <u>were</u>) covered with ice.
10. Each fork and spoon (<u>was</u>, were) lying in the sink.
11. Normal adults and children (requires, <u>require</u>) 1 gram of protein daily for every 2.2 pounds of body weight.
12. Neither the school nor the community halls (has, <u>have</u>) enough space to hold the college fair.
13. Both Julia and her sister (is, <u>are</u>) attending the University of Florida.
14. Your fielding and batting in Tuesday's game (was, <u>were</u>) much improved.

Compound Subjects

15. Both Ulysses S. Grant and Dwight D. Eisenhower (was, <u>were</u>) graduates of West Point.
16. Bacon and eggs (<u>is</u>, are) my favorite breakfast.
17. Every nook and cranny in Professor Nelson's study (<u>was</u> were) bulging with books.
18. Our electrician and plumber (<u>is</u>, are) Tony, our neighbor.
19. Neither Jenny nor her sisters (is, <u>are</u>) working at the camp.
20. Both my arms and legs (was, <u>were</u>) speckled with paint.

EXERCISE 4   Oral Practice
Read aloud the following items, adding *is* or *are* after each one. Then repeat the exercise using *was/were* and *has/have*.

1. you   are/were/have
2. Carrie   is/was/has
3. they   are/were/have
4. Jamie and Ken   are/were/have
5. the lion   is/was/has
6. either Mom or Dad   is/was/has
7. the price of tickets   is/was/has
8. each horse and cow   is/was/has
9. his choice of words   is/was/has
10. neither the cats nor the dog   is/was/has

EXERCISE 5   Writing Sentences
Write a sentence for each item in Exercise 4, using only present-tense verbs. Make sure each verb agrees with its subject. *Sample answers precede this chapter.*

EXERCISE 6   Time-out for Review
Number your paper 1 to 20. Find and write the <u>verbs</u> that do not agree with their subjects. Then write them correctly. If a sentence is correct, write *C* after the number.

1. The first telephone operators employed by the Bell Telephone Company <u>was</u> (were) young men who worked standing up.
2. Neither Kate nor Gwen <u>want</u> (wants) to join the volleyball team.
c 3. The first president born outside the 13 original states was Abraham Lincoln.
4. An essay and a lab report, unfortunately for me, <u>was</u> (were) due on the same day.
5. The walls of the Arizona state capitol <u>is</u> (are) made out of the porous rock tufa.
c 6. Bacon, lettuce, and tomato is my favorite sandwich.
7. Each tomato and squash <u>were</u> (was) grown in my own garden.
8. Most automobile trips in this country <u>is</u> (are) less than five miles long.

Subject and Verb Agreement

9. The slippery surface of the tennis court, not the wind, were [was] responsible for our terrible game.
10. Either Raleigh or Durham are [is] easily reached from the airport situated between the two cities.
11. Macaroni and cheese are [is] one of the easiest casseroles to make.
12. A thousand tons of meteor dust falls [fall] to Earth every day.
13. During midsummer certain leaves of the compass plant points [point] precisely north and south.
c 14. Neither the team members nor the coach was hurt in the plane accident.
15. The stamps on that envelope is [are] Australian.
c 16. Both taxi drivers and business executives have the highest statistical chance of getting ulcers.
17. Every aunt, uncle, and cousin of mine were [was] at the family reunion.
c 18. A person dressed in many layers stays warm even in very cold weather.
19. Either Ann or she are [is] willing to drive you.
20. Food, clothes, and shelter is [are] needed for the homeless.

Special Agreement Problems

There are some special agreement problems you should watch for when you write.

Indefinite Pronouns as Subjects. Indefinite pronouns have number. Some are singular, some are plural, and some can be either singular or plural.

> **8h** A verb must agree in number with an indefinite pronoun used as a subject.

Common Indefinite Pronouns	
SINGULAR	anybody, anyone, each, either, everybody, everyone, neither, no one, one, somebody, someone
PLURAL	both, few, many, several
SINGULAR/PLURAL	all, any, most, none, some

174

Agreement Problems

8h

A singular verb agrees with a singular indefinite pronoun, and a plural verb agrees with a plural indefinite pronoun.

SINGULAR   **Either** of the cars **is** a bargain.

PLURAL   **Both** of my umbrellas **have** holes in them.

The number of an indefinite pronoun in the last group in the box is determined by the object of the preposition that follows the pronoun.

SINGULAR   **Most** of my report **is** finished.
OR PLURAL
  Most of the deviled eggs **were** eaten.

EXERCISE 7 Making Verbs Agree with Indefinite Pronoun Subjects

Number your paper 1 to 20. Write the subject in each sentence. Then next to each one, write the form of the verb in parentheses that agrees with the subject.

1. None of the salad (has, have) been eaten.
2. Anyone in the junior class (is, are) eligible.
3. Some of the time (was, were) devoted to decorations.
4. A few of our dishes (was, were) broken during the move.
5. All of the coats in Kendall's Department Store (was, were) on sale last week.
6. Many of my friends (has, have) jobs.
7. Some of the football players (was, were) in poor shape.
8. No one in the group (likes, like) the idea.
9. Each of those raisins (was, were) once a juicy grape.
10. Not one of the pictures (was, were) clear.
11. Several of the snowplows (was, were) stalled.
12. Most of her lecture (was, were) very interesting.
13. None of the hamburgers (has, have) been cooked yet.
14. Somebody in English class (is, are) leaving me notes.
15. Both of the cars (needs, need) a new coat of paint.
16. Everyone in my neighborhood (is, are) outside today.
17. Neither of the goalies (was, were) able to stop the puck.
18. Any of the runners (is, are) capable of winning the award.
19. Most of my textbooks (has, have) covers on them.
20. Everybody in my homeroom (is, are) planning to help.

Subject and Verb Agreement

Subjects in Inverted Order. A subject usually comes before the verb in a sentence. For variety, however, a sentence will appear in *inverted order* with the subject following the verb or part of a verb phrase. Regardless of where a subject is in a sentence, the verb must agree with it.

8i ▶ The subject and the verb of an inverted sentence must agree in number.

There are several types of inverted sentences. *(See pages 32–33.)* When you are looking for the subject in an inverted sentence, turn the sentence around to its natural order. To make sense, you must occasionally drop *here* or *there* when putting the sentence into its natural order.

INVERTED ORDER	On the shores of the Ohio River **are** several large **cities**. [Several large *cities are* on the shores of the Ohio River.]
QUESTION	**Have** the **actors** been selected? [The *actors have* been selected.]
SENTENCES BEGINNING WITH *HERE* OR *THERE*	Here **is** the grocery **receipt**. [The grocery *receipt is* here.]
	There **are** many **mushrooms** in these hills. [Many *mushrooms are* in these hills.]

EXERCISE 8 Making Verbs Agree with Subjects in Inverted Order

Number your paper 1 to 20. Write the subject in each sentence. Then next to each one, write the form of the verb in parentheses that agrees with the subject.

1. On the top shelf (was, were) two small elephants carved out of teak.
2. Here (is, are) the two missing nails.
3. Where (is, are) the pickles?
4. There (is, are) 26 states in the nation with a city or town named Franklin.
5. (Was, Were) all the officers present at the meeting?
6. In the box (was, were) six black-and-white kittens.

Agreement Problems

8i–j

7. Here (comes, <u>come</u>) the <u>members</u> of our victorious basketball team!
8. (Is, <u>Are</u>) many <u>people</u> trying out for the spring play?
9. Here (<u>is</u>, are) an extra <u>blanket</u> for your bed.
10. In the last column of the newspaper (was, <u>were</u>) two <u>ads</u> for part-time employment.
11. When (<u>is</u>, are) <u>everyone</u> arriving?
12. In each classroom there (is, <u>are</u>) several new <u>desks</u>.
13. There (is, <u>are</u>) more <u>children</u> than adults at the block party.
14. (Was, <u>Were</u>) <u>you</u> ever in Rhode Island?
15. On the top of many New England barns (is, <u>are</u>) copper <u>weather vanes</u>.
16. (<u>Does</u>, Do) a red <u>sky</u> or a gray <u>sky</u> in the evening usually predict warm weather?
17. There (is, <u>are</u>) 35 million digestive <u>glands</u> in the human stomach.
18. In his arms (was, <u>were</u>) three large <u>bags</u> of laundry.
19. How (does, <u>do</u>) <u>Ellen</u> and <u>Paul</u> like their new school?
20. There (is, <u>are</u>) several hundred <u>kinds</u> of marble, differing in color and pattern.

Collective Nouns. A *collective noun*, such as *chorus*, *herd*, *family*, and *majority*, names a group of people or things. A collective noun may be either singular or plural—depending on how it is used in a sentence.

8j Use a singular verb with a collective-noun subject that is thought of as a unit. Use a plural verb with a collective-noun subject that is thought of as individuals.

The **orchestra is** playing a new symphony. [The orchestra is working together as a whole unit in this sentence. As a result, the verb is singular.]

The **orchestra are** taking their places in the pit. [The members of the orchestra are acting independently in this sentence—each one taking his or her own seat. As a result, the verb is plural.]

Words Expressing an Amount. Words that express amounts, measurements, or weights usually have a plural form but are

Subject and Verb Agreement

often considered to be a singular unit. Use a singular verb when these words tell *how much*.

8k ▶ A subject that expresses an amount, a measurement, or a weight is usually considered singular and takes a singular verb.

Six months is needed for this job.
Eight dollars was donated to the fund.
Two thirds of the garden **has** been planted.

If an amount, measurement, or weight is being thought of in its individual parts, then the verb must be plural. Use a plural verb when these words tell *how many*.

Six months have passed quickly.
Eight dollars were scattered on the table.
Two thirds of the seeds **have** been planted.

The Number Of, A Number Of. Although these expressions are very similar, one takes a singular verb and one takes a plural verb.

8l ▶ Use a singular verb with *the number of* and a plural verb with *a number of*.

The number of women scientists **has** increased greatly over the past 25 years. [singular]
A number of strange lights **were** noticed in the sky last night. [plural]

Singular Nouns That Have a Plural Form. Some words look plural because they end in *-s*. They are singular, however, because they name single things, such as one type of disease or one area of knowledge. Following are some examples.

USUALLY SINGULAR   civics, economics, gallows, gymnastics, mathematics, measles, molasses, mumps, news, physics, social studies

8m ▶ Use a singular verb with certain subjects that are plural in form but singular in meaning.

178

Agreement Problems

8k – m

Gymnastics is my favorite form of exercise.
Mumps is a very uncomfortable illness.

There are similar words, however, that are usually plural, and some others that can be either singular or plural—depending on how they are used in a sentence. Since it is difficult to tell what number these words are by looking at them, it is always best to check the dictionary.

USUALLY PLURAL   barracks, data, eyeglasses, media, pliers, scissors, shears, slacks, trousers

SINGULAR/PLURAL   acoustics, athletics, headquarters, politics

The **pliers are** rusted. [plural]

Politics is usually a controversial subject. [singular—the science of government]

Politics are on his mind day and night. [plural—political practices or policies]

NOTE: When a word that is usually plural is preceded by *pair of,* the verb is singular because it agrees with the singular noun *pair.*

PLURAL   Your **slacks are** pressed.
SINGULAR   Your **pair** of slacks **is** pressed.

EXERCISE 9   Making Subjects and Verbs Agree
Write the correct form of the verb in parentheses.

1. Three fourths of the orange crop (was, were) destroyed by the frost.
2. The news (was, were) not good.
3. The number of Charleston High students taking part in extracurricular activities (is, are) increasing.
4. The costume committee (is, are) arguing about where to store the costumes for the play.
5. My extra pair of glasses (is, are) broken too.
6. In 1820, two thirds of all the cloth produced in the United States (was, were) made in the home.
7. A growing number of people (is, are) redeeming coupons at the grocery store.
8. Miguel's group (plays, play) at all the school dances.
9. One hundred and fifty pounds (is, are) the average weight of the players on our football team.

Subject and Verb Agreement

10. My family (is, are) visiting relatives in Oklahoma.
11. About twenty-four inches of ribbon (is, are) needed to make the bow.
12. Fifty percent of the auditorium seats (was, were) reserved for parents.
13. A large number of students (has, have) the flu.
14. A herd of cows (is, are) capable of producing a ton of milk in less than a day.
15. (Is, Are) twenty-five dollars too much to pay for this used typewriter?
16. Thirty-four percent of all land in the United States (is, are) owned by the federal government.
17. The jury (is, are) still undecided about the verdict.
18. (Is, Are) physics a difficult subject?
19. The number of students taking Latin (has, have) been declining for a long time.
20. I think ten dollars (is, are) the registration fee.

Doesn't and Don't. *Doesn't* and *don't* are contractions. To avoid a mistake, always say the two words of a contraction separately when checking for agreement with a subject. Also keep in mind which contractions are singular and which are plural.

SINGULAR **does**n't, **has**n't, **is**n't, **was**n't
PLURAL **do**n't, **have**n't, **are**n't, **were**n't

8n The verb part of a contraction must agree in number with the subject.

Mr. Barry doesn't usually assign homework on Friday.
We don't know when they are arriving.

Subjects with Linking Verbs. A predicate nominative follows a linking verb and renames or identifies the subject. *(See page 10 for lists of linking verbs.)* Sometimes, though, a subject and its predicate nominative will not have the same number. Still, the verb always agrees with the subject.

8o A verb agrees with the subject of a sentence, not with the predicate nominative.

Agreement Problems

8n–p

Acorns are the squirrel's favorite food. [The plural verb *are* agrees with the plural subject *acorns*—even though the predicate nominative *food* is singular.]

The squirrel's favorite **food is** acorns. [In this sentence *is* agrees with the subject *food*—not with the plural predicate nominative *acorns*.]

NOTE: Whenever possible, you should avoid writing sentences in which the subject and the predicate nominative do not agree in number.

Titles. Many titles are composed of several words, some of which may be plural in form. A title, nevertheless, is singular and takes a singular verb because it is the name of one book or one work of art. Most multiword names of businesses and organizations are also considered singular.

8p → A title is singular and takes a singular verb.

Curious Facts by John May **contains** information about everything from advertising to zoos.

The **United Nations has** its headquarters in New York City.

EXERCISE 10 Making Subjects and Verbs Agree
Write the correct form of the verb in parentheses.

1. "Mushrooms" (is, are) the title of a poem by Sylvia Plath.
2. Yellow daisies (is, are) my favorite flower.
3. Adam (doesn't, don't) want to go camping with us.
4. The bell for third period (hasn't, haven't) rung yet.
5. The problem on our street (is, are) speeding cars.
6. The League of Women Voters (is, are) holding a debate for the congressional candidates.
7. Maria's chief concern at that moment (was, were) her lost skates.
8. Why (doesn't, don't) they like country music?
9. *Webster's Treasury of Relevant Quotations* (is, are) 658 pages long.
10. (Isn't, Aren't) the dishes done yet?
11. Those new tapes on the table (is, are) Robert's birthday present from the four of us.

Subject and Verb Agreement

12. It (<u>doesn't</u>, don't) seem like a good day for a picnic.
13. *Leaves of Grass* (<u>was</u>, were) one of Walt Whitman's greatest efforts.
14. This month's bills (hasn't, <u>haven't</u>) been paid yet.
15. (<u>Isn't</u>, Aren't) the duplicating machine working today?
16. The potholes in the road (is, <u>are</u>) a nuisance.
17. My brother (<u>isn't</u>, aren't) taking chemistry this year.
18. *Fruit Bowl, Glass, and Apples* (<u>is</u>, are) the name of a famous painting by Cézanne.
19. (<u>Hasn't</u>, Haven't) anyone started dinner?
20. Telephones (is, <u>are</u>) available in many styles.

EXERCISE 11 Oral Practice

Read aloud the following items, adding *is* or *are* after each one. Then repeat the exercise, using *doesn't/don't* and *wasn't/weren't*.

1. the flock of sheep — is/doesn't/wasn't
2. everyone in the room — is/doesn't/wasn't
3. *The Last of the Mohicans* — is/doesn't/wasn't
4. some of the roses — are/don't/weren't
5. a number of people — are/don't/weren't
6. mumps — is/doesn't/wasn't
7. the number of coins — is/doesn't/wasn't
8. one third of the test — is/doesn't/wasn't
9. the United States — is/doesn't/wasn't
10. most of the apples — are/don't/weren't

EXERCISE 12 Writing Sentences

Write a sentence for each of the items in Exercise 11, using only present-tense verbs. Make sure each verb agrees with its subject. *Sample answers precede this chapter.*

EXERCISE 13 Time-out for Review

Number your paper 1 to 20. Find and write the verbs that do not agree with their subjects. Then write them correctly. If a sentence is correct, write *C* after the number.

1. The first manufactured item ever exported by American merchants w~~ere~~ tar. *(was)*
2. Two presidents of the United States, George Washington and James Monroe, w~~as~~ unopposed in their elections. *(were)*
3. One of the largest tomatoes from the garden weighs two pounds. *(C)*
4. Two hundred and sixty dollars w~~ere~~ the cost of a Ford in 1925. *(was)*
5. A favorite fruit in the United States a~~re~~ bananas. *(is)*

182

Editing for Agreement

c 6. There are two word processors in the school library.
7. Both Missouri and Tennessee ~~touches~~ *touch* on eight other states.
8. John Steinbeck's novel *Of Mice and Men* ~~have~~ *has* been made into several movies.
c 9. Each year the United States loses billions of tons of soil through erosion.
10. At graduation there ~~was~~ *were* 2,000 people in the audience.
11. One fourth of all the energy in the United States ~~are~~ *is* used to heat and cool homes and other buildings.
c 12. The life expectancy of Americans in 1876 was about 40.
c 13. Orville Wright, who with his brother Wilbur invented the airplane, was badly injured in an airplane crash.
14. In 1910, a football team ~~were~~ *was* penalized 15 yards for an incompleted forward pass.
c 15. There was no public library in the United States in 1800.
16. In 1805, half of the Harvard students ~~was~~ *were* suspended after protesting against the terrible dormitory food.
17. In 1915, the average family income in the United States ~~were~~ *was* about $650 a year.
c 18. Is there any documented proof that Betsy Ross designed the American flag?
c 19. The practice of identifying baseball players by number was begun by the Cleveland Indians in 1916.
20. Two thirds of the orchestra members ~~plays~~ *play* two or more instruments.

Application to Writing

When you finish writing a report, an essay, or even a friendly letter, always reread it to check just for subject and verb agreement.

EXERCISE 14 **Editing for Subject and Verb Agreement**
Find and write the verbs that do not agree with their subjects in the following paragraphs. Then write them correctly.

Outer Space Litter

In addition to approximately 1,200 satellites now in orbit around the earth, there ~~is~~ *are* nearly 3,500 pieces of orbiting space debris. These include spent rockets, fragments of wrecked satellites, and miscellaneous nuts, bolts, and ceramic tiles. The

183

Subject and Verb Agreement

satellites, as well as the junk, is [are] cataloged and tracked by the North American Aerospace Defense Command, or NORAD.

There is [are] good reasons for monitoring this space trash. For one thing, even a chunk of metal as small as a grapefruit become [becomes] a deadly weapon if it falls to the earth. More frightening still, a piece of space litter showing up on a radar screen could easily be mistaken for an enemy missile.

The chances of real danger, however, is [are] slim. Of the 4,698 recorded objects now in orbit, some is [are] in "deep space." At approximately 3,000 miles up, atmospheric drag and gravitational pull is [are] minimal. The pieces closer to the earth fall out of orbit at a rate of more than one a day. Most of the pieces burns [burn] up on reentry. One of the most memorable exceptions were [was] *Skylab,* whose pieces landed in Australia in July 1979.

NORAD admits that some bits of space junk is [are] too small to be tracked regularly. A NORAD employee, for example, recently reported an orbiting glove!

CHAPTER REVIEW

Write the correct form of the verb in parentheses.

1. The quarterback and the halfback (has, **have**) worked together for weeks on that new play.
2. Each magazine and newspaper (**was**, were) returned to its place after study hall.
3. Neither the Harris brothers nor José (**is**, are) playing in today's game.
4. Approximately 26 miles (**is**, are) the distance run by Olympic marathon runners.
5. The committee (was, **were**) able to agree on a project.
6. The outcome of the class elections (**is**, are) being announced in the assembly today.
7. There (has, **have**) been three sites mentioned for the Junior Prom.
8. Mathematics (**has**, have) always interested me.
9. In the back of the drawer (was, **were**) the missing socks.
10. Sandra (**doesn't**, don't) look as though she has just finished jogging five miles.

Chapter Review

11. Most of the world's diamond supply (<u>comes</u>, come) from Africa.
12. A basket of oranges and grapefruit (<u>was</u>, were) sent to us from Florida.
13. Every stick, twig, and splinter of wood (<u>was</u>, were) gathered to keep the campfire going.
14. Neither radar nor unmarked police cars (has, <u>have</u>) been able to eliminate speeding on the freeway.
15. One of the giant galaxies (<u>is</u>, are) our own Milky Way.
16. Thanks to conservation forces, the buffalo population of the United States and Canada (<u>is</u>, are) up again.
17. In his yard (was, <u>were</u>) two fierce-looking bulldogs.
18. (Has, <u>Have</u>) they left for Pennsylvania yet?
19. Cheese and crackers (<u>is</u>, are) a nutritious snack.
20. Ten blocks (<u>is</u>, are) too far to walk in this rain.

MASTERY TEST

Number your paper 1 to 10. Write the <u>subject</u> in each sentence. Then next to each one, write the form of the <u>verb</u> in parentheses that agrees with the subject.

1. One of the oak <u>trees</u> in our backyard (<u>was</u>, were) struck by lightning in last night's storm.
2. The vivid <u>colors</u> of the rainbow (was, <u>were</u>) a breathtaking sight.
3. A <u>number</u> of umbrellas (was, <u>were</u>) left under the seats in the theater.
4. (Doesn't, <u>Don't</u>) <u>he</u> drive an old red Buick?
5. Either <u>Charlene</u> or <u>one</u> of her sisters (<u>is</u>, are) writing an advice column for the school newspaper.
6. The football <u>team</u> (<u>begins</u>, begin) practice two weeks before school starts.
7. The <u>craters</u> of the moon (is, <u>are</u>) visible through a telescope.
8. Three <u>fourths</u> of the auditorium (was, <u>were</u>) filled.
9. The <u>Guinness Book of World Records</u> (<u>is</u>, are) full of amazing statistics.
10. Neither of the morning <u>flights</u> (<u>is</u>, are) on schedule.

Chapter 9   Using Adjectives and Adverbs

OBJECTIVES

- To form and use correctly the comparative and superlative forms of regular and irregular adjectives and adverbs.
- To identify and be able to correct double comparisons.
- To use *other* and *else* correctly in comparisons.
- To identify and be able to correct illogical comparisons.
- To recognize and be able to correct double negatives.
- To use adjectives and adverbs correctly after action and linking verbs.
- Application: To identify and avoid common errors in the use of adjectives and adverbs.

MOTIVATIONAL ACTIVITY

Write the following sentences on the board.

For certain types of lubrication, machine oil is <u>good</u>.
For other types grease may be <u>better</u>.
For locks, however, graphite is <u>best</u>.

Then ask your students if they can see any reason for using *good, better,* and *best* in the preceding sentences. If they see the comparison of the different types of lubrication, they will understand the principle for the comparison of modifiers.

TEACHING SUGGESTIONS

Before you begin this chapter, you may want your students to review "Adjectives and Adverbs" on pages 14–18 in Chapter 1. In particular, you may want to point out the examples of the different positions of adjectives on pages 14 and 15. This short review should provide adequate background for this chapter.

In informal conversation it is sometimes permissible to use the superlative when comparing two people or things. Your students, nevertheless, need to know the formally correct form for most situations.

Comparison of Adjectives and Adverbs *(pages 187–191)*

A true test of your students' mastery of this material is their ability to use the comparative and superlative forms of modifiers correctly in sentences of their own. You may, therefore, want your students to write sentences that use the comparative and superlative forms they wrote for Exercise 2 on page 190. The ability to write the forms of these modifiers or pick out the correct form in an exercise is meaningless if your students cannot use such forms correctly in sentences.

Problems with Modifiers *(pages 191–197)*

Depending on the level of your various classes, you may want to be selective in choosing which parts of this section you want to teach. Most basic students should cover at least "Double Comparisons" *(page 191),* "Double Negatives" *(pages 193–194),* and "Adjective or Adverb?" *(page 195).*

Double Comparisons *(page 191)* Some of your students may be using double comparisons because they are unsure of whether to use *er* or *more* or *est* or *most.* You may be able to help these students by telling them to say the words aloud with the different endings. If a word becomes difficult to pronounce when *-er* or *-est* are added, then *more* or *most* should be used.

Double Negatives *(pages 193–194)* You may want to point out to your advanced students that in addition to negative words, there are also negative prefixes—such as *un (unkind), non (noncooperative),* and *dis (disclaim).* The prefix *in (inadequate),* meaning "not," sometimes appears in other forms—depending on the initial consonant of the word to which it is added: *il (illogical), im (immortal),* and *ir (irrational).*

Chapter 9 a

Using Adjectives and Adverbs

Illogical Comparisons *(page 193)* Along with this section, you should also teach the use of the apostrophe with possessive nouns on page 271. Students most often make illogical or unclear comparisons because they do not include the apostrophe. To make this point, show your students that the possessive can stand alone. The following example from page 193 in the student text is correct when an apostrophe is used, but the sentence becomes illogical without an apostrophe.

Football players' equipment is much heavier than baseball players'.

Adjective or Adverb? *(page 195)* The test of whether to use an adverb or an adjective is this: Does the word modify the verb or the subject? Show your students that in many sentences some form of the verb *be* can be substituted for linking verbs like *feel, look, smell,* and *taste*. If the sentence makes sense when the substitution is made, an adjective, not an adverb, is needed.

ADJECTIVE The lost child looked *anxious*. [The lost child was *anxious*. *Was,* a form of *be,* can be substituted for the linking verb *looked*.]

ADVERB The lost child looked *anxiously* around the large hall. [The lost child was *anxiously* around the large hall. *Was* cannot be substituted for the action verb *looked*.]

You may want to point out that some adverbs have two correct forms for each degree of comparison: without *-ly* and with *-ly (loud/loudly)*; without *more* and with *more* or *most: (slower, more slowly, slowest, most slowly)*.

Other Aspects of Modifiers *(Glossary of Usage)*

Along with this chapter, you may want to refer to the Glossary of Usage for the following items that pertain to modifiers.
a, an on page 202
anymore on page 204
anywhere on page 204
bad, badly on page 205
farther, further on page 210
fewer, less on page 211
good, well on page 211
kind of, sort of on page 213
most on page 216
some, somewhat on page 219
them, those on page 222
this here, that there on page 222
this, that, these, those on page 222
unique on page 223

ACTIVITIES FOR DIFFERENT ABILITIES

Basic Students

ACTIVITY 1 Comparison of Adjectives

Have your students fill each blank with the comparative and superlative forms of the following adjectives. Give them the following examples before they begin.

the sad, <u>sadder</u>, <u>saddest</u> story
the clever, <u>more clever</u>, <u>most clever</u> ad

1. the narrow ____, ____ bridge
2. the long ____, ____ book
3. the colorful ____, ____ costume
4. that old ____, ____ tree
5. the stubborn ____, ____ mule
6. the respectable ____, ____ gentleman
7. the clean ____, ____ room
8. the pretty, ____, ____ model
9. the beautiful, ____, ____ scenery
10. the many ____, ____ cartons

ACTIVITY 2 Double Negatives

To provide additional practice, write the following sentences on the board or duplicate them. Then have your students correct the mistake in each one.

1. I can't pick no more apples today.
2. When we saw Connie in her costume, we didn't hardly recognize her.
3. Ann hasn't never been on television before.
4. Our dog wasn't but half a mile from home when we found him.
5. I can't hardly wait for spring vacation.
6. He can't bear to say no to nobody.
7. Although the man looked suspicious, he hadn't done nothing wrong.

Chapter 9 b

Using Adjectives and Adverbs

8. We didn't have no blankets to keep us warm.
9. Mike shouldn't never take a second job.
10. There isn't hardly any air in your front tire.

ACTIVITY 3 Adjective or Adverb?
To provide additional practice, duplicate the following sentences. Then have your students find and correct each mistake.

1. Dad is progressing rapid and expects to be back to work next week.
2. Alice looks beautifully in her new outfit.
3. To be able to play the trumpet good is Daniel's ambition.
4. When I woke up this morning, I felt miserably.
5. Despite many misfortunes for the prince and for Tom, *The Prince and the Pauper* ends happy.
6. Jackson played good but had no defense against Washington's passing attack.
7. Whatever is in the oven certainly smells well.
8. The ball bounced crazy off the rim and then dropped through.
9. Marianne played her part perfect.
10. That dessert looks too well to eat.

Advanced Students

ACTIVITY 1 Using Comparisons
Divide your class into two teams. Have a student from Team A choose one of the following words and give either the comparative or the superlative form of that word. Then have the first student on Team B make up a sentence that uses the form of the modifier given. Keep score, proceeding as if you were having a spelling bee.

1. gentle
2. good
3. strong
4. difficult
5. much
6. sweet
7. heavy
8. trustworthy
9. early
10. cheerful

ACTIVITY 2 Spelling Changes with Comparisons
To reinforce the fact that a spelling change occurs when *er* or *est* is added to some adjectives, have your students write the comparative and superlative forms of the following words. (If they are unsure of the spelling, have them look up the words in the dictionary.) Then have your students write sentences that use both the comparative and the superlative forms of each adjective.

1. sad
2. pretty
3. scary
4. hot
5. thin
6. early
7. happy
8. friendly
9. heavy
10. hungry

ACTIVITY 3 Chapter Review
To provide additional practice, duplicate the following sentences. Then have your students write each sentence, correcting each mistake.

1. Of the two gardens, Mrs. Rand's is the most colorful.
2. I find maple sugar more sweeter than regular sugar.
3. Georgia is larger than any state east of the Mississippi.
4. Of the two songs, I think "God Bless America" is easiest to sing.
5. Because of the cold spring, we couldn't hardly harvest a crop of tomatoes before the first frost.
6. Jupiter is more larger than the first four planets put together.
7. Joy's backhand is better than her brother.
8. Dad thinks football is more exciting than any sport.
9. A fresh lemon doesn't taste too tartly for Jan.
10. Is it more easier to row a boat than to paddle a canoe?
11. Mrs. Taylor hasn't never approved my research topic yet.
12. Of the three routes to the lake, which one is more scenic?
13. Each spring the red-winged blackbird comes back to the Bay area earlier than any bird.
14. Don't you think it's more wiser to keep cats indoors?
15. The junior prom went good.
16. My mother's Thanksgiving dinner always tastes better than my sister-in-law.

Chapter 9 c

Using Adjectives and Adverbs

17. The roses in that vase smell so fragrantly.
18. This year's football team had a better record than any team we have ever had.
19. Laura always walks more faster than I do.
20. Mr. Jackson asked which of the two poems I liked best.

ACTIVITY 4 Writing Sentences
Have your students write five to ten sentences that make comparisons between two normally dissimilar objects—such as a house key and a textbook or a dog and a beach ball. Encourage your students to include several forms of comparison. Then have your students edit their sentences for any errors in comparison.

ADDITIONAL PRACTICE

Basic Students
  Teacher's Resource Book:
  pages 147–148
  Workbook: pages 101–108

Average Students
  Teacher's Resource Book:
  pages 149–150
  Workbook: pages 101–108

Advanced Students
  Teacher's Resource Book:
  pages 151–152

REVIEW EXERCISES AND TESTS

Student Text
  Diagnostic Test: page 186
  Chapter Review: pages 198–199
  Mastery Test: page 199

Teacher's Resource Book
  Chapter 9 Test: pages 25–26
  (Also available as spirit duplicating masters.)

ADDITIONAL ANSWERS

EXERCISE 2   Forming the Comparison of Modifiers *(page 190)*

1. warmer, warmest
2. more steadily, most steadily
3. heavier, heaviest
4. more spectacular, most spectacular
5. worse, worst
6. faster, fastest
7. greater, greatest
8. more easily, most easily
9. better, best
10. more quietly, most quietly
11. less, least
12. hungrier, hungriest
13. more, most
14. more special, most special
15. more outstanding, most outstanding

Chapter 9 d

9 Using Adjectives and Adverbs

For additional practice for this chapter, see the Teacher's Resource Book and the Workbook.

DIAGNOSTIC TEST

Number your paper 1 to 10. Then write the correct form of the modifier in parentheses.

1. Which of the two automobiles is (faster, fastest)?
2. We could not see the lighthouse very (good, well) because of the fog.
3. Which would you like to visit (more, most), Orlando, San Francisco, or Boston?
4. Of the two courses, I like this one (less, least).
5. Ken enjoys chess more than (any, any other) board game.
6. Bart, Aaron, and Lou had a contest to see who was the (stronger, strongest).
7. On a hot summer day, a tall glass of orange juice tastes (delicious, deliciously).
8. Which is (bigger, biggest), the Irish wolfhound or the Saint Bernard?
9. This test was (more harder, harder) than the one we took last week.
10. After a day at the beach, I was so sunburned I (couldn't hardly, could hardly) sleep.

Note: Misplaced and dangling modifiers are taught on pages 67–68 and 86.

Comparison

An adjective and an adverb have more than one form. The additional forms are used when two or more people or things are being compared. A coat, for example, can be *warm;* but it also can be *warmer* than the coat you had the year before, or the *warmest* coat you have ever had. The television set in your home might work *well;* but it also might work *better* than the last one you had, or the *best* of all the television sets you have ever had. This chapter will review the different forms of comparison, as well as some problems with comparisons.

COMPARISON OF ADJECTIVES AND ADVERBS

Most adjectives and adverbs have three forms to show degrees of comparison: the *positive,* the *comparative,* and the *superlative.*

> **9a** Most modifiers show degrees of comparison by changing form.

When no comparison is being made, the *positive* form is used. It is the basic form of an adjective or an adverb.

ADJECTIVE This tree is **tall.**
ADVERB Jerome works **efficiently.**

When two people or things are being compared, the *comparative* degree is used. Notice that *-er* is added to *tall* and *more* is used with *efficiently.*

ADJECTIVE This tree is **taller** than the oak next door.
ADVERB Jerome works **more efficiently** than Roy.

When more than two people or things are being compared, the *superlative* degree is used. Notice that *-est* is added to *tall* and *most* is used with *efficiently.*

ADJECTIVE This tree is the **tallest** tree in the neighborhood.
ADVERB Of all the people on the assembly line, Jerome works **most efficiently.**

Using Adjectives and Adverbs

EXERCISE 1   Determining Degrees of Comparison

Number your paper 1 to 10. Write the underlined modifiers in the following sentences. Then label the degree of comparison of each modifier—*positive*, *comparative*, or *superlative*.

S 1. Blue eyes are the <u>most sensitive</u> to light.
P 2. Hanover Street is too <u>narrow</u> for on-street parking.
C 3. First-class mail travels <u>faster</u> than parcel post.
S 4. *Our Town* was the <u>most professionally</u> performed high school play I have ever seen.
S 5. The <u>largest</u> chicken egg ever laid weighed more than one pound.
C 6. The brain of a Neanderthal person was <u>larger</u> than that of a modern person.
S 7. The harvest is the <u>most plentiful</u> of the last five years.
C 8. Which one of the two exercises is <u>easier</u> to do?
P 9. Drive <u>cautiously</u> on the icy roads.
C 10. I thought the history exam was <u>harder</u> than the math exam.

Regular and Irregular Comparison

Most adjectives and adverbs, like the ones used in the previous exercise, form their comparative and superlative degrees the same way. A few modifiers, however, form their comparative and superlative degrees irregularly.

Regular Comparison. The comparative and superlative forms of most modifiers are determined by the number of syllables an adjective or adverb has.

9b Add *-er* to form the comparative degree and *-est* to form the superlative degree of one-syllable modifiers.

POSITIVE	COMPARATIVE	SUPERLATIVE
thick	thicker	thickest
strong	stronger	strongest
fast	faster	fastest

Although most two-syllable modifiers form their comparative and superlative degrees by adding *-er* and *-est*, some use *more* and *most*, because they would sound awkward or would be impossible to pronounce if *-er* or *-est* were added. You

Comparison

9b–d

would never say, for example, "hopefuler." The *more* and *most* forms are also always used for adverbs that end in *-ly*.

9c ▶ Use *-er* or *more* to form the comparative degree and *-est* or *most* to form the superlative degree of two-syllable modifiers.

POSITIVE	COMPARATIVE	SUPERLATIVE
busy	busier	busiest
playful	more playful	most playful
often	more often	most often
brightly	more brightly	most brightly

NOTE: If you are not sure how to form the comparative and superlative of a two-syllable modifier, check the dictionary.

Modifiers with three or more syllables always form their comparative and superlative degrees by using *more* and *most*.

9d ▶ Use *more* to form the comparative degree and *most* to form the superlative degree of modifiers with three or more syllables.

POSITIVE	COMPARATIVE	SUPERLATIVE
talented	more talented	most talented
convenient	more convenient	most convenient
nervously	more nervously	most nervously

Less and *least* are used to form negative comparisons.

POSITIVE	COMPARATIVE	SUPERLATIVE
talented	less talented	least talented
nervously	less nervously	least nervously

Irregular Comparison. Entirely different forms are used to indicate the comparative and superlative degrees of a few modifiers.

POSITIVE	COMPARATIVE	SUPERLATIVE
bad/badly/ill	worse	worst
good/well	better	best
little	less	least
many/much	more	most

Using Adjectives and Adverbs

NOTE: Never add -er and -est to the comparative and superlative degrees of these irregular modifiers. For example, you would never use "worser" as the comparative form of *bad*.

EXERCISE 2 Forming the Comparison of Modifiers
Number your paper 1 to 15. Then copy each modifier and write its comparative and superlative forms.
Answers precede this chapter.

1. warm
2. steadily
3. heavy
4. spectacular
5. bad
6. fast
7. great
8. easily
9. good
10. quietly
11. little
12. hungry
13. many
14. special
15. outstanding

EXERCISE 3 Using the Correct Form of Comparison
Write the correct form of the <u>modifier</u> in parentheses.

1. The whale has the (slower, <u>slowest</u>) metabolism of all animals.
2. Which of the two routes to Salem is (<u>shorter</u>, shortest)?
3. That is the (quieter, <u>quietest</u>) humidifier I have ever heard.
4. Which of the two trees grows (<u>taller</u>, tallest), the redwood or the giant sequoia?
5. One of the (hardier, <u>hardiest</u>) of all the world's insects is the mosquito.
6. The *West Wind* is the (<u>more</u>, most) seaworthy of the two boats.
7. I read that the herring is the (<u>most</u>, more) widely eaten fish in the world.
8. Of the three movies, which one did you enjoy (more, <u>most</u>)?
9. Is milk (<u>heavier</u>, heaviest) than cream?
10. Which took you (<u>less</u>, least) time to write, your history report or your English composition?
11. A rat can go without water (<u>longer</u>, longest) than a camel.
12. Which of those two books did you like (<u>better</u>, best)?
13. I think my temperature is (<u>higher</u>, highest) now than it was an hour ago.
14. Of all the world's vegetables, lettuce is the (more, <u>most</u>) popular.
15. The weather is (<u>worse</u>, worst) this year than it was last year.

16. Charlene is the (friendlier, <u>friendliest</u>) of the group.
17. Goat's milk is used (<u>more</u>, most) widely throughout the world than cow's milk.
18. Of your three job interviews, which seemed (more, <u>most</u>) promising?
19. A hippopotamus can run (<u>faster</u>, fastest) than a man.
20. Of all the meats I have eaten, I like pork (less, <u>least</u>).
21. Which do you think are (<u>more</u>, most) comfortable to wear, slippers or sneakers?
22. The (more, <u>most</u>) delicious part of the meal was the vegetable appetizer.
23. Which is (<u>worse</u>, worst), losing your notebook or missing the school bus?
24. I think Corey is the (better, <u>best</u>) skater in the group.
25. My grandparents visit (<u>less</u>, least) frequently in the winter than during other parts of the year.

Problems with Modifiers

As you edit your written work, you should be aware of the following special problems with modifiers.

Double Comparisons. Use only *one* method of forming the comparative and superlative degrees of a modifier. Using both methods simultaneously results in a *double comparison*.

9e Do not use both *-er* and *more* to form the comparative degree, or both *-est* and *most* to form the superlative degree.

DOUBLE COMPARISON	This chicken is **more tastier** than usual.
CORRECT	This chicken is **tastier** than usual.
DOUBLE COMPARISON	This is the **most happiest** day of my life!
CORRECT	This is the **happiest** day of my life!

Other and Else in Comparisons. One or more people or things are often compared with other people or things. People or things, however, should never be compared with themselves.

9f Add *other* or *else* when comparing a member of a group with the rest of the group.

Using Adjectives and Adverbs

INCORRECT   That chair is older than any piece of furniture in our house. [Since the chair is a piece of furniture, it is being compared with itself.]

CORRECT   That chair is older than any **other** piece of furniture in our house. [By adding the word *other*, the chair is now being compared only with the other pieces of furniture.]

INCORRECT   Kim has shot more baskets this season than anyone on the team. [Since Kim is a player on the team, she is being compared with herself.]

CORRECT   Kim has shot more baskets this season than anyone **else** on the team. [By adding the word *else*, Kim is now being compared only with the other players on the team.]

EXERCISE 4   Correcting Mistakes in Comparisons

Write the following sentences, correcting each mistake.
Answers may vary.

1. Geese can fly ~~more~~ higher than some mountains.
2. Is the crow smarter than any ^other^ bird?
3. The ~~most~~ shortest route to the pond is through that meadow.
4. Which would you like ~~more~~ better, the $5,500 prize or the week in London with all expenses paid?
5. According to an article I read, the sailfish can swim faster than any ^other^ fish.
6. This assignment took me ~~more~~ longer to finish than last week's assignment.
7. Lloyd received more athletic awards than anyone ^else^ in the junior class.
8. The ball-point pen is the most common~~est~~ writing instrument used today.
9. That movie was ~~more~~ scarier than any other movie I have ever seen before.
10. Georgia is larger than any ^other^ state east of the Mississippi.
11. Who is the ~~more~~ safer driver, Connie or Mario?
12. My classmate Rosa can write poetry better than anyone ^else^ in the school.
13. Cape Horn is over a thousand miles ~~more~~ farther south than the Cape of Good Hope.

Problems with Modifiers

9g

14. I am ~~more~~ busier now than I have ever been before in my life.
15. The palms of the hands and the soles of the feet contain more sweat glands than any ^(other) part of the body.
16. Extending 30 miles from end to end, Figueroa Street in Los Angeles is one of the ~~most~~ longest streets in the United States.
17. Martin is the ~~most~~ happiest person I know.
18. Our oak trees were attacked by gypsy moths more than any ^(other) trees on our property.
19. My friend Suzuki can type faster than anyone ^(else) I know.
20. The trumpeter swan is larger than any ^(other) waterfowl in this country.

Illogical Comparisons. When you write a comparison, be sure you compare two or more similar things. When you compare different things, the comparison is illogical.

> **9g** Compare only items of a similar kind.

ILLOGICAL COMPARISON	Football players' equipment is much heavier than **baseball players.** [Equipment is being compared with baseball players.]
LOGICAL COMPARISON	Football players' equipment is much heavier than baseball players' **equipment.** [Now equipment is being compared with equipment.]
ILLOGICAL COMPARISON	The distance covered by the Nile is greater than the **Amazon.** [Distance is being compared with a river.]
LOGICAL COMPARISON	The distance covered by the Nile is greater than the **distance** covered by the Amazon. [Now distance is being compared with distance.]

NOTE: See pages 271–272 for more information about the use of an apostrophe with possessives.

Double Negatives. The following words are considered *negatives*. A double negative usually cancels itself out, leaving a positive statement.

193

Using Adjectives and Adverbs

9h Avoid using a double negative.

Common Negatives	
but (meaning "only")	none
barely	no one
hardly	not (and the contraction *n't*)
neither	nothing
never	only
no	scarcely

DOUBLE NEGATIVE   I do**n't** have **no** free time tonight.
CORRECT   I do**n't** have any free time tonight.

DOUBLE NEGATIVE   There is**n't hardly** any milk left.
CORRECT   There is **hardly** any milk left.

EXERCISE 5   Correcting Mistakes in Comparisons
Write the following sentences, correcting each mistake.
Answers may vary.

1. Because of the heavy winds, we could~~n't~~ hardly keep the boat from meeting the waves broadside.
2. China's population is greater than Russia**'s population**.
3. Isn't ~~nobody~~ **anybody** going to help me wash Floppy?
4. Egypt's history goes back farther than America**'s history**.
5. Our dog is larger than the ~~Roberts~~. **Robertses' dog.**
6. A palm tree doesn't have ~~no~~ **any** branches.
7. My sister's car is much smaller than my parents**'s car**.
8. We had~~n't~~ barely left the dock when we felt the first drops of rain.
9. I couldn't find ~~nothing~~ **anything** to wear to the costume party.
10. This year's team is more determined than last year**'s team**.
11. He never was much good at pitching; he couldn't catch ~~neither~~ **either**.
12. That was~~n't~~ hardly the answer I expected.
13. Flora's writing was almost as creative as Kenneth**'s writing**.
14. Doesn't ~~no one~~ **anyone** know the time?
15. I haven't ~~never~~ **ever** seen the Grand Canyon.
16. A raven's life span is approximately three times greater than a blue jay**'s life span**.
17. We could~~n't~~ barely see the moon through the thick clouds.

Problems with Modifiers

9h

18. Hospitality House has been the scene of more political meetings than any ^other^ hotel in our city.
19. There aren't any new courses being offered ~~neither~~ ^either^.
20. Our vegetable garden attracted more rabbits than the McBells', ^vegetable garden.^

Adjective or Adverb? In the grammar section of this book, you learned that an adjective modifies a noun or a pronoun. An adverb modifies a verb, an adjective, or another adverb. An adjective also follows a linking verb. Verbs such as *feel, look, smell,* and *taste* can be used as both linking verbs and action verbs. An adjective follows a linking verb; an adverb follows an action verb. *(See page 10 for lists of linking verbs.)*

ADJECTIVE	Tim's backpack felt very **heavy.** [*Felt* is used as a linking verb.]
ADVERB	Tim felt **blindly** for his flashlight. [*Felt* is used as an action verb.]
ADJECTIVE	The plant grew very **large.** [*Grew* is used as a linking verb.]
ADVERB	The plant grew **rapidly.** [*Grew* is used as an action verb.]

Good is always an adjective. *Well* is usually used as an adverb. *Well* is used as an adjective, however, when it means "in good health," "attractive," or "satisfactory."

ADJECTIVE	Earl is a **good** writer.
ADVERB	Earl writes **well.**
ADJECTIVE	Earl finally feels **well** again. [in good health]

EXERCISE 6 Choosing an Adjective or an Adverb
Write the correct form of the modifier in parentheses.

1. Measure the ingredients (accurate, <u>accurately</u>).
2. I think freshly squeezed orange juice tastes more (<u>delicious</u>, deliciously) than frozen.
3. For a beginner, Karen plays the violin (good, <u>well</u>).
4. After a slow start, Sean won the 5,000-meter race (easy, <u>easily</u>).

195

Using Adjectives and Adverbs

5. The toaster works (good, <u>well</u>) since Mom fixed it.
6. The detective (careful, <u>carefully</u>) watched the entrance of the office building.
7. This latex paint certainly covers the wall (good, <u>well</u>).
8. Considering the fact that our two best players were sick, we didn't do too (bad, <u>badly</u>) in the Simsbury game.
9. The note was written (beautiful, <u>beautifully</u>).
10. Roberta doesn't appear (<u>angry</u>, angrily) anymore.
11. To drive (good, <u>well</u>) is to drive as though you own the car, not the road.
12. I could not see the actors very (good, <u>well</u>) from where I was sitting.
13. He looked (<u>nervous</u>, nervously) as he gave his speech.
14. Ann researched her final term paper very (thorough, <u>thoroughly</u>).
15. A cold glass of milk always tastes (<u>good</u>, well) at lunch.
16. The coach spoke (calm, <u>calmly</u>) to the team at halftime.
17. Roasting turkey always smells (<u>good</u>, well) to me.
18. Though the band members have had only two rehearsals, they all played (good, <u>well</u>) today.
19. We won (easy, <u>easily</u>) against Newton.
20. I've looked (thorough, <u>thoroughly</u>) through the closet, but I still can't find my jacket.

EXERCISE 7 Time-out for Review

Number your paper 1 to 25. Rewrite the following sentences, correcting each mistake. If a sentence is correct, write *C* after the number.
Answers to 5, 9, 12, and 16 may vary.

1. A full-grown whale is larger than any ˄other animal that ever lived on Earth.
2. Which of the two peaks is the ~~highest~~ higher, Mount Rainier or Mount Hood?
C 3. Mrs. Reynolds pronounced each word on the spelling test distinctly.
4. Kim translated our French homework ~~easy~~ easily.
5. A teenager's appetite is often bigger than an adult/'s appetite.
6. When the truck finally came to a stop, it was~~n't~~ scarcely an inch away from our back fender.
7. Steven draws cartoons better than ˄anyone˄I know. else
8. Andrew didn't enjoy that movie ~~neither~~ either.
9. The ~~most~~ commonest way to catch a cold is via the hands.

196

Editing Modifiers

c 10. Is Route 67 or the Middlebury Turnpike the shorter route to the fairgrounds?
11. The sandpiper is probably seen on the beach more often than any ^other^ bird.
12. Our city's property-tax rate is higher than Richmond**'s tax rate**.
c 13. Home certainly looked good to me after being away.
c 14. Of the three major sports, which one do you enjoy watching most?
15. I think Australia raises more sheep than any ^other^ country.
16. Michael shouldn't have ~~never~~ tried to steal second base when there were two outs.
17. The ginkgoes, which are living fossils from ages past, are the ~~most~~ rarest trees.
18. Jennifer and her lab partner work ~~good~~ ^well^ together.
19. My cat is much larger than Kate**'s cat**.
c 20. After three years Cliff plays the piano very well.
c 21. Raccoons easily climb trees.
22. The day after Gene went skiing for the first time, he was so stiff he could~~n't~~ hardly move.
23. Our drama program is the ~~most~~ best in the county.
24. Which is ~~largest~~ ^larger^, Texas or Alaska?
c 25. Which one of these languages is more widely spoken, Chinese or English?

Application to Writing

When you write reports or compositions, particularly science reports, you will undoubtedly use comparisons. After you finish writing, always check to see that you have used the correct forms of comparison and that you have avoided the problems with comparisons.

EXERCISE 8 Editing for the Correct Use of Modifiers
Write the following paragraphs, correcting each mistake.
Answers may vary.

Like the Moon

Mercury is the planet ~~most~~ nearest the sun. It is ~~more~~ smaller than any ^other^ planet in the universe. Its diameter is about one-third that of Earth. Because of its smaller size, however, Mercury's gravity is much weaker than Earth**'s gravity**. One hundred kilograms on Earth, for example, would weigh only about 37 kilograms on Mercury.

197

Using Adjectives and Adverbs

Scientists hardly knew ~~nothing~~ [anything] about the surface of Mercury until *Mariner 10*, an unpiloted spacecraft, made flyby observations in 1974 and 1975. The photographs taken of about one third of Mercury turned out ~~good~~ [well]. They showed that Mercury's surface was similar to the moon[’s surface]. The rocky landscape on Mercury is marked by broad plains, a few large ringed basins, and highlands studded with ~~more~~ smaller craters. The plains were formed by lava. Basins were formed when rock masses from space collided ~~forceful~~ [forcefully] with Mercury. Caloris Basin, the ~~most~~ largest known on Mercury, has a diameter of 1,300 kilometers and is ringed by mountains 2 kilometers high. Most of the craters were formed when large, rocky masses smashed into the planet's surface.

CHAPTER REVIEW

Number your paper 1 to 25. Then write the following sentences, correcting each mistake. If a sentence is correct, write C after the number. *Answers to 6, 10, and 24 may vary.*

1. Which lasts ~~longest~~ [longer] in the refrigerator, milk or meat?
2. With so many low-flying planes overhead, we could~~n't~~ scarcely hear the guide.
3. Today donations to the scholarship fund climbed to their ~~most~~ highest level.
c 4. Which state grows the most apples — Washington, New York, or Virginia?
5. Does the movie end ~~happy~~ [happily]?
6. Our yard is much smaller than the Jacksons['s yard].
7. The library in our town is larger than any [other] library in the county.
8. This suit fits ~~good~~ [well] even though it's a hand-me-down.
9. The ~~most~~ largest snowflake on record measured eight inches in width.
10. Wasn't there ~~no one~~ [anyone] at the camp who could build a fire?
c 11. Which costs less, a dozen oranges or a dozen grapefruit?
c 12. When polishing the car, you must rub vigorously.
13. The Grand Coulee Dam produces more hydroelectric power than any [other] dam in the United States.
c 14. Thomas looked the car over well before he bought it.

198

Chapter Review

15. Which is the ~~largest~~ (largest) city south of the equator, Buenos Aires or Rio de Janeiro?
16. The banana has been called the most ancient~~est~~ fruit.
17. Dan can swim 300 yards ~~easy~~ (easily).
18. Flora earns better grades than anyone (else) in biology class.
c 19. Of all the planets, Jupiter has the shortest day.
20. We can~~'t~~ hardly wait to see the Whalers play again.
21. At 282 feet below sea level, California's Death Valley has a lower elevation than any (other) place in the United States.
c 22. I haven't been feeling well for a week now.
23. The animal with the ~~most~~ longest life span is generally conceded to be the Galápagos Islands tortoise.
24. My salary is smaller than Tim('s salary), but I enjoy my job more (than he does).
25. Which instrument is ~~more~~ (most) popular in the music department—the violin, the guitar, or the piano?

MASTERY TEST

Number your paper 1 to 10. Then write the correct form of the modifier in parentheses.

1. After the storm the ocean became (calm, calmly).
2. Which magazine has the (greater, greatest) circulation, *Reader's Digest* or *TV Guide?*
3. I think ice hockey is more exciting to watch than (any, any other) sport.
4. Covering a square block, the world's (largest, most largest) log cabin stands in Portland, Oregon.
5. Where would you like to live (more, most), in Maryland, Nebraska, or Oregon?
6. Which color do you like (better, best), blue or yellow?
7. Beefalo meat contains (less, least) fat and cholesterol than beef.
8. If you (haven't never, haven't ever) tasted bread pudding, you're in for a treat.
9. Of these four artists, whose paintings do you like (more, most)?
10. I hope one day to play the piano (good, well).

199

Glossary of Usage

OBJECTIVES
- To avoid various common usage errors.
- To use *lie* and *lay*, *rise* and *raise*, and *sit* and *set* correctly.
- To distinguish between words that sound the same but are spelled differently.

TEACHING SUGGESTIONS

You may want to refer to various entries in this glossary as you teach particular chapters.

Chapter 1: The Parts of Speech
Nouns and Pronouns
  both on page 207
  both, each on page 207
  former, latter on page 211
  kind, sort, type on page 213
  -self, -selves on page 218
  way, ways on page 223
Verbs
  ain't on page 203
  bring, take on page 207
  can, may on page 207
  can't help but on page 208
  discover, invent on page 209
  done on page 209
  had of on page 212
  have, of on page 212
  imply, infer on page 212
  learn, teach on page 213
  leave, let on page 213
  may be, maybe on page 216
  ought on page 217
  try to on page 223
Adjectives and Adverbs
  a, an on page 202
  a lot on page 204
  anymore on page 204
  anywhere on page 204
  farther, further on page 210
  irregardless on page 212
  kind of, sort of on page 213
Prepositions and Conjunctions
  among, between on page 204
  at on page 205
  beside, besides on page 207
  different from on page 208
  in, into on page 212
  nor, or on page 217
  of on page 217
  so on page 219

Chapter 4: Clauses
  as far as on page 205
  because on page 206
  being as on page 207
  like, as on page 214
  than, then on page 219
  what on page 223
  when, where on page 223
  where on page 224

Chapter 6: Using Verbs
  lie, lay on page 214
  rise, raise on page 218
  says on page 218
  shall, will on pages 218–219
  sit, set on page 219

Chapter 7: Using Pronouns
  that, which, who on page 221
  them, those on page 222
  who, whom on page 224

Chapter 8: Subject and Verb Agreement
  amount, number on page 204
  doesn't, don't on page 209

Chapter 9: Using Adjectives and Adverbs
  bad, badly on page 205
  double negative on page 209
  fewer, less on page 211
  good, well on page 211
  most on pages 216–217
  some, somewhat on page 219
  this here, that there on page 222
  this, that, these, those on page 222
  unique on page 223

Chapter 14: Spelling
  accept, except on page 203
  adapt, adopt on page 203
  advice, advise on page 203
  affect, effect on page 203
  all ready, already on page 203
  all together, altogether on page 203
  allusion, illusion on page 204
  a while, awhile on page 205
  capital, capitol on page 208
  coarse, course on page 208
  continual, continuous on page 208

Glossary of Usage

emigrate, immigrate on page 209
hear, here on page 212
hole, whole on page 212
its, it's on page 213
knew, new on page 213
loose, lose on page 216
passed, past on page 217
precede, proceed on page 217
principal, principle on page 218
respectfully, respectively on page 218
their, there, they're on page 222
theirs, there's on page 222
threw, through on page 222
to, too, two on page 222
weak, week on page 223
whose, who's on page 224
your, you're on page 224

ACTIVITIES FOR ALL ABILITIES

ACTIVITY 1 Glossary Review

For additional practice duplicate the following sentences. Then have your students find and correct each error.

1. If I had of taken a rest after school, I would feel fine now.
2. Less people attended the meeting this week than last week.
3. Your the one they want to see.
4. Lionel was kind of disappointed with the outcome of the election.
5. Everyone is ready accept Vincent.
6. Karen and myself are planning a joint experiment for chemistry class.
7. I can't help but think of all the good times we've had together.
8. When my sister travels on business, she hardly never packs much.
9. When I couldn't decide between the two hats, I bought the both of them.
10. Mom wants one of them quartz battery clocks for the den.
11. Doesn't anyone like these kind of hats any more?
12. Please take your books off of the kitchen table.
13. Why don't he know the way to Kit's house?
14. You should share these extra squashes between your many friends.
15. Mr. Franklin inferred that additional employees would have to be hired.

ACTIVITY 2 Writing Sentences

Write the following words on the board or duplicate them. Then have your students write a sentence for each word.

1. accept, except
2. advice, advise
3. all together, altogether
4. capital, capitol
5. emigrate, immigrate
6. loose, lose
7. precede, proceed
8. their, there, they're
9. to, too, two
10. your, you're

ADDITIONAL PRACTICE

Basic Students
Teacher's Resource Book: pages 153–154
Workbook: pages 109–114

Average Students
Teacher's Resource Book: pages 155–156
Workbook: pages 109–114

Advanced Students
Teacher's Resource Book: pages 157–158

REVIEW EXERCISES AND TESTS

Student Text
Glossary Review: pages 225–226
Standardized Test: pages 227–228

Teacher's Resource Book
Glossary Test: pages 27–28
(Also available as spirit duplicating masters.)
Workbook Unit Review: pages 115–116

Glossary of Usage

For additional practice for this section, see the Teacher's Resource Book and the Workbook.

January has 31 days. That is a correct statement. It would be incorrect to say that January has 25 days or 42 days. Unlike factual information, written or spoken English is often not a matter of correctness but of appropriateness in certain situations. For example, if the principal of your school asked you to be a tutor, you might say, "I would be happy to take part in the school's tutoring program." On the other hand, if friends asked if you wanted to join them for something to eat after a football game, you might say, "Count me in!" Each reply would be appropriate in its own situation.

LEVELS OF LANGUAGE

The region of the country in which you were raised has influenced your speech from the moment you began to talk. Each section of the country has a unique dialect and has its own particular colloquial expressions. People from the Midwest and people from the South, even though they can understand each other, speak quite differently. Ethnic background and education influence your speech as well.

All of these factors have contributed to the richness and the diversity of the English language today. These factors have also created the use of two different levels of the English language: *standard* and *nonstandard*.

Standard English

The term *standard English* refers to the rules and the conventions of usage that are accepted and used most widely by

English-speaking people throughout the world. Writers, television and radio personalities, government officials, and most public figures usually use standard English in both their written and spoken public presentations. Standard English, however, is different for formal and informal situations.

Formal English. Formal English has a wide range of applications. It is found in legal documents, business letters, and well-written compositions. Formal English, which is the standard for all written work, strictly follows conventional rules of grammar, usage, and mechanics, because a writer has time to think and edit. Formal English is not necessarily synonymous with stiffness and stuffiness, although words are sometimes used that would not normally be used in ordinary conversation. To maintain a formal tone of writing, writers also avoid contractions, colloquialisms, and common verbal expressions. The following example of formal English is the first part of Abraham Lincoln's *Gettysburg Address*.

> Four score and seven years ago our fathers brought forth on this continent a new nation conceived in liberty and dedicated to the proposition that all men are created equal. Now we are engaged in a great civil war testing whether that nation, or any nation so conceived and so dedicated, can long endure. We are met on a great battlefield of that war. We have come to dedicate a portion of that field as a final resting-place for those who here gave their lives that that nation might live . . .

Informal English. Informal English is used more often than formal English. This level of English, however, is not inferior to formal English, because it still follows the rules and the conventions of standard English. Informal English is merely used on other occasions. It is most often used in magazines, newspapers, advertising, and much of the fiction that is being written today. Informal English includes words and expressions that would sound out of place in formal writing. Even shortcuts, such as contractions, are often included. Informal English is also used by most educated people in their everyday conversations. The following example of informal English was written by Andy Rooney.

Glossary of Usage

> There are two kinds of savers. The first is the practical saver who keeps string, bags, and old aluminum foil as a practical matter. And then there's the sentimental saver. The sentimental saver can't stand the idea of throwing out any memory of his life.
> —ANDY ROONEY, *A FEW MINUTES WITH ANDY ROONEY*

Nonstandard English

Nonstandard English has many variations because it is influenced by regional dialects, as well as by other factors such as slang. Since nonstandard English lacks uniformity, always use standard English when you write. Nonstandard English, however, does appear in some literature when a writer wants to recreate the conversation of people from a particular locale. This, for example, was Mark Twain's purpose when he wrote the following passage from *Huckleberry Finn*.

> Looky here—mind how you talk to me; I'm a-standing about all I can stand now—so don't gimme no sass. I've been in town two days, and I hain't heard nothing but about you bein' rich. I heard about it away down the river, too. That's why I come. You git me that money tomorrow—I want it.
> —MARK TWAIN, *HUCKLEBERRY FINN*

GLOSSARY OF USAGE

The following glossary of usage covers common usage problems. As you go through the items in the glossary, notice that some of them refer to standard and nonstandard English. The glossary has been arranged alphabetically so you can use it as an easy reference tool.

a, an. Use *a* before a word beginning with a consonant sound and *an* before a word beginning with a vowel sound. Always keep in mind that this rule applies to sounds, not letters. For example, *an hour ago* is correct because the *h* in *hour* is silent.

I would like to live in **a** house in the country.
We planned **an** early departure.

Nonstandard English

accept, except. *Accept* is a verb that means "to receive with consent." *Except* is usually a preposition that means "but" or "other than."

I **accept** all your suggestions **except** this one.

adapt, adopt. Both of these words are verbs. *Adapt* means "to adjust." *Adopt* means "to take as your own."

If we **adopt** Jefferson High's regulations, we can **adapt** them to our particular needs.

advice, advise. *Advice* is a noun that means "a recommendation." *Advise* is a verb that means "to recommend."

I **advise** you to follow your parents' **advice**.

affect, effect. *Affect* is a verb that means "to influence." *Effect* is usually a noun that means "a result" or "an influence." As a verb *effect* means "to accomplish" or "to produce."

Was your decision **affected** by his comments?
What **effect** will his promotion have on you? [a noun]
The snowstorm **effected** a change in their plans. [verb]

ain't. This contraction is nonstandard and should be avoided in your writing.

NONSTANDARD   He **ain't** my favorite singer.
   STANDARD   He **isn't** my favorite singer.

all ready, already. *All ready* means "completely ready." *Already* means "previously."

The cast was **all ready** for opening night.
I have taken my SAT's **already**.

all together, altogether. *All together* means "in a group." *Altogether* means "wholly" or "thoroughly."

We should go to the landlord **all together** to present our mutual complaints.
Are you **altogether** sure that's the right thing to do?

203

Glossary of Usage

allusion, illusion. Both of these words are nouns. An *allusion* is "an implied or indirect reference; a hint." An *illusion* is "something that deceives or misleads."

> "He has the Midas touch" is an **allusion** to a legendary king who could turn everything he touched into gold.
> We can see motion in motion pictures only because of an optical **illusion**.

a lot. These words are often written as one word. There is no such word as "alot." *A lot* should be avoided in formal writing. (Do not confuse *a lot* with *allot,* which is a verb that means "to distribute by shares.")

INFORMAL	He gave us **a lot** of help.
FORMAL	He gave us **much** help.
	Was the scholarship money **allotted** evenly among the three winners?

among, between. Both of these words are prepositions. *Among* is used when referring to three or more people or things. *Between* is usually used to refer to two people or things.

> This subscription can be shared **among** the four of us.
> Divide the last piece of pizza **between** the two of you.

amount, number. *Amount* refers to a singular word. *Number* refers to a plural word.

> How did you feed such a large **number** of people with such a small **amount** of spaghetti?

anymore. Do not use *anymore* for *now* or *nowadays. Anymore* is usually used in a negative statement.

NONSTANDARD	The town's parks are very crowded **anymore**.
STANDARD	The town's parks are very crowded **now**.
STANDARD	Since you got a job, I don't see you **anymore**.

anywhere, everywhere, nowhere, somewhere. Do not add *s* to any of these words.

NONSTANDARD	That key must be here **somewheres**.
STANDARD	That key must be here **somewhere**.

Glossary of Usage

as far as. This expression is sometimes confused with "all the farther," which is nonstandard English.

NONSTANDARD   This is **all the farther** the bus will take us.
STANDARD   This is **as far as** the bus will take us.

at. Do not use *at* after *where*.

NONSTANDARD   Can you tell us **where** we're **at**?
STANDARD   Can you tell us **where** we are?

a while, awhile. *A while* is an expression made up of an article and a noun. It is used mainly after a preposition. *Awhile* is an adverb.

For **a while** no one said anything.
Let's rest **awhile** before we continue exercising.

bad, badly. *Bad* is an adjective and often follows a linking verb. *Badly* is used as an adverb. In the first two examples, *felt* is a linking verb.

NONSTANDARD   I have felt **badly** all week.
STANDARD   I have felt **bad** all week.
STANDARD   We need the rain **badly.**

EXERCISE 1   **Determining the Correct Word**

Number your paper 1 to 25. Then write each word in parentheses that correctly completes the following sentences.

1. After living in Florida, do you think you can (adapt, adopt) to the harsh winters in the North?
2. My brother is the manager of (a, an) hotel in Maine.
3. The team's chances of winning looked (bad, badly).
4. Have you seen my bowling shoes (anywhere, anywheres)?
5. The football team (adapted, adopted) a St. Bernard for its mascot.
6. In the book *Moby Dick,* many (allusions, illusions) are made to the Bible.
7. A large (amount, number) of toxic waste was found buried under the empty lot.
8. Did the Student Council (affect, effect) any changes in the cafeteria rules?

Glossary of Usage

9. Only a small (amount, <u>number</u>) of people turned out for the town meeting.
10. Please stay for (<u>a while</u>, awhile).
11. I sing so (bad, <u>badly</u>) that I don't even hum in public.
12. The graduation requirements are getting much tougher (anymore, <u>nowadays</u>).
13. Your rousing speech will (<u>affect</u>, effect) everyone at the rally.
14. Following Miguel's (<u>advice</u>, advise), we dressed warmly for the hike.
15. This is (all the farther, <u>as far as</u>) we can go.
16. Do you want (a, <u>an</u>) apple or (<u>a</u>, an) pear?
17. (<u>Somewhere</u>, Somewheres) there's a muffler you can (<u>adapt</u>, adopt) to your old car.
18. The ultimate (affect, <u>effect</u>) of the telethon will be that a larger (amount, <u>number</u>) of people will receive help.
19. The (allusions, <u>illusions</u>) the magician created were (all together, <u>altogether</u>) amazing.
20. Everyone in my house feels (<u>bad</u>, badly) (accept, <u>except</u>) my little brother.
21. I have (all ready, <u>already</u>) heard that you will (<u>accept</u>, except) the nomination for class president.
22. (<u>Between</u>, Among) you and me, I'd take Brenda's (<u>advice</u>, advise).
23. We were (<u>all ready</u>, already) to leave, but we had to wait for (<u>a while</u>, awhile) for Buddy.
24. The large (<u>amount</u>, number) of leftover food should be divided (between, <u>among</u>) all the workers.
25. I (advice, <u>advise</u>) you to take Milbury Road because River Road is full of potholes (anymore, <u>now</u>).

because. Do not use *because* after *the reason*. Use one or the other.

NONSTANDARD   The **reason** I fell is **because** I wasn't looking where I was going.
STANDARD   I fell **because** I wasn't looking where I was going.
STANDARD   The **reason** I fell is **that** I wasn't looking where I was going.

Glossary of Usage

being as, being that. These expressions should be replaced with *because* or *since*.

NONSTANDARD **Being that** the motor on the boat wouldn't start, I began to row.

STANDARD **Since** the motor on the boat wouldn't start, I began to row.

beside, besides. *Beside* is always a preposition that means "by the side of." As a preposition, *besides* means "in addition to." As an adverb, *besides* means "also" or "moreover."

Place the spoon **beside** the knife. [by the side of]

Besides my mother and my father, my grandparents will be there. [in addition to]

When our flight was canceled, we were given a night's stay in a hotel and breakfast **besides**. [also]

both. Never use *the* before *both*.

NONSTANDARD **The both** of them were absent today.
STANDARD **Both** of them were absent today.

both, each. *Both* refers to two persons or objects together, but *each* refers to an individual person or object.

Although **both** artists have equal talent, **each** has his own style.

bring, take. *Bring* indicates motion toward the speaker. *Take* indicates motion away from the speaker.

Please **take** these books to the English office and then **bring** the cart back to me.

can, may. *Can* expresses ability. *May* expresses possibility or permission.

Rita **can** type 80 words per minute.
May I take your hat and coat?

207

Glossary of Usage

can't help but. Use a gerund instead of *but*.

NONSTANDARD I **can't help but remember** our good times at school.

STANDARD I **can't help remembering** our good times at school.

capital, capitol. A *capital* is the chief city of a state. Also, names are written with *capital* letters, people invest *capital,* and a person can receive *capital* punishment. A *capitol* is the building in which the legislature meets.

We toured the **capitol** in Hartford, the **capital** of Connecticut.

coarse, course. *Coarse* is an adjective that means "loose or rough in texture" or "crude and unrefined." *Course* is a noun that means "a way of acting or proceeding" or "a path, road, or route." Also, people play the game of golf on a *course,* students take *courses* in school, and an appetizer is one *course* of a meal. *Course* is also the word used in the parenthetical expression *of course.*

The linen bedspread has a very **coarse** weave.
Choose the **course** you want to follow and stick to it.

continual, continuous. Both of these words are adjectives. *Continual* means "frequently repeated." *Continuous* means "uninterrupted."

The **continual** advertisements on TV are distracting.
The rainfall was heavy and **continuous.**

different from. Use this form instead of *different than. Different than,* however, can be used informally when it is followed by a clause.

INFORMAL Inés found life on her uncle's ranch **different than** she had expected.

FORMAL Inés found life on her uncle's ranch **different from** what she had expected.

STANDARD Her opinion about the political candidate is **different from** mine.

Glossary of Usage

discover, invent. Both of these words are verbs. *Discover* means "to find or get knowledge of for the first time." *Invent* means "to create or produce for the first time." Something that is discovered has always existed but been unknown. Something that is invented has never existed before.

> While some scientists were still **discovering** facts about the moon, other scientists were **inventing** a spaceship to take astronauts there.

doesn't, don't. *Doesn't* is singular and should be used only with singular nouns and the personal pronouns *he, she,* and *it. Don't* is plural and should be used with plural nouns and the personal pronouns *I, you, we,* and *they.*

NONSTANDARD	She **don't** live here anymore.
STANDARD	She **doesn't** live here anymore.
NONSTANDARD	Skiing **don't** appeal to me.
STANDARD	Skiing **doesn't** appeal to me.

done. *Done* is the past participle of the verb *do.* When *done* is used as a verb, it must have one or more helping verbs.

NONSTANDARD	I **done** my homework already.
STANDARD	I **have done** my homework already.

double negative. Words such as *hardly, never, no, not,* and *nobody* are considered negatives. Do not use two negatives to express one negative meaning. *(See page 194 for a list of negative words.)*

NONSTANDARD	I do**n't never** eat lunch in the cafeteria.
STANDARD	I do**n't** ever eat lunch in the cafeteria.
STANDARD	I **never** eat lunch in the cafeteria.

emigrate, immigrate. Both of these words are verbs. *Emigrate* means "to leave a country to settle elsewhere." *Immigrate* means "to enter a foreign country to live there." A person emigrates *from* a country and immigrates *to* another country. *Emigrant* and *immigrant* are the noun forms.

> In 1954, Grandfather **emigrated** from Germany.
> He **immigrated** to Israel.

Glossary of Usage

etc. *Etc.* is an abbreviation for a Latin phrase that means "and other things." Never use *and* with *etc*. If you do, what you are really saying is *"and and* other things." It is best, however, not to use this abbreviation at all in formal writing.

NONSTANDARD   To make the posters, we will need poster board, paint, **etc.**

STANDARD   To make the posters, we will need poster board, paint, **and other art supplies.**

farther, further. *Farther* refers to distance. *Further* means "additional" or "to a greater degree or extent."

Is the cabin much **farther?**
Further information will be sent to you next week.

EXERCISE 2 Determining the Correct Word

Number your paper 1 to 25. Then write each word in parentheses that correctly completes the following sentences.

1. The (continual, continuous) hammering, for over an hour, gave me a headache.
2. On the lower slopes of a mountain, the snow often forms into (coarse, course) crystals.
3. I (done, have done) what you suggested.
4. (Beside, Besides) apples we picked a dozen pears.
5. Mr. Crouse (could, couldn't) hardly walk in the snow.
6. (Bring, Take) the dog for a walk.
7. (Can, May) I have your attention, please!
8. The French meal consisted of six (coarses, courses).
9. There wasn't (anyone, no one) in my history class who could name the 13th president of the United States.
10. When scientists (discovered, invented) the transistor, a revolution in the electronics industry occurred.
11. We will meet at the golf (coarse, course) at noon.
12. Through the protected binoculars, we saw the partial solar eclipse and some sunspots (beside, besides).
13. (Both, Each) of the umpires had his own book of rules.
14. From the mountain peak, the climbers looked down on the (coarse, course) they had followed to the top.
15. Because I had (continual, continuous) interruptions, I didn't finish my homework until 11 o'clock.

Glossary of Usage

16. The principal will provide (farther, <u>further</u>) details about the field trip.
17. We climbed to the top of the dome in our state (capital, <u>capitol</u>).
18. Stacy (<u>doesn't</u>, don't) know which country he (<u>emigrated</u>, immigrated) from.
19. He (discovered, <u>invented</u>) a machine that is (<u>different from</u>, different than) anything I have ever seen before.
20. (Beside, <u>Besides</u>) a beach towel, please (<u>bring</u>, take) me a regular towel.
21. (Farther, <u>Further</u>) documents must be supplied before you can (emigrate, <u>immigrate</u>) to New Zealand.
22. (Being as, <u>Because</u>) you're going to the library anyhow, you can (bring, <u>take</u>) these books back.
23. (The both, <u>Both</u>) of you should have visited Dover, the (<u>capital</u>, capitol) of Delaware.
24. My dog (<u>doesn't</u>, don't) (<u>ever</u>, never) obey me.
25. (Being that, <u>Since</u>) you didn't come with anyone, why don't you sit (<u>beside</u>, besides) me.

fewer, less. *Fewer* is plural and refers to things that can be counted. *Less* is singular and refers to quantities and qualities that cannot be counted.

Fewer apples would make **less** applesauce.

former, latter. *Former* is the first of two people or things. *Latter* is the second of two people or things. (Use *first* and *last* when three or more are involved.)

For our book report, we had a choice of a novel or a biography. I chose the **former;** Beth chose the **latter.**

good, well. *Good* is an adjective and often follows a linking verb. *Well* is an adverb and often follows an action verb. However, when *well* means "in good health," "attractive," or "satisfactory," it is used as an adjective.

The plot of that book sounds **good.** [adjective]
I wish I could skate **well.** [adverb]
You don't look **well.** [adjective—"in good health"]

Glossary of Usage

had of. Do not use *of* after *had*.

NONSTANDARD   If I **had of** taken typing, I could type this term paper much faster.

STANDARD   If I **had** taken typing, I could type this term paper much faster.

have, of. Never substitute *of* for the verb *have*. When speaking, many people make a contraction of *have*. For example, someone might say, "We should've left sooner." Because *'ve* sounds like *of*, *of* is often substituted for *have* when written.

NONSTANDARD   I **could of** worked this weekend.

STANDARD   I **could have** worked this weekend.

hear, here. *Hear* is a verb that means "to perceive by listening." *Here* is an adverb that means "in this place."

From **here** I could **hear** everything they said.

hole, whole. A *hole* is an opening. *Whole* means "complete" or "entire."

The **hole** is so big that a **whole** orange can fit into it.

imply, infer. Both of these words are verbs. *Imply* means "to suggest" or "to hint." *Infer* means "to draw a conclusion by reasoning or from evidence." A speaker implies; a hearer infers. *Implication* and *inference* are the noun forms.

Julie's comment **implied** that what I had **inferred** from John's remarks was wrong.

in, into. Use *into* when you want to express motion from one place to another.

The apples **in** the bag should be put **into** the refrigerator.

irregardless. Do not substitute this word for *regardless*.

NONSTANDARD   I am going through with my plans, **irregardless** of the consequences.

STANDARD   I am going through with my plans, **regardless** of the consequences.

Glossary of Usage

its, it's. *Its* is a possessive pronoun. *It's* is a contraction for *it is*.

The jury defended **its** guilty verdict.
Since **it's** such a nice day, we should go swimming at Gull Pond.

kind, sort, type. These words are singular and should be preceded by *this* or *that*. *Kinds, sorts,* and *types* are plural and should be preceded by *these* or *those*.

Do you like **this kind** of flower?
Do you like **these kinds** of flowers?

kind of, sort of. Never substitute these expressions for *rather* or *somewhat*.

NONSTANDARD   That test was **kind of** hard.
STANDARD   That test was **rather** hard.

knew, new. *Knew,* the past tense of the verb *know,* means "was acquainted with." *New* is an adjective that means "recently made" or "just found."

I **knew** you would wear your **new** wool sportcoat for the class picture.

learn, teach. Both of these words are verbs. *Learn* means "to gain knowledge." *Teach* means "to instruct."

NONSTANDARD   Wanda **learned** me how to use the microwave oven.
STANDARD   Wanda **taught** me how to use the microwave oven.
STANDARD   I **learned** how to use the microwave oven by reading the instructions.

leave, let. Both of these words are verbs. *Leave* means "to depart." *Let* means "to allow" or "to permit."

NONSTANDARD   **Leave** me handle this matter for you.
STANDARD   **Let** me handle this matter for you.
STANDARD   We must **leave** the house at six to be on time for the concert.

Glossary of Usage

lie, lay. *Lie* means "to rest or recline." *Lie* is never followed by a direct object. Its principal parts are *lie, lying, lay,* and *lain*. *Lay* means "to put or set (something) down." *Lay* is usually followed by a direct object. Its principal parts are *lay, laying, laid,* and *laid*.

LIE   You should **lie** down and rest.
His suit was **lying** over the chair.
Last night I **lay** on the beach and looked at the stars.
I had just **lain** down when the telephone rang.

LAY   **Lay** the blanket at the foot of the bed.
Dad is **laying** the tiles in the kitchen himself.
Who **laid** the new roll of film in the sun?
I have **laid** the mousetrap near the door.

like, as. *Like* is a preposition that introduces a prepositional phrase. *As* is usually a subordinating conjunction that introduces an adverb clause. Although *like* is sometimes used informally as a subordinating conjunction, it should be avoided in formal situations.

INFORMAL   Jenny retold the story just **like** it had happened.
FORMAL   Jenny retold the story just **as** it had happened. [clause]
FORMAL   **Like** me, she registered to vote. [prepositional phrase]

EXERCISE 3 Determining the Correct Word

Number your paper 1 to 25. Then write each word in parentheses that correctly completes the following sentences.

1. From his confident manner, I (implied, <u>inferred</u>) that he had succeeded.
2. If we (<u>had</u>, had of) planted the seeds in April, we would have vegetables by now.
3. I could (<u>have</u>, of) put up the tent myself.
4. (Irregardless, <u>Regardless</u>) of what you say, I know I'm right.
5. Stand on the mark on the stage, just (like, <u>as</u>) I showed you.
6. When we spoke the other day, Lucinda (<u>implied</u>, inferred) that she would like to find a new job.
7. I want a TV that will work (good, <u>well</u>) for a long time.

214

Glossary of Usage

8. My tennis coach (learned, <u>taught</u>) me how to put a topspin on my backhand.
9. Don't put that (hole, <u>whole</u>) piece of garlic (in, <u>into</u>) the gravy!
10. (Leave, <u>Let</u>) me take your (knew, <u>new</u>) coat and hang it in the closet.
11. Did you (<u>hear</u>, here) the music (like, <u>as</u>) it was playing?
12. Don't you think that (hole, <u>whole</u>) is (kind of, <u>rather</u>) small for this button?
13. The bird has built (<u>its</u>, it's) nest right (hear, <u>here</u>) on the windowsill.
14. If the snow (<u>had</u>, had of) kept falling throughout the night, we would (<u>have</u>, of) been snowbound by morning.
15. Coach Greenberg (learned, <u>taught</u>) us how to dive gracefully (in, <u>into</u>) the water from the diving board.
16. The senator (<u>implied</u>, inferred) that lowering the tax rate would result in (<u>fewer</u>, less) city services.
17. (Irregardless, <u>Regardless</u>) of what anyone says, (its, <u>it's</u>) up to you to make the decision.
18. The soup tastes so (<u>good</u>, well) I hope you'll (learn, <u>teach</u>) me how to make it.
19. I (<u>knew</u>, new) that I would (<u>hear</u>, here) from you sooner or later.
20. If you (<u>leave</u>, let) early, please (leave, <u>let</u>) me know.
21. During the (hole, <u>whole</u>) time I was giving my speech, I didn't feel (good, <u>well</u>).
22. (<u>This</u>, These) kind of puzzle always leaves me (sort of, <u>somewhat</u>) frustrated.
23. We have (fewer, <u>less</u>) money (<u>in</u>, into) our account now than we have ever had before.
24. You should (<u>have</u>, of) been able to spot (<u>that</u>, those) type of sales pitch.
25. The newspaper would operate more efficiently if there were (<u>fewer</u>, less) members on (<u>its</u>, it's) executive board.

EXERCISE 4 Using *Lie* and *Lay* Correctly

Complete each sentence by writing the correct form of *lie* or *lay*.

1. Last night Shags __lay__ at the foot of my bed.
2. An unusual seashell was __lying__ half buried in the sand.

Glossary of Usage

3. Melinda carefully _laid_ the crushed rose on her dresser.
4. Kim _lay_ down and fell into a deep sleep.
5. Please _lay_ the wet towels across the clothes rack.
6. This fertile valley _lies_ between the mountains and the river.
7. The cheerleaders _laid_ their pom-poms on the ground.
8. When the mail comes, I always _lay_ it on the desk.
9. Your books have been _lying_ on the coffee table for two days.
10. Keith has _laid_ a mattress in the garage to use as a mat for his gymnastic routines.
11. The weary puppy was _lying_ in the corner of the room.
12. If Marcy _lies_ in the sun any longer, she will be badly burned.
13. Yesterday the workers were _laying_ the foundation to our new house.
14. Have you _laid_ your books by the door so you won't forget them tomorrow?
15. To ease his aching muscles, Jorge _lay_ in a tub of hot water for an hour.
16. Patty has _laid_ an old blanket over the broken springs in the backseat of her car.
17. He _laid_ a message on her desk.
18. I have _lain_ here for an hour, trying to fall asleep.
19. Why are you _laying_ the dog's leash on the counter?
20. Jeffrey _lay_ perfectly still, pretending he was asleep.

loose, lose. *Loose* is usually an adjective that means "not tight." *Lose* is a verb that means "to misplace" or "not to have any longer."

   I knew I'd **lose** that **loose** button.

may be, maybe. *May be* is a form of the verb *be*. *Maybe* is an adverb that means "perhaps."

   This **may be** your last chance to apply.
   Maybe you should see a doctor.

most. *Most* is either a pronoun or an adjective that modifies a noun or a pronoun. *Almost*, which means "nearly," is an adverb. Do not substitute *most* for *almost*.

NONSTANDARD   Brad finished **most** all the repair work on his car last night.
STANDARD   Brad finished **almost** all the repair work on his car last night.
STANDARD   **Most** students in my school enjoy gym classes.

nor, or. Use *neither* with *nor* and *either* with *or*.

Neither Tim **nor** his brother can come to dinner.
Either tulips **or** daffodils will look nice in that vase.

of. Prepositions such as *inside, outside,* and *off* should not be followed by *of*.

NONSTANDARD   Please take the towels **off of** the clothesline.
STANDARD   Please take the towels **off** the clothesline.

ought. Never use *have* or *had* with *ought*.

NONSTANDARD   I **hadn't ought** to eat this late.
STANDARD   I **ought not** to eat this late.

passed, past. *Passed* is the past tense of the verb *pass*. As a noun *past* means "a time gone by." As an adjective *past* means "just gone" or "elapsed." As a preposition *past* means "beyond."

In the **past,** time **passed** much slower for me. [*past* as a noun]
For the **past** several days, I have been driving **past** her house. [*past* as an adjective and then as a preposition]

precede, proceed. Both of these words are verbs. *Precede* means "to be, go, or come ahead of something else." *Proceed* means "to move along a course," "to advance," or "to continue after a pause or interruption."

In the procession the faculty **preceded** the members of the graduating class.
I think we should **proceed** with our plans for the class day picnic.

Glossary of Usage

principal, principle. As an adjective *principal* means "main" or "chief." As a noun *principal* means "the head of a school" or "leader." *Principle* is a noun that is synonymous with *law, truth, doctrine,* or *code of conduct.*

> Our **principal,** Mrs. Dobin, will be the **principal** speaker at the graduation ceremonies.
> Most of the moral **principles** that people live by are learned from their parents.

respectfully, respectively. *Respectfully* is the adverbial form of the noun *respect,* which means "high regard or esteem." *Respectively* means "in the order given."

> The man addressed the Queen **respectfully.**
> Phoenix, Santa Fe, and Albany are the capitals of Arizona, New Mexico, and New York, **respectively.**

rise, raise. *Rise* means "to move upward." *Rise* is never followed by a direct object. Its principal parts are *rise, rising, rose,* and *risen. Raise* means "to lift (something) up," "to increase," or "to grow." *Raise* is usually followed by a direct object. Its principal parts are *raise, raising, raised,* and *raised.*

> The sun will **rise** at 5:42 A.M. tomorrow.
> **Raise** the flag as everyone sings the national anthem.

says. Do not use *says,* the present tense of the verb *say,* when you should use the past tense *said.*

> NONSTANDARD   After Jim struck out, Paul **says,** "My turn!"
> STANDARD   After Jim struck out, Paul **said,** "My turn!"

-self, -selves. A reflexive or an intensive pronoun that ends in *-self* or *-selves* should not be used as a subject. (Never use "hisself" or "theirselves.")

> NONSTANDARD   Dad and **myself** are the only ones at home.
> STANDARD   Dad and **I** are the only ones at home.

shall, will. Formal English uses *shall* with first-person pronouns and *will* with second- and third-person pronouns. Today, however, *shall* and *will* are used interchangeably with *I*

Glossary of Usage

and *we,* except that *shall* is still used with first-person pronouns for questions.

Shall we take a vote on the amendment?
They **will** see you tomorrow.

sit, set. *Sit* means "to rest in an upright position." *Sit* is rarely followed by a direct object. Its principal parts are *sit, sitting, sat,* and *sat. Set* means "to put or place (something)." *Set* is usually followed by a direct object. Its principal parts are *set, setting, set,* and *set.*

Do you always **sit** in that chair?
Set the hot bread on the windowsill to cool.

so. *So* should not be used to begin a sentence.

NONSTANDARD	**So** what did she say then?
STANDARD	He had to complete the job, **so** he worked late. [coordinating conjunction]
STANDARD	Your story was **so** amusing. [adverb]

some, somewhat. *Some* is either a pronoun or an adjective that modifies a noun or a pronoun. *Somewhat* is an adverb that modifies an adjective or another adverb.

NONSTANDARD	Mom is **some** better today.
STANDARD	Mom is **somewhat** better today.

than, then. *Than* is usually a subordinating conjunction and is used for comparisons. *Then* is an adverb that means "at that time" or "next."

My report is shorter **than** yours.
We saw a movie, and **then** we got something to eat.

EXERCISE 5 Determining the Correct Word

Number your paper 1 to 25. Then write each word in parentheses that correctly completes the following sentences.

1. (Most, Almost) all the players felt that the umpire had been very fair.
2. Allison was embarrassed when she fell (off, off of) her horse.

Glossary of Usage

3. San Francisco is the (<u>principal</u>, principle) port of northern California.
4. Rosa's bedroom in the new apartment is much larger (<u>than</u>, then) the one she used to have.
5. Did Adams (<u>precede</u>, proceed) Jefferson as president?
6. Sandra Shaw, Monica Loez, and Lou Williams are the presidents of the sophomore, the junior, and the senior class, (respectfully, <u>respectively</u>).
7. You should tighten your (<u>loose</u>, lose) shoestring before you trip over it.
8. He lives by a strict set of (principals, <u>principles</u>).
9. (Shall, <u>Will</u>) you help me clean the garage?
10. Mark threw a pillow at Evan; (than, <u>then</u>) the fun began!
11. Neither the pilot (<u>nor</u>, or) the copilot was available for an interview.
12. The senators (<u>respectfully</u>, respectively) submitted their suggestions to the President.
13. The (<u>principal</u>, principle) will ask either Willie (<u>or</u>, nor) David to present the athletic award.
14. (<u>Shall</u>, Will) we look (<u>inside</u>, inside of) the box?
15. Randy and (myself, <u>I</u>) finished (most, <u>almost</u>) all our homework in study hall.
16. This car is (some, <u>somewhat</u>) larger (<u>than</u>, then) my car.
17. (May be, <u>Maybe</u>) we should find out what happened in the (passed, <u>past</u>).
18. Then my lawyer (says, <u>said</u>), "I will appeal if we (loose, <u>lose</u>) the case."
19. (Ourselves, <u>We</u>) and the Masons (<u>may be</u>, maybe) moving this spring.
20. The district attorney (preceded, <u>proceeded</u>) with the case as a matter of (principal, <u>principle</u>).
21. This puzzle is (some, <u>somewhat</u>) harder to do (<u>than</u>, then) the last puzzle we did.
22. In the (passed, <u>past</u>) several years, Lee and (myself, <u>I</u>) have become good friends.
23. Our letter to the (<u>principal</u>, principle) (<u>respectfully</u>, respectively) requested a meeting.
24. I think you should (precede, <u>proceed</u>) straight until you have (<u>passed</u>, past) the library.
25. If you put your (<u>loose</u>, lose) change in a jar, you won't (loose, <u>lose</u>) so much of it.

Glossary of Usage

EXERCISE 6 Using *Rise/Raise* and *Sit/Set* Correctly

Complete each sentence by writing the correct form of *rise/raise* or *sit/set*.

1. Please __set__ the lawn chairs by the pool.
2. Whenever the river __rises__ to a dangerous level, the citizens are evacuated from their homes.
3. Of course the biscuits haven't __risen__; you didn't add baking soda!
4. The day after his operation he was __sitting__ up in a chair.
5. The tide will __rise__ tonight at 6:49.
6. __Sit__ down and catch your breath.
7. The dancers stood in a long line and __raised__ their arms in unison.
8. Jamie is __sitting__ in the first row of the balcony.
9. Did you __set__ the carton of juice on the counter?
10. Last Sunday we all __sat__ on the floor and watched the Super Bowl.
11. When the curtain __rose__, the audience applauded.
12. The drum major __raised__ his baton, and the music began.
13. The price of gasoline has __risen__ again.
14. When you finish, __set__ the dishes in the sink.
15. The Persian cat has __sat__ in that same position in the sunlight for 15 minutes.
16. Had the sun __risen__ before you woke up this morning?
17. Balloons filled with helium always __rise__ to the ceiling.
18. Please __set__ that bowl of flowers on my desk.
19. When Joshua hit a home run, the fans __rose__ from their seats with a roar.
20. Have you __sat__ here very long?

that, which, who. These words are often used as relative pronouns to introduce adjective clauses. *That* refers to people, animals, and things and always begins an essential clause. *Which* refers to animals and things. *Who* refers to people.

> The movie **that** we saw last night was excellent.
>
> *Moby Dick*, **which** is required reading for all juniors, is about a giant white whale.
>
> Mr. Weissinger, **who** is the manager of the hardware store, is retiring next month.

221

Glossary of Usage

their, there, they're. *Their* is a possessive pronoun. *There* is usually an adverb, but sometimes it can also begin an inverted sentence. *They're* is a contraction for *they are.*

They're here for **their** annual checkup.
Your books are lying over **there** by the desk.

theirs, there's. *Theirs* is a possessive pronoun. *There's* is a contraction for *there is.*

There's our car, but where is **theirs**?

them, those. Never use *them* as a subject or a modifier.

NONSTANDARD	**Them** are the ones I want. [subject]
STANDARD	**Those** are the ones I want.
NONSTANDARD	Do you want **them** running shoes? [adjective]
STANDARD	Do you want **those** running shoes?

this here, that there. Avoid using *here* and *there* in addition to *this* and *that.*

NONSTANDARD	**That there** horse is very gentle.
STANDARD	**That** horse is very gentle.

this, that, these, those. *This* and *that* are singular and modify singular nouns. *These* and *those* are plural and modify plural nouns.

NONSTANDARD	I like **these** make of jeans.
STANDARD	I like **this** make of jeans.

threw, through. *Threw* is the past tense of the verb *throw. Through* is a preposition that means "in one side and out the other."

He accidentally **threw** the ball **through** the window.

to, too, two. *To* is a preposition. *To* also begins an infinitive. *Too* is an adverb that modifies a verb, an adjective, or another adverb. *Two* is a number.

We had **to** drive **two** miles before reaching a rest stop.
Go **to** the store before it is **too** late.

Glossary of Usage

try to. Use *try to* instead of *try and,* which is nonstandard.

NONSTANDARD   I will **try and** save you a seat.
STANDARD   I will **try to** save you a seat.

unique. *Unique* is an adjective that means "the only one of its kind." Because of its meaning, *unique* should not be written in the comparative or superlative degree.

NONSTANDARD   Charles has a **most unique** style of painting.
STANDARD   Charles has a **unique** style of painting.

way, ways. Do not substitute *ways* for *way* when referring to a distance.

NONSTANDARD   When the canoe overturned, we were still a long **ways** from shore.
STANDARD   When the canoe overturned, we were still a long **way** from shore.

weak, week. *Weak* is an adjective that means "not strong" or "likely to break." *Week* is a noun that means "a period of seven days."

I have felt sick and **weak** for over a **week** now.

what. Do not substitute *what* for *that*.

NONSTANDARD   The apartment **what** we looked at today was too small.
STANDARD   The apartment **that** we looked at today was too small.

when, where. Do not use *when* or *where* directly after a linking verb in a definition.

NONSTANDARD   Early in the morning is **when** it is best to pick roses.
STANDARD   Early in the morning is the best time to pick roses.
NONSTANDARD   Astronomy is **where** you study celestial bodies and their motion.
STANDARD   Astronomy is the study of celestial bodies and their motion.

Glossary of Usage

where. Do not substitute *where* for *that*.

NONSTANDARD I read **where** he will run for reelection.
  STANDARD I read **that** he will run for reelection.

who, whom. *Who*, a pronoun in the nominative case, is used as a subject or a predicate nominative. *Whom*, a pronoun in the objective case, is used mainly as a direct object, an indirect object, or an object of a preposition. *(See page 153.)*

Who delivers your newspaper? [subject]
From **whom** did you buy the canoe? [object of a preposition]

whose, who's. *Whose* is a possessive pronoun. *Who's* is a contraction for *who is*.

Whose car is in your driveway?
Who's writing a report on Robert Frost?

your, you're. *Your* is a possessive pronoun. *You're* is a contraction for *you are*.

I suppose **you're** looking for **your** umbrella.

EXERCISE 7 Determining the Correct Word

Number your paper 1 to 25. Then write each word in parentheses that correctly completes the following sentences.

1. (Whose, Who's) report was longer?
2. I never saw (them, those) photographs of myself before.
3. To (who, whom) did you send your application?
4. I read (where, that) since the sixteenth century, scientists have used diving bells to go underwater.
5. I had only gone a little (way, ways) on Route 56 when I had a flat tire.
6. (That, Those) brand of cough drops tastes like cherry.
7. I will try (and, to) see her today.
8. The crow, (which, who) sometimes lives to be 100 years old, has a longer life span than most other birds.
9. I noticed (where, that) you left work late.
10. The student (who, which) got the highest score was Ben.
11. I read in *Natural History* (where, that) unprovoked animals rarely attack humans.

Glossary Review

12. The sunglasses (what, <u>that</u>) I want are finally on sale at the mall.
13. (This here, <u>This</u>) tour will take you (threw, <u>through</u>) Italy, England, and Germany.
14. In Ceylon (theirs, <u>there's</u>) a species of wasp (what, <u>that</u>) builds a home six feet long.
15. (Their, There, <u>They're</u>) staying with us because (<u>their</u>, there, they're) house was damaged during the storm.
16. Going (threw, <u>through</u>) snow, (<u>this</u>, this here) old car performs quite well.
17. In August (their, <u>there</u>, they're) are jellyfish a little (<u>way</u>, ways) out in the bay.
18. (<u>Who</u>, Whom) is going (<u>to</u>, too, two) take the tickets at the door?
19. All last (weak, <u>week</u>) I worked on (that there, <u>that</u>) science report.
20. (Whose, <u>Who's</u>) taking care of (<u>your</u>, you're) dog?
21. (Them, <u>Those</u>) tangerines are (to, <u>too</u>, two) expensive.
22. I will try (and, <u>to</u>) drive you (their, <u>there</u>, they're) myself.
23. By accident he (<u>threw</u>, through) (<u>theirs</u>, there's) into the wastepaper basket.
24. (Your, <u>You're</u>) sure this computer is accompanied by a (<u>unique</u>, most unique) package of software, aren't you?
25. (That there, <u>That</u>) bridge is (to, <u>too</u>, two) (<u>weak</u>, week) (<u>to</u>, too, two) support more than one truck.

GLOSSARY REVIEW

Number your paper 1 to 25. Then write each <u>word</u> in parentheses that correctly completes the following sentences. (This exercise uses words from the entire glossary.)

1. At dusk we reached a high cliff and realized that was (all the farther, <u>as far as</u>) we could go that day.
2. Just (among, <u>between</u>) you and me, I didn't think the party was much fun.
3. How is rock music different (<u>from</u>, than) jazz?
4. (Being as, <u>Because</u>) clouds consist of condensed water, one cloud sometimes weighs several tons.

225

Glossary of Usage

5. Should we eat (<u>that</u>, those) kind of mushroom?
6. (Their, <u>There</u>, They're) are billions of stars in our galaxy alone.
7. Please (bring, <u>take</u>) the attendance report to the office and (<u>bring</u>, take) back a package of paper.
8. Did you (loose, <u>lose</u>) your bus pass?
9. The storm had little (affect, <u>effect</u>) on the shore (accept, <u>except</u>) to strew the beaches with driftwood and seaweed.
10. Carl Schultz and Jacob Riis (<u>emigrated</u>, immigrated) from Germany and Denmark, (respectfully, <u>respectively</u>).
11. If the Rams (<u>had</u>, had of) thrown (<u>fewer</u>, less) passes, they might (of, <u>have</u>) won the game.
12. Were you able to (learn, <u>teach</u>) your puppy to stay (<u>off</u>, off of) your new sofa?
13. Mary walked (in, <u>into</u>) the room; (than, <u>then</u>) everyone began to applaud.
14. Of (coarse, <u>course</u>), we will (<u>hear</u>, here) from Alicia in (<u>a while</u>, awhile).
15. (<u>Shall</u>, Will) I carry (them, <u>those</u>) boxes to the attic?
16. (Most, <u>Almost</u>) all of us have (all ready, <u>already</u>) seen that movie.
17. The price of oranges (<u>rose</u>, raised) last (weak, <u>week</u>) after the frost in Florida.
18. The (<u>continual</u>, continuous) ringing of (that there, <u>that</u>) telephone annoyed me.
19. The (farther, <u>further</u>) you read in this novel, the more (your, <u>you're</u>) going to like it.
20. (May be, <u>Maybe</u>) you should (<u>lie</u>, lay) down.
21. (<u>Doesn't</u>, Don't) Kimberly know (<u>who</u>, whom) (discovered, <u>invented</u>) the automobile?
22. The magician created many (allusions, <u>illusions</u>) during the (coarse, <u>course</u>) of his performance.
23. I read (<u>that</u>, where) a beautiful Greek statue was found (<u>in</u>, into) the coastal water off Crete.
24. The (<u>principal</u>, principle) reason for this reunion was to bring us (<u>all together</u>, altogether) at least one time.
25. You (<u>implied</u>, inferred) that I couldn't (adapt, adopt) (good, <u>well</u>) to the (knew, <u>new</u>) requirements.

STANDARDIZED TEST

USAGE

Directions: Each sentence may contain an underlined part that is unacceptable. On your answer sheet, fill in the circle containing the letter of the unacceptable part. If there is no underlined part requiring change, fill in *E*.

SAMPLE Ed and I have chosen foods with less calories. No error
              A B   C   D   E

ANSWER Ⓐ Ⓑ Ⓒ Ⓓ Ⓔ

E 1. None of the contestants appear calmer than she. No error
        A   B   C   D   E

A 2. Are there a whole herd of goats inside that fence? No error
        A   B   C   D   E

E 3. Whom do Ellen and he like more, Tamara or Leslie? No error
        A B   C   D   E

A 4. There is Carl and he lying on the beach beside Joe. No error
          A   B C   D   E

B 5. Kathleen fell over the cat because hardly no sun or light was
              A   B   C
        coming into the attic. No error
              D   E

D 6. "He who hesitates is lost," Cora said to Ben and I. No error
         A B   C   D   E

D 7. By noon I had already sold a large amount of books. No error
             A   B   C   D   E

B 8. Everyone whose answer is correct know his facts well.
                 A   B   C   D
        No error
        E

E 9. If Ramona or I were president, who do you think would
                   A B   C
        advise us? No error
          D   E

C 10. I took the skate with the loose blade to Mr. Liu to be fixed, and
          A   B
        he brings it back looking like a new skate. No error
           C   D   E

Directions: Each sentence is followed by five ways to write the underlined part of the sentence. Choose the best one. If the original way is best, choose *A*. Fill in the circle containing the letter of your answer.

SAMPLE   <u>Was all of the dishes broken</u> in the storm?
     A Was all of the dishes broken
     B Were all of the dishes broked
     C Was all of the dishes breaked
     D Were all of the dishes broken
     E Were all of the dishes breaked

ANSWER   Ⓐ Ⓑ Ⓒ ● Ⓔ

E 11. Mr. McKelvy <u>bought that there statue somewhere</u> in Asia.
    A bought that there statue somewhere
    B buyed that statue somewheres
    C bought that statue somewheres
    D buyed that there statue somewheres
    E bought that statue somewhere

B 12. <u>Since neither Kevin nor I were there</u>, they lost the game.
    A Since neither Kevin nor I were there,
    B Since neither Kevin nor I was there,
    C Since neither Kevin nor me was there,
    D Since neither Kevin nor me were there,
    E Since neither Kevin nor I were their,

C 13. Don't <u>leave your white cat lay</u> on the blue sofa, please.
    A leave your white cat lay
    B let your white cat lay
    C let your white cat lie
    D leave you're white cat lie
    E let you're white cat lie

A 14. <u>Is it really she whom</u> Ms. Hayashi interviewed?
    A Is it really she whom   **D** Was it really her whom
    B Was it really she who   **E** Is it really she who
    C Was it really her who

E 15. The place my family <u>like better is</u> the Hawaiian Islands.
    A like better is   **D** like best is
    B likes best are   **E** likes best is
    C likes better are

Unit 3

Mechanics

10 Capital Letters
11 End Marks and Commas
12 Other Punctuation

Chapter 10   Capital Letters

OBJECTIVES

- To capitalize the first word of a sentence and the first word of a line of poetry.
- To capitalize the words *I* and *O*.
- To capitalize all proper nouns and most proper adjectives.
- To capitalize certain titles of people and all works of art.
- To capitalize the salutations and closings of letters.
- Application: To learn and apply the rules of capitalization in all writing, in and out of school.

MOTIVATIONAL ACTIVITY

Write the following sentences on the board. Then ask your students if the sentences make sense.

The father is very tall. The baby is a little Taller.

The capital letter on "Taller," turns nonsense to sense. The baby's last name is Taller! This is just one example of the role that capital letters play in making written words easier to understand.

TEACHING SUGGESTIONS

One reason for drill in the mechanics of writing is to help students achieve an automatically correct application of the rules in all their writing. On a literature test or in a history report, students sometimes cannot understand why deductions from their grades are made for errors in capitalization, punctuation, or spelling. That is why it is so important that you stress that there are no separate languages called *literature* or *history*. Students write English, and they should write it correctly at all times.

To encourage your students to submit their best efforts, make editing a part of every writing assignment. Call time five minutes before the end of a class-writing or test period, and tell your students to check what they have already written. Occasionally return compositions for proofreading for about ten minutes the day after they have been written. This procedure allows students to check their work more objectively, since they are no longer concerned with the content. You also may want your students to exchange papers occasionally with a neighbor. For homework assignments, you could consider having a five-minute period at the beginning of class for editing papers before they are turned in. These practices, if used regularly, will emphasize the importance and the positive results of editing. Hopefully, your students will then begin to check their own work automatically—for all assignments and in all classes.

Also encourage your students to use this chapter as a reference source when editing their written work. In addition, you may want to review the rules for capital letters as the need for them arises in your students' writing.

Capitalization with quotations is covered in Chapter 12 on page 287, and capitalization for outlines is covered in Chapter 23 on page 543. These rules are placed in the chapters in which direct quotations and outlining are taught.

NOTE: There are 50 answers to both the Diagnostic Test and Mastery Test in this chapter.

Proper Nouns and Proper Adjectives *(pages 232–240)*

A review of proper nouns and proper adjectives on pages 3 and 14 respectively may be a good introduction to this section.

Titles *(pages 240–242)*

You may want to cover the rules for punctuating titles of works of art along with the rule for their capitalization. Underlining titles is covered on page 283, and quotation marks with titles is covered on pages 284–285.

Sample Board Sentences

Charles Dickens' absorbing novel, *The Tale of Two Cities*, comments on the behavior of British and Parisian citizens during the French Revolution. [proper nouns and proper adjectives]

The movie *Around the World in Eighty Days* won the Academy Award in 1956. [title and proper noun]

ACTIVITIES FOR DIFFERENT ABILITIES

Basic Students

ACTIVITY 1 Capital Letter Review

For additional practice duplicate the following sentences. Then have your students write each word that should begin with a capital letter.

Facts and Figures

1. "murder in the rue morgue" and "the gold bug" are two stories by edgar allan poe.
2. on august 1, 1876, colorado was admitted as the 38th state to join the united states.
3. in the midwest sudden and violent storms are a constant threat at harvest time.
4. the pentateuch is another name for the first five books of the old testament.
5. the great symbol of american independence, the liberty bell, was cracked on july 8, 1835.
6. c. w. ceram, a german archaeologist, has written several books about the discovery of ancient civilizations.
7. the superstition of groundhog day is an old one.
8. any scandinavian trip should include a stop in odense, denmark, the birthplace of hans christian andersen.
9. according to "know your money," a booklet put out by the united states secret service, counterfeit money is easily distinguishable from real money.
10. lewis and clark, explorers of the northwest, started their famous expedition in 1804 and returned to st. louis on september 23, 1806.
11. the first place on which the famous dutch explorer henry hudson set foot when he arrived in new york was coney island.
12. in 1500 b.c., in egypt, a shaved head was considered the ultimate in feminine beauty.
13. san francisco's golden gate bridge was completed in 1937.
14. anyone writing a letter to the *new york times* has a 1 chance in 21 of having the letter published.
15. the famous russian composer nicolai rimsky-korsakov, creator of the popular *scheherazade*, did not know how to read music until he was in his late teens.
16. wendell lewis wilkie, the republican candidate for the presidency in 1940, was originally named lewis wendell wilkie.
17. after protestants, catholics, and jews, there are more buddhists in the united states than members of any other religious group.
18. socrates, one of the most famous greek philosophers, never wrote down a single word of his teachings.
19. in 1818, in austria, the famous christmas carol "silent night" was written by a parish priest, in three hours on christmas eve.
20. according to the new york telephone company, of the approximately 400 million telephones in the world, more than one third are in the united states.

ACTIVITY 2 Capital Letter Review

For additional practice duplicate the following sentences. Then have your students write each word that should begin with a capital letter.

The Golden Spike

1. the first great link between the eastern and western parts of the united states was begun the year the homestead act was passed.
2. although a plan for a railroad from lake michigan to the pacific ocean was proposed to congress in 1844, the project was forgotten until 15 years later.

Capital Letters

3. theodore judah, an engineer from california, revived the plan with the help of leland stanford, mark hopkins, collin p. huntington, and other prominent californians.
4. with the support of president lincoln, congress granted money and land to the union pacific railroad company and the central pacific railroad company.
5. the union pacific began laying its tracks at council bluffs, iowa, and the central pacific started work at sacramento, california.
6. the progress of the central pacific section was slow because shipments of rails, tools, and machinery had to travel to california around cape horn or across the isthmus of panama.
7. when hundreds of buffalo were killed to provide food for the union pacific workers, the plains indians foresaw the end of their buffalo hunting.
8. destruction of the huge buffalo herds dealt a serious blow to the sioux, the comanche, the kiowa, and other tribes.
9. late in the spring of 1867, the two railroads finally met when the last wooden tie was laid at promontory, utah, near great salt lake.
10. when the famous golden spike was driven into this tie, the eastern and western parts of our country were connected, and people could travel from the atlantic ocean to the pacific in only seven days.

ACTIVITY 3 Capital Letters and Spelling
Play the game of ghosts, using only the names of geographical places, such as cities and states. The first player names a geographical location. The second player must then use the last letter of that geographical location for the first letter of his or her word. If the second player fails to do this, he or she is "out." For instance, the first player may say "Arkansas." Since the second player must begin his or her word with an *s*, he or she may say "Sioux City." If the third player cannot think of a city or a state that begins with *y*, he or she is "out."

ACTIVITY 4 Capital Letters and Dictionary Skills
Have your students skim through the dictionary until they have compiled a list of ten proper nouns. This exercise will reinforce the fact that proper nouns are listed in the dictionary. Then have your students use their words in sentences.

ACTIVITY 5 Writing Sentences
Have your students write a minibiography of someone they know. They should include the place of birth, nationality, and other important facts about the person's life. When they have finished, have them edit their work for the proper use of capital letters.

Advanced Students

ACTIVITY 1 Capital Letter Review
For additional practice duplicate the following paragraphs. Then have your students find and correct each word that is not capitalized and should be, and each word that is capitalized and should not be.

The Adventures of Alexander Selkirk
   The Story of Robinson Crusoe as told by Daniel Defoe was suggested by the adventures of a scotsman named Alexander Selkirk. Selkirk, whose father was a shoemaker and tanner, was born in fifeshire, scotland, in 1676. When he was 19, he was called before the members of his Church for misbehavior during the services, but he ran away to Sea and never returned to his home.
   In may 1703, he joined an expedition to the south seas as one of the Mates. The fictional Robinson Crusoe was shipwrecked on an Island near trinidad. The Island where Selkirk's adventures took place was really on the other side of the World, but his story is almost as exciting as Crusoe's.
   While on the voyage, Selkirk had a quarrel with his Captain and asked to be put ashore. His Ship, *cinque ports*, dropped him off at Juan Fernandez island, about 350 miles West of Valparaiso, chile. Selkirk became frightened at the

last minute and asked to return to the Ship, but the Captain refused and left him on the uninhabited Island.

Selkirk took little with him besides his clothing and bedding, a few weapons, a bible, and a kettle. The Author of *Robinson Crusoe* gave his fictional Hero a faithful friend named Friday, but the real-life Hero had no human companionship at all.

During his four years on the Island, he saw two boats anchor there for wood and water, but he was afraid to approach them because they were spanish. His Country and Spain were then at War, and he didn't want to be captured and sent to South America as a prisoner.

Fortunately, the weather on Juan Fernandez island was never severe. There was some frost in june and july, when it is Winter in the Southern hemisphere; but partly because of Ocean currents, it never was really cold there during the Winter or hot in the Summer.

Large numbers of goats lived on the Island, and Selkirk trained himself to run fast enough to catch them. He made his clothes and lined his house with goatskins. He also became skilled in capturing the giant turtles on the Beach. His food tasted terrible at first because he had no salt, but he soon learned to use the fruit of the Pimento Tree for flavoring.

Selkirk lived on the Island until he was found in January of the Year 1709 by captain Woodes Rogers of the british navy. Selkirk returned to england after his rescue but soon began sailing the Seas again. He died in 1721 while serving as a Mate aboard the ship *weymouth*.

ACTIVITY 2 Capital Letters and Library Skills

Give your students the following broad topics. Then have them go to the library and find a fact that pertains to each topic. Each fact should include a proper noun, a proper adjective, or a title.

1. basketball
2. literature
3. the planet Earth
4. firsts
5. winter
6. religion
7. languages
8. holidays
9. automobiles
10. a state

ACTIVITY 3 Writing Sentences

Have your students choose one of the facts they researched for Activity 2 and expand it by writing 10 to 15 sentences about that topic. Once they have finished, have them edit their sentences for the correct use of capital letters.

ADDITIONAL PRACTICE

Basic Students
  Teacher's Resource Book:
  pages 159-160
  Workbook: pages 117-122

Average Students
  Teacher's Resource Book:
  pages 161-162
  Workbook: pages 117-122

Advanced Students
  Teacher's Resource Book:
  pages 163-164

REVIEW EXERCISES AND TESTS

Student Text
  Diagnostic Test: page 230
  Chapter Review: pages 245-246
  Mastery Test: page 247

Teacher's Resource Book
  Chapter 10 Test: pages 29-30
  (Also available as spirit duplicating masters.)

10

Capital Letters

For additional practice for this chapter, see the Teacher's Resource Book and the Workbook.

DIAGNOSTIC TEST

Number your paper 1 to 10. Then write each word that should begin with a capital letter.

EXAMPLE   last fall my sister enrolled at wesleyan university.

ANSWER   Last, Wesleyan University

1. to reach the pennsylvania turnpike, drive south until you reach route 340.
2. while the northeast was having balmy weather, the rocky mountain states were being buried under a blizzard.
3. the national parks, such as yellowstone, are under the supervision of the department of the interior.
4. the main entrance to the metropolitan museum of art in new york city is on fifth avenue and eighty-second street.
5. last week she flew to south carolina on piedmont airlines to attend a conference.
6. if i take algebra II next year, i won't be able to take calculus.
7. for his oral presentation, bart read the poem "story from bear country."
8. recently queen elizabeth II and her husband visited several countries in africa.
9. did you see the football game between the dolphins and the cowboys on monday night?
10. yesterday we saw the play *the diary of anne frank*.

230

First Words

10a–b

This chapter and the two punctuation chapters that follow make up the Mechanics Unit of this textbook. The information in these chapters, if applied correctly, can make your writing flow smoothly—just as a mechanic can make your car run smoothly. On the other hand, using this information incorrectly will undoubtedly result in costly problems, such as misunderstanding and confusion on the part of the reader.

RULES FOR CAPITAL LETTERS

Before the printing press was invented, every letter in every word was a capital letter. Today capital letters have special uses that provide clues to help readers understand what is written. This chapter will review those uses.

First Words

Basically, capital letters are attention getters. They are taller and larger than lowercase letters. One important place to which they draw a reader's attention is the beginning of a new sentence or a new line of poetry.

10a Capitalize the first word in a sentence or a line of poetry.

SENTENCE **S**ome hailstones are bigger than baseballs.

LINES OF **A** bird came down the walk:
POETRY **H**e did not know I saw. —EMILY DICKINSON

NOTE: The first word of a direct quotation is also capitalized. *(See page 287.)* The first word of each topic in an outline is capitalized as well. *(See page 544.)*

I and *O*

Always capitalize these single-letter words.

10b Capitalize the pronoun *I*, both alone and in contractions. Also capitalize the interjection *O*.

231

Capital Letters

I   **I** sleep better if **I**'ve had some exercise that day.
O   I have a song to sing, **O**!   — W. S. GILBERT

NOTE: *Oh* is not capitalized unless it comes at the beginning of the sentence.

Proper Nouns

Beginning a noun with a capital letter can tell a reader that the noun is a proper noun — that it names a *particular* person, place, or thing.

10c   Capitalize proper nouns and their abbreviations.

Since there are so many proper nouns, they have been divided into the following groups to help you remember them easily.

Names of Persons and Animals. Capitalize the names of particular persons and animals.

PERSONS   **A**my, **E**rnest **W**arner, **N**orman **A**. **G**oldstein
ANIMALS   **M**uffin, **T**rigger, **L**assie, **L**ightning, **B**aron

Some surnames have two capital letters. In those names the letter following *De, Mc, Mac, O'*, and *St.* should be capitalized. Names, however, do vary. It is always best to ask individual people exactly how their names are spelled and capitalized.

De**N**ise, **M**c**N**air, **M**ac**D**uffee, **O**'**N**eil, **S**t. **C**lair

Abbreviations that follow a person's name should also be capitalized.

Margaret M. Perry, **M.D.**   Edward J. Lee, **Sr.**

Capitalize common nouns that are clearly personified.

All **N**ature wears one universal grin.   — HENRY FIELDING

Geographical Names. Capitalize the names of particular places, bodies of water, and celestial bodies.

STREETS, HIGHWAYS   **V**ine **B**rook **R**oad, **R**oute 6, **C**alifornia **F**reeway, **F**orty-second **S**treet [The second part of a hyphenated numbered street is not capitalized.]

Proper Nouns

10c

CITIES, STATES	**S**alt **L**ake **C**ity, **U**tah; **G**reat **F**alls, **M**ontana; **N**ashville, **T**ennessee
TOWNSHIPS, COUNTIES	**P**lymouth **T**ownship, **C**hickasaw **C**ounty
COUNTRIES	**P**oland, **N**igeria, **J**apan, **P**eru, **T**urkey
SECTIONS OF A COUNTRY	the **N**ortheast, the **M**idwest, the **S**outh [Compass directions do not begin with a capital letter: *Go east to Kent Road.*]
CONTINENTS	**N**orth **A**merica, **A**frica, **A**ustralia
ISLANDS	**S**anta **R**osa, **C**orsica, **H**awaiian **I**slands
MOUNTAINS	**M**ount **R**ainier, the **R**ocky **M**ountains
PARKS	**O**lympic **N**ational **P**ark, **K**enny **S**tate **P**ark
BODIES OF WATER	**A**rctic **O**cean, **L**ake **E**rie, **C**hesapeake **B**ay, **W**appapello **R**eservoir, **G**ulf of **M**exico
STARS	the **N**orth **S**tar, **S**irius, **V**ega, **A**ntares
CONSTELLATIONS	**L**ittle **D**ipper, **Q**ueen **C**assiopeia's **C**hair
PLANETS	**M**ercury, **S**aturn, **U**ranus, **E**arth [Do not capitalize *sun* or *moon*. Also, do not capitalize *earth* if it is preceded by *the*.]

NOTE: Capitalize words such as *street, island,* or *city* only when they are part of a proper noun.

The largest **l**ake in the **s**tate of **L**ouisiana is **L**ake **P**ontchartrain.

EXERCISE 1 Using Capital Letters

Number your paper 1 to 20. Then write the following items, using capital letters only where needed.

1. south of clay city
2. matthew r. royan, jr.
3. an island off the coast of massachusetts
4. the philippine islands
5. a port on the black sea
6. a city in kentucky
7. the big dipper
8. mississippi river
9. my dog jiggers
10. the southeast
11. lake louise
12. the united states
13. a lake near terre haute, indiana
14. the soviet union

233

Capital Letters

15. the <u>m</u>acgregors' house
16. <u>f</u>ifty-fifth <u>s</u>treet
17. a country in <u>e</u>urope
18. <u>n</u>ew <u>e</u>ngland
19. the <u>a</u>ndes <u>m</u>ountains
20. <u>o</u>ntario, <u>c</u>anada

EXERCISE 2 Using Capital Letters

Number your paper 1 to 10. Then write each <u>word</u> that should begin with a capital letter.

1. <u>tokyo</u> is on <u>honshu</u>, <u>japan's</u> largest island.
2. <u>did</u> you know that <u>france</u> is bordered by the <u>english channel</u> to the north?
3. <u>charon</u>, <u>pluto's</u> only moon, was discovered from the earth with the aid of a powerful telescope.
4. <u>no</u> fish can live in the <u>great</u> <u>salt</u> <u>lake</u> in <u>utah</u>.
5. <u>jacksonville</u>, <u>florida</u>, is on the <u>st. john's river</u>, 12 miles from the <u>atlantic</u> <u>ocean</u>.
6. <u>the</u> highest mountain in <u>africa</u> is <u>mount</u> <u>kilimanjaro</u>.
7. <u>in</u> a week the <u>o'malleys</u> will be leaving for <u>logan</u>, <u>ohio</u>.
8. <u>the</u> <u>bering</u> <u>strait</u> separates <u>alaska</u> and <u>siberia</u>.
9. <u>charleston</u>, an important seaport in the <u>south</u>, is the site of the oldest museum in the <u>united</u> <u>states</u>.
10. <u>the</u> <u>columbia</u> <u>river</u> flows through the state of <u>washington</u> and <u>british</u> <u>columbia</u>, <u>canada</u>.

Names of Groups and Businesses. Capitalize the names of organizations, businesses, institutions, government bodies, and political parties.

ORGANIZATIONS	the **N**ational **F**ootball **L**eague, the **H**umane **S**ociety, the **B**righton **C**ivic **A**ssociation, the **A**merican **M**edical **A**ssociation
BUSINESSES	**M**obil **O**il **C**orporation, **S**ears **R**oebuck and **C**ompany, **D**ouber and **A**ssociates
INSTITUTIONS	**P**erkins **S**chool for the **B**lind, **M**iddlebury **H**igh **S**chool, **G**reenwood **H**ospital [Words such as *school, college,* and *hospital* are not capitalized unless they are part of a proper noun.]
GOVERNMENT BODIES	**D**epartment of the **I**nterior, the **S**upreme **C**ourt, **C**ongress, **U**nited

Proper Nouns

	States **T**reasury, the **H**ouse of **C**ommons, the **B**ritish **P**arliament
POLITICAL PARTIES	the **R**epublican **P**arty, a **D**emocrat

Specific Time Periods, Events, and Documents. Capitalize days of the week, months of the year, civil and religious holidays, and special events. Also capitalize the names of historical events, periods, and documents.

DAYS, MONTHS	**S**unday, **S**aturday, **J**anuary, **D**ecember [Do *not* capitalize the seasons of the year.]
HOLIDAYS	**F**ourth of **J**uly, **V**eterans **D**ay, **Y**om **K**ippur
SPECIAL EVENTS	the **M**ardi **G**ras **P**arade, the **O**lympic **G**ames, the **S**uper **B**owl, the **N**ew **Y**ork **M**arathon
HISTORICAL EVENTS	the **B**oxer **R**ebellion, **B**attle of **B**ull **R**un, the **B**oston **T**ea **P**arty, the **V**ietnam **W**ar, the **A**tlantic **C**harter, the **N**ew **D**eal
PERIODS	the **V**ictorian **P**eriod, the **I**ndustrial **R**evolution, the **M**iddle **A**ges
DOCUMENTS	the **F**irst **A**mendment to the **U**nited **S**tates **C**onstitution, the **B**ill of **R**ights, the **F**ederal **R**eserve **A**ct, **T**reaty of **G**reenville

NOTE: Prepositions are not capitalized.

Nationalities, Races, Languages, and Religions. Capitalize the names of nationalities, races, languages, religions, and religious references.

NATIONALITIES	an **I**talian, an **A**merican, the **F**rench
RACES	**C**aucasian, **O**riental, **M**ongoloid
LANGUAGES	**E**nglish, **S**wahili, **P**olish, **H**ebrew
RELIGIONS	**B**aptist, **R**oman **C**atholic, **H**indu
RELIGIOUS REFERENCES	**J**ehovah, the **N**ew **T**estament, the **H**oly **S**pirit, the **K**oran, the **S**tar of **D**avid [Capitalize pronouns referring to the Diety. Do *not* capitalize *god* when it refers to a mythological god.]

235

Capital Letters

Other Proper Nouns. Capitalize other nouns that name specific places and things.

VEHICLES	*Columbia*, *Old Ironsides*, *Orient Express* [Names of vehicles are also italicized.]
AWARDS	**N**obel **P**eace **P**rize, the **C**y **Y**oung **A**ward
BRAND NAMES	**J**ello-**O** pudding, **C**amay soap, **K**odak film [The product itself is *not* capitalized.]
MONUMENTS, MEMORIALS	**M**ount **S**tate **M**onument, **L**incoln **M**emorial
BUILDINGS	**P**rudential **B**uilding, **K**ennedy **C**enter
SPECIFIC COURSE NAMES	**W**oodworking II, **A**rt I, **L**atin, **E**nglish, **C**hinese

NOTE: Unnumbered courses such as *history, home economics*, and *science* are not capitalized. Also, do not capitalize class names such as *junior* or *senior* unless they are a part of a proper noun, such as the *Junior Prom*.

EXERCISE 3 Using Capital Letters

Number your paper 1 to 20. Then write the following items, using capital letters only where needed.

1. biology and french
2. a college in the south
3. the aluminum company of america
4. campbell's chicken vegetable soup
5. the university of iowa
6. the social security act
7. the grace baptist church
8. the battle of bunker hill
9. a cadillac convertible
10. department of housing and urban development
11. the war of 1812
12. the magna carta
13. the house of representatives
14. thunder lake lodge
15. the guggenheim museum in new york city
16. a mother's day card
17. the old testament
18. spring and summer
19. baseball in yankee stadium
20. a republican in congress

Proper Nouns

EXERCISE 4 Using Capital Letters

Number your paper 1 to 10. Then write each word that should begin with a capital letter.

1. jeannette rankin was elected to the house of representatives by the republicans of montana in 1916.
2. the irish were the first europeans to make the potato a staple food.
3. have you found your warranty from the bulova watch company?
4. members of the farmington board of education will meet for a special session on friday.
5. the cathedral of cologne in germany took more than 300 years to build.
6. the declaration of independence is a popular exhibit at the national archives building in washington, d.c.
7. does winter officially begin before or after christmas?
8. the mormons, members of the church of jesus christ of latter-day saints, founded salt lake city, utah.
9. the golden gate bridge in san francisco is one of the longest suspension bridges in the world.
10. most immigrants who came to the united states between the civil war and world war I settled in large cities.

EXERCISE 5 Writing Sentences

Write six to ten sentences that describe your hometown. Include its geographical location, historical background, points of interest, and notable citizens. Be sure to capitalize all proper nouns. *Sample sentence:* Philadelphia's Franklin Institute, a museum of science and technology, is named after Benjamin Franklin.

EXERCISE 6 Time-out for Review

Number your paper 1 to 20. Then write each word that should begin with a capital letter.

Facts and Figures

1. the largest desert in the world is africa's sahara desert.
2. one of the first photocopiers was marketed by the rectigraph company of rochester, new york, in the early 1900s.
3. the sears tower in chicago is the world's tallest building; the world trade center in new york city is the second tallest.

237

Capital Letters

4. testing of the unmanned space shuttle *enterprise* ended on october 26, 1977, at andrews air force base.
5. the crash of the new york stock exchange in 1929 started the great depression in the united states.
6. volleyball was invented in 1895 by william g. morgan, who was the director of the young men's christian association in holyoke, massachusetts.
7. in 1958, two united states atomic submarines, the *nautilus* and the *skate*, made history by being the first ships to travel under the north pole.
8. the 16th amendment to the constitution, passed by congress in 1913, made income tax a fact of life.
9. the highest uninhabited point in the united states is mount mckinley in alaska; the lowest is death valley.
10. among the most widely spoken languages in the world today are chinese, english, and russian.
11. booker t. washington founded the tuskegee institute.
12. john glenn was the first american to orbit the earth.
13. the emancipation proclamation was issued on september 22, 1862, and became effective on january 1, 1863.
14. the united states census bureau may not share information about an individual with any other federal agency without the individual's permission.
15. eight signers of the declaration of independence were born in the british isles.
16. edna st. vincent millay published her first volume of poetry the same year she graduated from vassar college.
17. in 1982, william devries implanted the first permanent artificial human heart.
18. charles curtis, elected as herbert hoover's vice-president in 1928, was partly an american indian.
19. the first cadillacs cost $750 in 1903 — less than the original model t, which cost $850.
20. the metropolitan opera house in new york city is one of the largest opera houses in the world.

Proper Adjectives

A proper adjective is formed from a proper noun. Since proper nouns begin with a capital letter, most proper adjectives also begin with a capital letter.

Proper Adjectives

10d Capitalize most proper adjectives.

PROPER NOUNS **A**laska, **C**ongress, the **M**idwest, the **S**outh
PROPER ADJECTIVES **A**laskan oil, **C**ongressional session, **M**idwestern farms, **S**outhern accent

NOTE: When an adjective formed from *midwest* or *south* indicates a compass direction, no capital letter is used.

Do you feel a **s**outherly breeze?

Some proper adjectives keep the same form as the proper noun.

PROPER NOUN **F**lorida, **F**riday
PROPER ADJECTIVES **F**lorida oranges, **F**riday traffic

NOTE: A few proper adjectives have become so commonplace in our language that they are no longer capitalized.

china cup, plaster of **p**aris, **p**asteurized milk

Sometimes a proper adjective will be part of a hyphenated adjective. Capitalize only the part that is a proper adjective.

American-made cars   trans-**A**tlantic flight

Occasionally, however, both parts of a hyphenated adjective will be proper adjectives.

Indo-**E**uropean language   **A**fro-**A**merican art

EXERCISE 7   Capitalizing Proper Adjectives

Number your paper 1 to 10. Then write each <u>word</u> that should begin with a capital letter.

1. <u>the</u> <u>dallas</u>-<u>fort</u> <u>worth</u> <u>airport</u> in <u>texas</u> is among the largest commercial air terminals in the world.
2. <u>the</u> <u>february</u> forecast calls for more snow and colder-than-normal temperatures.
3. <u>the</u> first patent for a plow was granted to a <u>new</u> <u>jersey</u> farmer in 1797.
4. <u>the</u> <u>republican</u> leaders of <u>congress</u> will meet today to discuss the new tax proposal.
5. <u>among</u> examples of traditional <u>canadian</u> architecture are the <u>french</u>-style homes of <u>quebec</u>.

239

Capital Letters

6. in this hemisphere the largest english-speaking city south of miami, florida, is kingston, jamaica.
7. at detroit, michigan, we crossed the canadian-american border.
8. the poet t. s. eliot was born in the united states but later became a british citizen.
9. what is the roman numeral for *20?*
10. the austro-hungarian monarchy, also known as austria-hungary, was a european country from 1867 until 1918.

Titles

Capital letters emphasize the importance of titles of people and works of art.

10e ▸ Capitalize the titles of people and works of art.

Titles Used with Names of People. Capitalize a title showing office, rank, or profession when it comes before a person's name.

BEFORE A NAME   Have you met **D**r. Jordan of Highview Hospital?
Our regular **d**octor was out of town.

BEFORE A NAME   The featured speaker will be **C**ongresswoman Michaels.
Have you ever met the **c**ongresswoman from our district?

NOTE: Do *not* capitalize the prefix *ex-* or the suffix *-elect* when either is connected to a title.

ex-Senator Burton   Mayor-**e**lect Rodini

Titles Used Alone. Capitalize a title that is used alone when it is being substituted for a person's name in direct address. The titles for the United States *President, Vice-President,* and *Chief Justice,* and for the *Queen of England* are always capitalized when they stand alone.

USED AS A NAME   I'd like to call Asheville, **O**perator.
NOT USED AS A NAME   The **o**perator helped me place my call.

HIGH GOVERNMENT OFFICIAL	The **P**resident held a dinner for the visiting dignitaries.

NOTE: *President* and *vice-president* are capitalized when they stand alone only if they refer to the current president and vice-president.

> Was Dwight Eisenhower the **p**resident who preceded John Kennedy or Lyndon Johnson?

Titles Showing Family Relationships. Capitalize titles showing family relationships when they come before a person's name or when they are being substituted for a person's name in direct address.

BEFORE A NAME	When will **A**unt Kate and **U**ncle Harold arrive?
USED AS A NAME	I'll make dinner tonight, **M**om.

Titles showing family relationships should *not* be capitalized when they are preceded by a possessive noun or pronoun—unless they are considered a part of a person's name.

> My **g**randfather has raised sheep for thirty years.
> When is your **U**ncle Harley going to take us fishing?

Titles of Works of Art. Capitalize the first word, the last word, and all important words in the titles of books, newspapers, periodicals, stories, poems, movies, plays, musical compositions, and other works of art. Do *not* capitalize a preposition, a coordinating conjunction, or an article—unless it is the first word in a title.

> One chapter in Jack London's book ***The Call of the Wild*** is entitled "**T**he **S**ounding of the **C**all."
> I saw Rembrandt's painting ***The Polish Rider*** in the book ***The Story of Painting***.
>
> The reviewer for the ***Washington Post*** praised the production of Carson McCullers' play ***The Member of the Wedding*** at the Wilbur Theater. [The word *the* before the title of a newspaper or a periodical is usually *not* capitalized.]

Capital Letters

EXERCISE 8 Capitalizing Titles

Number your paper 1 to 10. Then write each word that should begin with a capital letter.

1. have you seen *chariots of fire*, the film that won the 1981 academy award for best picture?
2. my grandmother and jack's aunt usually spend the winter in st. petersburg, florida.
3. have you been hiking for very long, dad?
4. what are the responsibilities of the president of the simsbury athletic association?
5. the famous cherry trees in washington, d.c., were a gift to president taft from the mayor of tokyo, japan, in 1912.
6. my uncle charles is a test pilot for sikorsky aircraft, a division of united technologies corporation.
7. among james fenimore cooper's most popular novels are *the last of the mohicans* and *the pathfinder*.
8. as the president entered the room this morning, the band began to play "hail to the chief."
9. what has ex-senator sullivan been doing since he left office last january?
10. we found a sunday, october 10, 1971, issue of the *new york times* in the bureau drawer.

Letters

Capital letters are used at the beginning and at the end of a friendly letter and a business letter.

10f Capitalize the first word and all nouns in the salutation and the first word in the closing of a letter.

SALUTATIONS	**D**ear **A**unt **M**artha,	**M**y dear **D**r. **S**tone:
CLOSINGS	**Y**our affectionate niece,	**S**incerely yours,

NOTE: Place a comma after the salutation in a friendly letter and a colon after the salutation in a business letter. Place a comma after the closing in all letters.

EXERCISE 9 Writing a Letter

Write a letter to one of your state senators. In your letter request that some action be taken concerning a local problem or need. Be sure to capitalize the proper words in the salutation and the closing, as well as any other words that should begin with a capital letter. *(See pages 564–566 for the form of a business letter.)* *Answers will vary.*

EXERCISE 10 **Time-out for Review**

Number your paper 1 to 20. Then write each word that should begin with a capital letter.

Do You Know?

1. is neptune or uranus closer to earth?
2. did robert frost or ralph waldo emerson write the poem "stopping by woods on a snowy evening"?
3. does the most valuable player in the national football league win the jim thorpe trophy or the heisman trophy?
4. does buffalo or rochester lie at the east end of lake erie, on the niagara river?
5. is shea stadium in new york city or in cincinnati?
6. did franklin roosevelt or martin luther king, jr., say, "i have been to the mountain"?
7. is *the grapes of wrath* by john steinbeck about people from the southwest or people from new england?
8. did the treaty of versailles end the spanish-american war or world war I?
9. in which state is the grand canyon national park?
10. during president carter's term in office, who was his vice-president?
11. is the north star in the handle of the big dipper or the little dipper?
12. what famous author lived near walden pond from 1845 to 1847?
13. three of the railroads in monopoly are the reading, the pennsylvania, and the short line. what is the fourth?
14. what was the name of king arthur's wife?
15. is the acropolis located in athens or in sparta?
16. was christopher columbus' nationality italian or spanish?
17. were the incas or the aztecs conquered by cortes in 1519?
18. who was the first roman catholic president?
19. the united states and what other country were involved in the louisiana purchase?
20. what is the last name of the artist who painted the famous portrait *whistler's mother*?

Capital Letters

Application to Writing

An important part of your editing should be rereading your written work for errors in the use of capital letters. You can always find out whether a word should or should not be capitalized by checking the dictionary.

EXERCISE 11 Editing for Capital Letters

Number your paper 1 to 50. Then write all the words in the following paragraphs that should begin with a capital letter. Do not include words that are already capitalized.

Abigail Smith Adams

Even though abigail smith and john adams were married for 54 years, they spent much of their married lives apart from each other. Letter writing became their main source of communication. Since abigail was a lively observer of people and events, her letters provide a rich account of american history. They also reveal her as an outspoken supporter of women's rights.

In 1764, abigail and john were married. They moved to a little farm in massachusetts, which john had inherited from his father. A year later word came that the english parliament had passed the stamp act, which taxed the colonies. From then on, john became involved in matters of government, leaving abigail to manage the household.

From 1774 to 1776, john was in philadelphia with the continental congress. In their letters they shared news of everyday life and the events and ideas that were shaping history. Some of abigail's letters began "dear friend." In june of 1775, she wrote of hearing cannon fire from the battle of bunker hill. In march of 1776, she heard washington's cannons before the capture of dorchester heights. She and her children watched the english fleet sail out of boston after the boston tea party.

In the winter of 1789, the first national election, provided by the constitution, was held. George washington became president, and john adams became vice-president. In 1797, john adams became the second president of the united states. He and abigail moved into the white house in 1800. They were the first presidential family to live there. Later their oldest son, john quincy adams, also became president.

CHAPTER REVIEW

A. Number your paper 1 to 20. Then write the following items, using capital letters only where needed.

1. my dad's ford sedan
2. summer on cape cod
3. genesis, a book in the old testament
4. the wall street journal
5. west on bentley highway
6. maytag washers
7. the monroe doctrine
8. an egyptian tomb
9. the justice department
10. first presbyterian church
11. the panama canal
12. fifty-sixth street
13. american history, gym, spanish, and shop II
14. ex-governor o'keefe
15. the fourth of july
16. my sister barbara
17. a democrat from delaware
18. court of appeals
19. mexican-american border
20. notre dame university

B. Number your paper 1 to 25. Then write each word that should begin with a capital letter.

1. the hawaiian islands in the pacific are actually the tops of a 1,600-mile-long range of underwater mountains.
2. tell me, mom, will grandfather willis be able to spend thanksgiving with us this year?
3. the movie *lust for life* was based on the life of the famous dutch painter vincent van gogh.
4. before she wrote her first novel, *so big*, edna ferber worked for her hometown newspaper, the *appleton daily crescent*.
5. the first of the breed of morgan horses was a stallion named justin morgan.
6. i read an article about a woman from london who made a solo trans-atlantic voyage, sailing from the canary islands to the west indies.
7. my brother carlos was just promoted to captain in the fulton police department.
8. a speech by senator payne highlighted the graduation ceremony at western institute of technology.
9. after spending our two-week vacation in the midwest, we headed east to pennsylvania.
10. although the constitution states that a senator must be at least 30 years old, 29-year-old henry clay became a member of the senate in 1806.

Capital Letters

11. during my senior year, i'm going to take english history, spanish II, english, trigonometry, chemistry, and art II.
12. the most famous geysers are in yellowstone national park, on north island in new zealand, and in iceland.
13. the planets smaller than mars are pluto and mercury.
14. who wrote the poem "when lilacs last in the dooryard bloomed"?
15. when are your aunt etta and uncle harold leaving from wichita falls to visit their relatives in canada?
16. england and france fought in the hundred years' war.
17. about 1382, the english philosopher john wycliffe and his followers translated the bible from latin into english.
18. did mayor-elect barillos give an exclusive interview to a reporter from the *washington post*?
19. is quebec the only official french-speaking province in canada?
20. shakespeare's play *romeo and juliet* is set in the italian city of verona.
21. one saturday last spring my aunt, my brother, and i went to the zoo in central park.
22. did dr. morris ship his dog west on northwest airlines?
23. on june 1, 1954, congress changed the name of armistice day to veterans day.
24. does your high school have a soccer team?
25. king john of england signed the magna charta in 1215.

C. Write sentences that include each of the following words used as a proper noun. You may use several of the words in one sentence. *Sample sentence:*
Walk down Anawan Avenue to the First Community Bank.

1. avenue
2. bank
3. battle
4. bridge
5. church
6. college
7. company
8. doctor
9. high school
10. hotel
11. lieutenant
12. mayor
13. mother
14. ocean
15. park
16. president
17. senator
18. south
19. uncle
20. war

Chapter Review

MASTERY TEST

Number your paper 1 to 10. Then write each word that should begin with a capital letter.

1. william cullen bryant was editor of the *evening post*, a new york newspaper, for almost half a century.
2. is it time, grandmother, to pick up aunt harriet at the train station?
3. the yukon river flows through the heart of alaska's interior.
4. the period from about 500 to about 1500 in europe is known as the middle ages.
5. our history teacher joined the national geographic society.
6. oklahoma, arizona, and new mexico contain nearly half of the entire indian population of the united states.
7. who was president in 1945 when the united nations held its first meeting?
8. henry wadsworth longfellow was the first american commemorated by a bust in england's westminster abbey.
9. recently my brother became an agent for the federal bureau of investigation in washington.
10. it took leo tolstoy six years to write *war and peace*, a novel that contains over 500 characters.

Chapter 11   End Marks and Commas

OBJECTIVES

- To know the four different kinds of sentences and the end mark that follows each one.
- To place a period after most abbreviations.
- To use commas to separate items in a series, some adjectives before a noun, some compound sentences, certain introductory words, dates, addresses, salutations of friendly letters, and closings of all letters.
- To use commas to enclose nouns of direct address, parenthetical expressions, appositives, titles and degrees, and nonessential participial phrases and adjective clauses.
- Application: To use end marks and commas correctly in all writing.

MOTIVATIONAL ACTIVITY

To remind your students how essential end marks and commas are, duplicate the following paragraph, which is taken from "Prelude" by Albert Halper. Then have your students try to read the paragraph. Follow this with a class discussion about the importance that end marks and commas have in clear, understandable writing.

Then the *Times* truck which was a little late roared up and dropped a load we were waiting for I cut the strings and stacked the papers and when my father came over and read the first page he suddenly looked scared in his eyes there was that hunted look I had noticed a couple of days ago . . .

TEACHING SUGGESTIONS

After reviewing comma rules, some students tend to overuse commas in their writing. As a result, you may want to remind your students never to use a comma unless they know a reason for it. You might want to tell them, "When in doubt, leave it out." Following are some common places where students tend to add unnecessary commas.

BETWEEN A SUBJECT AND A VERB Higher members of the animal kingdom/absorb oxygen through gills or lungs.
BEFORE OR AFTER A SERIES Do you want spaghetti, meat loaf, or tuna casserole/for dinner?
BETWEEN AN ADJECTIVE AND A NOUN The decorative, old-fashioned/merry-go-round was the main attraction in the park.
AFTER A CONJUNCTION The Jamestown colony was located in a mosquito-infested swamp, and/hundreds of settlers died from malaria.
BETWEEN PAIRED WORDS OR PHRASES The crew was sure that land was near because of the numerous birds/and the cold south-southwestern wind.
BETWEEN A VERB AND A NOUN CLAUSE Ralph Waldo Emerson declared/that each man is a hero to somebody.

NOTE: There are 25 answers to both the Diagnostic Test and the Mastery Test for this chapter.

Commas *(pages 252–266)*

Heath Grammar and Composition has divided comma use into two sections: the single comma to separate and the double comma to enclose. The advantage to teaching commas in these two broad categories is that students are learning two basic rules instead of learning more than a dozen separate rules.

Commas That Separate *(pages 252–260)* With your basic students, you may want to point out that there is a second test that they can use to determine whether or not a comma should be placed between two adjectives preceding a noun. They should read the sentence, reversing the order of the adjectives. If the sentence sounds natural, a comma is needed.

COMMA NEEDED Below our window was a rushing, foaming brook. [*Foaming, rushing brook* sounds natural.]
NO COMMA NEEDED Did they buy that large brick house? [*Brick large house* does not sound natural.]

Chapter 11 a

End Marks and Commas

Commas That Enclose *(pages 260–265)* With your average and advanced students, you may want to point out that occasionally an appositive will be preceded by words such as *or, particularly, noteably,* and *especially.* These appositives should be punctuated like other appositives.

The European ibex, *or wild goat,* closely resembles the American mountain goat in its preference for mountainous areas.

Many animals, *notably the squirrel,* have become well adapted to city life.

Sample Board Sentences

Commas That Separate

Tadpoles grow hind legs first, grow front legs next, and then finally lose their tails. [series]

Some cacti produce beautiful, delicate flowers. [two adjectives]

Most animals remain on land, but a few are equipped for gliding. [compound sentence]

Although Beethoven had become completely deaf, he continued to compose his sublime music. [introductory element]

Commas That Enclose

A fly's taste buds, surprisingly enough, are located in its feet. [parenthetical expression]

Francisco Coronado, a Spanish explorer, brought the first horse to America in 1540. [appositive]

Huskies, warmed by their thick coats, can sleep in the snow. [nonessential element]

ACTIVITIES FOR DIFFERENT ABILITIES

Basic Students

ACTIVITY 1 Commas with Essential and Nonessential Elements

For additional practice duplicate the following sentences. Then have your students add commas where needed.

1. In the Sahara Desert where daytime temperatures can reach 130°F one can shiver from the cold at night.
2. Do you understand the agreement that you signed with your landlord?
3. Randy Adams substituting for the regular pitcher has already struck out three batters.
4. The bird that just landed at the feeder is a red-winged blackbird.
5. The senator who gave the opening remarks was an exceptionally good speaker.
6. A stone shaft marks the site of Sutter's Mill where James Marshall first discovered gold.
7. The loaf of bread sitting on the kitchen counter is homemade.
8. We couldn't see the Statue of Liberty hidden by a dense fog.
9. Closed-circuit television which is limited to a certain audience is used in schools, colleges, and theaters.
10. Hoover Dam which holds back Lake Mead has a reservoir capacity of over 31 million acre-feet.

ACTIVITY 2 Comma Review

For additional practice duplicate the following sentences. Then have your students add commas where needed.

Chemical Personalities

1. Last year chemistry was a required course but I found that I really enjoyed it.
2. I learned that chemical elements like people have distinct personalities.
3. Helium unlike many other elements will not readily combine with other substances.
4. This gas colorless and inactive was discovered on the sun in 1868.
5. After many years of searching by many scientists helium was finally found on Earth by Sir William Ramsay.
6. On November 11 1935 a helium balloon made history by carrying

End Marks and Commas

two men 13 miles up into the stratosphere.
7. Because of its light weight and nonexplosive properties helium was an excellent gas for use in dirigibles.
8. The use of helium would have prevented the tragic explosion of the *Hindenburg* on May 6 1937.
9. Another interesting chemical personality is neon the gas of many advertising signs.
10. Neon like helium will not readily combine with other substances.
11. Platinum though not a gas also resists chemical change.
12. This substance one of our rarest metals was once discarded by gold miners.
13. The miners you see did not wash the debris from the platinum.
14. Oh by the way platinum is now very expensive.
15. It is hard strong rustproof and resistant to acids.
16. Because of its many excellent qualities it now has varied industrial uses.
17. Platinum surprisingly enough is twice as heavy as lead.
18. I find this information quite interesting not at all dull.
19. Yes I now plan to major in chemistry in college.
20. Chemistry should be a good major for there is always a demand for qualified chemists in industry.

Advanced Students
ACTIVITY 1 Comma Review
For additional practice duplicate the following sentences. Then have your students add commas where needed.

The Horseless Carriage
1. As it puffed and chugged along the streets in 1895 the first gas-engined American automobile aroused people's curiosity fear and scorn.
2. In less than 50 years however the motorcar completely changed the lives of the American people.
3. The world's first automobile built by a French army officer in 1769 traveled 2 miles per hour and stopped every 200 feet.
4. Almost 80 years later Gurney an Englishman built a steam-powered carriage which he drove for 200 miles at an average speed of 15 miles per hour.
5. Steam carriages were used in England by 1830 but most people were afraid of them.
6. The first American motor vehicle developed in 1805 by Oliver Evans in Philadelphia Pennsylvania was a combination steam wagon and flatboat.
7. Although numerous models were developed in succeeding years steam-powered automobiles were never very popular.
8. The electric-powered car a vehicle completed in 1834 by Thomas Davenport was the most popular automobile in the United States before 1900.
9. Since the batteries needed recharging every 100 miles the silent fumeless electric cars soon lost favor.
10. Using a one-cycle engine Siegfried Marcus an Austrian invented the first gas-powered automobile in 1864.
11. In 1885 while Karl Benz of Germany was building a three-wheeled carriage with a gas engine Gottlieb Daimler was constructing a two-wheeled motorcycle.
12. The first men to make automobiles commercially René Panhard and Émile Levassor of France preferred to place engines in front to avoid the carriage effect.
13. Charles and Frank Duryea who had studied Benz's design built a successful gasoline-powered American automobile in 1893 and Elwood Haynes produced one in 1894.
14. With a vehicle using a two-cylinder four-horsepower engine Henry Ford joined the ranks of automotive pioneers in 1896.

Chapter 11 c

15. In the same year in Lansing Michigan Ransom Olds who had built steam carriages perfected an automobile with a six-horsepower engine.
16. In another 30 years there were over 17 million automobiles or horseless carriages in the United States.
17. Because hand labor was expensive American automobile makers adopted the methods of using interchangeable parts that Eli Whitney had devised.
18. The early automobiles nevertheless lacked windshield wipers brake lights bumpers and other such devices.
19. When Charles Kettering perfected the electric self-starter which eliminated the difficult unpleasant task of cranking he made driving more attractive than ever before.
20. The early automobile makers predicted the acceptance of automobiles but none of them could foresee the changes that would result from quantity production.

ACTIVITY 2 Writing Sentences
Have your students write a short letter to their state senator that suggests some improvement or change they think needs to be made in their city or neighborhood. When they have finished, have them edit their letter for the correct use of commas. (Refer your students to the proper form of a letter on page 565 of Chapter 24.)

ADDITIONAL PRACTICE
Basic Students
Teacher's Resource Book: pages 165–167
Workbook: pages 123–132
Average Students
Teacher's Resource Book: pages 168–170
Workbook: pages 123–132
Advanced Students
Teacher's Resource Book: pages 171–173

REVIEW EXERCISES AND TESTS
Student Text
Diagnostic Test: page 248
Chapter Review: pages 267–268
Mastery Test: page 269
Teacher's Resource Book
Chapter 11 Test: pages 31–32
(Also available as spirit duplicating masters.)

ADDITIONAL ANSWERS
EXERCISE 2   Writing Sentences *(page 251)*

Sample answers:
1. A musical group will play at the rally. (declarative)
2. Give us the name of a good musical group. (imperative)
3. Have you ever heard a better musical group? (interrogative)
4. This musical group is unbelievably good! (exclamatory)

EXERCISE 8   Writing Sentences *(page 259)*

Sample answers:
1. Janice wobbled, swayed, and slid awkwardly over the ice.
2. The energetic, active shovelers quickly cleared the snow away.
3. The fees at the animal clinic are low, but pet owners are required to pay immediately.
4. Before Nancy applied for a job, she took an aptitude test.
5. On November 8, 1984, we moved to 19 Parkside Avenue, Waltham, MA 02154.

11

End Marks and Commas

For additional practice for this chapter, see the Teacher's Resource Book and the Workbook.

> ### DIAGNOSTIC TEST
>
> Number your paper 1 to 10. Write each sentence, adding a comma or commas where needed. Then add an appropriate end mark.
>
> EXAMPLE   Yes Mr. Rogers your order is ready
> ANSWER   Yes, Mr. Rogers, your order is ready.
>
> 1. This afternoon I attended a Student Council meeting, studied in the library, and went to basketball practice.
> 2. The students waited in a long, winding line to enter the assembly hall.
> 3. Oh, I forgot to turn off the oven!
> 4. Do you know what time the movie starts at the Plaza, the theater at the mall?
> 5. Mark Twain, who is known for his wit and humor, was born in Florida, Missouri, on November 30, 1835.
> 6. Standing on the ferry's deck, Amanda watched the impressive New York skyline.
> 7. After you typed your report, did you proofread it?
> 8. Without the slightest warning, the lightning struck the tree in our front yard.
> 9. Before the start of any long-distance race, Cheryl warms up by stretching.
> 10. During the winter, days are much shorter than in the summer.

Sentences and End Marks

11a

Timothy Dexter, an American businessman, published a collection of his philosophical essays in 1802. Being somewhat eccentric, Dexter published his book without including a single mark of punctuation. When his first edition did not sell a single copy, Dexter decided to publish a second edition. This time he included punctuation—at the back of the book in an appendix. His second edition did not sell any better than his first edition.

Timothy Dexter's philosophical essays may have been extremely profound and insightful, but no one will ever know, because they were never read. Lack of proper punctuation or misuse of punctuation often results in misunderstanding on the part of a reader. In extreme cases, such as Timothy Dexter's, it may even lead to a lack of desire to read what has been written. This chapter will review end marks and commas—marks of punctuation that are essential for clear, easy-to-understand writing.

KINDS OF SENTENCES AND END MARKS

The purpose of all sentences is to communicate. Within this broad category, however, there are four kinds of sentences—each with a particular function. A sentence can be *declarative, imperative, interrogative,* or *exclamatory*. The end mark you use is determined by the function of the particular sentence.

The first function of a sentence is to make a statement or to express an opinion. The majority of sentences fall into this category.

> **11a** A **declarative sentence** makes a statement or expresses an opinion and ends with a period.

The following examples are both declarative sentences, even though the second example contains an indirect question.

In China bicycles are a common means of transportation.

I don't know what time the play starts. [The direct question would be, *What time does the play start?*]

The second function of a sentence is to give directions, make requests, or give commands. Generally *you* is the understood subject of these sentences.

249

End Marks and Commas

11b > An **imperative sentence** gives a direction, makes a request, or gives a command. It ends with either a period or an exclamation point.

If a command is said in a normal voice, it is followed by a period when written. If it expresses strong feeling, it is followed by an exclamation point.

> Meet me in the library. [normal voice]
> Don't touch the poison ivy! [emotional voice]

Occasionally an imperative sentence is stated as a question, but no reply is expected. Since the purpose of the sentence remains the same—to make a request—the sentence is followed by a period or an exclamation point.

> Will you turn the heat down before you go to bed.

The third function of a sentence is to ask a question—whether it is completely or incompletely expressed.

11c > An **interrogative sentence** asks a question and ends with a question mark.

> Do wild cattle still exist in some parts of the world?
> What? I couldn't hear you.

The fourth function of a sentence is to express strong feeling, such as excitement or anger. Avoid overusing this type of sentence, for it can very quickly lose its impact.

11d > An **exclamatory sentence** expresses strong feeling or emotion and ends with an exclamation point.

> You look wonderful!
> I've never been so scared in all my life!
> We're thrilled you will be there!

NOTE: Remember that an interjection can also be followed by an exclamation point. *(See page 21.)*

> No! Visitors are not allowed after nine o'clock.
> Yes! I would love to go.

Periods with Abbreviations

11b–e

EXERCISE 1 Classifying Sentences

Number your paper 1 to 10. Write an appropriate end mark for each sentence. Then label each one *declarative*, *imperative*, *interrogative*, or *exclamatory*.

D 1. In area Los Angeles is more than a third the size of Rhode Island.
IM 2. By Friday read the next two chapters in your textbook.
D 3. Mr. Kent asked Kate whether she had taken her SAT's.
IM 4. Turn down your radio! /.
IN 5. Did Toby drive you to school today?
E/D 6. We're going to miss the bus! /.
IN 7. Do you think the game will be delayed because of the storm?
IM 8. May I please have your attention. /!
E/D 9. There's smoke coming from the kitchen! /.
D 10. I don't know what he sent you for your birthday.

EXERCISE 2 Writing Sentences

Choose one of the following topics. Then write a declarative sentence, an imperative sentence, an interrogative sentence, and an exclamatory sentence about that topic. Label each sentence.

Sample answer for item 1 precedes this chapter.

1. a musical group   2. automobiles   3. a recent movie
4. television news shows   5. future space exploration

Periods with Abbreviations

Abbreviations can be very handy shortcuts when you are writing quickly. They save time when you are taking notes from reference books or on class lectures. Most abbreviations, however, should be avoided in formal writing.

11e Use a period after most abbreviations.

The following list contains some abbreviations that are acceptable in formal writing. Use the dictionary to find the spelling and the punctuation of other abbreviations.

TITLES WITH NAMES	Mr.	Ms.	Mrs.	Sgt.	Capt.	Lt.
	Gen.	Jr.	Sr.	Rev.	Dr.	Hon.
TIMES WITH NUMBERS	A.M.	P.M.	B.C.	A.D.		

251

End Marks and Commas

I am proud to introduce Dr. James T. Malone, Jr.

By about 2700 B.C., a strong and fairly centralized government had developed in Egypt.

If a statement ends with an abbreviation, only one period is needed at the end of the sentence. If an interrogative or an exclamatory sentence ends with an abbreviation, both a period and a question mark or a period and an exclamation point are needed.

Your bus leaves at 6:45 P.M.
Does your bus leave at 6:45 P.M.?

NOTE: Following are examples of a few abbreviations that should be written without periods. The state abbreviations used by the United States Post Office do not include periods.

CBS   FBI   FCC   TV   FM   PA   mph   km

EXERCISE 3   Writing Abbreviations

Write the abbreviations that stand for the following items. Be sure to include periods where needed. If you are unsure of the spelling or the punctuation of a particular abbreviation, look it up in the dictionary.

ft.   1. foot
St.   2. Street
oz.   3. ounce
Feb. 4. February
vol. 5. volume

NM   6. New Mexico
Maj. 7. Major
m   8. meter
F   9. Fahrenheit
UN   10. United Nations

COMMAS

As you review the specific rules for commas in this section, keep in mind that commas have basically only two purposes. They are used either to separate items or to enclose them.

Commas That Separate

Commas are needed to separate similar items that come together in a sentence. Without commas, a reader would not know where one item stopped and another item began. By clarifying your meaning with commas, you will ensure the

Commas That Separate

11f

reader's understanding. Following are some specific situations in which commas should be used to separate items.

Items in a Series. A series is three or more similar items listed in consecutive order. Words, phrases, or clauses can be written as a series.

> **11f** Use commas to separate items in a series.

WORDS Lemons, limes, and oranges are grown in California. [nouns]
Every Saturday morning I jog one mile, eat breakfast, and leave the house by eight. [verbs]

PHRASES My biology book must be in the cafeteria, in my locker, or in Dad's car.

CLAUSES Did he say when we should arrive, what we should bring, and who will be there?

When a conjunction connects the last two items in a series, a comma is optional. It is always better, however, to include the comma before the conjunction.

CONFUSING We served string beans, carrots and peas. [Were the carrots and peas served separately or mixed together?]

CLEAR We served string beans, carrots, and peas.

If conjunctions connect all the items in a series, no commas are needed.

> Every one of the volunteers worked quickly **and** efficiently **and** quietly.

NOTE: Some expressions, such as *franks and beans,* are thought of as a single item. If one of these pairs of words appears in a series, it should be considered one item.

> We were offered several kinds of sandwiches: ham and cheese, peanut butter and jelly, and tuna salad.

Adjectives before a Noun. A conjunction sometimes connects two adjectives before a noun. When the conjunction is omitted, a comma is sometimes used instead.

> We heard loud, strange sounds coming from the cellar.

End Marks and Commas

11g > Use a comma sometimes to separate two adjectives that directly precede a noun and that are not joined by a conjunction.

To help you decide whether a comma should be placed between two adjectives, you can use the following test. Read the sentence with *and* between the adjectives. If the sentence sounds natural, a comma is needed.

COMMA NEEDED   The dark, foggy night made driving difficult. [*Dark and foggy night* sounds natural.]

COMMA NOT NEEDED   The dark winter night made driving difficult. [*Dark and winter night* does not sound natural.]

COMMA NEEDED   That large, colorful hat is mine. [*Large and colorful hat* sounds natural.]

COMMA NOT NEEDED   That large Mexican hat is mine. [*Large and Mexican hat* does not sound natural.]

EXERCISE 4   **Using Commas to Separate**

Number your paper 1 to 20. Then write each series or each pair of adjectives, adding a comma or commas where needed. If a sentence does not need any commas, write *C* after the number.

EXAMPLE   I fed the dog made dinner and did my homework.
ANSWER   fed the dog, made dinner, and did my homework

1. The snow clogged the streets, paralyzed the traffic, and closed the airport.
2. The ear is one of the most intricate, complicated organs in the human body.
3. Pipelines have stretched through deserts, over mountains, under rivers, and through gorges.
c 4. Bears and woodchucks and prairie dogs sleep for months at a time when the weather is cold.
5. The hungry, tired hikers returned to camp at six o'clock.
6. Please tell me where I should go, whom I should see, and what message I should give.
7. The three main parts of the human circulatory system are the heart, the blood vessels, and the blood.
c 8. I like to go swimming on warm summer days.
9. The bicycle is a popular means of transportation in the Orient, in parts of Africa, and in the Near East.

Commas That Separate

11g–h

c 10. I painted a picture of the tall birch trees in Victoria Park.
11. A garnet is a hard, brittle gemstone.
c 12. You could paint your room off-white or yellow or green.
13. The specials on the menu were chicken and dumplings, turkey and stuffing, and meatloaf.
14. Large, flat riverboats carry cargo down the Mississippi to New Orleans.
15. I haven't decided if I should be a camp counselor, if I should work at the supermarket, or if I should take a Spanish course in summer school.
16. The large, stately building on Temple Street is being converted to a mall.
17. We drove to Yellowstone National Park, set up camp, and made day trips from there.
18. Philadelphia is an old, historic city in Pennsylvania.
19. Salt is used in manufacturing glass, soap, and washing compounds.
c 20. Did anyone find my blue wool sweater?

Compound Sentences. Placing a comma before a coordinating conjunction is one way to separate the independent clauses of a compound sentence. *And, but, or, nor, for,* and *yet* are all coordinating conjunctions. *(A semicolon can also be used between independent clauses. See pages 276–278.)*

> **11h** Use a comma to separate the independent clauses of a compound sentence if the clauses are joined by a conjunction.

Your dinner was delicious, but I can't eat another bite.
My birthday is in June, and my sister Kim's is in July.

No comma is needed in a very short compound sentence—unless the conjunction *yet* or *for* separates the independent clauses.

NO COMMA   I was sleeping but the phone awoke me.
COMMA   I understand, for I was frightened also.

NOTE: Do not confuse a sentence that has one subject and a compound verb with a compound sentence that has two sets of subjects and verbs. A comma is not placed between the parts of a compound verb.

255

End Marks and Commas

  COMPOUND SENTENCE I swam several laps in the pool**,** and Hank practiced his diving. [comma needed]

  COMPOUND VERB I swam several laps in the pool and practiced my diving. [comma not needed]

EXERCISE 5 Using Commas with Compound Sentences
Number your paper 1 to 10. Then write each sentence, adding a comma where needed. If a sentence does not need a comma, write *C* after the number.

1. These old photographs have faded**,** but the people in them are still recognizable.
c 2. During the 1840s, as many as 700 whaling ships would leave New England in a single year and stay away 4 or 5 years.
3. The price is right**,** yet I'm still uncertain.
4. The first basket used in basketball was a close-bottomed peach basket**,** and a ladder was used to retrieve the ball.
5. Rain may not fall for several years in parts of Africa**,** but certain plants are able to survive.
c 6. You were early and I was late.
c 7. King Arthur formed the Knights of the Round Table and served as their leader.
8. The girls' softball team practiced on Saturday**,** for the championship game was on Monday.
9. Ernest Hemingway's prose is precise and vivid**,** and his style has been imitated by a number of other writers.
10. The jigsaw can cut curves in wood**,** but the hacksaw is used exclusively for metal and other hard materials.

Introductory Elements. Certain introductory words, phrases, and clauses are separated from the rest of the sentence by a comma.

> **11i** Use a comma after certain introductory elements.

Following are examples of the introductory elements that should be followed by a comma.

  WORD **Now,** aren't you proud of yourself? [*No, oh, well, why,* and *yes* are other introductory

Commas That Separate

11i

words—unless they are part of the sentence: *Now is the time to act.*]

PREPOSITIONAL PHRASE **From the high mountaintop,** we could see the entire valley below us. [A comma comes after a prepositional phrase of four or more words. Do *not* place a comma after an introductory phrase that is followed by a verb: *Among the football players sat a young boy.*]

PARTICIPIAL PHRASE **Tipping his hat,** the gentleman greeted his friends.

ADVERB CLAUSE **When we get home,** let's go for a swim.

OTHERS **Besides Mary,** Lou is a good friend of mine.
In 1985, 120 acres of forest land were sold. [Commas are used in these sentences to prevent confusion.]

EXERCISE 6 Using Commas with Introductory Elements

Number your paper 1 to 20. Then write the introductory elements, adding a comma after each one. If a sentence does not need a comma, write *C* after the number.

1. Because my bicycle tire was flat this morning, I had to walk to school.
2. No, I didn't realize that the author George Eliot was a woman.
3. After baking, apples should be allowed to cool.
4. Although many states have an official flower, the United States does not have a national flower.
c 5. Around the huge indoor track raced the cyclists.
6. Unable to get his locker open, Roger went to the office.
c 7. From the balcony I could hear the actors quite well.
8. In June, January issues of some magazines are already being planned.
9. After a long drought, the prairie soaked up the welcome downpour.
10. Seeking a short way to India in order to import spices, Columbus made his first journey to America.
11. If you disregard the sun, the nearest star to the earth is more than four light-years away.

257

End Marks and Commas

12. Having paced herself carefully during the first part of the mile run, Alex made a strong finish.
c 13. From the barn came the loud hoot of an owl.
14. Well, you should do what you think is right.
15. After pruning, the shrubs look more attractive.
16. From now until next month, I will be working at Gary's Garage on the weekends.
17. Shining brightly above the horizon near sunrise or sunset, Venus is sometimes mistaken for a beacon.
c 18. By early tomorrow we will know the results of the tests.
19. In less than a week, I was creating my own programs on the school's new computer.
20. When a team wins four games in the World Series, it wins the world championship.

Commonly Used Commas. Probably a day does not go by in which you do not use commas in a date, in an address, or in a letter.

> **11j** Use commas to separate the elements in dates and addresses.

Notice in the following examples that a comma is used to separate the last item in a date or the last item in an address from the rest of the sentence.

> On Saturday, June 16, 1984, my older brother graduated from high school.

> Write to Hanson Studios, 400 Wellwyn Highway, Portland, Connecticut 06480, for free samples. [*No* comma is placed between the state and the ZIP code.]

NOTE: No commas are used when just the month and the year are given.

> Hawaii became a state in June 1959.

> **11k** Use a comma after the salutation of a friendly letter and after the closing of all letters.

SALUTATIONS	Dear Aunt Ruth,	Dear Cathy,
CLOSINGS	Sincerely yours,	Love,
	Yours truly,	Sincerely,

258

Commas That Separate

11j–k

EXERCISE 7 Using Commas Correctly

Number your paper 1 to 10. Then write each sentence, adding commas where needed.

1. On February 1, 1958, the nation's first satellite was launched from Cape Canaveral, Florida.
2. Write to the Office of Admissions, Heidelberg College, Tiffin, Ohio 44883, for a catalog.
3. When the horse stopped, Marty almost fell off.
4. At the last minute, he saw the tanker in the fog, turned the wheel sharply, and threw the engines into reverse.
5. On Thursday, August 14, 1986, I sent a check to Service Merchandise, P.O. Box 25130, Nashville, Tennessee 37202.
6. Leaping from the top shelf, the cat landed on the armchair.
7. On January 3, 1959, Alaska became the 49th state.
8. Between 1200 B.C. and 400 B.C., the Phoenicians established colonies on the Atlantic coast of Spain and Africa.
9. In Philadelphia, Pennsylvania, on January 1, 1976, the Liberty Bell was moved from Independence Hall to Liberty Bell Pavillion.
10. Melinda's sneakers, old and tattered, look comfortable.

EXERCISE 8 Writing Sentences

Write sentences that follow the directions below. Use commas where needed.
Sample answers precede this chapter.

1. Include a series of verbs that describe the actions of someone learning to skate.
2. Include before a noun two adjectives that are separated by a comma.
3. Include two independent clauses that are joined by the conjunction *but*.
4. Include an adverb clause at the beginning of a sentence.
5. Include today's date and your address.

EXERCISE 9 Time-out for Review

Write the following paragraphs, adding commas where needed. There are 20 commas.

A Person of Many Talents

   Benjamin Franklin was born on January 17, 1706, in Boston, Massachusetts. He was the 15th child and youngest son of a soap and candle maker. His formal schooling ended after two

259

End Marks and Commas

years, and the young Franklin was apprenticed to an older brother in his printing shop. Working long, hard hours, young Franklin still managed to educate himself. He taught himself grammar, algebra, geometry, navigation, and philosophy.

After a disagreement with his brother, Franklin moved to Philadelphia. Within a few years, he became a famous author and publisher, and throughout the following years, he became much more. He also established a reputation as a scientist, a statesman, an inventor, a businessman, a philosopher, an artist, and a humanitarian.

Commas That Enclose

Some sentences contain interrupting expressions. These expressions interrupt the flow of a sentence because they generally add information that is not needed to understand the main idea of a sentence. If one of these interrupting expressions comes in the middle of a sentence, two commas are needed to enclose the expression—to set it off from the rest of the sentence. If an interrupting expression comes at the beginning or at the end of a sentence, only one comma is needed.

Direct Address. Any name, title, or other word that is used to address someone directly is set off by commas. These interrupting expressions are called nouns of *direct address*.

> **11l** Use commas to enclose nouns of direct address.

> **Lance,** please answer the telephone.
> I understand**, Bart,** how much you want a car.
> Where are you going**, Meredith?**

Parenthetical Expressions. These expressions act as transitions or comments on the main idea of the sentence. When speaking, you naturally pause slightly—before and after a parenthetical expression.

> **11m** Use commas to enclose parenthetical expressions.

Following is a list of common parenthetical expressions.

Commas That Enclose

11l–n

Common Parenthetical Expressions		
after all	however	nevertheless
at any rate	I believe (guess,	of course
by the way	hope, know, think)	on the contrary
consequently	in fact	on the other hand
for example	in my opinion	therefore
for instance	moreover	to tell the truth

On the other hand, I like the arrangement of the song.
The class trip**, by the way,** was very enjoyable.
We were able to talk for a few minutes**, after all.**

NOTE: The parenthetical expressions listed in the box are set off by commas only when they interrupt a sentence.

COMMAS   The movie**, to tell the truth,** was rather boring.
NO COMMAS   It is always important **to tell the truth.**

Contrasting expressions, which usually begin with *not*, are also considered parenthetical expressions.

It is the high humidity**, not the high temperature,** that makes me uncomfortable.

Appositives. An appositive with its modifiers renames, identifies, or explains a noun or a pronoun in the sentence. *(See pages 56–57.)*

11n   Use commas to enclose most appositives and their modifiers.

Their car**, that old red convertible,** needs a new muffler.
I want a cat**, an orange-striped one like Morris.**

An appositive is *not* set off by commas if it identifies a person or a thing by telling which one or ones. Usually these appositives are names and have no modifiers.

My father was born in the year **1940.** [Which year?]
The book ***Moby Dick*** was made into a movie. [Which book?]

Adjectives, titles, and degrees in the appositive position are also set off by commas.

261

End Marks and Commas

    ADJECTIVES   Nylon**, strong and elastic,** is used for making parachutes.
    TITLES   Stephen R. Malory**, Sr.,** is my uncle.
    DEGREES   Gretchen Winters**, D.D.S.,** is president of the Cleveland Dental Association.

EXERCISE 10   Using Commas with Interrupters

Number your paper 1 to 10. Then write each sentence, adding commas where needed. If a sentence does not need any commas, write *C* after the number.

1. Alaskan brown bears, the longest of all bears, may grow to a length of nine feet.
2. The Dodo bird, clumsy and short-legged, had become extinct by the end of the seventeenth century.
3. Beth and her cousin Sue look as if they could be sisters. *(c)*
4. Tell me, Donald, how did you like the exhibit?
5. Helium, however, is not changed by heat.
6. Wolfgang Amadeus Mozart, famous all over Europe for his wonderful music, was buried in a pauper's cemetery.
7. I believe that Halley's Comet made its first recorded appearance in 240 B.C. *(c)*
8. The Amazon, not the Nile, is the largest river in the world.
9. By the way, Alan, are you going to the dance?
10. Most of Iceland's rivers, in fact, cannot be navigated.

Nonessential Elements. Like the other interrupters you have just reviewed, some participial phrases and clauses are not needed to make the meaning of a sentence clear or complete.

11o   Use commas to set off a nonessential participial phrase or a nonessential clause.

A participial phrase or a clause is nonessential only if it supplies extra, unnecessary information. To decide whether a phrase or a clause is nonessential, read the sentence without it. If the phrase or the clause could be removed without changing the basic meaning of the sentence, it is nonessential. A phrase or a clause that modifies a proper noun is almost always nonessential.

Commas That Enclose

11o

NONESSENTIAL PARTICIPIAL PHRASE	The Panama Canal**, completed in 1914,** is used by more than 12,000 ships a year. *[The Panama Canal is used by more than 12,000 ships a year.]*
NONESSENTIAL ADJECTIVE CLAUSE	Rhode Island**, which became the 13th state in 1790,** is the smallest state in the United States. *[Rhode Island is the smallest state in the United States.]*

An essential phrase or clause identifies a person or thing by answering the question *Which one?* Since an essential phrase or clause cannot be removed from a sentence, no commas are used. If the phrase or the clause was removed, the meaning of the sentence would be unclear or incomplete. An adjective clause that begins with *that* is always essential.

ESSENTIAL PARTICIPIAL PHRASE	The book **lying on the kitchen table** belongs to Sandy. *[The book belongs to Sandy.* The phrase is needed to identify which book.]
ESSENTIAL ADJECTIVE CLAUSE	The position **that you wanted** is already filled. *[The position is already filled.* The clause is needed to identify which position.]

NOTE: Nonessential and essential elements are also called *nonrestrictive* and *restrictive*.

EXERCISE 11 Using Commas with Nonessential Elements

Number your paper 1 to 20. Then write each sentence, adding a comma or commas where needed. If a sentence does not need any commas, write *C* after the number.

c 1. All runners who come in first or second in the trials will qualify for the finals.
2. Neon lights invented by Georges Claude in 1910 can produce different colors by using different gases.
3. The Pyramid of the Sun located near Mexico City has a larger base than that of the biggest pyramid in Egypt.
4. Carrots contain large amounts of vitamin A which is essential to good vision.
c 5. The left bank of a river is the bank that is to the left of a person looking downstream.
c 6. The town in which my mother was born is quite rural.

End Marks and Commas

c 7. The world history class that used to be taught by Mr. Brown will be taught by Ms. Volkman next year.
8. Raymond, who works after school at Rollins Press, is going to have the tickets printed for the spring concert.
9. The Taj Mahal, which is in India, is considered by many to be the most beautiful memorial in the world.
c 10. The car that you just bought is being recalled.
11. A centimeter, which is a unit of length in the metric system, is equal to approximately 0.39 inches.
c 12. The car parked in the driveway is my uncle's.
13. The stratosphere, which begins about 6 to 10 miles above the earth, often has an approximate temperature of −60°F.
c 14. A jogger burning off about 100 calories per mile would have to jog a mile a day for a year to shed 10 pounds.
c 15. The first woman who swam 100 yards in one minute flat was Helene Madison.
c 16. Please defrost the hamburger meat wrapped in foil.
17. The game of quoits, which was played many centuries ago, was the forerunner of horseshoes.
c 18. The sweater that you wanted is on sale at Harlow's.
19. The oldest unchanged national flag in existence is the flag of Denmark, dating back to the thirteenth century.
c 20. *Seven seas* is a figurative term that means "all the waters of the earth."

EXERCISE 12 Using Commas Correctly

Number your paper 1 to 10. Then write each sentence, adding a comma or commas where needed. If a sentence does not need any commas, write *C* after the number.

1. Walt Whitman, who grew up and was educated in Brooklyn, New York, is the author of *Leaves of Grass*.
2. The letters H, I, N, O, S, X, and Z are exactly the same upside down.
3. The Westport Action Committee, formed over a year ago, is responsible for many community improvements.
4. Without the help of Mrs. Reeve, our faculty adviser, we would not have had a class play.
c 5. The track meet that was scheduled for this afternoon has been canceled due to inclement weather.
6. The warbler darted, fluttered, and swooped through the branches of the plum tree.

Commas That Enclose

C 7. I just joined the YWCA that is located on High Street.
C 8. The movie *The Wizard of Oz* was recently shown on TV.
9. In the northern part of Sweden, for example, the sun shines 24 hours a day during part of the summer.
10. Starting in September, the Channel Eight local news, which comes on at six o'clock, will be an hour long.

EXERCISE 13 Using Commas Correctly
Write each sentence, adding a comma or commas where needed.

Hot Dogs
1. The hot dog is a medieval invention, but it has become a popular American food.
2. During the early nineteenth century, German immigrants brought the hot dog to the United States.
3. Hot dogs were first sold on Coney Island, New York, during the late nineteenth century.
4. Called dachshund sausages, they were sold without buns.
5. A vendor would hand a hot dog to a buyer, who would then hold it in his or her fingers.
6. Some vendors supplied customers with gloves for keeping their fingers clean, but this method proved to be too expensive for the vendors.
7. When buns were introduced at the 1904 St. Louis World's Fair, this problem was solved.
8. The term *hot dog*, however, was not coined at the Fair.
9. T. A. Dorgan, a sports cartoonist, went to a baseball game in New York to make some sketches of the game.
10. Because Dorgan couldn't spell *dachshund*, he used the label "Hot Dog" in his drawings. The name stuck.

EXERCISE 14 Time-out for Review
Number your paper 1 to 10. Then write each sentence, adding a comma or commas where needed. If a sentence does not need any commas, write *C* after the number.

Facts and Figures
1. Hares are often confused with rabbits, but hares usually have longer legs and longer ears.
C 2. The stripes that appear on the United States flag stand for the 13 colonies.
3. On January 6, 1912, New Mexico, the 47th state, entered the union.

265

End Marks and Commas

4. Indian paths, buffalo trails, and canoe routes served as roads for the first explorers who traveled in Oklahoma.
5. The New York Public Library, containing over nine million volumes, is one of the largest public libraries in the world.
6. Because the orangutan is awkward on the ground, it often travels through the forest by swinging from tree to tree.
7. Black holes in space, mysterious and awe-inspiring, may be the remains of collapsed stars.
8. Electro, a mechanical man, was exhibited in 1939 at the New York World's Fair.
9. Through his telescope Galileo discovered that the moon has both mountains and deep valleys.
10. When warm, moist air touches the surface of cool objects, the water vapor condenses into small drops of water or dewdrops.

Application to Writing

One step of your editing process should be to look for misused or missing commas.

EXERCISE 15 Editing for Commas
Write the following paragraphs, adding commas where needed. There are 25 commas.

Her Place in History

On May 14, 1804, about 40 men and a dog set out from St. Louis, Missouri, to explore the northwestern part of what is now the United States. The leaders of the expedition, Meriwether Lewis and William Clark, had been commissioned by President Thomas Jefferson. Over two years later, they brought back much information about the Louisiana Territory, which Jefferson had just purchased from France. On their long, dangerous trip, however, they received enormous help from Sacajawea, a young Indian woman.

As the expedition journeyed west, it was Sacajawea who was principal guide, who acted as interpreter, and who found food in the wilderness. Moreover, her presence with the expedition was a sign of peace to various Indian groups.

One of the strangest parts of the trip sounds like a made-up story. One day the explorers, wondering what to expect, approached a strange Indian tribe. Before anything happened, Sacajawea spotted the chief and recognized him as her long-lost brother. This was her own tribe, from which she had been captured many years before. Sacajawea's brother, according to Lewis' and Clark's journals, provided the expedition with horses, supplies, and important information that made it possible for the expedition to continue its search for the Pacific.

The success of Lewis and Clark opened the way for new exploration, but no one knows how successful they would have been if Sacajawea had not been along. Today some historians number Sacajawea among America's most important women.

CHAPTER REVIEW

A. Number your paper 1 to 10. Write an appropriate end mark for each sentence. Then label each one *declarative*, *imperative*, *interrogative*, or *exclamatory*.

- D 1. Corn is one of the largest farm crops in the United States.
- IN 2. Is the opossum related to the kangaroo?
- IM 3. Follow these directions carefully.
- D 4. I asked whether he had swum in the Great Salt Lake.
- D 5. I don't care for kumquats.
- E 6. We just won the championship game!
- IN 7. Why didn't you take that job?
- IM 8. Don't skate on that thin ice!
- E 9. That's the best news I've heard all week!
- IM 10. Will you turn off the lights when you're finished.

B. Number your paper 1 to 25. Then write each sentence, adding a comma or commas where needed. If a sentence does not need any commas, write *C* after the number.

1. From the bark of the birch tree, the Indians were building a watertight, portable boat.
2. Ernest Hemingway grew up in Oak Park, Illinois, but spent his summers in Michigan.
- C 3. The train arriving at 6:42 P.M. is from Chicago.

267

End Marks and Commas

4. By midnight the heavy, dense fog had descended on the highway, and traffic ground to a halt.
5. When Alexander Calder's huge mobiles are pushed by air currents, the delicately balanced sculptures move.
6. During Admiral Byrd's first expedition to the South Pole, he had to become accustomed to the long Antarctic nights.
c 7. A *palindrome* is a word or a sentence that reads the same backward as it does forward.
8. Three weeks before, Lola had applied for a summer job.
9. Paderewski, one of the greatest concert pianists of all time, was also a premier of Poland.
10. On September 21, 1784, the first daily newspaper in the United States was published in Philadelphia, Pennsylvania.
11. Well, have you decided what you're going to do?
12. Playing the part of Harry in the musical, Marvin Dawson is hilarious.
13. *A Tale of Two Cities*, which is set in Paris, France, is a historical novel.
14. The Milky Way, which appears in the sky as a hazy band, really contains millions of huge stars.
15. Florida's state bird is the mockingbird, and Maine's is the chickadee.
16. On the evening of October 22, 675 people attended the band concert in the auditorium.
c 17. To the bottom of the lake sank Jan's fishing pole.
18. Lake Superior, the largest body of fresh water in the world is also the deepest, the most northern, and the highest above sea level of the Great Lakes.
c 19. The rain stopped and we went out.
20. After I opened my savings account, I enjoyed watching the interest accumulate.
21. Tomorrow, by the way, is Uncle Fred's birthday.
22. The ocean waves, high and thunderous, smashed against the creaky, weather-beaten pier.
23. Steam, not gasoline, powered the first self-propelled road vehicles.
24. Before we leave, we must make a lunch, find our bathing suits, and pack the car.
25. We signed up for the course last month, but our names are still on the waiting list.

Chapter Review

MASTERY TEST

Number your paper 1 to 10. Write each sentence, adding a comma or commas where needed. Then add an appropriate end mark.

1. Before eating, the dog lapped up the bowl of water.
2. With only 20 seconds until the end of the game, Willie scored the winning basket!
3. Have you met Jamie Thorn, the new student from Evanston, Illinois?
4. The skunk is usually a quiet, well-behaved animal.
5. The mountain trail, steep and narrow, was a challenge for all climbers.
6. Carla Anderson, who has a scholastic average of 95, is eligible for the National Honor Society.
7. Next year I want to take trigonometry, not calculus.
8. Today's temperature, rising to 104 degrees, broke all previous records!
9. On February 27, 1807, Henry Wadsworth Longfellow was born in Maine.
10. When you parked the car, did you lock the doors?

Chapter 12   Other Punctuation

OBJECTIVES

- To use apostrophes correctly to form the possessive of nouns and indefinite pronouns.
- To use apostrophes correctly with contractions.
- To use apostrophes correctly to show joint and separate ownership.
- To use apostrophes correctly to form the plural of numbers, letters, symbols, and words that are used to represent themselves.
- To use semicolons correctly between the clauses of a compound sentence that are not joined by a conjunction, and between clauses that are joined by certain transitional words.
- To use semicolons correctly in sentences in which additional commas would be confusing.
- To use a colon correctly before a list of items and in certain special situations.
- To use underlining and quotation marks correctly with titles.
- To punctuate and capitalize direct quotations correctly.
- To use hyphens correctly when writing certain numbers and fractions, and to separate the parts of some compound nouns and adjectives.
- To use hyphens correctly with certain prefixes and the suffix *elect*.
- To use hyphens correctly to divide a word at the end of the line.
- To use dashes, parentheses, and brackets correctly to set off certain expressions.
- Application: To use all marks of punctuation correctly to ensure clarity and understanding in writing.

MOTIVATIONAL ACTIVITY

Since punctuating direct quotations is probably a weak area for your students, you may want to begin this chapter by having your students play the Name Game. Have them write quotations in which some word relates to the speaker's name. On the board give them the following examples before they begin.

"Everyone got more than I did," said Les.
"Do you want me to make the hamburgers?" asked Patty?
"I carry a spear in the school play," said Lance.

Have your students write as many quotations as they can, carefully following the punctuation and capitalization in the previous examples. Then have your students read some of their answers aloud. This simple, fun exercise should remind your students of the basic rules for punctuating and capitalizing direct quotations.

TEACHING SUGGESTIONS

NOTE: There are 30 answers to both the Diagnostic Test and Mastery Test for this chapter, if beginning and end quotation marks are counted separately.

Apostrophes *(pages 271–276)*

Because various standardized tests indicate that students generally have trouble with apostrophes, you may want to spend some extra time on this section. A major problem that students have is confusing the singular form of a possessive noun with the plural of the same noun. You may want to remind your students that an *of* phrase can be substituted for a possessive: the boys' locker room—the locker room *of the boys*. To check whether your students understand the difference between the two forms, have them write sentences that use the following words.

1. dogs, dog's
2. teachers, teacher's
3. computers, computer's
4. cars, car's
5. senators, senator's

With your basic students, you may want to omit the sections "Apostrophes to Show Joint and Separate Ownership" on pages 274–275 and "Apostrophes to Form Certain Plurals" on page 275.

Chapter 12 a

Other Punctuation

Semicolons and Colons *(pages 276–282)*

If your students know how to use a semicolon correctly, they will be able to eliminate a percentage of run-on sentences in their writing. Remind your students, however, that only closely related sentences should be joined by a semicolon. If there is ever any doubt, they should write two separate sentences.

You may want to review independent clauses and compound sentences, on pages 77 and 89, respectively before you begin this section. You may also want to put on the board some examples of compound sentences, and simple sentences with a compound verb. Placing a semicolon between the parts of a compound verb in a simple sentence is a common mistake that students make.

Exercise 8 on pages 279–280 asks students to supply both semicolons and commas. Learning to use a semicolon before a transitional word in a compound sentence is somewhat meaningless if students do not remember to add the comma as well.

With your basic students, you may want to omit the section "Semicolons to Avoid Confusion" on page 278.

Quotation Marks *(pages 284–293)*

You may want to try to teach punctuating and capitalizing direct quotations from a logical, common-sense approach, rather than from a formal rule approach. Write several quotations on the board. First ask your students where the quotation marks go. Then ask if the quotation begins a sentence. If it does, it must begin with a capital letter. Then ask them where any pauses occur. As in a regular sentence, a comma usually comes at a pause. Finally, look at the end of the sentence. Like a regular sentence, a quotation must end with an end mark. If your students can logically think through the punctuation of the basic sentence pattern of a direct quotation, the other rules should make more sense.

With your basic students, you may want to omit the section "Quotations within Quotations" on page 292. A reasonable goal for basic students would be the correct punctuation of a direct quotation.

Other Marks of Punctuation *(pages 293–298)*

The main section to emphasize with all classes is hyphens. Dashes, parentheses, and brackets could be omitted with your basic students.

Hyphens *(pages 293–295)* You may want to tell your students that most fractions are used as nouns; therefore, a hyphen is seldom used when writing a fraction.

As your students edit their written work, encourage them to check the spelling of compound nouns and compound adjectives in the dictionary. There is no sure way to know whether a compound noun, for example, is hyphenated or not.

Remind your students that whenever possible, they should avoid dividing a word at the end of a line. Hyphenated words—particularly words that are hyphenated incorrectly—slow a reader down and can create confusion or misunderstanding.

Dashes, Parentheses, and Brackets *(pages 296–298)* As you go over this section, warn your students against excessive use of these marks. These marks can play a useful role, as the text points out, but they can also be used as a stopgap when a student is not quite sure what mark to use.

Sample Board Sentences

Cells in the earthworm's skin are sensitive to sound. [apostrophe]

The whale's strange behavior could not be explained. [apostrophe]

Type O is the most common blood type; type AB is the rarest. [semicolon]

George Washington chose the site of the White House; however, he never lived there. [semicolon]

The ocean floor is divided into three main regions: the continental shelf, the slope, and the abyss. [colon]

Some reptiles—for example, the common toad, the alligator, and the

Chapter 12 b

Other Punctuation

mud turtle—may live 25 years or more. [dashes]

ACTIVITIES FOR DIFFERENT ABILITIES

Basic Students

ACTIVITY 1 The Possessive Form of Nouns

To provide additional practice, duplicate the following sentences. Then have your students correctly write each word that should show possession.

1. Has anyone seen Dicks saxophone?
2. My grandparents farm is about 20 miles outside of town.
3. The teams picture is in todays newspaper.
4. The coyotes howls could be heard for miles.
5. There will be a three weeks delay in the broadcast of the TV special.
6. The televisions report of the accident was very different from the newspapers version.
7. After several moments pause, I resumed my climb up the cliffs steep side.
8. The mud in beavers dams is held together by leaves, roots, and tough grasses.
9. In most tennis tournaments, the womens playoffs are held before the mens.
10. Every year the members of the Drama Club put on a hilarious skit, in which the boys play girls parts and the girls play boys parts.

ACTIVITY 2 Punctuating and Capitalizing Direct Quotations

To provide additional practice, duplicate the following quotations. Then have your students add capital letters, quotation marks, and other punctuation marks where needed.

Fish

1. all fish have certain characteristics in common Mrs. Adams told the class
2. she continued all fish have backbones and are cold-blooded
3. in addition she went on most fish breathe through gills
4. how do the gills work Allen asked
5. that's an excellent question Mrs. Adams exclaimed
6. answering Allen's question she said gills take up oxygen that is dissolved in water
7. Penny asked do fish actually swallow water
8. you're right Mrs. Adams explained as a fish opens its mouth, water passes into its mouth and over the gills
9. in the gills molecules of oxygen diffuse from the water into the blood she said
10. Mrs. Adams continued at the same time carbon dioxide passes out of the blood into the water

Advanced Students

ACTIVITY 1 Writing Compound Sentences

Have your students write compound sentences that follow the directions below.

1. Join the clauses with a comma and a conjunction.
2. Join the clauses with a semicolon only.
3. Join the clauses with a semicolon and the word *moreover*.
4. Join the clauses with a semicolon and the word *however*.
5. In the first clause, include a series of words. Then join the clauses with a semicolon.

ACTIVITY 2 Punctuating and Capitalizing Direct Quotations

To provide additional practice, duplicate the following quotations. Then have your students add capital letters, quotation marks, and other punctuation marks where needed.

Time

1. Bernard Berenson mused I wish I could stand on a busy corner, hat in hand, and beg people to throw me all their wasted hours
2. the present is a point just passed stated David Russell

Chapter 12 c

3. where does time go asked Austin Dobson ah, no, time stays and we go
4. time is a circus Ben Hecht commented that is always packing up and moving away
5. Brendan Francis said no yesterdays are ever wasted for those who give themselves to today
6. ordinary people merely think how they shall spend their time commented Arthur Schopenhauer a man of talent tries to use it
7. Thomas Mann stated time has no divisions to mark its passing there is never a thunderstorm to announce the beginning of a new month or year
8. an inch of time a Chinese proverb states cannot be bought by an inch of gold
9. was it Irene Peter who said living is entirely too time-consuming
10. time always moves on Theodore Haecker said one can take a step back in space and in other things, but never in time

ACTIVITY 3 Writing Sentences

Have your students write 10 to 15 sentences that explain what the following statement means to them: It is always darkest just before the dawn. Have them include at least one compound sentence joined with just a semicolon and one compound sentence joined with a semicolon and a transitional word. When they have finished writing, have them edit their work for the correct use of all punctuation.

ADDITIONAL PRACTICE

Basic Students
  Teacher's Resource Book: pages 174–176
  Workbook: pages 133–146

Average Students
  Teacher's Resource Book: pages 177–179
  Workbook: pages 133–146

Advanced Students
  Teacher's Resource Book: pages 180–182

REVIEW EXERCISES AND TESTS

Student Text
  Diagnostic Test: page 270
  Chapter Review: pages 299–300
  Mastery Test: page 300
  Standardized Test: pages 301–302

Teacher's Resource Book
  Chapter 12 Test: pages 33–34
  (Also available as spirit duplicating masters.)

Workbook
  Unit Review: pages 147–148

ADDITIONAL ANSWERS

EXERCISE 9   Writing Sentences *(page 280)*

Sample answers:
1. We have had ten inches of rain this week, and the river may overflow its banks.
2. I like baseball best; Roberto prefers football.
3. Your dinner was delicious; however, I am too full to eat any more.
4. The treasury is very low; therefore, we will have to raise money.
5. Julia plays the piano, the drums, and the bassoon; but she is best at the bassoon.

12 Other Punctuation

For additional practice for this chapter, see the Teacher's Resource Book and the Workbook.

DIAGNOSTIC TEST

Number your paper 1 to 10. Then write each sentence, adding apostrophes, semicolons, colons, hyphens, quotation marks, and other punctuation marks needed with direct quotations. Only a sentence with a speaker tag *(he said, she asked)* should be considered a direct quotation.

EXAMPLE Kate asked What time should we leave?
ANSWER Kate asked, "What time should we leave?"

1. "Did anyone take the dog for a walk?" Dad asked.
2. Silkworms are not worms; they are actually baby moths.
3. In a democracy there are three recognized rights for each human being: life, liberty, and the pursuit of happiness.
4. "Don't walk on the carpet with your muddy boots!" he shouted.
5. The chair from Marshall's Furniture Store hasn't arrived yet; however, we expect it very soon.
6. "The time has come," Miguel announced, "to take a vote."
7. The Johnsons' dog became the mother of four puppies last night around 9:30 P.M.
8. The shark does not have a single bone in its body; its skeleton is made of cartilage.
9. Seventy-five dollars was raised at the car wash; moreover, everyone had a good time.
10. "They're here," Mom called to us. "Are you ready?"

Apostrophes

Although end marks and commas are the most frequently used punctuation marks, you also need to know how to use the other marks of punctuation. A contraction without an apostrophe or a direct quotation without quotation marks, for example, can be as confusing to read as several sentences that run together without any end marks to separate them.

APOSTROPHES

This section will cover the use of the apostrophe with contractions, as well as with nouns and some pronouns to show possession.

Apostrophes to Show Possession

An apostrophe is used to signal to a reader that a noun and certain pronouns are showing possession.

The Possessive Forms of Nouns. The possessive of a singular noun is formed differently from the possessive of a plural noun.

12a Add **'s** to form the possessive of a singular noun.

To form the possessive of a singular noun, write the noun. Do not add or omit any letters. Then just add **'s** at the end.

dog + **'s** = dog's   Where is the dog**'s** leash?
Ben + **'s** = Ben's   We are meeting at Ben**'s** house.
dollar + **'s** = dollar's   Give me a dollar**'s** worth of nails.

Singular compound nouns and the names of most businesses and organizations form their possessive the way other singular nouns do.

The jack-in-the-box**'s** lid is stuck.
Macy**'s** Department Store is having a sale on shirts.

To form the possessive of a plural noun, begin by writing the plural form of the word—just as it is. Then look at the ending of the noun. That ending will determine how you form the possessive.

Other Punctuation

12b   Add only an apostrophe to form the possessive of a plural noun that ends in *s*.

If the plural noun ends in *s*, add only an apostrophe.

     parents + ' = parents'   The parents' open house is scheduled for Monday night.
     Adamses + ' = Adamses'   The Adamses' relatives are here.
     weeks + ' = weeks'   I get two weeks' vacation.

If a plural noun does not end in *s*, add *'s* to form the possessive —just as you would for a singular noun that does not end in *s*.

     women + 's = women's   Women's shoe sizes are different from men's.
     men + 's = men's
     geese + 's = geese's   The geese's honking was very loud.

NOTE: Do not confuse a plural possessive with the simple plural form of a noun.

    POSSESSIVE   The bears' cave was monitored by the forest ranger.
    PLURAL   Did you see any bears in the state forest?

EXERCISE 1   Forming the Possessive of Nouns

Write the possessive form of each noun. Then use five of the forms in sentences of your own.

1. brother's
2. editors'
3. Peter's
4. Joneses'
5. Denver's
6. hour's
7. men's
8. month's
9. life's
10. day's
11. president's
12. teachers'
13. plumber's
14. children's
15. mice's
16. town's
17. dime's
18. Cathy's
19. world's
20. boys'

Sample sentence: The editors' meeting lasted an hour.

EXERCISE 2   Using the Possessive of Nouns

Write each word in the following sentences that needs an apostrophe or an apostrophe and an *s*.

1. What is the assignment in Mr. Clark's class?
2. They had only a few minutes' conversation together.
3. When is Anne's birthday?
4. After a month's delay, they received the set of books.
5. Have you been inside the Petersons' apartment?
6. I just heard about your brother-in-law's new job.

272

Apostrophes

12b

7. All of the boxe**'s** lids are missing.
8. Are these men**'s** shirts?
9. Hanover**'s** Discount Store has some great buys.
10. The fair will be held in the children**'s** park on Kent Street.

The Possessive Forms of Personal Pronouns. Personal pronouns and the pronoun *who* show possession by changing form—*not* by adding an apostrophe.

Whose drawing do you like better, **his** or **mine**?

The following possessive pronouns do not include apostrophes.

Possessive Pronouns			
my, mine	his	its	their, theirs
your, yours	her, hers	our, ours	

NOTE: Do not confuse a contraction with a possessive pronoun. A possessive pronoun does not include an apostrophe, but a contraction does. *Its, your, their,* and *theirs* are possessive pronouns. *It's, you're, they're,* and *there's* are contractions. (See page 151.)

The Possessive Forms of Indefinite Pronouns. An indefinite pronoun forms its possessive the same way a singular noun does—by adding *'s*. (See page 7 for a list of common indefinite pronouns.)

Everyone**'s** ballot had been counted by midnight.
We should hold the meeting at someone**'s** home.

EXERCISE 3 Using the Possessive of Pronouns
Rewrite any incorrectly written possessive form of a pronoun. If a sentence is correct, write *C* after the number.

1. No one**'s** property was damaged in the storm.
c 2. Is it time for your dentist appointment?
c 3. Whose position did you fill at the supermarket?
4. These tickets are ours, but where are the**theirs**re's?
5. Does this count represent everyone**'s** vote?
6. You're submitting you're [your] application, aren't you?

273

Other Punctuation

    7. Mine was cooked longer than <u>her's</u>. *(hers)*
c 8. Yours is under this pile of papers.
    9. <u>Somebodys</u> notebook was left on my desk. *(Somebody's)*
  10. <u>There</u> snow tires are stored over there. *(Their)*

Other Uses of Apostrophes

An apostrophe has other uses besides showing possession.

Apostrophes with Contractions. An apostrophe takes the place of any missing letters in a contraction.

12c   Use an apostrophe in a contraction to show where one or more letters have been omitted.

    is n~~o~~t = isn't   there ~~i~~s = there's
    I h~~a~~ve = I've   let ~~u~~s = let's
    he w~~ill~~ = he'll   of ~~the~~ clock = o'clock

No letters are added or changed around in a contraction except in the contraction for *will not*, which is *won't*.

EXERCISE 4   **Writing Contractions**
Write the contraction for each pair of words.

1. have not	6. is not	11. I would	16. we will
2. we have	7. I am	12. has not	17. let us
3. that is	8. will not	13. you are	18. did not
4. I have	9. they are	14. does not	19. it is
5. there is	10. were not	15. who is	20. do not

Answers (margin):
1. haven't
2. we've
3. that's
4. I've
5. there's
6. isn't
7. I'm
8. won't
9. they're
10. weren't
11. I'd
12. hasn't
13. you're
14. doesn't
15. who's
16. we'll
17. let's
18. didn't
19. it's
20. don't

Apostrophes to Show Joint or Separate Ownership. Correctly used, apostrophes can identify joint or separate ownership. One apostrophe is used to show joint ownership. Two or more apostrophes are used to show separate ownership.

12d   Add 's to only the last word to show joint ownership. Add 's to each word to show separate ownership.

In the following example, the dog belongs to both Nancy and Dan. Therefore, an apostrophe is added to only Dan's name.

    Pumpkin is Nancy and Dan**'s** dog.

Apostrophes

12c–e

If one of the words showing joint ownership is a possessive pronoun, the noun must also show possession.

Pumpkin is Nancy**'s** and **his** dog.

In the following example, Nancy and Dan have separate reports; therefore, an apostrophe is added to both names.

Nancy**'s** and Dan**'s** reports are due tomorrow.

Apostrophes to Form Certain Plurals. An apostrophe and an *s* are used to form the plural of certain items and words.

12e Add *'s* to form the plural of numbers, letters, symbols, and words that are used to represent themselves.

Are those *3***'s** or *8***'s**?
Do not use *&***'s** in place of *and***'s** in your written assignments.

NOTE: *Although the items and the word* and *in the examples above are italicized, the 's in each sentence is not italicized. (See pages 282–283 for the use of italics.)*

EXERCISE 5 Using Apostrophes in Special Situations
Write each <u>letter</u> or <u>word</u> that needs an apostrophe or an apostrophe and an *s*.

1. Why <u>don't</u> you ever dot your <u>i's</u>?
2. <u>Cynthia's</u> and <u>David's</u> poems were the best two in the class.
3. I <u>haven't</u> heard if <u>they'll</u> be joining us.
4. Devon is Ellen and <u>John's</u> youngest daughter.
5. You must make a greater distinction between your <u>k's</u> and <u>h's</u>.
6. Paul and <u>Pat's</u> party will be held on Friday evening.
7. <u>Let's</u> leave no later than six <u>o'clock</u>.
8. <u>Andrea's</u> and his savings bond was purchased with money they received for their anniversary.
9. Avoid using <u>ah's</u> to connect sentences when you speak.
10. <u>Beth's</u> and <u>Jerry's</u> lab experiments produced opposite results.

EXERCISE 6 Time-out for Review
Number your paper 1 to 20. Rewrite any incorrectly written <u>letter</u>, <u>number</u>, or <u>word</u>. If a sentence is correct, write *C* after the number.

1. *Haven't* <u>Have'nt</u> you ever read any of John <u>Steinbeck's</u> novels?

Other Punctuation

2. The teachers' meeting is in the first room on the right.
3. All the students' books were stored in the school's basement during the summer.
4. Why isn't the band marching in the parade on Labor Day?
5. In the secret code, the 5's stood for e's.
c 6. My mother is a member of a women's softball team.
7. The attorney-at-law's hours are posted on his door.
8. My aunt's severance pay was equal to two months' wages.
9. Sue and Tad's cousin is the principal of the middle school.
10. There's a tag hanging from its collar.
c 11. Everyone's picture has finally been taken for this year's yearbook.
12. Pat's sunglasses were left in their car.
13. This wasn't anyone's decision but my own.
14. Sujata's and Simon's reports received the best marks in the class.
c 15. What is the coach's decision about the new team members?
16. The men's and women's volleyball tournament will be held on the town's outdoor court.
17. Dick's pitching will certainly improve the team's prospects this year.
18. Who's handing out programs for the drama club's performance tonight?
19. After a year's delay, work will finally begin on the girls' gymnasium.
c 20. The truck drivers' paychecks are ready to be distributed.

SEMICOLONS AND COLONS

A semicolon (;) and a colon (:) are similar in appearance, but they have different uses within a sentence.

Semicolons

Two independent clauses that are not properly joined together result in a run-on sentence. There are, however, several ways to separate the independent clauses of a compound sentence. Using a comma and a conjunction is one way. *(See pages 255–256.)*

Semicolons

Kim served spaghetti for dinner**, and** everyone enjoyed it.

Clauses in a compound sentence can also be joined by a semicolon when there is no conjunction.

Kim served spaghetti for dinner**;** everyone enjoyed it.

12f Use a semicolon between the clauses of a compound sentence when they are not joined by a conjunction.

The Julian calendar was very much like our own**;** every fourth year was a leap year with an extra day.

NOTE: Only clauses that are closely related should be joined by a semicolon. If two ideas are not closely related, put them in separate sentences.

JOINED — A terrible blizzard struck the mountain village**;** all telephone communication was cut off.

SEPARATED — A terrible blizzard struck the mountain village. The previous winter had been quite mild.

Semicolons with Transitional Words. Clauses in a compound sentence can also be joined by a semicolon and certain transitional words.

12g Use a semicolon between the clauses in a compound sentence when they are joined by certain transitional words.

The corn wasn't ripe**; in fact,** the only vegetables ready to be picked were the tomatoes.

Following is a list of common transitional words.

Common Transitional Words		
accordingly	furthermore	moreover
as a result	hence	nevertheless
besides	however	otherwise
consequently	indeed	that is
for example	in fact	therefore
for instance	instead	thus

277

Other Punctuation

NOTE: Some of the transitional words in the previous list can also be used as a parenthetical expression within a single clause. *(See pages 260–261.)*

Notice in the following examples that the semicolon comes before the transitional word, and a comma follows the transitional word.

> The sun was hot; **nevertheless,** a cool breeze was blowing in from the inlet.
>
> Our term papers are due on Friday; **however,** I passed mine in this morning.

Semicolons to Avoid Confusion. Occasionally a semicolon is substituted for a comma.

12h   Use a semicolon instead of a comma in certain situations to avoid confusion.

A semicolon is used instead of a comma between the clauses of a compound sentence if there are commas within a clause.

> Put away these books, magazines, and games; for we are having company tonight. [Normally a comma would come before a conjunction separating the clauses in a compound sentence.]

Semicolons are also used instead of commas between items in a series if the items themselves contain commas.

> I have a final exam on Thursday, May 29; Tuesday, June 21; and Friday, June 6. [Normally commas would separate the items in a series.]

NOTE: See Chapter 11 for rules for commas.

EXERCISE 7 Using Semicolons

Write the following sentences, adding semicolons where needed.

1. Vermont was not one of the original 13 colonies;it became the 14th state in 1791.
2. John intends to spend this afternoon at the lake;therefore, he will take his fishing pole.

Semicolons 12h

3. We bought ham, cheese, and lettuce; but we forgot the bread.
4. Women in ancient Egypt could own property; they could also work outside the home.
5. The seniors have not finished planning for the graduation ceremony; however, they have already selected a speaker.
6. You should bake an extra potato; otherwise, you might not have enough.
7. The color black absorbs heat; white reflects it.
8. That material will be fine; for instance, it won't wrinkle.
9. We have lived in Rochester, New York; Richmond, Virginia; and Brownsville, Texas.
10. Dry ice does not melt; it evaporates.

EXERCISE 8 Using Semicolons and Commas

Write the following sentences, adding semicolons and *commas* where needed.

1. Turtles don't have teeth their jaws form a sharp beak.
2. The river has risen a foot since last night as a result many families have been evacuated.
3. We fed the chickens the pigs and the cows but that was only the beginning of the morning's chores.
4. It has rained all day today consequently the picnic has been postponed.
5. The international date line is located entirely on the ocean hence all changes of date are made on a ship or on a plane.
6. Profits are down this year nevertheless the company has promised that there won't be any layoffs.
7. Some day I would like to visit Paris France Rome Italy and London England.
8. Andrew Jackson is on the twenty-dollar bill Ulysses S. Grant is on the fifty-dollar bill.
9. The weather was perfect during our entire vacation for example the temperature never went below 75 degrees.
10. The cornea of the human eye is transparent it allows light to enter the eye.
11. I prefer painting with watercolor acrylic and oil but I also use tempera.
12. Many kinds of articles go through an electroplating process they range from jet-engine parts to delicate jewelry.

279

Other Punctuation

13. The dentist can see you on Friday, May 2; Tuesday, May 6; or Thursday, May 8.
14. Two straight lines that intersect to form right angles are perpendicular; two straight lines that do not intersect are parallel.
15. I have two hours of homework to do; furthermore, I have to baby-sit for my younger brother.
16. Reptiles eat insects, rodents, and other animals; but this behavior contributes to a balance in nature.
17. A sea cucumber is an animal that usually looks like a cucumber; however, it changes shape while moving around.
18. I can't find my sneakers, my baseball cap, or my windbreaker; but I'll keep looking.
19. The National Honor Society was going to have a bake sale to raise money; instead, it held a car wash.
20. The heart of a human infant beats about 120 times per minute; an adult's heart beats about 70 times per minute.

EXERCISE 9 Writing Sentences
Write compound sentences that follow the directions below.
Sample answers precede this chapter.
1. Join the clauses with a comma and the conjunction *and*.
2. Join the clauses with a semicolon only.
3. Join the clauses with a semicolon and the word *however*.
4. Join the clauses with a semicolon and the word *therefore*.
5. In the first clause, include a series of words. Then join the clauses with a semicolon and the conjunction *but*.

Colons

The most common use of a colon is to signal a list of items that is about to follow in a sentence.

12i Use a colon before most lists of items, especially when a list comes after an expression such as *the following*.

The parrot family includes the following birds: the kea, the parakeet, the cockatoo, and the macaw.

A colon, however, never follows a verb or a preposition.

Colons

12i

NO COLON   Last fall we planted tulips, daffodils, and irises.
COLON   Last fall we planted three different flowers: tulips, daffodils, and irises.

NOTE: Commas separate items in a series. *(See page 253.)*

Colons are also used in several other situations.

BETWEEN HOURS AND MINUTES   4:15 P.M.
BETWEEN BIBLICAL CHAPTERS AND VERSES   Romans 6:23
BETWEEN PERIODICAL VOLUMES AND PAGES   *America* 157:12–15
AFTER SALUTATIONS IN BUSINESS LETTERS   Dear Sir:

EXERCISE 10   Using Colons

Number your paper 1 to 10. Then write each word or number that should be followed by a colon and add the colon. If a sentence does not need a colon, write *C* after the number.

1. Have you learned the following computer terms: *flowchart, modem,* and *debugging?*
c 2. Among the most intelligent animals are the chimpanzee, the gorilla, the dolphin, and the elephant.
3. When it is 1:00 P.M. in Miami, it is 11:00 A.M. in Denver.
4. Many reptiles are protected by law: turtles, alligators, crocodiles, and some snakes.
c 5. Three of the most populous cities in the world are Tokyo, London, and Peking.
6. The text of the church service, which starts at 10:45 A.M., is Proverbs 4:7.
c 7. Among the poets we have studied this year are Emily Dickinson, Robert Frost, and Carl Sandburg.
8. In *The Readers' Guide to Periodical Literature,* I found that the article on a future space station is in *Explorer,* 19:9-13.
9. These animals are considered endangered species: the Bengal tiger, the California condor, and the blue whale.
c 10. House wrens have been known to build nests in old shoes, hats, tin cans, and mailboxes.

EXERCISE 11   Time-out for Review

Write the following sentences, adding semicolons, colons, and *commas* where needed.

A Bit of Americana

1. Most of the potatoes grown in the United States come from three states: Idaho, Washington, and Maine.

281

Other Punctuation

2. William Faulkner won two Pulitzer Prizes;moreover he was awarded the Nobel Prize for Literature in 1949.
3. Lancaster,Pennsylvania;Princeton,New Jersey;and Annapolis,Maryland,have all been capitals of the United States.
4. By 1983, the Statue of Liberty was in need of extensive repairs;consequently,a citizens' group raised millions of dollars for its restoration.
5. The Liberty Bell in Independence Hall was first cast in London in 1752;it was recast in Philadelphia a year later.
6. North Carolina is a major textile,electronic equipment,and furniture producer;and it is also a rich agricultural state.
7. The first telephone directory, issued in 1878, was quite small;in fact,it included only about 50 names.
8. The first woman to become governor of Connecticut was Ella T. Grasso;she held office from 1975 to 1980.
9. Candidates for United States president must have three major qualifications:be at least 35 years old,be a "natural-born" citizen,and have lived in this country for at least 14 years.
10. One of the longest continuous borders in the world lies between the United States and Canada;it extends 3,987 miles.

UNDERLINING

Underlining is used as a substitute for italics. *Since you cannot write or type the way this sentence is printed, you should underline anything that should be in italics.* Letters, numbers, words, and titles should be underlined in certain situations.

12j Underline letters, numbers, and words when they are used to represent themselves. Also underline foreign words that are not generally used in English.

LETTERS, NUMBERS	The <u>a</u>'s and the <u>3</u>'s aren't showing up on the computer screen.
WORDS, PHRASES	I misspelled the word <u>aggressive</u> on the spelling test.
FOREIGN WORDS	Instead of using the abbreviation, Janice wrote <u>et cetera</u>.

Underlining

12j–k

NOTE: Only the *a* and the *3* in the first example are underlined — not the *'s*.

12k Underline the titles of long written or musical works that are published as a single unit. Also underline the titles of paintings and sculptures and the names of vehicles.

Long works include books, periodicals, newspapers, full-length plays, and very long poems. Long musical compositions include operas, symphonies, ballets, and albums. Vehicles include airplanes, ships, trains, and spacecraft. Titles of movies and radio and TV series should also be underlined.

Nathaniel Hawthorne wrote <u>The House of the Seven Gables</u>.

The <u>Mayflower</u> probably had three masts and two decks.

Have you seen this morning's edition of the <u>Chicago Tribune</u>? [*The* is generally not considered part of the title of a newspaper or a periodical.]

NOTE: See pages 240–241 for the capitalization of titles.

EXERCISE 12 Using Underlining

Write and underline each letter, number, word, or group of words that should be italicized.

1. Ernest Hemingway's book <u>The Old Man and the Sea</u> won the Pulitzer Prize for literature in 1953.
2. One of Winslow Homer's famous paintings is <u>Boys in a Pasture</u>.
3. There are four <u>i</u>'s and four <u>s</u>'s in the word <u>Mississippi</u>.
4. CBS's <u>60 Minutes</u> was among the first news programs in a magazine-type format.
5. Lorraine Hansberry's play <u>A Raisin in the Sun</u> was made into a movie.
6. The French word <u>franc</u> is an abbreviation for <u>Francorum Rex</u>, which means "King of the Franks."
7. The blast-off of the space shuttle <u>Challenger</u> transformed an overcast sky into a rosy dawn.
8. Have you ever heard Verdi's opera <u>Otello</u>?
9. The 1927 film <u>The Jazz Singer</u> ended the era of silent films.
10. On display at the Museum of Modern Art in New York City is Henry Moore's sculpture entitled <u>Family Group</u>.

Other Punctuation

QUOTATION MARKS

Have you ever stopped to think why novels and short stories almost always have conversation in them? One reason is that people talking to one another adds realism to fiction. Another reason is that authors use conversation to reveal important information, as well as characters' feelings, beliefs, and attitudes. It is, of course, impossible to write a conversation without knowing how to use quotation marks correctly.

It is also impossible to write a term paper without knowing how to use quotation marks. The purpose of a term paper is to state a thesis and then to support that thesis with facts. Many of these facts are the words of other people. Because these words belong to someone else, they must be written with quotation marks.

The most important thing to remember about quotation marks throughout this section is that they come in pairs. Quotation marks are placed at the beginning and at the end of uninterrupted quotations and certain titles.

Quotation Marks with Titles

In the last section, you learned that titles of long works of art and publications are underlined. Usually, however, these long works are composed of smaller parts. For example, a book has chapters, a magazine has articles, and an album has songs. When the titles of these smaller parts are written, they should be enclosed in quotation marks.

> **12l** Use quotation marks to enclose the titles of chapters, articles, stories, one-act plays, short poems, and songs.

Also put quotation marks around the titles of essays, compositions, episodes from a TV series, and movements from long musical compositions.

> Our homework assignment is to read the chapter "The Governor's Hall" in Hawthorne's <u>The Scarlet Letter</u>.
>
> After reading "The Next Step into Space" in <u>Newsweek</u>, I wanted to become an astronaut.
>
> Is Mary Austin's poem "The Grass on the Mountain" in our anthology <u>America Speaks</u>?

Quotation Marks

12l–m

EXERCISE 13 Using Quotation Marks with Titles

Write each title, adding quotation marks and underlining where needed.

1. Tomorrow we will discuss the article "Stalking the Stock Market" in <u>U.S. News and World Report</u>.
2. In 1899, Scott Joplin became famous when he wrote the ragtime song "Maple Leaf Rag."
3. One movement from Gustave Holst's orchestral suite <u>The Planets</u> is called "Uranus, the Magician."
4. "St. Helens May Erupt Again" was the lead story in the <u>Seattle Times</u>.
5. The short story "By the Waters of Babylon" by Stephen Vincent Benét takes place in a futuristic world.
6. Judy Garland sings "Somewhere over the Rainbow" in the movie <u>The Wizard of Oz</u>.
7. Evelyn Tooley Hunt's poem "Taught Me Purple" is included in the anthology <u>Modern American Poetry</u>.
8. Tonight I have to read the chapter "Atoms to Minerals" in our science book <u>Earth Science</u>.
9. "The Wit and Wisdom of Benjamin Franklin" was the title of Yvonne's English composition.
10. The soprano sang the aria "One Beautiful Day" from Puccini's opera <u>Madame Butterfly</u>.

Quotation Marks with Direct Quotations

Only a *direct quotation*—the exact words of a person—is enclosed in quotation marks. Quotation marks do not enclose an *indirect quotation*—a paraphrase of someone's words.

12m Use quotation marks to enclose a person's exact words.

> DIRECT QUOTATION   Pam said, "The meeting starts at four."
> INDIRECT QUOTATION Pam said that the meeting starts at four. [The word *that* often signals an indirect quotation.]

A one-sentence direct quotation can be written in any of three ways. It can be placed before a speaker tag or after a speaker tag. For variety a direct quotation can also be interrupted by a speaker tag. In all three cases, quotation marks enclose *only* the person's exact words. Notice in the third

285

Other Punctuation

sentence in the following examples that two sets of quotation marks are needed because quotation marks enclose only a person's exact words—not the speaker tag.

> BEFORE "Your dinner was excellent," Ken said.
> AFTER Ken said, "Your dinner was excellent."
> INTERRUPTED "Your dinner," Ken said, "was excellent."

Only one set of quotation marks is needed to enclose any number of sentences—unless the quotation is interrupted by a speaker tag.

Ken said, "Your dinner was excellent. I especially liked the roast potatoes. I've never eaten them cooked that way before." [Quotation marks are not needed after *excellent* and before *I* or after *potatoes* and before *I've*.]

EXERCISE 14 Using Quotation Marks with Direct Quotations

Write each sentence, adding quotation marks where needed. In this exercise, place a comma or an end mark that follows a quotation *inside* the closing quotation marks.

Friends

1. Katherine Mansfield said, "I always felt that the great comfort of friendship was that one had to explain nothing."
2. "Friendship will not stand the strain of very much good advice for very long," Robert Lynd stated.
3. "When people are friendly," a Chinese proverb says, "then even water is sweet."
4. "None is so rich as to throw away a friend," states a Turkish proverb.
5. Another Turkish proverb states, "He who seeks a faultless friend remains friendless."
6. Eleanor Roosevelt said, "Friendship with oneself is all-important. Without it one cannot be friends with anyone else in the world."
7. "Good friendships are fragile things," Ralph Bourne once said, "and require as much care as any other precious thing."
8. "Give and take makes good friends," states a Scottish proverb.
9. "Even from the best of human friends, I must not ask for more than he can give," said Alban Goodier.

Quotation Marks

10. E. W. Howe advised, "When a friend is in trouble, don't annoy him by asking if there is anything you can do. Think up something appropriate and do it."

Capital Letters with Direct Quotations. A capital letter begins a quoted sentence — just as it begins a regular sentence.

> **12n** Begin each sentence of a direct quotation with a capital letter.

"**H**e expects to win the nomination," she said.

She said, "**H**e expects to win the nomination." [Two capital letters are needed — one for the first word of the sentence and one for the first word of the quotation.]

"**H**e expects," she said, "to win the nomination." [*To* does not begin with a capital letter because it is in the middle of the quotation.]

EXERCISE 15 Using Quotation Marks and Capital Letters with Direct Quotations

Write each sentence, adding quotation marks and capital letters where needed. In this exercise place a comma or an end mark that follows a quotation *inside* the closing quotation marks.

1. John Keynes once said, "Ideas shape the course of history."
2. "To grow older is a new venture in itself," Goethe once wrote.
3. A German proverb reads, "Even the smallest eel hopes to become a whale."
4. "Attention is a hard thing to get from people," Francis A. Baker commented.
5. "Every calling is great," Oliver Wendell Holmes observed, "when greatly pursued."
6. "To change and to improve," a German proverb states, "are two different things."
7. "When you have to make a choice and don't make it," William James stated, "that is in itself a choice."
8. Gertrude Stein said, "The things I like most are the names of the states of the United States. They make music and they are poetry."
9. "People of many kinds ask questions, but few and rare people listen to answers. Why?" asked Janet Erskine Stuart.

Other Punctuation

10. "Little by little, in the long run, aspirations can realize themselves," Ruth Benedict said. "We work for that. We must count it our wealth."

Commas with Direct Quotations. A comma creates a pause in speech and a visual separation between a quotation and a speaker tag.

12o Use a comma to separate a direct quotation from a speaker tag. Place the comma inside the closing quotation marks.

Notice in the following examples that when the speaker tag follows the quotation, the comma goes inside the closing quotation marks.

"The storm is finally subsiding," David said. [The comma goes *inside* the closing quotation marks.]

David said, "The storm is finally subsiding." [The comma follows the speaker tag.]

"The storm," David said, "is finally subsiding." [Two commas are needed to separate the speaker tag from the parts of an interrupted quotation. The first comma goes *inside* the closing quotation marks.]

EXERCISE 16 Using Commas with Direct Quotations
Write each sentence, adding capital letters and commas where needed.

Proverbs
1. "The hand will not reach for what the heart does not long for," states a Welsh proverb.
2. A German proverb says, "When a person is happy, he does not hear the clock strike."
3. "Happiness is not a horse," a Russian proverb states. "You cannot harness it."
4. An Arabic proverb says, "He who has health has hope, and he who has hope has everything."
5. "Help your brother's boat across," states a Hindu proverb, "and your own will reach the shore."
6. "A person with little learning," a Burmese proverb says, "is like the frog who thinks its puddle a great sea."
7. A Russian proverb says, "A kind word is like a spring day."

Quotation Marks

12o–p

8. "In the eyes of its mother, every beetle is a gazelle," states a Moroccan proverb.
9. "One can pay back the loan of gold," a Malayan proverb says, "but one dies forever in debt to those who are kind."
10. "Better one word before," states a Welsh proverb, "than two after."

End Marks with Direct Quotations. A period follows a quotation that is a statement or an opinion—just as it does a regular sentence.

12p Place a period inside the closing quotation marks when the end of the quotation comes at the end of a sentence.

Carrie said, "The paper drive was a huge success." [The period goes *inside* the closing quotation marks.]

"The paper drive was a huge success," Carrie said. [The period follows the speaker tag, and a comma separates the quotation from the speaker tag.]

"The paper drive," Carrie said, "was a huge success." [The period goes *inside* the closing quotation marks.]

A quotation can also end with a question mark or an exclamation point. When it does, place the question mark or the exclamation point inside the closing quotation marks. Notice that the question mark goes *inside* the closing quotation marks in all three of the following examples.

Anita asked, "What time should I meet you?"

"What time should I meet you?" Anita asked. [A period follows the speaker tag.]

"What time," Anita asked, "should I meet you?"

The exclamation point also goes *inside* the closing quotation marks in the following three examples.

Eddie exclaimed, "Oh no, I just missed the bus!"

"Oh no, I just missed the bus!" Eddie exclaimed. [A period follows the speaker tag.]

"Oh no," Eddie exclaimed, "I just missed the bus!"

A quotation of several sentences, of course, can include various end marks.

289

Other Punctuation

"Why do you want to leave?" Hannah asked. "I'm having a wonderful time!"

The question marks and the exclamation points in the previous examples are placed inside the closing quotation marks because they are part of the quotation. Occasionally a question or an exclamatory statement will include a direct quotation. In such cases the question mark or the exclamation point goes *outside* the closing quotation marks.

Who said, "Go west, young man"? [The whole sentence is the question, not the quotation.]

I thought I was dreaming when the announcer said, "You win the trip to Hawaii"! [The whole sentence is exclamatory, not the quotation.]

NOTE: In the two previous examples, the end marks for the quotations are omitted.

EXERCISE 17 Using Commas and End Marks with Direct Quotations

Write each sentence, adding commas and end marks.

1. "The geometry test was very short," Bertha stated.
2. Dad inquired, "Who wants to go swimming today?"
3. "What's for dinner?" André asked.
4. "That light isn't bright enough for reading," he said.
5. "Do you want just a hamburger," the waiter asked, "or the hamburger platter?"
6. Roberta screamed, "Water is pouring into our basement!"
7. "I put a dime into the telephone," Bart explained, "but I didn't get a dial tone."
8. "You're driving too fast!" Sean shouted.
9. Did you say, "Mrs. Finton didn't assign any homework for tonight"?
10. "You sing marvelously!" Tanya exclaimed. "Have you ever taken lessons?"

EXERCISE 18 Time-out for Review

Write each sentence, adding capital letters, quotation marks, and other punctuation marks where needed.

Books

1. William Feather said, "Finishing a good book is like leaving a good friend."

Quotation Marks

2. "A book is like a garden carried in the pocket," declares a Chinese proverb.
3. "There is more treasure in books," Walt Disney stated, "than in all the pirates' loot on Treasure Island."
4. "A book is good, bad, or medium for me," remarked Lillian Hellman, "but I usually don't know the reasons why."
5. Theodore Haecker mused, "There are people who talk like books. Happily there are also books that talk like people."
6. "It may be said of books," Henry Van Dyke said, "that they are nothing but the echoes of echoing echoes."
7. "The worst thing about new books is that they keep us from reading the old ones," mused Joseph Joubert.
8. "What is a book? It is everything or nothing. The eye that sees it is all," stated Ralph Waldo Emerson.
9. "Just the knowledge that a good book is waiting at the end of a long day makes that day happier," said Kathleen Norris.
10. "I read prodigiously," Thomas Wolfe reflected. "Ten, twelve, fifteen books a day are nothing."

Other Uses of Quotation Marks

Long quotations in reports and conversations between two or more people in a story require some special applications of quotation marks.

Writing Dialogue. A dialogue is a conversation between two or more people. When writing dialogue, begin a new paragraph each time the speaker changes so that a reader will know who is speaking.

The following dialogue from *The Pearl* takes place between Kino and his wife. Each individual quotation follows the rules you have just studied, but each time the speaker changes, a new paragraph begins. Notice also that actions or descriptions of the two characters are sometimes included within the same paragraph in which each one speaks.

His hand strayed limply to the place where the pearl was hidden under his clothes. "They will find it," he said weakly.

"Come," she said. "Come!" And when he did not respond, "Do you think they would let me live? Do you think they would let the little one here live?"

Other Punctuation

> Her goading struck into his brain; his lips snarled and his eyes were fierce again. "Come," he said. "We will go into the mountains. Maybe we can lose them in the mountains."
> — JOHN STEINBECK

NOTE: An *ellipsis* (three dots) is used to indicate the omission of part of a quotation. If an ellipsis comes at the end of a sentence, it is followed by a period—making it four dots.

"Come," he said. "We will go into the mountains. . . ."

Quoting Long Passages. To support a point you have made in a research paper, you may want to quote a long passage from a book, a magazine, or another source. Rather than use quotation marks, as you do when you write a report, a dialogue, or a short passage, you set off the quoted passage from your text. When quoting a passage of five or more lines, skip two lines between your text and the first line of the quoted information. Then indent ten spaces along the left margin of the quoted passage. *(See page 555.)*

Quotations within Quotations. Occasionally a direct quotation will include a title or another quotation. A distinction is made between the two sets of quotation marks by using single quotation marks for one set. Use single quotation marks to enclose a quotation or certain titles within a quotation.

"The short story 'Safe and Soundproof' was written by Joan Aiken," Mr. O'Flannery informed us.

Jim told Greg, "Mom said, 'Call if you're going to be late.'"

A quotation within a quotation follows all the rules covered in this section. Notice, however, in the last example that the closing single quotation mark and the closing double quotation marks come together.

EXERCISE 19   Time-out for Review
Correctly rewrite the following dialogue between Kino and his wife Juana. Add punctuation, capitalization, and indentation where needed. *Slash (/) indicates indentation.*

From *The Pearl*

"Will they follow us?" she asked. "Do you think they will try to find us?" "They will try," said Kino. "Whoever finds us will take the pearl. Oh, they will try." / Juana said, "Perhaps the dealers were right, and the pearl has no value. Perhaps this has all been an illusion." Kino reached into his clothes and brought out the pearl. He let the sun play on it until it burned in his eyes. "No," he said, "they would not have tried to steal it if it had been valueless."

— JOHN STEINBECK

EXERCISE 20   Writing Dialogue
Write a brief imaginary conversation in which you speak with Neil Armstrong, the first astronaut to walk on the moon. Punctuate and indent the dialogue correctly.
Answers will vary.

OTHER MARKS OF PUNCTUATION

This section will cover hyphens, dashes, parentheses, and brackets.

Hyphens

Although a hyphen is used most often to divide a word at the end of a line, it has several other uses as well.

Hyphens with Numbers and Words.   Certain numbers and fractions are written with a hyphen.

> **12q**   Use a hyphen when writing out the numbers *twenty-one* through *ninety-nine*. Also use a hyphen when writing out a fraction that is used as an adjective.

Thirty-two people applied for the job.

The bill must receive a two-thirds majority of the vote.

A fraction used as a noun is *not* written with a hyphen.

I've already spent two thirds of my paycheck.

Hyphens with Compound Nouns and Adjectives.   Compound nouns and adjectives can be written in any of three ways. Some are written as one word and some as two separate words. Others are written with one or more hyphens. Since compound nouns and adjectives can take these different forms, it is always best to check the dictionary for the correct spelling.

Other Punctuation

12r   Use a hyphen to separate the parts of some compound nouns and adjectives.

    COMPOUND NOUNS   stand-in, attorney-at-law, send-off
    COMPOUND ADJECTIVES   long-term, third-class, face-to-face

NOTE: Compound adjectives are usually hyphenated only when they come before a noun. You should *never* hyphenate a compound adjective, however, that includes a word ending in the suffix *-ly*.

Hyphens with Certain Prefixes. Several prefixes and one suffix are always separated from their root words by a hyphen.

12s   Use a hyphen after the prefixes *ex-, self-,* and *all-* and before the suffix *-elect.*

     ex-governor, self-assured, all-around, mayor-elect

Also use a hyphen with all prefixes before a proper noun or a proper adjective.

     pre-World War I tension, pro-American film, mid-July sale

EXERCISE 21   **Using Hyphens**

Number your paper 1 to 10. Then correctly write each word that should be hyphenated. If no word in the sentence needs a hyphen, write *C* after the number.

1. Each person owns a one-third share of the company.
2. The United States Congress issued the first postage stamps in the mid-nineteenth century.
3. Enclose your check in the self-addressed envelope.
4. Is that an American-made car?
5. The team made an all-out effort to win the championship.
6. He has completed one-third of the crossword puzzle.
7. An ex-captain of Monroe High School's track team was a participant in the 1984 Olympics.
8. Have you met your new in-laws yet?
9. The mayor-elect held a press conference the day after he won the election.
10. The do-it-yourself frame kit was missing three nails.

Hyphens

12r–t

Hyphens to Divide Words. A hyphen is used to divide a word at the end of a line; however, you should try to avoid dividing words. If a word must be divided, use the following guidelines.

12t ▶ Use a hyphen to divide a word at the end of a line.

Guidelines for Dividing Words

1. Divide words only between syllables.
   signature: sig-nature or signa-ture
2. Never divide a one-syllable word.
   verse silk lung soup
3. Never separate a one-letter syllable from the rest of the word; for example, the following words should never be divided.
   DO NOT BREAK e-vent a-mong i-tem
4. Hyphenation after two letters at the end of a line is permissible, but a two-letter word ending should not be carried over to the next line.
   BREAK de-cay ex-pand re-lief
   DO NOT BREAK time-ly liv-er strick-en
5. Usually divide words containing double consonants between the double consonants.
   sum-mit lat-tice ham-mer fol-low
6. Divide hyphenated words only after the hyphens.
   hand-to-mouth daughter-in-law sixty-one
7. Do not divide a proper noun or a proper adjective.
   Bernstein Montana African Victorian

EXERCISE 22 Using Hyphens to Divide Words

Number your paper 1 to 20. Then write each word, adding a hyphen or hyphens to show where the word can be divided. If a word should not be divided, write *no* after the number.

1. rate no
2. handful
3. indent
4. happened
5. again no
6. bitter
7. lava
8. idol no
9. fault no
10. empty no
11. hamster
12. ten-foot
13. driven no
14. molasses
15. fast-food
16. infant
17. Rogers no
18. around no
19. moldy no
20. enactment

2. hand-ful
3. in-dent
4. hap-pened
6. bit-ter
7. la-va
11. ham-ster
14. mo-las-ses
16. in-fant
20. en-act-ment

295

Other Punctuation

Dashes, Parentheses, and Brackets

Dashes, parentheses, and brackets are used to separate certain words or groups of words from the rest of the sentence. Be careful that you do not overuse them or substitute them for other marks of punctuation, such as commas or colons. Each of these marks of punctuation has specific uses.

Dashes. Although dashes are used the way commas are, they indicate a greater separation between words than commas do. Dashes should be used in the following situations.

12u Use dashes to set off an abrupt change in thought.

> A number of sailboats—I counted ten—sailed across the inlet toward the ocean.
>
> Then we opened the old trunk—well, that's a story for another time.

12v Use dashes to set off an appositive that is introduced by words such as *that is,* *for example,* or *for instance.*

> Many popular house plants—for example, the spider plant and the philodendron—thrive in sunless rooms.
>
> Somnambulists—that is, people who walk in their sleep—should not be awakened suddenly.

12w Use dashes to set off a parenthetical expression or an appositive that includes commas. Also use dashes to call special attention to a phrase.

> The gentle, quiet koala—probably the most harmless animal in the world—lives almost entirely in the branches of the eucalyptus tree.
>
> Mr. Hall rehearsed separate groups—the strings, the woodwinds, and the brasses—and then the full orchestra.

12x Use dashes to set off a phrase or a clause that summarizes or emphasizes what has preceded it.

Dashes, Parentheses, Brackets

12u–z

The hot days, the cold nights, the mosquitoes—all these turned our camping trip into a disaster.

Swimming, singing, painting—Janet is outstanding in all of them.

NOTE: You can write or type a dash by placing two hyphens together.

Parentheses. Parentheses separate additional information or an explanation that is added, but not needed, from the rest of the sentence. Definitions and dates, for example, are sometimes put into parentheses.

12y Use parentheses to enclose additional information that is not needed in a sentence.

Almost all marsupials (pouched animals) live in Australia, New Guinea, and the islands of Australasia.

George Washington served two terms as president (1789–1797).

NOTE: A period follows a closing parenthesis that comes at the end of a sentence.

Brackets. Brackets have one basic use that you may need to know when writing a report or a term paper that includes quoted passages.

12z Use brackets to enclose an explanation within quoted material that is not part of the quotation.

Charles Wolcutt wrote, "Herman Melville seems to have started it [*Moby Dick*] as a sea adventure."

EXERCISE 23 Using Dashes and Parentheses
Write the following sentences, adding dashes and parentheses where needed.

1. Sparsely populated, mountainous, and ruggedly beautiful these words all describe the open country in Montana.
2. Several birds for example, the ostrich and the kiwi have lost the ability to fly.

297

Other Punctuation

3. Frogs, toads, and salamanders these are all classified as amphibians.
4. Each morning I have to feed the animals a horse, a dozen pigs, and a flock of chickens before breakfast.
5. The history assignment was to write I typed mine and explain three reasons for the Industrial Revolution.
6. Mercy Otis Warren poet, dramatist, and historian was the sister of James Otis, an activist and a statesman during the American Revolution.
7. The kitchen probably the last room I'll work on will be painted by next week.
8. Sara Teasdale (1884–1933) won the Columbia University prize for poetry for her collection entitled *Love Songs*.
9. Ampere, hertz, and volt all these are units of measurement that were named after scientists.
10. The quarterback tucked the ball under his arm oh, I can see you're not interested.

Application to Writing

As you write and edit your written work, keep in mind the punctuation marks covered in this chapter. Many of them provide you with opportunities for sentence variety. Instead of always writing a compound sentence with a comma and a conjunction, for example, you can occasionally write a compound sentence with a semicolon.

EXERCISE 24 Editing for Punctuation Marks
Write the following paragraphs. Add any needed punctuation.

Mohawks Climb High

American Indians Mohawks, to be precise have built virtually all of New York City's skyline. Mohawks were quickly recognized for their grace, agility, and balance; and many seem to have little fear of walking on narrow girders and beams at high altitudes. These qualities have earned Mohawks high-paying positions as riveters in many cities: New York, Boston, and Chicago.

In 1886, Mohawks first received recognition for their great skill; they participated in the construction of a long bridge spanning Canada's St. Lawrence River. Their reputation quickly spread; consequently, thousands were hired during

298

Manhattan's building boom (1920s – 1930s). They played a major role at various construction sites: the Empire State Building, Rockefeller Center, and other famous landmarks.

CHAPTER REVIEW

Write each sentence, adding punctuation where needed. Only a sentence with a speaker tag should be considered a direct quotation.

1. A string quartet has four instruments: the first violin, the second violin, the viola, and the cello.
2. "Faults are thick where love is thin," states a Danish proverb.
3. Sean bought new sneakers, a sweatshirt, and a headband; and any day now he plans to start jogging.
4. "Don't touch the casserole dish," John bellowed. "It's very hot."
5. The mule cannot reproduce itself; it is an offspring of a donkey and a horse.
6. During the summer our attic became unbearably hot; as a result, our landlord installed an exhaust fan.
7. Davy Crockett, famous hunter, pioneer, and frontier hero, was born in Limestone, Tennessee.
8. "Where is this month's issue of *Sports Illustrated*?" Jennifer inquired.
9. Everyone's help contributed to the governor-elect's victory.
10. Sue received the most votes in the election (142 in all).
11. Shells have been used for all sorts of curious things: money, ornaments, buttons, and horns.
12. Andrea told him, "My brother-in-law's farm was not affected by the early frost."
13. The price charged at nickelodeons (the first movie theaters) was often a dime, not a nickel.
14. *My Fair Lady* is a musical adaptation of George Bernard Shaw's play *Pygmalion*.
15. A meter is approximately 39.37 inches; a decimeter is approximately 3.94 inches.
16. "I will subtract points from your compositions if your *o*'s look like *a*'s," Mrs. Henderson said.
17. "When was the 'Star-Spangled Banner' adopted as the national anthem of the United States?" Amanda asked.
18. Gary's and Bill's photographs appeared in Sunday's paper.

Other Punctuation

19. In 1883, William Cody—he was famous as Buffalo Bill—helped form a traveling "Wild West Circus."
20. Back home the days were cool, moist, and cloudy; but here they are hot and sunny.
21. "Someone's umbrella," Mr. Harrington said, "was left under a seat in the auditorium last night."
22. A warm spring day, a quiet stream, and the trout jumping above the water—what more could a fisherman ask for?
23. The bus left St. Louis an hour late; nevertheless, we still made our connection in Chicago.
24. "It's almost five miles from the Carters' cabin to Silver Lake," Jeffrey informed us.
25. The taste buds can detect the following tastes: sweet, sour, bitter, and salty.

MASTERY TEST

Number your paper 1 to 10. Then write each sentence, adding apostrophes, semicolons, colons, hyphens, quotation marks, and other punctuation marks needed with direct quotations. Only a sentence with a speaker tag should be considered a direct quotation.

1. Water boils at 212°F; iron melts at 2,795°F.
2. "Meet me in the gym in 15 minutes," Jake said.
3. Vote for only one junior: Faye Ryan, Lionel Harris, or Pedro Torres.
4. "Watch out for that pothole!" Brad exclaimed.
5. Corn uses up the soil's strength; however, through crop rotation a farmer can renew the land's fertility.
6. "Everyone is leaving at eight sharp," Dad stated. "Make sure you are ready."
7. We learned about three national parks in California: Lassen Volcanic, Sequoia, and Yosemite.
8. The Evanses' plans aren't definite yet.
9. "Put the casserole in the oven at 325 degrees," explained the chef, "and cook it for one hour."
10. We don't have to hurry; the concert doesn't start until 7:45 P.M.

STANDARDIZED TEST

MECHANICS

Directions: Each sentence may contain a capitalization or punctuation error in one of the underlined parts. On your answer sheet, fill in the circle containing the letter of the part that has an error. If there is no error in an underlined part, fill in *E*.

SAMPLE To hear Queen Elizabeth and her son speak we
                      A   B   C   D
          turned on the radio. No error
                                E

ANSWER Ⓐ Ⓑ Ⓒ ● Ⓔ

B 1. On Mauritius, which is East of Madagascar, lived the
         A   B   C
   dodo bird. No error
        D   E

C 2. "Isn't Australia a continent" he asked. No error
       A   B   C   D   E

E 3. My aunt has seen Chaplin's movie *City Lights* ten
        A   B   C   D
   times. No error
         E

A 4. Our Congressman, Senator-elect Ray, and Mayor Silva
          A   B   C
   won two thirds of the votes. No error
        D   E

A 5. "Its Passover, a Jewish holiday," I said. No error
     A   B   C   D   E

C 6. At the Bateses' house, we ate broiled chicken, and
          A   B   C
   mashed potatoes and steamed broccoli. No error
          D   E

E 7. Electric-powered saws work well; however,
        A   B   C   D
   operators must be careful of the cord. No error
                                            E

D 8. Ian has three cats: Flo, Mo and Bo. No error
                 A   B   C D   E

E 9. I like Kim's tasty, hot Korean food. No error
         A   B   C   D   E

D 10. Our train, the *Chief*, arrived on time; theirs' was
           A   B   C   D
   late. No error
        E

Directions: Each sentence has one underlined part. After the sentence there are four ways to write the underlined part. Choose the best way. If the sentence is correct as it is, choose *A*. Fill in the circle containing the letter of your answer.

SAMPLE   Tom <u>dried the dishes, fed the dog; and then went to bed.</u>

    A dried the dishes, fed the dog; and then went to bed.
    B dried the dishes; fed the dog; and then went to bed.
    C dried the dishes, fed the dog and then went to bed.
    D dried the dishes, fed the dog, and then went to bed.

ANSWER Ⓐ Ⓑ Ⓒ Ⓓ

A   11. <u>After the History II and biology exams ended,</u> I sighed.

    A After the History II and biology exams ended,
    B After the History II and Biology exams ended.
    C After the history II and biology exams ended,
    D After the History II and Biology exams ended,

B   12. The bird kept <u>chirping, furthermore,</u> another joined in.

    A chirping, furthermore,
    B chirping; furthermore,
    C chirping, furthermore
    D chirping; furthermore

D   13. Did the group sing <u>*Yesterday, Ruby Tuesday,* or *Changes?*</u>

    A *Yesterday, Ruby Tuesday,* or *Changes?*
    B *Yesterday, Ruby Tuesday* or *Changes?*
    C "Yesterday," "Ruby Tuesday," or "Changes?"
    D "Yesterday," "Ruby Tuesday," or "Changes"?

D   14. Ben hauled the <u>wood, and then sawed it before</u> I left.

    A wood, and then sawed it before
    B wood, and then sawed it, before
    C wood; and then sawed it, before
    D wood and then sawed it before

C   15. The <u>college, offering the best program, is Crane I believe.</u>

    A The college, offering the best program, is Crane I believe.
    B The College offering the best program is Crane, I believe.
    C The college offering the best program is Crane, I believe.
    D The College, offering the best program, is Crane, I believe.

Unit 4

Vocabulary and Spelling

13   Vocabulary
14   Spelling

Chapter 13 Vocabulary

OBJECTIVES
- To use context clues to understand word meaning.
- To use prefixes, suffixes, and roots to understand word meaning.
- To identify synonyms and antonyms.
- To use etymologies to remember word meaning.
- To add at least 84 words to a working vocabulary.

MOTIVATIONAL ACTIVITY

Introduce students to the words they will be studying in this chapter with the following story. (You may either read it aloud or write it on a duplicating master.) Students should use the number clues provided to find the word from the list on page 322 that best fills each blank. The clues refer to the column number in which an appropriate word can be found. The answers are given in parentheses after the blanks.

My Neighbor Ran for Office

Manny Goldman lived next door to me for many years. He was a high-minded and high-spirited friend and neighbor, with __2__ (fervent) beliefs about right and wrong in government policies. He soon decided it was his __1__ (civic) duty to run for office and try to put his ideas into action. His enthusiasm and __1__ (buoyancy, compassion) and his __3__ (jovial) smile made him a favorite among voters, who also recognized that his policies would be __1__ (advantageous, beneficial) to the community. Manny always faced the issues squarely, while other candidates tried to __2__ (elude) them. His ideas were often at __4__ (variance) with his opponents', but he explained his positions clearly. He called for a return to __2__ (idealism) in politics, even though the practical realities of political life threaten to weaken ideals. His __1__ (compassion) for citizens less fortunate than he is and his __4__ (reverence) for the law helped him fulfill his __4__ (quest) and win his office.

TEACHING SUGGESTIONS

Word Meaning *(pages 304–318)*

Use the example of *interminable* on page 304 to show students how to use all of the suggestions for unlocking word meaning that are listed below it. First have them consult a dictionary and use the definition to think of a familiar synonym for the word (*endless* is probably the most familiar synonym). To demonstrate the next suggestion, write the sample sentence on the chalkboard and omit the word *interminable*. Ask students to supply other words that they might use to complete the sentence, focusing on the contrast suggested in the sentence between summer vacation—to which most students look forward eagerly—and exam week. Although supplying their own word may not result in a synonym for *interminable*, they will at least see that the supplied word conveys a more negative association than *summer vacation*. This clue about a negative connotation can be carried over into the next suggestion: dividing the word into smaller parts. Ask students to name the root of *interminable (term)* and to think of other familiar words that use this root. (Possibilities include *term* itself, *terminal*, *terminate*, and *exterminate*.) From these words students can deduce the meaning of *term (ending)*. Use the same process with the word's prefix. Have students think of other familiar words that begin with the prefix *in-* (examples include *indigestion*, *inconsistent*, *independent*). From these familiar words students can deduce the meaning of *in-* if they have forgotten it and put the whole word together.

To show how the last suggestion works in some cases, revise the sample sentence and write the new sentence on the chalkboard. We thought the week of exams preceding summer vacation was as interminable as a never-ending head cold.

This sentence contains an obvious synonym for *interminable*. For more prac-

Vocabulary

tice, ask students to revise the sentence so that it contains an obvious antonym. Exam week seemed as interminable as summer vacation will seem brief.

Context Clues *(pages 305–308)* Placing words in a familiar context will help students remember the words. After students have finished Exercise 1, have them turn to the list on page 322 and make three lists of words on their papers. One list should be called "Science Words," the second "Language and Literature Words," and the third "Social Studies and History Words." Have students work independently for the first five or ten minutes. Then have them work in pairs to see if they can increase the number of words in each list. Ask selected pairs to read their lists as you write them on the chalkboard. Others can then add words from their lists. The following lists include possibilities of words that your students might give.

Science Words
amorphous	habitat
antidote	hyperactive
asphyxiation	hypothermia
botany	intricate
buoyancy	inverse
carnivorous	metamorphosis
celestial	mirage
contour	spectrum
diagnosis	ultrasonic
eradicate	

Language and Literature Words
bibliography	irony
fallacy	literal
fluency	memoirs
illegible	thesis

Social Studies and History Words
affirmative	inaugurate
beneficial	infraction
civic	intervene
commemorate	judicious
decree	lenient
expatriate	mandatory
idealism	posterity
imperial	

Prefixes, Suffixes, and Roots *(pages 308–316)* Refer students to the chart on page 310. To help lock the meaning of each prefix in students' minds, ask the class to think of at least four more words that begin with each prefix. Students may use their dictionaries to find words. Remind them to check to make sure that the beginning letters are used as genuine prefixes. *Abash,* for example, does not begin with the prefix *ab-*.

EXAMPLES
ab- absence, abdicate, abduct, abjure
bi- biplane, bicentennial, bisect, biped

You can repeat the assignment with the prefixes from Greek (page 311), as well as with suffixes (pages 313–314) and roots (page 315).

Synonyms and Antonyms *(pages 317–318)* To help students understand the shades of differing meaning in synonyms, have them use the words from Exercise 6 to write two sentences for each number in the exercise. The first sentence should use the word that is in capital letters. The second sentence should use the synonym for that word and clearly show a variant in meaning.

EXAMPLE
I had a *premonition* that there would be a fire in our garage.
The principal issued a *forewarning:* Any student who misses four classes without a suitable explanation will be suspended.

Word Etymology *(pages 318–321)*

Divide the class into four groups based on the students' interest in one of the following general areas: music, math, literature, and science. Each group will have the task of reporting to the class on the etymologies of words from their subject area (see next page). Students in each group should decide which person will report on which word. When the work is complete, ask each group member to report to the whole class.

Chapter 13 b

Vocabulary

MUSIC	LITERATURE
pizzicato	poetry
staccato	comedy
legato	tragedy
sonata	alliteration
orchestra	prosody
crescendo	persona

MATH	SCIENCE
algebra	biology
geometry	botany
calculus	chemistry
triangle	physics
parallelogram	zoology
hypotenuse	astronomy

Increasing Your Vocabulary *(pages 321–322)*

In addition to the vocabulary notebook containing problematic words from this chapter, you may want students to keep a vocabulary notebook according to subject matter. The notebook should contain as many pages as the number of classes students are taking. Each page should be labeled with the course title. Over a period of a month, students should add words to the appropriate vocabulary list as they come across them in their other classes. Each page should contain at least fifteen words, with phonetic pronunciations copied from the dictionary and brief definitions.

ACTIVITIES FOR DIFFERENT ABILITIES

Basic Students

ACTIVITY 1 Suffixes
Write the following words on the chalkboard. Have students choose one of the suffixes on page 313 or 314 to form a different word.

1. personal (-ity)
2. wish (-ful)
3. hard (-en)
4. standard (-ize)
5. patriot (-ism)
6. self (-ish)
7. courage (-ous)
8. train (-able)
9. rare (-ity)
10. perform (-ance, -er)

ACTIVITY 2 Writing
Have students write a paragraph about a costume party. They should use and underline five words from the list on page 322 in their paragraphs.

Advanced Students

ACTIVITY 1 Vocabulary Stumpers
Every day for a period of several weeks, you may want to start class with the following activity. Have a student come to class prepared with a word chosen from the dictionary that the rest of the class is unlikely to know. Along with choosing the word, the student should also compose a sentence using one type of context clue from pages 305–306. The rest of the class should try to use the clue to guess the meaning of the word. At the end of the exercise, write the word on a 3 x 5 card and pin it with the others on the bulletin board.

ACTIVITY 2 Etymologies of Place Names
Have students each choose one local place name and, using the resources of the library or any other community source, prepare a short oral report explaining the derivation of the name.

ACTIVITY 3 Writing
Have students imagine they are television writers assigned to creating a new idea for a soap opera. The ideas they present to their producers should include:

1. a list of characters with brief descriptions and an explanation of how the characters are related to each other
2. possible entanglements in which the characters might find themselves
3. a story outline for the first episode

In their presentations, students should include at least ten words from the vocabulary list on page 322.

When the assignments are complete, have students read them to the class so

Vocabulary

that many different vocabulary words are offered in context.

ADDITIONAL PRACTICE

Teacher's Resource Book: pages 183–186
Workbook: pages 149–152

REVIEW EXERCISES AND TESTS

Student Edition
Chapter Review: pages 322–323

Teacher's Resource Book
Chapter 13 Test: pages 35–36
(Also available as spirit duplicating masters.)

13

Vocabulary

For additional practice for this chapter, see the Teacher's Resource Book and the Workbook.

The study of English is the study of words. Whether you are doing grammar exercises, writing a composition, reading Shakespeare's *Macbeth*, or carrying on a conversation, you are dealing with words. The more words you know, the more likely you are to do well in English—and in other subjects as well.

WORD MEANING

The English language contains so many words that to learn all of them would be a monumental task. There are several ways, however, to build your vocabulary so that you can express your ideas more clearly and effectively. Consider, for example, the word *interminable* in the following sentence.

We thought the week of exams preceding summer vacation was *interminable*.

If you had never seen the word *interminable* before, you could use any one of the four approaches that follow to determine its meaning—"having or seeming to have no end."

- Consult a dictionary.
- Try to figure out the meaning by looking carefully at the rest of the sentence.
- Divide the word into smaller parts to see if your knowledge of word parts leads to a definition.
- Search the sentence for an obvious synonym or antonym.

Context Clues

Most of the words you have learned up to now you have learned through context. The *context* of a word is the sentence, the surrounding words, or the situation in which the word appears. Sometimes the verbal context will give a straightforward definition, as in the following sentence.

A *mirage* is an optical illusion resulting from the bending of light rays by a layer of air that has varying density.

Generally, however, the context of a word gives clues to the word's meaning rather than an outright definition. Following are examples of some familiar types of context clues.

RESTATEMENT — The mayor had the support of the press in his *quest* for reform, his **search** for ways to govern the city better. [The word *search* is a restatement of *quest*. This restatement helps to define *quest* as "an act or instance of seeking; a pursuit."]

EXAMPLE — Mr. Agarwal spoke about *celestial* matters; I remember best his vivid **description of the Milky Way.** [By using the description of the Milky Way as an example, the writer makes clear the meaning of *celestial*—"relating to the sky or the visible heavens."]

COMPARISON — Joan Freitas recently completed her *memoirs,* a work **"rather like Agatha Christie's autobiography,"** she says. [The quotation helps to define *memoirs* as "a kind of autobiography" by making a comparison between Ms. Freitas' writing and Agatha Christie's autobiography.]

CONTRAST — Although the game seemed *frivolous* to me, **the children played it with great seriousness.** [The word *although* signals a contrast between the seriousness of the children and the seemingly frivolous game they were playing, suggesting that *frivolous* means "lacking in seriousness."]

Vocabulary

PARALLELISM She will *interrogate* the suspect; **I will question the witness.** [The parallel construction is a clue — but only a clue — that *interrogate* means "to question."]

EXERCISE 1 Using Context Clues

Write the letter of the word or group of words closest in meaning to the underlined word.

B 1. The winners were <u>exuberant</u>, while the losers were very downcast.
   (A) wealthy (B) enthusiastic (C) generous
   (D) heartbroken (E) intelligent

D 2. Lions are <u>carnivorous</u>; they prey on other animals.
   (A) handsome (B) trainable (C) endangered
   (D) flesh-eating (E) jungle-dwelling

A 3. The downtown area of the capital city has experienced a <u>renaissance</u>, a revival of the grandeur of the past.
   (A) rebirth (B) catastrophe (C) new name
   (D) decline (E) holiday

C 4. My cousin looked <u>gaunt</u>; he reminded me of the bony Ichabod Crane in "The Legend of Sleepy Hollow."
   (A) heavyset (B) dangerous (C) thin
   (D) self-confident (E) athletic

B 5. The decision was thoughtful and <u>judicious</u>, the kind of wise conclusion expected of the Supreme Court.
   (A) grand (B) sensible (C) extravagant
   (D) fast-paced (E) cruel

E 6. Students in <u>botany</u> examine the structure of a leaf, while in zoology they examine the anatomy of a frog.
   (A) chemistry (B) fossil study (C) biology
   (D) college (E) plant study

A 7. Frank's <u>dexterity</u>, which enables him to place skillful shots, also makes him a great dribbler in basketball.
   (A) manual skill (B) trickery (C) size (D) speed
   (E) awkwardness

C 8. Twenty-seven people cast <u>affirmative</u> votes, but a far larger number voted no.
   (A) strongly worded (B) local (C) positive
   (D) negative (E) important

Context Clues

B 9. The scene before us was as <u>tranquil</u> as a meadow on a quiet summer day.
(A) unusual (B) peaceful (C) fleeting (D) mournful (E) dramatic

E 10. Our committee considered a <u>spectrum</u> of choices, all the way from no prom at all to the biggest prom ever held.
(A) couple (B) scheme (C) limited group (D) duplication (E) range

A 11. Dr. Avery's <u>diagnosis</u>, her conclusion about the cause of my condition, was that I had nothing but a common cold.
(A) analysis (B) treatment (C) preference (D) annoyance (E) mistake

D 12. A flame that is kept burning forever, such as the one at President Kennedy's grave, is a <u>perpetual</u> flame.
(A) royal (B) bright (C) magnificent (D) continuous (E) memorial

C 13. His <u>apparel</u> consisted of a beige wool sweater, a blue cotton shirt, and blue jeans.
(A) suitcase (B) closet (C) clothing (D) good taste (E) appearance

E 14. The quarterback managed to <u>elude</u> two tacklers, just as he had gotten away from two others on the previous play.
(A) collide with (B) block (C) confuse (D) surprise (E) avoid

B 15. We had no <u>inkling</u>—not even a slight indication—that there would be an assembly on Friday.
(A) worry (B) hint (C) contract (D) improvement (E) dismissal

A 16. It is a story rich in <u>irony</u>; the results of many events in the plot are the opposite of what a reader expects.
(A) contradictions (B) strength (C) disputes (D) love (E) sadness

C 17. Although we expected <u>beneficial</u> results from the new law, we soon observed just the opposite—a higher crime rate.
(A) unhappy (B) distinct (C) favorable (D) dangerous (E) internal

C 18. Nothing is more <u>obstinate</u> than a mule, which seems to refuse to move just for the sake of refusing.
(A) remarkable (B) flexible (C) stubborn (D) humorous (E) worthless

Vocabulary

C 19. Children often learn their first words by naming <u>tangible</u> items—those that can be perceived by the sense of touch.
(A) imaginary (B) furry (C) material (D) orange (E) musical

D 20. He sent a <u>condolence</u> card to his friend; I expressed my regrets in person.
(A) written (B) postal (C) congratulatory (D) sympathy (E) thank-you

D 21. The Women's Rights National Historical Park in New York State <u>commemorates</u> the start of the women's rights movement in 1848.
(A) defines (B) organizes (C) signals (D) celebrates (E) questions

B 22. Although a jellyfish appears to be an <u>amorphous</u> mass as it moves through the water, the creature is actually shaped like a bell, a bowl, or an umbrella.
(A) marine (B) shapeless (C) fragile (D) floating (E) weightless

E 23. The lens of the eye, like the lens of a camera, produces <u>inverse</u> images—upside down and reversed right to left.
(A) clear (B) visual (C) negative (D) immediate (E) opposite

B 24. Historically, <u>infractions</u> of the law have been treated differently; in the United States today a thief is fined or sentenced, but in early Rome the victim sued the thief.
(A) victims (B) violations (C) codes (D) demands (E) courts

D 25. Edward Jenner's 1796 discovery of the smallpox vaccine was a major step toward <u>eradicating</u> smallpox.
(A) discovering (B) defining (C) creating (D) exterminating (E) confining

Prefixes, Suffixes, and Roots

Many English words are made up of smaller word parts. These word parts—prefixes, suffixes, and roots—typically come from Latin and Greek, although some are from Old English, French, and other languages. You will recall that a *root* is the part of a word that carries the basic meaning. A *prefix* is one or more syllables placed in front of the root to modify the meaning of the root or to form a new word. A *suffix*

Prefixes, Suffixes, and Roots

is one or more syllables placed after the root to help shape its meaning and often to determine its part of speech.

The English language contains hundreds of roots, prefixes, and suffixes. If you know even a few examples of each word part, you can increase your vocabulary significantly. Knowing, for instance, that the root *man* or *manu* means "hand" will help you figure out the definitions of such words as *manipulate, manual, manufacture,* and *manicure.* The following examples illustrate how the meaning of each word part contributes to the meaning of the word as a whole.

Word Parts with Latin Origins

WORD	PREFIX	ROOT	SUFFIX
collinear	col- (with)	-line- (narrow, elongated mark)	-ar (of, relating to)
discreditable	dis- (not)	-credit- (worthy of belief or praise)	-able (capable of)

Word Parts with Greek Origins

WORD	PREFIX	ROOT	SUFFIX
hypothermia	hypo- (less than normal)	-therm- (heat)	-ia (disease, condition)
sympathy	sym- (with)	-path- (suffering)	-y (state of)

Although word parts do not usually provide exact dictionary definitions, they do give you clues to the meaning of the word. Following are dictionary definitions of the previous examples.

> *collinear:* lying on or passing through the same straight line
> *discreditable:* disgraceful
> *hypothermia:* subnormal temperature of the body
> *sympathy:* act of sharing the feelings of another

By learning the prefixes, suffixes, and roots in the lists that follow, you will be able to determine the meaning of a number of unfamiliar words.

Vocabulary

Prefixes. A prefix may appear in a variety of words. Prefixes may have more than one meaning and more than one spelling. The prefix *in-*, for example, may mean *not, in,* or *into,* and may be spelled *il-* (*il*legal), *im-* (*im*mature), or *ir-* (*ir*resistible), according to the first letter of the root with which it is paired.

	Prefixes from Latin	
Prefix	**Meaning**	**Example**
ab-	from, away, off	ab + normal: differing from the average
bi-	two, occurring every two	bi + monthly: occurring every two months
circum-	around	circum + spect: careful to consider all consequences
com-, col-, con-	with, together	com + passion: sympathy with another's distress col + lect: bringing together into one body or place
contra-	against	contra + dict: resist or oppose in argument
dis-	do the opposite of, not	dis + engage: release from something that holds
ex-	out of, outside	ex + patriate: one who lives in a foreign country
in-, il-, im-, ir-	not, in, into	in + human: lacking pity, kindness, or mercy il + legible: not able to be read
non-	not	non + entity: something that does not exist or exists in imagination
ob-	in the way of, against	ob + noxious: objectionable
semi-	half in quantity or value	semi + annual: occurring twice a year
ultra-	beyond range or limit of	ultra + sonic: having frequency above human ear's audibility level

Prefixes

Prefixes from Greek

Prefix	Meaning	Example
a-, an-	not, without	a + symmetrical: lacking balanced proportions
dia-	through, across	dia + logue: conversation between two or more persons
dys-	impaired, bad	dys + function: impaired or abnormal functioning
hemi-	half	hemi + sphere: one of two half spheres
hyper-	excessively	hyper + critical: finding excessive fault with
meta-	beyond, change	meta + morphosis: change in appearance or character
para-	beside, acting as assistant	para + professional: trained aide assisting a professional
peri-	all around, surrounding	peri + scope: optical instrument for seeing around obstructed views
syn-, sym-	with, together	syn + onym: word with same or similar meaning to another word

EXERCISE 2 Combining Prefixes and Roots

Write the Latin or Greek prefix that has the same meaning as the underlined word or words. Then write the complete word defined after the equal sign.

EXAMPLE *half* + formal = suitable for moderately formal occasions

ANSWER semi—semiformal

1. *against* + vene = go or act contrary to   contra — contravene
2. *through* + meter = length of a straight line through the center of an object   dia — diameter
3. *not* + replaceable = unable to be substituted for   ir — irreplaceable
4. *impaired* + lexia = disturbance of the ability to read   dys — dyslexia

311

Vocabulary

5. *two* + plane = airplane with two main supporting surfaces placed one above the other   bi — biplane
6. *assistant* + medic = one who assists a physician   para — paramedic
7. *with* + phony = complex musical composition for an orchestra; harmony of sounds   sym — symphony
8. *excessively* + active = far more active than normal   hyper — hyperactive
9. *beyond the range of* + violet = located beyond the visible spectrum at its violet end   ultra — ultraviolet
10. *all around* + phery = outside boundary of something   peri — periphery
11. *change* + plasia = transformation of one tissue into another tissue   meta — metaplasia
12. *not* + typical = not conforming to a standard or type; not typical   a — atypical; non — nontypical
13. *from* + errant = deviating from that which is normal, usual, or correct   ab — aberrant
14. *around* + scribe = draw a line around something or form the boundaries of   circum — circumscribe
15. *in the way of* + stacle = something that or someone who stands in the way of   ob — obstacle

Suffixes. There are two kinds of suffixes. One kind, called an inflectional suffix (or grammatical suffix), changes the number in nouns *(office, offices)*, the form of comparison in modifiers *(simple, simplest)*, and the tense in verbs *(question, questioned, questioning)*. An inflectional suffix does not change either the essential meaning of the word or its part of speech.

More important to vocabulary study, however, is the second kind of suffix. This kind, called a derivational suffix, changes the meaning and very often the part of speech of the word to which it is added. Consider the word *agree*.

WITH NO SUFFIX	*agree:* verb
WITH *-MENT*	*agreement:* noun
WITH *-ABLE*	*agreeable:* adjective
WITH *-LY*	*agreeably:* adverb (*-ly* added to the adjective form)

As the previous examples show, some suffixes form nouns, some form adjectives, and some form verbs. The only common adverb-forming suffix is *-ly*. The following chart indicates a number of suffixes and the part of speech formed by each one.

Suffixes

Suffixes

Noun Suffix	Meaning	Example
-ance, -ence	action, process, instance of	further + ance: act of advancing
-cy	action, state, quality	buoy + ancy: quality of being able to float
-er	one that is, does, makes	reform + er: one that works for improvement by change
-ion	act, process, result, state	validate + ion: act or process of making legal
-ism	act, state, characteristic	colloquial + ism: the characteristic of familiar, informal conversation
-ity	quality, state, degree	objective + ity = expression of facts without distortion by emotions

Suffixes

Adjective Suffix	Meaning	Example
-able, -ible	capable of, fit for, tending to	perish + able: tending to spoil or decay
-ful	full of, having the qualities of	event + ful: full of occurrences
-ish	characteristic of, inclined to	book + ish: inclined to rely on book learning rather than experience
-less	not having, unable to act	defense + less: not having the means to protect oneself or another
-ous	full of, having the qualities of	advantage + ous: having superiority of position or condition
-some	characterized by action or quality	cumber + some: characterized by being unwieldy because of size and weight

Vocabulary

Suffixes

Verb Suffix	Meaning	Example
-ate	act on, cause to become	motive + ate: cause a person to act because of need or desire
-en	cause to be or have	length + en: cause to have longer dimension
-fy, -ify	make, form into, invest with	just + ify: show to be right or reasonable
-ize	become like, cause to be	crystal + ize: cause to form crystals

EXERCISE 3 Combining Suffixes and Roots

Write the suffix that has the same meaning as the underlined word or words. Then write the complete word defined after the equal sign. Make spelling changes if necessary.

EXAMPLE beauty + <u>make</u> = make attractive
ANSWER fy — beautify

1. confuse + <u>state</u> = state of being confused   ion — confusion
2. style + <u>characteristic of</u> = conforming to current fashion   ish — stylish
3. military + <u>cause to be</u> = cause to be equipped with armed forces and defenses   ize — militarize
4. fluent + <u>quality</u> = quality of speaking easily and well   cy — fluency
5. worry + <u>characterized by</u> = inclined to worry or fret   some — worrisome
6. meaning + <u>full of</u> = having purpose or significant quality   ful — meaningful
7. glory + <u>invest with</u> = give praise or honor   fy — glorify
8. regard + <u>not having</u> = without regard to; not giving attention to   less — regardless
9. knowledge + <u>tending to</u> = having intelligence   able — knowledgeable
10. active + <u>cause to be</u> = make productive or effective   ate — activate

Roots. Since a root carries the basic meaning of a word, it is important to know the common roots in English. Many of these roots came originally from Latin or Greek.

Sometimes a root may stand alone, as in the word *self.* A root may be combined with a prefix (*un*do), a suffix (*free*dom), or even another root word *(manuscript)*. The following chart contains some of the common Latin and Greek roots that are the basic elements of many English words.

Latin Roots

Root	Meaning	Examples
-cred-	believe	credulous, credible
-fid-	faith	fidelity, confide
-frag-, -fract-	break	fragile, fragment, fracture, infraction,
-grat-	thankful, pleasing	gratitude, congratulate
-mort-	death	mortuary, immortal
-omni-	all	omniscient, omnivorous
-ped-	foot	pedal, pedestrian
-port-	carry	portable, transport
-scrib-, -script-	write	scribble, inscribe, transcript, inscription
-vert-, -vers-	turn	divert, vertebra
-viv-, -vit-	live, life	vivid, revive, vitality

Greek Roots

Root	Meaning	Examples
-arch-	rule	monarch, matriarch
-bio-, -bi-	life	autobiography
-chron-	time	synchronize
-geo-	earth	geology, geometry
-graph-	write	graphic, photograph
-log-, -logy-	speech, reason, science	prologue, logic, ecology, meteorology
-mono-	alone, single	monotonous, monosyllable
-morph-	form	amorphous, metamorphic
-ortho-	straight, correct	orthodox, orthopedic
-poly-	many	polygon, polysyllabic
-soph-	wise	philosopher

Vocabulary

EXERCISE 4 Recognizing Latin and Greek Roots

Write the root of each of the following words. Then use the charts in this chapter to write a definition for each word. Refer to a dictionary if necessary.

EXAMPLE vitalize
ANSWER vit — cause to be lively or active

Sample answers:
1. ex<u>port</u> carry out of
2. in<u>cred</u>ible unbelievable
3. circum<u>scribe</u> draw a line around
4. im<u>ped</u>iment barrier
5. <u>mort</u>ify subdue, deaden
6. <u>grat</u>eful full of thanks
7. con<u>vert</u>ible changeable
8. in<u>scrip</u>tion something written
9. con<u>fid</u>ence faith, trust
10. an<u>arch</u>y absence of rule

EXERCISE 5 Using Prefixes, Roots, and Suffixes

Write the letter of the phrase closest in meaning to the word in capital letters. What you have learned in this chapter will help you determine the meaning of each capitalized word.

B 1. OMNIPRESENT (A) able to be carried anywhere (B) present in all places at all times (C) ruling all
A 2. ADVISABLE (A) fit to be done (B) full of suggestions (C) having realistic standards
A 3. CONTROVERSY (A) discussion of opposing views (B) expression of hostility (C) ability to turn around
A 4. SYSTEMIZE (A) cause to be in order (B) rank in importance (C) give rules
C 5. INSEPARABLE (A) consisting of layers (B) broken into two parts (C) not capable of being kept apart
A 6. MONOGRAPH (A) written account of a single thing (B) one handwritten name (C) unified program
B 7. IDEALISM (A) state of perfection (B) act of forming standards (C) one who seeks to make things better
C 8. HYPODERMAL (A) full of energy (B) able to triumph over odds (C) lying beneath an outer skin
B 9. PERIPHERY (A) one who walks across (B) external boundary of something (C) under the ground
A 10. INGRATITUDE (A) state of not being thankful (B) support for an enemy (C) ability to express thanks fully

316

Synonyms and Antonyms

A thorough understanding of synonyms and antonyms will help you expand your vocabulary. A *synonym* is a word that has the same or nearly the same meaning as another word. An *antonym* is a word that means the opposite or nearly the opposite of another word.

There are often a number of synonyms for a word. For example, some of the synonyms for the word *close* are *dense, compact,* and *thick.* Notice that these words do not share precisely the same meaning. Entries in dictionaries often explain the slight differences between synonyms. *(See page 345.)*

You are probably familiar with the specialized dictionary for synonyms, called a *thesaurus.* Generally a thesaurus is indexed to help readers find the synonyms they need. *(See page 358.)*

EXERCISE 6 Recognizing Synonyms

Write the letter of the word or group of words closest in meaning to the word in capital letters. Check your answers in a dictionary.

C 1. PREMONITION   (A) payment (B) ghost
   (C) forewarning (D) reward (E) greeting
D 2. DECREE   (A) quantity (B) loss (C) challenge
   (D) order (E) joke
A 3. RELINQUISH   (A) release (B) conquer
   (C) discourage (D) excite (E) announce
C 4. IMMATERIAL   (A) untidy (B) false
   (C) unimportant (D) wicked (E) substantial
B 5. CONTOUR   (A) journey (B) outline
   (C) gathering (D) agency (E) photograph
B 6. THESIS   (A) guess (B) hypothesis (C) debate
   (D) example (E) definition
E 7. HABITAT   (A) sleep (B) custom (C) yarn
   (D) promise (E) home
A 8. INTERVENE   (A) come between (B) withdraw
   (C) contact (D) construct (E) require
A 9. ASPHYXIATION   (A) suffocation (B) extension
   (C) loss (D) delivery (E) breathing
D 10. ANTIDOTE   (A) poison (B) story (C) opponent
   (D) cure (E) predecessor

317

Vocabulary

EXERCISE 7 Recognizing Antonyms

Write the letter of the word or group of words most nearly opposite in meaning to the word in capital letters. Check your answers in a dictionary.

D 1. INTRICATE   (A) local (B) complex (C) required (D) simple (E) flowery
C 2. PAUPER   (A) artist (B) doctor (C) millionaire (D) athlete (E) genius
E 3. RAUCOUS   (A) loud (B) entertaining (C) unusual (D) gleaming (E) quiet
A 4. DISCRETION   (A) carelessness (B) caution (C) argument (D) familiarity (E) accuracy
D 5. FERVENT   (A) noisy (B) inverted (C) savage (D) unemotional (E) forgotten
E 6. MANDATORY   (A) mass-produced (B) critical (C) hazardous (D) illegal (E) unnecessary
B 7. POSTERITY   (A) descendants (B) ancestors (C) fortune (D) encounter (E) relatives
B 8. PRELUDE   (A) symphony (B) postlude (C) soprano (D) permit (E) drama
C 9. LENIENT   (A) forgotten (B) casual (C) strict (D) upright (E) sly
D 10. REVERENCE   (A) nonfiction (B) simplicity (C) love (D) disrespect (E) glory

WORD ETYMOLOGY

The *etymology* of a word is the history of that word from its earliest recorded use. From the Greek word *psallein,* for example, meaning "to pluck or play a stringed instrument," came *psalmos,* "the twanging of a harp." That word became the Latin word *psalmus,* then the Old English *psealm.* Eventually, but still long ago, the word took its present form, *psalm,* "sacred song or poem." Dictionary entries often contain brief etymologies. *(See page 344.)*

Tracing Word Histories

Early invaders of England—the Romans, the Angles and Saxons, and the Norman French—all contributed words to the English language. The history of American English goes back to the arrival in the seventeenth century of the first English settlers.

Although most of the words in use in the United States today were brought to this country by English settlers, other cultural groups have contributed words to the American English language. The various American Indian languages, for instance, had a significant influence on place names in the United States. More than half of the states have names of Indian origin, as do countless counties, cities, and towns. For example, the names *Chicago, Omaha, Topeka, Wichita,* and *Seattle* all come from American Indian words, along with *Allegheny, Wabash, Niagara,* and *Susquehanna*. Other American Indian contributions include *pecan, succotash, squash, persimmon, raccoon,* and *opossum*.

Other languages contributed to American English as well. Some of these contributions are place names; others are words in use in everyday life, such as the names of food. The following words were donated to the English language by explorers, settlers, and visitors to this country.

SPANISH	Los Angeles, San Diego, pueblo, rodeo, tornado
FRENCH	Detroit, Baton Rouge, bureau, depot, prairie
GERMAN	Bismarck, Potsdam, frankfurter, noodle, hamburger
DUTCH	Brooklyn, Yonkers, boss, yacht, coleslaw
ITALIAN	Orlando, Syracuse, opera, pizza, spaghetti

Words with Unusual Origins

Words can come from literally anywhere. Some words come from names of people (*cardigan,* after the seventh Earl of Cardigan) or from literature (*newspeak,* or propagandistic language, in George Orwell's novel *Nineteen Eighty-Four*). Others have their origins in mythology (*odyssey,* a long voyage, after Homer's epic poem the *Odyssey*) or in place names (*tangerine,* after Tangier, Morocco, which exported the fruit). Still others are derived from words connected with historical events (*blitzkrieg,* "lightning war," a kind of warfare developed in World War II) and from many other sources. Words can be made up, like the word *googol,* meaning "the figure *1* followed by 100 *0*'s." This word was coined by the nephew of an

Vocabulary

American mathematician; or *Exxon*, a computer-created trade name. Following are additional examples of words with unusual origins.

Word	Meaning	Etymology
pasteurize	sterilize a substance	from Louis Pasteur, French chemist who discovered the process
scrooge	a miserly person	from Ebenezer Scrooge, a character in Charles Dickens' "A Christmas Carol"
jovial	good-humored, merry	from Jove (another name for Jupiter), supreme god in Roman mythology
cantaloupe	a melon with a reddish-orange flesh	from Cantalupo, former papal villa near Rome, Italy
oxford	a low shoe laced and tied over the instep	from Oxford, a city on the Thames River in England

EXERCISE 8   Recognizing Etymologies

Write the letter of the phrase that matches the etymology of the numbered word. Check your answers in a dictionary.

f 1. atlas
j 2. Braille
b 3. cheddar
i 4. hominy
h 5. leotard
g 6. plaza
a 7. Pollyanna
e 8. ultimatum
d 9. solar
c 10. Spartan

a. naive optimist; named after heroine of novel
b. cheese that originated in English village
c. self-disciplined; like citizens of Greek city
d. relating to sun; from Latin word for *sun*
e. final demand; from Latin word for *final*
f. book of maps; named for mythological giant
g. public square; word borrowed from the Spanish language
h. close-fitting garment; named for French gymnast
i. hulled corn; word of American Indian origin
j. writing system for blind; named for developer

Increasing Your Vocabulary

EXERCISE 9   Exploring Etymologies

Write the letter of the phrase that matches the etymology of the numbered word. Check your answers in a dictionary.

d 1. aghast
g 2. beneficiary
b 3. bibliography
h 4. catechism
j 5. civic
a 6. composite
f 7. fallacy
e 8. imperial
c 9. inaugurate
i 10. literal

a. made up of separate parts; from Latin word *componere,* meaning "put together"
b. list of written works; from two Greek words meaning "copying of books"
c. in Latin means "practice augury," which is to foretell from signs and omens; now means "induct into office"
d. struck with amazement and terror; derived from Old English word for *ghost*
e. from Latin word for *command* or *empire*
f. false idea; derived from Latin word for *deceive*
g. one who receives an advantage; from Latin word meaning "favor"
h. from Greek word *katechein,* meaning "teach"
i. "word for word"; from Latin word for *letter*
j. relating to a citizen or city; from Latin word for *citizen*

INCREASING YOUR VOCABULARY

Words are the tools of communication, and communication is a part of everyone's daily life. You can increase your knowledge of words by using a dictionary regularly and efficiently. Look up unfamiliar words that you read or hear. Read the definition, check the spelling, and look at the etymology of each word. Notice prefixes, suffixes, and roots. They can help you understand the meaning not only of the word you are looking up but also of other words.

A good way to add new words to your vocabulary is to keep a special notebook for difficult words. Write down new words and their meanings as you come across them. Review your list from time to time. By following this procedure, you can increase your vocabulary significantly.

Vocabulary

Vocabulary List

The following list contains words that you are likely to find in your reading. Since these words appeared earlier in the chapter, you should know most of them already. As you go over the list, try to define each word. If you are unsure of what a word means, look it up in the dictionary and enter the word in your vocabulary notebook.

Vocabulary List

advantageous	contour	illegible	mirage
affirmative	credulous	immaterial	nonentity
aghast	cumbersome	imperial	obstinate
amorphous	decree	inaugurate	pauper
antidote	dexterity	infraction	periphery
apparel	diagnosis	inhuman	perpetual
asphyxiation	discreditable	inkling	posterity
asymmetrical	discretion	interminable	prelude
beneficial	disengage	interrogate	premonition
beneficiary	elude	intervene	quest
bibliography	eradicate	intricate	raucous
botany	expatriate	inverse	relinquish
buoyancy	exuberant	irony	renaissance
carnivorous	fallacy	jovial	reverence
celestial	fervent	judicious	spectrum
circumspect	fluency	justify	thesis
civic	frivolous	lenient	tranquil
commemorate	habitat	literal	ultimatum
compassion	hyperactive	mandatory	ultrasonic
composite	hypothermia	memoirs	validation
condolence	idealism	metamorphosis	variance

CHAPTER REVIEW

A. Write the letter of the word or group of words closest in meaning to the word in capital letters.

E 1. AMORPHOUS   (A) untrustworthy (B) dying
   (C) curious (D) regretful (E) shapeless

Chapter Review

A 2. DISCRETION   (A) caution (B) difficulty (C) laughter (D) confusion (E) denial
E 3. INVERSE   (A) distant (B) careful (C) poetic (D) ancient (E) opposite
A 4. FERVENT   (A) emotional (B) ill (C) casual (D) hostile (E) sensible
D 5. INFRACTION   (A) illusion (B) vacancy (C) fulfillment (D) violation (E) increase
B 6. ULTIMATUM   (A) summit (B) final demand (C) community (D) perfection (E) verdict
C 7. FALLACY   (A) worthlessness (B) disgrace (C) false idea (D) deformity (E) necessity
D 8. ERADICATE   (A) accompany (B) intervene (C) supplement (D) uproot (E) employ
B 9. RENAISSANCE   (A) century (B) rebirth (C) surplus (D) romance (E) art
C 10. MANDATORY   (A) automatic (B) delightful (C) required (D) impossible (E) shrewd

B. Write the letter of the word or group of words most nearly opposite in meaning to the word in capital letters.

B 1. AFFIRMATIVE   (A) uncertain (B) negative (C) pleasing (D) timid (E) bold
A 2. ADVANTAGEOUS   (A) harmful (B) kind (C) plentiful (D) late (E) selfish
D 3. ILLEGIBLE   (A) straight (B) pronounceable (C) athletic (D) readable (E) correct
E 4. FRIVOLOUS   (A) hostile (B) encouraging (C) harmless (D) noisy (E) serious
B 5. RELINQUISH   (A) give in (B) keep (C) dislike (D) retreat (E) give up
E 6. IMMATERIAL   (A) invisible (B) hasty (C) unrecognized (D) formless (E) important
D 7. CIRCUMSPECT   (A) talkative (B) curious (C) disrespectful (D) daring (E) cheerful
D 8. JUDICIOUS   (A) sound (B) nonjudgmental (C) cooperative (D) unwise (E) law-abiding
D 9. OBSTINATE   (A) sturdy (B) impolite (C) certain (D) yielding (E) forgiving
A 10. ASYMMETRICAL   (A) balanced (B) similar (C) necessary (D) unequal (E) measured

Chapter 14 Spelling

OBJECTIVES
- To avoid spelling errors by observing spelling rules for *ie/ei, sede/ceed/cede*, plurals, and the addition of prefixes and suffixes.
- To practice spelling commonly misspelled words.

MOTIVATIONAL ACTIVITY

Ask each student to imagine that he or she is editor of a school newspaper. A newly appointed reporter turns in his first story (below). Pass out copies of the story. Ask students to read it carefully and find and correct all the spelling errors. Then have the class discuss ways to explain to the new reporter the importance of spelling conventions.

Cafeteria Food Fails Nutrishun Standards

1. It doesn't take a genious to see
2. that the food offered in the school
3. cafeteria places the health of
4. students in jepeordy. Since students
5. eat only one meal a day in the
6. cafateria, that meal should satisfy
7. at least one fourth of the minamum
8. daily requierments recommended
9. by the United States Department of
10. Agriculture. A test conducted last
11. simester, however, showed that the
12. meals fall short. A report from the
13. testing officials reccomended that
14. the school nigotate with the food
15. service company to improve the
16. standerds of the fare. A representa-
17. tive of the food copmany, Norm
18. Richter, has expressed willingness to
19. raise the food's standards in com-
20. pliance with the school's wishes.
21. Although the result may not make
22. the food less monatanous, we
23. should at least be seeing healthier
24. offerings in the cafateria next year.

Lines	Errors
headline	cafeteria, nutrition
1	genius
3	cafeteria
4	jeopardy
6	cafeteria
7	minimum
8	requirements
11	semester
13	recommended
14	negotiate
16	standards
17	company
22	monotonous
24	cafeteria

Students should then think of suggestions they can give this writer to improve his spelling. These suggestions might include the following:

1. Keep a spelling notebook in which you list words that give you trouble.
2. Spell words by syllables.
3. Consult a dictionary.
4. Use memory tricks such as the following:
   FAMILIAR The *liar* told a fami*liar* story.
   LABORATORY Important *labor* occurs in a *labor*atory.
5. Proofread your writing to find errors.

TEACHING SUGGESTIONS

Spelling Patterns *(pages 324–325)* You can explain the exceptions to the *ie/ei* rule in the list at the top of page 325 by grouping them in the following categories.

SHORT VOWEL SOUND
ancient
conscience

In almost all cases, a short vowel sound, such as the short *e* sound in *friend* and the short *i* sound in *kerchief*, is spelled with *ie*.

Nonpareil and *heifer* and words ending in *-feit* or *-eign* are exceptions.

-feit words	*-eign* words
forfeit	foreign
surfeit	sovereign
counterfeit	

LONG E SOUND
either   seize
leisure   weird
protein

These words belong to a group of stubborn exceptions; other words in this group are *codeine, caffeine, Keith,* and *O'Neill.*
LONG I SOUND
height

Except for three words, all syllables sounded as a long *i* take the *ei* spelling: *sleight, Fahrenheit, stein, seismic, kaleidoscope.* The *only* exceptions are *hierarchy, fiery,* and *hieroglyphic.*
SHORT A SOUND
their
heir

After students have completed Exercise 1, go over each answer and ask students to explain the rule (or the exception) by which he or she arrived at the proper spelling.
ANSWERS
1. long *a*
2. long *e*; no *c*
3. long *e*; no *c*
4. short *a* sound
5. long *a* sound
6. long *e*; no *c*
7. exception to short vowel rule: *-eign* word
8. long *e*; no *c*
9. long *e*; no *c*
10. long *e*; no *c*
11. long *e* after *c*
12. long *e*; no *c*
13. exception to long *e* rule
14. long *e* after *c*
15. long *e* after *c*
16. long *e*; no *c*
17. long *e*; no *c*
18. exception to long *e* rule
19. long *e* after *c*
20. exception to long *e* rule

Plurals *(pages 325–328)* Another common mistake among students is assuming that plurals ending in *a* are singular (phenomena, media, etc.). Read the following sentences to the class, asking students to choose the word that correctly completes the sentence.

1. Please file these (memorandum, memoranda) before leaving today.
2. The formation of hailstones is an interesting (phenomena, phenomenon).
3. The study was based on numerous (data, datum) that supported the scientist's hypothesis.
4. Principals from various schools met to compare their (curriculum, curricula).

Prefixes and Suffixes *(pages 328–330)* Many students are tempted to drop an *s* that is needed before adding the prefix *mis-*. They may also be tempted to add an unnecessary *s* when adding the prefix *dis-*. Remind students that the *s* is doubled only when the root word to which they are adding a prefix already begins with *s*.

mi*s*step but mismanage
di*s*satisfy but disappoint

Test students on these *mis-* and *dis-* words by reading them and asking students to spell them correctly.

1. disarray   6. mislead
2. mistake   7. misconduct
3. misshapen   8. dissimilar
4. disagree   9. misspeak
5. disservice   10. dissuade

ACTIVITIES FOR DIFFERENT ABILITIES
Basic Students
ACTIVITY 1 Homonyms and Other Tricky Spellings
You may wish to review and test students on the following terms from the Glossary of Usage (pages 200–226).

accept, except
advice, advise
affect, effect
all ready, already
all together, altogether
allusion, illusion
a while, awhile
coarse, course
hear, here
its, it's
knew, new
loose, lose
may be, maybe
passed, past

Chapter 14 b

Spelling

precede, proceed
principal, principle
than, then
their, there, they're
theirs, there's
threw, through
to, too, two
weak, week
whose, who's
your, you're

ACTIVITY 2 Drilling in Pairs
Pair students and have them drill each other on the words in the list of spelling demons on page 331. You may repeat this activity over a period of several days, having students do ten words at a time.

ACTIVITY 3 Writing Sentences
Have students choose ten words from the list of spelling demons on page 331 and use each in a sentence. Students may exchange papers and look for any other spelling errors that their classmates may have made.

ACTIVITY 4 Writing Paragraphs
Have students write a paragraph about a courtroom trial, using the plural forms of at least five words from Exercise 3 on page 326.

Advanced Students

ACTIVITY 1 Using Spelling Demons
Write the following sentences on the chalkboard. For each one, students should choose a word from the list on page 331 to replace the underlined word or expression. Tell them that they might have to change some words slightly (singular to plural or adjective to noun, for example).

1. The <u>king</u> ruled wisely and fairly. (sovereign)
2. One night, however, his soothsayer told him about an ancient <u>warning about the future</u>. (prophecy)
3. He said he would have to <u>give up</u> his throne. (forfeit)
4. According to the warning, a <u>general agreement</u> would force him to give up the <u>plush</u> life he lived at the palace. (consensus, luxurious)
5. The reasons related to the vast difference in the <u>monetary</u> conditions between the royal family and most of the populace. (financial)
6. When the king heard this, he decided to recommend a new law that would guarantee every citizen a <u>lowest possible</u> standard of decent living. (minimum)
7. The king decided not to raise <u>taxes</u> to accomplish this; instead he gave to his country most of his own great wealth. (tariffs)
8. The <u>lawmaking body</u> recognized the wisdom of the king's new law and passed it <u>without a single dissenting vote</u>. (parliament, unanimously)
9. The people were <u>ardent</u> about the new law, which <u>moved</u> wealth from the royal family to the very poor. (enthusiastic, transferred)
10. Because the king had taken advantage of <u>chance</u> to improve the lives of his countryfolk, he remained in power to the end of his days. (opportunity)

ACTIVITY 2 Proofreading Symbols
Have students write a paragraph about a concert. They should intentionally misspell at least five words. Then have students exchange papers and have each reader use the appropriate proofreading symbols (see "Appendix," page 614) to mark the spelling corrections. The most useful symbols will be those for inserting a letter, transposing letters, and deleting letters.

ACTIVITY 3 Writing Paragraphs
Have each student write a paragraph explaining one or more memory tricks he or she has devised to help remember the spelling of words. Have students read their paragraphs to the class, so that others can share the benefit of their peers' ideas and students can get a feeling for writing for an audience.

ADDITIONAL PRACTICE
Teacher's Resource Book: pages 187–190

Spelling

**REVIEW EXERCISES
AND TESTS**

Student Edition
 Chapter Review: pages 331–332
 Standardized Test: pages 333–334

Teacher's Resource Book
 Chapter 14 Test: pages 37–38
 (Also available as spirit duplicating masters.)

Chapter 14 d

14

Spelling

For additional practice for this chapter, see the Teacher's Resource Book.

Good spelling is a goal worth pursuing. If you have prepared a thoughtful or a carefully researched paper, it is well worth the time and effort to correct any misspellings in your paper. This chapter covers some of the techniques that will help you become a better speller.

SPELLING RULES

Improving your spelling requires practice and effort. Whether you are a good speller or a poor speller, you have to *want* to improve before you *will* improve. Once you make the commitment to improve, you will find that a knowledge of spelling rules will help.

Spelling Patterns

The following rules cover the spelling patterns for the long *e* sound and the *seed* sound.

Words with *ie* or *ei*. When the sound is long *e* ($\bar{e}$), the spelling is *ie* except after *c*.

Put *i* before *e*: believe   brief   niece   yield
Except after *c*: ceiling   conceit   deceive   receipt

When the sound is long *a* ($\bar{a}$), the spelling is *ei*.

Long *a* sound: freight   vein   feign   veil

Spelling Patterns

Although these rules generally apply, there are exceptions, such as the following words.

ancient	foreign	leisure	sovereign
conscience	forfeit	protein	their
either	height	seize	weird

NOTE: These rules do not apply if the *i* and the *e* are in different syllables.

be ing   happi er   re invest   sci ence

Words with the "Seed" Sound. The "seed" sound is spelled three ways: *-sede, -ceed,* and *-cede.*

1. Only one word in English ends in *-sede: supersede.*
2. Only three words end in *-ceed: exceed, proceed, succeed.*
3. All other words that end in the "seed" sound have the ending *-cede.* These words include *accede, concede, precede, recede,* and *secede.*

EXERCISE 1 Using Spelling Patterns

Write each word, adding either *ie* or *ei*.

1. w*ei*ght
2. s*ie*ge
3. br*ie*f
4. h*ei*r
5. v*ei*l
6. p*ie*rce
7. for*ei*gn
8. gr*ie*ve
9. y*ie*ld
10. rel*ie*ve
11. dec*ei*ve
12. hyg*ie*ne
13. l*ei*sure
14. rec*ei*ve
15. c*ei*ling
16. med*ie*val
17. retr*ie*ve
18. prot*ei*n
19. perc*ei*ve
20. *ei*ther

EXERCISE 2 Using Spelling Patterns

Write each word, adding *-sede, -ceed,* or *-cede.*

1. ex*ceed*
2. con*cede*
3. se*cede*
4. suc*ceed*
5. super*sede*
6. inter*cede*
7. pro*ceed*
8. ac*cede*
9. re*cede*
10. pre*cede*

Plurals

The following rules will help you spell the plural form of most nouns.

Regular Nouns. To form the plural of most nouns, add *s*.

SINGULAR	plumber	almanac	course	maze
PLURAL	plumbers	almanacs	courses	mazes

325

Spelling

To form the plural of nouns ending in *s*, *ch*, *sh*, *x*, or *z*, add *es*.

SINGULAR	atlas	sandwich	ash	reflex
PLURAL	atlases	sandwiches	ashes	reflexes

Nouns Ending in y. Add *s* to form the plural of a noun ending in a vowel and *y*.

SINGULAR	birthday	valley	buoy	buy
PLURAL	birthdays	valleys	buoys	buys

For a noun ending in a consonant and *y*, change the *y* to *i* and add *es*.

SINGULAR	body	salary	fantasy	charity
PLURAL	bodies	salaries	fantasies	charities

EXERCISE 3 Forming Plurals

Write the plural of each of the following nouns.

1. lawyers
2. journeys
3. taxes
4. inquiries
5. satires
6. deliveries
7. fees
8. delays
9. mosses
10. alleys
11. minorities
12. dishes
13. inequities
14. nephews
15. convoys
16. churches
17. comedies
18. vases
19. juries
20. eagles

Nouns Ending in o. Add *s* to form the plural of a noun ending in a vowel and *o*.

SINGULAR	studio	curio	stereo	kangaroo
PLURAL	studios	curios	stereos	kangaroos

Also add *s* to form the plural of a musical term ending in *o*.

SINGULAR	soprano	cello	trio	concertino
PLURAL	sopranos	cellos	trios	concertinos

Nouns ending in a consonant and *o* follow no regular pattern for plurals. They may end in either *s* or *es*.

SINGULAR	auto	ego	hero	embargo
PLURAL	autos	egos	heroes	embargoes

A number of words ending in a consonant and *o* form their plural with either *s* or *es*. The plural of *avocado*, for example, can be spelled *avocados* or *avocadoes*. The word *buffalo* has three acceptable plural forms: *buffalo*, *buffaloes*, and *buffalos*.

Plurals

When you are in doubt about the spelling of a plural, consult the dictionary. *(See page 343.)* If the dictionary shows more than one plural form, use the first form listed. If the dictionary shows no plural form, the plural of that word ends in *s* or *es*.

Nouns Ending in *f* or *fe*. To form the plural of some nouns ending in *f* or *fe*, simply add *s*.

SINGULAR	gulf	sheriff	fife	safe
PLURAL	gulfs	sheriffs	fifes	safes

For other nouns, change the *f* to *v* and add *s* or *es*.

SINGULAR	wife	half	loaf	self
PLURAL	wives	halves	loaves	selves

There is no sure way to tell which method should be used to form the plural of nouns ending in *f* or *fe*. If you are in doubt as to whether the *f* or *fe* changes, check the plural spelling in a dictionary.

Foreign Plurals. Some foreign words keep their original form.

SINGULAR	alumnus	genus	crisis	datum
PLURAL	alumni	genera	crises	data

Plurals of Numbers, Letters, Symbols, and Words Used as Words. Add an apostrophe and an *s* to form the plural of numbers, letters, symbols, and words used as words.

NUMBERS   Notice the odd *6*'s on these old coins.
LETTERS   Be sure to dot your *i*'s and cross your *t*'s.
SYMBOLS   The *+*'s and *$*'s are blurred.
WORDS AS WORDS   Underline all the *and*'s in this paragraph.

EXERCISE 4   Forming Plurals

Write the plural of each of the following nouns. Use a dictionary if necessary.

1. altos
2. echoes
3. photos
4. solos
5. shampoos
6. ratios
7. concertos
8. silos
9. cuckoos
10. potatoes
11. chiefs
12. wolves
13. chefs
14. tariffs
15. lives
16. alumnae
17. data
18. crises
19. 4's
20. then's

Spelling

Other Plural Forms. A number of familiar nouns form their plural in irregular ways.

SINGULAR	child	woman	tooth	foot	mouse	ox
PLURAL	children	women	teeth	feet	mice	oxen

Some nouns do not change form.

SINGULAR	deer	cattle	species	series	Swiss
PLURAL	deer	cattle	species	series	Swiss

Compound Nouns. The plurals of most compound nouns are formed in the same way that other noun plurals are.

SINGULAR	eyetooth	hourglass	stepchild
PLURAL	eyeteeth	hourglasses	stepchildren

In hyphenated compounds and in nouns of more than one word, the main word is often made plural.

SINGULAR	sister-in-law	hanger-on	poet laureate
PLURAL	sisters-in-law	hangers-on	poets laureate

EXERCISE 5 Forming Plurals

Write the plural of each of the following nouns.

1. moose
2. species
3. doorman
4. musk-ox
5. Chinese
6. railroad
7. stopwatch
8. by-product
9. son-in-law
10. bill of sale
11. headquarters
12. mayor-elect
13. chairwoman
14. venetian blind
15. counselor-at-law

Prefixes and Suffixes

A *prefix* is one or more syllables placed in front of a root to modify the meaning of the root or to form a new word. When you add a prefix, do not change the spelling of the root.

in + visible = invisible mis + step = misstep
co + operate = cooperate re + entry = reentry

A *suffix* is one or more syllables placed after a root to help shape its meaning. The spelling of the root does not change when the suffixes -*ness* and -*ly* are added.

keen + ness = keenness   total + ly = totally

Prefixes and Suffixes

When you add a suffix other than *-ness* and *-ly*, you may have to change the spelling of the root.

Words Ending in e. Drop the final *e* before a suffix that begins with a vowel.

   drive + ing = driving   believe + able = believable

Keep the final *e* before a suffix that begins with a consonant.

   hope + ful = hopeful   amaze + ment = amazement

If a word ends in *ce* or *ge*, however, and the suffix begins with *a* or *o*, keep the final *e*.

   notice—noticeable   courage—courageous

Following are some exceptions to these rules.

awe—awful	argue—argument	die—dying
true—truly	judge—judgment	dye—dyeing

EXERCISE 6   **Adding Prefixes and Suffixes**
Write each word, adding the prefix or the suffix shown. Remember to make any necessary spelling changes.

1. re + elect
2. scarce + ity
3. note + able
4. im + movable
5. mile + age
6. over + rule
7. pre + existing
8. care + ful
9. smile + ing
10. brave + ly
11. approve + al
12. imagine + ary
13. manage + able
14. argue + ment
15. actual + ly

Words Ending in y. Keep the *y* when adding a suffix to most words ending in a vowel and *y*.

   buoy + ant = buoyant   employ + ment = employment

For most words ending in a consonant and *y*, change the *y* to *i* before adding a suffix.

   icy + ly = icily   study + ous = studious

Following are some exceptions to these rules.

   SUFFIX BEGINNING WITH *i*   hurrying   thirtyish   specifying

   ONE-SYLLABLE ROOT WORDS   daily   paid   slyness   gaily   fryer

Spelling

EXERCISE 7 Adding Suffixes

Write each word, adding the suffix shown. Remember to make any necessary spelling changes.

1. friendly + ness
2. dizzy + ly
3. obey + ing
4. ply + able
5. forty + eth
6. carry + ing
7. child + ish
8. defy + ance
9. supply + er
10. hobby + ist
11. play + ful
12. rely + able
13. funny + est
14. spray + ed
15. day + ly

Doubling the Final Consonant. Sometimes you must double the final consonant when you add a suffix beginning with a vowel. Do so only if the root word satisfies *both* of the following conditions.

- The word must have only one syllable or must be stressed on the final syllable.
- The word must end in one consonant preceded by one vowel.

ONE-SYLLABLE WORD	step + ing stepping	tan + ed tanned	hot + est hottest
FINAL SYLLABLE STRESSED	transfer + ed transferred	permit + ing permitting	refer + al referral

Words Ending in c. When a word ends in *c* preceded by a single vowel, do not double the final consonant if the suffix begins with *e* or *i*. Instead, add *k* before the suffix. This keeps the *c* sound hard.

   mimic, mimicking   shellac, shellacked   panic, panicky

EXERCISE 8 Adding Suffixes

Write each word, adding the suffix shown. Remember to make any necessary spelling changes.

1. get + ing
2. plain + est
3. sad + en
4. picnic + ed
5. submit + ed
6. commit + al
7. propel + er
8. lug + age
9. recur + ing
10. swim + er
11. real + ist
12. occur + ed
13. stop + age
14. red + ish
15. win + er
16. proclaim + ed
17. frolic + ing
18. slim + est
19. wet + er
20. remit + ance

Chapter Review

Commonly Misspelled Words

The words in the following list are frequently used but commonly misspelled. Study them carefully.

Spelling Demons

accessory	enthusiastic	outrageous
acknowledgment	especially	paralysis
acquittal	fatigue	parliament
analysis	financial	pastime
annihilate	forfeit	perseverance
anxious	genius	personally
argument	illegible	prominent
barbecue	jeopardy	prophecy
biscuit	knowledge	referred
breathe	limousine	reminisce
cafeteria	losing	representative
carburetor	luxurious	semester
chaperon	matinee	sovereign
comparison	minimum	success
compel	monotonous	sufficient
conscientious	municipal	synonym
consensus	negotiate	tariff
delegate	noticeable	transferred
desperate	opportunity	treacherous
efficient	optimistic	unanimous

CHAPTER REVIEW

Write the letter preceding the misspelled word in each group. Then write the word, spelling it correctly.

1. (A) illegible (B) cellos (C) echoes (D) accessory (E) believeable [believable]
2. (A) acknowledgment (B) procede [proceed] (C) famous (D) sandwiches (E) either
3. (A) picnicker (B) selves (C) ilegible [illegible] (D) buoys (E) keenness
4. (A) eighth (B) decieve [deceive] (C) studios (D) dizzily (E) tariff

331

Spelling

5. (A) supersede (B) matinee (C) courageous
   (D) transfered [transferred] (E) totally
6. (A) loseing [losing] (B) dissatisfied (C) their (D) foreign
   (E) occurred
7. (A) breathe (B) sameness (C) leisure (D) halfs [halves]
   (E) argument
8. (A) mosses (B) argument (C) happier (D) conceit
   (E) outragous [outrageous]
9. (A) tarriff [tariff] (B) solos (C) analysis (D) sufficient
   (E) representative
10. (A) referred (B) icily (C) consciencious [conscientious]
    (D) efficient (E) counselors-at-law
11. (A) financial (B) jeopardy (C) noticable [noticeable] (D) 7's
    (E) protein
12. (A) municipal (B) accede (C) reelect (D) forfiet [forfeit]
    (E) truly
13. (A) delays (B) compell [compel] (C) submitted
    (D) knowledge (E) noticeable
14. (A) stubborness [stubbornness] (B) potatoes (C) monotonous
    (D) success (E) reminisce
15. (A) pastime (B) finally (C) stereos (D) exceed
    (E) recuring [recurring]
16. (A) deliveries (B) symonym [synonym] (C) hopeful
    (D) permitting (E) personally
17. (A) acquittal (B) perceive (C) annihilate
    (D) relyable [reliable] (E) anxious
18. (A) biscuit (B) driving (C) fiegn [feign] (D) juries
    (E) sizable
19. (A) retrieve (B) salarys [salaries] (C) cafeteria (D) reflexes
    (E) carburetor
20. (A) comparison (B) concensus [consensus] (C) minimum
    (D) wives (E) height
21. (A) mispell [misspell] (B) delegate (C) desperate
    (D) ancient (E) concede
22. (A) gulfs (B) heros [heroes] (C) niece (D) daily (E) awful
23. (A) amazement (B) hurrying (C) enthusiatic [enthusiastic]
    (D) changeable (E) stepping
24. (A) prominent (B) negotiate (C) judgment
    (D) icily (E) optomistic [optimistic]
25. (A) cooperate (B) panicy [panicky] (C) brief (D) specifying
    (E) employment

STANDARDIZED TEST

VOCABULARY AND SPELLING

Directions: Decide which underlined word in each sentence is misspelled. On your answer sheet, fill in the circle containing the same letter as your answer. If no word is misspelled, fill in *e*.

SAMPLE She remained <u>nonshalant</u> despite the <u>knowledge</u>
                           a   b
that she was in serious <u>financial</u> <u>jeopardy</u>. <u>No error</u>
                              c   d   e

ANSWER ⓐ ⓑ ⓒ ⓓ ⓔ

c 1. The <u>fatigued</u> defendant and his <u>anxious</u> family sobbed
           a   b
with relief after his <u>aquittal</u> as an <u>accessory</u> to the crime.
                         c   d
<u>No error</u>
  e

d 2. Two <u>prominent</u> <u>delegates</u> met with the <u>sovereign</u> to discuss
            a   b   c
the <u>tarrif</u> agreement. <u>No error</u>
      d   e

a 3. They have <u>sufficent</u> <u>opportunity</u>, <u>especially</u> during vacations,
                  a   b   c
to pursue their favorite <u>pastimes</u>. <u>No error</u>
                             d   e

a 4. Despite a <u>carbaretor</u> problem, the <u>luxurious</u> <u>limousine</u>
                  a   b   c
delivered the actor to the theater in time for the <u>matinee</u>.
                                                      d
<u>No error</u>
  e

e 5. Greeley was <u>optimistic</u> about being able to <u>negotiate</u> a
                     a   b
contract with an increased <u>minimum</u> wage for <u>municipal</u>
                              c   d
workers. <u>No error</u>
            e

b 6. As a <u>chaperon</u> at the <u>barbeque</u>, you are <u>personally</u>
              a   b   c
responsible for controlling any <u>outrageous</u> behavior.
                                    d
<u>No error</u>
  e

d 7. Hilda was <u>unanimously</u> elected class <u>representative</u> to the
                    a   b
student <u>parliament</u> for the coming <u>semestre</u>. <u>No error</u>
           c   d   e

333

c 8. After a <u>comparison</u> of the <u>biscuits</u> and rolls in the <u>cafeteria</u>,
         　　　　　a　　　　　　　b　　　　　　　　　　　　c
      the <u>consensus</u> was that they were equally tasty. <u>No error</u>
      　　　d　　　　　　　　　　　　　　　　　　　　　　　e

e 9. Would the <u>treacherous</u> King Mynoh <u>annihilate</u> the <u>desperate</u>
      　　　　　　　a　　　　　　　　　　　b　　　　　　　c
      Sushas, or would the <u>genius</u> of their queen save them?
      　　　　　　　　　　　　d
      <u>No error</u>
      　　e

a 10. Her <u>persaverance</u> and <u>enthusiastic</u> attitude contributed to
      　　　a　　　　　　　　　　b
      her <u>success</u> in overcoming the effects of the <u>paralysis</u>.
      　　　c　　　　　　　　　　　　　　　　　　　　　　　d
      <u>No error</u>
      　　e

Directions: Choose the word that is most nearly *opposite* in meaning to the word in capital letters. Fill in the circle containing the same letter as your answer.

SAMPLE   TRANQUIL   (a) vertical (b) agitated (c) ugly
         (d) calm   (e) witty

ANSWER ⓐ ● ⓒ ⓓ ⓔ

a 11. GAUNT   (a) fleshy (b) huge (c) ugly (d) ironic
       (e) tiny
b 12. FERVENT   (a) stubborn (b) unemotional (c) noisy
       (d) sincere (e) prompt
d 13. ASYMMETRICAL   (a) rough (b) smooth
       (c) shapeless (d) balanced (e) uneven
b 14. AMORPHOUS   (a) timid (b) structured (c) obscure
       (d) shapeless (e) huge
e 15. DISENGAGE   (a) interrupt (b) vow (c) validate
       (d) slice (e) connect
c 16. OBSCURE   (a) heavy (b) harmless (c) obvious
       (d) soft (e) pleasant
a 17. IMMATERIAL   (a) important (b) useless (c) flimsy
       (d) imaginative (e) recommended
c 18. OBSTINATE   (a) jovial (b) continuing (c) flexible
       (d) unyielding (e) idealistic
d 19. MANDATORY   (a) definite (b) required (c) human
       (d) optional (e) forceful
c 20. CIRCUMSPECT   (a) somber (b) forceful
       (c) adventurous (d) observant (e) cautious

334

Unit 5

Reference Skills

15 The Dictionary
16 The Library

Chapter 15   The Dictionary

OBJECTIVES

- To use unabridged and abridged dictionaries.
- To use the dictionary to find different kinds of entries, including biographical and geographical names.
- To explain the function of each part of a dictionary entry, including spelling, division into syllables, pronunciation, part-of-speech labels, inflected forms and derived words, etymologies, and multiple meanings and their labels.

MOTIVATIONAL ACTIVITY

As a general introduction to the subject of words and language, you may wish to have students read Bergen Evans's essay, "Now Everyone is Hip About Slang." One obvious theme of this essay is that language is always changing. Use this theme as the starting point for a discussion of changing language, focusing on the following questions.

1. How is the changing nature of language shown in the two sample entries for the word *silly* given on page 337? (Earlier definitions are given.)
2. How does the dictionary indicate the changes in word meaning? (by using labels such as *archaic* and *obsolete* that show the word's earlier meanings)
3. What are some examples of new words? (Students might provide examples of current slang or new technical terms. As students offer ideas, write them on the chalkboard.)
4. Do all these examples listed on the chalkboard already appear in the dictionary?
5. If not, is it likely that they will in the future? What kinds of tests must a word pass to become a dictionary entry? (Students will have to speculate about this, but they may suggest such things as use over a wide geographical area, precision of meaning, and use over a long period of time.)
6. What examples of dead slang can you think of? (Students can use the essay by Bergen Evans to find such examples as *square* and *hip*. Other examples may include *the cat's pajamas, neato, far out,* etc. Write all examples on the chalkboard.)
7. Are all the above examples in the dictionary?

TEACHING SUGGESTIONS

Kinds of Dictionaries *(pages 336–337)*

Have students choose a word to look up in both an abridged and an unabridged dictionary. Advise students to stay away from extremely common, simple words such as *go, see,* and *be* because their entries are often very long. Have students use the library to find the word in both kinds of dictionaries and answer the following questions about *each* entry.

1. Does the entry contain all of the nine parts listed at the bottom of page 337?
2. If not, which are missing?
3. How many different definitions are offered?
4. Is the pronunciation the same in both dictionaries?
5. Is the etymology the same in both dictionaries?

Information in a Dictionary *(pages 338–346)*

As a preview to the information in this section, have students use the work they completed in the previous exercise to help write their own dictionary entry. First have them make up a nonsense word. Then have them refer to the entry in the abridged dictionary that they used in the previous exercise to write an entry for their nonsense word that includes division into syllables, pronunciation (using the key in their classroom diction-

Chapter 15 a

ary), part of speech, inflected forms, a definition, derived words, and one synonym and one antonym. They should also use their made-up word in a sentence. Next have students exchange papers. Take turns going around the class having students read their partners' made-up words and trying to use them in sentences.

EXAMPLE OF MADE-UP ENTRY
flot·sy (flot' zē) *adj.* **-si·er, -si·est;** nervous, clumsy. **—flotsily** *adv* **—flotsiness** *n.* **—Syn.** clumsy **—Ant.** graceful

Special Sections *(pages 338-339)* Few students realize how valuable the dictionary is as a general reference work. In many cases, the charts and graphs alone contain a great deal of valuable information. To help students appreciate the diversity of information in a dictionary, have them make a list of all the charts and graphs in their dictionary and their page numbers. Under each one, they should list one fact they learned from the chart or graph.

Information in an Entry *(pages 339-346)* Students may need help learning how to locate idioms in a dictionary. First review the meaning of the word *idiom* (an expression whose literal meaning does not explain its meaning as used). Explain to students that the meanings of idioms can be found in a dictionary by identifying the key word in the idiom and searching for the idiom in the entry for that key word. Have students tell you what word they would look up to find the meanings of the following idioms.

1. nip and tuck (nip)
2. by a nose (nose)
3. in one ear and out the other (ear)
4. prick up one's ears (ear)
5. lie low (lie)
6. give up the ghost (ghost)
7. give in (give)
8. right off the bat (bat)
9. square off (square)
10. chip off the old block (chip)

ACTIVITIES FOR DIFFERENT ABILITIES
Basic Students
ACTIVITY 1 Using the Dictionary for Editing
Copy the following paragraph, line for line, on the chalkboard or on a duplicating master. Ask students to use their dictionaries to correct spelling, capitalization, and hyphenation mistakes. They should rewrite the paragraph correctly.

A Famous Misteak
There is an old addage: don't believe everything you read in the newspaper. One reason that newspapers are sometimes subject to errers. is that they must be put on the presses in a hurry. Readers expect their morning papers at the usaul hour. Few misteaks, thogh, have been as embarasing to the newspapers as the one that appeared in the chicago daily tribune in 1948. In that year, president harry Truman was running for reelection against thomas dewey. On election night, most experts thought Dewey was going to win easily. In order to meet the morning deadline, the chicago daily tribune decided to print the news that Dewey had won the election. The bold headline in the chicago paper, however, still read "Dewey Defeats Truman." In a famous photograph, Truman is shown holding up the newspaper with a broad grin on his face.

ACTIVITY 2 Imitation Words
Have students look up the word *buzz* in their dictionaries to find its etymology. Depending on the dictionary, either no etymology will be given or there will be a notation about the imitative sound of the word. Words like *buzz* are also sometimes called *echoic words* because they echo the meaning of the word. Have students think of other echoic words and then check the dictionary to see if any etymologies are given. Their echoic words might include *whack, clang, squeal, drip, sizzle, crackle,* or *boom.*

Chapter 15 b

The Dictionary

Advanced Students

ACTIVITY 1 Cognates
Ask students who are taking a foreign language to think of a word in that language that has a cognate in English. Write both the foreign and the English version of each word on the chalkboard. When you have about ten pairs, ask students to choose five words and look up the English version in a dictionary to discover the original source word.

ACTIVITY 2 Etymologies
Ask each student to skim a college dictionary to find one word with a Greek origin, one with a Latin origin, and one with an Old English origin. As each student reports his or her words to the class, write them in three columns on the chalkboard. When the lists are complete, ask students to generalize about the kinds of words borrowed from each source language, any recurring affixes associated with each source language, and any other characteristics that distinguish one group from another.

ADDITIONAL PRACTICE

Teacher's Resource Book:
pages 191–194

REVIEW EXERCISES AND TESTS

Student Edition
Chapter Review: pages 346–347
Teacher's Resource Book
Chapter 15 Test: pages 39–40
(Also available as spirit duplicating masters.)

ADDITIONAL ANSWERS

EXERCISE 2   Using Your Dictionary *(page 339)*

Answers refer to *Webster's New Collegiate Dictionary* (1981)

1. an American general, president of the Republic of Texas from 1836–1838 and 1841–1844 (special section)
2. 183.85 (main listing)
3. founder of the Mongol Dynasty in China (special section)
4. India (special section)
5. répondez s'il vous plaît (main listing)
6. nerve (main listing)
7. 1870 (special section)
8. Reserve Officers' Training Corps (main listing)
9. little one (main listing)
10. a monster with many snakelike heads (main listing)

EXERCISE 6   Tracing Word Origins *(page 344)*

Sample answers:

1. Our word *ambush* comes from the Old French word *embusche*, which was made up of *en-*, meaning "in," and *busche*, which meant "wood" or "bush."
2. The word *anthology* comes from the Greek word *anthologia; anthologia*, in turn, came from *anthos*, which means "flower," and *legein*, which means "to gather."
3. The word *circus* is the Latin word meaning "ring."
4. Our word *corner* derives from the Old French word *cornere*, which came from the Latin word meaning "horn," *cornu*.
5. The English word *delirium* comes from the Latin word *delirare*, which meant "to rave or be crazy." *Delirare* can be divided into *de-*, "out of," and *lira*, "furrow"; literally, *delirare*, which meant "to go out of the furrow."
6. Our word *error* comes from the Latin word *errare*, which meant "to wander."
7. *Glockenspiel* comes from the German words *Glocke*, "bell," and *Spiel*, "play."

8. Our word *iris* is the same as the Latin and Greek word that means "rainbow."
9. The English word *numb* is derived from the Old English word *numen*, which meant "taken or seized."
10. *Precarious* derives from the Latin word *precarius*, which meant "uncertain" or "obtainable by entreaty." *Precarius* in turn came from the Latin word *prex*, meaning "prayer."

15

The Dictionary

For additional practice for this chapter, see the Teacher's Resource Book.

Ever since Noah Webster published the *American Dictionary of the English Language* in 1828, both the dictionary and the English language have undergone numerous changes. There are many different kinds of dictionaries available today. They appear in a variety of sizes and cover a wide range of subject areas. Whether you are writing a literary essay, preparing a lab report, or filling out a college application form, the dictionary is one of your most valuable resource tools.

KINDS OF DICTIONARIES

Most libraries have a thick, heavy dictionary that usually sits open on a pedestal in the reference section. This large dictionary, containing over 500,000 words, is called *unabridged*, or unshortened. Unabridged dictionaries provide longer entries and more complete information than do smaller dictionaries. Listed below are some well-known unabridged dictionaries.

UNABRIDGED DICTIONARIES
Oxford English Dictionary
Random House Dictionary of the English Language, Unabridged Edition
Webster's New Third International Dictionary of the English Language

Shortened dictionaries are called *abridged*, *college*, or *school* dictionaries. They contain fewer words than unabridged dictionaries, and their definitions are usually shorter and more concise. They are also much easier to handle and contain most of the words you come across in your everyday

Kinds of Dictionaries

reading and conversation. The following list shows some popular abridged dictionaries.

COLLEGE *American Heritage Dictionary of the English Language*

Random House College Dictionary

Webster's New Collegiate Dictionary

SCHOOL *The Macmillan Dictionary*

Scott, Foresman Advanced Dictionary

Webster's New World Dictionary, Student's Edition

Read and compare the following entries. The first is from an abridged dictionary; the second is from an unabridged dictionary. Notice that each entry has the same features, but that the treatment in the unabridged dictionary is more thorough.

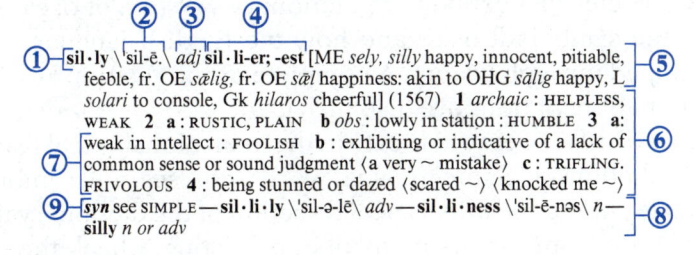

①—sil·ly \\'sil-ē.\\ ②③adj ④sil·li·er; -est [ME *sely, silly* happy, innocent, pitiable, feeble, fr. OE *sǣlig*, fr. OE *sǣl* happiness: akin to OHG *sālig* happy, L *solari* to console, Gk *hilaros* cheerful] (1567) **1** *archaic* : HELPLESS, WEAK **2 a** : RUSTIC, PLAIN **b** *obs* : lowly in station : HUMBLE **3 a** : weak in intellect : FOOLISH **b** : exhibiting or indicative of a lack of common sense or sound judgment ⟨a very ~ mistake⟩ **c** : TRIFLING, FRIVOLOUS **4** : being stunned or dazed ⟨scared ~⟩ ⟨knocked me ~⟩ ⑤⑥⑦ —*syn* see SIMPLE — **sil·li·ly** \\'sil-ə-lē\\ *adv* — **sil·li·ness** \\'sil-ē-nəs\\ *n* — **silly** *n or adv* ⑧⑨

By permission. From *Webster's Ninth New Collegiate Dictionary* © 1983 by Merriam-Webster Inc., publishers of the Merriam-Webster® Dictionaries.

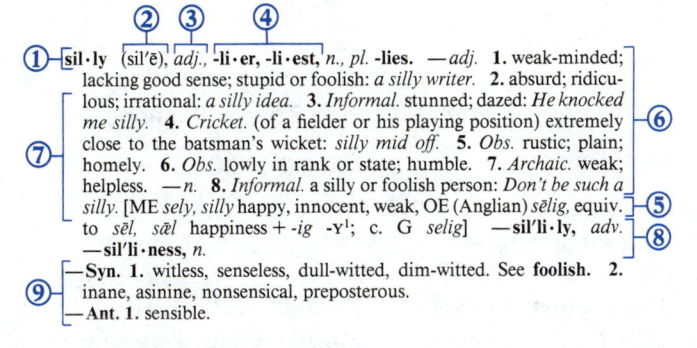

①—**sil·ly** ②(sil'ē), ③*adj.,* ④**-li·er, -li·est,** *n., pl.* **-lies.** —*adj.* **1.** weak-minded; lacking good sense; stupid or foolish: *a silly writer.* **2.** absurd; ridiculous; irrational: *a silly idea.* **3.** *Informal.* stunned; dazed: *He knocked me silly.* **4.** *Cricket.* (of a fielder or his playing position) extremely close to the batsman's wicket: *silly mid off.* **5.** *Obs.* rustic; plain; homely. **6.** *Obs.* lowly in rank or state; humble. **7.** *Archaic.* weak; helpless. —*n.* **8.** *Informal.* a silly or foolish person: *Don't be such a silly.* [ME *sely, silly* happy, innocent, weak, OE (Anglian) *sēlig*, equiv. to *sēl, sæl* happiness + *-ig* -Y¹; c. G *selig*] —**sil'li·ly,** *adv.* —**sil'li·ness,** *n.* ⑤⑥⑦⑧
—**Syn. 1.** witless, senseless, dull-witted, dim-witted. See **foolish. 2.** inane, asinine, nonsensical, preposterous. ⑨
—**Ant. 1.** sensible.

Reprinted by permission from *The Random House Dictionary of the English Language.* Copyright © 1967, 1966 by Random House, Inc.

1. word shown in syllables
2. pronunciation
3. part of speech
4. inflected forms
5. etymology
6. definitions
7. word used in a phrase or sentence
8. derived words
9. synonyms and antonyms

337

The Dictionary

INFORMATION IN A DICTIONARY

Dictionaries provide more than just the spelling or the definition of a word. Most dictionaries include biographical and geographical entries, foreign words and phrases, and an interpretation of signs and symbols, as well as other special features. The placement of these special features will vary from dictionary to dictionary. Knowing the content and organization of a dictionary will help you find the information you need.

Special Sections

Every dictionary includes information at the beginning called *front matter*. Front matter consists of charts, tables, and short articles that explain the dictionary's system of organization, the symbols it uses, and how the English language has developed through history. A complete pronunciation key and a list of abbreviations are also provided.

Most words are easy to locate in the main alphabetical listing of any dictionary. Some unusual words, phrases, and symbols, however, may appear in a special section of the dictionary that is separate from the main alphabetical listing. Check the dictionary's contents page to learn where these unusual entries are placed.

Entries Often Placed in Special Sections

Type of Entry	Examples
abbreviations	AFL-CIO, NAACP, C.O.D.
biographical names	Henry Ford, Marco Polo
charts, tables	Metric Conversion Table
colleges, universities	Duke University, Hope College
foreign words, phrases	monde, e pluribus unum
geographical names	Innsbruck, Transylvania
new words	microchip, lepton
signs, symbols	○ (clear weather), ✶ (snow)
style	punctuation, manuscript form

338

Special Sections

EXERCISE 1 **Learning about Your Dictionary**

Tell where each of the following is located in the dictionary you use most often by writing *front, back,* or *main alphabetical listing*. Answers refer to Webster's Ninth New Collegiate Dictionary (1983).

1. complete pronunciation key front, back
2. list of abbreviations used to identify the parts of speech front
3. explanation of how definitions are given for each word front
4. information about how language has developed front
5. biographical names back
6. geographical names back
7. symbols for the chemical elements main listing, back
8. foreign words and phrases main listing, back
9. metric conversion table main listing
10. explanation of the parts of a dictionary entry front

EXERCISE 2 **Using Your Dictionary**

Use your dictionary to answer the following questions. Next to each answer, indicate whether you found the answer in the *main listing* of the dictionary or in a *special section*.
Sample answers precede this chapter.

1. Who was Samuel Houston?
2. What is the atomic weight of tungsten?
3. According to Chinese history, who was Kublai Khan?
4. Where is Jodhpur?
5. What French words does the abbreviation *R.S.V.P.* stand for?
6. What does the combining form *neuro-* mean?
7. In what year did Charles Dickens die?
8. What does the abbreviation *ROTC* stand for?
9. What is the definition of the suffix *-ie*?
10. In Greek mythology what is the Hydra?

Information in an Entry

A dictionary is used mainly to check spelling, meaning, or pronunciation. Dictionaries, however, contain much more information about each word. They show how the word is correctly divided into syllables, the parts of speech it can function as, other forms of the word, the word's history, and often synonyms and antonyms for the word. Together, this

The Dictionary

information for each word is known as a *main entry*. The word itself is called an *entry word*.

Entry words are listed in alphabetical order. The following list shows some of the different types of entry words and the order in which they would appear in a dictionary.

Entries Placed in the Main Listing	
single word	ant
suffix	-ant
abbreviation	ant.
compound word	ant hill
prefix	anti-

Preferred and Variant Spellings. The entry word, printed in heavy type, shows the correct spelling of a word. Some words have more than one correct spelling. The *preferred spelling* is listed first. It is followed by the less common spelling, called the *variant*.

⎯⎯⎯⎯⎯⎯⎯⎯⎯ PREFERRED SPELLING

hon·or, *also, British,* **hon·our.**
⎯⎯⎯⎯⎯⎯⎯⎯⎯ VARIANT SPELLING

For some words the variant spelling is listed as a separate entry, in alphabetical order. The entry showing only the variant spelling does not include a full definition. Instead, it refers the reader to the preferred spelling.

⎯⎯⎯⎯⎯⎯⎯ PREFERRED SPELLING

rime, *var. of* RHYME.
⎯⎯⎯⎯⎯⎯⎯⎯⎯ VARIANT SPELLING

Always use the preferred spelling of any word in your writing.

EXERCISE 3 **Finding Preferred Spellings**

Each of the following words is a variant spelling. Using your dictionary, write the preferred spelling for each word.

EXAMPLE calory
ANSWER calorie

1. aeroplane   airplane
2. esthetic   aesthetic
3. copeck   kopeck
4. tsar   czar

Information in an Entry

5. practise practice
6. grey gray
7. saleable salable
8. odour odor
9. encyclopaedia encyclopedia
10. councillor councilor

Dividing Words into Syllables. When dividing a word at the end of a line, you will need to know how the word breaks into syllables. Most dictionaries use dots or empty spaces in the entry word to show these breaks, but writers must use hyphens. *(See pages 293–295.)*

EXAMPLES   op·po·nent   pa·rab·o·la   qual·i·fy

EXERCISE 4   Dividing Words into Syllables
Copy the following entry words from your dictionary to show how they are divided into syllables. Place a small dot between each break in the word.

EXAMPLE   fraternity
ANSWER   fra·ter·ni·ty

1. catastrophe ca·tas·tro·phe
2. simplicity sim·plic·i·ty
3. cordiality cor·dial·i·ty
4. ostentatious os·ten·ta·tious
5. mediator me·di·a·tor
6. dais da·is
7. demitasse demi·tasse
8. ecstatic ec·stat·ic
9. fluorescent flu·o·res·cent
10. collaboration col·lab·o·ra·tion

Pronunciation. Following the entry word is the phonetic spelling of the word, which shows how it is pronounced.

grad u a tion (graj′ū ā′shən), *n.* 1 a graduating from a school, college, or university. 2 ceremony of graduating; graduating exercises. 3 division into equal spaces. 4 mark or set of marks to show degrees for measuring. 5 arrangement in regular steps, stages, or degrees. — PHONETIC SPELLING

From SCOTT, FORESMAN ADVANCED DICTIONARY by E. L. Thorndike and Clarence L. Barnhart. Copyright © 1983, 1979, 1974 by Scott, Foresman & Co. Reprinted by permission.

The symbols used in the phonetic spelling are shown in a chart at the beginning of the dictionary. Most dictionaries also show a partial pronunciation key at the top or bottom of each right-hand page. This partial key provides easy reference for interpreting the phonetic symbols. Always consult the key if you are not sure how a word should be pronounced.

The Dictionary

PARTIAL PRONUNCIATION KEY

a hat	i it	oi oil	ch child		a in about
ā age	ī ice	ou out	ng long		e in taken
ä far	o hot	u cup	sh she	ə =	i in pencil
e let	ō open	ù put	th thin		o in lemon
ē equal	ô order	ü rule	ŦH then		u in circus
ėr term			zh measure	< = derived from	

From SCOTT, FORESMAN ADVANCED DICTIONARY by E. L. Thorndike and Clarence L. Barnhart. Copyright © 1983, 1979, 1974 by Scott, Foresman & Co. Reprinted by permission.

To find out how to pronounce the vowel in the second syllable of *graduation,* look for the symbol *ü* in the pronunciation key. You can see that it is pronounced like the *u* in *rule.* To distinguish one vowel sound from another, dictionaries include diacritical marks above the vowels. The letter *u,* for example, has three different sounds.

u as in c**u**p   **u** as in p**ù**t   **u** as in r**ü**le   ——— DIACRITICAL MARKS

The letter *u,* as well as the other vowels, is sometimes pronounced *uh.* This sound is represented by a symbol called a *schwa.* In the word *graduation,* the last syllable contains the schwa sound.

graj′ü ā′sh**ə**n   SCHWA

Phonetic spellings also contain accent marks to show which syllables are stressed. A heavy accent mark, called a *primary stress,* indicates which syllable receives the most emphasis. A *secondary stress* is marked with a lighter accent.

———— PRIMARY STRESS
graj′ü ā′shən
———— SECONDARY STRESS

If a word can be pronounced in more than one way, the dictionary will show each correct form. The first one shown, however, is preferred. In some dictionaries, only those parts of the word that differ in an alternate pronunciation are given.

ALTERNATE PRONUNCIATIONS   **ec·o·nom·ics** (ek′ə nom′iks. ē′kə-)
ei·ther (ē′ŦHər, ī′ŦHər)

From MACMILLAN DICTIONARY. Copyright © 1981 Macmillan Publishing Co., Inc.

Information in an Entry

Phonetic symbols and the placement of accent marks differ from dictionary to dictionary. Check the front of your dictionary to learn the symbols used in pronunciation.

EXERCISE 5 Using Pronunciation Keys
Number your paper 1 to 10. Using the pronunciation key on page 342, write the word that each phonetic spelling represents.

1. kə lam′ə tē   calamity
2. kal′sē əm   calcium
3. kal′kyə ləs   calculus
4. kə zü′   kazoo
5. kak′ē   khaki
6. kėr′tē əs   courteous
7. kən kėr′   concur
8. kon′krēt′   concrete
9. kən fesh′ən   confession
10. kul′chər   culture

calculus
confession
courteous
calamity
culture
khaki
calcium
concur
kazoo
concrete

Part-of-Speech Labels. Dictionaries use abbreviations to show what part of speech a word is. A list of abbreviations can usually be found at the beginning of the dictionary. If the word can be used as more than one part of speech, its most common usage will usually be listed first.

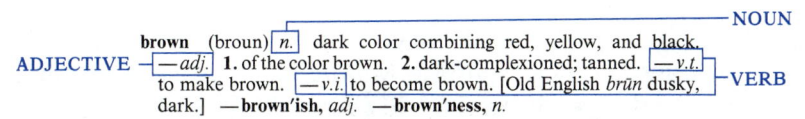

> **brown** (broun) *n.* dark color combining red, yellow, and black. —*adj.* **1.** of the color brown. **2.** dark-complexioned; tanned. —*v.t.* to make brown. —*v.i.* to become brown. [Old English *brūn* dusky, dark.] —**brown′ish,** *adj.* —**brown′ness,** *n.*

NOUN — *n.*
ADJECTIVE — *adj.*
VERB — *v.t.*, *v.i.*

From MACMILLAN DICTIONARY. Copyright © 1981 Macmillan Publishing Co., Inc.

Inflected Forms and Derived Words. A dictionary entry shows endings that change the form of the word but not its part of speech. This change in the form of a word is called *inflection*. Verbs, for example, can be inflected with *-ed* or *-ing* to change from one principal part to another. Adjectives can be inflected with *-er* or *-est* to show degree. Nouns can be inflected with *-s* or *-es* to make them plural. Most dictionaries show inflected forms only if they are formed irregularly.

Derived words are also formed by adding endings, but these endings change the part of speech of a word. For example,

343

The Dictionary

adding the suffix *-ly* to the noun *leisure* results in *leisurely*, which is an adjective or an adverb. Such derived words are listed at the end of a main entry.

                INFLECTED FORMS
                                                IRREGULAR

husk y[1] (hus′kē), *adj.* husk i er, husk i est, *n., pl.* husk ies. —*adj.*   PLURAL
1 big and strong. **2** dry in the throat; hoarse; rough of voice: *a husky cough.* **3** of, like, or having husks. —*n.* INFORMAL. a big, strong person. [<*husk*, noun] —**husk′i ness,** *n.*
                                                                 DERIVED WORD

From SCOTT, FORESMAN ADVANCED DICTIONARY by E. L. Thorndike and Clarence L. Barnhart. Copyright © 1983, 1979, 1974 by Scott, Foresman & Co. Reprinted by permission.

Etymologies. The etymology of a word is an explanation of its history and origin. The most recent source of the word is listed first. Dictionaries often use abbreviations to stand for the languages from which a word has developed. Symbols that stand for "derived from" (<) or "equal to" (=) are commonly used in an etymology. Check the front of your dictionary for an interpretation of abbreviations and symbols.

pa·tient (pā′shənt) *adj.* **1.** Capable of bearing affliction with calmness: *"My uncle Toby was a man patient of injuries."* (Sterne). **2.** Tolerant; understanding. **3.** Persevering; constant: *a patient worker.* **4.** Capable of bearing delay and waiting for the right moment. —*n.* One under medical treatment. [Middle English *pacient*, from Old French *patient*, from Latin *patiēns*, from the present participle of *patī*, to suffer.] —**pa′tient·ly** *adv.*   ETYMOLOGY

Reprinted by permission from *The American Heritage Dictionary of the English Language.* Copyright © 1981 by Houghton Mifflin Company.

The etymology for *patient* can be translated as follows: The word *patient* comes from the Middle English word *pacient*, which was derived from the Old French word *patient*. *Patient* was derived from the Latin word *patiens*, which is the past participle of *pati*, meaning "to suffer."

EXERCISE 6   Tracing Word Origins
Use your dictionary to discover the etymology for each of the following words. Then choose five etymologies and write their translations. Use the example for *patient* as a model.
Sample answers precede this chapter.

1. ambush
2. anthology
3. circus
4. corner
5. delirium
6. error
7. glockenspiel
8. iris
9. numb
10. precarious

Information in an Entry

Multiple Meanings. Many words have more than one meaning. Usually dictionaries will list the most common meaning first. Some dictionaries, however, list meanings in historical order, showing the oldest meaning first.

Dictionaries use labels to point out some differences in meaning. These are called restrictive labels, since they restrict the meaning of the word to a certain geographic area, a certain subject area, or a certain level of usage.

bat·ter·y (bat'ər ē) *pl.,* **-ter·ies.** *n.* **1.** *Electricity,* cell or group of cells producing and storing direct current by means of a chemical reaction. **2.** group of things that are similar or related to one another and are assembled or used as a unit: *a battery of lights, to run through a battery of tests.* **3.** *Military.* **a.** two or more guns or other weapons operating as a unit. **b.** these guns or other weapons together with the men and equipment for them. **c.** the men operating these weapons. **4.** *Law.* unlawful beating, touching, or physical constraint of another person. Distinguished from **assault. 5.** *Baseball.* pitcher and the catcher who is receiving his pitched balls. **6.** *Archaic.* platform or fortification on which artillery is mounted. [French *batterie* beating, from *battre* to beat, from Latin *battuere.*]

— SUBJECT LABELS

— USAGE LABEL

From MACMILLAN DICTIONARY. Copyright © 1981 Macmillan Publishing Co., Inc.

Synonyms and Antonyms. The last part of an entry is sometimes a list of synonyms (words with similar meanings) and antonyms (words with opposite meanings). Some dictionaries also include explanations of how the various synonyms and antonyms convey differing shades of meaning.

EXERCISE 7 Recognizing Multiple Meanings

Use the following entry for *project* to write the definition that suits the use of the underscored word in each sentence.

proj ect (*n.* proj'ekt; *v.* prə jekt'), *n.* **1** a proposed plan or scheme: *a project for better sewage disposal.* See **plan** for synonym study. **2** an undertaking; enterprise: *a research project.* **3** a special assignment planned and carried out by a student, a group of students, or an entire class. **4** group of apartment houses built and run as a unit, especially as part of public housing. —*v.t.* **1** plan, contrive, or devise: *project a tax decrease.* **2** throw or cast forward: *A cannon projects shells.* **3** cause to fall on a surface: *project a shadow. Motion pictures are projected on the screen.* **4** cause to stick out or protrude. **5** draw lines through (a point, line, figure, etc.) and reproduce it on a line, plane, or surface. **6** make a forecast for (something) on the basis of past performance. —*v.i.* stick out; protrude: *The rocky point projects far into the water.* [< Latin *projectum* thrown forward < *pro-* forward + *jacere* to throw] —**pro ject'a ble,** *adj.*

From SCOTT, FORESMAN ADVANCED DICTIONARY by E. L. Thorndike and Clarence L. Barnhart. Copyright © 1983, 1979, 1974 by Scott, Foresman & Co. Reprinted by permission.

EXAMPLE The committee proposed plans for a new <u>project</u>.
ANSWER a proposed plan or scheme

The Dictionary

1. Since our science <u>project</u> was awarded first prize, we did not have to take the final exam. _{n. 3}
2. After looking over last year's budget, our class treasurer <u>projected</u> the expenses for next year. _{v.t. 6}
3. The government has approved a plan to renovate the city's housing <u>projects</u>. _{n. 4}
4. As we <u>projected</u> the slides on the screen, Melissa started the story. _{v.t. 3}
5. The lifeguard station <u>projects</u> far above the water so that nothing can obstruct the view of the swimming area. _{v.i.}

CHAPTER REVIEW

Using the dictionary entries on page 347, write the answers to the following questions.

1. What is a variant spelling for *pajamas*?   pyjamas
2. In what year was Thomas Paine born?   1737
3. What are the two synonyms for the adjective *pale*?   pallid, wan
4. What are the inflected forms of *pal*?   palled, palling
5. What is the preferred spelling of *palaeo-*?   paleo-
6. What is the meaning of *palaeo-*?   See below.
7. What does the abbreviation *pal.* stand for?   paleontology
8. What is the usage label for *painkiller*?   informal
9. What is the capital of Pakistan?   Islamabad
10. Which of the definitions for *painter* refers to boating?   painter[2]
11. What is the plural of *palazzo*?   palazzi
12. How does *Paleolithic* divide into syllables?   Pa·le·o·lith·ic
13. What words are derived from *painful*?   painfully, painfulness
14. Should the noun *paintbrush* be hyphenated?   no
15. From what language is the word *pal* originally derived?   Sanskrit
16. Where in the United States does the painted bunting live?   southern U.S.
17. How many different parts of speech can *pale* be used as?   See below.
18. What is the translation of the etymology for *pajamas*?   See below.
19. Which definition of the noun *palate* applies to the following sentence? _{n. 2}

    The homemade maple syrup pleased my <u>palate</u>.
20. Which syllable receives a primary stress in *painstaking*?   first

   6. old; early; paleolontological
  17. three (noun, verb, adjective)
  18. <u>Pajamas</u> comes from the Hindustani word <u>pajama</u>, which comes from the Persian words <u>Pai</u>, "leg," and <u>jamah</u>, "garment."

Paine (pān), *n.* Thomas, 1737–1809, American writer on politics and religion, born in England.

pain ful (pān′fəl), *adj.* **1** causing pain; unpleasant; hurting: *a painful illness, a painful duty.* **2** involving much trouble or labor; difficult. —**pain′ful ly,** *adv.* —**pain′ful ness,** *n.*

pain kill er (pān′kil′ər), *n.* INFORMAL. a drug that relieves or lessens pain.

pain less (pān′lis), *adj.* without pain; causing no pain. —**pain′less ly,** *adv.* —**pain′less ness,** *n.*

pains tak ing (pānz′tā′king), *adj.* **1** very careful; particular; scrupulous. **2** marked or characterized by attentive care; carefully done. —**pains′tak′ing ly,** *adv.*

paint brush (pānt′brush′), *n.* **1** brush for putting on paint. **2** Indian paintbrush.

painted bunting, a small bright-colored finch of the southern United States, the male of which has a purple head, red breast, and green back; nonpareil.

paint er[1] (pān′tər), *n.* **1** person who paints pictures; artist. **2** person who paints houses, woodwork, etc. [< Old French *peinteur,* ultimately < Latin *pictorem* < *pingere* to paint]

paint er[2] (pān′tər), *n.* a rope, usually fastened to the bow of a boat, for tying it to a ship, pier, etc. [probably < Middle French *pentoir* hanging cordage < Latin *pendere* to hang]

paint er[3] (pān′tər), *n.* puma. [variant of earlier *panter* panther]

paint ing (pān′ting), *n.* **1** something painted; picture. **2** act of one who paints. **3** art of representation, decoration, and creating beauty with paints.

Pai ute (pī yüt′, pī üt′), *n., pl.* **-ute** or **-utes.** **1** member of a tribe of American Indians living in Utah, Nevada, California, and Arizona. **2** language of this tribe.

pa ja ma (pə jä′mə, pə jam′ə), *n.* pajamas. —*adj.* of or having to do with pajamas: *pajama tops.*

pa ja mas (pə jä′məz, pə jam′əz), *n.pl.* **1** sleeping or lounging garments consisting of a jacket or blouse and loose trousers fastened at the waist. **2** loose trousers worn by Moslem men and women. Also, **pyjamas.** [< Hindustani *pājāmā* < Persian *pāe* leg + *jāmah* garment]

Pak i stan (pak′ə stan, pä′kə stän), *n.* country in S Asia, west of India. 80,171,000 pop.; 310,000 sq. mi. (802,900 sq. km.) *Capital:* Islamabad. See **Bangladesh** for map.

pal (pal), *n., v.,* **palled, pal ling.** —*n.* a close friend; comrade; partner. —*v.i.* associate as pals [< Romany, variant of *pral* brother < Sanskrit *bhratr*]

pal., paleontology.

palaeo-, *combining form.* a variant form of **paleo-.**

pal ate (pal′it), *n.* **1** roof of the mouth. The bony part in front is the hard palate, and the fleshy part in back is the soft palate. **2** sense of taste: *The new flavor pleased his palate.* **3** a liking; relish: *have no palate for danger.* [< Latin *palatum*] —**pal′ate less,** *adj.* —**pal′ate like′,** *adj.*

pa laz zo (pä lät′sō), *n., pl.* **-zi** (-sē). palace, mansion, or large town house in Italy. [< Italian]

pale[1] (pāl), *adj.,* **pal er, pal est,** *v.,* **paled, pal ing.** —*adj.* **1** without much color; whitish: *When you have been ill, your face is sometimes pale.* See synonym study below. **2** not bright; dim: *a pale blue.* —*v.i.* turn pale. —*v.t.* cause to become pale. [< Old French < Latin *pallidum* < *pallere* be pale. Doublet of PALLID.] —**pale′ly,** *adv.* —**pale′ness,** *n.*
Syn. *adj.* **1 Pale, pallid, wan** mean with little or no color. **Pale** means without much natural or healthy color: *He is pale and tired-looking.* **Pallid** suggests having all color drained away, as by sickness or weakness: *Her pallid face shows her suffering.* **Wan** emphasizes the faintness and whiteness coming from a weakened or unhealthy condition: *The starved refugees were wan.*

pale[2] (pāl), *n., v.,* **paled, pal ing.** —*n.* **1** a long, narrow board, pointed on top, used for fences; picket. **2** boundary; restriction: *outside the pale of civilized society.* **3 beyond the pale,** socially unacceptable; improper: *His rude behavior at the party was beyond the pale.* **4** an enclosed place; enclosure. **5** district or territory within fixed bounds or subject to a particular jurisdiction. **6** a broad vertical stripe in the middle of an escutcheon. —*v.t.* build a fence around; enclose with pales or a fence. [< Old French *pal* < Latin *palus* stake. Doublet of POLE[1].]

paleo-, *combining form.* **1** old; ancient; prehistoric, as in *paleography.* **2** early or earliest, as in *Paleocene.* **3** that is a branch of paleontology; paleontological, as in *paleobotany.* Also, **palaeo-.** [< Greek *palaio-* < *palaios* ancient]

Pa le o lith ic (pā′lē ə lith′ik), *adj.* of or having to do with the earliest part of the Stone Age. Paleolithic tools were crudely chipped out of stone.

Chapter 16   The Library

OBJECTIVES

- To locate works of fiction according to alphabetical order.
- To locate works of nonfiction using the Dewey decimal system.
- To locate works of fiction and nonfiction using the Library of Congress classification system.
- To use author, title, subject, cross-reference, and analytic cards in the card catalog to find books.
- To use general and specialized references, including encyclopedias, biographical references, atlases, almanacs, and specialized dictionaries to find information.
- To use the *Readers' Guide to Periodical Literature* to find magazine articles.
- To find material in the vertical file.

MOTIVATIONAL ACTIVITY

There is no better motivation for using the library than a genuine interest in the subject of research. You can help students complete the work in this chapter with just that motivation by taking some time at the start to have students complete an inventory of interests. As the chapter progresses, students can use a subject from their personal inventory as the basis for their library work. Reproduce the following questionnaire on a duplicating master, leaving sufficient room for students to list as many items as possible to complete each sentence.

Inventory of Interests

A. School Subjects
  1. My favorite subjects are . . .
  2. Within those subjects, areas of special interest to me include . . .
  3. For other classes, I have prepared reports on . . .
  4. Some of the interesting people I have learned about in school include . . .
  5. The period in history that interests me the most is . . .

B. Outside Interests
  1. Outside of school, I have become good at . . .
  2. Television shows that seem to hold my interest are usually about . . .
  3. Clubs I have belonged to include . . .
  4. The kinds of books I enjoy reading are mainly . . .
  5. My favorite magazines are . . .
  6. Inside those magazines, I like to read about . . .

C. Careers
  1. The careers of my family members include . . .
  2. When I was younger I wanted to become a . . .
  3. Now the careers that interest me the most include . . .
  4. The people I admire the most work in such careers as . . .
  5. I can prepare for my chosen career by . . .

D. Arts and Entertainment
  1. My favorite musicians are . . .
  2. My favorite authors are . . .
  3. The movies that I enjoy the most are usually about . . .
  4. The sporting events I most like to attend are . . .
  5. The games I enjoy playing include . . .

This would be a good time for students to start writing folders for the year. They should put their completed "Inventory of Interests" in these folders. These subjects will prove useful for future composition assignments.

TEACHING SUGGESTIONS

Library Arrangement *(pages 348–355)*

Have students choose one of the authors they named in part D, number 2 in their "Inventory of Interests." Then have them go to the library and find one book *by* the author and one book *about* the author or his or her works. For each book, have students supply the identifying ma-

Chapter 16 a

terial the library uses to shelve the book properly (label, call number, etc.).

The Card Catalog *(pages 352–355)* Ask students to use the card catalog to list the exact subject headings under which they might find books on the following topics. (Possible answers are provided.)
1. the Boston Massacre (U.S. history—revolutionary period)
2. underwater photography (photography—marine)
3. the Prairie style of architecture developed by Frank Lloyd Wright (Wright, architecture—Prairie School)
4. Einstein's general theory of relativity (Einstein, physics—relativity)
5. how police solve crimes (criminology, police)

Reference Materials *(pages 356–361)*

Introduce students to the three-part *Encyclopaedia Britannica (EB)* with the following exercise. First have students choose a subject from their inventory of interests. Next ask them to find that subject in *EB* and write a paragraph answering the following questions about what they find. (If they are unable to find information on one subject from their inventories, they should try another until they find something.)
1. Was the subject covered in both the *Micropaedia* and the *Macropaedia*?
2. How much space was given to the article in the *Micropaedia*? How much, if any, in the *Macropaedia*?
3. Was the article in the *Micropaedia* signed by an author? Was the article in the *Macropaedia* signed?

As a follow-up to this assignment, ask students to find the same subject in a different encyclopedia and write a paragraph explaining which encyclopedia would prove more useful to someone researching this subject. Their paragraph should include specific reasons why one encyclopedia would be more useful than another.

Specialized References *(pages 356–360)* For practice with almanacs and yearbooks, students can create a trivia game. Have them copy the following ten categories on a piece of paper.

Weather Statistics
Cities
Sports
Colleges and Universities
Astronomy
Money
Historic Dates
Agriculture
Foreign Countries
Celebrities

Then have each student use an almanac or yearbook to find one trivia question for each category and write it on an index card, indicating the category at the top of the card. They should write the answer to the question on the back of the card, noting the source and page number on which the answer can be verified. Divide the class into two teams, keeping the cards from each team separate. Read a question from one team to the other team. If the second team cannot answer the question, the first team wins a point. If the second team answers correctly, it wins the point. You can keep track of the running score in a corner of the chalkboard.

Reference Materials about Language and Literature *(pages 360–361)* For a more in-depth study of these reference materials, have students find the answers to the questions in Exercise 9. After each answer they should indicate the title of the source in which they found it.

ACTIVITIES FOR DIFFERENT ABILITIES

Basic Students

ACTIVITY 1 Finding Books
To make sure students can find their way around the library, have them write the title of a book from the shelves in each of the ten main categories of the Dewey decimal system. In addition to the title, they should write the book's call number.

ACTIVITY 2 Readers' Guide
Using the excerpt on page 359, talk through the first entry to explain what

The Library

each part of the entry means (title, author, illustrated, *Science News* magazine, volume 124, pages 202–203, September 24, 1983). Then choose other entries in the excerpt and have students explain the meaning of each part.

ACTIVITY 3 Research Guide
Have students write a step-by-step explanation of how they would go about finding information in the following sources:
1. encyclopedia
2. card catalog
3. *Readers' Guide*
4. specialized dictionary

Advanced Students

ACTIVITY 1 Newspaper Index
Have students use a community library if necessary to find three recent news stories on the space shuttle. They should indicate the issue of the paper as well as the section, page, and column number.

ACTIVITY 2 Using References about Language and Literature
Have each student think of and write *one* of the following:
1. the first line of their favorite poem
2. their favorite quotation
3. the title of their favorite short story
4. their favorite play

Next pair students and have them give their partners the information they have written down. It is the partner's duty to use a literary reference work to find whichever of the following is relevant.
1. the title and author of the poem
2. the author and source of the quotation
3. the author of the short story and the title of a collection in which it appears
4. the author of the play

ACTIVITY 3 A Working Bibliography
Have students use their interest inventory or any other ideas to think of a subject they would genuinely like to know more about and possibly write a research paper on later. Then have them use the library's resources to compile a bibliography with at least five entries in each of the following categories.
1) encyclopedia articles
2) books
3) magazine articles

ADDITIONAL PRACTICE

Teacher's Resource Book: pages 195–198

REVIEW EXERCISES AND TESTS

Student Edition
Chapter Review: page 362

Teacher's Resource Book
Chapter 16 Test: pages 41–42
(Also available as spirit duplicating masters.)

ADDITIONAL ANSWERS

EXERCISE 6 Understanding Catalog Cards *(page 355)*

Title Card

```
        A Tolkien bestiary
828     Day, David.
TOL        A Tolkien bestiary.
        New York: Ballantine Books, 1984.
        287 p.; illus.
        ISBN 0-345-28283-3
```

Subject Card

```
        TOLKIEN, JOHN RONALD REUEL
         — CHARACTERS
828     Day, David.
TOL        A Tolkien bestiary.
        New York: Ballantine Books, 1984.
        287 p.; illus.
        ISBN 0-345-28283-3
```

EXERCISE 7 Understanding the *Readers' Guide* *(pages 359–360)*
1. eight
2. Testing; Unauthorized Use
3. "Plugging into a World of Help"
4. *Money*
5. I. Peterson
6. choosing software
7. Computer literature; Computers — Bibliography; Publishers and Publishing — Computer Literature
8. 1983
9. "Scheme to Foil Software Pirates"
10. Computers — Security Measures

EXERCISE 9 Understanding Literary Reference Works *(page 361)*

Sample answers:
1. *A Dictionary of Literary Terms*
2. *Short Story Index*
3. *Familiar Quotations*
4. *Twentieth Century Authors*
5. *Ottemiller's Index to Plays in Collections*

CHAPTER REVIEW *(page 362)*
1. that part of the mind that reacts to the outside world and mediates between the *id* and the *superego*
2. in southeast Canada between New Brunswick and Nova Scotia
3. 1861
4. two atoms of hydrogen and one atom of oxygen
5. Answers will vary.
6. Some possibilities include *rebellious, opposed, unruly, ungovernable, refractory, willful,* and *headstrong*.
7. a mathematical theory that develops strategies for decision-making based on making the most of gains and limiting losses
8. composing music
9. Alberta
10. Gwendolyn Brooks

16

The Library

For additional practice for this chapter, see the Teacher's Resource Book.

Whether you are researching a subject for U.S. History or deciding which kind of stereo equipment to buy, the library holds the information to answer your questions. Magazines, books, newspapers, and pamphlets are available on every imaginable subject. Most libraries today also contain nonprint materials, such as records, filmstrips, videotapes, and computer software. This chapter will help you discover the library's rich resources.

LIBRARY ARRANGEMENT

There are two systems of organization that libraries use to arrange the thousands of books in their stacks. Most school and local libraries use the Dewey decimal classification system. This system can organize up to 30,000 titles. Larger libraries, including those at most colleges and universities, use the Library of Congress system. This system is capable of arranging millions of books.

The Dewey Decimal Classification System

In the Dewey decimal classification system, works of fiction and nonfiction are shelved in separate sections.

Fiction. Works of fiction are arranged by the author's last name. In some libraries they are also marked with the symbol *F* or *Fic*. The following rules will help you locate works of fiction.

Library Arrangement

- Two-part last names are alphabetized by the first part of the name. (**Van** Doren, **O**'Hara, **Mc**Carthy)
- Names beginning with *Mc* and *St.* are alphabetized as if they began with *Mac* and *Saint*.
- Books by authors with the same last name are alphabetized by the author's first name.
- Books by the same author are alphabetized by title, skipping *a, and,* and *the*.
- Numbers in titles are alphabetized as if they were written out. (1001 = One Thousand and One)

EXERCISE 1 Finding Fiction

Using the Dewey decimal system, list the following fiction books in the order you would find them on the shelves.

1 *The Uninvited* by Dorothy Macardle
8 *Drums Along the Khyber* by Duncan MacNeil
6 *Sushita* by Graham McInnes
4 *The Vanishing Gunslinger* by William Colt MacDonald
9 *Breaking Smith's Quarter Horse* by Paul St. Pierre
5 *School Spirit* by Tom McHale
7 *Upside-Down* by Denis Mackail
3 *Aunt Bel* by Guy McCrone
10 *The White Buffalo* by Richard Sale
2 *Groves of Academe* by Mary McCarthy

Nonfiction. In the Dewey decimal classification system, nonfiction books are assigned a number according to their subject.

Main Subject Areas in the Dewey Decimal System	
000–099	General Works (reference works)
100–199	Philosophy
200–299	Religion
300–399	Social Sciences (law, education, economics)
400–499	Language
500–599	Science (mathematics, biology, chemistry)
600–699	Technology (medicine, inventions)
700–799	Fine Arts (painting, music, theater)
800–899	Literature
900–999	History (biography, geography, travel)

The Library

There are ten subdivisions within each main subject area. Following are the subdivisions for literature.

800–899 Literature				
800–809	General		850–859	Italian
810–819	American		860–869	Spanish
820–829	English		870–879	Latin
830–839	German		880–889	Greek
840–849	French		890–899	Other

These subdivisions are broken down even further with the use of decimal points and other identifying symbols. The following books are shelved numerically under the literature subdivision English Literature, 820–829.

Title	Call Number
How Shakespeare Spent the Day	Bradley 821.91208 CON
English Tragedy	Bentley 822.008 B446d
English Comedy	Thorndike 822.09 T393ec
The Development of English Drama	Thorndike 822.09 T393t
Contemporary Irish Poetry	Brown 822.331 B813h

The numbers identifying a book form the *call number*. In addition to the call number, some nonfiction works carry a special label to show the section of the library in which they are shelved. *B* or *92* (short for *920* in the Dewey decimal system), for example, indicates that a work is a biography or an autobiography.

Biographies and autobiographies are usually in a section of their own. They are arranged in alphabetical order according to the subject of the book, not the author. Books about the same person are arranged according to the author's last name.

Library Arrangement

Other works often given special labels are listed in the following chart.

CATEGORIES	SPECIAL LABELS
Juvenile books	J or X
Reference works	R or REF
Records	REC
Filmstrips	FS

EXERCISE 2 Understanding the Dewey Decimal System
Using the list of classifications on page 349, write the subject numbers for each of the following books.

EXAMPLE *Basic Concepts of Biology*
ANSWER 500–599

Answers for Exercise 4 also appear below.

900-999 1. *Buccaneers of the Pacific* E
600-699 2. *Doctor in the Zoo* R
400-499 3. *Spanish Step-by-Step* P
900-999 4. *Berlin: A Handbook for Travellers* D
700-799 5. *Painting Sharp Focus Still Lifes* N
500-599 6. *In the Wake of the Whale* Q
500-599 7. *Physics for Nonscientists* Q
300-399 8. *China and U.S. Foreign Policy* J
200-299 9. *Gateway to Judaism* B
100-199 10. *Way to Wisdom: An Introduction to Philosophy* B

EXERCISE 3 Using the Dewey Decimal System
Using the Dewey decimal system, arrange the following call numbers in the order they would appear on the shelves.

6 1. 563.782
      D168
2 2. 127.046
      N31x
3 3. 127.406
      L42g
7 4. 719.628
      F97p
9 5. 857.09
      D22t

8 6. 719.628
      P81m
1 7. 127.04
      R14q
10 8. 857.91
      A12s
5 9. 563.78
      G18l
4 10. 563.078
      L79d

351

The Library

The Library of Congress System of Classification

The Library of Congress system uses letters instead of numbers and has 20 main categories. Unlike the Dewey decimal system, the Library of Congress system does not separate fiction and biography from other kinds of works. A book *about* Mark Twain, for example, would be shelved with novels *by* Mark Twain.

Main Categories in the Library of Congress System

A	General works	L	Education
B	Philosophy, religion	M	Music
C	Sciences of history	N	Fine Arts
D	Non-American history and travel	P	Language and literature
		Q	Science
E	American history	R	Medicine
F	U.S. local history	S	Agriculture
G	Geography, anthropology	T	Technology
		U	Military science
H	Social sciences	V	Naval science
J	Political science	Z	Library science

These 20 main categories are divided into smaller divisions with the use of a second letter. QB, for example, refers to the general category of science with a focus on philosophy. Further subdivisions are made by using numbers and letters.

EXERCISE 4 **Understanding the Library of Congress System** Using the classifications for the Library of Congress system, write the first letter of the call number for each of the books listed in Exercise 2.

EXAMPLE *Basic Concepts of Biology*
ANSWER Q

Answers appear with Exercise 2.

The Card Catalog

The card catalog contains cards for every book in the library. Most books have three cards in the catalog: an author card, a

The Card Catalog

title card, and a subject card. The cards are arranged alphabetically. While any of these cards will help you locate the book you need, the author card contains the fullest information. When you want a book by a particular author, look under the author's last name in the card catalog.

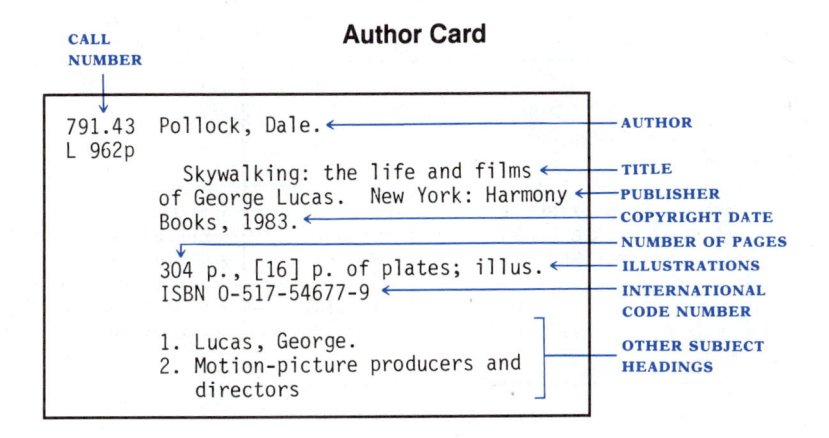

Author Card

```
CALL
NUMBER

791.43   Pollock, Dale.  ←──────────── AUTHOR
L 962p
           Skywalking: the life and films ←── TITLE
         of George Lucas.  New York: Harmony ←── PUBLISHER
         Books, 1983. ←────────────── COPYRIGHT DATE
                                              NUMBER OF PAGES
         304 p., [16] p. of plates; illus. ←── ILLUSTRATIONS
         ISBN 0-517-54677-9 ←──────── INTERNATIONAL
                                              CODE NUMBER
         1. Lucas, George.                    OTHER SUBJECT
         2. Motion-picture producers and      HEADINGS
            directors
```

Use title cards when you know the title but not the author. These cards are alphabetized by the first word in the title except *a*, *an*, and *the*.

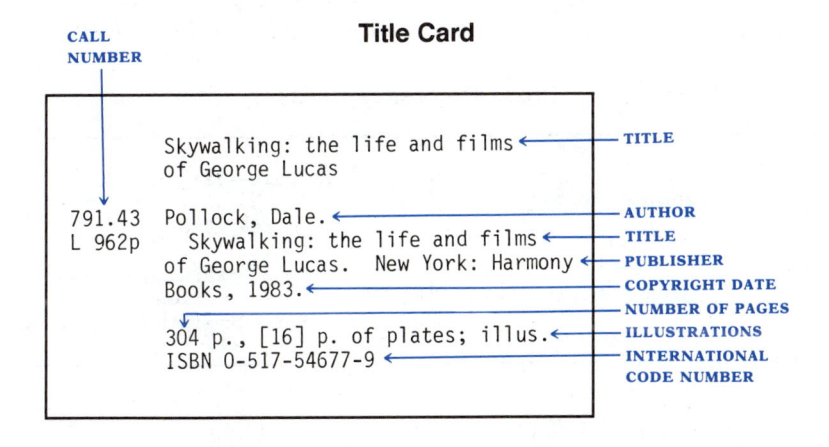

Title Card

```
CALL
NUMBER

         Skywalking: the life and films ←── TITLE
         of George Lucas

791.43   Pollock, Dale. ←──────────── AUTHOR
L 962p     Skywalking: the life and films ←── TITLE
         of George Lucas.  New York: Harmony ←── PUBLISHER
         Books, 1983. ←────────────── COPYRIGHT DATE
                                              NUMBER OF PAGES
         304 p., [16] p. of plates; illus. ←── ILLUSTRATIONS
         ISBN 0-517-54677-9 ←──────── INTERNATIONAL
                                              CODE NUMBER
```

Subject cards are helpful when you do not know the author or the title of a book. At the top of each card, the subject is

The Library

printed in capital letters. These cards are arranged alphabetically according to the first main word in the subject heading. Subject headings under *History,* however, are filed in chronological order.

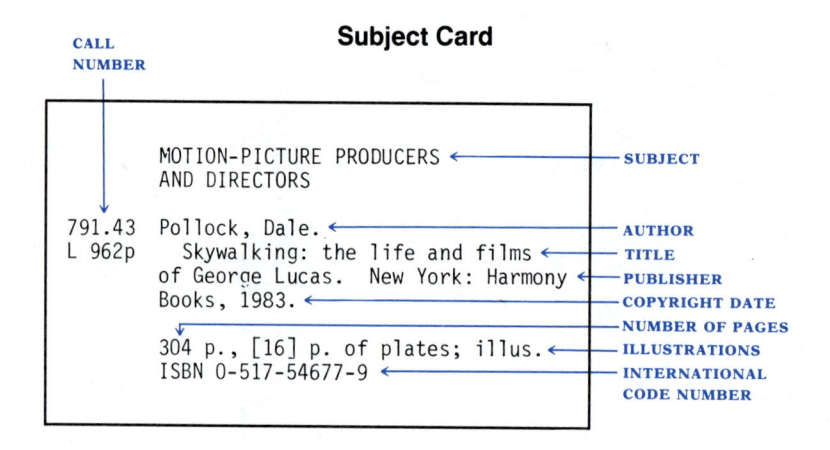

Subject Card

```
                    MOTION-PICTURE PRODUCERS      ← SUBJECT
                    AND DIRECTORS
          791.43    Pollock, Dale.                ← AUTHOR
          L 962p      Skywalking: the life and films  ← TITLE
                    of George Lucas.  New York: Harmony ← PUBLISHER
                    Books, 1983.                  ← COPYRIGHT DATE
                                                    NUMBER OF PAGES
                    304 p., [16] p. of plates; illus. ← ILLUSTRATIONS
                    ISBN 0-517-54677-9            ← INTERNATIONAL
                                                    CODE NUMBER
```

Labels on left: CALL NUMBER

In addition to the three cards provided for each book, the card catalog also has "see" and "see also" cards. These are called *cross-reference cards* because they refer you to other listings in the catalog. The "see" card tells you that the subject you have looked up is under another heading. The "see also" card lists more subjects you could look up for additional titles.

Cross-Reference Cards

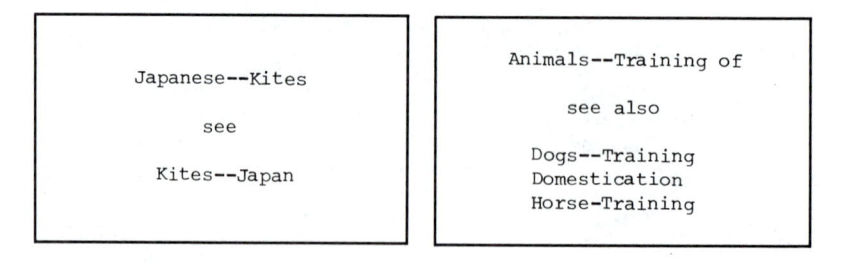

```
       Japanese--Kites              Animals--Training of

            see                          see also

       Kites--Japan                 Dogs--Training
                                    Domestication
                                    Horse-Training
```

Another type of card in the catalog is called an analytic card. This type of card shows you what separate works are contained within a collection.

The Card Catalog

Analytic Card

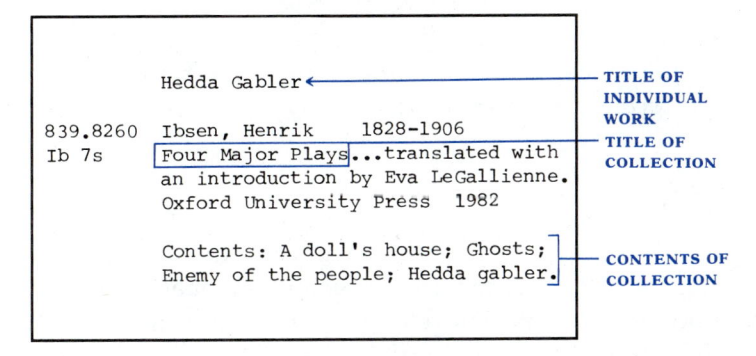

```
           Hedda Gabler←                    ─── TITLE OF
                                                INDIVIDUAL
 839.8260  Ibsen, Henrik    1828-1906           WORK
 Ib 7s     Four Major Plays...translated with ─ TITLE OF
           an introduction by Eva LeGallienne.  COLLECTION
           Oxford University Press  1982

           Contents: A doll's house; Ghosts; ┐
           Enemy of the people; Hedda gabler.┘── CONTENTS OF
                                                COLLECTION
```

Most catalogs use word-by-word alphabetizing rather than letter-by-letter. The entry *New Zealand* for example, would come before *newspaper*.

EXERCISE 5 Understanding the Card Catalog

Write the first three letters you would look under to find each of the following in the card catalog.

1. cable television tel
2. *Handbook of Nature Study* han
3. James Baldwin bal
4. vegetable gardening gar
5. the supreme court sup
6. Japanese paper folding pap
7. home video recorders vid
8. the plays of Arthur Miller mil
9. gorilla family groupings gor
10. *The Sound and the Fury* sou

EXERCISE 6 Understanding Catalog Cards

Use the information on the following author card and write a title and a subject card for this book.

Answers precede this chapter.

```
   828    Day, David
   Tol
          A Tolkien bestiary.
       New York: Ballantine Books, 1984.

       287 p.; illus.
       ISBN 0-345-28283-3

       1. Tolkien--Characters
       2. Tolkien--Illustrations
```

355

The Library

REFERENCE MATERIALS

Most libraries have a separate section for reference materials. Since these materials cannot be taken from the library, most reference rooms provide a study area.

Encyclopedias

Encyclopedias contain general information about a variety of subjects. Subjects are arranged in alphabetical order in each volume. Since some encyclopedias include a list of further readings at the end of each article, they are good sources to use at the beginning of your research.

GENERAL
ENCYCLOPEDIAS
Collier's Encyclopedia
Compton's Encyclopedia
Encyclopaedia Britannica
The Random House Encyclopedia
World Book Encyclopedia

The most recent edition of the *Encyclopaedia Britannica* offers a three-part organization. The first volume, called the *Propaedia,* is an overview of the rest of the work and a guide to users of the encyclopedia. The next 10 volumes are called the *Micropaedia.* The *Micropaedia* contains short articles with references to longer articles in the remaining 19 volumes. These last volumes are called the *Macropaedia.* The *Macropaedia* is the place to look for in-depth articles on your subject.

Specialized References

Specialized references provide specific information about a wide variety of subjects.

Specialized Encyclopedias. Specialized encyclopedias are available on almost every subject. Since they concentrate on one particular subject area, they provide more information than general works do.

SPECIALIZED
ENCYCLOPEDIAS
Encyclopedia of Modern Art
Encyclopedia of Animal Care
Encyclopedia of Religion

Reference Materials

Biographical References. These reference works contain information about notable people. The entries are arranged alphabetically. Some works contain only a paragraph of information, while others contain a long article about each person. All include such essential information as birth and death dates and the reason why a person is famous. The following excerpt is from *Who's Who in America, 1983.*

> GIFFORD, FRANK NEWTON, broadcast journalist; b. Santa Monica, Calif., Aug. 16, 1930; s. Weldon Wayne and Lola (Hawkins) G.; student Bakersfield Jr. Coll., 1948-49; B.A., U. So. Calif., 1952; m. Astrid Naess; children—Jeffery, Kyle, Victoria; m. 2d, Astrid Naess Lindley, Mar. 1978. Mem. N.Y. Giants, profl. football team, 1952-65; sports reporter CBS Radio, N.Y.C., 1957-59; Nat. Football League pre-game show host CBS-TV Network, N.Y.C., 1959-62; sports reporter WCBS-TV, N.Y.C., 1962-71; reporter ABC Radio Info., N.Y.C., 1971-77; sports corr. ABC TV Network, N.Y.C., 1971-77. corr. Eyewitness News, N.Y.C., 1971—; host The Superstars Series. Dir. sports writers and broadcasters Spl. Olympics, 1972-75; Bd. dirs. Nat. Soc. for Multiple Sclerosis, 1973-78. Named Sportsman of Yr., Cath. Youth Orgn., 1964; elected to Nat. Football Found. Hall of Fame, 1975, Pro Football Hall of Fame, 1977; recipient Gil Hodges Meml. sports award Cath. Med. Center, 1976, Adam award Men's Fashion Assn. Am., 1976, Emmy award for outstanding sports personality, 1977. Author: Frank Gifford's NFL-AFL Football Guide, 1968, rev. edits., 1969, 70; Frank Gifford's Football Guide Book, 1966; (with Charles Mangel) Gifford on Coverage, 1976.

BIOGRAPHICAL REFERENCES	*Current Biography* *Who's Who* *Who's Who in America* *Encyclopedia of American Biography* *Webster's Biographical Dictionary* *New Century Cyclopedia of Names*

Atlases. These books of maps include much information about the various regions of the world. Special-purpose maps or charts and tables show a region's cities, population, climate, products, and resources.

ATLASES	*Goode's World Atlas* *The World Book Atlas* *The Times Atlas of the World* *Hammond Medallion World Atlas* *National Geographic Atlas of the World* *Rand McNally International World Atlas*

Almanacs and Yearbooks. Since these reference works are published once a year, they are reliable sources for current information on a wide range of subjects. Some are organized

The Library

chronologically while others are arranged by topic. The following excerpt is from *The World Almanac & Book of Facts*.

Hurricane Names in 1984

U.S. government agencies responsible for weather and related communications have used girls' names to identify major tropical storms since 1953. A U.S. proposal that both male and female names be adopted for hurricanes, starting in 1979, was accepted by a committee of the World Meteorological Organization.

Names assigned to Atlantic hurricanes, 1984 — Arthur, Bertha, Cesar, Diana, Edouard, Fran, Gustav, Hortense, Isidore, Josephine, Klaus, Lili, Marco, Nana, Omar, Paloma, Rene, Sally, Teddy, Vicky, Wilfred.

Names assigned to Eastern Pacific hurricanes, 1984 — Alma, Boris, Cristina, Douglas, Elida, Fausto, Genevieve, Hernan, Iselle, Julio, Kenna, Lowell, Marie, Norbert, Odile, Polo, Rachel, Simon, Trudy, Vance, Wallis.

The WORLD ALMANAC & BOOK OF FACTS, 1984 edition, copyright © Newspaper Enterprise Association, Inc., 1981, New York, NY 10166.

ALMANACS AND YEARBOOKS
Information Please Almanac
The World Almanac & Book of Facts
Guinness Book of World Records
Britannica Book of the Year
Collier's Year Book

Specialized Dictionaries. In addition to the abridged and unabridged dictionaries discussed in Chapter 15, the library has a number of specialized dictionaries. A dictionary of synonyms and a thesaurus are just one type of specialized dictionary. These books provide a list of synonyms and will help you make exact word choices.

SPECIALIZED DICTIONARIES
Roget's Thesaurus in Dictionary Form
Webster's New Dictionary of Synonyms
Harvard Dictionary of Music
Dictionary of Biology

Readers' Guide to Periodical Literature. Researchers keep track of the thousands of newspaper and magazine articles published each year with the help of indexes. Most indexes are arranged alphabetically by subject matter and author. *The Readers' Guide to Periodical Literature,* an index containing references to more than 175 magazines, can help you locate articles on almost any subject. It is issued in paperback once a month in February, July, and August and twice a month during the rest of the year. Notice the numerous cross-references and abbreviations in the following excerpt.

Reference Materials

ALPHABETICAL SUBJECT LISTINGS

Computer languages
    Computer languages: in search of a better bug finder. I. Peterson. il *Sci News* 124:202-3 S 24 '83   What is the LOGO language? il *Consum Rep* 48:617 N '83
Computer literacy *See* Computer—Study and teaching
Computer literature

CROSS-REFERENCES

    See also
      Computers—Bibliography
      Publishers and publishing—Computer literature
    A how to for have-nots [work of M. Crichton] il por *Time* 122:57 O 24 '83

MAGAZINE ISSUE

Computer networks
    See also
      American Telephone & Telegraph Co
      Information storage and retrieval systems
Computer printers *See* Computers—Print-out equipment
Computer program languages *See* Computer languages
Computer programming
    See also
      Booksellers and bookselling—Computer programming
      Computer service industries
      Computers—Operating systems
    Hex/ASCII/decimal conversion chart. L. Solomon. il *Comput Electron* 21:68 O '83
    How to peek into a ROM cartridge [VIC-20 plug-in programs] H. McGoff. il *Comput Electron* 21:52-3 O '83

ABBREVIATIONS EXPLAINED AT FRONT OF BOOK

    Program the world in your classroom. S. Horowitz. il *Sch Update* 116:TE7 O 14 '83
    Synonyms for word processing [Electronic thesaurus] E. E. Mau. il *Comput Electron* 21:76-7 O '83
    Testing
    The computer as teacher. il *Consum Rep* 48:614-17 N '83
    Plugging into a world of help [money management software] G. M. Taber. il *Money* 12:149-50+ O '83

ALPHABETICAL SUBHEADINGS UNDER SUBJECT

    Solving the software dilemma [choosing software] S. Miastkowski *Esquire* 100:167 O '83
    Unauthorized use
    Scheme to foil software pirates [weak bit scheme of Adi Shamir and others] G. Kolata. *Science* 221:1279 S 23 '83
Computer science *See* Computers
Computer security *See* Computers—Security measures

From Readers' Guide to Periodical Literature. Copyright © 1983 by The H. W. Wilson Company. Material produced by permission of the publisher.

Newspaper articles are listed in a general work called the *Newspaper Index.* Some large newspapers, however, publish their own index to help you locate articles that have appeared in their columns. For example, the *New York Times Index* will refer only to articles that have been in the *New York Times.*

EXERCISE 7   Understanding the *Readers' Guide*

Using the excerpt from the *Readers' Guide* above, write the answers to the following questions.
    Answers precede this chapter.

1. How many articles are listed under the subject heading Computer Programming?
2. What are the two subheadings listed under Computer Programming?

359

The Library

3. Under the subheading Testing, what is the title of the article about money-management software?
4. In what magazine does the article in question 3 appear?
5. Who is the author of the article "Computer Languages: In Search of a Better Bug Finder"?
6. What is "Solving the Software Dilemma" about?
7. What subjects have articles on computer literature?
8. In what year were the articles in this excerpt published?
9. What is the title of the article about unauthorized use in computer programming?
10. Under what subject heading would articles about computer security be listed?

The Vertical File. In addition to books and magazines, libraries also store pamphlets, catalogs, newspaper clippings, and other printed matter in special filing cabinets known as the vertical file. Items are kept in file folders and arranged by subject.

EXERCISE 8   Using Specialized References

Review pages 356–360. Then write one source, other than a general encyclopedia, where you could find the following.
Sample answers:
1. the life of news commentator Edward R. Murrow   biographical reference
2. an article in the *New York Times* newspaper   New York Times Index
3. the population of the African country Chad   atlas
4. a magazine article on the latest advances in automobiles   Readers' Guide
5. a pamphlet on rules of the road   vertical file

Reference Materials about Language and Literature

For your English course, you may be required to use reference works specifically focused on the subjects of language and literature. Following are some of these materials.

SPECIALIZED DICTIONARIES	*Webster's Dictionary of Synonyms*
	Roget's International Thesaurus
	A Dictionary of Literary Terms
	Wood's Unabridged Rhyming Dictionary
SPECIALIZED ENCYCLOPEDIAS	*Cassell's Encyclopedia of World Literature*
	Reader's Encyclopedia of American Literature
	Encyclopedia of World Literature in the 20th Century

Reference Materials

BIOGRAPHICAL REFERENCES
Contemporary Authors
Twentieth Century Authors
British Authors of the Nineteenth Century
Contemporary Poets of the English Language
Black American Writers Past and Present: A Biographical and Bibliographical Dictionary

A handbook can explain literary terms, give plot summaries, or describe characters.

HANDBOOKS
American Authors and Books
The Oxford Companion to English Literature
Penguin Companion to European Literature
Crowell's Handbook of Contemporary American Poetry

A book of quotations can tell you the source of a particular quotation.

BOOKS OF QUOTATIONS
Familiar Quotations
The Home Book of Quotations
Dictionary of Quotations

Indexes are useful when you are looking for a specific poem, short story, or play. An index will list the books that contain the selection you are looking for.

INDEXES
Granger's Index to Poetry
Ottemiller's Index to Plays in Collections
Short Story Index
Play Index

EXERCISE 9 Understanding Literary Reference Works

After each question write the name of one source you could use to find the answer.
Sample answers precede this chapter.
1. What does the term *stream of consciousness* mean?
2. Where could you find a short story by Tillie Olson titled "I Stand Here Ironing"?
3. Who wrote, "Simplify, simplify, simplify"?
4. In what year was the twentieth-century American writer Dorothy Parker born?
5. Where could you find the title of a publication that includes the play *Rosencrantz and Guildenstern Are Dead?*

361

The Library

CHAPTER REVIEW

A. Following is a list of library resources. After the proper number on your paper, write the best resource for finding the answer to each question.

    A card catalog   F index
    B general encyclopedia   G atlas
    C specialized encyclopedia   H almanac
    D biographical reference   I *Readers' Guide*
    E specialized dictionary   J vertical file

E   1. What do psychologists mean by the term *ego*?
G   2. Where is the Bay of Fundy?
D   3. In what year was actress Lillian Russell born?
C   4. What is the structure of a water molecule?
I   5. What is the name of one magazine article on the Environmental Protection Agency?
E   6. What are two synonyms for *recalcitrant*?
C   7. What is the game theory of mathematics?
D   8. For what is Charles Ives famous?
G   9. In what province of Canada is Banff National Park?
F   10. Who wrote the poem called "We Be Cool"?
J   11. Where in the library can you find a catalog of camping outfitters in your area?
H   12. Where was the lowest temperature on Earth recorded?
A   13. How many novels by Pearl S. Buck does your library have?
H   14. What record album sold the most copies last year?
B   15. What impact did the printing press have on the number of people who learned to read?
B or E   16. In the game of soccer, what does the word *volley* mean?
F   17. Cordelia appears in which Shakespearean play?
B or E   18. What is the chemical formula for vitamin C?
J   19. What is the tuition at Rutgers University in New Jersey?
H   20. How many Americans won gold medals in the 1984 summer Olympic Games?

B. Use the resources of your library to answer the first ten questions.
Answers precede this chapter.

Unit 6

Composition

17 Words and Sentences
18 Clear Thinking
19 Paragraphs
20 Expository Essays
21 Other Kinds of Essays
22 The Summary
23 Research Papers
24 Business Letters

Composition Overview

The composition unit has been planned to help young writers master the *composing process* with its four main stages: prewriting, writing, revising, and editing. To accomplish this goal, the unit contains the following:
- a variety of strategies for generating subject ideas
- brainstorming activities for listing supporting details
- guidelines for organizing supporting material, reinforced at appropriate points in the unit
- step-by-step instruction in shaping prewriting notes into a first draft
- clear, consistent, and manageable guidelines for revision
- editing checklists for preparing a final draft
- comprehensive summary charts at the end of chapters as guides for students' independent writing

The Structure of the Composition Unit

The self-contained chapters in the composition unit may be taught in any order. The order in which they appear in the book, however, provides a strong foundation for learning by proceeding from identification and analysis of rhetorical concepts and models to step-by-step instruction in all stages of the composing process, with a special emphasis on purpose and audience. The following chart summarizes the pedagogical development of the composition unit.

Chapters	Analysis	Writing/Revising Practice	Step-by-Step Writing Process
17 Words and Sentences	X	X	
18 Clear Thinking	X	X	
19 Paragraphs	X	X	X
20 Expository Essays	X	X	X
21 Other Kinds of Essays	X	X	
22 The Summary	X	X	X
23 Research Papers	X	X	X
24 Business Letters	X	X	X

All Chapters conclude with a Chapter Review, a set of exercises or composition assignments that call for application of the material covered in the chapter. All composition chapters also contain two features designed to encourage creativity and independence. One is Writing Extra, placed strategically in the chapter to reinforce a concept. The focus of all the Writing Extra features in grade 11 is thinking skills. The other feature, On Your Own, challenges students to apply the composing skills they have just learned to independent research and writing activities. Although both the Writing Extra and On Your Own features are optional, they effectively extend the instruction in the chapter to develop both fluency and independence.

Suggestions for Evaluation

Research has shown time and again that abundant writing practice is one key to mastery of the writing process. To help balance the need for numerous writing activities with the limited time available for evaluation, researchers and practitioners have developed several useful evaluation methods that not only reduce assessment time but also improve the quality of the evaluation.

Analytic Scoring For all relevant chapters, the Teacher's Edition provides analytic scoring charts. Each chart isolates the most important features of the chapter and assigns each a maximum point value. A numerical score for a composition can easily be tabulated from these charts, and brief notes explaining any point value lower than the maximum will help guide the student to a further revision if required.

Holistic Scoring Once you have a clear idea of the general range of writing ability in your class, you can use holistic scoring. In contrast to analytic scoring, holistic evaluation considers the composition as a whole, without isolating specific elements within it. Holistic scoring also emphasizes the relative quality of a work — its value in comparison with others from the same class — rather than its conformity to an idealized standard of composition. The following steps will help you use holistic scoring effectively in your classroom.

1. Read the first batch of papers and choose from them five papers that represent the following values: (1) excellent, (2) good, (3) average, (4) below average, (5) poor.
2. Copy these papers and keep them as a guide for future use.
3. With every new assignment, lay these original papers across your desk.
4. Read each new paper very quickly, focusing on how well the paper as a whole accomplishes the purpose of the assignment.
5. Add the new papers to the pile each belongs in. Place an easily erased pencil mark on papers about which you have some doubt and re-read them after you have finished all the others.
6. Assign a number (1–5) or letter grade to each paper according to the pile you placed it in.

To achieve the anonymity usually associated with holistic scoring, ask students to write their names on the back of the paper so that you will not know the writer until after you have read the composition.

Peer Evaluation The success of peer evaluation depends in large measure on how specific the evaluation criteria are. Limit the students' focus to three points at most and be sure to have students comment on strong as well as weak elements in their peers' work. The Teacher's Edition includes detailed instruction in peer evaluation.

Self-Evaluation The numerous checklists throughout the student text provide effective self-evaluation guides.

A final word: You do not need to evaluate every composition. You may have students choose only two to four of their compositions to submit for full and complete evaluation by you.

Chapter 17 Words and Sentences

OBJECTIVES

- To use specific words whose connotations match the intended meaning.
- To use figurative language to appeal to readers' imaginations.
- To eliminate clichés.
- To write concise sentences by avoiding redundancy, empty expressions, and wordiness.
- To use sentence-combining techniques to write sentences of varied lengths.
- To write sentences with varied structures and beginnings.
- To revise faulty coordination and subordination.
- To break up rambling sentences.
- To revise faulty parallelism.
- To avoid overuse of the passive voice.

MOTIVATIONAL ACTIVITY

Writing is a process of making choices. To help students approach the composition unit with this in mind, have them complete the following activity.

Students should imagine they are on the Board of Tourism for the city of Chicago, Illinois. Their job is to prepare a paragraph of no more than five sentences that will be included in a publicity brochure. The purpose of the brochure is to attract tourists to Chicago. The brochure will be on display in travel agencies around the country. Students should choose the most appropriate information from the following fact sheet to include in their paragraph.

Fact Sheet on Chicago

Sears Tower is the world's tallest building.
O'Hare Airport is the busiest in the country.
Chicago has a larger Polish population than Warsaw, Poland.
Miles of continuous parks line the city's waterfront on Lake Michigan.
Harold Washington, the city's first black mayor, was elected in 1983.
The Art Institute has one of the world's most extensive collections of impressionist paintings.
Water Tower Place is a luxurious atrium shopping mall.
Elevated trains form a loop over the heart of the business district.
Chicago has world famous museums, including the Museum of Science and Industry, Natural History Museum, Adler Planetarium, and Shedd Aquarium.

After students have completed their work, have them read their paragraphs to the class and explain why they made the choices they made. After each reading, have the rest of the class comment on how effective the choices were in relation to the *purpose* of the paragraph and its intended *audience*. Finally, have students place their paragraphs in their writing folders for later revision.

TEACHING SUGGESTIONS

Word Choice *(pages 364–370)*

Specific Words *(pages 365–367)* Have students search their work from the Motivational Activity for general words that could be replaced with livelier, more specific words. After students have revised their paragraphs, ask for volunteers to read both versions aloud to the class.

Figurative Language *(pages 367–370)* You can extend the previous activity by asking students to come up with a slogan for Chicago that will appear on the cover of the brochure. The slogan should contain a personification, simile, or metaphor. Carl Sandburg's poem "Chicago," which contains a series of personifications, may give students some ideas.

For practice in writing extended metaphors, have students choose one item from the first column below and one item from the second and develop a point-by-point comparison between the two; refer them to the extended metaphor on page 368 as a model. (Students should also be free to think of two items on their own; the lists are merely suggestions.)

COLUMN 1	COLUMN 2
school	a good meal
growing up	a stage play
travel	a familiar face
family	an admired rival
friendship	a good book
nature	a surprise party

Concise Sentences *(pages 370–374)*

Have students write a sentence on each of the following topics:

something they have learned in a science, health, or social-studies class
something they have seen on television
a character in a book
a detailed description of the weather outside
the quality they admire most in people and why it is important

When students have finished the first draft of their sentences, have them count the number of words in each and write that number after each sentence. They should then trade papers with a classmate and try to revise the classmate's sentences, eliminating at least three words from each. You may also want to remind students to look especially carefully for redundancy, empty expressions, and wordiness.

Sentence Variety *(pages 374–382)*

For more emphasis on the writing process as a series of choices, choose five students' revisions from Exercise 15 to duplicate on a spirit master and distribute to the class. Have students examine the alternate ways of creating a variety of sentence structures.

Faulty Sentences *(pages 382–389)*

Students should be reminded that while faulty parallelism is confusing to a reader, effective parallelism often makes an eloquent expression. Read the following sayings to the class to demonstrate the eloquence of parallelism. Ask students to identify the parallel elements and also to explain the meaning of the saying.

1. Some books are undeservedly forgotten; none are undeservedly remembered. — W. H. Auden
2. The weak in courage is strong in cunning. — William Blake
3. Write injuries in dust, benefits in marble. — Benjamin Franklin
4. We are never so ridiculous through what we are as through what we pretend to be. — La Rochefoucauld

ACTIVITIES FOR DIFFERENT ABILITIES

Basic Students

ACTIVITY 1 Word Power

Have students brainstorm a list of food products with attention-getting names while you write the names on the board. When your list includes about twenty items, ask students to comment on the message each name sends to a potential customer. In short, what purpose were the manufacturers trying to accomplish by naming the product as they did? What impression do the names make on the consumer? As a follow-up, ask students to make up their own name for a new breakfast cereal and write a short paragraph explaining the sales value of the name.

ACTIVITY 2 Writing Sentences

After students have completed Exercise 3, have them use the words they chose in sentences. The result should be five pairs of sentences. In each pair, one sentence will contain the specific word with a positive connotation; the other will contain the specific word with a negative connotation.

Advanced Students

ACTIVITY 1 Figurative Language

You may wish to introduce students to the device of allusion. An allusion is a reference made to a famous person, place, event, or literary work in an effort to illustrate an idea. For example, if a writer is trying to describe a handsome high school boy, he might say, "He was the Robert Redford of Richton High."

Words and Sentences

OTHER EXAMPLES

The dinner table argument was a reenactment of the Battle of New Orleans.

If we the people do not exercise our right to vote, then we the people will perish.

He was the Captain Ahab of our small town, alienated from humans and nature.

Ask students to write sentences with an allusion to each of the following:

1. a famous line from Shakespeare
2. a world leader
3. an entertainment personality
4. a famous place or event

ACTIVITY 2 Experimenting with Style

Ask students to copy a paragraph from a book by their favorite writer and read the paragraph to the class. Following each reading, discuss the individual style of the writer, pointing to such qualities as sentence complexity or brevity, diction, tone, and so forth. Then ask each student to write a paragraph on a subject of his or her choice, imitating the style of a favorite author. The paragraph may take the form of a parody.

ADDITIONAL PRACTICE

Teacher's Resource Book: pages 199–206
Workbook: pages 153–158

REVIEW EXERCISES AND TESTS

Student Text
Chapter Review: pages 389–390

Teacher's Resource Book
Chapter 17 Test: pages 43–44
(Also available as spirit duplicating masters.)

ADDITIONAL ANSWERS

EXERCISE 1 Choosing Specific Words *(page 365)*

Sample answers:

1. horse, wolf
2. famished, starving
3. haltingly, gradually
4. glide, sway
5. shouted, quipped
6. novel, textbook
7. creak, clatter
8. witty, hilarious
9. alluring, eye-catching
10. unconventional, extraordinary

EXERCISE 3 Thinking of Words with Different Connotations *(page 366)*

Sample answers:

1. hum, screech
2. aroma, odor
3. chanted, croaked
4. gaze, leer
5. strolled, shuffled
6. pat, grab
7. dined, gobbled
8. sedan, rattletrap
9. invigorating, numbing
10. outfit, tatters

EXERCISE 4 Translating Inflated Language *(pages 366–367)*

Sample answers:

1. The candidate made a mistake.
2. Students who fail mathematics courses must repeat these courses until they pass.
3. Work as hard as you can so that by the weekend you've made up for the time lost on Tuesday.
4. It is best to follow your own standards of behavior and let others follow theirs.

Words and Sentences

EXERCISE 6   Eliminating Clichés *(page 369)*

Sample answers:
1. Six-month old Emily is the gleam in her father's smile.
2. Suddenly we decided to go out.
3. In her new dress, she looked as delicate as a butterfly.
4. The answer is obvious.
5. The running back was as powerful as Niagara Falls.
6. After a good night's sleep, I felt as fresh as autumn air.
7. Let's get started.
8. Avoid clichés like a herd of stampeding buffalo.
9. Denise is very spoiled and expects everything to be done for her without any effort on her part.
10. Looking for Tony's contact lens on the football field was like trying to see a white rabbit against a snowbank.

EXERCISE 7   On Your Own *(page 370)*

Sample answer:
The sky, blue and bright just a few minutes before, turned a threatening gray, and huge raindrops began to splatter on the forest floor.
Like soldiers fleeing a losing battle, the disappointed picnickers hurried to the dry shelter of their cars.
The tree trunks huddled together under their leafy umbrellas and shuddered at each fresh gust of wind.

EXERCISE 11   On Your Own *(page 374)*

Sample answers:
1. Dessert is a sweet after meals.
2. The Fourth of July is America's Birthday.
3. Noon is midday.

Chapter 17 d

17

Words and Sentences

For additional practice for this chapter, see the Teacher's Resource Book and the Workbook.

Words and thoughts go hand in hand. If a word you choose is vague, the thought it expresses will be equally fuzzy. Similarly, a carelessly structured sentence will reflect a carelessly conceived thought. This chapter will help you polish your words and sentences so that they reflect your exact meaning.

WORD CHOICE

As you read the following passage, notice how the choice of words brings the picture into sharp focus.

> Then, after six years, she saw him again. He was seated at one of those little bamboo tables decorated with a Japanese vase of paper daffodils. There was a tall plate of fruit in front of him, and very carefully, in a way she recognized immediately as his "special" way, he was peeling an orange.
> — KATHERINE MANSFIELD, "A DILL PICKLE"

The precise language in Mansfield's paragraph helps the reader's imagination picture the scene. Choosing words that create strong images will bring your writing to life.

Specific Words

In the following pairs of examples, specific words replace general words and create a more precise meaning.

GENERAL VERB	Juanita **went** out of the room.
SPECIFIC VERB	Juanita **tore** out of the room.
GENERAL NOUN	Do you want to see the **movie**?
SPECIFIC NOUN	Do you want to see the **thriller**?
GENERAL ADJECTIVE	Sarina's voice is **beautiful**.
SPECIFIC ADJECTIVE	Sarina's voice is **velvety**.
GENERAL ADVERB	Martin played the drums **well**.
SPECIFIC ADVERB	Martin played the drums **passionately**.

In addition to their literal meaning, or *denotation*, most specific words have meanings that come from the emotions or ideas you associate with them. This level of meaning is called *connotation*. The connotation of a word is often either positive or negative.

GENERAL WORD	leader
SPECIFIC WORDS	chief, president, director [positive]
	tyrant, dictator, ringleader [negative]

17a Use **specific words** with **connotations** that suit your meaning.

EXERCISE 1 Choosing Specific Words

Number your paper 1 to 10. Then write two specific words for each of the following general words.
Sample answers precede this chapter.

1. animal
2. hungry
3. slowly
4. move
5. said
6. book
7. sound
8. funny
9. attractive
10. unusual

EXERCISE 2 Choosing Appropriate Connotations

Write the word with the more appropriate connotation.

1. The fabric used to make this dress is (artificial, fake).
2. In the morning the ocean appeared (dead, motionless).
3. We walked slowly through the (dead, calm) summer air.
4. Carol was annoyed by the (hum, drone) of the fan.
5. Lynn and Kurt (abandoned, left) the canoe when they realized that it was caught between two sharp rocks.
6. Barbara Day, a candidate for the Senate, stressed that she is (tough, inflexible) on environmental issues.

Words and Sentences

7. At the audience's request, the singer (<u>extended</u>, prolonged) his performance.
8. Before speaking to the other members of the royal family, the queen took a (swig, <u>drink</u>) of water.
9. The Olympic gold medalist (<u>wept</u>, sobbed) when the official put the award over his head.
10. With a sly grin, Father continued the (narrative, <u>tale</u>) he had begun last night.

EXERCISE 3 Thinking of Words with Different Connotations

Choose five of the following general words and write two specific words for each. One should have a positive connotation; the other should have a negative connotation.
Sample answers precede this chapter.

      EXAMPLE   inactive
POSSIBLE ANSWER   calm [positive]   idle [negative]

1. noise   3. sang   5. walked   7. ate   9. cold
2. smell   4. look   6. touch   8. car   10. clothing

Writing Extra

Some writers tend to use inflated language—words with many syllables that sound impressive but that do not communicate as effectively as simple, everyday words. Avoid using long words that you think will impress your reader.

EXERCISE 4 Translating Inflated Language

The following sentences are loaded with inflated language. Reword each one as a short, direct sentence.
Sample answers precede this chapter.

EXAMPLE   The governor has availed herself of every opportunity to enlarge her knowledge of recently published economic theories.

TRANSLATION   The governor has studied recent economic theories.

1. The candidate was the victim of incorrect thinking and made a misstatement.
2. Students who cannot successfully function in a mathematical learning situation must be reprocessed until they acquire this vital skill.

3. Maximize your work-load output so that the neutralization of the effect of the short work day on Tuesday is accomplished by the time of the weekend's arrival.
4. Experience has shown that a suitable course of conduct is to adhere to one's own standards of behavior and allow others the opportunity to operate according to theirs.

Figurative Language

Literal language uses words to express their exact, direct meaning. When literal language is inadequate, writers use *figurative language,* or figures of speech. Figurative language uses words in an unusual way, inviting readers to use their imaginations.

LITERAL LANGUAGE	The maple trees seem more colorful than before, and the fields show a bright red color.
FIGURATIVE LANGUAGE	The maple wears a gayer scarf, the field a scarlet gown. —EMILY DICKINSON

In the figurative example, the maple trees and field are described as persons who have put on brightly colored items of clothing. Although trees and fields do not really wear clothing, the figurative language helps the reader picture the scene.

17b Use **figurative language** to make ideas vivid for your readers.

Personification. This figure of speech transfers human qualities to lifeless objects or ideas.

PERSONIFICATION The sunny skies smiled on the poor farmer's crops.

Trouble knocked on the door.

The flashing warning lights way at the top boasted the skyscraper's height and bullied the tiny airplane.

Skies and skyscrapers cannot smile or boast, and trouble—an idea—cannot knock at the door. By giving things and ideas human qualities, however, you invite the reader to see them in a new and vivid way.

Words and Sentences

Similes and Metaphors. The two most common figures of speech are similes and metaphors. Both create a vivid impression through the use of fresh comparisons. Similes use the word *like* or *as* to compare two essentially different things. Metaphors imply a comparison without using *like* or *as*.

SIMILE   Think of the storm roaming the sky uneasily like a dog looking for a place to sleep.
—ELIZABETH BISHOP

METAPHOR   The kitchen was the great machine that set our lives running; it whirred down a little only on Saturdays and holy days.   —ALFRED KAZIN

In the preceding examples, Elizabeth Bishop uses *like* to compare a storm to a restless dog. Alfred Kazin, without using *like* or *as*, compares his kitchen to a great, whirring machine.

The following examples make the same comparison.

SIMILE   The trees, **like a dark mansion,** soon appeared.

METAPHOR   **A dark mansion of trees** soon appeared.

Extended metaphors, as their name implies, stretch a comparison by mapping out a set of parallel qualities between two essentially different things. In the following extended metaphor, a lake is compared with an eye.

EXTENDED METAPHOR   A lake is the landscape's most beautiful and expressive feature. It is the earth's eye, looking into which the beholder measures the depth of his or her own nature. The trees next to the shore are the slender eyelashes which fringe it, and the wooded hills and cliffs around are its overhanging brows.
—HENRY DAVID THOREAU, "THE WATERS OF WALDEN"

Onomatopoeia. Another way to stir the reader's imagination is to use words that reveal their meaning through their sound. Following are examples of onomatopoeia.

| sizzle | giggle | sputter | squish | splash | crackle |
| thump | trickle | drip | ooze | rip | whisk |

Figurative Language

Clichés. Some figures of speech have been used so often that they no longer create a mental image. Words and phrases that have been dulled by overuse are called clichés. Avoid using clichés in your writing. The following are clichés.

hungry as a wolf	crystal clear	pretty as a picture
sweet as pie	cool as ice	smooth as satin

EXERCISE 5 Identifying Figures of Speech

Identify the figure of speech underlined in the sentence by writing *simile*, *metaphor*, *personification*, or *onomatopoeia*.
(S)   (M)   (P)   (O)

- O   1. The child <u>slurped</u> her melting popsicle.
- P   2. Dawn <u>embraced</u> the frosty land <u>with arms</u> of warmth.
- O   3. Brakes <u>screeched</u> and sirens <u>whined</u>.
- S   4. Worries pounded her head <u>like angry waves</u>.
- M   5. Time <u>is a taskmaster whipping us on</u>.
- S   6. The leaves of the trees were <u>like huge fans</u> cooling us.
- M   7. The <u>ice age</u> of technology <u>is thawing</u>, and a <u>new world</u> of computers <u>is blossoming</u>.
- P   8. The <u>thirsty</u> sand <u>drank up</u> the desert shower in minutes.
- S   9. <u>Like a swan through water</u>, the skater glided across the ice.
- O   10. The explorers trod on to their destination, <u>slashing</u> their way through the dense vegetation.

EXERCISE 6 Eliminating Clichés

Revise each sentence to eliminate the underlined cliché. Replace each cliché with fresh figurative language or specific literal words.
Sample answers precede this chapter.

1. Six-month old Emily is <u>the apple of her father's eye</u>.
2. <u>On the spur of the moment</u>, we decided to go out.
3. In her new dress, she looked <u>as pretty as a picture</u>.
4. The answer is <u>as plain as the nose on her face</u>.
5. The running back was <u>as tough as nails</u>.
6. After a good night's sleep, I felt <u>as fresh as a daisy</u>.
7. Let's <u>get the show on the road</u>.
8. Avoid clichés <u>like the plague</u>.
9. Denise is very spoiled and expects everything to be <u>served on a silver platter</u>.
10. Looking for Tony's contact lens on the football field was <u>like trying to find a needle in a haystack</u>.

Words and Sentences

EXERCISE 7 On Your Own
Using precise, literal language, write one sentence describing the approach of a storm. In a second sentence, describe the same scene by using a simile. In a third sentence, describe the approaching storm with personification. Exchange papers with a classmate and compare your figures of speech.
Sample answer precedes this chapter.

CONCISE SENTENCES

Like gardeners good writers weed their work to display it at its best advantage. A sentence overgrown with extra words is hard for a reader to follow.

17c   Keep your sentences concise by eliminating needless words and phrases.

Redundancy

One way to keep your sentences concise is to eliminate unnecessary repetition, or redundancy. Notice how the following sentences are improved with the redundancy trimmed away.

REDUNDANT   Lynn shouted loudly to warn her brother of the dangerous risk.
CONCISE   Lynn shouted to warn her brother of the danger.

REDUNDANT   The poverty-stricken beggar wore tattered, worn-out clothes.
CONCISE   The beggar wore tattered clothes.

EXERCISE 8 Eliminating Redundancy
Revise each sentence by eliminating the redundant words or phrases.
Sample answers:

Talking Sense

1. Our five senses link us to the external world. ~~outside of our bodies~~.
2. Messages received by our eyes travel ~~instantaneously~~ to our brain at lightning-fast speed.
3. Except for primates most mammals see only in black and white, ~~not in color~~.

370

Concise Sentences

17c

4. Animals that have large outer ears ~~on the outside of their heads~~ gather sounds more effectively than humans.
5. In humans and animals, these sounds travel through a narrow ~~in width~~ channel that leads to the inner ear.
6. Although we cannot see the ~~invisible~~ particles that activate our sense of smell, they are all around us.
7. Our taste buds ~~that we use for tasting~~ are linked with our sense of smell.
8. If you are holding your nose, you cannot tell the difference ~~or distinguish~~ between the taste of an apple and a potato.
9. At first touch, intense cold feels the same as intense heat ~~when you first feel it.~~
10. We also have inner senses, including a thirst center inside the brain, which tells us when we ~~are thirsty and~~ crave water.

Empty Expressions

Empty expressions are phrases that add no meaning to a sentence. You should eliminate these entirely or replace them with single words or concise phrases.

EMPTY **Due to the fact that** it was a legal holiday, schools were closed last Monday.
CONCISE Because of the legal holiday, schools were closed last Monday.

EMPTY **It seems as if** advertisers often try to appeal to buyers' emotions.
CONCISE Advertisers often try to appeal to buyers' emotions.

EMPTY **There is** something I want to tell you.
CONCISE I want to tell you something.

Empty Expressions	
on account of	due to the fact that
what I want is	the reason that
it seems as if	the thing is that
it is/was	there is/are/was/were
because of the fact that	I believe/feel/think that

371

Words and Sentences

EXERCISE 9   Eliminating Empty Expressions

Revise each sentence to eliminate the empty expression. *Answers may vary.*

EXAMPLE   It can be said that the Western is a typically American kind of movie.

POSSIBLE ANSWER   The Western is a typically American kind of movie.

The West on Film

1. ~~There was~~ A movie called *The Great Train Robbery*, made in 1903, ~~that~~ was the first Western.
2. It was different from today's movies ~~due to the fact that~~ because it was only 11 minutes long.
3. ~~On account~~ Because of their natural settings and low cost of producing, Westerns became very popular.
4. ~~It was~~ In the 1920s ~~that~~ some of the best movies made were Westerns, including *The Spoilers* and *The Virginian*.
5. ~~There were~~ Some Westerns made in the 1930s ~~that~~ were true epics, such as the movies *Drums along the Mohawk* and *Stagecoach*.
6. ~~On account of~~ Gene Autry began the trend of the singing cowboy ~~began~~ in the 1940s.
7. ~~I feel that~~ Most of these early Westerns were unrealistic.
8. ~~The fact is that~~ Realistic Westerns did not begin until the 1950s.
9. ~~One movie worth pointing out is~~ *Broken Arrow*, ~~which~~ was the first Western since silent films to sympathize with the Native Americans.
10. ~~Due to the fact that~~ Since color photography was advancing, many Westerns in the late 1950s were great spectacles.

Wordiness

In the English language, one idea can often be expressed in a number of ways — in a phrase, in a clause, or in a single word. Look for the most economical way to express your meaning. Constructions that use more words than necessary are called *wordy*. Notice how each of the following wordy sentences can be reduced to a more economical package.

WORDY   Sailors aboard a submarine perform their tasks **in a routine manner.** [prepositional phrase]

CONCISE   Sailors aboard a submarine perform their tasks **routinely.** [adverb]

Concise Sentences

WORDY	On a typical day, each sailor stands two watches **consisting of four hours each.** [participial phrase]
CONCISE	On a typical day, each sailor stands two **four-hour** watches. [adjective]
WORDY	A sailor **who is on watch** may be assigned to the engine room, the radio, the periscope, or the bridge. [adjective clause]
CONCISE	A sailor **on watch** may be . . . [prepositional phrase]

or

A sailor **standing watch** may be . . . [participial phrase]

WORDY	The galley, **which is the kitchen of a ship,** is busy every hour of the day and night. [adjective clause]
CONCISE	The galley, **the kitchen of a ship,** is busy . . . [appositive phrase]
WORDY	Food **that is plentiful** is a must on every submarine. [adjective clause]
CONCISE	**Plentiful** food is a must . . . [adjective]

EXERCISE 10 Reducing Wordy Sentences

Revise each sentence by shortening the underlined phrase or clause. *Answers may vary.*

The End of War

1. The Civil War, ~~which was~~ fought between 1861 and 1865, ended at the Appomattox Courthouse in Virginia.
2. The general ~~who led~~ *leading* the Union forces was Ulysses S. Grant.
3. Robert E. Lee, ~~who was~~ a former classmate of Grant's at West Point, led a major part of the Confederate forces.
4. They met in a farmhouse ~~that was~~ near the battle site.
5. There they talked ~~in a brief manner~~ *briefly* about happier days.
6. Grant and Lee agreed to peace terms ~~that were honorable~~ *honorable*.
7. The soldiers ~~in the Confederacy~~ *Confederate* could return home.
8. They could take with them the animals, ~~used for farming~~ *farm*, such as horses and mules, that they had used as mounts.
9. As Lee mounted his horse after signing the agreement, General Grant saluted him by raising his hat, *weatherbeaten* ~~which was weather-beaten~~.
10. Lee, ~~who was~~ a great gentleman, raised his tailored hat in turn and rode off.

373

Words and Sentences

EXERCISE 11 On Your Own

Define each of the following in a sentence using no more than the number of words indicated.

    EXAMPLE   aunt (6)
POSSIBLE ANSWER   An aunt is a parent's sister.
Sample answers precede this chapter.

1. dessert (8)   2. the Fourth of July (7)   3. noon (6)

SENTENCE VARIETY

Readers can "hear" what they are reading. If a passage has sentences of varying lengths and patterns, the resulting rhythm is natural and pleasing. If all the sentences follow the same pattern, the rhythm becomes dull and tiresome. The variety of sentences in the following passage holds the reader's interest.

> I was too young to be other than awed and puzzled by Doc Marlowe when I knew him. I was only 16 when he died. He was 67. There was that vast difference in our ages and there was a vaster difference in our backgrounds. Doc Marlowe was a medicine-show man. . . . He would come out after the entertainment and harangue the crowd and sell bottles of medicine for all kinds of ailments. I found out all this about him gradually, toward the last, and after he died. When I first knew him, he represented the Wild West to me, and there was nobody I admired so much.
> — JAMES THURBER, "DOC MARLOWE"

17d Vary the length and structure of your sentences.

Sentence Combining

One way to achieve sentence variety is to combine short, choppy sentences into longer ones that read more smoothly. Combining related ideas into one sentence can also help clarify your point. In the following sentences, the reader might not understand how both ideas could be true.

Kathleen missed her family. She was having a good time at camp.

Note: Additional practice for sentence combining is on pages 73–74 and 94–95.

Sentence Variety

17d

When the sentences are combined, however, the meaning becomes clear.

> Although Kathleen missed her family, she was having a good time at camp.
>
> or
>
> Although she was having a good time at camp, Kathleen missed her family.

Notice that the emphasis in the two sentences is different. When you combine sentences, choose the way of combining that best expresses your meaning.

Combining Sentences with Phrases. In the following examples, short sentences are combined into a longer sentence that includes at least one phrase.

A. Polar explorers wear heavy parkas. These parkas have hoods. The hoods have drawstrings.

Polar explorers wear heavy parkas **with drawstring hoods.** [prepositional phrase]

B. The drawstrings help keep the person warm. They prevent warm air around the head from escaping.

The drawstrings help keep the person warm, **preventing warm air around the head from escaping.** [participial phrase]

C. Balaclavas keep the face warm. Balaclavas are tight-fitting woolen head masks.

Balaclavas, **tight-fitting woolen head masks,** keep the face warm. [appositive phrase]

EXERCISE 12 Combining Sentences with Phrases

Combine each set of short sentences, using the models above. The letter in brackets indicates which model to use. Remember to use commas correctly.

In Cold Regions

1. Caribou skin₍, a warm and waterproof material,₎ is used for sleeping bags. ~~Caribou skin is a warm and waterproof material~~. [C]
2. Well-balanced diets ~~are carefully selected. They consist~~ of fats, carbohydrates, and proteins₍,₎ ~~They~~ are ₍carefully₎ selected before an expedition sets off. [A]

375

Words and Sentences

3. Arctic explorers burn up energy quickly~~, They require~~ ,requiring 1,000 more calories per day than their usual intake. [B]
4. To survey new areas, explorers today use special planes, with ~~These planes have~~ skis for landing~~/They land~~ on ice. [A]
5. Temperatures at night can reach 40 degrees below zero, making ~~The temperatures make~~ the oil in a propeller plane as thick as tar. [B]
6. Mechanics must drain the oil before nightfall, warming ~~They warm~~ it up in the morning before putting it back in the plane. [B]
7. Glaciologists, people who study ice formations, now go to Antarctica and brave the climate that threatened the early explorers. ~~Glaciologists are people who study ice formations.~~ [C]
8. Experts ~~go to Antarctica to study. These experts are~~ in biology, geophysics, meteorology, and geology, go to Antarctica to study. [A]
9. Scientists believe that great reserves of oil and other minerals ~~are there. They believe these resources~~ lie beneath the ice cap. [A]
10. These people are highly dedicated, enduring ~~They endure~~ great loneliness as they study and learn. [B]

Combining Sentences by Coordinating. Ideas of equal importance can be joined in one sentence with the use of coordinating conjunctions *(and, but, or, for, yet,* and *so).* The resulting sentences will contain compound elements.

A. "Mississippi Rag" is an early example of ragtime piano music. "Harlem Rag" is an early example of ragtime piano music.

"Mississippi Rag" and "Harlem Rag" are early examples of ragtime piano music. [compound subject]

B. Scott Joplin performed ragtime. Scott Joplin composed ragtime.

Scott Joplin **performed and composed** ragtime. [compound verb]

C. Joplin's piano rags were influenced by show music. They were influenced by a popular dance called the cakewalk.

Joplin's piano rags were influenced **by show music and a popular dance called the cakewalk.** [compound object of a preposition]

Sentence Variety

D. Ragtime melodies were hard to sing. Most rags were written without words.

Ragtime melodies were hard to sing, **so** most rags were written without words. [compound sentence]

E. Ragtime rhythms are syncopated. They are energetic.

Ragtime rhythms are **syncopated and energetic.** [compound predicate adjective]

F. Scott Joplin was a famous ragtime composer. Thomas Turpin was a famous ragtime composer.

Two famous ragtime composers were **Scott Joplin and Thomas Turpin.** [compound predicate nominative]

EXERCISE 13   Combining Sentences by Coordinating

Combine the following pairs of sentences, using the models on pages 376–377. The model and the conjunction to be used are provided in brackets.

EXAMPLE   A high fever was a symptom of the bubonic plague. Swollen glands were a symptom of the bubonic plague. [A—*and*]

ANSWER   A high fever and swollen glands were symptoms of the bubonic plague.

The Plague

1. The plague reached London in 1592 through wharves, *and* ~~It reached London through~~ river mouths. [C—*and*]
2. Rats from ships carried fleas, *and* ~~The~~ fleas spread germs throughout the city. [D—*and*]
3. To avoid infection, public meeting places *and theaters* were closed. ~~Theaters were closed~~. [A—*and*]
4. Shakespeare's plays could not be performed, *but* ~~He~~ continued to write plays during the plague. [D—*but*]
5. Home remedies against the plague were creative, *but* ~~They were~~ ineffective. [E—*but*]
6. The only medicines were herbs, *or* ~~The only medicines were~~ spices. [F—*or*]
7. One out of every ten people died, *and* ~~Many~~ more were ill or disabled. [D—*and*]
8. The only people who could flee the dreaded disease were the wealthy, *and* ~~The only people who could flee the dreaded disease were~~ the titled. [F—*and*]

377

Words and Sentences

9. The plague has been called the Black Death. Its victims got black spots all over their bodies. [D—*because*] *(because inserted)*
10. The danger passed for a while in 1594. The plague swept the city again in 1603. [D—*but*] *(but inserted)*

Combining Sentences by Subordinating. Ideas of unequal importance can be combined into one sentence with the technique of subordinating. To use this technique, change the less important idea into a subordinate clause. The following words are often used to begin subordinate clauses. *(See page 80 for a complete list of subordinating conjunctions.)*

RELATIVE PRONOUNS		SUBORDINATING CONJUNCTIONS	
who	that	after	because
whom	which	until	whenever
whose		unless	although

The following examples show how two ideas can be combined by subordinating.

A. Sunspots look like dark blotches on the sun. They are 2,000 degrees cooler than the surrounding surface.

Sunspots, **which are 2,000 degrees cooler than the surrounding surface,** look like dark blotches on the sun. [adjective clause]

Astronomers use special reflecting devices to observe the sun and its spots. They know the danger of looking directly at the sun.

Astronomers, **who know the danger of looking directly at the sun,** use special reflecting devices to observe the sun and its spots. [adjective clause]

B. Sunspots have a fiery temperature of 4,000 degrees. They are cooler than the rest of the sun's surface.

Although they are cooler than the rest of the sun's surface, sunspots have a fiery temperature of 4,000 degrees. [adverb clause]

Sunspots can interfere with radio communications. They hurl electrically charged particles into space.

Because they hurl electrically charged particles into space, sunspots can interfere with radio communications. [adverb clause]

378

Sentence Variety

EXERCISE 14 Combining Sentences by Subordinating

Combine each pair of sentences. Use the models on page 378 as indicated in the brackets.
Answers may vary.

Sun and Stars

1. The largest sunspots stretch across one third of the visible sun, which ~~This~~ is a distance ten times the earth's diameter. [A—*which*]
2. The outermost layer of the sun, which is called the corona, reaches a temperature of one million degrees. ~~It is called the corona.~~ [A—*which*]
3. Although it is usually invisible, the corona can be seen during an eclipse. ~~Usually it is invisible.~~ [B—*although*]
4. Sunspots, which can affect the earth's weather, ~~can affect the earth's weather. They~~ occur in cycles of 11 years. [A—*which*]
5. Some spots disappear in a few hours, while others last several weeks. [B—*while*]
6. The sun, which is expected to burn for another 5,500 million years, ~~The sun~~ is about halfway through its life cycle. [A—*which*]
7. The medium-sized sun will last longer than more massive stars because massive stars burn up their fuel at a very fast rate. [B—*because*]
8. The Crab nebula, which was first observed in China on July 4, 1054, ~~The Crab nebula~~ is made up of the gaseous leftovers of a supernova explosion. [A—*which*]
9. The center of the Crab nebula, where a neutron star flashes 30 times a second, intrigues astronomers. ~~There~~ [B—*where*]
10. A red giant, which is typically 100 times larger than our sun, is a star in the first stages of its death. ~~A red giant is typically 100 times larger than our sun.~~ [A—*which*]

Varying Sentence Structure

The sentence-combining techniques you have just studied will help you achieve a variety of sentence types. Strive for a mixture of the four basic sentence types. *(See pages 89–94.)*

SIMPLE   Pups show their obedience to other dogs by rolling over on their sides or backs. [one independent clause]

COMPOUND   Most pups will let an older dog dominate them, but some insist on being the boss. [two or more independent clauses]

379

Words and Sentences

COMPLEX Very young pups can be hurt by older dogs because they do not yet know the rules of showing obedience. [one independent clause and one or more subordinate clauses]

COMPOUND-COMPLEX After a pup reaches the age of four months, it has learned the social rules, and an owner can safely leave it with an older dog. [two or more independent clauses and one or more subordinate clauses]

EXERCISE 15   Varying Sentence Structure

The following paragraph contains only simple sentences. Using the combining techniques of coordinating and subordinating, revise the paragraph so that it contains a mixture of simple, compound, complex, and compound-complex sentence structures.

Sample answer:

Daily Rhythms

Humans experience a lull in energy level in the middle of the day. Lower mammals often pursue quiet activities in the early afternoon. Animals spend early morning and early evening hours in active feeding. They reserve the early afternoon hours for grooming and play. People all over the world slow down after lunch. Many make mistakes during this period. Eating lunch is not believed to be the cause of the slowdown. In some tropical climates, shops and businesses close down during the midday siesta period. In nonindustrial countries workers rest from their strenuous activities and stay inside talking or mending tools. Activity begins to pick up by late afternoon in both humans and animals. Some scientists believe these patterns stem from a body clock. All creatures carry a body clock within them.

Varying Sentence Beginnings

The most natural way to begin a sentence is with the subject. If all the sentences in a passage begin this way, however, the writing is monotonous. You can achieve variety by beginning your sentences in different ways. The following examples show several ways to begin sentences.

Sentence Variety

SUBJECT	**Grant Wood** was born in 1892 on a farm in Iowa.
ADVERB	**Gradually** he began sketching the animals and scenery of his farm home.
ADJECTIVE	**Industrious,** he worked odd jobs to buy art supplies.
INFINITIVE PHRASE	**To learn his craft,** he studied at the Handicraft Guild in Minneapolis.
PARTICIPIAL PHRASE	**Taking the first job offered him,** Wood worked as a caretaker in a morgue to pay expenses while studying art.
PREPOSITIONAL PHRASE	**In later years** he studied in Chicago and Paris.
ADVERB CLAUSE	**Although he studied in Europe,** Wood developed a distinctly American style and continued to paint the landscapes and people of his childhood.

Revised sentences should begin with underlined words.

EXERCISE 16 Varying Sentence Beginnings

Vary the beginnings of the following sentences. Use as openers the construction or part of speech suggested in brackets.

A New Game

1. Most sports have a long history because they were played in one form or another by the ancients. [adverb clause]
2. You need to look back no further than 1891 to find the beginnings of basketball. [infinitive phrase]
3. Dr. Arthur Gulick, a YMCA leader, began looking for a new sport in that year. [prepositional phrase]
4. Dr. Gulick wanted a sport that could be played indoors to fill the gap between football season and baseball season. [infinitive phrase]
5. He also wanted a sport without much body contact, believing that rugby and soccer were too rough. [participial phrase]
6. He went to Dr. James Naismith for help in developing the new game. [prepositional phrase]
7. Dr. Naismith went to work on the problem immediately. [adverb]
8. The game of basketball was created after much careful thinking. [prepositional phrase]

381

Words and Sentences

9. The first official game was played on January 20, 1892.
[prepositional phrase]
10. Basketball has become one of the world's most popular spectator sports, although the first game was clumsy and confused. [adverb clause]

EXERCISE 17 On Your Own

Write five to ten sentences that explain what you plan to do when you graduate from high school. Read them over when you have finished and revise them as necessary to include a variety of sentence lengths, structures, and beginnings. Include at least one compound sentence, one complex sentence, and one sentence that does not begin with the subject.
Answers will vary.

FAULTY SENTENCES

Good writers reread everything they write, asking, "Is this really what I mean? Will my reader understand this?" If they find a problem, they rework their sentences, adding words, eliminating phrases, or correcting mistakes. Always read over your sentences with a critical eye.

17e ▶ Revise sentences with **faulty coordination, faulty subordination,** or **faulty parallelism.** Avoid **rambling sentences** and overuse of **passive voice.**

Faulty Coordination and Faulty Subordination

The techniques of coordination and subordination can add variety to your sentences and clarify your ideas. If you use the wrong conjunction, however, the resulting sentence can leave a reader puzzling over the relationship between ideas.

FAULTY COORDINATION   I liked the movie, and I thought the acting was poor.

PRECISE COORDINATION   I liked the movie, **but** I thought the acting was poor.

or

I liked the movie; **however,** I thought the acting was poor.

Faulty Coordination and Subordination

17e

NOTE: See pages 276–277 for a review of how to use a semicolon to join independent clauses.

Coordinating words have different meanings. Some show similarity, some show contrast, and some show result. The following chart lists some common coordinators according to their use.

TO SHOW SIMILARITY	TO SHOW CONTRAST	TO SHOW RESULT
and	but	so
both/and	yet	therefore
not only/but also	however	consequently
just as/so also	instead	thus
besides	on the other hand	hence
indeed	still	accordingly
furthermore	or, nor	as a result
moreover	nevertheless	for this reason

Faulty coordination can also result if you try to combine two unrelated ideas. To correct this problem, express the ideas in separate sentences.

FAULTY COORDINATION — Developing your own photographs can be fun, and my friend Gail has her own darkroom.

CORRECT — Developing your own photographs can be fun. My friend Gail has her own darkroom.

Another problem arises if you coordinate ideas that are not of equal importance. Subordination is the proper technique for such a situation. To subordinate correctly, change the less important idea into a phrase or a dependent clause.

FAULTY COORDINATION — Toby broke a drinking glass, and she was washing the dishes.

CORRECT — **Washing dishes,** Toby broke a drinking glass. [phrase]

CORRECT — **As she was doing the dishes,** Toby broke a drinking glass. [subordinate clause]

The following guidelines will help you correct problems in coordination and subordination.

383

Words and Sentences

17f

Correcting Faulty Coordination and Faulty Subordination

1. Use the connecting word that best shows the relationship between your ideas (similarity, contrast, result).
2. Express unrelated ideas in separate sentences.
3. If the ideas are of unequal importance, express the less important idea in a phrase or a subordinate clause.
4. Always express your most important idea in an independent clause.

EXERCISE 18   Correcting Coordination and Subordination
Using the guidelines above, revise each sentence.
Sample answers:

Dancing Bees

1. Bees use no words, ~~and~~ yet they communicate to one another.
2. After ~~A~~ female, worker bee finds food, ~~and~~ she returns to the hive to let the other bees know.
3. She dances in a circle; ~~nevertheless,~~ accordingly, this dance is called a round dance.
4. As the bee dances in a circle, ~~and~~ the other bees follow her movements, keeping their antennae close to her body.
5. ~~Because~~ One of the other bees leaves and finds the same feeding spot, because she has learned from the dancer where the food is.
6. The newly fed bee returns to the hive, ~~yet~~ and she also begins a dance.
7. The process continues, ~~and~~ until many bees have learned of the feeding spot.
8. ~~Because~~ The other bees hold their antennae close to the dancer's body, because she carries the scent of the food.
9. The bees pick up the scent; ~~nevertheless,~~ consequently, they are able to trace down the food when they leave the hive.
10. In the dance movements, a bee can communicate the direction and distance of the food, ~~and~~ Scientists have charted these dances carefully.

Rambling Sentences

Readers need to digest ideas one at a time. If too many phrases or clauses are used in one sentence, the main point becomes lost. Avoid "overfeeding" your readers by breaking up one long, rambling sentence into several shorter ones.

384

Rambling Sentences

17f

RAMBLING   For a long time, one phone company controlled all the telephone services in the United States, and people rented phones for use in their homes and businesses, but in 1983 the government ruled that other phone companies should be allowed to offer their services, and now consumers have many choices, including whether to buy a phone or rent one and whether to use a cordless phone or one that remembers phone numbers or one that has push buttons or a rotary dial, and many people are now enjoying a wide variety of telephone services.

IMPROVED   For a long time, one phone company controlled all the telephone services in the United States, and people rented phones for their homes and businesses. In 1983, however, the government ruled that other phone companies should be allowed to offer their services. Now consumers have many choices, including whether to buy a phone or rent one. They can choose a cordless phone or one that remembers phone numbers or one that has push buttons or a rotary dial. Many people are now enjoying a wide variety of telephone services.

EXERCISE 19   Correcting Rambling Sentences

Revise the following rambling sentences by breaking them into shorter sentences. Add capital letters and punctuate where needed.

Sample answers:

1.

December on State Street in Chicago is a hectic time. ~~for~~ Holiday shoppers crowd the streets and stores. ~~and~~ Even though the street was turned into a mall that allows buses only, traffic on surrounding streets is still congested, especially when bad weather makes the roads slippery, however, ~~yet~~ The hectic feeling adds to the holiday excitement. ~~and~~ The store windows with their animated scenes re-create fanciful wonderlands, and volunteer musicians collecting money for charity play carols on the street corners.

Words and Sentences

2.

Singing in a choir or glee club is a rewarding experience for several reasons, one of them is that singing in itself is such a pleasurable feeling, especially when you need to let off steam or unwind from tension. When you add the pleasure of singing with others, you enjoy a double pleasure by working with your friends and choirmates to form rich harmonies and stay on pitch. When you finally have rehearsed a piece long enough, the pleasure of hearing yourself in the polished choir adds yet a third delight.

3.

Working part-time has its pros and cons, yet on the whole it is a good experience. It helps you practice discipline in your schedule, since you need to find time to do homework and still have fun. The extra money comes in handy for saving for the future or spending on special purchases, and you learn skills that may help you find another job when you are out of school.

4.

Certain colors are known to have certain effects on people, and knowledge of these effects is often used in planning color-coded devices. In traffic lights, red is used to signal, "Stop!" because red has the effect of alerting people. Green, which tends to calm people down, is used for, "Go ahead; everything is clear."

5.

The word *bonanza* is a Spanish word that means "fair weather at sea." *Bonanza* signifies good luck for sailors, travelers, and fishers. The word was also used in gold-rush days in Nevada in the 1850s. When miners found a rich vein of gold they would shout "Bonanza!" This expression then gradually came to mean that someone has struck it rich.

Faulty Parallelism

A sentence with parallelism uses the same grammatical construction to express similar ideas. Parallelism, as its name suggests, points out parallels that help a reader group certain ideas together. Faulty parallelism occurs when similar ideas are expressed in different grammatical constructions.

Faulty Parallelism

FAULTY   Jeffrey's hobbies are playing the piano and to work on cars. [one gerund phrase; one infinitive phrase]

PARALLEL   Jeffrey's hobbies are **playing the piano** and **working on cars.** [two gerund phrases]

FAULTY   This plant needs a small amount of water and to be directly in the sunlight. [noun and infinitive phrase]

PARALLEL   This plant needs a small **amount** of water and direct **sunlight.** [two nouns]

FAULTY   Jessye Norman's voice is clear, colorful, and with a heavenly quality. [two adjectives and a prepositional phrase]

PARALLEL   Jessye Norman's voice is **clear, colorful,** and **heavenly.** [three adjectives]
or
Jessye Norman's voice **is** clear and colorful and **has** a heavenly quality. [two verbs]

EXERCISE 20 Correcting Faulty Parallelism

Revise each sentence so that the grammatical constructions are parallel. *Answers may vary.*

1. Her eyes were violet and ~~with a~~ soft ~~look~~.
2. I want to stick to my diet and ~~that I~~ exercise every day.
3. The city was a symphony of noises: trains clattering, ~~the beeps~~ beeping of horns, cars buzzing on the freeways, and ~~overhead there were~~ airplanes roaring overhead.
4. Eating out is more expensive than ~~to eat~~ eating at home.
5. To surprise his mother and ~~hoping~~ to make her laugh, Roberto appeared at the back door in a disguise.
6. To keep the peace, to uphold human rights, and ~~feeding~~ to feed the hungry — these are the goals for which nations strive.
7. My best friend is sympathetic, and understanding, and acts like a sister to me.
8. Ellen likes to fish, ~~to~~ ride her bicycle, and run.
9. Cross-country skiing and ~~to swim~~ swimming are good exercise for the heart, lungs, and legs.
10. Carla wanted driving lessons and ~~that~~ someone to inform her about buying a car.

387

Words and Sentences

Passive Voice

The passive voice places emphasis on the receiver of the action rather than on the doer. *(See pages 133–135.)*

PASSIVE The sandwich was eaten by me.
ACTIVE I ate the sandwich.

In some cases the doer of the action is missing entirely from a passive construction.

PASSIVE The decision was made to add two extra hours to the school day.

When you wish to place emphasis on the receiver of the action, the passive voice is proper and useful.

Miguelina was named the top student by her peers.
Sandy was elected class president.

Overuse of the passive voice, however, drains writing of vitality. Use the active voice whenever possible.

17g ▶ Avoid overusing the **passive voice.** Whenever possible, use the **active voice.**

EXERCISE 21 Changing Passive Voice to Active Voice
Revise each sentence by using the active voice instead of the passive voice.

EXAMPLE The speech was rehearsed carefully by me, but still I was nervous.
ANSWER I rehearsed my speech carefully, but still I was nervous.

1. A cake was baked by Mr. Gianelli. / baked a cake.
2. It was decided by the Student Council to cancel the spring dance. [T, decided]
3. A lie was told by Tracy about how the paint was spilled. [told a lie]
4. The conclusion reached by me is that friendships are worth working at. [I reached]
5. The illness was diagnosed by the doctor as the 24-hour flu. [doctor, illness]
6. An experiment was assigned by the chemistry teacher. [T, assigned an experiment.]
7. Computers are used by a space shuttle to monitor all its systems. [A space shuttle uses]

Passive Voice

17g

8. ~~The bed was made and~~ the room ~~was cleaned by Mark~~.
   _{↑Mark made}   _{cleaned↑}

9. The ~~musical was rehearsed~~ for weeks ~~by the acting club~~ before it was performed.
   _{↑acting club rehearsed the↑}

10. ~~The decision was made by~~ Congress to lower the speed limit on highways to 55 miles per hour.
    _{made the decision↑}

EXERCISE 22   On Your Own
Write a paragraph-long description of the most unusual character you have ever met. Then exchange papers with a classmate and comment on the following questions.
Answers will vary.

1. Are there any sentences with faulty coordination or faulty subordination?
2. Are there any rambling sentences?
3. Are there any sentences with faulty parallelism?
4. Has the passive voice been overused?

CHAPTER REVIEW

A. Specific Words
Revise each sentence to eliminate the problem indicated in brackets.   *Sample answers:*

1. The ~~food~~ was sizzling on the grill. [general noun]
   _{steak}
2. A long-distance runner needs to have three ~~things~~: patience, stamina, and determination. [general noun]
   _{qualities}
3. "Watch out for that car!" he ~~said~~. [general verb]
   _{screamed}
4. The happy father ~~bolted~~ his baby son in the car seat, and the family set out on their vacation. [wrong connotation]
   _{fastened}
5. Knowing how happy her parents would be, Ellen ~~boastfully~~ told them she had a part in the school play. [wrong connotation]
   _{proudly}

B. Figurative Language
Identify the figure of speech used in each sentence by writing *simile*, *metaphor*, *personification*, or *onomatopoeia*.
_{S   M   P   O}

M   6. Jill pranced by with the air of a well-bred racehorse.
O   7. The mountain stream gurgled and splashed.
S   8. The storm, like a bird of prey, swooped down on the town.
P   9. The mountains bared their teeth to the weary climbers.
M   10. Luck is a fickle friend.

389

Words and Sentences

C. Effective Sentences

Revise each sentence to eliminate the problem indicated in brackets. *Answers may vary.*

11. The ~~restless~~ child slept uneasily. [redundancy]
12. ~~Due to the fact that~~ Because my car had a flat tire, I took the subway downtown. [empty expression]
13. ~~What I am trying to say is that~~ With the right attitude, failure can be educational. [empty expression]
14. Julie, ~~a friend of mine, who is a person~~ My friend who loves animals, has two dogs and two cats. [wordiness]
15. The report that I am working on, ~~which is~~ about undersea minerals ~~that are under the sea~~, is due on Friday. [wordiness]
16. ~~Stephen looked~~ Looking through his rearview window, ~~He~~ Stephen turned on his blinker to change lanes. [needs combining with a phrase]
17. Carlos and Burton made the honor roll. ~~Burton made the honor roll.~~ [needs combining with coordination]
18. Marion ran in to mail a letter at the post office, while Georgia waited in the car. [needs combining with subordination]
19. Suzanne wanted to stay longer at the party, ~~and~~ but she knew her parents would worry. [faulty coordination]
20. Letter writing is a lost art, ~~and~~ T̸hat's really a shame, because the process of writing letters is a pleasant one. ~~since~~ Ø̸ne can sit alone and reflect on recent happenings, and think about the best way to explain and describe those happenings, ~~and~~ A̸fter a letter is written, the experiences it relates are set in the writer's mind, ~~but~~ N̸ow the telephone has taken the place of pen and paper. [rambling]
21. The high school years are a time for learning, making friends, and ~~to prepare~~ preparing for later life. [faulty parallelism]
22. I learned A lesson ~~was learned by me~~ the hard way. [misuse of passive]
23. The ~~reason that the~~ player was ~~disqualified and~~ benched because ~~was that~~ he lost his temper and threw the bat. [empty expression and redundant]
24. Our senator gave A speech ~~was given by our senator~~ at graduation, and handed out Diplomas ~~were handed out by him~~. [misuse of passive and needs combining]
25. We played Parcheesi ~~A game was played by us~~ to pass the time. [general noun and misuse of passive]

390

Chapter Summary

Words and Sentences

Word Choice
1. Use specific words with connotations that suit your meaning.
2. Use figurative language to enliven writing.
3. Avoid clichés.

Concise Sentences
4. Express your meaning in as few words as possible by
   - eliminating redundancy.
   - avoiding empty expressions.
   - revising wordy sentences.

Sentence Variety
5. Vary the length of your sentences. Combine sentences to avoid too many short, choppy sentences in a row.
6. Use a mixture of simple, compound, complex, and compound-complex sentences.
7. Vary the beginnings of your sentences.

Faulty Sentences
8. Revise faulty sentences by
   - eliminating instances of faulty coordination and faulty subordination.
   - breaking up rambling sentences.
   - using parallel constructions.
9. Avoid overusing the passive voice. Use the active voice whenever possible.

Chapter 18   Clear Thinking

OBJECTIVES

- To distinguish between facts and opinions and use each appropriately in writing.
- To avoid hasty generalizations.
- To replace platitudes and empty rhetoric with specific examples and information.
- To detect the following logical fallacies and avoid them in writing:
  attacking the person instead of the issue
  the fallacy of either-or
  the fallacy of non sequitur
  confusing chronology with cause and effect
  false analogy
  begging the question and circular reasoning.

MOTIVATIONAL ACTIVITY

To preview some of the problems in logical thinking that will be covered in this chapter, ask students to imagine that they are trying to persuade a friend to go see a movie at the Franklin Theater, but the friend offers several arguments against going. Ask how the students would counter each of the following arguments:

1. The movies that the Franklin Theater shows are never very good. (Students should recognize that there might be exceptions: hasty generalization.)
2. How can I trust your judgment in movies? You didn't even make the honor roll! (Students should recognize that there is not necessarily any connection between good grades and taste in movies: attacking the person instead of the issue.)
3. Sorry. If I spend the money, I'll never save enough to afford a car. (Students should recognize that the price of one movie admission would not greatly influence the ability to purchase a car: either-or fallacy.)
4. No thanks. The day after I went to the Franklin the last time, I fell and sprained my ankle. The Franklin brings me bad luck! (Students should recognize that just because the friend fell *after* going to the Franklin does not mean the Franklin had any part in *causing* the fall: confusing chronology with cause and effect.)

Point out that logical thinking is especially important in persuasion. One idea or viewpoint must be measured against another, and the logic with which a viewpoint is expressed will affect how a reader makes up his or her own mind. Also, recognizing logical flaws in opposing viewpoints is a good way to build a stronger case for one's own viewpoint.

TEACHING SUGGESTIONS

Facts and Opinions *(pages 392–395)*

The opinions of many people are formed relatively early in life, shaped in large part by the opinions of people close to them. To help students learn how to develop opinions from facts instead of from imitation, have them develop an opinion on the basis of each of the following facts:

1. Fact: Most countries that have lower-than-average literacy also have lower-than-average life expectancy.
   Possible opinion: Widespread education could lead to longer life expectancies, since people could learn how to take care of their health.
2. Fact: Stroking a pet often lowers a person's blood pressure.
   Possible opinion: People with high blood pressure should get a pet.
3. Fact: In the past year, fourteen accidents have happened at the intersection of Crawford and Blake roads; there are no stop signs at this intersection.
   Possible opinion: Stop signs should be placed at the intersection of Crawford and Blake roads.

Clear Thinking

You can continue this assignment by having students brainstorm a list of facts and develop an opinion based on each.

Generalizations *(pages 395–399)*

Developing generalizations is an essential part of the writing process. Explain to students that the material they write in response to Exercise 4 can serve as the basis for compositions. They may wish, therefore, to add their work from Exercise 4 to their permanent writing folders.

Platitudes *(pages 398–399)* Students often use platitudes as a substitute for facts in their writing. To help students avoid this problem in later composition assignments, refer them to their Inventory of Interests in their writing folders. (See Teaching Suggestions for Chapter 16.) Have students choose three of the subjects that interest them the most. They should then prepare a fact sheet on each subject with the help of library resources. For each subject, they should find at least ten facts. Students should record information in their own words, and also note the source from which they took their information. These sheets should then be filed in the students' writing folders for use in future writing assignments.

Fallacies *(pages 400–407)*

Many logical fallacies appeal to emotion rather than reason. In argument, both reason and emotion are useful, but reason is the most persuasive. Excessive appeals to emotion can actually weaken an argument, since a listener or reader can conclude that there are insufficient reasonable arguments in favor of a position.

To demonstrate the power of appeals to emotion, have each student bring in a copy of a magazine advertisement and be prepared to explain what emotions the advertiser is appealing to. Students should also explain what, if any, appeals to reason the advertisement makes. Finally, students should identify any logical fallacies that the advertisements contain.

ACTIVITIES FOR DIFFERENT ABILITIES

Basic Students

ACTIVITY 1 Facts and Opinions

On each of the following subjects, have students write one sentence expressing a fact and one expressing an opinion.

1. government
2. fast-food restaurants
3. cars
4. exercise
5. books

ACTIVITY 2 Generalizations

Have students revise the following hasty generalizations by replacing or modifying the underlined word with a more moderate, limiting word.

1. *All* artists are temperamental.
2. There are *never* enough check-out clerks in supermarkets.
3. Pollsters can *always* predict the outcome of elections.
4. Television shows are *totally* insensitive to elderly people.
5. *None* of the movies based on books are as good as the books themselves.

Advanced Students

ACTIVITY 1 Developing Logical Reasons

Have students think of a situation in which they have argued about some issue—for example, trying to persuade their parents to allow them special privileges or arguing with a friend about politics. Then have them write a realistic dialogue between the conflicting parties in which each arguer offers reasons for his or her point of view. After completing the assignment, students should examine all the reasons on both sides and look for examples of illogical thinking.

ACTIVITY 2 Using Specific Examples

Have students choose one of the following proverbial generalizations and write a draft of an essay supporting or refuting it. Stress the importance of using specific examples, incidents, and other kinds of supporting details.

1. A stitch in time saves nine.
2. Virtue is its own reward.
3. Time heals all wounds.

Chapter 18 b

Clear Thinking

ADDITIONAL PRACTICE
Teacher's Resource Book: pages 207–210
Workbook: pages 159–160

REVIEW EXERCISES AND TESTS
Student Text
Chapter Review: page 408
Teacher's Resource Book
Chapter 18 Test: pages 45–46
(Also available as spirit duplicating masters.)

ADDITIONAL ANSWERS

EXERCISE 2   Supporting Opinions with Facts *(page 394)*

Sample answers:
1. A four-day workweek would allow people to spend more time with their families.
2. Sweets can cause tooth decay.
3. There are more museums, shops, and theaters in the city than in the country.
4. Such a law would make more people become involved in the election process.
5. Better grades would result.
6. Cats do not require as much work as dogs do.
7. Most cars today tend to be relatively small and fuel-efficient.
8. This new party would offer voters an alternative to the established Democratic and Republican parties.
9. Fall is a time when many plants die.
10. The costs of health care have risen dramatically.

EXERCISE 4   Drawing Sound Generalizations *(pages 396–397)*

Sample answers:
1. Younger brothers often try to copy their older brothers.
2. Many family gatherings are marked by reminiscing.
3. Most tests produce anxiety.
4. Some television shows are about police officers.
5. Most homework assignments help you understand the subject.
6. Most computers are becoming easier to use.
7. Some friendships are more difficult than others.
8. Many politicians have a background in law.
9. Some science-fiction movies offer little more than special effects.
10. Most athletes know the importance of daily training.

EXERCISE 6   Eliminating Platitudes and Empty Rhetoric *(page 399)*

Sample answer:
   The computer revolution is bringing about great changes in the way we work and conduct our lives. Forward-looking young people will take advantage of the computer courses offered in high schools, trade schools, and colleges to prepare themselves for living and working in the future. Those who fail to learn about computers will be at a disadvantage in the job market of the future.

EXERCISE 7   On Your Own *(page 399)*

Sample answer for item 1:
   Adults are often wiser than teenagers. Because they have lived longer than teenagers, adults have had a greater chance to test out the world and see how it works, and they can base their judgments and values on their own experience. For example, since

their parents no longer support them financially, adults generally have more experience with finding employment and budgeting money than do teenagers. While a person of any age can still learn new things, adults generally have gained more knowledge and wisdom than have teenagers.

EXERCISE 8 Recognizing the Fallacy of Ad Hominem *(pages 400–401)*

Sample answers:
1. Doyle's divorces do not reflect on his ability to make plans for the new library.
2. Carr's dietary preferences have little to do with her qualifications for the office of governor.
3. Osaki's skill as a tennis player does not assure that he will be able to make the city run efficiently.
4. That De Passo's family doesn't speak English is no reflection on her ability to be class president.
5. Monroe's conviction record does not disqualify his ideas on crime prevention.
6. Mayor Goldsmith's age does not necessarily mean that his mind is closed to new ideas.
7. That Silver was fired from his television job for tardiness does not necessarily mean that his views on television violence are inaccurate.
8. That a person plays the lottery does not necessarily mean that his ideas on taxes and the economy are unsound.
9. Martin's skill as a hostess does not assure that she will be an effective diplomat.
10. The kind of car Davis drives does not necessarily reflect on his ability to be a union representative.

EXERCISE 9 Finding Alternatives in Either-or Statements *(page 402)*

Sample answers:
1. You may have lost the race because you pulled a muscle.
2. Someone might have been at home but was unable to answer the telephone.
3. You may have been unable to vote in one election because you had not lived in the neighborhood long enough to register.
4. Police and fire departments may find ways of saving money without sacrificing the quality of home protection.
5. You may care about your future and still prefer to have your hair at its present length.
6. You may do other things in your life that show your compassionate side.
7. I may get another scholarship.
8. They might be trying to lose weight by dieting.
9. In spite of not being captain, I might play because I enjoy the game.
10. You may choose to remain silent instead of tell the truth.

EXERCISE 10 Detecting Non Sequiturs *(page 403)*

Sample answers:
1. The dessert might be made of fruit or other low-calorie ingredients.
2. The sweater might carry a designer label that increases the price without adding to the quality.
3. Many people from small towns are not gossipy.
4. Just because a piece is beautiful does not mean that it has to be difficult to play.
5. Arturo could have been the best candidate for the job.
6. Sonia's looks have little to do with how good a class president she would be.
7. There could have been a city-wide power failure.
8. The car might have a flat tire.

Clear Thinking

9. Snobbishness is a trait shared by rich and poor.
10. Only two students might have deserved an A.

EXERCISE 11 Supplying Logical Causes *(page 404)*

Sample answers:
1. The earthquake could have been caused by the usual factors and coincidentally happened after the rocket took off.
2. I may have studied well for the test.
3. The car may have had a serious problem before it was driven to the gas station.
4. I may not have been studying enough.
5. Tony may have been ill.
6. I may be getting a cold.
7. Someone else may just as easily have been responsible.
8. I may have prepared better for this speech than for any previous one.
9. The illness may have run its course.
10. I sleep late because I'm tired from the day's activities and something in those activities may have given me a backache.

EXERCISE 12 Identifying the Flaws in False Analogies *(pages 405–406)*

Sample answers:
1. Cats and dogs, while similar in some ways, are different enough so that what works for one does not necessarily work for the other.
2. Although both typewriters and computers have keyboards, a computer is much more complex than a typewriter.
3. The kind of technology that allows people to go into outer space is different from medical technology.
4. The existence of lots of fish in the sea does nothing to lessen the importance of this dance to you.
5. Human behavior is too complex to be compared to the behavior of birds.
6. You must consider many more factors when you buy a car than when you buy milk.
7. People are all the same species, while animals who are natural enemies are not.
8. Math and English require different learning skills.
9. Paying for a major purchase on credit is not as easy as counting.
10. Helen's ability to afford a car has nothing to do with my financial situation.

EXERCISE 13 Identifying Unproved Assumptions *(page 407)*

Sample answers:
1. First show that the tax is unfair.
2. Show that the laws in the last administration were successful in protecting the environment.
3. Show that it is necessary to send troops into the country.
4. Show that the number of ambitious students in the United States has decreased.
5. First prove that the workers are poor.

EXERCISE 14 Understanding Circular Reasoning *(page 407)*

Sample answers:
1. I oppose the capture of wild animals because I oppose the capture of wild animals.
2. My choice is Senator Everyman because he is the candidate of my choice.
3. The movie was fascinating because it was fascinating.
4. Veterinarians must love animals because veterinarians love animals.
5. Performing in front of an audience is hard because it is hard.

18

Clear Thinking

For additional practice for this chapter, see the Teacher's Resource Book and the Workbook.

Many brilliant ideas begin as dim hunches. They travel through a maze of logical steps and problems in the mind before they emerge as clear ideas. Writing is one way to direct your hunches and half-formed thoughts through this mental maze. Putting your thoughts on paper helps you see where your thinking is clear and logical and where it is muddy or illogical. This chapter will show you how to avoid the traps of illogical thinking.

FACTS AND OPINIONS

Like scientists, writers try to verify their hunches with tests. If a statement can be proved, it is a *fact*.

18a A **fact** is a statement that can be proved. An **opinion** is a judgment that cannot be proved.

One way to test a fact is to look for confirmation of it within your own experience. You can, for example, test the following statement against your own experience.

FACT   Thanksgiving falls on the fourth Thursday of November.

Some statements cannot be verified by your own observation and experience. Consider the following sentence.

FACT   The first Thanksgiving was celebrated in the colonial settlement of Plymouth, Massachusetts.

Since you were not part of that settlement, you cannot use your own experience to verify this statement. You can, however, consult a history book to check the place of the first Thanksgiving. Consulting reliable authorities is the second way to verify facts.

18b Use your own experience and reliable authorities to verify facts.

Opinions, unlike facts, can never be proved. They are judgments that vary from person to person. Some opinions, however, are more sound than others. Sound opinions are as valuable as facts in any discussion or composition about important issues. The soundest opinions are those that can be backed up with facts.

OPINION   People should wear seat belts. [Fact Backing Up Opinion: The National Safety Council estimates that 14,000 lives per year could be saved if people wore seat belts.]
OPINION   Chocolate tastes better than vanilla. [No facts are available to back up statement.]

Opinions that cannot be supported with facts should be qualified, or limited, so that they express a strictly personal viewpoint. Instead of asserting that chocolate tastes better than vanilla, for example, you could confidently assert that *you* prefer chocolate to vanilla.

18c Back up your opinions with facts. If no facts are available, qualify your opinion to show that is a personal preference.

Learn to recognize opinions in what you read and what you write. Check every opinion for facts that back it up. The following words are often used in statements of opinion.

Opinion Words		
should	good, better, best	probably
ought	bad, worse, worst	might
can	beautiful	perhaps
may	terrible	maybe

Clear Thinking

EXERCISE 1   Identifying Facts and Opinions

Indicate whether each sentence expresses a fact or an opinion by writing *F* for fact and *O* for opinion. If you are in doubt about a sentence, verify it by checking in the library or asking a reliable authority.

O 1. May is the most beautiful month of the year.
F 2. Harper Lee wrote *To Kill a Mockingbird*.
O 3. Mark Twain's best novel is *The Adventures of Huckleberry Finn*.
O 4. The government should provide funds for developing solar power.
F 5. Solar power uses the sun's energy.
O 6. People ought to limit their television viewing to two hours a day.
O 7. We probably caught so many fish last Saturday because we used a new kind of bait.
F 8. Light travels faster than sound.
O 9. Swimming is a better sport than jogging.
F 10. Swimming provides less stress to the body than jogging.

EXERCISE 2   Supporting Opinions with Facts

For each opinion given, write one fact that could be used to back it up.

   EXAMPLE   Students should do their homework.
   POSSIBLE   One penalty for not doing homework is
   ANSWER   a low grade.
   Sample answers precede this chapter.
1. The workweek should be four days rather than five.
2. People ought to avoid eating too many sweets.
3. The city is much more interesting and exciting than the countryside.
4. There should be a law requiring people to vote.
5. Students should concentrate on learning, not socializing.
6. Cats make better pets than dogs.
7. Big luxury cars are becoming extinct.
8. We need a third major political party in this country.
9. Fall is a melancholy time of year.
10. The government needs to spend more money on health care.

EXERCISE 3 On Your Own

Think of one opinion you hold strongly about your school, job, or family life and write it on your paper. Then list three facts that you could use to back up your opinion. Exchange papers with a classmate and discuss the following two questions about each other's supporting facts.
Answers will vary.

- Is each supporting fact verifiable?
- Can it be verified from your own experience, or would you need to consult a reliable source?

If any statements are not verifiable facts, rework them until they are.

GENERALIZATIONS

To understand new experiences, people naturally tend to generalize on the basis of past experiences. Suppose you receive an invitation to Susan's birthday party. Every year for the past six years, you have had a miserable time at Susan's birthday party, so you assume that this year will be no different. You are drawing a general conclusion based on the particular parties you have attended.

Generalizing is a useful reasoning tool. When not done carefully, however, generalizing can cause you to overlook important exceptions, leaving you with a false or misleading conclusion.

Hasty Generalizations

To draw a conclusion based on particular experiences, you need to be sure that you have examined *enough* particular experiences. If you had been to only one of Susan's parties, for example, you would not have sufficient experience to conclude that the next party would be dull. Even if you had been to many of her parties, but were the only person who did not have a good time, you could not logically conclude that her parties are failures. Similarly, if three of her parties were fun and three were dull, you could not reasonably conclude that the next party would be dull.

Clear Thinking

A sound generalization, then, depends on three factors: (1) a sufficient number of experiences, (2) verification of your experiences by others, and (3) explainable exceptions. Hasty generalizations lack one or more of these three factors. Consider the following hasty generalizations.

> HASTY GENERALIZATION — All dogs are loyal and obedient. [Has the writer examined enough dogs to conclude that they all share these traits?]
>
> HASTY GENERALIZATION — Eating strawberries results in a rash. [Does everyone who eats strawberries break out in a rash?]
>
> HASTY GENERALIZATION — The space program has been a complete success. [Were there no exceptions, such as loss of life and failure to accomplish missions successfully?]

All of these hasty generalizations can be made more sound by limiting them to some, many, or most cases instead of *all* cases.

> LIMITED GENERALIZATIONS — **Many** dogs are loyal and obedient.
>
> Eating strawberries results in a rash for **some** people.
>
> **Most** of the space program has been a success.

18d ▶ Avoid **hasty generalizations** by limiting generalizations to some, many, or most cases.

Even many sound generalizations are, at best, theories. Beware of such words as *all, total, complete, every, always, never,* and *none*.

EXERCISE 4 Drawing Sound Generalizations

For each topic, write a generalization based on your own past experience. Limit your generalization with a word like *some, many,* or *most*.

> EXAMPLE school dances
> POSSIBLE ANSWER Most school dances have a theme.
> *Sample answers precede this chapter.*

1. younger brothers
2. family gatherings
3. tests
4. televisions shows

Hasty Generalizations

18d

5. homework
6. computers
7. friendships
8. politicians
9. science-fiction movies
10. athletes

Writing Extra

The reasoning process that leads from the particular to the general is called *induction*. For example, if you concluded after climbing several mountains that the temperature is cooler at the tops of mountains than at the bases, you would be using induction. The opposite of induction, called *deduction*, begins with a general idea known to be true and then proceeds with the application of the general idea to a particular idea. The following is an example of deduction.

GENERAL TRUTH	All normal dogs are creatures with four legs.
PARTICULAR	King is a normal dog.
CONCLUSION	Therefore, King is a creature with four legs.

The conclusion in a deduction is valid only if the statements on which it is based are true. If either the general statement or the particular statement is false, then the conclusion is false.

FALSE STATEMENT	All creatures with four legs are normal dogs.
PARTICULAR	My cat Ajax is a creature with four legs.
FALSE CONCLUSION	Therefore, my cat Ajax is a normal dog.

EXERCISE 5 Using Deduction

Practice your deductive reasoning skills by writing the conclusion for each of the following deductive steps.

1. All choir members are people who sing well.
   Jody is a choir member.
   Therefore, _Jody is a person who sings well._
2. Aerobic exercises are good for the heart and lungs.
   Jumping rope is an aerobic exercise.
   Therefore, _jumping rope is good for the heart and lungs._
3. All postal workers are employees of the civil service.
   Ms. Williams is a postal worker.
   Therefore, _Ms. Williams is an employee of the civil service._

Clear Thinking

4. All national parks are lands owned by the government.
   Yosemite is a national park.
   Therefore, <u>Yosemite is land owned by the government</u>.
5. People who are not in the armed services are civilians.
   Alfonso is not in the armed services.
   Therefore, <u>Alfonso is a civilian</u>.

Platitudes

Platitudes are dull, overused generalizations. A person who uses platitudes offers a simple saying as the solution to a problem rather than careful thought. How many times have you heard or read the following platitudes?

PLATITUDES   Boys will be boys.
             Life isn't a bed of roses.
             Every cloud has a silver lining.

Platitudes are a form of empty rhetoric, language meant to sound grand and important but lacking in specific ideas. Clear thinking is specific. Compare the two paragraphs that follow. The first is filled with the hot air of platitudes and empty rhetoric. The second is firmly anchored to specifics.

USE OF PLATITUDES AND EMPTY RHETORIC

We can learn much about our wide, wonderful world by studying those gentle giants the gorillas. Their family groupings provide a mirror image of our own human families. Their communications with one another are an eye-opening study for humans. How much poorer our world would be without our hairy friends the mountain gorillas.

USE OF SPECIFICS

Dian Fossey's 15-year study of gorillas in the wild has provided a wealth of information about this endangered species. Gorillas live in family groups consisting of 1 silverback, an adult male leader; 1 blackback, an immature male; 3 or 4 adult females who are bonded for life to the silverback; and 3 to 6 juveniles under 8 years of age. Their social interactions are

Platitudes

18e

complex. They communicate a wide range of emotions and information—from contentment to reprimands to fear—in clearly distinctive sounds. Fossey's work also included recommendations for saving the species, whose remaining members now number only 242.

18e Replace **platitudes** and **empty rhetoric** with specific examples and information.

EXERCISE 6 Eliminating Platitudes and Empty Rhetoric
Rewrite the following paragraph. Replace the platitudes and empty rhetoric with specific examples and information from your own knowledge and experience.
Sample answer precedes this chapter.

Preparing for the Future

We live in an ever-changing world. All around us there are great changes in communication, transportation, and lifestyles. Young people preparing for careers in the world of tomorrow must be flexible and ready to meet the new and exciting challenges head-on. Getting a head start at learning the modern technologies will help the go-getters find their ideal job. Undoubtedly, however, some people will fall between the cracks and lag behind in the great race to the future.

EXERCISE 7 On Your Own
Choose one of the following hasty generalizations. Rewrite the statement until it is a limited generalization with which you agree. Then write a paragraph supporting your limited generalization, using specific examples and information to make your point.
Sample answer for item 1 precedes this chapter.
1. All adults are wiser than teenagers.
2. Life in big cities is thoroughly unbearable.
3. Life in a small town is always quiet and boring.
4. High school dropouts always end up in jail.
5. Once a person breaks the law, you can never again trust him or her to be a responsible citizen.
6. All parents hate loud rock music.

Clear Thinking

FALLACIES

A fallacy is an error in logic. Some fallacies seem convincing at first glance. When you examine them closely, however, they crumble into nonsense. Some of the most common fallacies are outlined in the following pages. As you think and write, test your ideas to be sure you have not fallen into one of these traps.

> **18f**   Avoid **fallacies** in your thinking and writing.

Attacking the Person Instead of the Issue

The Latin name for this fallacy is *argumentum ad hominem*. It means "argument against the man." Writers who commit this fallacy sidestep the real issue and instead try to slur the character of their opponent.

AD HOMINEM FALLACY   Candidate William Young's proposal for a new highway is filled with potential problems. Young does things at the last minute, and his proposal was probably thrown together too quickly. He suffered from this problem in college, too, where he failed two courses. [That Young does things at the last minute and failed two college courses does not necessarily mean that his proposal is faulty.]

This example argues from an irrelevant, negative character trait. Using positive but equally irrelevant personal qualities as the basis for an argument is also illogical.

AD HOMINEM FALLACY   Joe Brian is a good father and a friendly neighbor, so I know he's right about the new school proposal. [Brian's goodness as a father and neighbor is no assurance that his views about the school are right.]

EXERCISE 8   Recognizing the Fallacy of Ad Hominem

For each statement, write one sentence that explains the fallacy. Use the bracketed explanations above as a model.
Sample answers precede this chapter.

1. Sam Doyle, twice divorced, wants us to believe that his plan for the new library is worthy.

2. Madeline Carr is a health-food person. Do we want to elect her to the serious office of governor?
3. John Osaki, a great tennis player and a great guy, knows how to make our city run efficiently.
4. Ellen DePasso would not be a good class president; her family does not even speak English.
5. Scott Monroe is an ex-convict. Can we believe his ideas about crime prevention?
6. Mayor Goodsmith's policy on city jobs is out-of-date; he's 73 years old, and times have changed.
7. Reuben Silver's views on television violence are highly suspect because he was fired from his job at WLIT-TV for showing up late to work.
8. My opponent's position on the issue of new taxes gambles on an improvement in the economy, a carry-over, no doubt, from his own favorite pastime of playing the lottery.
9. Eliza Martin is a gracious hostess. Surely she would make a fine diplomat.
10. Ben Davis should not be a union representative because he drives a foreign car.

The Fallacy of Either-Or

Too often thinkers assume that there are only two sides to every question. Between two opposite points of view on an issue, there are usually a number of alternative viewpoints. Notice how the following statements ignore alternatives between the two extremes.

EITHER-OR FALLACY — Either you support the wilderness bill, or you favor killing baby seals. [There may be people who want to save seals but who want a slightly different wilderness bill.]

EITHER-OR FALLACY — Either you study for tomorrow's test, or you will never get into college. [A student may do poorly on the test but still have good enough grades and test scores to go to college.]

Although the words *either . . . or* are often used in this fallacy, be ready to detect the fallacy when it is expressed in other words.

Clear Thinking

EITHER-OR FALLACY If you do not paint your house when it needs painting, you obviously do not care about your property. [A person may care very much but be unable to paint the house for reasons of money, health, or weather.]

EITHER-OR FALLACY I had to buy this record; it was on sale today only. [Missing the sale and saving to buy the record at a later date might be more sensible.]

EXERCISE 9 Finding Alternatives in Either-or Statements

For each statement, write one sentence that offers an alternative to the choices given in the either-or fallacy. Use the bracketed statements on pages 401–402 as a model.
Sample answers precede this chapter.

1. If you lose a race in the last forty yards, it is because you lack courage.
2. If no one is answering the telephone, then there must be no one at home.
3. If you have not voted in every election, you have ignored your responsibilities as a citizen.
4. Either we raise taxes, or the police and fire departments cannot keep our homes secure.
5. If you care about your future, then you will get a haircut before your job interview.
6. By refusing to be a volunteer in the hospital, you show your lack of compassion.
7. If I don't get that scholarship, my future is ruined!
8. If people suddenly lose weight, then there must be something worrying them.
9. Unless I am captain of the soccer team, I will be too depressed to play.
10. Either you tell the truth all the time, or you are a liar.

The Fallacy of Non Sequitur

Non sequitur is a Latin phrase meaning "it does not follow." Like the either-or fallacy, the non sequitur omits reasonable alternatives. The conclusion drawn in a non sequitur does not necessarily follow from the evidence.

NON SEQUITUR Debbie got the most votes; she must be the best-qualified candidate for the job. [Debbie

Fallacies

NON SEQUITUR   may have waged the best campaign and won, but another candidate may have been better qualified.]

NON SEQUITUR   Because Bill was more nervous at the auditions than Frank, Bill deserves to get the part. [How nervous one is at an audition is not as important as how good an actor that person is.]

NON SEQUITUR   Louisa didn't call me; she must not like me anymore. [Louisa may have been busy or ill.]

EXERCISE 10   Detecting Non Sequiturs

For each non sequitur, write one sentence that explains why the conclusion is illogical. Use the bracketed explanations on pages 402–403 as models.
Sample answers precede this chapter.

1. This dessert is delicious; it must be loaded with calories.
2. This sweater is very expensive; it must be of high quality.
3. Because Becky comes from a small town, she tends to be gossipy.
4. That piece you were playing on the piano was beautiful. It must be very difficult to play.
5. Arturo landed a summer job as a lifeguard at the pool. He must know the right people.
6. Sonia is a very attractive girl, so she should run for class president.
7. The lights went out; we must have blown a fuse.
8. The car was left at the side of the road. It must have had engine trouble.
9. Katy's family is rich, so she tends to be snobbish.
10. Only two students received *A*'s from Mr. Hanson last term; he must be a hard grader.

Confusing Chronology with Cause and Effect

A fallacy results when something that happens *after* an event is assumed to be the *result* of that event. In many cases the relationship between the two events is merely coincidental. The Latin name for this fallacy is *post hoc, ergo propter hoc*. In English these words mean "after this; therefore, because of this."

Clear Thinking

CAUSE-EFFECT FALLACY Since I went to sleep right after watching the movie, the movie must have caused my nightmares. [Other problems could have been bothering you; simply because the movie came before your nightmares does not mean it caused them.]

CAUSE-EFFECT FALLACY Every time I attend a game, my team loses. I must have a bad effect on them. [A likelier explanation is that you happen to go to the games in which the team plays poorly or is facing a particularly tough opponent.]

EXERCISE 11 Supplying Logical Causes
In each sentence, a time sequence is confused for a cause and its effect. For each one write a more likely cause of the second event. Use the bracketed explanations above as models.
Sample answers precede this chapter.

1. Right after the rocket blasted off, an earthquake shook the area. The blast must have caused the quake.
2. I rubbed my lucky charm before taking the test; that must explain why I did so well.
3. The attendant at that last gas station didn't seem to pay attention to what he was doing. That is why the car is backfiring now.
4. Ever since Ms. Barnes became principal, I have gotten poor grades. She is to blame.
5. After our last conversation, Tony stopped calling me. I must have said something to offend him.
6. I felt a headache coming on after swimming. The chlorine in the water must have irritated my sinuses.
7. I saw a stranger walking down my street last night. This morning the tape deck in my car was missing. The stranger must have taken it.
8. I left my note cards at home, so I had to give my speech without them. It was the best speech I have ever given. Speaking without the note cards resulted in a much better performance.
9. It's spring. The patient feels better. The arrival of spring caused the patient's health to improve.
10. Whenever I sleep late, I wake up with a backache.

Fallacies

False Analogies

Analogies are useful tools. They help you understand ideas or experiences that might otherwise be difficult to grasp. Suppose, for example, that you were trying to persuade your mayor to make bicycle lanes in your city. You might help the mayor understand your view by using an analogy like the following.

ANALOGY   Depriving bicycle riders of bicycle lanes is like depriving pedestrians of sidewalks.

An analogy sheds light on an idea or experience by comparing it to something else that is similar in many ways.

A false analogy attempts to compare two things that are not enough alike to be logically compared.

FALSE ANALOGY   I can't complete my book report on time. After all, Rome wasn't built in a day. [Although completing the book report and building Rome both involve an effort, the size of the effort is so dramatically different that the analogy is illogical.]

FALSE ANALOGY   Regina will probably make the cheerleading squad. Her sister did. [Regina and her sister, although probably similar in some ways, may have different levels of athletic ability.]

Analogies, when they compare things that are truly similar, can enrich and clarify writing. Avoid using analogies as proofs, however, since what is true about one thing is not necessarily true about something similar.

EXERCISE 12   Identifying the Flaws in False Analogies

For each false analogy, write one sentence that explains the flaw in reasoning. Use the bracketed explanations above as models.

Sample answers precede this chapter.

1. Obedience training should work with cats; after all, it works with dogs.
2. Anyone who can use a typewriter can use a computer.
3. If our technology is advanced enough to put humans into outer space, we ought to be able to wipe out all diseases.
4. Don't feel bad about not getting a date for the dance; there are lots of fish in the sea.

405

Clear Thinking

5. Just as birds of a feather flock together, so do people of similar types find each other.
6. There's no reason for any American to buy a foreign car; you don't leave your state to buy milk.
7. Just as some animals are natural enemies, some people can just never get along.
8. If you can pass English with A's and B's, you can do as well in math.
9. Buy this color television on credit; it's as easy as counting *1, 2, 3*.
10. I should be able to buy my own car; Helen's parents let *her* buy one.

Begging the Question

Underlying many thoughts and arguments are some basic assumptions. A critical thinker challenges these hidden assumptions before taking the thought too seriously.

Building an argument on an unproved assumption is called *begging the question*. In the following examples, all of the assumptions offered as facts need to be proved before the argument is logical.

BEGGING THE QUESTION The irresponsible attitudes of today's youth are the main cause of juvenile delinquency. [First prove that today's youth have irresponsible attitudes.]

BEGGING THE QUESTION The government's excessive spending on weapons is a waste of taxpayers' money. [First show that the spending is excessive by proving that the government could and should spend less.]

Begging the question is a form of *circular reasoning*. In the last example, "excessive spending" and "waste of money" mean the same thing. What the sentence is actually expressing is simply this: The government wastes taxpayers' money on weapons because that spending is a waste of taxpayers' money. This kind of reasoning is meaningless because it goes around in circles. Notice the circular reasoning used in the following example.

Fallacies

CIRCULAR REASONING — My doctor must be smart because he made it through medical school. [Translation: My doctor must be smart because he's a doctor.]

EXERCISE 13 Identifying Unproved Assumptions

For each example of begging the question, write one sentence that identifies the assumption that needs to be proved first. Use the bracketed explanations on page 406 as models.

Sample answers precede this chapter.

1. The unfair tax on automobiles should be abolished.
2. The laws that successfully protected the environment in the last administration should be renewed in the present administration.
3. The necessary course of sending troops into the country will solve the bitter conflict.
4. The decrease in the number of ambitious students in the United States is endangering our society.
5. Big businesses should share their profits with their poor workers.

EXERCISE 14 Understanding Circular Reasoning

Translate each circular statement so that its lack of logic becomes clear. Use the bracketed translation on page 406 as a model.

Sample answers precede this chapter.

1. I oppose the capture of wild animals because I believe animals should be allowed to live in the wild.
2. I am going to vote for Senator Everyman because he is the candidate of my choice.
3. The movie was fascinating because it held my attention.
4. Veterinarians must love animals because if they didn't, they wouldn't be veterinarians.
5. Performing in front of an audience is hard because it's a real challenge to get up in front of people.

EXERCISE 15 On Your Own

Read the editorial page of your local newspaper or favorite magazines. Look for arguments that commit one of the fallacies described on pages 400–407. Copy (or clip out if the paper or magazine is yours) any arguments containing fallacies and bring them to class. Be prepared to explain the flaw in thinking.

Answers will vary.

Clear Thinking

CHAPTER REVIEW

Identify each statement by writing one of the following terms.

- A fact
- B opinion
- C non sequitur
- D platitude
- E false analogy
- F hasty generalization
- G cause-effect fallacy
- H either-or fallacy
- I begging the question
- J circular reasoning
- K ad hominem (attacking the person)

H 1. Either we ban violence on TV, or we become a more violent nation.
A 2. In the year 1976, the United States was 200 years old.
B 3. Mozart's piano music is more beautiful than Chopin's.
D 4. Love will heal the suffering's wounds.
E 5. Psychiatrists cannot really help people, because you can lead a horse to water but you cannot make it drink.
C 6. Lynn Dole is a feminist, so we have to doubt the accuracy of her report on crime.
J 7. Matt is on a diet because he needs to control what he eats.
A 8. Although the moon appears to shine, it is only reflecting light, not radiating it.
J 9. The unsolvable puzzle had no answer.
H 10. If I don't make the team, then I'll never be good at anything.
C 11. I can't find my wallet; there are too many thieves around these days.
F 12. All younger brothers try to imitate their older brothers.
G 13. I always gain weight in the winter. Cold weather must make me feel hungrier.
B 14. The Student Council ought to sponsor a writing contest.
D 15. Life is a learning experience.
F 16. All fire fighters are courageous people.
I 17. The cruel justice of the sentence should worry every member of society.
K 18. Ron Jones's opinion on nuclear power does not count; he dropped out of college.
E 19. Just as swallows return to Capistrano, a criminal will return to the scene of a crime.
G 20. After going over to Marilyn's for dinner, I broke out in a rash. I must be allergic to her cats.

Chapter Summary

Clear Thinking

Facts and Opinions
1. A fact is a statement that can be proved. An opinion is a judgment that cannot be proved.
2. Use your own experience and reliable authorities to verify facts.
3. Back up your opinions with facts. If no facts are available, qualify your opinion to show that it is a personal preference.

Generalizations
4. Avoid hasty generalizations by limiting generalizations to some, many, or most cases, rather than all cases.
5. Replace platitudes and empty rhetoric with specific examples and information.

Logical Fallacies
6. Avoid fallacies in your thinking and writing. Watch especially for
    - attacking the person instead of the issue.
    - the fallacy of either-or.
    - non sequiturs.
    - confusing chronology with cause and effect.
    - false analogies.
    - begging the question and circular reasoning.

Chapter 19 Paragraphs

OBJECTIVES

- To explain the function of the elements within a paragraph, including topic sentence, supporting sentences, and concluding sentence.
- To explain the function of chronological order and a consistent point of view in narrative paragraphs.
- To explain the function of spatial order, sensory details, and figurative language in descriptive paragraphs.
- To identify various methods of developing an expository paragraph.
- To describe the tools of persuasion in a paragraph expressing an opinion.
- To identify the most logical order of development for various kinds of paragraphs.
- To follow the prewriting steps that shape a general idea into an organized plan for a paragraph.
- To write the first draft of a paragraph, revise it, and edit it.

MOTIVATIONAL ACTIVITY

Attitude is a critical factor in determining the success of writing. You may therefore wish to begin this chapter with an exploration and discussion of students' attitudes toward writing. The following activity will give students an opportunity to express themselves honestly and will also help establish a tone of support in the classroom for writing efforts.

Pass out an index card to each student. Ask the students to use the card to express how they feel about writing—whether they like or dislike it, and why they have that particular attitude. Tell students not to put their names on the cards. Collect the cards and read them all to the class. (Most of them will no doubt express a negative—usually anxious—attitude about writing.) Seeing how others feel about writing will help students realize that writing is a challenge to most people, not only to themselves. Hold a brief discussion about why students feel as they do, and impress upon them the value of helping one another by serving as readers for their peers' writing.

TEACHING SUGGESTIONS

Paragraph Structure *(pages 410–415)*

Use the first paragraph in Exercise 1 to demonstrate the way in which the topic sentence of a paragraph limits the subject and raises certain expectations in the reader's mind. The broad subject, the northern lights, is introduced in the first part of the topic sentence. The rest of the topic sentence limits that broad subject to the various forms in which the northern lights appear. Ask students to comment on what they would expect in the rest of the paragraph from the following topic sentences, all about the same broad subject.

The aurora borealis, or northern lights, has appeared again and again in folklore. (It raises expectations that the rest of the paragraph will provide specific examples of the aurora's appearance in folklore.)

The aurora borealis, or northern lights, is most often seen in certain locations. (It raises expectations that the rest of the paragraph will name the locations from which the northern lights can be seen.)

The aurora borealis, or northern lights, usually appears in connection with sunspot activity. (It raises expectations that the relation between the northern lights and the activity of sunspots will be explained.)

Kinds of Paragraphs *(pages 415–433)*

In addition to the four main purposes named on page 415, writers may also have a more specific purpose, such as to entertain, teach a moral lesson, sell, or inspire. You can use the models on pages 416 and 417 to demonstrate this variety of purposes. For example, the narrower narrative purpose of "A Long Shot," page 416, is to amuse.

Ask students to name the specific purpose of each of the following kinds of writing:

Chapter 19 a

Paragraphs

1. a human-interest story in a newspaper
2. a story of an automobile accident in a brochure published by the National Safety Council
3. a letter to a restaurant owner relating the story of rude treatment by an employee
4. a diary entry
5. notes kept for a science project

Descriptive Paragraphs *(pages 419–422)* Just as an awareness of *purpose* can generate writing ideas, an awareness of *audience* can also inspire ideas. To help students think of ideas for descriptive paragraphs, have them list as many possible answers to each of the following questions. Students should label this exercise "Subject Ideas for Descriptive Writing" and add it to their writing folders.

1. What people, places, or things would very young children be interested in?
2. What places that I've visited would a person from another country be interested in reading about?
3. What things would my best friend be interested in reading a description of?
4. What people, places, and things would my grandparents find interesting?
5. What would I like to read about?

Expository Paragraphs *(pages 423–428)* The ten methods of paragraph development shown on pages 423–424 can be used to generate ideas for expository paragraphs. The following questions are based on various methods of development. Have students choose five questions and list at least three subject ideas under each.

1. What subjects can I explain with facts and examples?
2. What subjects can I explain by outlining steps in a process?
3. What subjects can I explain by giving a set of directions?
4. What can I explain with incidents?
5. What do I know how to define?
6. What items or subjects can I compare and contrast?
7. What subjects can I explain with the use of analogy?
8. What subjects can I explain by breaking them into parts?
9. What can I explain the cause and/or effect of?
10. What can I explain by showing various groupings of items or ideas?

After students have completed this activity, they should title their work "Subject Ideas for Expository Writing" and add it to their writing folders.

Persuasive Paragraphs *(pages 429–433)* Effective persuasive paragraphs are built on a solid core of factual knowledge, even though they express an opinion. To help students develop ideas for persuasive paragraphs that move beyond personal preferences, have them answer the following questions built on the knowledge and experience they are acquiring in their classes in school.

1. What facts have I learned in science or biology class that have led to a respect for the environment? Why should people take care of their environments?
2. What facts have I learned in history class that show that a concern for equal rights is important in good government? What opinions can I base on these facts?
3. What facts have I learned in health and physical education that show how one's behavior can effect one's health? What opinions can I base on these facts?
4. What facts have I learned in my vocational classes that show the necessity for safety precautions around tools and machines? What opinions can I base on these facts?

When students have answered these questions, have them title their work "Subject Ideas for Persuasive Writing" and add it to their writing folders.

ACTIVITIES FOR DIFFERENT ABILITIES

Basic Students

ACTIVITY 1 Peer Work
Writing an expository paragraph according to a set of directions is a good task for

Paragraphs

basic students. For example, you might have students explain the requirements for obtaining a driver's license. Give them a list of specific points to cover, such as age requirement, written test, and road test. As part of the prewriting work, pair students and have one talk through the directions while the other takes notes. Then have students exchange roles.

ACTIVITY 2 Editing
Have students begin a personalized editing checklist. Across the top of their papers, they should write the following headings: Grammar, Usage, Spelling, Capitalization, Punctuation. Starting with their final assignment for this chapter, they should list all errors they made in each category. As the term progresses, students should continue to add errors to their checklists. Patterns will emerge, and students will be better able to watch for certain mistakes.

Advanced Students
ACTIVITY 1 Tone
Introduce the concept of a familiar as opposed to an impersonal tone. With a familiar tone, a writer uses speechlike patterns and often writes from a first-person point of view. With an impersonal tone, the writer keeps his or her personality separate from the subject at hand. Ask students to experiment in both styles in two separate paragraphs on the same general subject.

ACTIVITY 2 Writing Practice
Have students write a draft of each kind of paragraph (narrative, descriptive, expository, and persuasive). When they have finished their drafts, have them choose *one* draft only to revise and polish into a final assignment for your evaluation. When preparing this draft, they should aim for a superior quality of writing. They should save their other drafts in their writing folders as possible starting points for longer compositions.

ADDITIONAL PRACTICE
Teacher's Resource Book: pages 211–218
Workbook: pages 161–168

REVIEW EXERCISES AND TESTS
Student Text
  Chapter Review: pages 444–445
Teacher's Resource Book
  Chapter 19 Test: pages 47–48
  (Also available as spirit duplicating masters.)

ADDITIONAL ANSWERS
EXERCISE 6 Using Transitions *(page 417)*
Sample answer:

   My mother once described me as an accident waiting to happen. I suppose she was right. Two years ago I kept a weather station as part of a science project. One day we had a heavy rainfall, and I went outside to check the cup that was collecting rain. Then, carrying the cup, I ran back into the house to measure the rainwater. I slipped on the wet floor, and the glass cup broke in my hand. As soon as I wrapped my finger in a cold washcloth, my mother rushed me to the emergency clinic. When we arrived, we found that we would have to wait an hour in the waiting room before the doctor could see me. Finally, after numbing my finger, the doctor put stitches in it, where they stayed for a week. A tiny scar on the fourth finger of my left hand is now my reminder to be more careful.

EXERCISE 9 Listing Sensory Details *(page 421)*
Sample answer for item 1:
1. smell of gas and oil
   brightly-colored tanks

Paragraphs

car bumpers glittering in the sun
sounds of car engines
oil-spotted cement

EXERCISE 15   Analyzing a Persuasive Paragraph *(pages 432–433)*
1. decline of the grizzly population from 400 to 200, and decline in the size of grizzly litters
2. Sample answer: Since the 1960s, when the dump closings began, the grizzly population has declined from 400 to 200, with the number of breeding-age females at a risky 29.
3. Richard Knight, a biologist of the U.S. Fish and Wildlife Service, and John and Frank Craighead, bear experts
4. If the grizzly population were not already in decline, the hands-off policy might have some merit.
5. Answers will vary.

EXERCISE 18   Choosing and Limiting a Subject *(page 436)*
Sample steps for one subject:
a. subject: cars
b. brainstorming list:
   - Cars need regular maintenance.
   - The cost of major repairs is much greater than the cost of regular maintenance.
   - Even standard maintenance is not cheap.
   - Many of my friends do their own basic maintenance.
   - There are courses in school on auto mechanics.
   - The new smaller, fuel-efficient cars are becoming popular.
   - Japanese carmakers recognized the U.S. market for smaller cars before American carmakers.
c. subject that is too broad: cars
   What about cars? car maintenance [more limited subject]
   What about car maintenance? how to change the oil filter [suitably limited subject]

EXERCISE 19   Listing Supporting Details *(pages 436–437)*
Sample answer for item 1:
1. I got lost on my way to the party and was an hour late.
   I was nervous about going to the party by myself.
   I met the person who eventually became my best friend.
   Once inside, I realized I knew more people than I thought.

EXERCISE 20   Arranging Details in Logical Order *(page 438)*
Sample answer for item 1 of Exercise 19:
1. what happened at the last party I attended
   I was nervous about going to the party by myself.
   I got lost on my way to the party and was an hour late.
   Once inside, I realized I knew more people than I had thought.
   I met the person who eventually became my best friend.
   (chronological order)

Paragraphs

EXERCISE 22 Writing the Body of an Expository Paragraph *(page 440)*

Sample answer:

   Many high-rise building managers have found an inexpensive way to make the wait for elevators seem shorter. They began to look for solutions when they received complaints from building users that the elevators took too long to arrive. The managers looked into adding more elevators but found the expense to be too great. Finally they hired experts to tell them how they could solve the problem. The experts told them to install mirrors near the elevators. As soon as the mirrors were in place, the level of complaints dropped off dramatically. Humans apparently find endless fascination in watching themselves in mirrors.

CHAPTER REVIEW, Part B *(page 445)*

You may wish to use the following evaluation forms.

Evaluation Form for Narrative Paragraphs

	POINT VALUE	STUDENT SCORE
1. suitably limited subject	10	____
2. strong topic sentence (sets the scene and makes the narrative purpose clear)	10	____
3. events in chronological order	10	____
4. unity	10	____
5. coherence	10	____
6. transitions	10	____
7. consistent point of view	10	____
8. strong concluding sentence	10	____
9. paragraph revised	10	____
10. paragraph edited	10	____
Total Score		____

Evaluation Form for Descriptive Paragraphs

	POINT VALUE	STUDENT SCORE
1. suitably limited subject	10	____
2. strong topic sentence (suggests an overall impression of the subject)	10	____
3. specific details, sensory words, and striking comparisons	10	____
4. logical order	10	____
5. unity	10	____
6. coherence	10	____
7. transitions	10	____
8. strong concluding sentence	10	____
9. paragraph revised	10	____
10. paragraph edited	10	____
Total Score		____

Paragraphs

Evaluation Form for Expository Paragraphs

	POINT VALUE	STUDENT SCORE
1. suitably limited subject	10	____
2. strong topic sentence (stating factual main idea)	10	____
3. appropriate method of development	10	____
4. appropriate method of organization	10	____
5. unity	10	____
6. coherence	10	____
7. transitions	10	____
8. strong concluding sentence	10	____
9. paragraph revised	10	____
10. paragraph edited	10	____
	Total Score	____

Evaluation Form for Persuasive Paragraphs

	POINT VALUE	STUDENT SCORE
1. suitably limited subject	10	____
2. strong topic sentence (states an opinion)	10	____
3. opinion supported with facts, examples, or reasons	10	____
4. clear organization	10	____
5. unity	10	____
6. coherence and transitions	10	____
7. reasonable approach (moderate language, opposition's good points conceded)	10	____
8. strong concluding sentence	10	____
9. paragraph revised	10	____
10. paragraph edited	10	____
	Total Score	____

Chapter 19 f

19

Paragraphs

For additional practice for this chapter, see the Teacher's Resource Book and the Workbook.

A paragraph is a block of thought. In a long piece of writing, each paragraph rests on the preceding block until an entire structure of thoughts is built. A solid paragraph, however, can also stand alone.

> **19a** A **paragraph** is a group of related sentences that present and develop one main idea.

PARAGRAPH STRUCTURE

A paragraph that stands alone has three main parts: a topic sentence, a body of supporting sentences, and a concluding sentence. Notice how each part helps develop the idea in the paragraph that follows.

An Experimental Car

TOPIC SENTENCE: STATES MAIN IDEA
The X-1000, which was designed in 1956, looked something like a supersonic jet fighter on wheels.

BODY OF SUPPORTING SENTENCES: DEVELOPS MAIN IDEA WITH SPECIFICS
It had a retractable bubble canopy over the cockpit and fenders suspended in such a way that they resembled jet fuel pods. There were twin air coolers up front and an exposed after-cooler on the rear deck.

CONCLUDING SENTENCE: ADDS A STRONG ENDING
The X-1000 was an interesting try, but it is doubtful that it really forecast the look of the future.

—HENRY B. LENT, *THE X CARS*

In your reading you will no doubt find variations in paragraphs. Some, for example, may imply the main idea rather than state it directly. In some the main idea may be expressed in two sentences instead of one. Some paragraphs that are part of a longer piece of writing may not require a concluding sentence. Good writers adapt the form of their paragraphs to the needs of the message they are conveying. Paragraphs that stand alone, however, are usually more effective when they have a clearly stated topic sentence, a body of supporting sentences, and a concluding sentence that completes the thought.

Topic Sentence

The topic sentence often comes at the beginning of a paragraph. It may, however, come in the middle or at the end of a paragraph. Although its placement may vary, its purpose and character are always the same.

Topic Sentence

A topic sentence
1. states the main idea.
2. limits the main idea to one aspect of the subject that can be covered in one paragraph.
3. is more general than the sentences that develop it.

EXERCISE 1   Identifying Topic Sentences

Read the following paragraphs. Then copy the topic sentence of each.

1. Northern Lights

The aurora borealis, or northern lights, appears in many forms. Sometimes it looks like a faint green curtain in the sky, fading in and out of view. Sometimes it appears in white, yellow, or red, like a glowing arc in the sky. At other times it has little form at all. Instead, it appears as a foglike cloud shimmering in the far northern skies. Whatever form it takes, the aurora with its quiet mystery is always a sight to be remembered.

Paragraphs

2. Color Blindness

For every thousand men, about 80 have some form of color blindness. The numbers are smaller for women — only four in every thousand have some color-vision problem. Color blindness is an inherited problem. Eye doctors have learned these facts about color blindness, but they are still uncertain about its cause. It is believed to be related to an abnormal condition in the eye's color receivers, called cones. In some cases it may result from a problem in the optic nerve. Although most people with color-vision problems can adjust to seeing the world in shades of gray, doctors and scientists continue to study the problem in hopes of identifying its cause precisely.

—FRANKLYN M. BRANLEY, *COLOR* (ADAPTED)

3. Jobs and Concrete Thinking

The architect is a good example of a person who must be able to visualize solid objects or structures. Civil engineers, who build bridges and highways, work with solids of three-dimensional objects; so do mechanical engineers who design and build machines. The diemaker, who makes patterns and molds, must be able to visualize the finished product his or her die will produce. The sculptor, too, must be able to "see" the finished statue in his or her imagination. Surgeons must have a clear picture in mind of the structure of that part of the body on which they are operating. The same is true of the builder, the mechanic, the dressmaker, the fashion designer —anyone whose job deals with shapes and solids. They all need an aptitude for concrete thinking.

—GEORGE FRANCIS BARTH, *YOUR APTITUDES*

4. A Stately Name

Most people would probably like to have an important place named after them and their family, but William Penn, the Quaker, was an exception. King Charles II of England owed Penn's father, Admiral William Penn, a large sum of money. In partial settlement King Charles granted a large tract of land to William Penn in the colonies. Penn suggested the name *Sylvania* for the new colony, which means "woodland." King Charles, over the protests of the humble Penn, added the prefix *Penn* in honor of the admiral. Now every map of the United States remembers the early founder in the name *Pennsylvania*.

—*WORLD ALMANAC AND BOOK OF FACTS* (ADAPTED)

Supporting Sentences

A topic sentence raises expectations and questions in the reader's mind. The function of the supporting sentences in a paragraph is to meet those expectations and answer those questions with specifics.

> **19c** **Supporting sentences** develop or support the topic sentence with specific details, events, facts, examples, or reasons.

As you read the following topic sentence, think about what you expect from the rest of the paragraph and what questions you want answered.

TOPIC SENTENCE
The eruption of Mount St. Helens in May of 1980 and the ashfall that followed took an awesome toll on the region's wildlife.

If you are like most readers, you expect the rest of the paragraph to provide some facts or statistics. You probably have such questions in your mind as "Which animals were affected? How many died?" The supporting sentences answer these questions.

SUPPORTING SENTENCES
The blast itself and the superheated volcanic flows accounted for more than 67,000 deaths of birds and mammals, including 6,000 black-tailed deer, 11,000 hares, and nearly 28,000 forest and sage grouse. These numbers, unfortunately, are only the beginning. By the time the tons of ash had fallen in the area, nearly one and a half *million* creatures had died, with the greatest toll in the bird families. As the fiery hot flows reached the rivers below, even more wildlife was destroyed. Rivers became boiling hot, and about eleven million

CONCLUDING SENTENCE
salmon and other fish were killed. A whole year of desolation passed before signs of life began, little by little, to reappear in this devastated region.

(SOURCE: THOMAS AND VIRGINIA AYLESWORTH, *THE MOUNT ST. HELENS DISASTER*)

Paragraphs

EXERCISE 2 Identifying Supporting Sentences

Copy the following three topic sentences on your paper. After each one write the numbers of the sentences that support it.

Topic Sentences
- **A.** The average life span of mammals in the wild varies greatly. 2, 5, 7
- **B.** Groups of animals are known by special names. 3, 8, 10
- **C.** The young and the old in animal groups are often identified by different names. 1, 4, 6, 9

1. A baby fish is called a fingerling.
2. Asian elephants live to be 40 years old.
3. A group of larks is called an exaltation.
4. *Elver* is the name for a young eel.
5. The chimpanzee, polar bear, gorilla, and rhinoceros have an average life span of 20 years.
6. A baby kangaroo is called a joey.
7. Kangaroos live only seven years.
8. A group of kangaroos is called a mob.
9. Young cows, elephants, and whales are called calves.
10. Hounds in a group are called a cry or a pack.

Concluding Sentence

The main purpose of the concluding sentence is to complete the paragraph. Without it a paragraph could hang in midair, leaving the reader expecting more. Most good concluding sentences are more general than the supporting sentences.

19d A **concluding sentence** adds a strong ending to a paragraph. It may restate the main idea, summarize the paragraph, evaluate the supporting details, or add an insight.

The following paragraph, without a concluding sentence, leaves the reader "hanging."

Famous Names

Many people in show business trade the names they were born with for names with more audience appeal. Woody Allen, for example, was born Allen Konigsberg. Michael Landon's original name was Eugene Orowitz. Cher shortened her name from Cherilyn Sarkisian. Stevie Wonder was born with the name Stevland Morris.

Concluding Sentence

19d – e

If you add a concluding sentence to the paragraph, however, the reader will feel satisfied that the thought is complete.

> Although their families and longtime friends probably still call these performers by their original names, the world knows them only by their stage names.

EXERCISE 3 Writing Concluding Sentences
Write two more possible concluding sentences for the preceding paragraph on performers' names. *Sample sentence:* The made-up names of many performers are typical of the fantasy world of entertainment.

EXERCISE 4 On Your Own
The following sentences are the body of a paragraph. Read them carefully. Then write a suitable topic sentence and a strong concluding sentence for the paragraph. *Sample topic sentence:* A driving test can be nerve-racking, but these simple tips may help you.

> Before taking your driving test, try to relax by breathing deeply. When you are called for your test, be confident. Take your time getting ready. Adjust the mirrors and seats, buckle your seatbelt, and take some more deep breaths. During the exam itself, do exactly what your examiner tells you. Once you are on the road, watch for all signs, especially speed limits in school zones. Also, remember to use your blinker for all turns. *Sample concluding sentence:* If you relax and concentrate, you'll soon be a licensed driver.

KINDS OF PARAGRAPHS

There are four main purposes in writing: to tell a story, to describe, to explain, and to persuade. Each kind of writing uses special tools to help accomplish its purpose. You can learn these tools by studying the four different kinds of paragraphs.

Narrative Paragraphs

If your writing purpose is to tell what happened, you will be writing *narration*. Narration is used in letters, news stories, short stories, novels, histories, and biographies.

19e A **narrative paragraph** tells a real or imaginary story with a clear beginning, middle, and ending.

Paragraphs

Paragraph Development. The topic sentence in a narrative paragraph sets the scene, captures the reader's attention, or sets the story in motion. The supporting sentences then tell the story. The concluding sentence gives the outcome of the story. Notice how the following narrative paragraph develops the story.

A Long Shot

TOPIC SENTENCE: SETS THE SCENE

SUPPORTING SENTENCES: RELATE EVENTS ONE BY ONE

CONCLUDING SENTENCE: GIVES THE OUTCOME OF THE STORY

At a track in England some years ago, a mounted policeman was helping to get the race horses into their starting positions. At the cry "They're off!" the policeman's horse broke with the field, and the astonished bobby found himself desperately trying to pull in his mount. The best he could do, however, was to slow him down to third place. On the stretch the horse began to fight it out with one of the official entries. Despite the policeman's efforts to pull out of the race, he came in second, a scant neck behind a horse ridden by Freddy Archer, one of England's greatest jockeys.

— READER'S DIGEST

The supporting sentences in the body of a narrative paragraph are the events that make up the story. They are usually presented in the order in which they happened, called chronological order. To help readers understand the time order of events, writers use transition words and phrases.

19f Use **chronological order** and **transitions** to organize your narrative.

19g

Some Transitions Used for Chronological Order

after	later	immediately	on Tuesday
before	when	as soon as	last month
during	until	at last	by afternoon
finally	suddenly	first, second	yesterday
while	then	meanwhile	following
next	at noon	last night	the next day

Narrative Paragraphs

19f–g

The transitions in the paragraph below are in heavy type.

D-Day and After

Operation OVERLORD, the invasion of France, began at 3 A.M. **on June 6, 1944, after six weeks** of rugged air assaults on Hitler's fortifications in northern France. Almost three million men aided by 11,000 airplanes and innumerable craft of all kinds were ready to support a landing in Normandy. In spite of bad weather, the first troop carriers with 176,000 men anchored off the Normandy beaches. **After** grave losses, a million Allied soldiers were fighting in Normandy **two weeks later. By July 24,** Allied troops had captured 1,500 square miles of Normandy and Brittany. **On July 25,** General George S. Patton's very mobile Third Army swept after the Germans, turning their retreat into a rout. Paris was retaken **on August 25,** and **two days later** de Gaulle installed himself as president of a provisional French government.

—C. L. VER STEEG AND R. HOFSTADTER, *A PEOPLE AND A NATION*

EXERCISE 5 Using Chronological Order

Write the following events in chronological order.

- 4 • I came into the house to measure the rainwater I collected.
- 1 • I kept a weather station for a science project two years ago.
- 3 • I went to check the cup to see how much rain we had had.
- 9 • The doctor numbed my finger and then gave me stitches.
- 6 • I wrapped a cold washcloth around my bleeding finger.
- 5 • I slipped on the wet floor, and the cup broke in my hand.
- 2 • We had a heavy rainfall.
- 7 • My mother rushed me to the emergency clinic.
- 10 • The stitches were removed after a week.
- 8 • We had to spend an hour in the waiting room.

EXERCISE 6 Using Transitions

Using the following topic sentence and concluding sentence, write a paragraph with the events from Exercise 5. Add transitions where needed to show how the events are related in time. *Sample answer precedes this chapter.*

TOPIC SENTENCE My mother once described me as an accident waiting to happen.

CONCLUDING SENTENCE A tiny scar on the fourth finger of my left hand is now my reminder to be more careful.

417

Paragraphs

Point of View. The person whose "voice" is telling the story in narrative writing is called the narrator. A *first person narrator* is directly involved in the story and uses such personal pronouns as *I, we, us,* and *our.* In contrast, a *third person narrator* stands back from the story and tells what happens to others, using such third person pronouns as *she, he, they, their,* and *his.* These different narrative styles are called *points of view,* because they indicate through whose eyes the story is being told. Once a point of view is chosen, it should be used consistently throughout the narrative.

19h Use **first person** point of view if you are a character in the story. Use **third person** point of view if you are reporting what happened to others.

FIRST PERSON **I** bounded up the three flights of stairs to **my** apartment, hardly noticing the strain on **my** legs.

THIRD PERSON **Michelle** bounded up the three flights of stairs to **her** apartment, hardly noticing the strain on **her** legs.

EXERCISE 7 Identifying Points of View
Indicate the point of view in each of the following sentences by writing *first person* or *third person.*

third 1. Jane Austen was now 25 years old, and hitherto her life had been a happy one.—David Cecil, *A Portrait of Jane Austen*

first 2. One summer, along about 1904, my father rented a camp on a lake in Maine and took us all there for the month of August.—E. B. White, "Once More to the Lake"

first 3. I feel a lot better today, but I guess I'm still a little angry that all the time people were laughing and making fun of me because I wasn't so smart.—Daniel Keyes, "Flowers for Algernon"

third 4. Mary Cochran went out of the rooms where she lived with her father, Doctor Lester Cochran, at seven o'clock on a Sunday evening.—Sherwood Anderson, "Unlighted Lamps"

first 5. The thousand injuries of Fortunato I had borne as I best could; but when he ventured upon insult, I vowed revenge.—Edgar Allan Poe, "The Cask of Amontillado"

Descriptive Paragraphs

19h–i

third   6. Richardson pulled up his horse and looked back over the trail, where the crimson serape of his servant flamed amid the dusk of the mesquite.—Stephen Crane, "Horses—One Dash"

third   7. Mike Woods, the last American hope for an Olympic speed-skating medal, knew the game was over when he felt the pain searing in his legs with 10 laps to go in the 10,000 meters.—John Husar, *Chicago Tribune*, February 19, 1984

first   8. All around me the mountains rose like black clouds in the night, and only by looking straight heavenward could I see anything of the dim afterglow of sunset.—Erskine Caldwell, "Warm River"

first   9. I rattled and clanked my way home in the crowded subway.

first   10. Before I had made a halt in this small birch forest, I and my dog had passed through a grove of towering aspens.—Ivan Turgenev, "The Tryst"

Descriptive Paragraphs

Writing that helps a reader picture a person, an object, or a scene is called description. Strikingly unusual characters, objects, and scenes, as well as more common people, things, and places, can come to life for readers through writing that appeals to their senses.

19i   A **descriptive paragraph** paints a vivid picture of a person, an object, or a scene.

Paragraph Development. The topic sentence of a descriptive paragraph will depend on the writer's overall impression of the subject. For example, two writers viewing the same sunny scene might write the following two different topic sentences.

POSITIVE OVERALL IMPRESSION   The sun glowed outside, inviting everyone indoors to leave what they were doing.

NEGATIVE OVERALL IMPRESSION   The sun fell in burning streaks through the trees, disturbing all who had no choice but to be in the streets.

Paragraphs

The supporting sentences in a descriptive paragraph show the details that make up the overall impression. To *show* rather than tell means to use *sensory words* to make readers see, hear, taste, smell, and feel the subject. The concluding sentence reinforces the overall impression. Notice the development of the following descriptive paragraph.

TOPIC SENTENCE: STATES MAIN IDEA AND OVERALL IMPRESSION

SUPPORTING SENTENCES: GIVE SENSORY DETAILS

CONCLUDING SENTENCE: REINFORCES OVERALL IMPRESSION

About 15 miles below Monterey, on the wild coast, the Torres family had their farm, a few sloping acres above a cliff that dropped to the brown reefs and to the hissing white waters of the ocean. Behind the farm the stone mountains stood up against the sky. The farm buildings huddled like the clinging aphids on the mountain skirts, crouched low to the ground as though the wind might blow them into the sea. The little shack, the rattling, rotting barn were gray-bitten with sea salt, beaten by the damp wind until they had taken on the color of the granite hills. Two horses, a red cow and a red calf, half a dozen pigs and a flock of lean, multi-colored chickens stocked the place. A little corn was raised on the sterile slope, and it grew short and thick under the wind, and all the cobs formed on the landward sides of the stalks.

— JOHN STEINBECK, "FLIGHT"

In the third sentence of the paragraph, Steinbeck compares the farm's appearance on the mountain to that of small insects (aphids) clinging to plants. Such a comparison, that uses *like* or *as* to compare essentially different things, is called a *simile*. A similar device is a *metaphor*. A metaphor implies a comparison without using *like* or *as*.

METAPHOR   Finally catching me out of breath, she tagged me with her fly swatter hand.

Similes and metaphors are examples of *figurative language*. *(See page 368.)* Along with sensory details, they bring a description to life.

19j ▸ Use **sensory details** and **figurative language** to develop descriptive paragraphs.

Descriptive Paragraphs

EXERCISE 8 Identifying Overall Impressions

Write *positive* or *negative* to indicate the type of overall impression conveyed by each topic sentence.

positive   1. The door was solid walnut carved with patterns more intricate than anyone would bother with today.
positive   2. The town was peaceful on Sunday morning.
negative   3. The room was filled with glaring light and shouting people.
positive   4. The desk was the worse for wear, yet it retained great charm.
negative   5. A pack of dogs roamed through the night as frighteningly as wolves in search of prey.

EXERCISE 9 Listing Sensory Details

For each subject, list five sensory details you could use to develop a descriptive paragraph. In each answer, include details that appeal to at least three of the five senses.
Sample answer for item 1 precedes this chapter.

EXAMPLE   a bakery shop
POSSIBLE   • smell of freshly baked bread
ANSWERS   • smooth feel of glass counter top
           • shelves of pastries in fancy shapes
           • sound of cash register ringing
           • taste of brownies, cut up and offered as samples

1. a gas station
2. a hospital
3. a dance
4. a stream
5. a library
6. your room
7. a city street corner
8. a dandelion
9. a concert
10. an airport

Spatial Order and Transitions. A writer of description is like a tour guide, leading the reader's eye from point to point. Using spatial order as the method of organization helps the reader see where each detail fits into the larger picture. Spatial order arranges details according to their location.

Transitions used with spatial order are like fingers pointing the way. Without them the reader would not know which way to look. The following chart shows the different types of spatial order and the transitional "pointers" used with each type.

Paragraphs

19k

Spatial Order	Transitions
top to bottom (or the reverse)	higher, lower, above, below, underneath, on top of, at the top (bottom), in the middle, at the base, from the ground, above the earth, atop
side to side	at the left (right), in the middle, next to, beside, at one end, at the other end
inside out (or the reverse)	within, in the center, on the outside, inside, further outside
near to far (or the reverse)	north, south, east, west, beyond, close by, around, in the distance, further, at the edge, on the horizon, behind, in front of, nearby

Many descriptive paragraphs use a unique spatial order rather than one of those shown in the chart. With this type of order, the writer describes details in the order in which they are observed, rather than in a set pattern such as top to bottom. Transitions make clear to the reader the unique order a writer has chosen.

EXERCISE 10 Identifying Spatial Order and Transitions
Copy the following paragraph on your paper. Underline all the transitional words and phrases. Then indicate the type of spatial order the description follows by writing *top to bottom, side to side, inside out, near to far,* or *unique* (or the reverse of one of these).

The City Park   bottom to top

    The lagoon in the center of Lincoln Park is like a mirrored floor reflecting the alternating layers of city and country above it. <u>On the surface of the lagoon</u>, afternoon idlers paddle around in bright yellow boats, their laughs and splashes muted by the windy day. <u>Overhead</u> the trees rise and arch, rustle and sway. <u>Above the tree line</u>, the city skyscrapers thrust their sleek gray heads, lording over the bending trees. <u>Still higher</u>, though, the white clouds race and billow, reminding all who stop to notice that some heights are beyond the reach of concrete and steel.

Expository Paragraphs

Paragraphs that explain are called expository paragraphs. In school you write expository paragraphs on essay tests and in reports. On the job you will write expository paragraphs to convey information. Whenever your purpose is to explain, you will be writing exposition.

> **19l** An **expository paragraph** explains, gives a set of directions, or informs.

Paragraph Development. There are many different ways to develop an expository paragraph. The topic sentence and the questions it raises usually hold the key to the best method of explaining. Study the following examples of expository topic sentences.

1. Symphony orchestras are part of the backbone of cultural life in cities around the world.

    QUESTIONS RAISED How are they part of the backbone? In what cities?
    WAY TO EXPLAIN   facts and examples

2. Rehearsing an orchestra is a painstaking process.

    QUESTION RAISED What is this process?
    WAY TO EXPLAIN   steps in a process

3. Young people can often try out for a symphonic training orchestra.

    QUESTION RAISED How does a person go about trying out?
    WAY TO EXPLAIN   set of directions

4. I began to appreciate how hard musicians work when I attended a rehearsal of the Seattle Symphony Orchestra.

    QUESTION RAISED What happened to make you appreciate musicians?
    WAY TO EXPLAIN   incident

5. Most orchestral music from the seventeenth century is contrapuntal.

    QUESTION RAISED What does *contrapuntal* mean?
    WAY TO EXPLAIN   definition

Paragraphs

6. The violin and cello belong to the same family of instruments, but each plays a different role in the symphony orchestra.

   QUESTIONS RAISED   How are they alike? How are they different?
   WAY TO EXPLAIN   comparison and contrast

7. The violins, flutes, and trumpets in an orchestra are like the sopranos in a choir.

   QUESTION RAISED   How are they like soprano singers?
   WAY TO EXPLAIN   analogy

8. Every symphony orchestra has four main groups of musical instruments.

   QUESTION RAISED   What are the four groups?
   WAY TO EXPLAIN   analysis

9. After Beethoven, symphonies were never the same.

   QUESTION RAISED   How did Beethoven change symphonies?
   WAY TO EXPLAIN   cause and effect

10. There are many different types of instrumental ensembles.

    QUESTION RAISED   What makes one type different from another?
    WAY TO EXPLAIN   classification

EXERCISE 11   Identifying Ways to Explain
Write the method of development used in each of the following paragraphs. Use the listing on pages 423–424 as a guide.

1. steps in a process

The death of a star is a spectacular event. The squeezed core of the star can no longer contain the enormous pressure that has built up within it. So, suddenly, like some great cosmic jack-in-the-box, this pressure pushing outward causes the unstable star to erupt. The star explodes with unimaginable power. After a life that has spanned millions of years, the death of a large star, from its final collapse to its violent disintegration, takes only a few minutes.

Expository Paragraphs

2. definition

Astronomers call exploding large stars supernovas. The ancients, who observed and described such events, believed they were witnessing the appearance of a new star, or nova. Today we recognize that what the ancients actually saw with their unaided eyes were not new stars being born but large, old stars dying. The term *super* refers to something great, or large, and so the name *supernova*. Supernovas shine with a brilliance many billions of times brighter than our sun. Therefore, were a supernova to appear in a neighboring part of our galaxy, it would be clearly visible even in daytime.

3. facts and examples

At least three appearances of supernovas have been recorded in history. The most recent, in 1604, was observed and described by the German astronomer Johannes Kepler and the Italian Galileo Galilei. Before that, the Danish astronomer Tycho Brahe witnessed one in 1572. Still earlier, Chinese astronomers noted the occurrence of a similar event in the constellation Taurus, the Bull, in the summer of the year A.D. 1054. Today, more than 900 years later, evidence of the supernova described by the Chinese is still visible.

4. analogy

The vast distances of space may be easier to understand if we reduce their scale. Think of the sun as an orange; then the earth would be a mere grain of sand, circling at a distance of 30 feet. Pluto, the farthest planet in our solar system, would be another grain of sand, orbiting the sun ten city blocks away. The sun's nearest neighbor, Alpha Centauri, would be another orange, 1,300 miles distant. On this scale the whole Milky Way becomes a bundle of 200 billion oranges that are about 2,000 miles apart.

5. classification

If we could soar out into the Cosmos in an intergalactic spaceship, we would see hordes of galaxies, and they would have different shapes. Most of them, including the Milky Way and Andromeda, would appear to be great spirals whirling in space. Edwin Hubble studied hundreds of galaxies and classified them by form. He divided galaxies into four main types; elliptical, spiral, barred spiral, and irregular.

— PARAGRAPHS FROM FRANCINE JACOBS, *COSMIC COUNTDOWN*

Paragraphs

Logical Order and Transitions. The best way to organize an expository paragraph depends on its method of development. If the supporting details are events, steps in a process, or a set of directions, chronological order is usually the most logical. *(See page 416.)* If the supporting details analyze a subject by showing what it is made of, spatial order is usually the clearest. *(See pages 421–422.)* Most expository paragraphs, however, use order of importance or developmental order.

19m **Order of importance** arranges details in the order of least to most or most to least important, interesting, or sizable.
Developmental order arranges ideas of equal importance in a way that shows the development of the writer's thoughts.

Transitions tell the reader how ideas are related. The following transitions are widely used with order of importance. With the exception of *more/most important,* they may also be used with developmental order.

19n

Transitions for Order of Importance	
first, second, third	furthermore
more/most important	also
one reason	in addition
to begin with	besides
finally	therefore

In the following expository paragraphs, the transitions are printed in heavy type. The first paragraph uses order of importance, moving from the most widely spoken to the least widely spoken language. The second paragraph uses developmental order; transitions show the relationship of details of equal importance.

World Languages

In the world today, there are more than 195 languages that each have more than one million speakers. **Topping the list** in number of speakers is Mandarin, a Chinese language spoken by 740 million people. The **next most** widely spoken language is English, with 403 million speakers. **Following** English is Russian. Two hundred and seventy-seven million

Expository Paragraphs

people speak the Great Russian dialect alone. **Slightly behind Russian in numbers** is Spanish, which is spoken by 266 million people. **Nearly as many** people—264 million—speak Hindi, the main language of India. All the other languages of the world have **fewer** than 200 million speakers. The wealth of world languages is a tribute to the rich diversity of our planet.

Meditating with Yoga

A student of Yoga can learn to meditate by practicing three activities. **One** is called "watching inwardly." In this exercise the student tries to watch all the words, pictures, and thoughts that come to mind as if they were on a screen. A **second** exercise for meditating is called "seeing simply." This activity calls for looking at objects without attaching a word to them. A chair, **for example,** should be experienced for its shape and color, rather than classified quickly as something to sit on. A **third** activity, called "following the breath," moves in stages—from concentrating on gentle breathing, to watching inwardly, and **finally** to keeping the mind quiet. People who use these techniques often feel refreshed and energetic afterward, as if they had taken a rest from the worries and pressures of their lives.

EXERCISE 12 Identifying Methods of Organization

Identify the type of order used in each paragraph by writing *chronological, spatial, order of importance,* or *developmental.*

1. chronological

What *is* time? This seemingly simple question has puzzled the world's great thinkers for centuries, from Plato and Galileo to Descartes, Newton, and Einstein. In the seventeenth century, Sir Isaac Newton could say only that "time is that which passes," and in the twentieth century Dr. Albert Einstein concluded that "time is what a clock measures." Today's scientists are still unable to agree on a definition that suits them. Engineer and philosopher Buckminster Fuller says that "time is something we wait in."

2. spatial

The world is divided into 24 standard time zones. The zero zone is centered on a line running north and south through Greenwich, England. The time zones east of Greenwich have time later than Greenwich time, and those to the west have earlier times. There is an hour difference in each time zone.

Paragraphs

3. order of importance

Amateur, or ham, radio operators listen regularly to stations that broadcast the exact time. First of all, they wish to record precisely the times of their contacts with other operators, some of whom may be halfway around the world. More important, they must be sure to keep their own broadcast exactly on frequency. The penalty for straying outside one's assigned frequency could be loss of license to operate. So part of the ham operator's "housekeeping" duties include tuning in a station he or she knows is precisely on its assigned frequency and checking equipment against it.

4. developmental

To determine the distance to objects, bats "measure" the time it takes a signal to travel to the object and back. The chief contribution of humans to the system nature developed for bats was to build better clocks and couple them with stronger echo signals. Some of these signals are sound waves, or *sonar*, which stands for "*so*und *na*vigation *r*anging" and describes a system used mainly to locate submarines. Others are radio waves, or *radar*, which stands for "*ra*dio *d*etection *a*nd *r*anging" and is used to probe the distant planets as well as to catch speeders on the highway. Whether sonar or radar, the principles are just the same as those used by bats.

— PARAGRAPHS FROM JAMES JESPERSEN AND JANE FITZ-RANDOLPH, *TIME AND CLOCKS FOR THE SPACE AGE* (ADAPTED)

Writing Extra

Advertisers often use specious arguments to persuade you. A specious argument is one that seems attractive at a glance but which is fallacious when examined. *(See pages 400–407.)*

EXERCISE 13 Detecting Specious Arguments

Identify the fallacy in the following by writing *begging the question, false analogy, non sequitur,* or *circular reasoning.*

1. Use Pearly-White toothpaste or get lost in the crowd. non sequitur
2. Getting a loan from us is as easy as counting 1-2-3! false analogy
3. Blondes have more fun! non sequitur
4. Princess cosmetics can help you look 20 years younger. begging the questi
5. Buy this new can opener because without it you'll be opening cans the old-fashioned way. circular reasoning

Persuasive Paragraphs

If you write a letter to a friend about a movie you have seen, your purpose may be to convince him or her to accept your opinion of the movie. If you write to your school newspaper about the school's requirements, your purpose is to sway students, teachers, and administrators to share your view. Any time your purpose is to state and support an opinion, you are writing persuasion.

> **19o** A **persuasive paragraph** states an opinion and uses facts, examples, reasons, and the opinions of experts to convince readers.

In all kinds of writing, an awareness of your readers helps you target your message so that it can be easily understood. In persuasive writing awareness of your audience is especially important, since some of your readers may hold views very different from your own. The challenge of persuasive writing is to win your readers over to your way of thinking.

Paragraph Development. The topic sentence in a persuasive paragraph asserts an opinion, not a fact. *(See pages 392–393.)* The job of the supporting sentences is to back up the opinion. The most reliable kinds of support are facts, examples, reasons, and the opinions of experts on the subject. Backing up your original opinion with more of your *own* opinions would probably not be persuasive, but the opinions of experts are hard to dispute.

Organization is especially important in persuasive writing. Usually the points made in persuasive writing vary in importance or strength. For this reason much persuasive writing is organized in order of importance. *(See pages 426–427.)* In the following persuasive paragraph, the transitions are printed in heavy type.

College and Jobs

TOPIC SENTENCE: ASSERTS AN OPINION

People facing a decision about college should understand the relation between college and jobs. **First of all,** many good jobs do not require a college education. The Department of Labor estimated that 80 percent of the

429

Paragraphs

SUPPORTING SENTENCES: OFFER FACTS, EXAMPLES, AND STATISTICS TO BACK UP OPINION

CONCLUDING SENTENCE: DRIVES HOME THE MAIN POINT

new jobs in 1983 required vocational or technical training, but not a college degree. **Second,** even in some jobs that usually require a college degree, people with drive and determination can often succeed without a college degree. President Harry Truman, for example, never attended college. **Most important,** most recent college graduates who hoped to find work related to their field of study have been unable to do so. In the 1970s, 75 percent of the social-science majors and 66 percent of the humanities majors wound up as either sales-people or clerical workers. Although there are many good reasons for going to college — including studying a favorite field, making new friends, and broadening your outlook on life — college is no guarantee of a satisfying job in the future.

EXERCISE 14 Using Transitions in a Persuasive Paragraph
The transitions used by the writer of the following paragraph have been left out. Rewrite the paragraph, inserting transitions from the following list at the points marked with a caret (∧).

Sample answers:

Transitions

2 in the first place   4 furthermore   1 although
5 finally   3 moreover

What is a Volcano?

"What is a volcano?" is a familiar question. An often given answer is that a volcano is a burning mountain from the top of which issue smoke and fire. Such a statement, ∧ it does express the popular idea of a volcano, held even today, contains few elements of truth. ∧ No burning in the sense of combustion, such as in the burning of wood, occurs in a volcano. ∧ Volcanoes are not necessarily mountains. ∧ The activity takes place not always at the summit but more commonly on the sides. ∧ The "smoke" is not smoke but condensed steam, mixed frequently with dust particles, and the "fire" is the reflection of the red-hot material on the vapor clouds above the volcano.

— FRED BULLARD, *VOLCANOES IN HISTORY, IN THEORY, IN ERUPTION*
(ADAPTED)

Persuasive Paragraphs

19p

The Tools of Persuasion. The best arguments appeal to reason rather than to emotion. Clear thinking is the most important persuasive tool. *(See Chapter 18 for a review of errors in logic.)* Another important tool is *credibility,* or believability. Writers of persuasion try to convince their readers that they are reasonable, logical people whose opinions are worth considering. The following techniques will help you write effective persuasive paragraphs.

19p

Tools of Persuasion

1. Check your logic for flaws in your thinking.
2. Back up your opinions with facts and examples, not more opinions.
3. Use polite and reasonable language rather than emotionally charged words.
4. If the opposition has a good point, admit it, but then show why it failed to convince you.
5. Refer to experts who agree with your position.

Notice the tools of persuasion at work in the following paragraph.

Hands Off Our Wildlife

TOPIC SENTENCE: ASSERTS AN OPINION

The current hands-off approach to wildlife management in our national parks is the best policy for the future of our preserves. Earlier policies included direct human intervention.

USE OF EXAMPLE

In Yellowstone National Park, for example, the elk population declined from 12,000 in 1956 to 4,000 in 1968 as a result of shootings and relocations. Park officials shot or moved elk to prevent a suspected overgrazing of the range.

USE OF EXPERT'S OPINION

Douglas Houston, a biologist for the National Park Service, has concluded in a detailed study that the elk population was never the problem.

POLITE LANGUAGE ACKNOWLEDGES FIRE FIGHTERS' GOOD INTENTIONS

Instead, it was the attempts of well-meaning humans to put out all forest fires that reduced the grazing range of elks. Tall trees saved from these fires prevented shorter aspen trees—a

431

Paragraphs

ADMISSION OF A GOOD POINT HELD BY THE OPPOSITION

favorite food of elks — from getting enough sun to grow and flourish. Although some hands-off policies seem cruel, such as refusing medicine to a herd in the grips of an epidemic, they at least acknowledge that nature has its own system of maintaining balance. Diseases, harsh winters, and fires are threats to the current animal populations, but they are part of the natural cycle and should be allowed to run their course. Only then will the parks of the future retain their undisturbed richness and beauty.

CONCLUDING SENTENCE: MAKES A FINAL APPEAL

EXERCISE 15 **Analyzing a Persuasive Paragraph**
Read the following draft of a paragraph that opposes a strict hands-off policy. Then answer the questions that follow it.
Sample answers precede this chapter.

Wildlife Needs a Hand

The current hands-off approach to wildlife management in our national parks is too extreme and represents a real danger to the animals. In Yellowstone National Park, for example, the hands-off policy called for closing the garbage dumps, which had become favorite feeding grounds for the grizzlies. Since the 1960s, when the cruel dump closings began, the grizzly population has declined from 400 to 200, with the number of breeding-age females at a risky 29. Richard Knight, a biologist of the U.S. Fish and Wildlife Service, has found that the average litter size of grizzlies has decreased since then, and the average age when a female gives birth to her first litter has risen. Both of these changes result in a population decline. Bear experts John and Frank Craighead blame the park service for not closing the dumps more gradually and giving the grizzlies a chance to readapt to finding food in the wild. If the grizzly population were not already in decline, the hands-off policy might have some merit. For now, however, we should offer supplemental feedings. We cannot afford to continue the mistakes of the past and further endanger this magnificent symbol of our national parks.

1. List two facts used as support in this paragraph.
2. Revise the sentence in this paragraph that uses emotional language to refer to the dump closings.

3. To what experts does the writer refer?
4. Copy the sentence in which the author admits that the opposition might have a good point if circumstances were different.
5. Reread the paragraph on page 431. Which side of the issue are you on? Explain your position in two or three sentences.

EXERCISE 16 On Your Own
Review pages 429–432. Then, using the following questions as a starting point, think about subjects on which you could write a paragraph. Write down ideas as you think of them.
Answers will vary.
1. What has happened to me, my friends, or my family recently that would make a good story?
2. What person, object, or scene that I know well could I describe vividly? What impression do I have of this subject?
3. What skills or knowledge do I have that I could explain?
4. What opinions do I hold that I could defend with the tools of persuasion?

THE PROCESS OF WRITING PARAGRAPHS

The writing process moves from discovering ideas to write about to polishing a final draft for others to read. The activities involved in this process can be grouped into four main stages: prewriting, writing, revising, and editing. In each stage of the process two goals remain constant. One is to be true to your *purpose* in writing. The other is to know your *audience* and anticipate their needs in understanding your message.

Prewriting

Prewriting includes all of the planning steps that come before writing the first draft. Like any undertaking, writing is easier if it is carefully planned in advance. Some writers give as much as 80 percent of their writing time to prewriting.

Finding Ideas. The first step in prewriting is to discover ideas to write about. During this step let your mind range freely over your interests, skills, experience, and knowledge. Try to remember what you have read recently or seen on television that

Paragraphs

sparked some interest in you. To help loosen up your mind, try the following activity. There are no right or wrong answers, so relax and let your mind lead you from one thought to the next.

EXERCISE 17 Discovering Ideas by Writing a Personal Profile

Write a personal profile as a way to find ideas. Copy the following items on your paper and jot down whatever comes to your mind about each one. Save your work for Exercise 18.
Answers will vary.

My birthplace was . . . .
My current home is . . . .
My job is . . . .
The last good movie I saw was . . . .
The last good book I read was . . . .
My nickname is . . . .
My favorite performer is . . . .
My personal heroes are . . . .
Nobody knows I am . . . .
The one thing I dislike in people is . . . .
My future plans include . . . .
My best subjects in school are . . . .
My hobbies are . . . .
One thing I know better than most people is . . . .
The best time in my life was . . . .
If I have learned one thing in life, it is . . . .

Choosing and Limiting a Subject. Once you have explored your knowledge and interests, you are ready to choose a subject from your list of ideas. At this stage you should begin to think about the purpose of your writing. Do you want to tell a story, describe a scene, explain a factual subject, or offer an opinion? When you have decided on a purpose, use the following guidelines to choose one subject from your ideas.

19q

> **Guidelines for Choosing a Subject**
>
> 1. Choose a subject that interests you.
> 2. Choose a subject that will interest your audience.
> 3. Choose a subject you know enough about now or can learn enough about later to cover adequately.

Prewriting

19q–r

One way to test possible subjects against these guidelines is to brainstorm. *Brainstorming* means writing down everything that comes to mind when you think of your subject. If, as you are jotting down notes, you find yourself becoming bored with the subject, you should go on to another one. You should also search for another subject if you can think of only two or three things to write down. If you can write between five to ten items on a subject you enjoy, you are ready for the next stage: limiting your subject.

Suppose from your personal profile you discovered that you know more about photography than most people. Your brainstorming notes might look like the following.

SUBJECT   Photography
BRAINSTORMING NOTES
- how to develop a picture
- how to build a darkroom
- capturing action shots
- working as a sports photographer for the school paper
- the time I ruined film
- the best kind of paper to use
- different kinds of lenses
- how to take a light reading
- the time I got trampled taking pictures of a tackle during a football game

As you look over your notes, you may notice that three items relate specifically to sports photography, a more limited subject than the general subject of photography. To narrow your subject even further, until it is a manageable size for a paragraph, ask yourself the following questions.

19r

Steps in Limiting a Subject

SUBJECT THAT IS TOO BROAD	Photography
Ask yourself	What type?
MORE LIMITED SUBJECT	Sports photography
Ask yourself	What about it?
SUITABLY LIMITED SUBJECT	Skills needed to be a good sports photographer

435

Paragraphs

When you can no longer find an answer to the question "What about it?" you have found a suitably limited subject. By that time you will have expressed in one phrase what your paragraph will be about.

EXERCISE 18   Choosing and Limiting a Subject
Number your paper 1 to 5, leaving ten blank spaces after each number.

a. After each number, write a possible subject for a paragraph. You may wish to use ideas from the personal profile you made in Exercise 17.
b. On the lines after each subject, brainstorm to measure your interest and knowledge of that subject.
c. Circle the two subjects that interest you the most. Limit each subject by following the steps on page 435, making sure to express in one phrase what the paragraph will be about.

Sample steps for limiting one subject precede this chapter.

Listing Supporting Details. With your subject suitably limited, you are ready to brainstorm once again for details that will develop the subject. The following chart lists the types of supporting details used with the four kinds of paragraphs.

19s

Types of Supporting Details	
Narrative paragraphs	Events *(See pages 416–417.)*
Descriptive paragraphs	Sensory details *(See pages 419–420.)*
Expository paragraphs	Facts, examples, reasons, comparisons/contrasts, definitions *(See pages 423–424.)*
Persuasive paragraphs	Facts, examples, reasons, opinions of experts *(See page 429.)*

EXERCISE 19   Listing Supporting Details
Write each of the following subjects and purposes on your paper. Under each one write a list of four supporting details that would develop the subject. Make sure that the type of detail matches the writing purpose. Save your work for Exercise 20.   *Sample answer for item 1 precedes this chapter.*

Prewriting

19s

EXAMPLE	LIMITED SUBJECT	skills needed to be a sports photographer
	PURPOSE	expository
	DETAILS	• agility • knowledge of sports • knowledge of basics of good photography • ability to write captions

1. **SUBJECT** what happened at the last party I attended
   PURPOSE narrative
2. **SUBJECT** how the school bus schedule should be improved
   PURPOSE persuasive
3. **SUBJECT** the decor in my favorite restaurant
   PURPOSE descriptive
4. **SUBJECT** the importance of relaxation
   PURPOSE expository
5. **SUBJECT** how to put together an attractive outfit
   PURPOSE expository

Organizing Details in a Logical Order. The last step in the prewriting stage is to arrange your list of supporting details in a logical order. The following chart reviews the methods of organization commonly used in the four types of paragraphs.

Types of Paragraphs	Methods of Organization
Narrative	Chronological (time) order
Descriptive	Spatial (location) order
Expository	Mainly order of importance or developmental order, but in some cases chronological and spatial order
Persuasive	Mainly order of importance

Following is the list of supporting details on the subject of sports photography, arranged in order of importance. The list proceeds from the most important skill to the least important.

437

Paragraphs

LIMITED SUBJECT   skills needed to be a sports photographer
PURPOSE   expository
DETAILS
- knowledge of basics of good photography
- knowledge of sports
- agility
- ability to write captions

EXERCISE 20   **Arranging Details in Logical Order**
Using your notes from Exercise 19, organize the details under each subject in logical order. Below your list indicate which method of organization you have used. Save your work for Exercise 21.

Sample answer for item 1 of Exercise 19 precedes this chapter.

Writing

The next stage of the writing process is writing the first draft. The main goal of this stage is to transform your notes into a clear topic sentence, a body of supporting sentences, and a concluding sentence that completes your thought.

Writing the Topic Sentence. The following chart outlines the steps for writing a clear topic sentence.

> **Steps for Writing a Topic Sentence**
>
> 1. Look over your prewriting notes.
> 2. Express your main idea in one sentence.
> 3. Rewrite that sentence until it makes your writing purpose clear and controls all your supporting details.

Notice how a topic sentence for the paragraph on sports photography is rewritten until it follows all of the guidelines in the chart.

FAULTY TOPIC SENTENCE   Once when I was taking pictures of a football game, I was trampled in a tackle. [suggests to the reader that the paragraph will tell the rest of the story and be a narrative paragraph]

Writing

19t-u

FAULTY TOPIC SENTENCE — Being a good sports photographer requires a knowledge of both sports and photography. [fails to control the supporting details of agility and writing ability]

STRONG TOPIC SENTENCE — A good sports photographer needs several important skills to do the job well. [makes the expository purpose clear and controls all the supporting details]

EXERCISE 21 Writing Topic Sentences
Using the organized lists of details from Exercise 20, write a topic sentence for each subject. Use the steps on page 438 as a guide. *See below.*

Writing the Paragraph Body. After you have written a topic sentence, the next step is to turn your organized list of supporting details into the smoothly flowing sentences of a paragraph body. Use the following steps.

19u

Steps for Writing the Paragraph Body

1. Write a complete sentence for each detail on your list.
2. Combine sentences that seem to go together.
3. When necessary, add transitions to help one sentence lead smoothly into the next.

Notice how the prewriting notes on sports photography become smooth sentences when transitions are added.

LIMITED SUBJECT — Skills needed to be a sports photographer
PURPOSE — expository
DETAILS
- knowledge of basics of good photography
- knowledge of sports
- agility
- ability to write captions

Becoming a Sports Photographer

A good sports photographer needs several important skills to do the job well. **The most important** is the ability to take good pictures, which includes a knowledge of lighting, composition, and color. **Next in importance** is knowledge of the

Sample topic sentence for item 1 of Exercise 19:
I didn't think I'd have a good time at Sharon's party, but things turned out differently from what I'd expected.

439

Paragraphs

sports he or she will be covering. This is important because a good photographer needs to anticipate the dramatic moments in a game and be ready to shoot when they happen. **Another** useful skill is agility, the ability to move around quickly and avoid being caught in the action. **Finally,** good writing abilities are also required, since the sports photographer is often called upon to write captions for pictures that appear in newspapers or magazines.

EXERCISE 22 Writing the Body of an Expository Paragraph
Write the body of an expository paragraph using the notes provided. Include the topic sentence and concluding sentence on your paper. Save your work for Exercise 23.
Sample answer precedes this chapter.

TOPIC SENTENCE Many high-rise building managers have found an inexpensive way to make the wait for elevators seem shorter.

DETAILS
- managers received complaints from building users that the elevators take too long to arrive
- managers looked into adding more elevators but found the expense too great
- managers hired experts to help solve the problem
- experts suggested installing mirrors near the elevators
- level of complaints dropped off dramatically

CONCLUDING SENTENCE Humans apparently find endless fascination in watching themselves in mirrors.

Writing the Concluding Sentence. After you have written the topic sentence and supporting sentences, look over your paragraph and write a concluding sentence that will serve one or more of the following purposes.

> **19v**
>
> **Concluding Sentence**
>
> A concluding sentence may
> - restate the main idea in fresh words.
> - summarize the paragraph.
> - evaluate the supporting details.
> - add an insight to show the importance of the main idea.

Revising

19v – w

The supporting sentences of a paragraph will suggest an appropriate concluding sentence. The details of the paragraph on sports photography, for example, are clear enough without a concluding sentence that summarizes them. A concluding sentence with any of the other three purposes, however, might be appropriate. Read the paragraph on sports photography on pages 439–440 with each of the following sentences as a possible concluding sentence.

CONCLUDING SENTENCES

Each of these skills is important to anyone wanting to become a professional sports photographer. [restates main idea]

Of these skills the first will likely take the most time to acquire. [evaluates details]

The fast action of sports provides photographers with a special challenge not found in other types of photography. [adds an insight]

EXERCISE 23   Writing Concluding Sentences
Write two more possible concluding sentences for the paragraph you wrote in Exercise 22. *Sample sentence:* Building managers saved money, and people no longer became impatient waiting for elevators.

Revising

In the revising stage of the writing process, writers look at their work with the fresh eye of a person who has never seen it before. In this way they can see what might be confusing to readers and try to correct any weaknesses.

Checking for Unity and Coherence. As you look over your paragraphs, check to make sure that each supporting sentence relates clearly to the topic sentence. If you find one that strays, cross it out. The result will be a paragraph with *unity*.

19w   Achieve **unity** by making sure all the supporting sentences relate directly to the topic sentence.

Readers may also be confused by a paragraph that lacks *coherence*. In a paragraph without coherence, the connections between sentences are not smooth.

441

Paragraphs

19x

> **Tips for Achieving Coherence**
>
> 1. Check your organization to make sure each detail fits logically into your method of organization.
> 2. Repeat key words occasionally.
> 3. Use synonyms in place of some key words.
> 4. Use pronouns in place of key words.
> 5. Check the transitions you used to show how your ideas are related. Add any that would link your thoughts.

EXERCISE 24 Revising for Unity and Coherence

Copy the following draft of a paragraph on a sheet of paper, leaving two spaces between lines. Then revise the paragraph, following the instructions listed after it.

Training to Become a Jockey

Many horse lovers dream of becoming a jockey in thoroughbred horse racing, but the training period is long and difficult, and the competition is fierce. First of all, jockeys must be excellent riders and must weigh no more than 108 pounds. Would-be jockeys need to be at least 16 years old before they can be placed in a training program with a thoroughbred horse owner. ~~Once an 11-year-old girl raced a trotter in harness racing and broke a track record.~~ During this training period, would-be jockeys are taught the fundamentals of racing and grooming the sometimes high-strung horses. ~~Would-be jockeys~~ *They* must train from one to three years and ride 40 winners before being considered apprentice jockeys. Only then can they race with experienced jockeys. *Finally,* ~~Would-be~~ *apprentice* jockeys must be licensed by a racing authority. ~~Many former jockeys become trainers.~~ With hard work, determination, and a little luck, a ~~would-be jockey~~ *horse lover* can become one of the handful of jockeys who run for the roses.
— BOB AND MARQUITA MCGONAGLE, *CAREERS IN SPORTS* (ADAPTED)

1. Find two sentences in the paragraph that stray off the point and destroy the paragraph's unity. Cross them out.   *See above.*
2. Cross out *would-be jockeys* in the sixth sentence and replace it with a pronoun.
3. Add a transition to the eighth sentence to show its relation to the seventh sentence.

4. Cross out *would-be* in the eighth sentence and replace it with another word.
5. Cross out *would-be jockey* in the last sentence and replace it with a phrase from the topic sentence.

Revision Checklist. Use the following checklist to revise your paragraphs step by step.

19y

Revision Checklist

Checking Your Paragraph
1. Do you have a strong topic sentence?
2. Do you have adequate and appropriate supporting sentences?
3. Does your paragraph have unity?
4. Does your paragraph have coherence?
5. Did you use transitions?
6. Do you have a strong concluding sentence?

Checking Your Sentences
7. Do your sentences have variety? *(See pages 374–381.)*
8. Did you combine sentences that go together? *(See pages 374–378.)*
9. Are sentences in your paragraph concise? *(See pages 370–373.)*
10. Have you avoided faulty sentences in your paragraph? *(See pages 382–388.)*

Checking Your Words
11. Did you use specific words with appropriate connotations? *(See pages 364–365.)*
12. Did you use figurative language where appropriate? *(See pages 367–369.)*

Editing

The final stage in the writing process is editing. A paper free of errors will let your reader concentrate on your message. Use the following editing checklist to polish your final draft. You may wish to use the proofreading symbols on page 614 when you edit.

Paragraphs

19z

> **Editing Checklist**
> 1. Are your sentences free of errors in grammar and usage?
> 2. Did you spell each word correctly?
> 3. Did you capitalize and punctuate correctly?
> 4. Did you use correct manuscript form? *(See pages 611–612.)*
> 5. Is your handwriting or typing clear?

EXERCISE 25 **On Your Own**

Review pages 433–444. Then using what you have learned about prewriting, writing, revising, and editing, write a paragraph on a subject of your choice.
Answers will vary.

CHAPTER REVIEW

A. Read the paragraph below and answer the questions that follow it.

Computerized Paper Routes

<u>A number of news agents are now using computers to schedule their delivery rounds.</u> One company in England has 3,500 customers, and each morning and each evening the paper carriers receive printed delivery lists. Each list is personalized and takes account of the day of the week and the papers ordered. The main benefits of the system include increased accuracy, reduced clerical work and wastage of papers, and a reduction in the number of outstanding paper bills. The customers get their papers earlier, and the news agent has a little longer in bed each morning!
— ROBIN BRADBEER, PETER DE BONO, AND PETER LAURIE,
THE BEGINNER'S GUIDE TO COMPUTERS

1. Write the topic sentence of this paragraph. *underlined above*
2. Is this example paragraph narrative, descriptive, expository, or persuasive? *expository*
3. Are the supporting sentences events, sensory details, or facts? *facts*

Chapter Review

19z

    4. Is this paragraph organized in chronological, spatial, or developmental order?   developmental

    5. What gives this paragraph unity?   All sentences relate to the topic sentence.

B. Using what you have learned about prewriting, writing, revising, and editing, write a paragraph on one of the following subjects or on one of your own choosing. Use the Steps for Writing a Paragraph on page 446 as a guide.

Evaluation suggestion precedes this chapter.

Subjects for a Narrative Paragraph
1. meeting someone who changed your life
2. a misunderstanding
3. driving the car for the first time by yourself
4. a case of mistaken identity
5. a moment of triumph

Subjects for a Descriptive Paragraph
6. your favorite shirt or blouse
7. a run-down, old building
8. a parade
9. a dance
10. the view from your window

Subjects for an Expository Paragraph
11. how a computer can help with schoolwork
12. casualties at the battle of Antietam
13. how to tune up a car
14. how to qualify for the Olympics
15. your plans for the first year after high school

Subjects for a Persuasive Paragraph
16. seeing movies on TV compared to seeing them in a theater
17. requiring offenders of drunk-driving laws to serve time as crossing guards
18. allowing students to choose the courses they will take
19. classes every student should take to be able to handle life well
20. whether or not robots should replace workers in some factories

445

Steps for Writing

Paragraphs

✓ **Prewriting**
  1. Find ideas by examining your interests, knowledge, and experience. *(See pages 433–434.)*
  2. Determine the purpose and audience of your paragraph. *(See page 434.)*
  3. Choose a subject and limit it. *(See page 434.)*
  4. Brainstorm a list of supporting details. *(See pages 435–436.)*
  5. Arrange your details in logical order. *(See pages 437–438.)*

✓ **Writing**
  6. Write a topic sentence appropriate for your purpose. *(See pages 438–439.)*
  7. Use your prewriting notes to write the supporting sentences. *(See pages 439–440.)*
  8. Add a concluding sentence. *(See pages 440–441.)*

✓ **Revising**
  9. Using the appropriate checklist on page 447 and the Revision Checklist on page 443, check paragraph structure, unity, coherence, sentences, and words.

✓ **Editing**
  10. Using the Editing Checklist on page 444, check your grammar, usage, spelling, mechanics, and neatness.

Checklist for Revising

Paragraphs

✓ **Narrative Paragraphs**
1. Does your topic sentence set the scene and make your narrative purpose clear?
2. Do the supporting sentences tell the story event by event?
3. Did you use chronological order with appropriate transitions?
4. Is your point of view consistent?
5. Does the concluding sentence give the outcome or make a point about the story's meaning?

✓ **Descriptive Paragraphs**
1. Does your topic sentence make a general statement that suggests an overall impression of the subject?
2. Do the supporting sentences supply sensory details?
3. Did you use figurative language?
4. Did you use spatial order and appropriate transitions?
5. Does your concluding sentence reinforce the overall impression?

✓ **Expository Paragraphs**
1. Does your topic sentence state a factual main idea and make your purpose clear?
2. Did you use an appropriate method of development?
3. Did you use an appropriate method of organization and transitions?
4. Does your concluding sentence complete your thought?

✓ **Persuasive Paragraphs**
1. Does your topic sentence assert an opinion?
2. Do your supporting sentences use tools of persuasion?
3. Did you use logical order with appropriate transitions?
4. Does your concluding sentence make a final appeal?

Chapter 20 Expository Essays

OBJECTIVES

- To define an expository essay as one that explains a factual subject or personal insight.
- To explain the purpose of the three parts of an essay—introduction, body, and conclusion.
- To identify the thesis statement and tone in the introduction of an essay.
- To follow the prewriting steps—which include choosing and limiting a subject, listing supporting details, and outlining—to shape a subject idea into an organized plan for an essay.
- To write the first draft of an essay, including the thesis statement, introduction, body, conclusion, and title.
- To revise and edit the first draft.

MOTIVATIONAL ACTIVITY

Publication is an excellent motivator. As an introduction to this chapter, tell students that their final essays will be published in one of two class magazines. One will include essays explaining a personal insight; the other will contain essays on factual subjects. Specific instructions for preparing these magazines will appear in the later section entitled Editing.

TEACHING SUGGESTIONS

Essay Structure *(pages 448–456)*

Begin the discussion of essay structure by having three students read the model essay on page 449 aloud, each taking one paragraph. (Using three students will reinforce the three-part form of the essay.) After the reading, ask students whether the ideas in each paragraph are general or specific. (The first paragraph is a general description, explaining what one hears and sees from a variety of locations. The second paragraph contains a number of differing specific patterns that one might see; this specificity is one mark of supporting details. The final paragraph is once again general and makes an appeal to emotions.)

The Body of an Essay *(pages 453–455)*
For an extension of the outlining offered on page 454 and to help students clearly see the structure of the model essay on pages 453–454, work with the class to write a detailed outline of this essay on the board. You may wish to start by writing the following skeleton and asking students to fill it in. (Answers students might suggest are provided in parentheses.)

Introduction—paragraph 1
Body—paragraphs 2 and 3
   I. How the computer planned a master strategy
      A. Programed to look ahead
      B. (Programed to consider various moves)
      C. (Programed to select best move)
      D. Remembered moves from previous games
   II. How the computer developed from a poor player into a championship player
      A. (Early failures)
      B. Storage of winning strategies on magnetic tape
      C. (Comparison of board patterns with those stored on tape)
      D. Later successes
Conclusion—paragraph 4

Prewriting *(pages 456–467)*

Finding Ideas *(pages 457–458)* In addition to the activities offered on pages 457–458 for finding ideas, you may wish to use the following suggestions.

1. Refer students to the work already in their writing folders, particularly the sheets entitled "Inventory of Interests" and "Subject Ideas for Expository Writing." (See Teaching Suggestions for Chapters 16 and 19.)
2. Divide the class into small discussion groups. Each member of each group

Expository Essays

should be prepared to give three possible essay subjects and explain briefly what he or she would say about them. The other members of the group should ask questions about the subjects and tell the writer which one he or she would be most interested in reading about.

Listing Supporting Details *(pages 460–461)* If students are writing an essay on a factual subject, encourage them to undertake some research to make sure that their coverage is adequate. Although they need not make footnotes, they should cite their sources informally by referring to the author and the title in their essays (for example, "In her book *The Guns of August*, Barbara Tuchman points out that . . . "). Remind students that if they use the author's exact words, they should use quotation marks. For specific instruction in notetaking, refer students to pages 608–609 in the Appendix.

Writing *(pages 468–477)*

While writing an outline is a valuable step in preparing to write an essay, students should realize that they are not bound to follow their outlines exactly. In the actual process of writing, students might think of more material to add or discover a better way of organizing their ideas than that indicated on the outline. Encourage students to let the writing process itself generate ideas.

Revising *(pages 477–479)*

To stress the importance of looking at compositions with a fresh eye before revising, collect the students' first drafts and keep them for at least two days. When you return them, ask students to clear their minds and pretend they have never heard anything about the subject they have written on. Then have them read their papers silently. When they finish, have them write a paragraph explaining the strengths of the draft and another paragraph pointing out some weaknesses. They should then use their own suggestions to write another draft before moving on to the Revision Checklist on page 479.

You can use the Revision Checklist for peer evaluation. Divide the class into groups of three students. Each member of the group will focus on a different level of the Revision Checklist. Reviewer A, for example, comments only on the questions under "Checking Your Essay" in the Revision Checklist. Reviewer A then passes the paper and his or her comments on to Reviewer B, who focuses on the questions under "Checking Your Paragraphs." Again his or her comments are passed along with the paper to the final reviewer, who comments on "Checking Your Sentences and Words."

Editing *(pages 479–480)*

You may wish to refer students to the section on proofreader's marks in the Appendix (page 614) to make their editing job proceed more smoothly.

To prepare the class magazines, give each student a duplicating master on which to copy his or her essay. When the essays are duplicated, divide them according to their subject matter (factual or personal) and have the class participate in collating the essays. You may also wish to have a student with artistic ability prepare a cover for each publication on another duplicating master. Be sure to include a table of contents that lists the title of each essay and the writer's name. The final magazines can be bound with staples or brads.

ACTIVITIES FOR DIFFERENT ABILITIES

Basic Students

ACTIVITY 1 Choosing a Subject
For their first expository essay, have students choose a subject from personal experience. (See suggested topics on page 482.) You may also want to limit the length of students' essays to three or four paragraphs to ensure greater control over the subject matter.

ACTIVITY 2 Revising and Editing
Before students make a final version of

Chapter 20 b

Expository Essays

their essays, review each student's work and select sentences that demonstrate a problem common in your class. Duplicate these sentences and go over them in class. Then return the students' essays and give students another chance to revise and edit their work on the basis of the discussion.

Advanced Students

ACTIVITY 1 Tone
To help students establish versatility in tone, have them reread the essay beginnings on pages 450–451. Two of the three selections are on the general subject of names. Using that subject as a starting point, ask students to write three separate paragraphs about names, their own or anyone else's. One paragraph should have a direct, or impersonal, tone. The second should have a comic tone, and the third, a reflective tone.

ACTIVITY 2 Writer's Roundtable
After the essays are completed, divide students into discussion groups. Each student should be prepared to tell the rest of the group which parts of writing the essay were the hardest for him or her, and which parts came easily. For the hard parts, the other students in the group should offer advice from their own experience. After the meetings, ask each student to write a short paragraph explaining what he or she learned from the discussion.

ADDITIONAL PRACTICE

Teacher's Resource Book: pages 219–222
Workbook: pages 169–174

REVIEW EXERCISES AND TESTS

Student Text
  Chapter Review: pages 480–482
Teacher's Resource Book
  Chapter 20 Test: pages 49–50
  (Also available as spirit duplicating masters.)

ADDITIONAL ANSWERS

EXERCISE 2 Listing Supporting Points *(page 455)*

Sample answer for item 1:
I look forward to weekends for three main reasons.
  I. Break from school
 II. Time to see friends
III. Family outings

EXERCISE 5 Finding Ideas by Asking Yourself Questions *(page 457)*

Sample answer for item 1:
I know a lot about baseball statistics and how they are compiled.
I know how to play the trumpet and how to read music.
I'm an expert Monopoly player, and I could explain my winning strategies.

EXERCISE 6 Finding Ideas from Reading and other Sources *(page 458)*

Sample answer for item 1:
the industrial revolution
the tenements in the cities
how labor unions became organized
pioneer women

EXERCISE 8 Limiting a Subject *(page 460)*

Sample answer for item 1:
1. I would like to explain the relationship between user and computer.

Expository Essays

2. My readers probably have all had some experience with a computer, so they know the basic facts about how computers operate.
3. The tone best suited to my essay is casual.
4. The insight I would like to express is that despite their mechanical nature, computers can become like persons in the eyes of their users.
5. With the right programing, a computer can seem almost like a person with whom the user can develop a relationship.

EXERCISE 9   Listing Supporting Details *(page 461)*

Sample answer for item 1:
sense of independence a car gives its driver
responsibility involved in driving
mobility
necessity of earning money to pay for gas
age necessary for obtaining a driver's license

EXERCISE 11   Outlining *(page 466)*

Sample answer:
  I. Officials and events receiving 21-gun salute
     A. President — salute followed by "Hail to the Chief"
     B. Visiting heads of state or members of royal family
     C. Salute to the flag
 II. Officials receiving 19-gun salute
     A. Secretary of defense and secretaries of Army, Navy and Air Force — arrival and departure
     B. Vice-president — arrival only
     C. Speaker of the House — arrival only
III. Officials receiving 17-gun salute
     A. Generals and admirals — arrival and departure
     B. Chairpersons of committees of Congress — arrival only

EXERCISE 13   Writing a Paragraph Definition *(page 467)*

Sample answer:
   Friendship is the state of liking someone, of enjoying that person's company and wanting to do nice things for him or her. A friend is not blind to your faults; rather he or she sees them clearly but accepts and likes you anyway. Flattery and friendship are not the same thing; a flatterer tells you what you want to hear, while a friend tells you the truth.

EXERCISE 14   Identifying Problems in Thesis Statements *(page 469)*

Sample answers:
1. The sentence does not include all supporting points (21- and 19-gun salutes).
2. It is too broad: it does not mention gun salutes at all.
3. It uses the empty phrase "In this essay I will explain . . . "
4. It does not include 17-gun salutes.
5. The sentence uses the empty phrase "this paper will be about. . . ."

EXERCISE 17   Experimenting with Essay Beginnings *(pages 471–472)*

Sample answers:
Background information
   Certain people these days are quick to criticize television on several grounds. They object, first of all, to violence on TV. They object to the unrealistic portrayal of women

Chapter 20 d

Expository Essays

and minorities on television. They object to the frequent and annoying commercials that blast from the set, and they criticize writers and producers for a generally low quality of television programing. However, although television has been described as a "vast wasteland," the best TV shows can be as stimulating as a great book or a great movie.

Personal incident

At a very young age, I watched a TV show about a girl about my age—blind, deaf, and wild with frustration—who tore around her house, bit her mother, and shook her head around and around in fury. I watched mesmerized as a teacher came to live with her and her worried family, and I watched the girl stand by a water pump with her teacher as the first realization of the word *water* began to dawn in her mind. The child was Helen Keller, and the images of that show, *The Miracle Worker*, have remained in my memory ever since. Although television has been described as a "vast wasteland," the best TV shows can be as stimulating as a great book or a great movie.

EXERCISE 18 Identifying Techniques for Achieving Coherence *(pages 474–475)*

1. transitional word
2. repeated word
3. pronoun
4. transitional word
5. transitional word
6. transitional word
7. repeated word
8. transitional word
9. earlier idea in new words
10. earlier idea in new words

EXERCISE 19 Writing a Concluding Paragraph *(page 477)*

Sample answer:

Belle Boyd supported the position of the Confederacy, while Emma Edmonds upheld the cause of the Union. Despite this major conflict of beliefs, these women shared strong similarities in character. While spying for opposing sides during the Civil War, both demonstrated rare courage and intense loyalty. Belle Boyd and Emma Edmonds exemplify the word *hero* and will be remembered for their unselfish dedication to their ideals.

CHAPTER REVIEW *(pages 480–482)*

Part A

1. The Smokey Bear Program has been effective because it accomplishes the three goals of any successful information campaign.
2. direct
3. by providing background information
4. in addition to
5. developmental order
6. The topics of the supporting paragraphs—creating awareness, providing motivation, and guiding actions—are developed in the order in which they are mentioned in the last sentence of the introduction.
7. although
8. more general
9. Because Smokey's keepers know they have a good thing, it is very likely that your children and your grandchildren will be just as familiar as you are with Smokey's famous warning—"Only you can prevent forest fires!"
10. All paragraphs and sentences relate to the main idea presented in the topic sentence; the paragraphs and sentences are presented in logical order and are smoothly connected.

Chapter 20 e

Expository Essays

Part B
You may wish to use the following evaluation form.

Evaluation Form for Expository Essays

	POINT VALUE	STUDENT SCORE
1. appropriate subject for an essay, suitably limited	10	_____
2. title	10	_____
3. strong introduction	10	_____
4. strong thesis statement	10	_____
5. logical organization	10	_____
6. unity	10	_____
7. coherence and transitions	10	_____
8. strong conclusion	10	_____
9. essay revised	10	_____
10. essay edited	10	_____
	Total Score	_____

20
Expository Essays

For additional practice for this chapter, see the Teacher's Resource Book and the Workbook.

An essay is a composition of three or more paragraphs that present and develop one main idea. If the writer's purpose is to explain a factual subject or a personal insight into a subject, the essay is called expository.

20a An **expository essay** explains a factual subject or personal insight.

ESSAY STRUCTURE

A complete piece of writing, whatever its length, has the same basic parts: an introduction, a body, and a conclusion. The structure of an essay can, therefore, be compared to the structure of a paragraph.

20b

Paragraph Structure	Essay Structure
topic sentence that expresses the main idea of the paragraph	introductory paragraph that includes a thesis statement expressing the main idea of the essay
body of supporting sentences	body of supporting paragraph(s)
concluding sentence	concluding paragraph

448

Introduction

20a–c

In the following short essay, the three parts are labeled. The main idea is expressed in the thesis statement.

Voice of Restless Autumn

THESIS STATEMENT — Most birds migrate in silence, but not geese.

INTRODUCTION — Whether you are walking down a city street, standing in a suburban backyard, or working in a rural wood lot, you know when geese fly over. First you hear that distant gabble, a faint clamor that seems to echo from the whole sky. You search the sky, and the gabble comes closer. Then you see them, flying high, making a V almost like a pencil line of dots.

BODY — You listen and watch, and the flight is so high it seems almost leisurely. If the V is close in formation, it is almost certainly Canada geese. If it is a looser V, rippling and waving, or if it is a long line like one leg of the V, it more likely is the less common snow geese. Whichever type of geese it is, the flock's gabbling is like the voice of restless autumn. The flight moves on and on, over the hills and the towns and the cities, to the far horizon and still beyond, southward. Only that restless echo, faint and haunting, remains.

CONCLUSION — Geese are footloose as the autumn wind, and they follow the sun. There is something both exhilarating and faintly sad in the echo of their going. Maybe it is the freedom song of the skies. Whatever it is, it haunts the earthbound heart.

— HAL BORLAND, *BOOK OF DAYS* (ADAPTED)

Introduction

Just as a warm-up routine readies an exerciser's body for the workout, the introduction to an essay prepares the reader's mind for the ideas that follow. In addition to arousing the reader's interest in the subject, the introduction establishes the tone of the essay and presents the thesis statement.

20c ▶ **Tone** is the writer's attitude toward his or her subject and audience.

Expository Essays

20d   The **thesis statement** states the main idea of the essay and makes the writer's purpose clear.

The chart below summarizes the purposes of an introduction.

20e

> **Introduction**
>
> The introduction of an essay
> 1. captures the reader's attention.
> 2. establishes the tone.
> 3. contains the thesis statement.

Many introductory paragraphs build toward the thesis statement, which comes last in the paragraph. A thesis statement, however, may appear anywhere in the introduction. There are many different types of tone that an essay can have, since the tone reflects the writer's feeling about the subject and audience. Notice the different tone in each of the following introductions and the placement of the thesis statement.

DIRECT TONE   In 1962, a former checkers champion lost a game of checkers for the first time in eight years. His opponent was an IBM Model 7094 electronic computer. The computer won fairly, without coaching from the sidelines. THESIS STATEMENT — Of perhaps the greatest significance was the fact that the computer learned to play just as a human being learns—from experience, observation, and a consideration of the problems involved.

— WILLIAM VERGARA, *SCIENCE IN THE WORLD AROUND US*

THESIS STATEMENT — Every few months somebody writes me and asks if I will give him a name for his dog. Several of these correspondents in the past year have wanted to know if I would mind the COMIC TONE use of my own name for their spaniels. Spaniel owners seem to have the notion that a person could sue for invasion of privacy or defamation of character if his name was applied to a cocker without written permission. One gentleman

Thesis Statement

20d–e

even insisted that we conduct our correspondence in the matter through a notary public. I have a way of letting communications of this sort fall behind my roll-top desk. It has recently occurred to me, however, that this is an act of evasion, if not, indeed, of plain cowardice. I have therefore decided to come straight out with the simple truth that it is as hard for me to think up a name for a dog as it is for anybody else. The idea that I am an expert in the business is probably the outcome of a piece I wrote several years ago, incautiously revealing the fact that I have owned 40 or more dogs in my life. This is true, but it is also deceptive. All but five or six of my dogs were disposed of when they were puppies, and I had not gone to the trouble of giving to these impermanent residents of my house any names at all except Shut Up! and Cut That Out! and Let Go!

—JAMES THURBER, "HOW TO NAME A DOG"

THESIS STATEMENT

REFLECTIVE TONE

In the dim beginnings, before I ever thought consciously of writing, there was my own name, and there was, doubtless, a certain magic in it. From the start I was uncomfortable with it, and in my earliest years it caused me much puzzlement. Neither could I understand what a poet was, nor why, exactly, my father had chosen to name me after one. Perhaps I could have understood it perfectly well had he named me after his own father, but that name had been given to an older brother who died and thus was out of the question. Why, however, hadn't he named me after a hero, such as Jack Johnson, or a soldier like Colonel Charles Young, or a great seaman like Admiral Dewey, or an educator like Booker T. Washington, or a great orator and abolitionist like Frederick Douglass? Again, why hadn't he named me (as so many Negro parents had done) after President Teddy Roosevelt?

—RALPH ELLISON, *SHADOW AND ACT* (ADAPTED)

451

Expository Essays

EXERCISE 1 Recognizing Thesis Statements and Tone
Write the thesis statement from each of the following introductory paragraphs. Then indicate the tone of each by writing *direct, comic,* or *reflective.*

1. comic

Cheese, like oil, makes too much of itself. It wants the whole boat to itself. It goes through the hamper, and gives a cheesy flavor to everything else there. You can't tell whether you are eating apple pie or German sausage, or strawberries and cream. It all seems cheese. There is too much odor about cheese. —JEROME K. JEROME, "THE ODOR OF CHEESE"

2. direct

At a time when President George Washington and Secretary of State Thomas Jefferson were discouraged and felt that their plans for a new capital of the country were doomed to failure, a black surveyor stepped forward and saved the situation. It was through his remarkable talents that the city of Washington, D.C., was finally laid out and completed. Outstanding astronomer, mathematician, and surveyor—this was Benjamin Banneker of colonial times.
 —LOUIS HABER, "BENJAMIN BANNEKER"

3. reflective

There are many reasons for going to the moon, above and beyond simply learning the answers to our age-old questions and learning how to survive there. Scientific research involving the moon, the earth, and outer space can all be done advantageously from our natural satellite. There is another forceful reason for colonizing the moon. Humans seem destined to explore the solar system and maybe even space beyond those several hundred millions of miles. As we begin such explorations, the moon should prove its worth in precious metals. It is truly a stepping-stone to our future as travelers in our universe. The same powerful drive that led Columbus west and Galileo to look upward through his primitive telescope will send people outward from the tiny planet they once thought the center of the universe. We will not make the trip in one jump—at least not at first. We will do it slowly and cautiously, and the moon is only our first step before we run across the millions of miles of deep space.
 —D. S. HALACY, JR., "STEPPING-STONE TO THE FUTURE"

The Body of an Essay

20f

The paragraphs that make up the body of an expository essay develop the main idea expressed in the thesis statement. They are called supporting paragraphs because they provide the specific details necessary to back up, or support, the main idea. Each supporting paragraph develops one main, supporting point.

20f | The **supporting paragraphs** in the body of an essay develop the main idea expressed in the thesis statement.

The following is the complete essay about the computer checkers champion. The introduction, which you have already read, is repeated here. Notice that each paragraph in the body develops one supporting point that expands on and clarifies the thesis statement.

Can a Computer Learn from Experience?

INTRODUCTION

In 1962, a former checkers champion lost a game of checkers for the first time in eight years. His opponent was an IBM Model 7094 electronic computer. The computer won fairly, without coaching from the sidelines.

THESIS STATEMENT

Of perhaps the greatest significance was the fact that the computer learned to play just as a human being learns—from experience, observation, and a consideration of the problems involved.

FIRST SUPPORTING PARAGRAPH

The machine "looked ahead" some 20 moves and employed strategy worthy of a champion. Yet, the scientist who programmed the computer, Dr. Arthur L. Samuel, was not a great player himself. He could not and did not plan the winning strategy. The computer had been "taught" to look ahead, "consider" various moves and countermoves, and select the move that would most probably lead to victory. In addition, the computer remembered favorable and unfavorable moves and positions from previous games, avoiding those that had turned out poorly.

453

Expository Essays

SECOND SUPPORTING PARAGRAPH When the machine first learned to play, it was a pretty poor player — even a young child could have beaten it. Little by little, however, it stored away on magnetic tape the sequence of moves that led to the capture of the opponent's pieces and to the "kinging" of its own pieces. In picking a move, it compared the existing board setup with patterns stored away in its memory and picked the move most likely to annoy the opponent. Because a roll of tape can remember a large number of moves, the computer's play improved mightily with each game. After several thousand games, the machine was able to beat good amateurs, including the man who taught it to play!

CONCLUSION This, of course, was the reason that the computer had been taught the game. Far from being a stunt, it showed how an intellectual pursuit can be reduced to computer science. It demonstrated and tested some of the methods by which a computer can be taught to learn from its own experience and assume ever more challenging tasks in the modern world.

— WILLIAM VERGARA, *SCIENCE IN THE WORLD AROUND US* (ADAPTED)

A simple outline of this essay about the computer shows how the supporting paragraphs develop the main idea expressed in the thesis statement.

THESIS STATEMENT Of perhaps the greatest significance was the fact that the computer learned to play just as a human being learns — from experience, observation, and a consideration of the problems involved.

I. How the computer learned the game and planned a master strategy
II. How the computer developed from a poor checkers player into a championship checkers player

Conclusion

20g

EXERCISE 2 Listing Supporting Points

Copy each thesis statement on your paper. Then list three supporting ideas that could serve as the basis for supporting paragraphs in the body of an essay. Use simple outline form (Roman numerals) to list the points.
Sample answer for item 1 precedes this chapter.

1. I look forward to weekends for three main reasons.
2. Major spectator sports are strongly associated with certain seasons of the year.
3. Of all the celebrities whose faces cover national magazines, three stand out above all the rest in the admiration they inspire.
4. My high school has many different clubs that serve the interests of a wide variety of students.
5. If I could have been born in another era of history, I would like to have lived during the Revolutionary War era.
6. Most television shows can be classified in one of three main categories.
7. Several movies in recent years have had robots or computers as characters.
8. Becoming an adult has its advantages and disadvantages.
9. The animal that best symbolizes the United States is the _____. *(Fill in the blank with your choice.)*
10. Each of my closest friends has a distinct personality.

Conclusion

After the warm-up of the introduction and the vigorous workout in the body, the conclusion provides a cool down for the reader. The main idea has been developed with specifics, and now the writer returns to more general comments to complete the essay. The length of the conclusion depends on the length of the essay. In most short essays, one paragraph is sufficient to wrap up the thoughts.

20g ▸ The purpose of the **conclusion** is to complete the essay and drive home the main idea.

The following paragraph ends D. C. Halacy, Jr.'s essay on the moon as a stepping-stone to the future. *(See the introduction on page 452.)*

Expository Essays

CLINCHER SENTENCE

We will go to the moon because it is there—and because there are strong reasons for going—and staying. Our forebears colonized a New World on our own planet. Some of us will be the first citizens of the moon, the vanguard of humans' conquest of outer space. The magic of the dream now is that it is at hand. Unlike Keppler, Goddard, and the others who could only foresee, we *go* to the moon, land on the moon, and look *up* to see from whence we came. Then we shall live on the moon.

Notice how the last sentence gives emphasis to the author's main idea. It fixes in the reader's mind the idea that we will colonize the moon. A sentence in the conclusion that reinforces the main idea is called a *clincher sentence*.

EXERCISE 3 On Your Own
The most common place to find essays today is in newspapers and magazines. In newspapers they are usually found in regular columns written by the same person every day, often on the editorial or opinion page. In magazines they can take the form of editorials or short articles. Over the next week, check your local newspaper and favorite magazines for short essays. When you find one you like, copy it (or clip it out if the paper or magazine belongs to you) and bring it to class. Be prepared to identify the essay's introduction, tone, thesis statement, supporting ideas offered in the body, and conclusion.
Answers will vary.

PREWRITING

Writing, like other forms of communication, is highly individualized. Even if you and all your classmates were assigned the same essay subject, no two essays would come out exactly the same. Every writer brings his or her own experience, knowledge, and views to a subject, and every writer finds a unique way of using that background and expressing those views. In the prewriting stage of the writing process, focus on yourself—your interests, your areas of special knowledge, and your views.

Finding Ideas

The first step in prewriting is to find ideas to write about. Some writers simply begin to write, jotting down anything that comes to mind on any subject. This method is called *free writing*. The only requirement in free writing is that you keep your pen or pencil moving. For many people this process unlocks ideas that can be turned into essay subjects.

Other writers ask themselves questions about their interests and skills. Then they write down everything that comes to mind about each question. Some writers vary this process by skimming magazines and books and asking themselves questions about what they read. All of these techniques can help you find a subject to write about. The following exercises will give you practice in using each technique.

EXERCISE 4 Finding Ideas by Free Writing

Using the starter line provided, write freely for five minutes. No one will see this paper; it is for your eyes only. You do not need to worry about complete sentences or proper punctuation. Just write. If you cannot think of anything else to write, just write "I can't think of anything else to write" until another idea comes into your mind. Save your notes for Exercise 7.

STARTER LINE   Subjects on television, in books, or in school that always seem to hold my attention are . . .

Answers will vary.

EXERCISE 5 Finding Ideas by Asking Yourself Questions

Copy the following questions on your paper, leaving ten blank lines after each one. Then write all answers that come to mind. Save your work for Exercise 7.
Sample answer for item 1 precedes this chapter.

1. At what activities am I an expert? What skills do I have? What could I explain to others about these activities or skills?
2. Whom do I most admire? What did this person do to earn my admiration?
3. What places have I been to that people might like to know about?
4. Someone once said, "Growing old just happens, but growing up takes work." How have I worked at growing up?
5. Who among my friends and family seem most happy? What do the happiest people I know seem to have in common?

Expository Essays

EXERCISE 6   Finding Ideas from Reading and Other Sources
Copy the following questions on your paper, leaving ten blank lines after each one. Then write all answers that come to mind. Save your work for Exercise 7.
Sample answer for item 1 precedes this chapter.

1. What have I been reading about in history class that interests me?
2. What have I been reading about in science or other classes that interests me?
3. What research projects have I worked on in past grades?
4. What did I read about in magazines lately that caught my attention?
5. Which of the following Chinese proverbs has a special meaning for me? What incidents in my life support or contradict the message in that proverb?
   a. A single kind word keeps one warm for three winters.
   b. A false friend is worse than an open enemy.
   c. A good talker does not equal a good listener.

Choosing and Limiting a Subject

The more enthusiastic a writer is about a subject, the better the essay that writer will produce. As you choose a subject from the many possible ideas you discovered, consider first and foremost which subject will interest you the most. Use the following guidelines when choosing a subject.

20h

> **Guidelines for Choosing an Essay Subject**
> 1. Choose a subject that you would enjoy writing about.
> 2. Choose a subject that will interest your readers.
> 3. Choose a subject you know enough about now or can learn enough about later to develop adequately in a short essay.
> 4. Choose a subject that reveals an insight about yourself or about your world.

Limiting your subject is the next step. A subject that is too broad will probably result in a poorly organized, overgeneralized essay. A narrow subject, on the other hand, will take on a

Choosing and Limiting a Subject

20h–i

sharp, clear form as you develop it with specifics. Limit your subject by asking yourself the following questions.

20i

> **Questions for Limiting a Subject**
>
> 1. What about the subject of my essay do I want to explain to my readers?
> 2. Who are my readers? What do they need to know to understand my subject?
> 3. What kind of tone is best suited to the message I wish to express?
> 4. What insight or understanding can I draw from the subject I chose?
> 5. How can I express the main idea of my essay in one sentence?

Suppose the subject you chose was one you learned about in your history class: women spies during the Civil War. You can limit this subject by answering the preceding five questions.

Answer to question 1: I would like to explain the similarities and the differences between Belle Boyd (South) and Emma Edmonds (North).
Answer to question 2: Since my readers may not have heard of these women, they need some background information.
Answer to question 3: The tone best suited to my subject is serious.
Answer to question 4: People who serve causes they believe in are motivated by a variety of forces.
Answer to question 5: In their similarities and differences, Belle Boyd and Emma Edmonds reveal the variety of motivations that lead people to serve causes they believe in.

EXERCISE 7 Choosing a Subject

Using your notes from Exercises 4, 5, and 6 or any fresh ideas, make a list of ten possible subjects for an expository essay. Review the guidelines on page 458 and put a check next to the one subject that comes closest to following all four guidelines. Then limit your subject by using the questions above. Save your work for Exercise 12.

Answers will vary.

Expository Essays

EXERCISE 8 Limiting a Subject

Copy each subject. Then after each one, answer the five Questions for Limiting a Subject on page 459.
Sample answer for item 1 precedes this chapter.

1. computers
2. my favorite movie
3. becoming an adult
4. first impressions
5. manners these days

Listing Supporting Details

With your subject limited, you can move on to listing details that will help you explain it. Use the technique of brainstorming to help you think of details. *Brainstorming* means writing down everything that comes to mind when you think about your subject. The details you list should include any of the following types of supporting details that are appropriate to your subject.

20j

Types of Supporting Details Used in Expository Essays		
facts	analogies	comparisons/contrasts
examples	incidents	steps in a process
reasons	definitions	causes and effects

The following brainstorming notes are on the limited subject of the similarities and differences between Belle Boyd and Emma Edmonds. Notice that the details are not yet arranged in any logical order.

LIMITED SUBJECT   the similarities and differences between Belle Boyd and Emma E. Edmonds

- Belle Boyd — 17 years old
- Belle Boyd — fun-loving, adventurous, warm-hearted
- Emma Edmonds decided to become a spy when the man she loved was killed
- Boyd was spy for the South; Edmonds for the North
- both young and highly independent

Listing Supporting Details 20j

- both passionately committed to their causes
- Boyd became spy after her home was attacked
- Edmonds was a master of disguise
- disguised herself as a peddler to penetrate lines at Yorktown
- Boyd delivered messages to J. E. B. Stuart and Stonewall Jackson
- Boyd's cheerfulness led her to sing "Maryland, My Maryland" when she was imprisoned
- George McClellan interviewed Edmonds for her job as spy
- Edmonds faced many hardships—enemy fire and disease
- both worked as nurses
- Edmonds's best work was to identify five Confederate spies
- used different methods—Boyd was a charmer; Edmonds, a masquerader
- Belle Boyd was inspired by Rose O'Neal Greenhow in Washington, D.C.
- Boyd's greatest success was helping Confederates recapture Front Royal
- Boyd surrounded by gaiety; knew how to make people admire her
- Edmonds helped a dying Confederate soldier

EXERCISE 9 Listing Supporting Details
Use the technique of brainstorming to list at least five supporting details for each of the following subjects.
Sample answer for item 1 precedes this chapter.

1. the car as a symbol of growing up
2. moviemakers' attitude toward creatures from outer space: fear or friendship?
3. how the world has changed since you were a child
4. the qualities you look for in a friend
5. the role of music in your life
6. your ideas for a perfect high school
7. your favorite daydream
8. weather and moods
9. what makes a movie enjoyable or interesting
10. your dream vacation

461

Expository Essays

Outlining

Most of the activities associated with prewriting are for the benefit of the writer. They help the writer collect his or her thoughts and focus them on one main idea. As a writer moves toward writing the first draft, however, *audience* becomes an important consideration. The writer must think, "Now that I know pretty well what I am going to write about, how can I make it clear to my readers?" One of the most important steps in making ideas clear to readers is organizing them logically.

Many writers find that the best way to organize supporting details is to *outline* them. The outlining process involves two steps: grouping notes into categories, and arranging those categories in a logical order with letters and numbers.

20k   Organize your notes in an **outline** that shows how you will cover the **main topics, subtopics,** and **supporting details** of your subject.

Grouping Notes into Categories. Finding categories calls for asking yourself what one detail on your list has in common with another. Scan your list of supporting details to see what categories you can create. The groupings that follow show the categories made from the list of details on pages 460–461.

Similarities
- both young and highly independent
- both worked as nurses
- both passionately committed to their causes

Belle Boyd's story
- at 17 years of age, became spy after her home was attacked
- Belle Boyd—fun-loving, adventurous, warmhearted
- Boyd delivered messages to J. E. B. Stuart and Stonewall Jackson
- Boyd's cheerfulness led her to sing "Maryland, My Maryland" when she was imprisoned
- Belle Boyd was inspired by Rose O'Neal Greenhow in Washington, D. C.
- Boyd's greatest success was helping Confederates recapture Front Royal

- Boyd surrounded by gaiety; knew how to make people admire her
- Boyd was a charmer

Emma Edmonds's story
- Edmonds decided to become spy when man she loved was killed
- Edmonds was a master of disguise
- disguised herself as a peddler to penetrate lines at Yorktown
- George McClellan interviewed Edmonds for her job as spy
- Edmonds faced many hardships—enemy fire and disease
- Edmonds's best work was to identify five Confederate spies
- Edmonds was a masquerader
- Edmonds helped a dying Confederate soldier

Arranging Categories in Logical Order. The categories you create from your prewriting notes are the main topics that you will use as support for your thesis statement. The next step is to arrange these topics in logical order. The following chart shows four common ways to organize ideas.

Methods of Organization

CHRONOLOGICAL ORDER	Items are arranged according to when they happened in time.
SPATIAL ORDER	Items are arranged according to their location.
ORDER OF IMPORTANCE	Items are arranged in order of importance, interest, or degree.
DEVELOPMENTAL ORDER	Items are arranged in a logical progression, in which one idea grows out of another.

The most logical arrangement for the categories about Belle Boyd and Emma Edmonds is probably developmental order, a common pattern for a comparison/contrast essay. If a Roman numeral is assigned to each category, a simple outline for this essay would appear as follows.

Expository Essays

    I. Similarities
   II. Belle Boyd's story
  III. Emma Edmonds's story

  Once your main categories are arranged logically and assigned Roman numerals, you can continue the outlining process by grouping and arranging the items *within* each category. This time each grouping is assigned a capital letter.

MAIN TOPIC	I. Similarities
SUBTOPICS	A. Young independent women
	B. Nursing
	C. Commitment to cause
MAIN TOPIC	II. Belle Boyd's story
SUBTOPICS	A. Personality
	B. Reasons for becoming spy
	C. Methods she used
	D. Greatest success
MAIN TOPIC	III. Emma Edmonds's story
SUBTOPICS	A. Reasons for becoming spy
	B. Methods she used
	C. Greatest success
	D. Dangers she faced

  The final step in outlining is to add supporting points under the subtopics if necessary. These are assigned Arabic numerals. If your supporting points can be broken down further, you can use lowercase letters to show the breakdown. The pattern that follows is the correct form for an outline.

    I. (Main topic)
      A. (Subtopic)
        1. (Supporting point)
        2. (Supporting point)
          a. (Detail)
          b. (Detail)
      B. (Subtopic)
        1. (Supporting point)
          a. (Detail)
          b. (Detail)
        2. (Supporting point)
        etc.

When you have finished your outline, ask yourself the following questions to check its form.

> **Questions for Checking an Outline**
> 1. Did you use Roman numerals for main topics?
> 2. Did you use capital letters for subtopics?
> 3. Did you use Arabic numerals for supporting points?
> 4. If your supporting points can be broken down, did you use lowercase letters?
> 5. If you include subtopics under topics, do you have at least two?
> 6. If you include supporting points under subtopics, do you have at least two?
> 7. If you break down your supporting points, do you have at least two details in the breakdown?
> 8. Does your indentation follow the model on page 464?
> 9. Did you capitalize the first word of each entry?
> 10. Are your main topics and each group of subtopics expressed in parallel forms? *(See page 464.)*

A final outline for the essay on Boyd and Edmonds might look like the following.

  I. Similarities
     A. Young women, highly independent
     B. Nursing
     C. Commitment to cause
 II. Belle Boyd's story
     A. Personality
        1. Fun-loving nature, adventurous, warmhearted
        2. Ability to charm and make people admire her
     B. Reasons for becoming spy
        1. Attack on home
           a. How she handled attacking officers
           b. How she gathered intelligence
        2. Inspiration of Rose O'Neal Greenhow
     C. Methods she used
     D. Greatest success: Recapture of Front Royal

Expository Essays

III. Emma Edmonds's story
    A. Reasons for becoming a spy
    B. Methods she used
    C. Greatest success
        1. Disguise as Southern country boy
        2. Identification of five Confederate spies
    D. Dangers she faced
        1. Enemy fire
        2. Disease on scouting missions

EXERCISE 10 Grouping Ideas into Categories

The following prewriting notes are on the subject of official military salutes for important leaders. Write three categories into which you can group the ideas. Then list the ideas under the proper category. All but one item should fit into one of the three categories you create. Save your work for Exercise 11.

Categories: I — Officials/events receiving 21-gun salute; II — 19-gun salute; III — 17-gun salute

- I • President receives 21-gun salute on arrival and departure
- II • Vice-President receives 19-gun salute on arrival only
- I • visiting heads of state or members of royal family receive 21-gun salute on arrival and departure
- III • generals and admirals receive 17-gun salute on arrival and departure
- II • Speaker of the House receives 19-gun salute on arrival only
- III • chairperson of a committee of Congress receives 17-gun salute on arrival only
- II • secretary of defense and the secretaries of the Army, Navy, and Air Force receive 19-gun salute on arrival and departure
- I • salute to the flag is 21 guns followed by national anthem
- I • President's salute is followed by "Hail to the Chief"
- • biggest salute is to the Union on the Fourth of July: 50-gun salute, one for each state

EXERCISE 11 Outlining

Following the steps on pages 462–465, use the categories you created in Exercise 10 to make an outline. The outline should show three main topics, with at least two subtopics under each one. The main topics and subtopics should be organized in logical order. Save your work for Exercises 14 and 15.

Sample answer precedes this chapter.

Outlining

EXERCISE 12 On Your Own
Using your work from Exercise 7, brainstorm a list of supporting details on your chosen subject and organize them into an outline. Save your work for Exercise 21.
Answers will vary.

Writing Extra

Developing an essay that defines a concept or uses definitions as support requires the ability to see similarities and differences among related ideas. The obvious way to define a concept is to say what it *is*, but good writers will take a broader outlook and consider every angle. For example, they might also say what it *does*, what it *is like or unlike*, and what it *is not*.

Study the following paragraph definitions.

WHAT IT IS AND WHAT IT IS LIKE	Patience, like charity, is long-suffering and kind. It is, moreover, the most practical of the virtues. For, with its aid and sustenance, all calamities can be endured, all fulfillments bearably and even hopefully awaited. Then, if the fulfillments do not come, patience itself has
WHAT IT DOES	become a habit, and it renders the lack of fulfillment less hard to take. —IRWIN EDMAN
WHAT IT IS NOT	The bullfight is not a sport in the Anglo-Saxon sense of the word, that is, not an equal contest or an attempt at an equal contest between a
WHAT IT IS AND WHAT IT IS LIKE	bull and a man. Rather it is a tragedy: the death of the bull, which is played, more or less well, by the bull and the man involved and in which there is danger for the man but certain death for the animal. —ERNEST HEMINGWAY

EXERCISE 13 Writing a Paragraph Definition
Choose one of the following ideas. Then write a one-paragraph definition that tells what it is or is not, what it is like or unlike, and what it does. *Sample answer precedes this chapter.*

friendship	boredom	comedy
flattery	democracy	conservation
jealousy	freedom	physical fitness

467

Expository Essays

WRITING

The second main stage of the writing process is writing the first draft. During this stage you will use your outline and other prewriting notes to express your thoughts in smoothly flowing sentences and paragraphs. You may also discover new ideas as you write. As long as these ideas relate directly to your main idea, feel free to include them, revising your outline as needed. Remember that a first draft need not be polished, but it should include all the parts of an essay: an introduction with a thesis statement, a body of supporting paragraphs, and a conclusion.

Writing the Thesis Statement

Working on your thesis statement first will help you keep your thoughts on target as you write the rest of your essay. Use the steps shown in the following chart to write an effective thesis statement.

20n

> **Steps for Writing a Thesis Statement**
>
> 1. Look over your prewriting notes, especially your outline and the questions you answered to limit your subject. *(See page 459.)*
> 2. Express your main idea in one sentence.
> 3. Revise your sentence until it controls all your main topics.
> 4. Avoid such expressions as "In this paper I will . . ." or "This essay will be about . . ."

Reread the prewriting notes and outline on Belle Boyd and Emma Edmonds on pages 462–463 and 465–466. Then study the problems in the following thesis statements.

WEAK THESIS STATEMENTS   Belle Boyd and Emma Edmonds used different methods in their spying missions. [too specific: does not control details about similarities and other differences between them]

Everyone has unique reasons for serving a cause of great importance. [too general: does not even mention the women by name]

Writing the Thesis Statement

20n

In this essay I will explain the similarities and differences between Belle Boyd and Emma Edmonds. [You want your reader to concentrate on the subject, not on you as you begin writing your essay.]

The following thesis statement is appropriately specific and controls all the supporting details.

STRONG THESIS STATEMENT
Both Belle Boyd for the Confederacy and Emma Edmonds for the Union served their causes bravely, but each was unique in her reasons for being a spy and in her methods.

EXERCISE 14 Identifying Problems in Thesis Statements
Reread the prewriting notes on official military salutes and the outline you wrote for Exercises 10 and 11 on page 466. Copy the following thesis statements on your paper, skipping a line after each one. On the blank line, explain in one sentence what is wrong with the thesis statement. Use the models on pages 468–469. *Answers precede this chapter.*

1. Lesser officials receive a 17-gun salute on arrival.
2. All over the world, countries have a set method for welcoming important people.
3. In this essay I will explain the different kinds of military salutes given to important leaders.
4. Some officials are greeted with a 21-gun salute, while others receive only a 19-gun salute.
5. This paper will be about official military salutes.

EXERCISE 15 Writing a Thesis Statement
Review the Steps for Writing a Thesis Statement on page 468. Then, using your outline from Exercise 11, write a thesis statement for an essay about official military salutes.
Sample answer: The number of guns saluting an official or event is a sign of rank and status.

Writing the Introduction

In many short essays, the thesis statement is the final sentence of the first paragraph. The sentences that precede it get the reader interested in the subject and set the tone of the essay. Use the following suggestions to help you write the introduction of your essay.

Expository Essays

20o

> **Suggestions for Beginning an Essay**
> 1. Begin with an incident that shows how you became interested in your subject.
> 2. Begin by giving some background information.
> 3. Begin with an example or incident that catches the reader's attention.

Depending on where you place it, you may need to revise your thesis statement to work it smoothly into your introduction. Notice how the thesis statement about Boyd and Edmonds on page 469 was revised to make it flow smoothly.

INTRODUCTION   Picture a 17-year-old girl, her eyes bright with adventure and daring. Her dark-blue dress and white sunbonnet attract attention as she scurries between the cross fire of Confederates and Federals to deliver a message to Stonewall Jackson's troops near Front Royal, Virginia. This was Belle Boyd, the most famous spy for the South during the War between the States. Next picture another young woman, her face blistered and her eyes red from the disguise she uses to penetrate the Confederate lines at Yorktown, Virginia. This was Emma Edmonds, a master masquerader and a spy for the Union in

THESIS STATEMENT   the Civil War. Both young women served their causes bravely, but each was unique in her reasons for being a spy and in her methods.

EXERCISE 16   Identifying Essay Beginnings

Read each introductory paragraph that follows. Then write *personal incident, background information,* or *attention-getting example* to indicate how the essay begins.

1. *personal incident*

When I was a child seven years old, my friends, on a holiday, filled my pockets with coppers. I went directly to a shop where they sold toys for children; and being charmed with the sound of a whistle . . . I voluntarily offered and gave all my money for one. I then came home and went

470

whistling all over the house, much pleased with my whistle but disturbing the family. My brothers and sisters and cousins, understanding the bargain I had made, told me I had given four times as much for it as it was worth. They put me in mind what good things I might have bought with the rest of the money and laughed at me so much for my folly that I cried in vexation. The reflection gave me more distress than the whistle gave me pleasure. This however was afterwards of use to me. The impression continued in my mind so that often, when I was tempted to buy some unnecessary thing, I said to myself, "Don't give too much for the whistle"; and I saved my money. — BENJAMIN FRANKLIN, "THE WHISTLE" (ADAPTED)

2. personal incident

From all available evidence, no black man had ever set foot in this tiny Swiss village before I came. I was told before arriving that I would probably be a "sight" for the village; I took this to mean that people of my complexion were rarely seen in Switzerland, and also that city people are always something of a "sight" outside the city. It did not occur to me — possibly because I am an American that there could be people anywhere who had never seen a black person.

— JAMES BALDWIN, "STRANGER IN THE VILLAGE"

3. background information

In 1876, Mark Twain published *The Adventures of Tom Sawyer* and in the same year began what he called "another boys' book." He set little store by the new venture and said that he had undertaken it "more to be at work than anything else." His heart was not in it — "I like it only tolerably well as far as I have got," he said, "and may possibly pigeonhole or burn the manuscript when it is done." He pigeonholed it long before it was done and for as much as four years. In 1880, he took it out and carried it forward a little, only to abandon it again. He had a theory of unconscious composition and believed that a book must write itself: the book that he referred to as "Huck Finn's Autobiography" refused to do the job of its own creation and he would not coerce it.

— LIONEL TRILLING, "HUCKLEBERRY FINN"

EXERCISE 17 **Experimenting with Essay Beginnings**
Read the following thesis statement. Then write two different introductory paragraphs that include the thesis statement. The first should provide background information; the second

Expository Essays

should use a personal incident. You may revise the thesis statement as needed to work it into each paragraph.

THESIS STATEMENT Although television has been described as a "vast wasteland," the best TV shows can be as stimulating as a great book or a great movie.

Sample answers precede this chapter.

Writing the Body

The outline you wrote is for the body of your essay. Each Roman numeral (main topic) in your outline should correspond to one paragraph in the essay body. Use your outline to help you draft the body of your essay, moving from point to point in the same order as the outline. Be sure to include all the ideas you listed in your outline.

As you write the body of your essay, you will need to use transitions and other techniques to connect your thoughts and make your essay read smoothly. Following is a partial list of some common transitions used with various methods of organization. *(For other lists of transitions, see pages 416, 422, and 426.)*

20p

Common Transitions

CHRONOLOGICAL ORDER	SPATIAL ORDER	ORDER OF IMPORTANCE	DEVELOPMENTAL ORDER
first, second	above	first, second	furthermore
then	below	more important	besides
at first	right	most important	however
immediately	beyond	the least/most	nonetheless
as soon as	east	the largest	despite
after	inside	besides	another
finally	behind	another	in addition

Using transitions will help give your essay *coherence*, the quality that makes each sentence seem connected to the one before it. Other tips for achieving coherence are listed in the chart that follows.

Writing the Body

20p–q

20q

> **Tips for Achieving Coherence**
> 1. Repeat a key word from an earlier sentence.
> 2. Use new words to repeat an idea from an earlier sentence.
> 3. Use a pronoun in place of a word used earlier.
> 4. Use transitional words and phrases.

Notice how the outline from pages 465–466 on Boyd and Edmonds can be turned into a coherent body of an essay. Words and phrases that aid coherence are in heavy type.

FROM I IN OUTLINE
The similarities between the two spies emphasize some of the qualities that helped them carry out their work. **Both** were young women and as such aroused less suspicion than young men might have. **Both** were highly independent, driven by a belief that an individual can make a difference. **Both** served as nurses and **so** knew how to talk easily to soldiers. **Both** were **also** passionately committed to their cause.

FROM II IN OUTLINE
The two spies' differences, **however**, point out the variety of motivations that lead people to give of themselves for a **cause** they believe in. Belle Boyd, for example, was fun-loving, adventurous, and warm-hearted. When Union troops overtook **her** hometown of Martinsburg, Virginia, and threatened to burn down her house, Boyd appealed to the chivalry of the commanding officer. So effective were her **appeals** that the officer not only saved her house but also assigned Union soldiers to protect it! Surrounded by admiring enemy troops, **she** soon picked up valuable information and began her career as a spy. Her most useful tool was her **warm-heartedness** and **charm**, which made people admire and trust her. Boyd redoubled her efforts when she learned of the glamorous Rose O'Neal Greenhow, spying for the South in Washington, D.C. Using her **charm**

473

Expository Essays

to obtain information and her courage to cross enemy lines, Boyd delivered secret information to General J. E. B. Stuart and General Stonewall Jackson. Her aid was instrumental in allowing the South to recapture an important bridge near Front Royal and take 3,000 prisoners along with valuable supplies. Although the danger Boyd faced on her missions was serious, her **powers to charm** protected her from harm and, on the whole, glamour and gaiety surrounded her.

FROM III IN OUTLINE

Emma Edmonds, **on the other hand,** spent her life as a spy in grueling, exacting labor. **She** first decided to become a spy when the man she loved, a Union soldier, was shot and killed. General George McClellan interviewed her and finally, despite her slight build, enlisted her service in the Union cause. **In all** she made 11 trips through enemy lines, adopting difficult and sometimes painful disguises. **Some** required that she shave her head; some required that she learn different dialects. **All** required quick thinking to avoid a fatal slip that would betray her disguise. **Her last assignment** was her highest achievement. Disguised as a Southern boy wanting to become a Confederate spy, she was able to identify five spies working for the Confederacy. In the two years she served as a spy, she faced **danger** constantly—not only in the form of enemy fire but also in the form of disease and hardship on her mission scouting for enemy troops.

EXERCISE 18 **Identifying Techniques for Achieving Coherence**

The following paragraphs are from a 1959 essay about space flight. Some of the techniques for achieving coherence are underlined and numbered. Next to the proper number on your paper, indentify the technique being used by writing *transitional word, repeated word, earlier idea in new words,* or *pronoun.* Answers precede this chapter.

Writing the Conclusion

The (1) <u>first</u> and by far the most delightful of the experiments that I was allowed to sample was weightlessness, officially known as the zero-gravity experiment. I became weightless in a modified Convair 131-B transport plane named *How High the Moon,* in which experiments are conducted by Major Edward L. Brown, a psychologist and pilot at the Aero Medical Laboratory of Wright Field, Ohio. In a satellite, people become (2) <u>weightless</u> as soon as they go into orbit because the centrifugal force throwing them outward, the result of their enormous velocity, exactly balances the inward pull of gravity. To duplicate (3) <u>this</u> situation, at least briefly, *How High the Moon* is put through a precise maneuver. (4) <u>First</u> it is power-dived from about 12,000 feet until it reaches an air speed of 285 mph. (5) <u>Then</u> it is sharply pulled up into a steep 30-degree climb. For the (6) <u>next</u> 15 seconds, the plane arcs through the air like a lobbed tennis ball, as weightlessly as if in orbit. Inside, everybody and every object that is not securely tied down (as the pilots are) rises eerily and floats aimlessly about.

Lying facedown on the padded floor of the plane as it began to pull up from its dive, I was pressed flat by a force of $2\frac{1}{2}$ G's ($2\frac{1}{2}$ times the force of gravity), which made my body "weigh" 500 pounds. I remember wishing the (7) <u>G's</u> would go away. I felt as if I were a lizard to whom the feat of rising must seem just barely possible but not worth the effort. Then, (8) <u>gradually</u>, (9) <u>the heavy hand of gravity</u> relaxed its pressure until it vanished. Gently, inexorably, I floated off the floor.

I was astonished to find that the world of weightlessness actually feels more natural than our customary gravity controlled realm. Free floating at zero G seems to give simultaneous buoyancy to both body and spirit. I remember grinning ridiculously at the others in the plane as I discovered (10) <u>the new world</u>. It was hard to remember or to care which was "up" and which was "down." Never again will ceilings be the same for me.

—WARREN R. YOUNG, "WHAT IT'S LIKE TO FLY IN SPACE"

Writing the Conclusion

The conclusion of an essay is a good place to present or restate the insight you wish to express. Refer to your prewriting notes, especially the questions you answered to limit your subject. You may find that a detail not used in the introduction

Expository Essays

or body of your essay can be used in the conclusion. Remember that the conclusion, like the introduction, is usually more general than the specific ideas in the essay body. The following are all good ways to end an essay.

20r

> **Ways to End an Essay**
>
> 1. Summarize the essay or restate the thesis in new words.
> 2. Refer to ideas in the introduction to bring the essay full circle.
> 3. Appeal to the reader's emotions.
> 4. Draw a conclusion based on the specifics in the essay body.

The following conclusion to the essay on Boyd and Edmonds restates the thesis. Notice that details about Boyd and Edmonds not used elsewhere in the essay are used in the conclusion. The last sentence, the *clincher*, makes a strong ending and fixes the main idea in the reader's mind.

> Two young women: One blazes with the spirit of high adventure and, on her capture and imprisonment, joyously sings, "Maryland, My Maryland," The other, while still disguised as a peddler, takes time out from her mission against the Confederacy to lighten the final hours of a dying Confederate soldier. Both women deserve their place in history. Enemies in their beliefs and contrasts in their methods, Belle Boyd and Emma Edmonds both demonstrate the independent spirit of American heroes and heroines.

Writing a Title. The final step in writing the first draft is to think of a suitable title for your essay. Many titles are taken from words and phrases in the essay itself. Choose a title that will make your readers want to read the essay. For the essay on Boyd and Edmonds, for example, you might first think of the title "Boyd and Edmonds." A more interesting title, however, would be "Two Female Fighters of the Civil War."

20s A good title should make your readers curious enough to want to read on.

Revising

20r–t

EXERCISE 19 Writing a Concluding Paragraph
Reread the introduction and body of the essay on Boyd and Edmonds on pages 470 and 473–474. Then write an alternative concluding paragraph. Make your concluding paragraph appeal to the reader's emotions. *Sample answer precedes this chapter.*

EXERCISE 20 Thinking of Titles
Make a list of five possible titles for the essay about Boyd and Edmonds. *Sample answers:* Spies above Suspicion; Emma and Belle: Civil War Spies; Women in Disguise; Civil War Secrets; Women of Valor

EXERCISE 21 On Your Own
Using your outline from Exercise 12, write the first draft of an introduction, body, and conclusion. (Remember to write your thesis statement first by following the steps on page 468.) Think of a good title for your essay and write it at the top. Save your paper for Exercise 22.
Answers will vary.

REVISING

The purpose of revising is to make your first draft clearer for readers. Putting your essay aside for a time will help you see it with fresh eyes when it is time to revise it.

Checking for Unity, Coherence, and Emphasis

Good writers keep the reader's mind focused on the main point. They do this by eliminating any idea that strays from the main point. When all the supporting details in an essay keep to the main idea expressed in the thesis statement, the essay is said to have unity.

20t In an essay with **unity,** each paragraph is directly related to the thesis statement.

Good writers also guide the thoughts of their readers by using logical order and clear transitions. The resulting essays are said to have coherence, the quality that creates a tightly woven fabric of ideas.

Expository Essays

20u ▶ **In an essay with coherence, the ideas are logically organized and smoothly connected.**

Emphasis is another characteristic of good essays. In many essays, one supporting point is more important than the others. The writer may show the importance of this point by devoting more space to it than to the other ideas. Another way to show emphasis is to use order of importance organization and transitional words that make the relative importance of the points clear.

20v ▶ **An essay with emphasis shows the relative importance of its supporting points.**

The following questions will help you check your essay for unity, coherence, and emphasis.

20w ▶

Checking for Unity, Coherence, and Emphasis

Checking for Unity
1. Does every paragraph in the essay relate to your main idea?
2. Does every sentence in each paragraph support the topic sentence?

Checking for Coherence
1. Are the paragraphs in the body of your essay presented in logical order? *(See pages 463–465.)*
2. Do your transitions smoothly connect paragraphs? *(See page 472.)*
3. Are the sentences *within* each paragraph presented in logical order?
4. Did you use the techniques for achieving coherence? *(See page 473.)*

Checking for Emphasis
1. Do your transitional words show the relative importance of your ideas?
2. Does the amount of space you gave to the ideas in your essay reflect their relative importance?

Revision Checklist

Use the following checklist to help you revise your essay.

> **Revision Checklist**
>
> **Checking Your Essay**
> 1. Do you have a strong introduction that sets the tone and captures attention?
> 2. Does your thesis statement make your main idea and purpose clear?
> 3. Does your essay have unity, coherence, and emphasis?
> 4. Do you have a strong concluding paragraph?
> 5. Did you add a title?
>
> **Checking Your Paragraphs**
> 6. Does each paragraph have a topic sentence? *(See page 411.)*
> 7. Is each paragraph unified and coherent? *(See pages 441–442.)*
>
> **Checking Your Sentences and Words**
> 8. Are your sentences varied? *(See pages 374–381.)*
> 9. Are your sentences concise? *(See pages 370–373.)*
> 10. Did you avoid faulty sentences? *(See pages 382–388.)*
> 11. Did you use specific words with correct connotations? *(See page 365.)*
> 12. Did you use figurative language? *(See pages 367–369.)*

EXERCISE 22 On Your Own

Use the Revision Checklist to make a final revision of the essay you wrote for Exercise 21. Save your paper for Exercise 23.
Answers will vary.

EDITING

The final stage in the writing process is editing. Most writers find that they cannot concentrate on everything at one time. For this reason they focus on their main idea, organization, and coherence during the writing and revision stages. They save the mechanical details for the editing stage. The following checklist will help you edit your work. You may want to use the proofreading symbols on page 614 as you edit.

Expository Essays

20y

> **Editing Checklist**
> 1. Are your sentences free from errors in grammar and usage?
> 2. Did you spell every word correctly?
> 3. Did you use capital letters where needed?
> 4. Did you punctuate your sentences correctly?
> 5. Did you use correct manuscript form in your essay? *(See pages 611–612.)*
> 6. Is your typing or handwriting clear?

EXERCISE 23 On Your Own
Use the Editing Checklist to edit your essay from Exercise 22.
Answers will vary.

CHAPTER REVIEW

A. Read the following essay and answer the questions below it.

   In 1984, Smokey the Bear, one of the best known symbols in the history of advertising, celebrated his 40th year as the national symbol of forest fire prevention. Smokey is credited with reducing forest fires by 50 percent since 1944, with resulting savings in human life, wildlife, and timber. The Smokey Bear program has been effective because it accomplishes the three goals of any successful information campaign. These are creating awareness, providing motivation, and guiding actions.
   Awareness is measured by recognizability and Smokey has certainly become a well-known character since he first appeared on a poster dressed in dungarees and a campaign hat, pouring water on a campfire. Surveys show that 98 out of 100 people know who he is, and that most know what he stands for. The Smokey Bear program goes beyond the familiar posters. In addition to television spots, the campaign uses personal appearances by forest rangers dressed as Smokey, Tournament of Roses parade floats, and a giant Smokey Bear balloon. Smokey gets so much mail that he has his own ZIP code (20252), and his commercial use is regulated by an act of Congress.

Motivation would appear to be no problem, for who wouldn't want to prevent forest fires? Actually, one fire of every four *is* started deliberately. If Smokey is even 75 percent successful in motivating us to prevent forest fires, however, his success rate is higher than that of the seat belt campaign.

Sixty percent of all forest fires result from careless human actions. (Only 9 percent are started by lightning.) What we have, then, in an average year is about 76,000 careless acts that result in forest fires. No one knows how many near-misses occur, but Smokey's success in guiding actions is not bad when one considers the millions of people who live in and visit forested areas.

Although there is room for improvement, Smokey's record in shaping a desired behavior is the envy of the advertising world. Because Smokey's keepers know they have a good thing, it is very likely that your children and your grandchildren will be just as familiar as you are with Smokey's famous warning—"Only you can prevent forest fires!"

—LARRY DOOLITTLE, "ONLY HE CAN PREVENT FOREST FIRES" (ADAPTED)

Answers precede this chapter.

1. What is the thesis statement of this essay?
2. Which word would you use to describe the tone of the essay: *reflective, comic,* or *direct?*
3. How does the introductory paragraph capture the reader's attention before presenting the thesis statement?
4. Find one transition in paragraph 2 and write it on your paper.
5. What method of organization is used in the supporting paragraphs: chronological order, spatial order, order of importance, or developmental order?
6. How does the last sentence in the introduction prepare the reader for the type of logical order used in the supporting paragraphs?
7. What transition word is used in the first sentence of the conclusion?
8. Is the conclusion of this essay more general or more specific than the introduction?
9. What is the clincher sentence?
10. What gives this essay unity and coherence?

Expository Essays

B. Write an essay on one of the following subjects or a subject of your choice. Use the Steps for Writing Expository Essays on page 483 as a guide.
Evaluation suggestion precedes this chapter.

Subjects Based on Personal Experience
1. rules you live by
2. the art of compromising
3. tips for job interviews
4. what you would do with a million dollars
5. the similarities and differences between students in your grade and those in the next lower grade
6. a celebrity you would like to be and why
7. an important moment in your life
8. skills needed to play your favorite sport
9. the character of your neighborhood
10. the power of advertising
11. the similarities and differences between the music you like and the music your parents enjoy
12. the quality of prime-time television programming
13. the most valuable classes you have taken in school
14. the advantages and disadvantages of being the oldest child
15. winter, spring, and summer vacations: Are these breaks in the school year really necessary?

Subjects Based on Outside Learning
1. similarities and differences between the Articles of Confederation and the Constitution of the United States
2. the interconnectedness of the ecosystem
3. the life cycle of a star
4. similarities and differences between the Spanish and English languages
5. themes in early American literature
6. the discovery of the ancient city of Troy
7. how a radio works
8. the bubonic plague
9. how triangulation is used to measure distances
10. Dr. Martin Luther King's policy of peaceful resistance
11. the political influence on the Olympic Games
12. the Alaskan Eskimo culture
13. new laws and restrictions against smoking
14. the psychological effects of regular exercise
15. the origins of breakdancing

Steps for Writing

Expository Essays

✓ **Prewriting**
1. Find ideas by asking yourself questions and by reading. *(See page 457.)*
2. From a list of possible subjects, choose one. *(See page 458.)*
3. Limit your subject by asking yourself questions about your audience, tone, and focus. *(See page 459.)*
4. Brainstorm a list of supporting ideas. *(See pages 460–461.)*
5. Organize your list of ideas into an outline. *(See pages 462–466.)*

✓ **Writing**
6. Write a thesis statement. *(See pages 468–469.)*
7. Write an introduction that includes your thesis statement. *(See pages 469–470.)*
8. Use your outline to write the paragraphs in the body. *(See pages 472–473.)*
9. Use connecting devices to link your thoughts. *(See pages 472–474.)*
10. Add a concluding paragraph. *(See pages 475–476.)*
11. Add a title. *(See page 476.)*

✓ **Revising**
12. Using the Revision Checklist, revise your essay for structure, well-developed paragraphs, unity, coherence, emphasis, and varied and lively sentences and words. *(See page 479.)*

✓ **Editing**
13. Using the Editing Checklist, check your grammar, spelling, mechanics, and manuscript form. *(See page 480.)*

Chapter 21   Other Kinds of Essays

OBJECTIVES

- To explain the purpose of descriptive, persuasive, and critical essays and to identify the function of the elements within each type.
- To select appropriate descriptive details and to organize them logically.
- To develop strong arguments with facts, examples, concessions, reasonable language, and expert testimonials and to organize these arguments logically.
- To differentiate a literary review from a critical essay.
- To develop a critical topic with specific details from a work of literature and to organize those details effectively.
- To write the first drafts of descriptive, persuasive, and literary essays; to revise and edit these drafts.

MOTIVATIONAL ACTIVITY

In preparation for writing a literary essay, have students choose, read, and study a short literary work. Ask students to write an informal paper discussing what the work means to them. Although this paper should not be evaluated, students should keep it in their writing folders for future reference.

TEACHING SUGGESTIONS

Descriptive Essays *(pages 484-490)*

Except in travel literature, description is rarely used entirely in an extended work of prose. Instead it serves other rhetorical purposes—as a scene-setting device in narration, background information in exposition, or an emotion-arousing device in persuasion. To show students the use of description in other modes, have them choose one of the following writing tasks as a prewriting activity for descriptive essays.

1. Write a paragraph-length advertisement describing a new jacket or stereo. The overall purpose is to persuade a reader to buy it.
2. Write a paragraph-length description of a new jacket or stereo. The overall purpose in this case is exposition—to explain how the item is different from others of its kind.
3. Write a paragraph-length description of a typical city street. The purpose is to set the scene for a story that takes place there.

Persuasive Essays *(pages 490-500)*

As a prewriting activity *after* students have chosen a subject for their own essays, have students write a working thesis statement that clearly expresses which side of the issue they are on. Then have them write, in class, two paragraphs from the *opposing* point of view. Encourage them to try earnestly to imagine they really believe what they are writing, even though it is in opposition to their own stated position. The effort to advocate an opponent's side will help when students write their real essays; they will know which points to concede, and they will better understand the reasons people hold opposing views. They will also know which of the opposition's arguments are the strongest and need the most attention to overcome.

Developing and Organizing Strong Arguments *(pages 496-499)* Refer students to the two essays about Bigfoot (pages 491-496). Ask students to name specific pieces of evidence or testimony included in one essay but omitted in the other. (Answers may include the 1884 capture, the publication of Patterson's book, and the explanations of experts regarding the size of the prints.) Point out to students that such omissions are examples of selective use of evidence. The strongest appeals to reason are those that do not omit evidence but instead try to show its strength or weakness. In appeals to emotion, however, selective evidence can be useful as long as it is not used to distort purposely.

Chapter 21 a

Literary Essays *(pages 500-508)*

Students are likely to have some difficulty in narrowing their subjects for a critical essay. In addition to the questions offered on page 505 for analyzing fiction, you may wish to distribute the following questions.
1. Choose a minor character from the work and explain why the author included that character. What role does that character serve in the work?
2. Compare and contrast two characters in the work.
3. Is there any humor in the work? If so, how does the author achieve humorous effects?
4. How do the characters change from the beginning to the end of the work? What, if anything, do they learn?
5. What other works like this one have you read? How is this work similar? How is it different?
6. How does the dialogue in the work help reveal the characters?
7. Choose one key incident from the work and use it to explain the larger meaning of the work.

ACTIVITIES FOR DIFFERENT ABILITIES
Basic Students
ACTIVITY 1 Descriptive Essays
To help students think of specific details, have them answer the following questions:
Objects
1. What are the dimensions of the object (length, breadth, height)?
2. What shape is the object?
3. What colors are in the object?
4. What textures does the object have?
5. To what can the object be compared?

Places
1. When you are in this place, what do you see when you look around you?
2. What colors catch your eye?
3. What sounds do you hear in this place?
4. What specific things or people help make this place come alive?
5. What smells or feelings do you associate with this place?

People
1. Describe the facial features of your subject.
2. Describe your subject's hair.
3. Describe your subject's build.
4. Does your subject have some unique manner of walking or talking?
5. How does your subject dress?

ACTIVITY 2 Persuasive Essays
The essays on Bigfoot (pages 491-496) provide sufficient information for students to use in expressing their own position on the issue. Have them write a short essay in which they argue for or against the existence of Sasquatch, based on the evidence in these two essays.

ACTIVITY 3 Literary Essays
You may wish to have the entire class write on the same literary work. As part of the prewriting work, engage the class in a discussion of the work, raising the questions on page 505. After the first drafts are written, duplicate three or four of them and distribute them to the class to show a range of viewpoints about the work's meaning. Then give all students a chance to revise their essays based on any new insights they gained from seeing other students' ideas.

Advanced Students
ACTIVITY 1 Persuasive Essays
Encourage students to carry out research to gather support for their opinions. Use the model essays on Bigfoot to show how sources can be worked into a composition even without formal citations.

ACTIVITY 2 Literary Essays
Although students should base their writing on their own responses to the literary work they have chosen, you may suggest that they use the library to find criticism of their chosen work. They can then agree or disagree with a critic's interpretation, always backing up their views with specific details from the work itself.

Other Kinds of Essays

ADDITIONAL PRACTICE
Teacher's Resource Book:
pages 223–234
Workbook: pages 175–178

REVIEW EXERCISES AND TESTS
Student Text
  Chapter Review: page 509
Teacher's Resource Book
  Chapter 21 Test: pages 51–52
  (Also available as spirit duplicating masters.)

ADDITIONAL ANSWERS

EXERCISE 1 Recognizing Descriptive Details *(pages 487–488)*

1. "burdened with cameras, binoculars, and tape recorders"
2. bobbing corks
3. Accept any three: sights—porpoises circling, humans bobbing like corks, pale green haze of the surface layers; sound—clicks of the porpoises' sonic emissions.
4. Accept any three: shifts in underwater topography, movement of sand bars, coral buildup, wrecked ship.
5. orange
6. in an orderly line
7. voices of the dolphins, and crashes and splashes as the dolphins leap
8. ink-black
9. snow
10. perfume on a spring day

EXERCISE 5 Analyzing a Persuasive Essay *(pages 494–496)*

1. Most of the so-called evidence that these creatures exist has some flaw that seriously weakens its reliability.
2. It explains why people might be inclined to believe any evidence, however questionable, that Bigfoot exists.
3. The uncertainty of the shooting speed of Patterson's film is too serious a flaw to be overlooked.
4. Because it shows that some filmed evidence *is* fake, it makes the reader question the reliability of Patterson's film. However, the author does not say Patterson's film is fake.
5. Probably. If he hadn't written the book, his motives could not be suspected.
6. tracks enlarged by melting of snow; bear tracks that are actually two footprints rather than one giant footprint; hoaxes
7. Just because the sounds are unknown it does not follow that the sounds were made by Sasquatch.
8. The fact that a one-time believer has given up indicates that there must not be any creatures to find.
9. No. In the last paragraph, the author says that there is not firm evidence that Bigfoot does not exist.
10. Answers will vary.

EXERCISE 6 Listing Pros and Cons *(pages 498–499)*

Sample answer for item 1:

1. *Pros:* A moon colony could be a launching point for space exploration; it could help us monitor Earth's weather; it would establish U.S. presence there. *Cons:* It would have little direct benefit to people on Earth; colonization should be an international effort; future plans in space need to be thought about more carefully.

Other Kinds of Essays

EXERCISE 7 Organizing Persuasive Ideas *(page 499)*

Sample answer:

Thesis statement: While colonizing the moon may be possible in the future, at the present time it would not be a wise step for the United States to take by itself.

I. Colonization in space should be an international effort.
   A. Benefits of sharing space technology
   B. Peace more likely with international cooperation
II. It would have little direct benefit to people on Earth.
   A. Enormous financial burden
   B. Resources diverted from more important projects
III. Future plans in space need to be thought about more carefully.
   A. Not enough knowledge about conditions on the moon
   B. Concerns about safety of colonists

EXERCISE 9 Detecting Bias *(page 500)*

Sample answer:

Any factory owner wants to produce products at the lowest possible cost. For this reason a factory owner would tend to be biased in favor of money-saving strategies, such as the use of robots as expressed in View 1. This bias might tend to overlook important factors that do not relate to cost cutting. Workers, on the other hand, are obviously interested in keeping their jobs. A worker such as the one whose ideas are expressed in View 2 might tend to be prejudiced against cost-cutting measures, however practical, if they mean a reduction in the number of employees.

EXERCISE 10 Analyzing a Critical Essay *(page 504)*

1. the mention of Santiago's physical hardship and loss of most of the fish
2. despite, however
3. his going 84 days without catching a fish, Manolin's being forbidden to fish with him, his distance from shore, the depths of his baits, his catching a giant fish
4. Sample answer: Unlike the ordinary people, Santiago is willing to go as far as it takes to reach for greatness.
5. The people realize that the victorious struggle with the fish was more important than the loss of the fish to sharks.
6. affirms, victorious struggle, greatness
7. also
8. The essayist parallels the relationship between ball players and their fathers with that of Manolin and Santiago.
9. Although the loss of the great fish to the scavenging sharks is tragic, the old man's endurance in his struggle and triumph in the capture override the tragedy.
10. Joe DiMaggio

EXERCISE 11 Developing Supporting Details *(pages 506–507)*

1. positive
2. Sample answer: friendly, informal language; image of clear water; image of the calf with mother
3. farming
4. references to cleaning the pasture and fetching the little calf
5. looking forward to them
6. Sample answer: He decides he might stay long enough for the enjoyment of watching the water clear; he wants to share the experience—"You come too."
7. informal

Chapter 21 d

Other Kinds of Essays

8. Sample answer: The language is simple; the sentence in parentheses is an afterthought.
9. The narrator of the poem seems to be addressing some specific person he knows and likes, but the poet also seems to be asking the reader to come along.
10. Sample answer: The speaker seems to take joy in the sights around him. He wants to share them with someone else.

CHAPTER REVIEW *(page 509)*

You may wish to use the following evaluation forms.

Evaluation Form for Descriptive Essays

	POINT VALUE	STUDENT SCORE
1. suitably limited subject	10	____
2. strong thesis statement (suggests an overall impression of the subject)	10	____
3. supporting paragraphs with sensory details	10	____
4. logical organization	10	____
5. title	10	____
6. unity and coherence	10	____
7. transitions	10	____
8. strong concluding paragraph	10	____
9. essay revised	10	____
10. essay edited	10	____
	Total Score	____

Evaluation Form for Persuasive Essays

	POINT VALUE	STUDENT SCORE
1. title and suitably limited subject	10	____
2. strong thesis statement (states opinion)	10	____
3. supporting paragraphs using facts, examples, incidents, and reasons	10	____
4. logical order	10	____
5. opposition's good points conceded	10	____
6. unity and coherence	10	____
7. transitions	10	____
8. strong concluding paragraph	10	____
9. essay revised	10	____
10. essay edited	10	____
	Total Score	____

Evaluation Form for Literary Essays

	POINT VALUE	STUDENT SCORE
1. title identifying focus of essay	10	_____
2. introduction identifying author and work	10	_____
3. thesis statement expressing interpretation	10	_____
4. interpretation developed with specifics from the work	10	_____
5. logical order	10	_____
6. unity and coherence	10	_____
7. transitions	10	_____
8. strong concluding paragraph	10	_____
9. essay revised	10	_____
10. essay edited	10	_____
	Total Score	_____

21

Other Kinds of Essays

For additional practice for this chapter, see the Teacher's Resource Book and the Workbook.

Reading an essay is like opening a door to a new world. Beyond that door might be a scene or a person so vividly described that it will long remain in your memory. An essay may also invite you into a world of ideas and opinions—fresh, carefully reasoned arguments that make you stop and think. An essay on a literary subject—a poem, short story, or novel—may open new doors of understanding and appreciation.

When you write essays, then, you extend an invitation to readers to enter your world and see things as you see them. Whether you are describing, persuading, or analyzing a work of literature, your goal is to open new doors of thought—for yourself and for your readers.

DESCRIPTIVE ESSAYS

The purpose of a descriptive essay is to re-create for your reader a memorable scene, object, or person. The essay's central idea is the writer's one main impression of the subject. This overall impression is brought to life by vivid, descriptive details.

21a A **descriptive essay** paints a vivid picture that expresses one main impression of a person, an object, or a scene.

Descriptive Essays

21a–b

Essay Structure

A typical descriptive essay has an introduction that includes the thesis statement, a body of supporting paragraphs that provides vivid details, and a conclusion that reinforces the overall impression of the subject. The introduction and conclusion are usually more general than the body. The following chart summarizes the structure of a descriptive essay.

21b

> **Structure of a Descriptive Essay**
>
> 1. The **introduction** captures the reader's attention and contains the **thesis statement**. The thesis statement expresses one main impression of the subject.
> 2. The **body of supporting paragraphs** brings the picture to life by using specific details and words that appeal to the senses.
> 3. The **conclusion** reinforces the overall impression by summarizing the specific details or by making a vivid comparison.

The main parts of the following descriptive essay are labeled for you. As you read it, look for the specific details that bring the scene to life.

Watching the Dolphins

INTRODUCTION

THESIS STATEMENT

We stand in the hot sun, burdened with cameras, binoculars, and tape recorders, watching the dolphins. Their play is joyous and unrestrained, like everything else they do. Their life absorbs us. We feel alert and expectant ourselves as their energy rises to meet us. We are studying the dolphins, but we wish to join them.

FIRST BODY PARAGRAPH

Late in the afternoon, we go in with them. Entering their world, we begin to understand it through our experience. Our weight lifts from us; we become more playful—weaving, dipping, bobbing like corks in the calm swells. The visibility is good; we see each other and the porpoises circling around us in the pale green

485

Other Kinds of Essays

haze of the surface layers. Time slows beneath the surface and is measured by our breathing. As we relax in the water, accept it, the porpoises come closer. We hear the fine sonic wash of their emissions clicking over our skin.

SECOND BODY PARAGRAPH The porpoises play most of the afternoon. Sometimes the play is unrestrained and vigorous, sometimes specific and ritualized. The bay, the home of the school of porpoises for the last five centuries, is reexplored daily. Minor shifts in underwater topography, the subtle movements of sand bars, the buildup of corals are investigated and probed. Shifting currents and floating sands have uncovered part of an old wrecked ship. Several young adult porpoises dive down through the dark water to investigate. Tuning their sonar, they make out the outlines of the rusting metal. With high-pitched whistles, they communicate this new find on the bottom to friends on the surface.

THIRD BODY PARAGRAPH The sun grows fat and misshapen as it reaches the horizon, spreading its orange light on the darkening water. First one, then another small group detach from the playing school and move out toward the open sea. They return and others move toward the fishing grounds in an effort to get the others to follow. For no reason apparent to us, the entire school decides it's time to leave. As if in answer to a signal, they leave the bay in a broad, orderly line and head out to sea.

FOURTH BODY PARAGRAPH We watch the school fishing in the orange-cast light of the rising moon. They are working out from an undersea shelf line, spread along a broad front, echolocating, keeping in voice contact as they sweep the depths. The porpoises move at high speed, leaping out of the water and crashing back into it, the sound of their splashing a signal of location and distance. . . . In the moonlight the broad, leaping, diving front of porpoises is an image out of a dream, as if the spirit of the sea itself is seeking its reflection. They time their leaps and dives so that the school is synchronized along a broad front, combining its collective information in order to find the fish. Suddenly the pattern breaks and the porpoises converge, almost instantaneously, at a single spot. They have found a school of fish and as the pattern breaks, mothers, infants, adults, yearlings dive into the ink-black water, echolocating, turning, twisting, catching the seething mass of fishes that whips the water, making the foam like snow in the darkness.

CONCLUSION
I have stroked and swum with and looked at these creatures, and felt their essence rise to meet me like perfume on a spring day. Touched by it, I felt gentler myself, more open to the possibilities that existed around me. There may be only one way to begin to learn from them — and that is to begin. We would not be harmed by returning to the roots that once nourished us, which still, unseen, link together all life that lives and feels and thinks and dies on this, our common planet.

— JOAN MCINTYRE, *MIND IN THE WATERS* (ADAPTED)

EXERCISE 1 Recognizing Descriptive Details

Reread the preceding essay and write short answers to the following questions. *Answers precede this chapter.*

1. What details in the introduction suggest that the watchers are weighed down?
2. To what are the watchers compared in the first body paragraph when they first enter the water?
3. Name three details that appeal to the senses in the first body paragraph.
4. Name three underwater sights that the dolphins explore in the second body paragraph.
5. What color dominates the scene in the third and fourth body paragraphs?
6. In what kind of pattern do the dolphins leave the bay?

Other Kinds of Essays

7. What sounds do you hear when you are reading the fourth body paragraph?
8. What color is the water into which the feeding dolphins dive?
9. To what is the sea-foam compared in the fourth body paragraph?
10. In the conclusion, to what is the essence (essential nature) of the porpoises compared?

Selecting and Organizing Descriptive Details

Since your goal in writing description is to create one main impression, the details you choose should all contribute to that impression. The dolphin watchers in the essay on pages 485–487, for example, may have been sunburned from their morning observations. Such a detail, however, would not contribute to the overall feeling of joyousness at the nearness of the dolphins. To help you select details that will support the overall impression expressed in your thesis statement, use the following brainstorming questions.

21c

> **Questions for Selecting Descriptive Details**
>
> 1. What sights and sounds contribute to the overall impression of your subject?
> 2. What smells, tastes, or textures contribute to the overall impression?
> 3. What comparisons (similes and metaphors) would help a reader understand the overall impression? *(See page 368.)*

When you have listed between 10 and 15 supporting details that contribute to the main impression of your subject, you are ready for the next step in writing a descriptive essay. That step is to arrange your details in logical order. Many descriptions use spatial, or location, order. Details arranged in spatial order can move from top to bottom (or the reverse), from side to side, inside out (or the reverse), or from near to far (or the reverse). A writer may also present details in the order that

Descriptive Essays

21c–d

they strike him or her. Using this special type of spatial order requires using carefully chosen transitions to make your organization clear.

> **21d** Spatial order arranges details according to their location, using transitions to lead the reader's eye from point to point.

Descriptive details can also be organized chronologically, especially if the subject is a scene at different times of the day. The essay on dolphins uses *chronological order* as it records the dolphins' activities from late afternoon to early evening. *Order of importance* and *developmental order* are also suitable for description. *(See pages 426–427.)* In all types of order, transitional words and phrases make the relationship of the details clear to the reader. *(See pages 416, 422, and 463 for lists of transitions.)*

EXERCISE 2 Selecting Descriptive Details
Copy the following thesis statements. After each one, use your imagination to list one sight, one sound, one smell, and one feeling or texture that could contribute to the overall impression suggested in the thesis statement.
Sample answer for item 1 appears below.

1. The costume party was like a scene out of a science-fiction movie.
2. The lawyer held the jury spellbound as he used his entire body to add to the dramatic effect of his closing statement.
3. At midnight the railroad station was a study in loneliness.
4. The 1962 Mustang convertible glistened with the pride of its owner.
5. After visiting the aquarium, I felt as if I had taken an underwater voyage through the murky and mysterious deep.
6. The construction site was buzzing with activity.
7. The art museum is a sanctuary of peace.
8. Whenever I'm stuck in rush-hour traffic, I feel as if four walls are closing in around me.
9. Stargazing on a summer night is a fascinating experience.
10. The crowd at the football stadium was tense in anticipation of a victory.

1. sight — E.T. costume   smell — pizza
   sound — laughter   texture — metallic cloth from costume

Other Kinds of Essays

EXERCISE 3 Organizing Descriptive Details
The following details describe a robot called the Mobot Mark IV. They are not in any order. Use the details to complete the outline that follows them. Assign each detail a capital letter and place it in a logical position in the outline.

I–A • robot slightly resembles a human from the waist up
I–B • torso is a plain metal box containing the computer hardware
II–A • arms extend from the shoulders as on humans
III–A • television eyes look like a capless can of floor wax lying on its side
II–B • arms are flexible tubing with elbow joint
III–B • television eyes mounted on a swiveling base that connects to beams rising from the shoulders
II–C • hands are padded metal with the ability to grip
III–C • above eyes are shiny disks that look like the lights doctors wear on their heads
I–C • torso is mounted on wheels for mobility

    I. Torso
   II. Arms
  III. Eyes

EXERCISE 4 On Your Own
For practice in developing the skill of description, use your imagination to design your own robot of the future. Make a list of descriptive details that would help your reader picture just what you see. Then organize your notes into an outline and save your work for use in the Chapter Review. *(See pages 462–466 for help with outlining.)*
Answers will vary.

PERSUASIVE ESSAYS

An essay of opinion, or persuasive essay, usually serves one of two general purposes. The purpose may be to win the reader over to the writer's way of thinking, or it may be to persuade the reader to take action—to write to a senator, to vote a certain way, to boycott or buy a certain product.

Persuasive Essays

21e A **persuasive essay** states an opinion on a subject and uses facts, examples, and reasons to convince readers.

The subjects of persuasive essays can range widely, from issues and concerns of personal and community life to the great debates of philosophy. Whatever their subjects, good persuasive essays stimulate thought and shed new light on difficult issues.

Essay Structure

The chart that follows shows the function of each main part of a persuasive essay. In addition to following the guidelines in the chart, a persuasive essay should be free of fallacies. *(See Chapter 18.)*

21f

Structure of a Persuasive Essay

1. The **introduction** presents the issue and contains the thesis statement, which expresses the author's opinion on the issue.
2. The **body of supporting paragraphs** presents reasons, facts, statistics, incidents, and examples that support the author's opinion.
3. The **conclusion** provides a strong summary or closing that drives home the author's opinion.

As you read the following persuasive essay, notice how each element serves its persuasive purpose.

Bigfoot: The Evidence Mounts

INTRODUCTION: PROVIDES BACKGROUND INFORMATION ON ISSUE

For centuries before white settlers came to the area, Indians in what is now Washington, Oregon, and northern California sighted—time after time—a 7-to-8-foot-tall humanlike creature covered with hair. It had broad shoulders and 3-foot-long arms and walked on two legs. The Indians named this creature Sasquatch, but it is now known to us mainly as

Other Kinds of Essays

THESIS STATEMENT: STATES AUTHOR'S OPINION

Bigfoot. Since 1811, others have also testified to seeing a creature of the same general description. For many years scientists were doubtful that such a creature existed. Now, however, the evidence seems both reliable and abundant that gorillalike creatures do exist in the forested mountains of our Northwestern states.

FIRST BODY PARAGRAPH: PROVIDES EVIDENCE TO CONTRADICT SKEPTICS' POINT

Skeptics argue that the widespread publicity surrounding Bigfoot feeds the public's imagination and leads to unreliable sightings that are then offered as evidence. This view however, does not explain the sightings recorded before the spread of publicity. As early as 1884, a Canadian newspaper published an account—later confirmed by another source—of an actual capture of one of these mysterious creatures. The creature is believed to have died in transit. Altogether, researchers have accumulated reports of 1,000 sightings. They also have many reports, photographs, and plaster casts of footprints measuring up to 18 inches long and 8 inches wide. Traces of hair that cannot be identified as belonging to any known animal have also been collected. Although some sightings and reports of tracks have been hoaxes, some of them seem to be genuine, and their details correspond convincingly. Three fairly recent "proofs" of the existence of Bigfoot stand out from the others.

SECOND BODY PARAGRAPH: PRESENTS ONE SPECIFIC EXAMPLE OF A SIGHTING

On June 6, 1978, two engineers were in the northern Cascades in Washington surveying land at an altitude of 4,000 feet above sea level. Suddenly they both saw a large creature totally covered with brown hair walking on two legs toward a dense timbered area. Skeptics until then, these two men are now certain that they saw a Sasquatch. Since these men were just out doing their jobs rather than actively searching for proof that Bigfoot does exist, their story is believable.

492

Persuasive Essays

THIRD BODY PARAGRAPH: PRESENTS ONE SPECIFIC EXAMPLE OF A TAPE RECORDING

Six years earlier, another piece of evidence was carefully examined and found to be genuine. This was a tape recording of a voice presumed to belong to a Bigfoot. It was made by journalist Alan Berry in the High Sierras of northern California. Experts who studied the tape agreed that it had not been tampered with in any way. They also agreed that the range of the sounds, despite their humanlike quality, could have been produced only by a creature with a vocal tract larger than that of a human.

FOURTH BODY PARAGRAPH: PRESENTS MOST CONVINCING EVIDENCE—FILM

Perhaps the most persuasive evidence is a film of a Bigfoot taken in the Bluff Creek Valley of northern California in October of 1967. Roger Patterson and his partner Bob Gimlin were searching for a creature in an area of frequent track sightings. When they did finally see one, they were taken by surprise, but Patterson began to roll his movie camera and got 20 feet of color film. Gimlin, meanwhile, tried to subdue the horses who were presumably scared by the creature's strong odor. The film shows a female creature covered with hair and walking on two legs. Patterson and Gimlin were also able to get one plaster cast of a footprint from this animal. Patterson's film has been shown widely—to scientists, to special-effects experts, and to skeptics—and no one has yet been able to find anything in it to suggest a hoax.

ADMITS AN AREA OF CONTROVERSY REGARDING FILM

The one area of dispute regarding the film is the speed at which it was shot. Patterson cannot remember whether he shot it at 16 frames per second (fps) or 24 fps. If it was shot at 16 fps, the creature simply could not have been a disguised human, for no human could walk the way it does. If it was shot at 24 fps, the picture could have been a human posing as a Bigfoot. However, the special-effects experts believe that such an acting job would be virtually impossible to perform so convincingly.

REFERS TO EXPERTS FOR SUPPORT

Other Kinds of Essays

CONCLUSION: CITES REPUTABLE EXPERTS WHO AGREE WITH AUTHOR'S OPINION

These recent findings, along with a half-mile trail of 1,089 tracks in Bossburg, Washington, which show one crippled foot, are leading highly respected scientists to admit that an apelike creature might exist in North America. Even the skeptic John Napier, curator of the primate collection at the Smithsonian Institution, admitted the Bossburg tracks "could conceivably be the footprints of an unknown member of the human family." Respected journals are now accepting articles about Bigfoot, and reputable universities and organizations, including the National Wildlife Federation, are providing funding for research. The Army Corps of Engineers now lists these creatures in its official *Washington Environmental Atlas*, although it adds that their existence is still "hotly disputed." Skeptics no doubt will continue to disregard the sightings and other evidence until this elusive creature is actually captured and held up for display to the scientific community.

FINAL SENTENCE RESTATES AUTHOR'S OPINION

Many who wish to save the creature this trouble, however, are convinced right now that harmless, gorillalike animals share nature's bounty with us right here in the United States.

EXERCISE 5 Analyzing a Persuasive Essay

The essay that follows takes another view of the evidence about Bigfoot. Read it carefully and answer the questions that follow it. The paragraphs are numbered for easy reference.

Bigfoot Evidence Inconclusive

(1) The search for Bigfoot or Sasquatch is at best well-intentioned and at worst a sign of the lengths people will go to attract tourists and sell newspapers and books. Most of the so-called evidence that these creatures exist has some flaw that seriously weakens its reliability.

(2) The most controversial piece of "evidence" is the Patterson film, showing what appears to be a female Sasquatch walking upright as it heads for cover. Patterson was out specifically to capture proof of the existence of this creature.

With such a single-minded purpose, he would have been studiously prepared, one would assume, to present proof that would be unquestionable once obtained. His confusion over the speed at which the film was shot throws a shadow over the film's reliability. If the film was shot at 24 frames per second, the walking pattern of the creature would be indistinguishable from that of a human. Although it is true that experts have found no fakery in the movie—as they did in a later film in which stitching could be seen at the joints of the "animal"—the uncertainty of the shooting speed is too large a flaw to be overlooked.

(3) Another factor that makes Patterson's film suspicious is the possible profit motive. Patterson had written what anthropologist Myra Shackley calls a "flamboyant journalistic paperback" titled *Do Abominable Snowmen of America Really Exist?* Reports of an acutal photograph of the creature would only help the sales of Patterson's book. Because he could stand to gain so much from sudden publicity, his motives have been questioned as seriously as the film itself.

(4) Other often-cited pieces of evidence are footprints. One noted scientist explains that the sun can melt animal tracks and that they appear larger than they really are when they melt. Another plausible explanation is that bears sometimes step over their forefoot track with a hind foot, making the track seem very large. The club-footed print found in Washington, while striking indeed, could have been an exceedingly clever hoax.

(5) Alan Berry's tape recording reveals no major flaw, except that experts who have tried to determine the creature's height from its vocalizations cannot arrive at a consistent answer. They conclude, then, that several creatures of different sizes are recorded on that tape. That is one interpretation. Another is that the sounds, although originating from unknown sources, are not necessarily those of Sasquatch.

(6) Even Peter Byrne, who ran the Bigfoot Information Center in The Dalles, Oregon, decided to stop his search for these creatures in 1980 when he had not succeeded in proving their existence. The inquiring mind should be open to convincing evidence; and, at least for now, there is no compelling evidence to show without a doubt that the creatures do *not* exist. At the same time, no evidence is sufficiently flawless to prove that an unclassified creature *does* exist. Future researchers, if they wish to have their findings treated seriously, should take every precaution to keep their motives

Other Kinds of Essays

strictly scientific. If reliable, untainted evidence becomes available, the case for Bigfoot will stand on solid ground. Until then, the scientists should withhold their judgment and tourists should hold on to their money.

Answers precede this chapter.

1. What is the thesis statement of this essay?
2. What bearing does the motive to attract tourists and sell newspapers and magazines have on the controversy surrounding Bigfoot?
3. Summarize the main point of paragraph 2 in one sentence.
4. What effect does the example about the faked movie have on the reader? Does the author come out and say that because one movie was known to be fake, Patterson's movie might also be fake?
5. If Patterson had not written the book described in paragraph 3, would you be more likely to trust his movie? Explain your answer.
6. What three explanations for the footprints are offered in paragraph 4?
7. In paragraph 5 the author shows the non-sequitur reasoning of those who believe the tape recording captures the sounds of Sasquatch. *(See page 495.)* Copy and complete the following sentence to show your understanding of the non sequitur:
   Just because the sounds are unknown, it does not follow that _____.
8. How does the detail about Peter Byrne in the concluding paragraph strengthen the author's argument that Bigfoot does not exist?
9. Does the author of this essay believe that Bigfoot does *not* exist? How do you know?
10. Reread the essay on pages 491–494. Based on what you have read, what is your opinion of the evidence for the existence of Bigfoot? State your views in one paragraph.

Developing and Organizing Strong Arguments

The introduction and conclusion of a persuasive essay often appeal to the reader's emotions. If the tone of the emotional appeal is sincere and reserved, such an approach can strengthen the force of the argument. If, on the other hand, the appeal is inflamed with loaded words and overcharged emotions, the writer may succeed only in sharpening the lines that divide opinions. Of the following two ways of expressing the same idea the second is more persuasive.

EMOTIONAL LANGUAGE The gym in our school is a useless mess; it should be closed down.

REASONABLE LANGUAGE The gym in our school needs new lighting and other improvements that would make it a pleasant place to exercise and compete.

Developing an Argument. The body of a good persuasive essay relies on appeals to reason instead of appeals to feelings. The best tools for building a strong argument are specific facts and examples and logical ideas. The following guidelines will help you build the body of your persuasive essay into a strong, logical argument.

Guidelines for Building an Argument

1. List both pros and cons (and positions in-between) in your prewriting notes and be prepared to address the opposing views point by point.
2. Use facts and examples rather than more opinions, since facts and examples are hard to dispute.
3. If the opposition has a good point, admit it. Then show why it does not change your overall opinion. Such an admission, called *conceding a point*, will strengthen your believability.
4. Use polite and reasonable language rather than words that show bias or overcharged emotions.
5. Refer to well-respected experts and authorities who agree with your opinion.

Organizing an Argument. As you think about how to organize the points in your argument, you may find that you have a choice of several logical arrangements. The two essays about Bigfoot, for example, both use *order of importance*. In the first essay, the pieces of evidence are arranged in order of least to most important. In the second essay, the evidence is presented in order of most to least important. The essays could also have

Other Kinds of Essays

been arranged in *chronological order,* presenting the earliest findings first and proceeding to the most recent findings. *Spatial order,* in which details are arranged according to the location of the evidence, would also have been possible. Order of importance is the most effective in these essays, however, since the writers can make their emphasis clear and show how they have evaluated each piece of evidence.

Whichever method of organization you use, remember to guide your reader through your thoughts with transitions. *(See pages 416, 422, 426, and 463 for lists of transitions.)* The following are transitional words that are especially useful when conceding a point or showing contrasting ideas.

21h

Transitions Showing Contrast or Concession

while it is true that	nonetheless
although	granting that
admittedly	still
nevertheless	despite
on the other hand	of course
however	instead

EXERCISE 6 Listing Pros and Cons

Copy each of the following thesis statements on your paper. Under each one, list three facts, examples, reasons, or incidents that support the thesis statement (pros) and three that disprove it (cons). Save your work for Exercise 7.

Sample answer for item 1 precedes this chapter.

1. The United States should colonize the moon as soon as possible.
2. A sense of humor is the most valuable trait a person can have.
3. When a movie wins an Academy Award, it does not necessarily mean the movie is of a high quality.
4. Radios should not be allowed at beaches.
5. Drivers who commit two moving violations within one year should have their licenses revoked for two years.
6. Even though they may contain fossil fuels, our wilderness areas should be completely preserved.
7. Every American citizen should learn to speak a second language.

8. Every student should be required to take a course in computer programming.
9. Even if the prices might be higher in some cases, Americans should buy American-made goods.
10. The only road to success is hard work.

EXERCISE 7 Organizing Persuasive Ideas
Choose one subject from Exercise 6 and decide which side of the issue you are going to support. Then complete the following assignment.   *Sample answer precedes this chapter.*

1. Write a thesis statement expressing your view about the subject. (Or, if you agree with the thesis statement given in the text, copy it.)
2. List the three ideas that support your position in the order of least to most important, leaving three blank lines after each one.
3. Assign each of your three points a Roman numeral as in an outline.
4. Add at least two supporting points under each of the Roman numerals to complete the outline in the following form.

   I. (Your least important point)
     A. (First supporting point)
     B. (Second supporting point)
  II. (Your more important point)
     A.
     B.
III. (Your most important point)
     A.
     B.

EXERCISE 8 On Your Own
One way to find ideas for persuasive essays is to skim the *Readers' Guide to Periodical Literature*. Often the titles of the magazine articles listed in the guide will suggest subjects about which there is debate or controversy. Use the *Readers' Guide* to find at least three good subjects for a persuasive essay. Then write a possible thesis statement for each one. Save your work for the Chapter Review.

Answers will vary.

Other Kinds of Essays

Writing Extra

As you look for expert opinions to help you back up a thesis statement, make sure you take into account the possibility of bias. *Bias* is a leaning toward one side of an issue based more on personal feelings or interests than on objective evidence. Bias is not necessarily a fault, and few experts are without it completely. Being able to recognize it, however, is an important skill. It will help you "consider the source" of an argument and respond accordingly.

EXERCISE 9   Detecting Bias

Following are two views on the use of robots in industry. Write a paragraph explaining the possible bias in each of the views. *Sample answer precedes this chapter.*

View 1: Factory owner

Robots should be used whenever possible in assembly-line work. They can do some jobs five times faster than humans. If you average out their cost over the number of working hours you can get from them, their "pay" is about one-third of the average pay of human workers. In the long run, the efficiency of robots will create a healthier economy and thus more jobs.

View 2: Factory worker

Robots should not be allowed to take jobs away from human workers. Although the development and use of robots might create jobs for engineers who design and build them, the workers displaced by robots are still without jobs. Even though robots may cost less in the long run than human workers, they will never be able to come up with new ideas to improve a product's quality.

LITERARY ESSAYS

There are two main types of essays about literature. The simpler type is the book review, in which the writer briefly summarizes the contents of a book and offers an overall opinion of the book. The second type is the critical essay, in which the writer analyzes and interprets a work of literature. To *interpret* a literary work means to state and explain your personal understanding of the author's meaning. The following pages in this chapter will help you learn the skills of writing a critical essay.

> **21i** A **critical essay** offers an intepretation of a work of literature and uses persuasive techniques to convince readers that the interpretation is sound.

Essay Structure

Like other essays the critical essay has an introduction, a body of supporting paragraphs, and a conclusion. The following chart summarizes the function of each part of a critical essay.

21j

> **Structure of a Critical Essay**
>
> 1. The **title** identifies which aspect of the work the essayist will focus on.
> 2. The **introduction** identifies the author and the work being analyzed. It contains a **thesis statement**, which expresses the essayist's interpretation.
> 3. The **body of supporting paragraphs** offers details from the work to back up the interpretation expressed in the thesis statement. In fiction these details include events, narration, and dialogue. In poetry they include figures of speech, rhythms, and sound in addition to events and literal meanings.
> 4. The **conclusion** summarizes, clarifies, or adds an insight to the interpretation.

Writers of critical essays usually assume that their readers have already read the work being analyzed. A strict summary of a book would therefore not be appropriate in a critical essay. The main purpose of the supporting details is to explain the essayist's interpretation, not to summarize or retell the story or poem. The following guidelines include three other special requirements that a critical essay writer should meet.

Other Kinds of Essays

21k

Special Features of Critical Essays

1. Assume that your readers have read the work you are analyzing.
2. Use the present tense to discuss the literary work.
3. Use third-person point of view. Avoid using *I* to make your interpretative points.
4. Cite the sources of quotations. If all your quotations are from a single source, give the page of the quotation in parentheses directly following the quotation. *(See the model essay on pages 502–504.)* If your quotations are from two or more sources, fully cite the source of each quotation with footnotes, endnotes, or parenthetical citations. *(See pages 554–558.)*

As you read the following critical essay on *The Old Man and the Sea*, notice the three main parts in the essay structure and the special features.

TITLE: IDENTIFIES FOCUS

INTRODUCTION: AUTHOR AND TITLE IDENTIFIED

THESIS STATEMENT

FIRST BODY PARAGRAPH: USES SPECIFIC DETAILS FROM THE BOOK TO INTERPRET THE OLD MAN'S SEPARATENESS

Hope in *The Old Man and the Sea*

In Ernest Hemingway's novel *The Old Man and the Sea*, the main character, Santiago, endures severe physical hardships in his fight with the great marlin. He also suffers a painful loss when sharks eat most of the great fish on the long journey back to shore. Despite the suffering and loss, however, the novel is affirmative and hopeful, stressing the power of humans to reach for greatness and to inspire greatness in others.

From the beginning, Santiago is set apart from the other fishermen. While the others have had good catches, the old man has gone without catching a fish for 84 days. The sail on his skiff "looked like the flag of permanent defeat" (p. 1). Manolin, the boy who brings him coffee, has been forbidden by his parents to fish any longer with the unlucky old man. Once out at sea, the old man's separation grows even

Literary Essays

greater. While the other boats hug the shore, Santiago goes out far. While the other fishermen let their baits drift with the current, Santiago's go straight down and deep. Straining himself to fish at greater depths and farther distances than the others, Santiago catches the biggest fish he has ever seen. Born to be a fisherman, the old man pushes himself to become a *great* fisherman. His adversary, the fish, was born to avoid capture, and it too makes a noble effort to fulfill its destiny.

SECOND BODY PARAGRAPH: INTERPRETS THE OLD MAN'S WILLINGNESS TO GO OUT SO FAR

Reaching for greatness, although rewarded by the capture of the marlin, comes with a price. If the old man had not been willing to go out so far, he would not have been able to catch the fish. Because he goes out so far, however, he cannot expect to avoid the shark attack. All he can do is fight it. Long before it happens, he anticipates it. In his simple way, Santiago understands that the circumstances that allow for greatness carry within them the risk of loss. Even the bare skeleton of the fish, however, inspires awe in all who observe it. Their awe affirms that the victorious struggle, not the tragic consequences that may follow, is the real measure of greatness.

THIRD BODY PARAGRAPH: OFFERS DETAILS OF CONVERSATION THAT REVEAL THE THEME OF CONTINUITY

Affirmation and hope is also the theme of the old man's relationship with Manolin. Early in the book, Santiago and Manolin talk of greatness in baseball—in Joe DiMaggio and Dick Sisler. They also talk of the fathers of these great players, implying a continuity of greatness from one generation to another. At the end of the book, Manolin decides to fish with Santiago once again, saying, "You must get well fast, for there is much that I can learn, and you can teach me everything" (pp. 138–139). The old man has had his moment; he has strained and captured greatness. Now, after learning from his elder, Manolin will carry on.

Other Kinds of Essays

CONCLUSION: RESTATES THESIS AND ADDS ANOTHER STRONG PIECE OF EVIDENCE

Although the loss of the great fish to the scavenging sharks is tragic, the old man's endurance in his struggle and triumph in the capture override the tragedy. Before the fateful 85th day, Manolin tells Santiago that the Yankees lost a game. "That means nothing," the old man replies. "The great DiMaggio is himself again." So it is with Santiago: He lost the game but pushed himself until he became all that he was able to be. With Manolin to carry on, the old man is ultimately undefeated.

EXERCISE 10 Analyzing a Critical Essay

Reread the preceding essay and write answers to the following questions. *Answers precede this chapter.*

1. What details in the introduction of the essay suggest that other interpretations of the book's meaning could be offered?
2. What transitions are used in the thesis statement?
3. What five details in the first body paragraph are used to show Santiago's separation from other people?
4. Using your own words, write a sentence explaining how the essayist interprets Santiago's separation.
5. How does the essayist explain the reaction of people who see the bare skeleton?
6. What words in the last sentence of the second body paragraph refer to key ideas in the thesis statement?
7. What is the transition in the first sentence of the third body paragraph?
8. What parallel does the essayist draw in the third body paragraph?
9. What sentence in the conclusion of this essay restates the thesis statement?
10. To whom is Santiago compared in the conclusion?

Developing and Organizing a Critical Essay

The most important guide in interpreting a work of literature is your own response to what you read. For example, although *The Old Man and the Sea* contains pain and sadness,

Literary Essays

21l–m

the writer of the model essay felt the final message of the novel was one of hope. Your job as a critical essayist is to find those details in a work of literature that support your interpretation of the work's meaning. Then you must arrange the details in a logical order.

Once you have identified your response to a work of literature, you can begin retracing your steps and searching for the specifics that molded your response. The questions that follow will help you pinpoint the specifics in fiction and poetry that add up to an overall interpretation.

21l Questions for Analyzing Fiction (Novels and Short Stories)

1. Who are the main characters? What in their actions and speech makes me admire or dislike them? What are their strengths and weaknesses?
2. What is the conflict in the story? How does the main character come out of the conflict?
3. How does the setting contribute to or reflect the characters' problems?
4. From what point of view is the story told? *(See page 418.)* How does the point of view affect my response to the work?
5. Are there any recurring words and ideas that contribute to an overall theme?
6. Taking the characters, plot, setting, theme, and point of view all together, what do I think the author is saying about humans and life?

21m Questions for Analyzing Poetry

1. What is the literal meaning of the poem?
2. What imagery and figures of speech are used in the poem? How do they affect the feeling created by the poem?
3. What rhythms and rhyme scheme are used in the poem? How do they affect the feeling created by the poem?
4. What is the total effect of the language and the poetic devices used in the poem? What meaning does the poem have for me?

Other Kinds of Essays

In a short essay, you cannot cover all the elements that contribute to a literary work's overall effect. Instead you must limit your subject to one or two aspects of the work that interest you the most. You may choose to focus only on theme, for example, or you may develop an interpretation of one main character, explaining why he or she behaves in a certain way. Once you have narrowed your subject, you can begin to gather together the details you need to persuade readers that your interpretation is sound.

The most common ways to organize critical essays are *order of importance* and *developmental order*. In each, transitions help the reader follow the logic of the interpretation. A literary essay may also be organized according to the location of details in the work. You may, for example, analyze details in the order of their appearance in the work, from beginning to middle to end. This form of organization is a variant of *chronological order*. (See page 463.)

EXERCISE 11 **Developing Supporting Details**

Read the following poem and answer the questions that follow it. Save your work for Exercise 13.

The Pasture

I'm going out to clean the pasture spring;
I'll only stop to rake the leaves away
(And wait to watch the water clear, I may)
I shan't be gone long.— You come too.

I'm going out to fetch the little calf
That's standing by the mother. Its so young
It totters when she licks it with her tongue.
I shan't be gone long.— You come too.

—ROBERT FROST

Answers precede this chapter.

1. What kind of feeling does this poem leave you with, positive or negative?
2. List three details that contribute to the overall feeling you identified in number 1.
3. How does the speaker in this poem make a living?
4. List two details that support your answer to number 3.
5. Does the speaker seem to be looking forward to the chores or dreading them?

6. List two details in the poem that support your answer to number 5.
7. How would you describe the tone of this poem, formal or informal?
8. List two details that support your answer to number 7.
9. To whom is the speaker in this poem extending an invitation to come along?
10. Why, in your opinion, did the poet write this poem? What was his purpose? Write two or three sentences to explain your interpretation.

EXERCISE 12 Analyzing the Organization of a Critical Essay
The following essay was written by a high school student. Read it carefully and answer the questions that follow it. The paragraphs are numbered for easy reference.

NOTE: The writer uses brackets to indicate words she inserted in quotations for clarity. *(See page 297.)*

Phineas's Escape

(1) Although Phineas, in John Knowles's novel *A Separate Peace*, is a self-assured, carefree person on the outside, a closer look reveals that these attributes actually are linked to his escape from reality. Escape may bring to mind a physical act of running or hiding. As Phineas's behavior shows, however, escape can mean refusing to accept an unpleasant fact or idea, refusing to accept reality.

(2) Finny's escape from reality begins at the most ordinary, everyday level. He escapes such small unpleasant realities of life as bad weather: "There was no bad weather in his philosophy" (p. 120). He also evades the rules and regulations at Devon (p. 16).

(3) More important than these are Finny's efforts to escape the harsh realities of war. For Phineas, the war does not exist. His escape route involves a theory, part of his "philosophy" again (p. 120), that the whole war was made up. Confident that there will indeed be a 1944 Olympics, Finny begins Gene's intensive training program. Eventually he draws Gene "increasingly away . . . into a world inhabited by just himself and [Gene], where there [is] no war at all, just Phineas and [Gene] alone among all the people of the world, training for the Olympics of 1944" (p. 119). The real source of

Other Kinds of Essays

Phineas's theory is his leg injury, which prevents him from enlisting. Since he cannot participate in the war, the war does not exist for him.

(4) Most important is Finny's effort to escape the truth about his fall from the tree. He refuses to believe that Gene, his best friend, bounced the limb and caused his crippling fall. When Gene tries to confess, Phineas refuses to listen and tells Gene to "go away" (p. 62). Inside he knows the truth, but by shutting out Gene's confession, he tries to escape its pain.

(5) Although Phineas finally admits the truth about the war, he never accepts the truth about the accident. The other seniors arrange a hearing to expose the guilty party. When Leper appears and begins to tell exactly what he saw, Phineas even then refuses to acknowledge what really happened. He rises and walks away from the congregation, from the truth, from reality, in a last attempt at escape. In an ironic way, he finally succeeds, for as a result he finds a separate peace.

—LYNN HARRIS, STUDENT WRITER

1. Copy the thesis statement of this essay. *underlined on page 508*
2. What method of organization is used in this essay? *order of importance*
3. What transitions highlight the method of organization? *See below.*
4. Which one of the following elements is the focus of this essay: theme, plot, characters, setting? *characters*
5. Use the essay to copy and complete the following outline.
   - I. Escape from small unpleasant realities
     - A. Bad weather
     - B. Rules and regulations at Devon
   - II. Escape from the harsh realities of war
     - A. "Philosophy" that war was made up
     - B. Gene's training
     - C. Leg injury that prevents enlistment
   - III. Escape from truth about accident
     - A. Refusal to believe
     - B. Response to Gene's confession

3. more important, most important

EXERCISE 13   On Your Own

Review your work from Exercise 11. Using your answer to question 1, 5, 7, 9, or 10, write a possible thesis statement for an essay on "The Pasture." Then list as many supporting details as you can find and arrange them in logical order. Save your work for the Chapter Review.
Answers will vary.

CHAPTER REVIEW

Evaluation suggestion precedes this chapter.

A. Write a descriptive essay on one of the following subjects or on one of your own choosing. (You may use your work from Exercise 4.) Use the Steps for Writing Essays on page 510.

1. a pep rally
2. a dark alley
3. a kite contest
4. an auto show
5. the place you work
6. a factory you have seen or visited
7. your childhood hideaway
8. a space station
9. a victory celebration
10. sunrise at the beach or a lake

B. Write a persuasive essay on one of the following subjects or on one of your own choosing. (You may use your work from Exercise 8.) Follow the Steps for Writing Essays on page 510.

1. Should the minimum wage be raised or lowered?
2. Are movies getting better or worse?
3. the role of television in electing a president
4. the role of television in informing people
5. protecting the environment
6. life in outer space
7. clothing: too much concern or too little?
8. movie stars as role models
9. growing up in the computer generation
10. At what age does a young person become an adult?

C. Write a critical essay on one of the following literary works or on one of your own choosing. (You may use your notes from Exercise 13.) Use the Steps for Writing Essays on page 510.

Fiction
Hitchhiker's Guide to the Galaxy by Douglas Adams
Maltese Falcon by Dashiell Hammett
Lost Horizon by James Hilton
The Grapes of Wrath by John Steinbeck
Dr. Jeckyll and Mr. Hyde by Robert Louis Stevenson

Poetry
"Nora" by Gwendolyn Brooks
"First Sight" by Philip Larkin
"Sky Diver" by Adrien Stoutenberg
"Street Window" by Carl Sandburg
"When I Heard the Learn'd Astronomer" by Walt Whitman

Steps for Writing

Essays

Prewriting
1. Find ideas by asking yourself questions and reading for inspiration. *(See page 457.)*
2. From a list of possible subjects, choose one and limit it. *(See pages 458–459.)*
3. Brainstorm a list of supporting ideas. *(See page 460.)*
4. Organize your list of ideas into an outline. *(See pages 462–466.)*

Writing
5. Write a thesis statement. *(See pages 468–469.)*
6. Write an introduction that includes your thesis statement. *(See pages 469–470.)*
7. Use your outline to write the paragraphs in the body. *(See pages 472–473.)*
8. Use transitions and other connecting devices to link your thoughts. *(See pages 472–474.)*
9. Write a concluding paragraph. *(See pages 475–476.)*
10. Add a title. *(See page 476.)*

Revising
11. Does your essay have all of the elements shown in the appropriate checklist on page 511?
12. Does your essay have unity, coherence, and emphasis? *(See pages 477–479.)*
13. Do your sentences have variety? *(See pages 374–381.)*
14. Are your sentences concise and free of faulty constructions? *(See pages 370–373 and 382–388.)*
15. Did you use precise, vivid words? *(See page 364.)*

Editing
16. Check for errors in grammar or usage.
17. Check your spelling, capitalization, and punctuation.
18. Did you use manuscript form? *(See page 611.)*
19. Is your handwriting or typing clear?

Checklists for Revising

Essays

✓ **Descriptive Essays**
1. Does your thesis statement express one main impression of your subject?
2. Do the supporting paragraphs in the body supply details that appeal to the senses?
3. Did you select details that support the overall impression you are trying to create?
4. Did you use logical order with appropriate transitions?
5. Does your concluding paragraph summarize the overall impression?

✓ **Persuasive Essays**
1. Does your thesis statement express an opinion?
2. Do your supporting paragraphs use facts, examples, incidents, and reasons?
3. Did you concede the opposition's good points?
4. Did you use logical order and appropriate transitions?
5. Does your concluding paragraph make a strong final appeal?

✓ **Literary Essays**
1. Does your title identify which aspect of the work you focus on?
2. Does your introduction identify the author and the work being analyzed?
3. Does your thesis statement express your interpretation of a limited aspect of the work?
4. Did you develop your interpretation with specifics from the work?
5. Did you use logical order and appropriate transitions?
6. Does your conclusion summarize or add an insight?

Chapter 22   The Summary

OBJECTIVES

- To identify the features of a summary.
- To understand the vocabulary and recognize the main ideas of the work being summarized.
- To write a summary by condensing and paraphrasing the original piece of writing.
- To revise the summary, checking for accuracy and conciseness and using a revision checklist.
- To edit the summary using an editing checklist.

MOTIVATIONAL ACTIVITY

As a warm-up activity and as an exercise in separating the main idea from unnecessary details, have students write a one-paragraph plot summary of a movie, book, or story most of them know well. Ask several students to read their completed summaries aloud. Then ask the listening students to comment on (a) whether the summaries excluded anything important, and (b) whether the summaries included any unnecessary information.

TEACHING SUGGESTIONS

The Features of a Summary *(pages 512–516)*

Students may be interested to know that there are several kinds of widely used summaries. One is the abstract, used mainly to distill the information in a long research project, especially a dissertation. A journal called *Dissertation Abstracts* prints these summaries so that researchers can quickly discover dissertations they might want to consult. Another kind of summary is the news brief, a capsule version of a longer story, printed on a separate page of the newspaper so that readers can skip the longer article and still have an idea of the story's essence. Informal summaries are used in many periodicals in the table of contents. Following the title of the article, these short summaries, often only one sentence long, serve to entice the reader to read the whole article. Another familiar kind of summary is found in the movie listing at the back of a television guide.

Although the formal summary is less common than the informal summary, the techniques required to write a formal summary will serve students well as they prepare research papers—in which they must summarize information from sources—and when they study for exams.

You may wish to have students bring in an example of one type of summary named above or any other kind they can think of. After they share their summary with the class, students should be prepared to explain the purpose of the summary.

Prewriting *(pages 517–520)*

You may wish to duplicate and distribute the following worksheet for students to use as they prepare their summaries.
Title, Author, and Source of Original
Number of Words or Pages _____
Definitions of Unfamiliar Words
(Leave five to ten lines blank.)
Main Ideas
(Leave five to ten lines blank.)

Writing *(pages 521–526)*

After students have written their drafts, have them prepare a chart like the one on page 522 that shows how they condensed the original material. This will help clarify the condensing and paraphrasing processes involved in summarizing.

Using Your Own Words *(pages 524–525)*

Have each student write a paraphrase of some familiar piece of writing, such as the Gettysburg Address. Duplicate a few of these paraphrases so that students can appreciate the different ways of expressing the same ideas. Then ask students to compare their paraphrases to the original for general effec-

Chapter 22 a

The Summary

tiveness of the writing. Paraphrases are often less effective pieces of writing than the original, since paraphrases are derivative and imitative. However, paraphrasing is a useful tool in note-taking and summarizing.

Revising and Editing (pages 526–527)

Have students exchange papers and use the checklists on pages 526 and 527 to evaluate each other's work. They should make suggestions in writing for revising and editing.

ACTIVITIES FOR DIFFERENT ABILITIES

Basic Students

ACTIVITY 1 Recognizing the Main Idea

For more practice in identifying the main point of a piece of writing to be summarized, have students think of titles for the following excerpts:

Brain paragraph, page 518

Earth/moon comparison, page 519

All paragraphs in Exercise 4, pages 519–520

ACTIVITY 2 Summarizing a Textbook Selection

Summarizing is a valuable way to prepare for tests. To demonstrate this, have students summarize a selection from a textbook on which they soon expect to be tested. The textbook should be one that they are using in another class.

Advanced Students

ACTIVITY 1 Abstracts

Young writers sometimes have difficulty condensing what they themselves have written. To encourage the development of the objectivity necessary for summarizing, have students prepare an abstract of an essay or research project they have previously completed.

ACTIVITY 2 A Classroom Reader's Digest

Using the summaries students developed for Exercises 2, 5, 8, 10, and 11, publish a digest of the articles for classroom sharing. Ask each student to copy his or her work on a duplicating master, indicating precisely the title, author, and source of the original work. Then duplicate and distribute the publication, keeping a master file of the originals in the classroom so that students can compare the originals to the summaries.

ADDITIONAL PRACTICE

Teacher's Resource Book: pages 235–238

Workbook: pages 179–180

REVIEW EXERCISES AND TESTS

Student Text

Chapter Review: pages 527–528

Teacher's Resource Book

Chapter 22 Test: pages 53–54

(Also available as spirit duplicating masters.)

ADDITIONAL ANSWERS

EXERCISE 1 Analyzing a Summary (pages 514–516)

1. yes
2. three
3. four
4. their behavior aimed at frightening attackers and the gorilla Koko's use of sign language
5. plant-eating
6. ethologists
7. their strong family ties
8. 47

The Summary

9. 22
10. yes

EXERCISE 3 Understanding Vocabulary *(pages 517–518)*

Sample answers:
1. profitable
2. devices used to communicate with a computer
3. acting together
4. at the same time
5. supply
6. wild dog of Australia
7. wild
8. kind of mammal in which the newborn young are carried in a pouch on the female's body
9. animals
10. original inhabitants of an area

EXERCISE 6 Condensing *(pages 522–523)*

Sample answers:
1. To develop a sense of humor, concentrate on listening appreciatively and seeing the humor in situations rather than cracking jokes.
2. First try to see the funny side of yourself and things around you. If you make a real effort, you will recognize humor more easily.
3. If you associate with people who have a sense of humor, you will learn from their actions and attitudes.
4. Learn the different kinds of humor that appeal to different people. People's backgrounds often influence the kinds of things they think are funny.
5. By studying cartoons and printed jokes, you will discover that surprise and exaggeration are often important elements in humor. Look in your own experiences for situations that would make good cartoons or jokes.

EXERCISE 7 Paraphrasing *(pages 524–525)*

Sample answers:
1. Most kinds of pollution are removed from the environment by natural processes.
2. Wind scatters the pollutants as they are released, and the heavier materials fall to the earth because of gravity.
3. As floating particles come together, they form a mass that falls because of its larger size.
4. Many air pollutants combine chemically with oxygen; these new compounds are removed from the air more quickly than the original pollutants.
5. Precipitation picks up many pollutants and carries them down to the ground, where trees and grasses filter out particles and some gases.
6. Sunlight causes a chemical reaction in some gases; the particles that result from these reactions are heavier than the gases and drop to the earth.
7. As long as they can keep up with the amount of material released, natural processes can clean the air.
8. Air pollution occurs when too much contaminant is released to be removed by natural processes.
9. People can help prevent air pollution by reducing the amount of pollutants before they actually enter the atmosphere.
10. This can be done by separating the pollutants from the exhaust before it is emitted into the atmosphere or by changing the pollutants to harmless forms that can then be released.

Chapter 22 c

CHAPTER REVIEW *(pages 527-528)*

Sample answer:

Scientists predict that in the future robot technology will play a significant part in running homes. In specially designed solar dwellings, robot sun trackers may rotate the home so that it can make maximum use of the sun's energy for generating heat and electricity. Radio-controlled robots may one day perform many routine household tasks, such as locking doors, cooking, and mowing lawns. Such a household robot, called the Mechanical Servant, exists right now. Run by a computer that its owner programs, the Mechanical Servant can move, grasp objects, and speak 250 words.

22

The Summary

For additional practice for this chapter, see the Teacher's Resource Book and the Workbook.

The formal summary, sometimes called a précis, is a very practical form of writing. It condenses writing from a longer piece into a much shorter, easily readable piece that contains only the essential information. Its brevity and concise style make the summary a valuable aid for professionals and students alike. Summarizing a chapter of your history text, for example, is a good way to prepare for a test. Business people often summarize long reports to save others time. Usually no more than one third the length of the original work, the summary saves reading time by directing the reader to the main ideas and by omitting most of the details.

22a The **summary** is a concise condensation of a longer piece of writing, covering only the main points of the original.

THE FEATURES OF A SUMMARY

Unlike the essay, the summary does not include personal comments, interpretations, and insights. It is a straightforward reworking—in condensed form—of the original piece of writing. It omits details that are unnecessary to an understanding of the main ideas. Although it presents the main ideas in the same order as the original, it uses new words to express them. The challenge of writing a good summary is to be true to the original and at the same time to use your own words in a smooth, easy-to-follow style.

Read the following original piece of writing and then study the features of the summary that condenses its information.

The Features of a Summary

22a

ORIGINAL   Many of you have dreamed of someday becoming an astronaut. What an adventure it must be to travel on a space flight! Being an astronaut, however, is also hard work. It involves years of training and special preparation. It is not the right job for everyone.

There will be a demand for three different types of astronauts to travel aboard the space shuttle. The qualifications are different for each.

To be a space-shuttle pilot, you have to have a bachelor's degree in engineering, biology, a physical science, or math. It would be even better if you had a master's degree or a doctorate. You are also required to have 1,000 hours of pilot-in-command flying time in high performance jet planes. You have to pass rigorous spaceflight physical exams. Your height must be between 64 and 74 inches.

If you want to be a space-shuttle mission specialist, you need a bachelor's degree in one of the same fields mentioned for the pilot. In addition you must have either a minimum of three years' work experience in one of these fields or an advanced degree (master's or doctorate). Ability to pass the spaceflight physical exam is also required. Is height a factor? For mission specialists height requirements are different. You can be between 60 and 75 inches.

You may be best qualified to be a payload specialist. These people have either knowledge related to specific experiments to be conducted on the shuttle flight or experience in handling special types of equipment. Often the payload specialist is not a regular astronaut but receives about 150 hours of special training before going on a flight.

All astronauts are required to have good eyesight (it's okay to wear glasses) and excellent hearing. [298 words]

—ANN ELWOOD AND LINDA WOOD, *WINDOWS IN SPACE* (ADAPTED)

The Summary

SUMMARY   Three different types of astronauts work aboard the space shuttle, and each must have special training. The pilots must have a college degree in one of the sciences or math, in addition to extensive flying experience. Excellent health and a height between 64 and 74 inches are also required. Mission specialists must have extended work experience or an advanced college degree. Excellent health is also required, but height restrictions are looser. Payload specialists, who run experiments or monitor equipment, need knowledge related to their work as well as 150 hours of training. Everyone on the shuttle must have good eyesight and hearing. [102 words]

Read the summary a second time, looking for the following specific features.

22b   Features of a Summary

1. A summary is usually no more than one third the length of the original.
2. A summary provides the main ideas of the original, omitting all of the details except a few vital ones.
3. A summary presents the main ideas in the same order as the original.
4. The summary expresses the main ideas of the original in the summary writer's own words.

EXERCISE 1   Analyzing a Summary

Read both the original piece and the summary that follows it. Then write answers to the numbered questions.

ORIGINAL   From the beginning Hollywood has been fascinated by wild beasts—elephants, tigers, lions, apes, rhinos, and any other species that could be worked into a film. Few Hollywood adventures with wildlife have had much connection with the real thing, however. Filmmakers generally swing to one extreme or to

The Features of a Summary

22b

another: Either they make wild animals seem tamer than they are, or they make them seem wilder than they are.

Two species that have gotten bad reputations because of the latter habit are the gorilla and the wolf. Until recently, the movies have pictured both as villains of the worst dye. It is part of movie folklore that gorillas are vicious animals, dangerous when they are encountered, always ready to attack humans, and consistently displaying a mean streak. As for wolves, it is an equally old movie tradition that they are utterly savage killers who have no redeeming qualities and who destroy other animals and attack humans out of sheer blood lust.

Hollywood can hardly be blamed for these attitudes, since they reflect an old, established image of both species. It is only in relatively recent years that ethologists—scientists who study animals in their native environments—have made a concerted effort to change the old images because of observations in the wild.

Those observations have shown that the gorilla is a gentle animal that eats only vegetation, avoids contact with humans whenever possible, and poses no threat unless it is attacked. The breast-beating and roaring that seem so ferocious are actually just an effort by the gorilla to scare possible attackers away by a bluff. In addition, the gorilla is one of the most intelligent animals known; a captive gorilla named Koko has been taught dozens of words (which are "spoken" by sign language) and is said to have an intelligence quotient of 60 to 90.

As for the wolf, observers describe it as an animal that is no more vicious than any other predator, that does not attack humans unless provoked, and that has strong family ties. Rather than being a totally destructive killer, the wolf is described by scientists who have studied its behavior as a useful creature who

The Summary

helps to maintain the strength of the species on which it preys because it kills only the animals that are least equipped to survive.

— EDWARD EDELSON, *GREAT ANIMALS OF THE MOVIES*

SUMMARY   Hollywood moviemakers tend to represent wild animals as either more gentle or more ferocious than they actually are. The gorilla and the wolf are usually shown as vicious animals that are ready to attack humans unprovoked. This view reflects long-held attitudes that have only recently been discovered to be false. Scientists studying the gorilla in the wild have found that they are gentle, plant-eating creatures that avoid attack when possible. Studies have also shown the gorilla to be an intelligent animal. The wolf, according to observers, is no more violent than any other predator, and it does not attack humans without cause. Because it attacks the weakest members of its prey, the wolf strengthens the species it preys upon and serves a useful purpose.

Answers precede this chapter.
1. Is the summary one third the length of the original?
2. To how many sentences are the first three paragraphs in the original reduced in the summary?
3. To how many sentences are the last two paragraphs in the original reduced in the summary?
4. What two details about gorillas are not in the summary?
5. What adjective in the summary replaces the clause "that eats only vegetation" in the original?
6. What technical word in the third paragraph of the original is omitted in the summary?
7. What detail about wolves is omitted in the summary?
8. How many words are in the last sentence of the original?
9. How many words are in the last sentence of the summary?
10. Does the summary present the main ideas in the same order as the original?

EXERCISE 2 On Your Own

Look through magazines for short articles you could summarize. Choose one article of interest and save it for Exercise 5.
Answers will vary.

PREWRITING

When you write a paragraph or an essay, your task is to develop your main idea into a full composition. When you write a summary, your task is to reduce the material. You need to retrace the author's steps, locating the main ideas. In addition, you need to translate the original work into your own words. In the process of writing summaries, you will use several different skills to help you accomplish your purpose. In the prewriting stage of this process, your main goal is to understand thoroughly the original work.

Understanding Vocabulary

A good summary must be accurate. To make sure you accurately state the main ideas of the original work, you may first need to look up unfamiliar words. Writing a synonym for a new word or writing a definition in your own words will help lock the word's meaning in your mind.

22c For each unfamiliar word in a passage, write a definition in your own words or find a familiar synonym.

EXERCISE 3   Understanding Vocabulary
Use your dictionary to look up the numbered, underlined words in each of the following two paragraphs. For each word, write a synonym or a definition in your own words.
Sample answers precede this chapter.

Computer Games

One of the most immediately appealing and (1) <u>lucrative</u> applications of computers is the development and support of games. Even in research environments, one finds, in fact, a keen interest in developing games—from chess to target practice to Star Trek. The student computer centers at colleges all over the country host students playing games with names like "galaxy," and "adventure." Some of the games are regular social events, with several players at different (2) <u>terminals</u>, (3) <u>interacting</u> (4) <u>simultaneously</u> to hunt, zap, and even occasionally help one another as part of the action. Creative students also contribute by adding new games to the available (5) <u>repertoire</u>.

— JOSEPH DEKEN, *THE ELECTRONIC COTTAGE*

The Summary

The Dingo

When white settlers first went to Australia, (6) <u>dingos</u> were (7) <u>feral</u>, living in a way similar to that of wolves, hunting in packs, and feeding on the numerous (8) <u>marsupial</u> (9) <u>fauna</u>. The (10) <u>aborigines</u> acquired their animals by stealing puppies and rearing them in their households. As house dogs, they were loyal and faithful and generally as trustworthy as fully domesticated breeds of dogs. They were in addition much prized for the services they could render in hunting.

— RICHARD AND ALICE FIENNES, *THE NATURAL HISTORY OF DOGS*

Recognizing the Main Idea

The most important skill in summarizing is distinguishing between main ideas and supporting ideas. To help you identify the main ideas, ask yourself, "Which idea is more general than all the others?" In some cases the answer to this question will be the thesis statement of an essay or the topic sentence of a paragraph. In other cases, however, the main idea may be implied rather than stated directly. If the main idea is implied, try to phrase a statement that expresses it. Study the following examples.

MAIN IDEA STATED
> Your brain is constantly guarded by a complicated mechanism known as the blood-brain barrier. This is a system that protects the central nervous system from harmful chemicals by blocking their entry into the brain. Much remains to be learned about the blood-brain barrier, but some scientists hope that they may learn enough about it to help in the treatment of brain disorders and to influence sleep, learning, emotions, and other processes that are controlled by the brain. If scientists can alter the chemicals that enter and are rejected by the brain, they will have a powerful tool, indeed.
>
> — MARGARET HYDE, EDWARD MARKS, JAMES WELLS, *MYSTERIES OF THE MIND*

The main idea of this paragraph is stated directly in the first sentence, which is the topic sentence. The other sentences provide supporting details, including a description of what the

Recognizing the Main Idea

22d

barrier does and how scientists hope to use what they learn about it to treat brain disorders.

MAIN IDEA IMPLIED

The surface area of the moon is about 1/14 that of Earth, and just about the size of the continent of Africa. The diameter of Earth is a little less than 4 times the diameter of the moon, and its volume is about 49 times that of the moon. If Earth and the moon had the same density, Earth would weigh about 49 times its satellite. However, the moon is somewhat less dense and weighs only 1/81 as much as Earth. Lest we underestimate this weight, it amounts to about 70 million trillion tons. Actually, *mass* is the correct word, instead of *weight*. Because of its smaller mass, the moon has a surface gravity only 1/6 that of Earth. On the moon a 180-pound astronaut will thus weigh only 30 pounds, although his mass will be the same as on Earth.

— D. S. HALACY, JR., *COLONIZATION OF THE MOON*

In this paragraph, all of the sentences are equally specific. The general idea is implied: *By all significant measurements, the moon is much smaller than Earth.* All the sentences contain supporting details that expand on this implied main idea.

22d Find the **main ideas** in a passage by identifying the most general statements or by expressing an **implied main idea** in your own words.

EXERCISE 4 Recognizing Main Ideas

Write the main idea of each paragraph. If the main idea is stated directly, copy it from the paragraph. If it is implied, write a sentence that expresses the main idea.

1.

The Saxons have left their name in many parts of the south of England. Essex, Sussex, and Middlesex were the lands of the East, South, and Middle Saxons. The great King Alfred, who lived in the ninth century, was King of Wessex (the West

The Summary

Saxons), but he spoke of his people as the "Anglekin," or English folk. In his lifetime both Angles and Saxons began to call all their land England.

2.

When Julius Caesar came to Britain in 55 B.C., the Thames River already had its name. It means "dark" and so also do the river names *Tame, Teme,* and *Tamar,* all coming from the same origin. The river name *Wye* means "winding," and *Wey* means the same. *Trent* means "wandering" or "flooding"; *Stour* (probably) means "strong." *Darwen, Derwent, Darent,* and *Dart* all come from a Celtic word meaning "oak trees" and tell of the forests through which these rivers flowed.

2. *Sample answer:* A river's characteristics were often the inspiration for its name.

3.

Wherever the British have settled all around the world, they have often longed for the sights and sounds of home. These they could not have, but a familiar name could be had at once, and this was often their choice. <u>There is hardly a town in Britain without a namesake overseas.</u> The Pilgrims in America began this naming, but Canadians, Australians, and New Zealanders have all done it too. There are at least 16 towns outside Britain called Cambridge, 20 called Oxford, 20 called Chester, and over 30 called Richmond.

4.

<u>A popular source of inspiration for naming has been wildlife.</u> America has dozens of towns with names like Beaver City, Elkton, Eagleton, and so forth, all coined in the same spirit that produced Beverly (from an old spelling of *beaver*) and Otterburn in England. The big city of Buffalo was actually named after an Indian chief of that name, but the city's name still comes indirectly from the buffalo. Canada is very rich in these animal names: Red Deer, Caribou Mountains, Great Bear Lake, Beaverlodge, and many more.

— ALL PARAGRAPHS FROM *HOW PLACE NAMES BEGAN,* C. M. MATHEWS (ADAPTED)

EXERCISE 5 **On Your Own**

Using the article you chose in Exercise 2, complete the following tasks. Save your work for Exercise 8. *Answers will vary.*

1. Look up all unfamiliar words and write a synonym or a definition in your own words for each.
2. Make a list of the main ideas in the article.

WRITING

Once you understand all the words and the main ideas of a selection, you are ready to write the first draft of your summary. Your task is to rewrite the original by condensing it and putting it in your own words. Referring to your prewriting notes, you will structure your summary by adding to the main idea or ideas the essential supporting ideas in condensed form.

Condensing

One way to condense, or shorten, a passage is to omit repetition and such details as examples, incidents, and descriptions. Another way is to reduce sentences, clauses, and phrases to short phrases or even single words. Combining two or more sentences into one concise sentence is one effective way to reduce the number of words. *(See pages 374–378.)* Study the following example. (The sentences are numbered for easy reference.)

ORIGINAL (1) One might assume that if few tadpoles can survive in small puddles, frogs should deposit their eggs in larger bodies of water such as lakes. (2) Lakes are certainly more stable than puddles in the road; they rarely dry up. (3) In large, permanent bodies of water, however, tadpoles may have to compete with many species for the organic food on which they depend. (4) Also, large lakes are often nutrient-poor, since sunlight cannot penetrate to their bottoms, permitting photosynthesis and plant growth. (5) Finally, lakes usually support fish that would prey on relatively defenseless tadpoles. (6) Indeed, tadpoles and fish very rarely occur together. (7) To escape aquatic predators, some tadpoles that live in tropical streams actually crawl up wet rocks and out of the water, or they burrow into leaf matter at the edge of streams. (8) Clearly, large bodies of water are not a preferred habitat.

—RICHARD WASSERSUG, "WHY TADPOLES LOVE FAST FOODS"

521

The Summary

SUMMARY   (1) Puddles make better homes for tadpoles than do large, more stable lakes. (2) In lakes tadpoles might have to compete with other species for food. (3) Lakes are also poor in nutritious plants because of the way they block the sunlight. (4) Finally, lakes are home to many fish that could prey on tadpoles or force them to find shelter on rocks or in leaves.

The following chart shows how information from the original paragraph is recast in the summary, sometimes by combining ideas from two sentences into one. Notice that the summary states the main idea in the first sentence and then presents the important supporting ideas in the same order as the original.

Original Sentence	Summary Sentence
2 and 8 (main idea)	⟶ 1
1	⟶ omitted: unnecessary detail
3	⟶ 2
4	⟶ 3
5 and 7	⟶ 4
6	⟶ omitted: unnecessary detail

22e Condense information from the original by omitting repetition and unnecessary details and by reducing two or more sentences to one. Present the main ideas and the important supporting ideas in the same order as the original.

EXERCISE 6 Condensing

Condense each paragraph in the following passage to no more than two sentences. Write those sentences next to the number of the paragraph. *Sample answers precede this chapter.*

(1) You can develop a sense of humor. You may never turn into a wit—the kind of person who can crack jokes all day—but that isn't necessary. It is more important for you to

Condensing

22e

learn to be an appreciative audience and to learn to see the humor in various situations.

(2) Perhaps the first thing you need to do is to begin looking for things that are funny in yourself and in the people and things around you. If you have a sour outlook on life, very little will ever seem funny to you. You have to shake yourself up a bit and say, "Look, let's take off these dark glasses and see what there is around here that is funny." Then you may see or hear something that will give you a great big laugh. Looking for humor and being alert to instances where it is likely to be present will help you detect it more readily, even if it is a joke on you.

(3) Second, it will help you a great deal to be around people who have a good sense of humor. You will notice what they think is funny. You will hear them say funny things, which you might even apply yourself in a similar situation. You will also begin to pick up their attitude toward things in general. They will teach you to see the funny side of things.

(4) Third, you might want to make a little study of just what it is that makes people laugh. Even if you apply this only to your own friends, you will discover this interesting fact: Different kinds of humor appeal to different people. What seems funny to one will not seem funny to another. One reason for this is difference in background and vocabulary. For instance, someone who has been reared on a farm might tell a joke about farm animals, which would mean absolutely nothing to someone who had been reared in the city and knew nothing about farm animals and their habits. Certainly, city people tell jokes about things that require a city background to understand.

(5) Fourth, you can study the cartoons or jokes that are printed in some of the leading magazines. Why are they considered funny? What is humorous about them? You will soon find that the element of surprise is likely to be present. Often a person or an animal is pictured as doing something ridiculous or unusual. Frequently you find everyday situations exaggerated to such an extent that they become funny. After you have analyzed these cartoons and jokes, be on the lookout for incidents that you think might make good cartoons, or for a conversation that might make a good joke. It will be an interesting experiment, and it will help to make you humor-conscious.

—VIRGINIA BAILARD AND RUTH STRANG, *WAYS TO IMPROVE YOUR PERSONALITY*

The Summary

Using Your Own Words

When you define unfamiliar words and condense, you will need to rephrase ideas from the original work in your own words. This technique is called *paraphrasing*. In a paraphrase you must include all of the author's ideas, even though you rewrite them in your own words. A paraphrase, therefore, is likely to be approximately the same length as the original. Two methods will help you rewrite information from the original in your own words. One is replacing words in the original with synonyms. (Remember to use the dictionary for help with difficult words.) The second is varying the structure of the original sentences. *(See pages 374–381.)*

22f ▸ **Paraphrase the original work by using synonyms and by varying sentence structure.**

Notice how the following paraphrase uses new words and a different sentence structure.

ORIGINAL   When Robert Mugabe was elected prime minister on April 18, 1980, nearly a century of exploitation and unrepresentative government came to an end for Zimbabwe's people.

PARAPHRASE   Robert Mugabe's election as prime minister of Zimbabwe on April 18, 1980 marked the end of almost a century of unfair use and undemocratic rule of the country's citizens.

The synonyms used in the paraphrase are *almost* for *nearly; unfair use* for *exploitation; undemocratic* for *unrepresentative; rule* for *government;* and *citizens* for *people.* The original sentence is a complex sentence. The paraphrase is a simple one.

EXERCISE 7   Paraphrasing

Paraphrase each of the following sentences by using synonyms and by varying sentence structure. Look up unfamiliar words.
Sample answers precede this chapter.

Clearing the Air

1. Nature provides a process to remove practically every known pollutant from its atmosphere.
2. As contaminants are discharged, wind causes all materials to disperse; gravity brings the heavier substances to the ground.

Paraphrasing

22f

3. As lighter particles, which remain afloat, collide and coagulate with each other, they increase in size and then fall.
4. Oxygen in the air reacts with many pollutants, changing them to a form that is more readily removed.
5. Rain and snow absorb and carry down many substances; trees and grasses act like large filters that collect particles and some gases.
6. Sunlight causes some gases to react chemically and form particulate matter that can settle down.
7. Nature can provide the cleansing function as long as the natural process can keep up with the quantities of material discharged.
8. Air becomes polluted when excess quantities of material are discharged and exceed nature's cleansing capabilities.
9. To prevent air-pollution conditions, people can assist by abating the contaminants prior to their discharge into the atmosphere.
10. This can be accomplished by separating the pollutants from exhaust prior to emission, or by converting them to innocuous products that may then be discharged.

—RICHARD T. SHEAHAN, *FUELING THE FUTURE: AN ENVIRONMENT AND ENERGY PRIMER*

EXERCISE 8 On Your Own
Using your notes from Exercise 5, write a summary of the article you chose in Exercise 2. Use the techniques of condensing and paraphrasing. Save your work for Exercise 10.
Answers will vary.

Writing Extra

Some kinds of condensing call for the skills of classifying and generalizing. Consider the following sentence.

> A devastating blizzard with 65-mile-per-hour winds blasted **Iowa, Wisconsin, Illinois, and Minnesota,** leaving 17 inches of snow on the ground and snowdrifts up to 10 feet.

One way to condense this sentence is to try to classify some of the specific details into one larger and more general category. The states hit by the blizzard, for example, share a common geographic region, the Midwest. Although the specific

The Summary

details are omitted in the following condensed sentence, the main idea about the location of the states is still present.

A winter storm with high winds and heavy snowfalls blasted **several Midwestern states.**

EXERCISE 9   Classifying Details in Large Categories
Write a condensed version of each sentence by classifying the underlined details in one group.   *Answers may vary.*

1. A 17-year-old boy and two girls, one 16 and the other 15, became local heroes when they rescued a drowning child.   *Three teenagers*
2. Most doctors recommend the eating of broccoli, carrots, cauliflower, zucchini, and celery to reduce calories.   *vegetables*
3. The dealer on Fifth Street only sells Toyota, Honda, and Subaru automobiles.   *Japanese*
4. Ted's photographs are mostly of birds, seals, and wildcats.   *wild animals*
5. Jo's Records is open until six Monday through Friday.   *weekdays*

REVISING

The main goals of revising are to check the accuracy of your summary against the original and to reduce your first draft to the most concise version possible. Use the following checklist.

22g

Revision Checklist

1. Compare your summary to the original. Are the ideas presented accurately?
2. Are the ideas in your summary presented in the same order as they appear in the original?
3. Count the number of words in your summary. Is your summary no more than one third the length of the original? If not, condense your work further by repeating the steps you took to condense the original. *(See page 529.)*
4. Did you use your own words and vary the sentence structure of the original?
5. Did you use transitions and other connecting devices to make your summary flow smoothly? *(See page 472.)*

Revising and Editing

22g–h

EXERCISE 10   On Your Own
Using the Revision Checklist, revise the first draft of your summary from Exercise 8. Save your work for Exercise 11.
Answers will vary.

EDITING

The final step in writing a summary is to edit it for accuracy in spelling, grammar, punctuation, and manuscript form. The following checklist will help you edit your work. You may wish to use the proofreading symbols on page 614 when you edit.

22h

> **Editing Checklist**
> 1. Are your sentences free of errors in grammar and usage?
> 2. Did you spell each word correctly?
> 3. Did you capitalize and punctuate correctly?
> 4. Did you use manuscript form? *(See pages 611–612.)*
> 5. Is your handwriting or typing clear?

EXERCISE 11   On Your Own
Using the Editing Checklist, edit the summary you revised in Exercise 10.
Answers will vary.

CHAPTER REVIEW

Write a summary of the following passage. Use the Steps for Writing Summaries on page 529 as a guide.
Sample answer precedes this chapter.

Robots at Home

   Robotized homes—ones not requiring constant attention by their owners—are a distinct possibility in the next century. Glass-domed solar houses are already on the design boards of imaginative architects. In such a house, the round living quarters could be engineered to rotate under the dome to take advantage of the sun's energy, which can be converted to heat and electricity. Electronic robot sun trackers would keep the house facing directly into or away from the sun, as

527

The Summary

desired by the owners. Inside this future home, other robotic devices would perform such chores as raising and lowering curtains, locking doors automatically at night, sliding doors open and shut, and switching TV channels at the command of the owner's voice.

A number of robotics engineers predict the time will come when rented or purchased radio-controlled robots will take care of household tasks like cooking, sweeping, lawn mowing, bed making, and even baby-sitting. Indeed, certain specialty companies offer what they call "domestic androids" right now. One such firm sells a 180-pound, five-foot-two-inch-tall Mechanical Servant, which has 36-inch-long tubular arms with functioning elbows, wrists, and tri-pincer (three-fingered) hands.

The Mechanical Servant has an "on-board" computer that the homeowner can program with a hand-held set of push buttons. The robot is charged with electrical power from a wall outlet. Once its program has been set and activated, radio commands go out in sequence to its mobile wheels and to servos in its arms and wrists. The Mechanical Servant's standard household functions include answering the door when guests arrive, announcing visitors (it has a preprogrammable 250-word vocabulary), adjusting thermostats, vacuuming rugs, dusting, serving drinks and snacks on a tray, polishing floors, and monitoring the home for fire, smoke, or unauthorized intruders.

—DAVID C. KNIGHT, *ROBOTICS, PAST, PRESENT, AND FUTURE*

Steps for Writing

Summaries

Prewriting
1. Read the original work once to understand the general idea.
2. Reread the work, writing down unfamiliar words.
3. Look up each unfamiliar word and write a synonym for it or a definition in your own words.
4. Read the work a third time, writing down the main ideas in the order in which they are presented.
5. Determine the length of the original work. Count words if the original is a short selection; count lines or pages if it is a long selection.

Writing

6. Present the main ideas and essential supporting ideas in the same order in which they appeared in the original.
7. Condense the original to approximately one third its length by
   a. omitting unnecessary details.
   b. combining ideas from several sentences into one.
   c. replacing long phrases, clauses, and sentences with shorter phrases or single words. *(See pages 370–373.)*
8. Restate ideas from the original in your own words by
   a. using synonyms.
   b. varying sentence structure. *(See pages 379–380.)*

Revising

9. Use the Revision Checklist on page 526 to check for accuracy and length.

Editing

10. Use the Editing Checklist on page 527 to check your grammar, usage, spelling, mechanics, and manuscript form.

Chapter 23   Research Papers

OBJECTIVES

- To follow the prewriting steps — which include finding ideas, choosing and limiting a subject, gathering information, evaluating sources, taking notes and summarizing, organizing notes, and outlining — to shape a subject idea into an organized plan for a research paper.
- To write the first draft of a research paper, including the thesis statement, introduction, body, and conclusion.
- To use sources smoothly and cite them accurately.
- To use the correct form for footnotes and bibliographies.
- To revise the research paper using a revision checklist.
- To edit the research paper using an editing checklist.

MOTIVATIONAL ACTIVITY

By now students should have a number of subject ideas in their writing folders. They also have some notes about books, specialized references, and magazines on some of their favorite subjects. Encourage students to look over the material in their folders to find a subject for their research papers. They should also try to think of a few ideas in addition to those listed in their writing folders. When they have three possible subjects, they may be able to choose the best one by completing the following questionnaire about each.

QUESTIONNAIRE FOR CHOOSING A SUBJECT

1. For how long have you been interested in this subject?
2. How did you become interested?
3. How would you rate your current knowledge of this subject?
   a. expert b. know more than most people c. know a little d. know almost nothing
4. If you chose c or d above, are you willing to start from the beginning in your research and devote the necessary time to learn about this subject? If not, choose another subject.
5. Are you already familiar with some books and/or articles on the subject? If so, what are their authors and titles?
6. Does your school or local library have these materials? Does it have other materials on this subject?
7. Do you know any people you could interview for information on this subject? If so, who are they and how can you get in touch with them?
8. When you have finished a research paper on this subject, will you have satisfied an intellectual curiosity or will you have discovered some practical information that you can put to use? Explain.
9. Name several people you know who might be interested in reading your finished report on this subject. Why would each be interested?
10. On a scale of 1 to 10, how do you rate your interest in this subject?

When the students have finished questionnaires for three subjects, have them compare the answers. This comparison should give students an indication of which of the three subjects interests them most and is the most practical topic for a research paper. Students thinking this carefully about a subject before undertaking a research project are likely to have a high motivation for completing it successfully.

TEACHING SUGGESTIONS

Prewriting *(pages 531–546)*

One useful technique for helping students determine what information they need to acquire is to have them try to write a draft of the research report as if it were an essay — based solely on the students' knowledge. This activity forces students to try to organize their thoughts, to measure what they already know about a subject, and to recognize categories of information they lack.

To make sure students proceed on their research projects at a reasonable pace, you may wish to set a date for each of the following checkpoints:

Choosing and Limiting a Subject (Students should hand in limited topics suitable for their research subjects.)

Gathering Information (Students should hand in their working bibliographies; form is not important at this stage.)

Evaluating Sources (Students should hand in an annotated version of their bibliographies, including comments about possible weaknesses in the sources.)

Taking Notes and Summarizing (Students should hand in their note cards, bound in a rubber band.)

Outlining (Students should hand in their outlines and their working thesis statements.)

Choosing and Limiting a Subject *(pages 532-534)* After students have submitted their limited subjects, prepare a list of all the subjects without identifying the writers who chose the subjects. Leave three lines after each subject. Post the list and ask students to sign up, one at a time, for papers they would like to read. Each student should write his or her name after three different subjects. Each subject should have a total of three readers, so if three names are already listed after a subject, students should choose another subject to read about.

In this way, each paper will have a guaranteed audience of three readers besides you, and each student will have a chance to read and comment on three papers.

Gathering Information *(pages 534-535)* Remind students that many books contain a bibliography listing the works the author consulted or suggesting items for further reading. Such bibliographies are often excellent sources of ideas for additional references for the students' own papers. In their evaluation notes for each book they consult, students should indicate whether the book includes such a listing. They should also check the school and local library to see if any of the books or magazine articles listed in the bibliography are available to them.

Evaluating Sources *(pages 535-537)* Introduce the terms *primary sources* and *secondary sources*. (Primary sources are original records of events made by persons who lived at the time of the events. They are often firsthand or eyewitness accounts. Examples of primary sources are letters, documents, autobiographies, newspaper accounts from the time, artifacts, pictures taken or painted at the time, and diaries. Secondary sources are materials written by people who have studied the primary sources. These include such works as reference books, biographies, and textbooks.)

Students seem to understand that errors can occur in secondary sources, but they should also know that a source is not necessarily reliable just because it is a primary source. As an exercise in evaluating sources, have students rank the following sources on the subject of unidentified flying objects (UFOs) in the order of most to least credible. For each source, they should indicate whether it is primary or secondary. They should also give reasons for their ranking order.

an eyewitness account of a UFO in the sky from a farmer

a recorded radar blip of an unidentified object

an Air Force pilot's report of an unidentified object seen through the airplane's windshield

a newspaper account of the Air Force pilot's report

an article in a magazine called "Strange But True" about a UFO landing in Utah

a book written by a person who believes that all UFOs are hoaxes or imaginings

a pamphlet published by a respected planetarium explaining UFOs

a photograph of a UFO

a sketch of a UFO

Research Papers

Taking Notes and Summarizing *(pages 538–540)* As students are taking notes on their subject, they will begin to synthesize the material they are reading and summarizing. Encourage students to jot their own ideas and questions on note cards as those ideas occur to them, but remind them to make clear the distinction between their own thoughts and the thoughts of the source's author. You may wish to recommend that they keep two different colored pens or pencils on hand, so that they can use a second color for their own thoughts and easily distinguish them later from borrowed material. Alternatively, they might write "my idea" or "my thought" in parentheses after those insights that are their own.

Also remind students to distinguish between paraphrases of a source and direct quotations. They should always use quotation marks for the latter type of note.

Organizing Your Notes and Outlining *(pages 541–546)* When students have completed their outlines, the groups of three readers that were suggested earlier (see *Choosing and Limiting a Subject*) might check their peers' outlines, commenting on organization and adequacy of the supporting points. However, although peer evaluation and consultation are valuable in many instances, at this final stage of the prewriting work your individual attention to the students is most important. Much of the success of the paper depends on how well the notes are sorted into groups and how well the ideas are arranged. Because each subject is different and has its own special requirements, you might schedule a conference with each student to assure that he or she has organized the material well and is generally progressing competently with the paper. So that you have a chance to read and evaluate the outlines before the conferences, have students submit them a day or two in advance.

Writing *(pages 546–560)*

Many writing experts recommend that the first draft of a composition be written quickly. Well-organized research and note cards should make this possible for high school juniors. Rather than interrupting the flow of their thoughts as they are writing to worry about the correct footnote form, students may benefit from using the following technique. As they write their first draft, have them indicate each borrowed idea with a superscript, and then keep track of each citation on a separate piece of paper by writing the superscript, the source's identifying number, and the number of the page from which the information was taken. You may wish to put the following blank model on the board, or prepare blank forms on a duplicating master and distribute them to the students.

CITATION   SOURCE NO.   PAGE NO.
1
2
3
etc.

Using and Citing Sources *(pages 554–560)* Students should not use quotations indiscriminately. They must not lose their own voice in the research paper by presenting a patchwork of other people's words. Remind students that direct quotations should be used instead of their own words in the following circumstances:

1. If the source's author has expressed an idea in a particularly succinct or eloquent way.
2. If you have already made a point in your own words but you wish to show that your ideas are confirmed by respected authorities.

Revising *(pages 560–561)*

After students have finished a quick first draft, recommend to them that they look over *all* of their note cards again. Chances are that they did not find a use for every single card, and that is perfectly acceptable. They may, however, have overlooked something that on second glance seems to add an important or interesting point to the paper. During the revising stage, students should not be content to focus only on the more me-

Chapter 23 c

chanical aspects of their work; they should review their entire research efforts to make sure they have ended up at the point to which all their research directed them.

Peer evaluation at this point is helpful. Students may become so engrossed in their work that they lose sight of a reading audience. Using the review groups set up earlier (see suggestions under *Choosing and Limiting a Subject*), have students share their latest draft with their readers. Each reader should answer the following questions about the three papers he or she reads. The reviewers' written comments should then be passed along to the writer of the paper, who should consider them when doing the revision.

1. What are two aspects of this paper that seem especially strong?
2. Are there any questions you wanted answered that the paper did not answer? If so, what are they?
3. Is there anything in the paper you did not readily understand? If so, what was it?

You may wish to allow extra time for the revising stage to allow students to move beyond the basic mechanics of a research report and try to incorporate all the features of good writing. To this end, you may give students the following checklist to use *after* they have satisfied the revisions called for by peer evaluation and the checklist on page 561.

REFINEMENT CHECKLIST

1. Does your introduction capture attention and raise the reader's curiosity?
2. Is your language simple and direct instead of stilted and formal?
3. Does your conclusion add a meaningful ending, or does it merely repeat ideas already stated clearly?
4. Is there anything in your report that is not cited with a superscript that you borrowed from a source? If so, cite the source.
5. Have you done everything you can think of to add interest to your writing?

Editing *(pages 561–562)*

You may wish to have *one* of the reviewers for each paper read the final draft with an eye for editing errors. Errors should be noted in pencil, with proofreading symbols where appropriate. (See page 614 in the Appendix.)

ACTIVITIES FOR DIFFERENT ABILITIES

Basic Students

ACTIVITY 1 Note-taking

For more directed instruction in note-taking, refer students to pages 608–609 in the Appendix.

For practice in note-taking, have all the students use the same source, such as a magazine article or a short section of a textbook, as the basis for a note-taking exercise. Give them assignments such as the following, which are based on a history textbook:

1. Make a note card briefly defining the term *Great Depression*. Use your own words. Base your explanation on the information in Chapter 30.
2. Choose one passage from Chapter 30 that you would like to quote exactly if you were doing a research paper on the Great Depression. Explain why you would use the author's exact words rather than expressing the idea in your own words.
3. List the steps the New Deal took to help working people. State the information as briefly as possible without leaving out important information.

ACTIVITY 2 The First Draft

Students may have some difficulty asserting a voice of their own in their writing, possibly depending too heavily on their sources. To encourage the students to assert the expertise they gained from their research, have them follow their outlines and write one draft without any citations or quotations. The purpose of this exercise is to have them use their own words entirely to make their points, even if they are not able to include all the specific facts or figures they have re-

Research Papers

corded on their note cards. In the next draft, they can expand their ideas by using cited material.

Advanced Students

ACTIVITY 1 Formulating Hypotheses
By eleventh grade, advanced students should be using research to supplement and support their *own* thinking on a subject. Encourage students to formulate a working hypothesis *before* they begin extensive note-taking. Encourage them also to add a persuasive edge to their thesis; they should not merely summarize the available information, but should instead try to interpret that information with the goal of developing a unique viewpoint. To accomplish this end, you may want to limit the subjects students write on to areas of genuine controversy, reminding students that on most interesting issues there are more than two simple sides.

ACTIVITY 2 Bibliography
College-bound students should recognize that the preparation of a bibliography is in itself a research project. The true purpose of a bibliography is to compile in one source a list of readings for further study, not merely to record the handful of sources cited in a short report. To supplement the bibliography of works cited, ask students to prepare a more extensive bibliography by adding the following minimum entries:

5 books
5 magazine or journal articles
5 articles in general or specialized encyclopedias
1 primary source

ADDITIONAL PRACTICE

Teacher's Resource Book:
pages 239–242
Workbook: pages 181–186

REVIEW EXERCISES AND TESTS

Student Text
Chapter Review: page 562
Teacher's Resource Book
Chapter 23 Test: pages 55–56
(Also available as spirit duplicating masters.)

ADDITIONAL ANSWERS

EXERCISE 4 Limiting a Subject *(page 534)*

Sample answer for item 1:
1. black Americans
    What about black Americans?
       their struggle for equal rights
    What about their struggle for equal rights?
       leaders of the movement
    What about leaders?
       Rosa Parks's contribution to the struggle for equal rights

EXERCISE 8 Taking Notes and Summarizing *(page 540)*

Sample answer:

Assateague study   2

  —Assateague National Seashore: 200 ponies
  —divided between Virginia and Maryland
  —studied by Dr. Ronal Keiper of Penn. Univ.
    in 1976
  —17 bands; 3–26 ponies in each
  —social structure: "one dominant stallion
    leading a number of mares and their foals"
  —attempts of stallions to steal mares from
    other bands—fights   p. 90

EXERCISE 9 Creating Categories *(page 542)*

Sample answer:
1. musical instruments—d, f, h, i
2. phonographs—b, g, j
3. stereoscopes—a, c, e

EXERCISE 12 Outlining *(page 545)*

Sample answer:
People 100 years ago had both sights and sounds to entertain them at home.
  I. Stereoscope
      A. Description
      B. Capacity to show three dimensions
      C. Popular views
 II. Musical instruments
      A. Piano and organ
      B. Banjos and accordions
      C. Player piano
III. Phonograph
      A. Early development
      B. Reactions of people to demonstration
      C. Popularity of windup style phonograph

Research Papers

EXERCISE 14   Revising Thesis Statements *(page 547)*

Sample answers:
1. Although all dogs share common characteristics, dogs descended from the wolf are different in some ways from those whose ancestors were jackals.
2. Male dogs in the wild observe special rules of etiquette toward certain other animals.
3. Many dogs have been taught valuable skills and are a great help to society.
4. Domestic dogs retain several physical and emotional traits of puppyhood that wolves lose when they mature.
5. Trainers use their own special skills and the dogs' instincts to help in the training process.

EXERCISE 16   Recognizing Transitions *(page 554)*

1. Atlantis
2. most significantly
3. however
4. Accept any two: for example, the most glaring, however
5. theories about Atlantis

EXERCISE 17   Using Sources *(pages 556–557)*

Sample answers:
1. Early skydivers showed off their daring "before breathless crowds at country fairs."
2. The first to demonstrate a parachute was Louis Sébastien Lenormand, in 1783. In Paris in 1797, André Jacques Garnerin descended in a parachute from a height of 3,000 feet. "Garnerin went on to exhibit his jumps at ever increasing heights in various countries, leaping 8,000 feet in England in 1802."
3. The modern parachute is more reliable than earlier ones for many reasons: An important development, undoubtedly not considered in the early parachutes, is the use of numerous pieces of fabric. These are cut, sewn, and arranged to confine a possible tear to the section in which it starts. The apparatus (parachute and suspension lines) is assembled in a pack. The rip cord that releases the parachute may be operated manually, or automatically via a timing device, or by a line attached to an aircraft.
   All of these improvements have taken some of the dare and risk out of skydiving.
4. With a parachute "resembling an oversized umbrella," Garnerin jumped 3,000 feet.
5. The parachute used to leave a supersonic plane opens after the pilot's seat, the pilot, and the parachute are ejected by a rocket charge. The seat drops off.

EXERCISE 18   Preparing Footnotes *(pages 559–560)*

[1] Mike Jahn, <u>How to Make a Hit Record</u> (Scarsdale: Bradbury Press, 1976), p. 26.
[2] Hans Fantel, "How to Choose a CD Player," <u>New York Times</u>, 1 April 1984, Sec. H, p. 27, col. 4.
[3] Jack Egan, "Pop Records Go Boom," <u>New York</u>, 31 Oct. 1983, p. 54.
[4] William E. Butterworth, <u>Hi Fi: From Edison's Phonograph to Quadrophonic Sound</u> (New York: Four Winds Press, 1977), p. 43.
[5] Norman Eisenberg, "Sound Recording and Reproduction," <u>Collier's Encyclopedia</u>, 1980 ed.
[6] "The Right Way to Take Care of Records," <u>Glamour</u>, Oct. 1983, p. 68.

EXERCISE 19   Preparing a Bibliography *(page 560)*

Butterworth, William E. <u>Hi Fi: From Edison's Phonograph to Quadrophonic Sound</u>.
   New York: Four Winds Press, 1977.

Egan, Jack. "Pop Records Go Boom." <u>New York</u>, 31 Oct. 1983, p. 54.
Eisenberg, Norman. "Sound Recording and Reproduction." <u>Collier's Encyclopedia</u>. 1980 ed.
Fantel, Hans. "How to Choose a CD Player." <u>New York Times</u>, 1 April 1984, Sec. H, p. 27, col. 4.
Jahn, Mike. <u>How to Make a Hit Record</u>. Scarsdale: Bradbury Press, 1976.
"The Right Way to Take Care of Records." <u>Glamour</u>, Oct. 1983, p. 68.

CHAPTER REVIEW *(page 562)*

You may wish to use the following evaluation form.

Evaluation Form for Reports

	POINT VALUE	STUDENT SCORE
Structure		
1. title	5	_____
2. introduction	10	_____
3. thesis statement	5	_____
4. body	20	_____
5. conclusion	10	_____
Sources		
6. sufficient number	5	_____
7. used appropriately	10	_____
8. correct footnote form	5	_____
9. correct bibliography form	5	_____
Revising and Editing		
10. report revised	10	_____
11. report edited	10	_____
12. correct manuscript form	5	_____
Total Score		_____

23

Research Papers

For additional practice for this chapter, see the Teacher's Resource Book and the Workbook.

When you write an essay, you express your own ideas about your chosen subject. When you write a *research paper,* or report, you piece together the ideas and views of others. You find these ideas and viewpoints by researching what experts have said or written on your subject. The conclusion you draw from this research determines how you will present the various pieces of information.

23a A **research paper** is a composition based on research drawn from books, periodicals, and interviews with experts.

Since the main purpose of a research paper is to convey information, you will be using the skills of expository writing. In addition, you will use your library skills to help you find information in books and magazines. *(You may wish to review Chapters 15 & 16 on library skills.)* In the course of taking notes from library sources, you will also draw on the skills of summarizing and paraphrasing. *(See pages 521–524.)* Developing the skills to write effective research papers will help you in your present and future schooling. It will also help you in the business world, where reports are widely used to convey the information needed for important decisions.

PREWRITING

In some ways writing a research paper is like hunting for the pieces of a puzzle and trying to fit them together. Since you must collect pieces of information from a number of different sources, keeping good track of all the pieces becomes very important. The right supplies can help you organize your research as you go along. These include a folder with pockets, index cards, paper clips, and rubber bands. When you are finally ready to begin piecing your information together, your well-organized notes will make the job easier.

Finding Ideas

Letting your mind run free is the best way to find ideas to write about in a research paper. Sometimes, however, you may feel that you have run out of ideas. The following exercises will fuel your imagination and help you think of at least 20 possible subjects for a research paper.

EXERCISE 1 Finding Ideas from Personal Experience
Ask yourself the following questions and write answers to them. *Answers will vary.*

1. Where have I been that I would like to know more about?
2. What trick, stunt, or special effect always makes me wonder, "How did they do that?"
3. What characteristics make the part of the country I live in unique?
4. What additional information would I like to have about my hobbies?
5. What famous person, past or present, do I admire?
6. If I had to give up all but one modern invention (telephone, car, television, for example), which one would I keep and why?
7. With what animals have I had first-hand experience?
8. What subjects interest my three closest friends?
9. Among the people I know, who has the most interesting job? What about it is interesting?
10. What machines do I know how to operate?

Research Papers

EXERCISE 2 Finding Ideas from Outside Sources

Ask yourself the following questions and write answers to them. *Answers will vary.*

1. What topics in my history class would I like to know more about?
2. Who is my favorite author?
3. What books or poems have I read and enjoyed in English class this year?
4. What current events would I like to understand better?
5. What region of the world would I like to know more about?
6. What recent television shows have had interesting or informative subjects?
7. What have I learned about in recent weeks from a newspaper or magazine article?
8. What natural disasters have happened in the past five years?
9. What people are making headlines today? Who interests me the most?
10. What recent movies have been made about interesting subjects?

Choosing and Limiting a Subject

Once you have discovered five to ten possible ideas for a research paper, the next step is to choose one. The following guidelines will help you choose a good subject.

23b

> **Guidelines for Choosing a Subject**
>
> 1. Choose a subject you would like to know more about.
> 2. Choose a subject that would interest your readers.
> 3. Choose a subject that can be covered adequately in a research paper approximately 2,000 words (7 typed pages) long.
> 4. Choose a subject on which there is likely to be sufficient information in the library.

The last guideline calls for making a preliminary check of the library's card catalog and some recent issues of the *Readers'*

Choosing and Limiting a Subject

23b–c

Guide to Periodical Literature. If you do not find at least two books and two magazine articles on your subject, you should probably try another subject.

Some subjects are so broad that they require whole books to be covered adequately. Within these broad subjects, however, are specific areas that could be covered in a shorter research paper. The subject of oceans, for example, is too broad for a short paper. Contained within that subject, though, are such specific subjects as "efforts to mine the ocean for gold," or "how tidal waves form," or "how the Gulf Stream current affects climate." Any of these would be a suitable subject for a research paper.

One good way to help you limit your subject to a manageable size and a sharp focus is to ask yourself a series of "what about" questions. Study the following example.

BROAD SUBJECT	the lost city of Atlantis
FIRST QUESTION	*What about* Atlantis?
MORE LIMITED	myth versus reality
SECOND QUESTION	*What about* myth versus reality?
MORE LIMITED	recent theories that attempt to explain Atlantis as a real place
THIRD QUESTION	*What about* these recent theories?
SUITABLY LIMITED	the strengths and weaknesses of the theory that places Atlantis on the Aegean island of Thera

Most suitably limited subjects need more than one or two words to express their focus. Continue limiting your subject until you can express in a phrase or partial sentence what the focus of your research paper will be.

23c Limit your subject by asking "What about (the subject)?" until you can express the focus of your research paper in a phrase or partial sentence.

EXERCISE 3 Choosing a Subject

Decide which of the following subjects are suitable for a short research paper and which are too broad. Indicate your answer by writing *suitable* or *too broad* for each subject.

too broad 1. science
too broad 2. tennis

533

Research Papers

suitable   3. how the ancient structure of Stonehenge marks the passing of time
suitable   4. campaign issues of the last presidential election
too broad   5. ownerless pets
suitable   6. rules of the waterways for boaters
too broad   7. Japan
too broad   8. galaxies
suitable   9. three causes of the Civil War
suitable   10. distress signals on the land, on the sea, and in the air

EXERCISE 4   **Limiting a Subject**
For each broad subject listed, write a series of "what about" questions until you have arrived at a suitably limited subject. Use the model on page 533 as a guide.
Sample answer for item 1 precedes this chapter.
1. black Americans
2. earthquakes
3. television
4. baseball
5. American writers

Gathering Information

With your limited subject clearly in mind, you can begin the process of gathering the information you need for your research paper. The first step is to write out five to ten guide questions that will help you find the specific information you will need.

If you had decided to write a paper on the recent theory of Atlantis that places it on the island of Thera, your guide questions might include the following:

- How did the story of Atlantis get started?
- What historical sources contain information about Atlantis that could confirm or deny the recent theory?
- What evidence does the Thera theory rest on?
- In what ways is the recent theory weak?
- What people were involved in forming this theory?
- What are some other theories about Atlantis?
- Why has it been so difficult to prove that Atlantis existed?

Gathering Information

23d

Once you have a list of guide questions, you should place them in your folder for future use. You will then be ready to gather information from the library, using the following steps.

> **Steps for Gathering Information**
>
> 1. Begin by consulting a general reference work such as an encyclopedia or a handbook to gain an overview of your subject. You will also often find a list of additional sources at the end of these articles.
> 2. Use the subject catalog in the library to find more books on your subject.
> 3. Use the *Readers' Guide to Periodical Literature* to find magazine articles on your subject.
> 4. Use a newspaper index to find newspaper articles on your subject.
> 5. Make a list of all available sources on your subject. Include the author, title, publisher and location, date of publication, and call number. For magazines, include the name and the number and date of the issue.
> 6. Assign each source on your list a number with which you can identify it in your notes.

EXERCISE 5 Gathering Information

Use the library to list five sources for each of the following subjects. At least two sources for each subject should be magazine articles. Assign each source an identifying number, and be sure to include all the information named in step 5 in the Steps for Gathering Information.
Answers will depend on library materials available.
1. space-shuttle flights in the last year
2. trends in science-fiction movies
3. training a thoroughbred horse for the Kentucky Derby
4. how meteorologists predict hurricanes
5. where clothes designers find their ideas for new fashions

Evaluating Sources

Before you can begin using your sources effectively, you need to survey each one for its usefulness and reliability. A book that has an old publication date might in some cases be

Research Papers

too outdated for your purposes. A magazine article might have too strong a bias because of the nature of the magazine itself. *(See page 500.)* To screen your sources and find the most current, accurate, and objective information on your subject, use the following evaluation checklists.

23e

Checklist for Evaluating Books

1. What is the publication date? If it is more than a few years old, do you think the book will be missing too much new information?
2. Who is the author? What are his or her credentials? (You can find these by reading the notes on the book jacket or by looking the author up in a biographical reference work such as those mentioned on pages 357 and 361 of the library chapter.)
3. Is there anything in the author's background that might suggest a biased viewpoint?
4. Check the table of contents and the index. Is there information on your limited subject in the book?

23f

Checklist for Evaluating Magazine and Newspaper Articles

1. When was the article published? If it was published more than a few years ago, do you think it may be missing important new information?
2. Who is the author? Who are his or her credentials? (You can usually find these in a note at the bottom of the first or last page of the article.)
3. Does the magazine or newspaper appeal to a special interest group that may have a biased viewpoint on your subject? (For example, a magazine called *Saving the Planet* would probably have a bias toward preserving the environment at all costs. One called *Industrial Progress*, on the other hand, might have a bias toward serving the needs of business rather than serving the needs of the environment.)
4. Does the article contain specific information on your limited subject?

Evaluating Sources

23e–f

After you have screened your sources, you may find that you can rely fully on only a few of them. Three to five good sources are better than ten or more questionable ones. Quality, not quantity, is the key.

EXERCISE 6 Evaluating Sources

Each of the following sources is on the subject of automobile safety. Each source suffers from one of the weaknesses listed below. Write the weakness of each source.

Weaknesses

A probably outdated
B probably biased
C lack of strong author credentials
D does not relate to the subject

A 1. *Paving the Way to Safety*, a book published in 1954, by Winston S. Martinsberg, director of Consumer Safety for the city of Atlanta, Georgia.

B 2. "Airbags Not the Answer," an article in *Auto Executives*, published in 1984, written by William O'Donnely, vice president of Zephyr Motors, Inc.

D 3. "Passenger Safety on Public Transportation," an article in *City News*, written by Caroline Levy, executive director of the Federal Safety Commission, published in 1982

C 4. "Tips for Safe Driving," an article published in *Modern Family* magazine, written in 1983 by Randolph Sutton, a free-lance writer with a varied background in science, sports, and law

A 5. *Building a Safe Car*, a book by Gregory Francis, professor of engineering at State University, published in 1972

Writing Extra

Books and magazine articles are only as perfect as the people who write and produce them. Despite the care that most authors take in researching their material, errors occasionally occur. The best way to confirm the accuracy of the information in a source is to check it against another source. If at least two books or articles contain the same basic facts, you can probably rely on their accuracy.

Research Papers

EXERCISE 7 **Checking Facts**

The following paragraph contains three errors. Find two sources in the library in which to check the information. Rewrite the paragraph with the correct information.

Jeanette Rankin was a crusader for women's rights and for world peace. She was born in Montana in ~~1808~~ [1880]; and after attending school and college, she decided to devote her life to public service. For six years she traveled around the country speaking on behalf of women's rights. In her home state of Montana, women won the right to vote in ~~1916~~ [1914], in large part because of Rankin's efforts. Rankin soon went on to national politics and became the ~~second~~ [first] woman ever elected to Congress. Throughout her career she stood for human rights and peace at all costs.

Taking Notes and Summarizing

Before you begin studying your evaluated sources and taking notes, you should review the guide questions you wrote at the beginning of your research. They will direct you to the information you need in each source. Once you are ready to start taking notes, bring out the index cards from your folder. As you begin taking notes, write the identifying number of each source in the upper right-hand corner of the note card. In the upper left-hand corner, identify the aspect of your subject that you are taking notes on. The label you use for each aspect of your subject should correspond in most cases to one of your guide questions. Notes taken to answer the guide question *How did the story of Atlantis get started?*, for example, might be labeled *Source of the Atlantis Story*. Avoid taking notes on information that has nothing to do with your guide questions. If you find information that is unrelated to your questions but that should be included in your research paper, identify the new aspect of your subject on the card and add it to your guide questions. As you take notes, keep the goals of note-taking in mind.

23g The goals of note-taking are to summarize main points in your own words and to record quotations that you might use in your research paper.

Taking Notes and Summarizing

23g

The following paragraphs are from the *New York Times,* August 29, 1979. The writer of the paper on the lost city of Atlantis has assigned this source the identifying number *4*. Read the paragraphs carefully and compare them to the sample note card that follows.

A Greek researcher says he has determined the exact whereabouts of the legendary island-continent of Atlantis and has brought together many recent conflicting theories as to its location. His theory has some similarities to the story by Plato, who some 24 centuries ago first wrote about a "lost continent" with an advanced civilization.

Vasilos Paschos says Atlantis was a continent larger than Asia in the area now occupied by the Atlantic Ocean. He says it had a population of about 60 million and had colonies in Latin America and the Middle East. He says that after the continent sank, around 6500 B.C., the colonies on the islands of Crete, Delos, and Thera, sometimes called Santorini, became what he calls the new Atlantis. This area was largely destroyed by volcanic eruption around 1450 B.C.

Sample Note Card

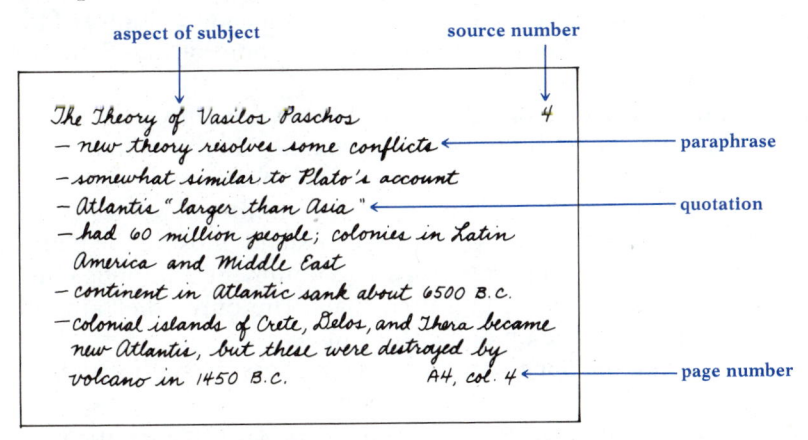

aspect of subject — The Theory of Vasilos Paschos

source number — 4

- new theory resolves some conflicts ← paraphrase
- somewhat similar to Plato's account
- Atlantis "larger than Asia" ← quotation
- had 60 million people; colonies in Latin America and Middle East
- continent in Atlantic sank about 6500 B.C.
- colonial islands of Crete, Delos, and Thera became new Atlantis, but these were destroyed by volcano in 1450 B.C.   A4, col. 4 ← page number

If you include more than one note on a card, be sure that all of the notes are closely related and are on a single aspect of your subject. Writing unrelated notes on one card will make it difficult to sort your cards later. As you finish with each source, clip all the note cards from that source together with a paper clip. Be sure that each separate card carries the identifying number in the upper right-hand corner.

Research Papers

EXERCISE 8 Taking Notes and Summarizing

The following excerpt is on the subject of feral, or untamed, horses. Assume it is from page 90 of a source that has been assigned the identifying number *2*, and make a note card for it. Identify the aspect of the subject being discussed. Then summarize the main points in your own words and record any good quotations. *(See pages 285–290 on the use of direct quotations.)* Use the sample note card on page 539 as an example.
Sample answer precedes this chapter.

Until the early 1970s, very little was known about the feral horses of North America, but scientists have since studied them in a variety of habitats, from Sable Island off the coast of Nova Scotia to the Grand Canyon in Arizona. The island horses or ponies are probably best known; they are much easier to study than the more far-ranging horses of the West. About 200 ponies live on Assateague, a 37-mile-long island that is situated partly in Maryland and partly in Virginia. Assateague is a National Seashore, managed by the National Park Service, and its Virginia portion is a National Wildlife Refuge. About 50 feral ponies live in the Maryland part of the island and belong to the park service. The other 150 live on the Virginia portion and are allowed to graze in the refuge, although they are owned by the Chincoteague Volunteer Fire Department. It annually auctions off some of the young to raise money.

In 1976, Dr. Ronal Keiper of Pennsylvania University began studying the feral ponies of Assateague. He found that there were 17 groups, or bands, of horses on the island, 4 on the upper part and 13 on the lower. The number of ponies in the bands varied from 3 to 26. Large or small, most of the bands had the same social structure: one dominant stallion leading a number of mares and their foals. The only other kind of group was made up of bachelor males.

During the spring-summer mating season, stallions try to steal mares from other stallions, and any stallion that already possesses mares fights to keep them. An intruder uses his body, neck, and head to force a mare away from her herd. Sometimes he succeeds, although an abducted mare frequently tries to rejoin her band. More often the intruder is challenged by the band's stallion. There is a fight with both horses rearing on their hind legs, biting, squealing, and pawing, and the intruder flees.

—LAWRENCE PRINGLE, *FERAL: TAME ANIMALS GONE WILD*

Organizing Your Notes

When you have finished reading and taking notes from your sources, your guide questions will help you organize your note cards into categories of information. Notice how the following categories on the subject of Atlantis are related to the questions that guided the research. *(See page 534.)*

CATEGORY 1 General Information: the nature of the problem and various attempts at explaining Atlantis
CATEGORY 2 Plato's story of Atlantis
CATEGORY 3 The strengths of the Thera theory
CATEGORY 4 The weaknesses of the Thera theory
CATEGORY 5 The difficulties in proving Atlantis existed

> **23h** Group your notes into three or more main categories of information.

After determining the appropriate categories for your research, sort your note cards into these categories and clip each group together. If some of these cards do not fit into your categories, clip them separately. You may find a use for these notes in writing the introduction or conclusion of your research paper.

Writing a Working Thesis Statement. After you have taken notes on your subject, you should know enough about it to write a rough draft of a thesis statement. *(See pages 538–539.)* This *working thesis statement* will establish the purpose and the main idea of your research paper and help you organize the information you collected. The following is a working thesis statement for the research paper on Atlantis. Notice how this thesis statement is drawn from the categories of information above.

WORKING THESIS STATEMENT A recent theory that places the lost city of Atlantis on the island Thera has strengths and weaknesses.

When you write the first draft of your research paper, you can revise your working thesis statement as needed.

Research Papers

EXERCISE 9 Creating Categories

Number your paper 1 to 3, skipping four lines after each number. Next to the numbers, write three main categories into which the following pieces of information can be grouped. Then write the letter of each item that belongs in the category. Save your work for Exercises 10 and 12. *Answers precede this chapter.*

SUBJECT home entertainment 100 years ago

a. stereoscope let people look into eyepieces and see pictures that were three-dimensional
b. phonograph was being developed in the late 1800s
c. stereoscope looked like a set of binoculars with racks behind the eyepieces, where pictures were inserted
d. player piano was introduced around 1900
e. people liked to look at three-dimensional pictures of Yellowstone, Alaska, Scandinavia, and disaster pictures from the Johnstown, Pennsylvania, flood of 1889
f. player piano was like a large music box operated by foot pedals
g. some people fainted when they saw an early demonstration of the phonograph because they couldn't believe that sounds could be reproduced
h. accordions and banjos were also popular musical instruments at that time
i. many people had a piano or an organ
j. windup phonograph was most popular kind in early 1900s

EXERCISE 10 Writing a Working Thesis Statement

Using your notes from Exercise 9, write a working thesis statement for the research paper on home entertainment 100 years ago. Save your work for Exercise 12. *Sample answer:* People 100 years ago had both sights and sounds to entertain them at home.

Outlining

The final step in the prewriting stage is to organize your notes into an *outline* of your research paper. The categories you made for your note cards will be the basis for your outline. Look over the categories and your working thesis statement and decide which type of order is most appropriate for your subject. (See page 472.) *Chronological order,* for example, is the best type of order for a research paper on a historical subject or on the steps in a process. *Spatial order* is sometimes useful for a research paper that describes or analyzes something. *Order of importance* and *developmental order* are perhaps the most common types of organization for research papers. Once you have chosen the best method of organization, you can begin outlining.

23i Begin the **outline** of your research paper by deciding on a method of organization and assigning your categories Roman numerals accordingly.

The categories on the lost city of Atlantis were arranged in developmental order. Notice that each category is phrased in a form parallel to all the others.

    I. Plato's story of Atlantis
   II. Strengths of the Thera theory
  III. Weaknesses of the Thera theory

An outline organizes the material for the body of a research paper. You may choose, therefore, to save one or two of your main categories for use in the introduction and the conclusion. The person writing on Atlantis, for example, outlined three of the categories on page 541, saving the other two categories for the introduction and conclusion of the paper.

After you establish your main topics, the next step is to go back over your notes and begin adding subtopics (capital letters) and supporting points (Arabic numerals) to fill out the outline.

23j Use your note cards to add **subtopics** and **supporting points** to the skeleton of your outline.

Use the following outline on Atlantis as a model for outlining your research paper. Notice that each group of subtopics and supporting points is also phrased in parallel form.

WORKING THESIS STATEMENT   A recent theory that places the lost city of Atlantis on the island Thera has strengths and weaknesses.

Research Papers

MAIN TOPIC   I. Plato's story of Atlantis
  SUBTOPIC   A. Setting
SUPPORTING   1. Date
    POINTS   2. Location
                     3. Type of civilization
               B. Description
                     1. Circles within circles
                     2. Palaces
               C. Downfall
          II. Strengths of Thera theory
              A. Location, size, and shape
              B. Volcanic eruption
              C. Buried city
         III. Weaknesses of Thera theory
              A. Insufficient proof of Minoan seafaring strength
              B. Discrepancy in dates
                   1. Gap of 8,000 years
                   2. Attempts to explain gap

When you have finished your outline, check its form by using the checklist on page 465.

EXERCISE 11   Completing an Outline

Use the following list of unsorted items to complete the outline that follows it.

List of unsorted items

- 234 pounds with backpack
- Liquid spices to prevent particles from floating in low gravity
- Need for furniture shaped to match the natural slouch of floating astronauts
- Space furniture
- Weight
- Supplies oxygen
- Furniture for eating
- Moisture readded in space by astronauts' squirting water into meal's plastic container
- Metal surfaces for magnetic meal plates

SUBJECT   Space Equipment

    I. Space foods
       A. Liquid spices to prevent particles from floating . . .
          1. Salt
          2. Pepper
          3. Sugar
       B. Dehydrated meals
          1. Moisture removed on Earth
          2. Moisture readded in space . . .
   II. Space furniture
       A. Furniture for rest
          1. Effect of low gravity on sitting
          2. Need for furniture shaped to match . . .
       B. Furniture for eating
          1. High tables to account for upward-floating astronauts
          2. Metal surfaces for magnetic meal plates
  III. Space suits
       A. Weight
          1. 234 pounds with backpack
          2. 484 pounds with manned maneuvering unit
       B. Life-support abilities
          1. Provides cooling system
          2. Supplies oxygen
          3. Maintains proper air pressure

EXERCISE 12   Outlining

Using your work from Exercises 9 and 10 on page 542, write a simple outline showing three main topics (Roman numerals) with at least three subtopics (capital letters) under each. Copy your working thesis statement above the outline. Check to be sure that your outline follows the correct form. Save your work for Exercise 15.   *Sample answer precedes this chapter.*

EXERCISE 13   On Your Own

Review what you have learned about prewriting on pages 531–544. Then find and limit a subject for a research paper. Use the library to gather information from at least three sources and take notes on cards from each source. Organize

your information into categories. Write a working thesis statement. Then use your categories to write an outline of the body of your research paper. Save your work for Exercise 20.
Answers will vary.

WRITING

As you write the first draft of your research paper, you begin fitting the pieces of your research puzzle into a well-formed whole. Your goals at this stage are to present your ideas smoothly and to work the information from your sources into the flow of your paper.

Writing the Thesis Statement

The *thesis statement* expresses the main idea and controls the entire research paper. It is helpful, therefore, to begin writing the first draft of your research paper by revising your working thesis statement. When you write your introduction, you can work your thesis statement into the appropriate spot. Use the guidelines below to revise your thesis statement.

23k

> **Guidelines for a Thesis Statement**
> 1. A thesis statement should make the main point of your research paper clear to a reader.
> 2. A thesis statement should be broad enough to cover all the main topics listed in your outline.

The following main topics are for a research paper on becoming a master craftsman in eighteenth-century America.

    I. Acquiring an apprenticeship
   II. Serving as an apprentice
  III. Becoming a master: independence

You might write the following working thesis statement.

WORKING THESIS STATEMENT   Serving as an apprentice in eighteenth-century America meant placing your life in the hands of the master.

Writing the Thesis Statement

23k

This thesis statement is weak because it is too narrow. It does not control all of the main topics listed in the outline. A better thesis statement would be the following.

REVISED THESIS STATEMENT Becoming a master craftsperson in eighteenth-century America involved acquiring and serving an apprenticeship which was often a difficult time for the apprentice.

EXERCISE 14 **Revising Thesis Statements**

Each of the following thesis statements fails to control all the main topics listed in the outline accompanying it. Rewrite each statement so that it is broad enough to cover all the main topics. *Sample answers precede this chapter.*

A Dog's Life

1. Dogs descended from the wolf are different from those whose ancestors were jackals.
    I. Differences in potential to be trained
    II. Differences in loyalty
    III. Similarities
2. Male dogs in the wild observe certain rules of etiquette toward female dogs and young puppies.
    I. Refusal to attack female dog
    II. Refusal to attack puppies
    III. Refusal to attack other animals that live in their home territory
3. Guide dogs provide a sightless owner with complete freedom of movement and are a great help to society.
    I. Accomplishments of guide dogs
    II. Accomplishments of police dogs
    III. Accomplishments of working dogs on farms and ranches
4. Domestic dogs retain several physical traits of puppyhood that wolves lose when they mature.
    I. Curly tails
    II. Floppy ears
    III. Emotional attachment to mother figure
5. A trainer can use a dog's instincts to help in the training process.
    I. Importance of praise
    II. Importance of right equipment
    III. Pack and den instincts

Research Papers

EXERCISE 15 Revising a Working Thesis Statement
Using your work from Exercise 12, revise your working thesis statement if it does not cover all the main topics in your outline. *Answers will vary.*

Structuring the Research Paper

As you write your first draft, keep in mind the structure of a good research paper. The following chart shows each part of a research paper and the purpose it serves. Note the special features.

The Structure of a Research Paper

Parts	Purpose
title	• suggests the subject of the research paper
introduction	• captures attention • provides necessary background information • contains the thesis statement
body	• supports the thesis statement with information drawn from research • contains well-developed body paragraphs
conclusion	• brings the research paper to a close by restating the thesis or referring to earlier ideas with fresh emphasis

Special Features

footnotes	• give credit to other authors for words and ideas • appear at the bottom of pages
bibliography	• lists sources used in preparing the research paper • appears at the end of paper

When you prepare your first rough draft, indicate each borrowed word, idea, or fact with a number above the line in which it appears. Be sure to keep track of the source and page number from which each borrowed detail is taken. In the next draft, you can go back and prepare the footnotes or endnotes and bibliography in their correct form.

The following sample research paper shows how each element in the structure of a research paper contributes to the whole. The numbers above the line refer readers to the proper footnote.

TITLE Atlantis Rediscovered?

INTRODUCTION:
BACKGROUND
INFORMATION For hundreds of years people have wondered whether the sunken city of Atlantis was myth or reality. Speculations about Atlantis and efforts to locate it have given rise to some 50,000 books on the subject.[1] Over the centuries theorists have placed the lost city in virtually all parts of the world, even in highly unlikely areas. These include "southern Sweden, the Caucasus mountains, Southern America, Ceylon, Algiers, and the western bulge of Africa."[2] Evidence used to support these various theories includes ruins found by digging, strange migration patterns of eels,[3] and photographs of underwater stones that are believed to "bear the mark of human handiwork."[4]

FOOTNOTES

[1] "Greek Backs Plato Theory on Where to Find Atlantis," New York Times, 29 August 1979, Sec. A, p. 4, col. 3.

[2] Willy Ley, Another Look at Atlantis (Garden City: Doubleday, 1969), p. 9.

[3] Otto Muck, The Secret of Atlantis, trans. Fred Bradley (New York: Times Books, 1976), p. 88.

[4] Craig R. Whitney, "Soviet Scientist Says Ocean Site May Be Atlantis," New York Times, 21 May 1979, Sec. A, p. 14, col. 1.

Research Papers

THESIS STATEMENT

In recent years the theory that has received the most attention links the lost city of Atlantis to the real-life ancient Minoan culture on the Aegean islands of Crete and Thera.

MAIN TOPIC I FROM OUTLINE

The original and only written source of the Atlantis story is writings of the Greek philosopher Plato, who lived between 427 and 347 B.C. He relates the story of a powerful, seagoing civilization that lived about 9500 B.C. on a continent called Atlantis in front of the Strait of Gibraltar. With their mighty power, the Atlanteans began conquering nearby peoples, including Athenians and Egyptians, and their might continued to grow.[5] Plato describes in very specific detail the island home of these people, painting a picture of a kingdom built in circles within circles, each separated by a canal. He also describes palaces of unbelievable beauty housing temples to Poseidon, the king.[6] Plato says that in the height of their glory, the Atlanteans' island home was swept by sudden floods and earthquakes

---

[5] Plato, *Timaeus*, trans. R.G. Bury (Cambridge: Harvard University Press, 1961), pp. 41-43.

[6] Plato, *Critias*, trans. R.G. Bury (Cambridge: Harvard University Press, 1961), pp. 281-295.

Structuring the Research Paper

and in a single day and night sank into the depths of the sea.[7]

MAIN TOPIC II FROM OUTLINE

The Minoans and their island home fit some of the descriptions Plato offers. Although the center of the empire was on Crete, other Minoans lived on Thera. Thera is part of a circular group of islands about 100 kilometers north of Crete. The location, size, and shape of this island group match those same features of Plato's Atlantis. Most significantly, scientists now know that a volcano that erupted

BORROWED WORDS IN QUOTATION MARKS

on Thera threw "about four times the volume of pumice and cinders into the atmosphere as Krakatoa did in 1883."[8]

In 1967, diggings on the island of Thera uncovered a prehistoric Minoan city buried in the layers of volcanic ash.[9] The

BORROWED INTERPRETATION CITED WITH NOTE

cataclysmic explosion created killer waves that reached nearby Crete and weakened or destroyed the Minoans' all-important harbors. With their naval strength cut off, the Minoan empire faded.[10]

SHORTENED NOTES

[7] Plato, *Timaeus*, p. 43.

[8] Ley, p. 13.

[9] Cokie Roberts and Steven V. Roberts, "Atlantis Recaptured," *New York Times Magazine*, 5 September 1976, p. 12.

[10] "Was Atlantis an Island in the Mediterranean?" *The UNESCO Courier*, May 1976, p. 29.

Research Papers

MAIN TOPIC III FROM OUTLINE

Many important details in the story of the Minoans, however, do not even come close to matching Plato's story of Atlantis. Some scholars, for example, do not believe that the Minoan culture was ever a very powerful seagoing empire. The most glaring difference between the stories, however, is the date of the volcanic eruption, which scientists place at about 1450 B.C. Plato's version relates a catastrophe that happened 8,000 years earlier. Atlantis expert A. G. Galanopoulous explains this disagreement by arguing that in the centuries-long process of transmitting the Atlantis story, all the numbers were mistakenly multiplied by ten.[11] Most scientists, whether they believe in the reality of Atlantis or accept it as a myth, agree that no advanced civilization could have existed as early as 9500 B.C.

CONCLUSION

The Thera-Crete theory about Atlantis suffers from the same fundamental problem as all the others. The problem is Plato's original account, with its own perplexing contradictions. Many people believe that Plato made up the story of Atlantis as a fable to show how warlike peoples are punished for their deeds. As far as we

---

[11] Edwin S. Ramage, "Perspectives Ancient and Modern," in _Atlantis: Fact or Fiction?_. ed. Edwin S. Ramage (Bloomington: Indiana University Press, 1978), p. 41.

know, no other written source relates the Atlantis story, even though extensive written accounts of other ancient happenings do exist. Of the 50,000 volumes on Atlantis, those that take Atlantis as a reality attempt to squeeze their theories into the confusing shape of Plato's original story. For now, the mystery is still unsolved, but the age-old quest for the city beneath the sea will no doubt continue into future ages.

Bibliography

"Greek Backs Plato Theory on Where to Find Atlantis." New York Times, 29 August 1979, Sec. A, p. 4, cols. 3-4.

Ley, Willy. Another Look at Atlantis. Garden City: Doubleday, 1969.

Muck, Otto. The Secret of Atlantis. Trans. Fred Bradley. New York: Times Books, 1976.

Plato. Critias. Trans. R.G. Bury. Cambridge: Harvard University Press, 1961.

----------. Timaeus. Trans. R.G. Bury. Cambridge: Harvard University Press, 1961.

TEN HYPHENS SHOW WORK BY THE SAME AUTHOR AS ABOVE

Ramage, Edwin S. "Perspectives Ancient and Modern." In Atlantis: Fact or Fiction? Ed. Edwin S. Ramage. Bloomington: Indiana University Press, 1978, pp. 3-45.

Roberts, Cokie, and Steven V. Roberts. "Atlantis Recaptured." New York Times Magazine, 5 September 1976, pp. 12-13 + 34-37.

"Was Atlantis an Island in the Mediterranean?" The UNESCO Courier, May 1976, p. 29.

Whitney, Craig R. "Soviet Scientist Says Ocean Site May Be Atlantis." New York Times, 21 May 1979, Sec. A, p. 14, col. 1.

Research Papers

As you are fleshing out your notes into a smoothly written paper, remember to use transitions to connect your ideas. They will serve as guideposts to readers as they follow your thoughts.

23m

Ways to Connect Ideas

1. Use transitional words and phrases such as *first, second, most important,* and *finally.* (See pages 416, 422, 426, and 472 for lists of transitions.)
2. Repeat key words or phrases from earlier sentences or paragraphs.
3. Use pronouns in place of nouns used earlier.

EXERCISE 16 Recognizing Transitions
Answer the following about the research paper on Atlantis.
Answers precede this chapter.
1. What key word in the thesis statement is repeated in the first sentence of the second paragraph?
2. What transition in the third paragraph points to the most important fact about Thera?
3. What transition in the fifth paragraph signals a change in the direction of thought about the Thera theory?
4. Find two other transitions in the fifth paragraph.
5. To what ideas in the introduction do the words *all the others* in the conclusion refer?

Using and Citing Sources

The ideas and words of authors are protected by law. Failure to give proper credit for borrowed words, ideas, and facts is called *plagiarism,* a serious and unlawful offense. All borrowings must be cited in your research paper with a footnote that gives credit to the original author. All books, articles, and other sources you used in preparing your research paper must be listed in a bibliography.

Using Sources. Besides giving proper credit to sources, you should also try to work borrowed ideas smoothly into your own writing. The suggestions that follow show five good ways to use sources in your paper.

Using and Citing Sources

23n

Tips for Using Sources

1. Use a quotation to finish a sentence you have started.

    EXAMPLE   Photographs taken in 1977 of underwater stones are believed to "bear the mark of human handiwork."[1]

2. Quote a whole sentence.

    EXAMPLE   "The absence of human skeletons from the city indicates that the inhabitants had advance warning of the oncoming of the volcano and had time to evacuate the island."[2]

3. Quote five or more lines from your source. (Start the quotation on a new line after skipping two lines and indenting ten spaces. You do not need quotation marks for such an extended quotation. A colon is usually used in the sentence that introduces the quotation.)

    EXAMPLE   Here is how Plato describes the downfall of Atlantis in the dialogue called *Timaeus:*

    > Afterwards there occurred violent earthquakes and floods. In a single day and night of misfortune, all your warlike men in a body sank into the earth, and the island of Atlantis in like manner disappeared in the depths of the sea.[3]

4. Quote just a few words.

    EXAMPLE   According to Plato, "in a single day and night"[4] Atlantis was destroyed.

5. Paraphrase information from a source.

    EXAMPLE   "Although many have dismissed Atlantis as a myth, some 50,000 volumes have been written trying to describe and locate it." [original]
    Speculations about Atlantis and efforts to locate it have given rise to 50,000 books on the subject.[5] [paraphrase]

Research Papers

EXERCISE 17 Using Sources

Read the following excerpt about parachutes. Use it as a source to complete the assignment that follows it.

Parachutes Past and Present

The principle and construction of the parachute might seem pretty elementary in these days of advanced aerodynamic technology. Early experiments with the devices, however, were feats of considerable daring, usually performed before breathless crowds at country fairs. Louis Sébastien Lenormand of France was the first to demonstrate his rustic canopy parachute in action. In 1783, he leaped from a high tower to a safe landing. Fourteen years later an excited crowd of Parisians gathered in the Parc Monceau to watch André Jacques Garnerin rise to an altitude of 3,000 feet in the basket of a balloon, abruptly cut the suspension cord, and descend gracefully to Earth with a parachute resembling an oversized umbrella. Garnerin went on to exhibit his jumps at ever increasing heights in various countries, leaping 8,000 feet in England in 1802.

The first parachutes were of canvas, later replaced by silk, and then nylon, which is used today. An important development, undoubtedly not considered in the early parachutes, is the use of numerous different pieces of fabric. These are cut, sewn, and arranged to confine a possible tear to the section in which it starts. The apparatus (parachute and suspension lines) is assembled in a pack. The rip cord that releases the parachute may be operated manually, or automatically via a timing device, or by a line attached to an aircraft. The first man to jump from a plane was Captain Albert Berry of the U.S. Army in 1912. Enormous parachutes helped the *Apollo 14* space capsule land in 1971. Perhaps the most extraordinary parachute is that used for getting out of an aircraft moving at supersonic speeds. In this case, the entire seat goes along—pilot, seat, and parachute are ejected by a rocket charge. Eventually, the seat is left behind and the parachute opens automatically, cutting the pilot's speed as he or she descends.   — CAROLINE SUTTON, *HOW DID THEY DO THAT?*

Sample answers precede this chapter.

1. Write a sentence about early experiments with parachutes. End your sentence with a quotation.
2. Write three sentences about Lenormand and Garnerin. One sentence should be a direct quotation.

Using and Citing Sources

23o-p

3. Write a paragraph about modern parachutes that includes an extended quotation of five lines or more. Be sure to indent the quoted lines correctly and remember that quotation marks are not necessary.
4. Write a sentence describing Garnerin's parachute that quotes just a few words from the source.
5. Write two sentences paraphrasing the information about parachutes used to leave supersonic aircraft.

Citing Sources. Notes that tell the original source of words or ideas you have used in your research paper are called *citations*. *Footnotes* are one type of citation. A very similar type is the *endnote*. Instead of identifying sources at the bottom, or foot, of the page, endnotes come at the end of the paper, after the conclusion but before the bibliography. A third type of citation is the *parenthetical citation*. Parenthetical citations are contained in the paper itself, in parentheses directly following the borrowed material. If you use parenthetical citations, include the same information in parentheses as you would in a footnote or endnote.

23o
Cite the sources of information you include in your research paper by using **footnotes, endnotes,** or **parenthetical citations.**

Use the following guidelines to determine what information should be cited.

23p

Citing Sources

1. Cite the sources of direct quotations. Use direct quotations only when the author's original wording makes the point more strongly or interestingly than you could by using your own words.
2. Cite the sources of ideas you gained from research, even though you express the ideas in your own words.
3. Cite the sources of figures and statistics you use.
4. Do not cite facts or ideas that are common knowledge.

The form for footnotes and endnotes is the same. In the research paper itself, following borrowed material, a number

Research Papers

refers readers to the footnote or the endnote with the same number. *(See the research paper on pages 549–553.)* Each footnote or endnote includes three important pieces of information that a reader would need in order to find the original source: the author and title, publication information, and the page number.

Correct Form for Footnotes and Endnotes

GENERAL REFERENCE WORKS	[1] Charlotte E. Goodfellow, "Atlantis," <u>World Book Encyclopedia</u>, 1983 ed. [2] "Atlantic States," <u>World Book Encyclopedia</u>, 1983 ed.
BOOKS WITH A SINGLE AUTHOR	[3] John S. Bowman, <u>The Quest for Atlantis</u> (Garden City: Doubleday, 1971), p. 38.
BOOKS WITH MORE THAN ONE AUTHOR	[4] Katherine E. Wilkie and Elizabeth R. Mosely, <u>Atlantis</u> (New York: Messner, 1979), p. 22.
ARTICLES IN MAGAZINES	[5] Thomas Fleming, "Solving the Lost-Continent Mystery," <u>The Reader's Digest</u>, Aug. 1978, p. 131.
ARTICLES IN NEWSPAPERS	[6] Craig R. Whitney, "Soviet Scientist Says Ocean Site May Be Atlantis," <u>New York Times</u>, 21 May 1979, Sec. A, p. 14, col. 1.
INTERVIEWS	[7] Personal interview (*or* Telephone interview) with Professor Stan Harrison, Department of Classics, Harperstown College, 23 April 1986.

For repeated references to a work already cited, you can use a shortened form of footnote. The author's last name and the page number are enough to refer to a work already fully cited. If you have cited more than one work by the author, include the title in the shortened footnote.

REPEATED REFERENCES	[1] Ley, p. 17. [2] Plato, <u>Timaeus</u>, p. 13.

Sources cited in notes or mentioned in the research paper must also be listed in a *bibliography*.

23q A **bibliography** is an alphabetical listing of sources used in a research paper. It appears at the end of the research paper.

Bibliography entries differ from footnotes in four main ways: (1) The first line is not indented, but the other lines are. (2) The

Using and Citing Sources

author's last name is listed first. (3) Periods are used in place of commas, and parentheses are deleted. (4) No specific page reference is necessary. Bibliography entries would be listed in alphabetical order (according to the first word of the entry) on a separate page at the end of your research paper.

Correct Form for a Bibliography

GENERAL REFERENCE WORKS	Goodfellow, Charlotte E. "Atlantis." <u>World Book Encyclopedia</u>. 1983 ed. "Atlantic States." <u>World Book Encyclopedia</u>. 1983 ed.
BOOKS WITH A SINGLE AUTHOR	Bowman, John S. <u>The Quest for Atlantis</u>. Garden City: Doubleday, 1971.
BOOKS WITH MORE THAN ONE AUTHOR	Wilkie, Katherine E., and Elizabeth R. Mosely. <u>Atlantis</u>. New York: Messner, 1979.
ARTICLES IN MAGAZINES	Fleming, Thomas. "Solving the Lost-Continent Mystery." <u>The Reader's Digest</u>, Aug. 1978, pp. 128–133.
ARTICLES IN NEWSPAPERS	Whitney, Craig R. "Soviet Scientist Says Ocean Site May Be Atlantis." <u>New York Times</u>, 21 May 1979, Sec. A, p. 14, col. 1.
INTERVIEWS	Harrison, Stan. Telephone interview. 23 April 1984.

Additional examples of footnotes and other guidelines for citing sources are included in the Appendix on pages 615–617.

EXERCISE 18 Preparing Footnotes

Use the information in each item to write a footnote for the source. Use the model footnotes on page 558 as a guide.
Answers precede this chapter.

1. Book title: How to Make a Hit Record
   Place of publication: Scarsdale, New York
   Author: Mike Jahn
   Date of publication: 1976
   Page number: 26
   Publishing company: Bradbury Press

2. Author: Hans Fantel
   Title of newspaper article: How to Choose a CD Player
   Date of newspaper: April 1, 1984
   Name of newspaper: New York Times
   Location of article: Section H, page 27, column 4

Research Papers

3. Name of magazine: New York
   Author of article: Jack Egan
   Date of magazine: October 31, 1983
   Page of quoted material: 54
   Title of article: Pop Records Go Boom

4. Publishing company: Four Winds Press
   Place of publication: New York, New York
   Author of book: William E. Butterworth
   Title of book: Hi Fi: From Edison's Phonograph to Quadrophonic Sound
   Date of publication: 1977
   Page number: 43

5. Name of encyclopedia: Collier's Encyclopedia
   Title of article: Sound Recording and Reproduction
   Author of article: Norman Eisenberg
   Date of encyclopedia: 1980

6. Name of magazine: Glamour
   Date of magazine: October 1983
   Page number of article: 68
   Title of article: The Right Way to Take Care of Records

EXERCISE 19   Preparing a Bibliography
Use the information from Exercise 18 to prepare a bibliography for a research paper on records. Remember to alphabetize the entries and follow the format shown on page 559.
Answers precede this chapter.

EXERCISE 20   On Your Own
Review what you have learned about writing the first draft of a research paper on pages 546–559. Using your outline from Exercise 13 revise your working thesis statement as needed. Then write the first draft of a research paper, being sure to use and cite sources smoothly and accurately. Save your work for Exercise 21.
Answers will vary.

REVISING

The following checklist will help you revise your research paper.

Revising

23r

> **23r**
>
> **Revision Checklist**
>
> **Checking Your Research Paper**
> 1. Does your introduction contain background information and a well-worded thesis statement?
> 2. Does the body of your research paper support the thesis statement?
> 3. Did you use and cite sources correctly?
> 4. Did you use transitional devices?
> 5. Does your research paper have unity? *(See page 478.)*
> 6. Does your research paper have coherence? *(See page 478.)*
> 7. Is your emphasis clear? *(See page 478.)*
> 8. Does your conclusion add a strong ending?
> 9. Does your research paper have a bibliography?
> 10. Does your research paper have a title?
>
> **Checking Your Paragraphs**
> 11. Does each paragraph have a topic sentence? *(See page 411.)*
> 12. Is each paragraph unified and coherent? *(See pages 441–442.)*
> 13. Does one paragraph lead smoothly into the next?
>
> **Checking Your Sentences and Words**
> 14. Are your sentences varied? *(See pages 374–381.)*
> 15. Are your sentences concise? *(See pages 370–373.)*
> 16. Did you use specific words with appropriate connotations? *(See page 365.)*

EXERCISE 21   On Your Own
Using the Revision Checklist, revise the research paper you wrote for Exercise 20. Save your paper for Exercise 22.
Answers will vary.

EDITING

Using sources requires special care in the editing process. The following checklist will help you polish your research paper. You may wish to use the proofreading symbols on page 614 when you edit.

561

Research Papers

23s

Editing Checklist

1. Are your sentences free of errors in grammar and usage?
2. Did you spell each word correctly?
3. Did you capitalize and punctuate correctly?
4. If you quoted a source, did you use the exact words, just as the author wrote them? Did you put them in quotation marks? *(See pages 285-290.)*
5. Does your footnote or endnote form match that in the models on page 558?
6. Does your bibliography form match the model bibliography on page 553?
7. Did you use correct manuscript form? *(See page 559.)*
8. Is your handwriting or typing neat and clear?

EXERCISE 22   On Your Own
Using the Editing Checklist, edit your research paper from Exercise 21. *Answers will vary.*

CHAPTER REVIEW

Write a research paper on one of the following subjects or on one of your own. Use the Steps for Writing Research Papers on page 563 as a guide. *Evaluation suggestion precedes this chapter.*

1. how to prepare for a career in law
2. the role of wolves in the arctic environment
3. the reasons for the stock-market crash of 1929
4. modern submarines
5. how computers compose music
6. the musical career of Seiji Ozawa
7. the steps in obtaining a pilot's license
8. dolphin communications
9. how stunts are performed in movies
10. fear of flying in planes and how to overcome it
11. the effects of a full moon on human behavior
12. the Salem witch trials
13. the American photographer Ansel Adams
14. why some classical works of literature have been banned
15. the services provided by Ronald McDonald houses

Steps for Writing

Research Papers

Prewriting
1. After listing possible subjects, choose one and limit it. *(See pages 532–533.)*
2. Make a list of questions to guide your research. *(See pages 534–535.)*
3. Gather information from books, magazines, newspapers, and interviews with experts. *(See page 535.)*
4. Use note cards for taking notes and summarizing your sources. *(See pages 538–539.)*
5. Organize your notes by finding categories. *(See pages 541–542.)*
6. Write a working thesis statement. *(See page 541.)*
7. Use your working thesis statement and note categories to outline the body of your research paper. *(See pages 542–544.)*

Writing

8. Revise your working thesis statement as needed. *(See pages 546–547.)*
9. Write your first draft, including an introduction, body, and conclusion. *(See pages 548–553.)*
10. Avoid plagiarism by using and citing sources carefully. *(See pages 554–559.)*
11. Add a title.

Revising

12. Using the Revision Checklist, check your research paper for structure, unity, coherence, emphasis, well-developed paragraphs, and varied and lively sentences and words. *(See page 561.)*

Editing

13. Using the Editing Checklist, check your grammar, spelling, mechanics, manuscript form, and footnote and bibliography form. *(See page 562.)*

Chapter 24 Business Letters

OBJECTIVES

- To use the modified-block or block form of business letters with a proper heading, inside address, salutation, body, closing, and signature.
- To address a business envelope properly.
- To write a letter of request.
- To write an order letter.
- To write a letter of complaint.
- To write a letter of application.

MOTIVATIONAL ACTIVITY

Ask students to imagine they are the owners of a pet store seeking a part-time employee to help out with sales and deliveries. They have advertised in the newspaper and have received, among others, the following letters from prospective employees. (Copy the letters on the board or on duplicating masters.)

LETTER 1

> 2220 South Park
> Chicago, IL 60698
> [Today's Date]

The Fish Tank
367 Wilson Road
Chicago, IL 60677

Dear Sir or Madam:

I am writing in response to your ad in last Sunday's paper for a part-time worker in your pet store. My past experience working with animals includes volunteering at the Animal Shelter, taking care of neighbors' pets while the neighbors are on vacation, and training my own dog. I have also been a member of Junior Achievement and have worked as a team leader to sell our products in the school store.

I am a junior in high school and would be free to work after school on weekdays and all day Saturday if necessary. My home phone number and other information are included in the enclosed résumé.

Thank you for your consideration. I will be looking forward to hearing from you soon.

> Sincerely,
>
> *Matt Teller*
>
> Matt Teller

LETTER 2

Dear Pet Stor Owner,

I read our ad in the paper the other day and would like to have the job at you're stor, seeing as how I like animals and need to earn some souny. I've all ready did some work with animals at the shelter, and I've took care of my ~~nieghbors~~ neighbors pets when they went on vacation, I also am in jr. achievement. Plus I trained my own dog. I go to high school but I could work after school and on Saterday, my home phone is 555-7890 and I hope you will call me for the job.

> your friend,
> Bob Singleberry

Ask students to compare the contents of the two letters; help them discover that the qualifications of the two applicants are identical. Then ask them to decide which applicant they would choose and why. The point of the activity is to impress students with the tremendous impact a letter has as a representative of the person who writes it.

TEACHING SUGGESTIONS

Using the Correct Form *(pages 564–566)*

Have students revise Letter 2 above so that it is written well and conforms to the proper form for a business letter. They should use their own names and addresses. They should also keep in mind that they are competing for this job with Matt Teller (the author of Letter 1) and should therefore try to make their letter stand apart from his in style, even though their qualifications are the same.

Chapter 24 a

Business Letters

Types of Business Letters *(pages 566–573)*

For some stimulating activities that provide practice in various types of business letters and also encourage creativity and research, have the students choose one or more letter-writing projects from the following suggestions:

LETTERS OF REQUEST
1. a letter from George Washington to Congress requesting additional supplies for the winter at Valley Forge
2. a letter to NASA from an astronaut on a space station requesting some of the comforts of home
3. a letter from Dorothy to the Wizard of Oz requesting items on behalf of her friends the tin woodsman, the cowardly lion, and the scarecrow

ORDER LETTERS
1. a letter from a citizen of the twenty-second century ordering merchandise from a catalog
2. a letter from a nineteenth-century citizen ordering home remedies displayed at a carnival attraction
3. a letter from an American colonist ordering goods made in England in the eighteenth century

LETTERS OF COMPLAINT
1. a letter from a computer to its owner complaining about being overworked
2. a letter from a factory worker in the early twentieth century complaining about working conditions
3. a letter of complaint to a television station for predicting the outcome of an election before polling places in all parts of the country were closed

LETTERS OF APPLICATION
1. a letter from J. S. Bach applying for a job as a church organist and composer
2. a letter from Albert Einstein applying for admission to college
3. a letter from Christopher Columbus applying to King Ferdinand and Queen Isabella for funds to finance a voyage of exploration

ACTIVITIES FOR DIFFERENT ABILITIES

Basic Students

ACTIVITY 1 Preparing Drafts
To help students concentrate on one item at a time in a business letter, have them first write the body of the letter without worrying about the correct format. They should follow the usual writing steps: listing ideas, organizing ideas, and then writing a first draft with smooth transitions. Only when they are satisfied with the body should they go back and put the other elements of the business letter in place.

ACTIVITY 2 Order Letters
Bring mail-order catalogs containing order blanks to class. Tell students to write a letter ordering one or more items from a catalog, assuming that they have lost the order blank. To help them identify the information they need to include in their letters, have them check the order blanks to see what kinds of information are requested there.

Advanced Students

ACTIVITY 1 Writing Letters of Opinion
Have students write and submit letters of opinion on a school- or community-related subject to the school newspaper.

ACTIVITY 2 Evaluating Letters of Opinion
Have students bring in letters to the editor on some controversial issue from newspapers. Ideally, several of the letters should express a range of views on the same controversy. Duplicate the letters and have students evaluate each of them for effectiveness, using such criteria as logic, use of facts and examples, reasonableness of language, and correctness of writing style.

ADDITIONAL PRACTICE

Teacher's Resource Book: pages 243–246
Workbook: pages 187–188

Business Letters

REVIEW EXERCISES AND TESTS

Student Text
 Chapter Review: pages 573–574
 Standardized Test: pages 575–576

Teacher's Resource Book
 Chapter 24 Test: pages 57–58
 (Also available as spirit duplicating masters.)

ADDITIONAL ANSWERS

EXERCISE 2 Writing an Order Letter *(page 572)*

Sample answer:

18 Carlin Lane
Newark, DE 19713
November 8, 1986

Order Department
Wilson's Farm Stand
11 Milford Road
Fish Creek, WI 54212

Dear Sir or Madam:

Please send me the following items from your catalog:

2 lbs. country cheddar cheese, #37, @ $4.79/lb.	$9.58
1 lb. smoked summer sausage, #42, @ $3.89/lb.	$3.89
2 cheese gift packs, #33, @ $5.00 each	$10.00
shipping and handling	$3.00
	$26.47

I have enclosed a check for $26.47.

Sincerely,
Sally Jo Lewis
Sally Jo Lewis

EXERCISE 3 Revising a Letter of Complaint *(page 572)*

Sample answer:

   Several weeks ago I used your photo-developing service to have some pictures developed through the mail. Last week I received a set of prints that are not mine. I received someone else's prints by mistake, and someone else probably has mine.

   I sent my negatives on July 10. The receipt number from the mailing envelope is 53-76891. The pictures I received have the number 53-76981. I am returning these pictures with this letter. I hope very much that you will be able to track down my prints as soon as possible. Please let me know at your earliest convenience what has happened to my pictures. I have already paid for these pictures, so if they are not found, I will request a refund of my money. Thank you for your help.

Chapter 24 c

Business Letters

EXERCISE 4 Writing a Letter of Application to a School *(page 572)*
Sample answer:

>188 Landis Avenue
>Battle Creek, MI 49015
>April 3, 1986

Director of Undergraduate Admissions
Grand Rapids Junior College
Grand Rapids, MI 49502

Dear Sir or Madam:

    I am a junior in high school and I am interested in the possibility of attending your school. Please send me a catalog of programs and courses, information on tuition and financial aid, and an application form. Although I have not yet decided on a major, I would appreciate receiving any special information you have on the program in communications. Thank you very much.

>Sincerely,
>
>*Charles Boucher*
>Charles Boucher

EXERCISE 5 Writing a Letter of Application for a Job *(page 573)*
Sample answer:

>32B Adams Street
>Oak Mill, Indiana 47240
>May 20, 1986

Mr. Frank McGoy
Senior Librarian
Oak Mill Public Library
1181 Payne Street
Oak Mill, Indiana 47240

Dear Mr. McGoy:

    I am writing to apply for the position of clerk available in your library. A résumé is enclosed. Although I have never had a paying job before, I did volunteer work at Oak Mill Hospital, where I enjoyed helping the patients and staff. I will be available any time after June 6 to begin work, and I can arrange to come in and meet you in person during afternoons or weekends. I hope to hear from you soon.

>Sincerely,
>
>*Marla Garvey*
>Marla Garvey

Chapter 24 d

24

Business Letters

For additional practice for this chapter, see the Teacher's Resource Book and the Workbook.

The ability to write clear and direct business letters is important to students, consumers, and workers. Students use the business letter to apply to colleges or universities, to request information, and to find a job. Consumers use business letters to order merchandise and to register complaints. People at work write business letters to communicate important information and decisions. In this chapter you will learn the correct form for business letters and some tips for writing simply and clearly.

USING THE CORRECT FORM

One important quality of a good business letter is neatness. A neat, easy-to-read letter assures that your request or message will be readily understood. Remember the following tips when you write business letters.

Tips for Neatness in Business Letters

1. Use white paper, preferably 8½ by 11 inches in size.
2. Leave margins at least one inch wide.
3. Type whenever possible.
4. If you type your letter, type your envelope.
5. Fold your letter neatly to fit the envelope.

The form of business letters varies somewhat, although the six parts remain the same. Following is one correct form for a business letter called the block style. In the block style the paragraphs are not indented.

Form for Business Letters

Block Style

heading

                                        113 King Drive
                                        Rowland, NC   28383
                                        April 26, 1986

inside address

Customer Service
Winston Foods
36 Everly Lane
Omaha, NE 68122

salutation

Dear Sir or Madam:

body

_____
_____
_____
_____
_____
_____
_____
_____

closing

                                        Yours truly,

                                        Peggy Feiser

signature

                                        Peggy Feiser

Correct Form for Envelope

```
Peggy Feiser
113 King Drive
Rowland, NC 28383


                      Customer Service
                      Winston Foods
                      26 Everly Lane
                      Omaha, NE   68122
```

Business Letters

24a > The parts of a business letter are the heading, inside address, salutation, body, closing, and signature.

All sample letters in this chapter use modified-block style. In modified block style, the heading, closing, and signature are positioned at the right, as in block style. In modified block style, however, the paragraphs are indented.

HEADING	Write your full address, including the ZIP code. Write the name of your state in full or use the two-letter postal abbreviation. Write the date.
INSIDE ADDRESS	Write the receiver's address two to four lines below the heading. Include the name of the person if you know it, using *Mr., Ms., Mrs., Dr.,* or other title. If the person has a business title, such as *Manager,* write it on the next line. Use the same way of identifying the state that you used in the heading.
SALUTATION	Start two lines below the inside address. Use *Sir or Madam* if you do not know the name. Otherwise use the person's last name preceded by *Mr., Ms., Mrs.,* or other title. Use a colon after the salutation.
BODY	Start two lines below the salutation. Double-space a single paragraph. For longer letters single-space each paragraph, skipping a line between paragraphs.
CLOSING	Start two or three lines below the body. Line up the closing with the left-hand edge of the heading. Use a formal closing such as *Sincerely yours,* or *Yours truly,* followed by a comma.
SIGNATURE	Type your name four or five lines below the closing. Then sign your name in the space between the closing and your typed name.

TYPES OF BUSINESS LETTERS

Business letters are written for a variety of purposes. Four of the most common types are given on the following pages.

24b Use business-letter form for letters of request, order letters, letters of complaint, and application letters.

Letters of Request

Notice how the form for business letters is used to request information.

Letter of Request

```
                                    3508 Dobson Street
                                    Bellwood, PA 16617
                                    June 11, 1986


United States Soccer Federation
350 Fifth Avenue
New York, NY   10001


Dear Sir or Madam:

     Some friends and I are interested in forming
a soccer team. We would eventually like to
be able to compete in league play.  Please
send me information about soccer teams in
our area of Pennsylvania.  If possible, include
the name and number of a person I can contact
in this area.

     We would also appreciate receiving the
guidelines for equipment standards and rules
and regulations that you publish.  If you have any
other information that you think would help
us as we start our team, please send that
also.

     Thank you for your help.


                            Sincerely,
                            Michael Langston
                            Michael Langston
```

Business Letters

Order Letters

Some catalogs and advertisements include an order blank to use when ordering merchandise. If no such blank is available, use business-letter form to order what you want. Be sure to include the order number, price, quantity, and size of the item you want. If you are sending a check or money order (never send cash), identify the amount enclosed in the letter.

Order Letter

```
                                    1456 Highcrest Drive
                                    Harrison, GA 31035
                                    October 14, 1986

Autos Etc., Inc.
388 Millicent Street
Eastman, GA 31023


Dear Sir or Madam:

    Please send me the following items from
your 1986 fall catalog:

    1   cassette case, #478-2A          $11.95
    2   vinyl seatcovers (for
        bucket seats), #532-6T
        @ $12.50 each                    25.00

        shipping and handling             4.30
                                        $41.25

A check for $41.25 is enclosed.

                          Sincerely,

                          Robert Stambley
                          Robert Stambley
```

Letters of Complaint

Most companies with which you do business are ready to help you if you have a problem with their service or product. A polite letter explaining the problem and offering a reasonable solution will probably bring the desired results. Write a letter of complaint as soon as you are aware of the problem. A long delay may make a suitable adjustment difficult or impossible.

Letter of Complaint

```
                                333 Meadow Lane
                                Long Valley, NJ 07843
                                May 17, 1986


Customer Adjustment Department
Sports Togs, Ltd.
1264 Hogan Avenue
Chicago, IL 60689

Dear Sir or Madam:

    I ordered and received a warm-up suit
from your company last week. I washed it
according to the laundering instructions on
the label. When I took it out of the dryer,
however, I found that the stitching around
the waist of the sweat pants had unravelled.
I believe I must have received a faulty
pair of pants, for the sweatshirt was
as good as new after the washing.

    I have enclosed the sweat pants in this
package along with a photocopy of the invoice
and cancelled check. Please send me a new pair
of pants in the same size (medium) and
color (blue).

    Thank you for your attention.

                                Yours truly,

                                Ty Gunnison
                                Ty Gunnison
```

Business Letters

Writing Extra

You can use business form to write a letter expressing an opinion to public figures such as mayors, senators, or school-board members. Like a letter of complaint, a letter of opinion should use a polite and reasonable tone. Courtesy sometimes calls for addressing the public figure in a set style. The models below show the correct form for addressing certain public officials.

President of the United States

INSIDE ADDRESS	The President The White House Washington, D.C. 20013
SALUTATION	Dear President _____:

United States Senator

INSIDE ADDRESS	The Honorable (senator's name) Senate Office Building Washington, D.C. 20013
SALUTATION	Dear Senator _____:

United States Representative

INSIDE ADDRESS	The Honorable (representative's name) House Office Building Washington, D.C. 20013
SALUTATION	Dear Mr. (or Ms.) _____:

Governors and mayors are also referred to as "The Honorable" in the inside address.

EXERCISE 1 Writing a Letter to a Public Official

Write a letter to the president of the United States or to your senator or representative. Express an opinion on a policy of the current administration. You may agree with the administration's policy, or you may disagree with it. Keep your letter short and to the point. Use facts instead of more opinions to back up your point of view. *Answers will vary.*

Application Letters

If you are applying for admission to a school, a neat and correct letter will make a good impression. *(See page 629 for a job application letter.)* When applying for admission to a college, university, or special program, the application letter resembles a letter of request.

Letter of Application to a School

```
                                    2243 Waverly Avenue
                                    Detroit, MI 48201
                                    January 28, 1986


Director of Admissions
Middletown Community College
303 S. Haverford Street
Detroit, MI 48233

Dear Sir or Madam:

    I am interested in applying for admission to
your school in the fall of 1987. I am particularly
interested in the classes you offer in computer
science.

    Please send me information about your school,
including information about tuition and financial aid.
If you have any special information on your
computer-science program, please send that also.
I would appreciate receiving an application form
if one is required. Thank you very much.

                              Sincerely,

                              Ray Sheperd
                              Ray Sheperd
```

Business Letters

EXERCISE 2   Writing an Order Letter
Use the following information to order merchandise from a catalog. Unscramble the information in the inside address and write it in the proper order. Use your own name and address and today's date. Add $3.00 for shipping and handling. Use modified-block style.   *Sample answer precedes this chapter.*

INSIDE ADDRESS	Order Department, Fish Creek, Wisconsin, Wilson's Farm Stand, 11 Milford Road, 54212
MERCHANDISE	2 lbs. country cheddar cheese, #37, $4.79/lb. 1 lb. smoked summer sausage, #42, $3.89/lb. 2 cheese gift packs, #33, @ $5.00 each

EXERCISE 3   Revising a Letter of Complaint
The body of the following letter uses an inappropriate tone for a complaint. Rewrite the letter, correcting the mistakes and revising the tone so that it is polite but firm.   *Sample answer precedes this chapter.*

   Somewhere, some family is wondering why your developing service sent them snapshots of my graduation. I'm certainly wondering why I received pictures of a child's birthday party with people I have never seen before in my life. You obviously can't read numbers or names, or else you wouldn't have sent me the wrong pictures.

   I sent my negatives in on July 10. The receipt number from the mailing envelope is 53-76891. The pictures I received have the number 53-76981. As you know, I've already forked over the money for these pictures, and if I don't get the right pictures in the mail within one week, I will report you to the Better Business Bureau.

EXERCISE 4   Writing a Letter of Application to a School
Choose a school, college, or university you might wish to attend. Write a letter requesting a catalog, information about tuition and financial aid, and an application form. You can find the addresses of colleges and universities in the back of a college dictionary. Address the letter to The Director of Undergraduate Admissions.   *Sample answer precedes this chapter.*

Chapter Review

EXERCISE 5 Writing a Letter of Application for a Job
Write a letter answering the following newspaper advertisement. Use the letter on page 629 as a model.
Sample answer precedes this chapter.

Full-Time Summer Position Available:
Library Clerk

Oak Mill Public Library seeks full-time clerk to check out and shelve books. No experience necessary, but applicants should like working with people. Send résumé and cover letter to Mr. Frank McGoy, Senior Librarian, Oak Mill Public Library, 1181 Payne Street, Oak Mill, Indiana 47240.

EXERCISE 6 On Your Own
Write a letter to the manager of your favorite store. Explain why you enjoy shopping at that store. Use the telephone directory and other resources to find the correct address and ZIP code of the store you choose. *Answers will vary.*

CHAPTER REVIEW

Use the following address to write each of the four letters described. Then make one sample envelope. Use the Steps for Writing a Business Letter on page 574 as a guide.

>Goodwin's Antique Auto Museum
>4215 E. Seventh Avenue
>Concordia, Kansas 66909

1. Write a letter requesting information for a school research paper on antique autos.
2. Write a letter ordering the following merchandise from Goodwin's spring 1986 gift-shop catalog: 2 packages of Model-T note cards, #31, @ $4.50 each; 2 "Made In America" bumper stickers, #43, @ $2.50 each. Include $2.00 for shipping and handling.
3. Write a letter of complaint about rude treatment that you received from a Goodwin employee when you visited the museum last week.
4. Write a letter in which you apply for a part-time job as a tour guide at the museum.

Look for the six parts of a business letter and a correctly addressed envelope with a return address.

Steps for Writing

Business Letter

1. Gather the information you need to explain your request, order, complaint, or application accurately.
2. Follow the Tips for Neatness on page 564.
3. Use the proper form for the heading, inside address, and salutation. *(See pages 565–566.)*
4. Express your message briefly and courteously, following the correct form for the body of the letter. *(See pages 565–566.)*
5. Use the correct form for the closing and signature. *(See pages 565–566.)*
6. Check your letter for errors in grammar, usage, spelling, and mechanics.
7. Keep a copy of your letter.
8. Address the envelope correctly. *(See page 565.)*

STANDARDIZED TEST

COMPOSITION

Directions: Decide which description below best fits each sentence. Fill in the circle containing the letter of your answer.

A if the sentence contains a word with an inappropriate connotation
B if the sentence contains a cliché
C if the sentence is not concise
D if the sentence contains faulty coordination, faulty subordination, or faulty parallelism
E if the sentence contains none of the above

SAMPLE   Due to the fact that it snowed, our plane was delayed.

ANSWER   Ⓐ Ⓑ Ⓒ Ⓓ Ⓔ

D 1. The two-hour parking limit is strictly enforced; furthermore, you had better move your car before five o'clock.
A 2. Ms. Dubois always incites us to speak French in class.
C 3. In Mexico the Mayas and then the Toltecs preceded the Aztecs, who were the people who were conquered by Spain.
E 4. Although *VI* looks like an abbreviation for Virginia, it is actually the official abbreviation for the Virgin Islands.
D 5. Whispering nervously, stepping carefully, and with our flashlights shining, we entered the abandoned old house.
A 6. Because Uncle Louis used his money carefully and wisely, his stinginess helped him to enjoy life.
C 7. It was in 1928 that a fierce hurricane killed 1,836 people living near Lake Okeechobee, Florida.
B 8. After baseball practice Jan arrived home hungry as a wolf.
D 9. Because the eggs are kept warm continuously, the male and female birds take turns sitting in the nest.
C 10. The soapy plate slipped from his hands and broke into dozens of pieces that scattered all over the floor everywhere.
B 11. The lake water was crystal clear; nevertheless, we failed to spot anything remotely resembling the fabled sea monster.
E 12. The editors of the school newspaper desperately needed a typewriter that worked and a person who could type.
A 13. Mercury was named for the messenger of the Roman gods since it whirls about the sun at 30 miles per second.

575

E 14. The entire ninth grade conspired to make the fair a success.
B 15. Carla, pleased as punch, bowed to the applauding audience.

Directions: Reword each sentence as directed and make any other changes required by the revision. Then choose the phrase that must be included in the revised sentence. Fill in the circle containing the letter of your answer.

SAMPLE It was a day for swimming, sunning, and napping on the beach.
Change *napping* to *a nap*

A a swim, sunning,
B to take a swim, sun oneself,
C a swim, a sunbath,
D taking a swim, sunning

ANSWER Ⓐ Ⓑ Ⓒ Ⓓ

D 16. Many people think that rabbits are rodents. They are wrong. Begin with *Although*.

A rodents; they
B rodents, but they
C rodents, and they
D rodents, they

A 17. Ben is a gifted artist, and he wants to design textiles. Begin with *A gifted artist*.

A artist, Ben
B and Ben wants
C artist, and Ben
D artist; Ben

B 18. To be true to oneself is not necessarily to be selfish. Begin with *She declared that being*.

A to be selfish necessarily
B being selfish
C to be necessarily selfish
D oneself necessarily

B 19. Later it was discovered by Liz that the dog had eaten the pizza. Change *it was discovered* to *discovered*.

A Later there was
B Later Liz
C Liz discovered that later
D That later Liz

C 20. There was an attempt yesterday to overthrow the present government of Fortlandia that ended in failure. Begin with *An attempt*.

A Fortlandia, which
B Fortlandia, but it
C Fortlandia ended
D Fortlandia, ending

576

Unit 7

Test Taking

25 Standardized Tests

Chapter 25   Standardized Tests

OBJECTIVES

- To identify synonyms and antonyms.
- To determine the relationship between words in pairs on an analogy test.
- To complete sentences with the word or words that make sense in context.
- To master strategies for answering reading-comprehension questions.
- To identify sentence errors on tests of standard written English.
- To master sentence rephrasing.
- To write a 20-minute essay.

MOTIVATIONAL ACTIVITY

Have students prepare a bibliography of materials that include advice on or practice in preparing for standardized tests, especially the ACT and the SAT.

TEACHING SUGGESTIONS

Vocabulary Tests *(pages 579–590)*

Begin by referring students back to Chapter 13, "Vocabulary." To give them more practice with synonyms and antonyms, have students match five pairs of synonyms and five pairs of antonyms in the following lists.

1. affirmative
2. beneficial
3. circumspect
4. immaterial
5. intricate
6. lenient
7. obstinate
8. prelude
9. raucous
10. relinquish

a. release
b. cooperative
c. strict
d. positive
e. introduction
f. significant
g. quiet
h. harmful
i. complex
j. cautious

ANSWERS
Synonyms   1–d; 3–j; 5–i; 8–e; 10–a
Antonyms   2–h; 4–f; 6–c; 7–b; 9–g

Analogies *(pages 582–586)* Remind students that the word order in an analogy must be the same in the answer as it is in the capitalized pair. Also, it is the relationship between words, not a possibly shared meaning, that counts in an analogy.

Each of the following extra practice items is designed so that the *type* of analogy is the same in all the possible answers, but the *order* of the relationship matches the order of the capitalized pair in only one answer.

1. SOLE:SHOE::(A) mouthpiece:telephone (B) car:tire (C) desk:drawer   *A*
2. SLEET:HAZARD::(A) illness:germs (B) toil:fatigue (C) blush:embarrassment   *B*
3. PAINTER:ROLLER::(A) scalpel:surgeon (B) writer:typewriter (C) hammer:carpenter   *B*
4. WRITER:NOVEL::(A) potter:bowl (B) opera:composer (C) movie:director   *A*
5. TELEPHONE:COMMUNICATE::(A) transport:airplane (B) heat:radiator (C) hose:irrigate   *C*
6. CABIN:DWELLING::(A) car:hatchback (B) stove:appliance (C) mammal:dog   *B*
7. KITCHEN:SINK::(A) screen:television (B) salad:lettuce (C) hand:clock   *B*
8. FOODSTUFFS:FARMER::(A) toolmaker:hammer (B) baker:pastry (C) timber:logger   *C*
9. INSTITUTION:GOVERNMENT::(A) paint:watercolors (B) novels:books (C) soccer:sports   *A*
10. BASEBALL:BAT::(A) racket:ball (B) pins:bowling ball (C) paddle:Ping-Pong ball   *B*

Reading Comprehension Tests *(pages 591–594)*

For practice in selecting suitable titles, refer students to the following list of model paragraphs found on earlier pages. Then list students' suggestions for titles for each paragraph. When you have about five titles for each paragraph, discuss the merits of each title.

Mount St. Helens, Chapter 19, page 413
All paragraphs in Exercise 11, Chapter 19, pages 424–425
All paragraphs in Exercise 12, Chapter 19, pages 427–428

Standardized Tests

Astronaut passage, Chapter 22, page 513
Passage in Exercise 1, Chapter 22, pages 514–516
Brain barrier paragraph, Chapter 22, page 518
Moon vs. Earth paragraph, Chapter 22, page 519
All paragraphs in Exercise 4, Chapter 22, pages 519–520
Passage in Exercise 6, Chapter 22, pages 522–523

Tests of Writing Ability *(pages 594–604)*

After students have completed Exercise 8, have them rewrite the sentences in paragraph format, correcting any errors.

After students have completed Exercise 9, have them identify the kind of error in the underlined part of any incorrectly written sentence.

(ANSWERS)
1. misplaced modifier
2. quotation interrupted by speaker tag
3. pronoun agreement
4. redundancy
5. no error
6. faulty parallelism
7. need for present participle
8. pronoun usage (nominative case needed)
9. no error
10. interrupting phrase needs to be set off with commas

As students are working on Exercise 10, have them write out the revised sentence on a separate sheet of paper so that they can see which phrase they must use in the revision.

ACTIVITIES FOR DIFFERENT ABILITIES

Basic Students

ACTIVITY 1 Analogies
Although students may at first have difficulty with this task, encourage them to try to write their own analogy questions with which they can test their classmates. The process of composing their own analogies will lock the understanding of relationships in their minds. To make their task as simple as possible, refer students to the list of types of analogies on page 583 and have them think of a capitalized pair of words that fits each. Then have them think of three possible answers, one correct and two that represent a different type of analogy.

ACTIVITY 2 The 20-Minute Essay
Encourage students to allow a block of time for each stage of the writing process. You may wish to suggest the following:
Read and understand question—2 minutes
Jot down ideas and plan—6 minutes
Write the essay—9 minutes
Revise and edit—3 minutes

Advanced Students

ACTIVITY 1 Improving Essay Answers
Have students bring in an essay test that they have taken in another class. Then ask them to revise the essay according to the guidelines on page 603.

ACTIVITY 2 Preparing for the SAT
Divide students into small study groups and provide each group with a sample page from a book designed to help students prepare for standardized tests. By circulating around the room and sitting in for a few minutes with each group, show students how to ask questions and work as a group to help one another prepare. After about 15 minutes, have the class as a whole discuss what they learned about working in a study group.

ADDITIONAL PRACTICE

Teacher's Resource Book: pages 247–252

REVIEW EXERCISES AND TESTS

Student Text:
  Chapter Review: pages 604–606
Teacher's Resource Book:
  Chapter 25 Test: pages 59–60
  Postbook Test: pages 61–68
  Standardized Tests: pages 69–80
  (Also available as spirit duplicating masters.)

Chapter 25 b

25

Standardized Tests

For additional practice for this chapter, see the Teacher's Resource Book.

Standardized tests are an important part of your school experience. They will probably help determine your future education and your career. A standardized test measures your academic progress, skills, and achievement.

Your best preparation for any standardized test is to work conscientiously in all your school courses, read widely, and learn the rules of test taking. The following strategies will help you achieve success when you take standardized tests.

Strategies for Taking Standardized Tests

1. Read the test directions carefully. Answer sample questions to be sure you understand what the test requires.
2. Relax. Although you can expect to be a little nervous, concentrate on doing the best you can.
3. Preview the whole test by quickly skimming. This will give you an overview of the kinds of questions on the test.
4. Plan your time carefully, allotting a certain amount of time to each part of the test.
5. Answer first the questions you find easiest. Skip those you find too hard, coming back to them later if you have time.
6. Read all choices before you choose an answer. If you are not sure of the answer, eliminate choices that are obviously wrong. Making an educated guess is generally wise.
7. If you have time, check your answers. Look for omissions and careless errors on your answer sheet.

VOCABULARY TESTS

Standardized vocabulary tests measure your understanding of the meaning of words and the way they are used in sentences. The tests often contain one or more of the following kinds of questions. A synonym question asks you to find a word similar in meaning to another word. An antonym question asks you to find a word opposite in meaning to another word. An analogy question requires that you figure out a relationship between two sets of paired words. A sentence-completion question asks you to fill in a blank with a word that makes the best sense in the context of the sentence.

Synonyms and Antonyms

Synonym questions require you to recognize words that are nearly the same in meaning, such as *agree* and *consent*. Antonym questions require you to recognize words that are most nearly opposite in meaning, such as *evident* and *obscure*. On both synonym and antonym tests, you must find a word or a group of words that is most nearly the same or most nearly the opposite in meaning to a word in capital letters.

Try to find a synonym for *fidelity* among the list of choices in the following synonym question.

FIDELITY   (A) pleasantness   (B) purity
(C) faithlessness   (D) sympathy   (E) loyalty

The answer is *loyalty*. No other choice is acceptable. Neither *pleasantness, purity,* nor *sympathy* is a synonym for *fidelity*. *Faithlessness* is an antonym, not a synonym, for *fidelity*.

Now try to find an antonym for *hostile* among the list of choices in the following antonym question.

HOSTILE   (A) quick-tempered   (B) friendly
(C) sorry   (D) antagonistic   (E) generous

If you chose *friendly,* you are correct. With antonym and synonym questions, you must pay close attention to the directions and then check your answers. It is all too easy to choose a synonym — *antagonistic,* in this case — when you are working on an antonym test, or an antonym on a synonym test.

579

Standardized Tests

Some questions ask you to find *either* a synonym *or* an antonym among the list of choices. Keep in mind that there is only *one* correct answer. Before you make your final selection, skim the list of choices for a synonym, then for an antonym, for the word in capital letters.

In the following question, look for a word that is *either* a synonym *or* an antonym for *prompt*. Use the same strategies you would use to answer a synonym or an antonym question.

PROMPT   (A) organized   (B) tidy   (C) distant   (D) tardy   (E) active

If you chose *tardy,* an antonym for *prompt,* you are correct.

Always consider every choice carefully before you make your final selection. Although you may not know the meaning of every lettered word on the test, you may find that a prefix, root, or suffix provides a clue.

EXERCISE 1   Recognizing Antonyms

Write the letter of the word or group of words most nearly opposite in meaning to the word in capital letters.

B   1. DUBIOUS   (A) hidden   (B) certain   (C) talented   (D) anxious   (E) economical

E   2. AFFIRMATIVE   (A) unwise   (B) relevant   (C) ancient   (D) mischievous   (E) negative

C   3. JEER   (A) taunt   (B) forfeit   (C) praise   (D) repeat   (E) cancel

C   4. STEADFAST   (A) faithful   (B) slow   (C) disloyal   (D) immovable   (E) arrogant

A   5. POTENT   (A) powerless   (B) disorderly   (C) resentful   (D) brave   (E) clumsy

A   6. SOMBER   (A) cheerful   (B) inventive   (C) energetic   (D) inconsiderate   (E) sad

D   7. CORRUPT   (A) eroded   (B) vicious   (C) foolish   (D) upstanding   (E) faded

E   8. PERPETUAL   (A) trustworthy   (B) everlasting   (C) shy   (D) productive   (E) temporary

B   9. FRIVOLOUS   (A) noisy   (B) serious   (C) outrageous   (D) uncommon   (E) reckless

C   10. OPTIMISTIC   (A) humble   (B) proper   (C) gloomy   (D) outstanding   (E) unjust

Vocabulary Tests

B 11. GENTEEL (A) tragic (B) impolite (C) unreliable (D) lazy (E) fearful
E 12. PASSIVE (A) unfriendly (B) doubtful (C) narrow (D) submissive (E) active
D 13. HAPHAZARD (A) lucky (B) clever (C) aimless (D) planned (E) distant
C 14. CONTEMPTIBLE (A) modern (B) stormy (C) admirable (D) intelligent (E) peaceful
A 15. LUSTROUS (A) dull (B) wicked (C) inaccurate (D) candid (E) glossy
E 16. BENEFICIAL (A) tearful (B) clumsy (C) honest (D) accidental (E) harmful
B 17. SUPERFLUOUS (A) small (B) necessary (C) lovely (D) gradual (E) marginal
D 18. TRANQUIL (A) subtle (B) appropriate (C) grave (D) troubled (E) virtuous
B 19. PROFANE (A) word-for-word (B) sacred (C) inoperative (D) discouraging (E) wealthy
A 20. JUDICIOUS (A) unwise (B) illegal (C) blissful (D) truthful (E) incomplete

EXERCISE 2 Recognizing Synonyms and Antonyms
Write the letter of the word or group of words most nearly the same *or* most nearly the opposite in meaning to the word in capital letters.

D 1. INVERSE (A) payable (B) poetic (C) artificial (D) opposite (E) fragrant
E 2. GAUNT (A) strange (B) artistic (C) courageous (D) unlikely (E) fleshy
A 3. LULL (A) pause (B) melody (C) evaluation (D) absence (E) boat
A 4. PARLEY (A) discussion (B) argument (C) bet (D) grain (E) illness
C 5. BLISS (A) mistake (B) sleepiness (C) sorrow (D) question (E) confusion
C 6. FRAUDULENT (A) disordered (B) warm (C) honest (D) elegant (E) diverse
D 7. METROPOLIS (A) clock (B) measurement (C) chemical (D) city (E) engraving

581

Standardized Tests

A 8. TOLERABLE (A) unbearable (B) prejudiced (C) sharp (D) unequal (E) affordable
E 9. VALISE (A) room (B) floor covering (C) doorway (D) cabinet (E) hand luggage
B 10. PREMONITION (A) apprentice (B) warning (C) guess (D) revival (E) cliff
E 11. RIVALRY (A) ceremony (B) hazard (C) confusion (D) signature (E) cooperation
C 12. QUEST (A) gossip (B) answer (C) search (D) essence (E) appearance
A 13. DEVOUT (A) religious (B) affectionate (C) laughable (D) corroded (E) sticky
D 14. FICKLE (A) sour (B) dislocated (C) sly (D) constant (E) dishonest
B 15. CELESTIAL (A) foreign (B) heavenly (C) famous (D) sporty (E) imprisoned
A 16. HECTIC (A) quiet (B) inclusive (C) neglectful (D) lacking (E) revolving
E 17. APPAREL (A) certainty (B) ghost (C) equality (D) device (E) clothing
E 18. ERADICATE (A) joke (B) dismiss (C) lengthen (D) compress (E) exterminate
C 19. CARNIVOROUS (A) hungry (B) festive (C) meat-eating (D) villainous (E) alert
B 20. DEMURE (A) spoiled (B) immodest (C) breathless (D) honest (E) following

Analogies

Analogy questions test your skill at figuring out relationships between words. Your first step on an analogy question is to decide how the first two words are related. In the analogy *sand:beach,* for example, the relationship of the two words is part-to-whole. Your next step is to find the pair of words among the choices that shows the same kind of relationship as that of the first pair. Identify the correct answer in the following analogy.

SAND : BEACH :: (A) common : unusual (B) page : book (C) plumber : wrench (D) halibut : fish (E) flood : destruction

582

The answer is *page:book*. It contains the only part-to-whole relationship among the choices given. The other choices are incorrect. The relationship of *common:unusual* is word-to-antonym, not part-to-whole. *Plumber:wrench* is a worker-to-tool relationship. *Halibut:fish* is an item-to-category relationship, and *flood:destruction* is a cause-to-effect relationship.

Sometimes analogies are written in sentence form and ask you to select the word that best completes the analogy. Following is an example of such an analogy.

Outcome is to *result* as *choice* is to ____.

(A) wish (B) vote (C) selection (D) standard
(E) suggestion

The first two italicized words, *outcome* and *result,* are synonyms. Therefore, the correct answer must be a synonym for *choice*—that is, *selection.*

Knowing some of the common types of analogies will help you figure out word relationships. The following chart lists types of analogies and examples.

Common Types of Analogies	
Analogy	**Example**
word : synonym	legal : lawful
word : antonym	ruthless : merciful
part : whole	carburetor : engine
cause : effect	overproduction : glut
worker : tool	electrician : pliers
worker : product	playwright : drama
item : purpose	fence : enclose
item : category	lobster : crustacean

EXERCISE 3 Verbal Analogies

Write the letter of the word that is related to the *third* italicized word in the same way that the second italicized word is related to the first.

EXAMPLE   *Dachshund* is to *dog* as *python* is to ____.
(A) mammal (B) scorpion (C) eagle
(D) snake (E) earthworm

ANSWER   (D)

583

Standardized Tests

B 1. *Writer* is to *pencil* as *carpenter* is to ____.
    (A) construction (B) hammer (C) electricity
    (D) house (E) wrecker

E 2. *Generous* is to *miserly* as *trustworthy* is to ____.
    (A) uncomfortable (B) boring (C) ridiculous
    (D) serious (E) undependable

A 3. *Hull* is to *ship* as *chassis* is to ____.
    (A) automobile (B) wheel (C) accelerator
    (D) framework (E) building

B 4. *Consensus* is to *agreement* as *narrative* is to ____.
    (A) argument (B) story (C) bookbinding
    (D) patriotism (E) athletics

C 5. *Miner* is to *gold* as *journalist* is to ____.
    (A) typewriter (B) press box (C) news (D) steel
    (E) columnist

D 6. *Tear* is to *sew* as *break* is to ____.
    (A) fragile (B) piece (C) shatter (D) glue (E) mold

C 7. *Evergreen* is to *fir* as *deciduous* is to ____.
    (A) forest (B) conservation (C) maple (D) north
    (E) leaf

A 8. *Computer* is to *keyboard* as *bicycle* is to ____.
    (A) handlebars (B) tricycle (C) maintenance
    (D) color (E) transportation

C 9. *Scientist* is to *research* as *legislator* is to ____.
    (A) mayor (B) democracy (C) lawmaking
    (D) history (E) politician

D 10. *Expel* is to *admit* as *praise* is to ____.
    (A) applaud (B) disallow (C) demand
    (D) disapprove (E) eliminate

EXERCISE 4 Recognizing Analogies

Write the letter of the word pair that has the same relationship as the word pair in capital letters.

D 1. OVEN : CHEF :: (A) dentist : drill (B) patient : doctor
    (C) job : typist (D) kiln : potter (E) pump : gasoline

D 2. EXTINCT : DINOSAUR :: (A) contemporary : new
    (B) flower : petals (C) marsupial : kangaroo
    (D) outdated : stagecoach (E) enjoyable : book

A 3. SONG : BALLAD :: (A) poem : haiku (B) scene : drama
    (C) flight : bird (D) desert : dry (E) novel : plot

Analogies

C 4. MAGNIFICENT : SPLENDID :: (A) spectacular : scenery
(B) dreary : exciting (C) saturated : drenched
(D) client : attorney (E) diamond : gorgeous

C 5. EAVES : ROOF :: (A) road : driver (B) forest : tree
(C) steps : staircase (D) germ : bacteria (E) pen : ink

D 6. KNOLL : MOUNTAIN :: (A) fox : rabbit
(B) rock : pebble (C) rat : rodent (D) creek : river
(E) role : actor

E 7. HABITAT : HOME :: (A) cockpit : airplane (B) sty : pig
(C) Earth : moon (D) principal : school
(E) sovereign : monarch

A 8. PEACOCK : PLUMAGE :: (A) chinchilla : fur
(B) arm : hand (C) cup : saucer (D) parrot : mimic
(E) leather : wallet

B 9. RIVALRY : COMPETITION :: (A) mystery : solution
(B) secret : covert (C) glittering : gem
(D) general : specific (E) victory : team

D 10. FARMER : CROPS :: (A) bus : driver (B) wet : rain
(C) metal : welder (D) contractor : buildings
(E) tent : camper

C 11. REIN : HORSE :: (A) wolf : howl (B) ask : answer
(C) leash : dog (D) antenna : roof (E) tie : knot

D 12. RETINA : SIGHT :: (A) water : dissolve (B) light : dark
(C) paper : ink (D) film : photography (E) touch : hand

C 13. EVADE : AVOID :: (A) chuckle : scowl (B) match : fire
(C) donate : give (D) forget : recall (E) cry : tears

B 14. GOAL : SOCCER :: (A) game : tennis
(B) home run : baseball (C) penalty : hockey
(D) aim : archery (E) parachute : skydiving

A 15. DYNASTY : RULER :: (A) country : president
(B) chess : pawn (C) team : spirit (D) yeast : dough
(E) cash : money

E 16. CHORUS : SINGING :: (A) lock : key (B) oral : spoken
(C) whole : part (D) imperial : empire (E) cast : acting

A 17. TEACHER : INSTRUCTOR :: (A) doubt : uncertainty
(B) book : student (C) school : building
(D) coach : team (E) adult : child

B 18. LUNAR : SOLAR :: (A) foolish : proud (B) moon : sun
(C) exploration : explorer (D) particle : matter
(E) shy : timid

Standardized Tests

E 19. COVE:LAKE:: (A) river:source   (B) stone:rock
(C) peninsula:water   (D) state:county   (E) bay:ocean
E 20. BRONZE:STATUE:: (A) magazine:cover
(B) house:attic   (C) foundation:base
(D) egg:chicken   (E) wool:rug

Sentence Completion

Sentence-completion questions require you to supply a missing word or words that will best complete a sentence. These questions demand skill in figuring out meanings from context. *(See pages 305–306.)* Sentence-completion questions deal with a variety of subjects, but they do not require that you have prior knowledge of these subjects. You can determine answers from context alone, often by noticing key words that appear in the sentences.

Following is a typical sentence-completion item. Complete the sentence by choosing the most appropriate word from the list of choices.

> The two state representatives have little in common either personally or politically; they are about as ____ as two officeholders can be.
> (A) dissimilar   (B) farfetched   (C) philosophical
> (D) moderate   (E) commendable

The answer is *dissimilar*. The key words in the sentence that give a clue to the answer are *little in common*. The other choices—*farfetched, philosophical, moderate,* and *commendable*—do not make sense in the context of the sentence.

Some sentence-completion questions have two blanks in the same sentence. Find the correct answer in this example.

> After the ____ of a strong rally late in the ball game, we were doubly ____ that our team had lost.
> (A) lack . . . surprised   (B) threat . . . amused
> (C) dispute . . . annoyed
> (D) excitement . . . disappointed
> (E) skill . . . doubtful

The answer is *excitement . . . disappointed*. The key words in the sentence that help you determine this answer are *strong rally* and *lost*. *Lack . . . surprised* would make sense only if the team had won. In *threat . . . amused,* the word *threat* seems reasonable, but the word *amused* does not. In *dispute . . . annoyed* and *skill . . . doubtful,* the meanings are incorrect in the context of the sentence.

EXERCISE 5   Sentence Completion
Write the letter of the word or group of words that best completes each of the following sentences.

C 1. While Aztec history can be reconstructed largely from written records, Toltec history is a curious mixture of fact and ___.
   (A) reality   (B) fossil   (C) legend   (D) conflict
   (E) history

E 2. Circus clowns sometimes walk on ___ to make themselves appear very tall.
   (A) tightropes   (B) unicycles   (C) pogo sticks
   (D) trapezes   (E) stilts

B 3. Although this is basically a ___ store, it occasionally sells goods at wholesale discounts to both consumers and other stores.
   (A) grocery   (B) retail   (C) chain   (D) successful
   (E) downtown

A 4. Sheila is always cheerful, buoyant, and positive; she has a real ___ for life.
   (A) zest   (B) outlook   (C) mood   (D) thesis
   (E) concern

C 5. Postage stamps often ___ important events and well-known people in a nation's history.
   (A) realize   (B) outline   (C) commemorate
   (D) reward   (E) define

D 6. Boats returning to harbor from open water use buoys as ___; they must keep red or even-numbered buoys on the right, and black or odd-numbered buoys on the left.
   (A) sails   (B) anchors   (C) targets   (D) guides
   (E) docks

B 7. Preserving historical buildings often extends to the ___ of other structures, such as covered bridges.
   (A) building   (B) restoration   (C) photographing
   (D) dilapidation   (E) purchase

Standardized Tests

E 8. Computers have introduced Americans to a specialized vocabulary, a whole ___ of terms to describe the new technology.
(A) word (B) printing (C) mirage (D) perimeter (E) array

D 9. A ___ at the end of the book lists dozens of other sources of information on the Comanches and Apaches.
(A) table of contents (B) footnote (C) preface (D) bibliography (E) binding

E 10. Even good typists may ___ letters in certain words, such as the *he* in *the (teh)* and the *an* in *can (cna)*.
(A) delete (B) repeat (C) obscure (D) erase (E) transpose

B 11. Yesterday the temperature reached 105°F, and the ___ weather is expected to continue.
(A) pleasant (B) sweltering (C) stormy (D) wintry (E) invigorating

A 12. Mexico City is one of the most ___ cities in the world, with more people than New York City, Hong Kong, or London.
(A) populous (B) civilized (C) remarkable (D) exotic (E) scenic

C 13. The opposing team led 47-0 at halftime, causing our coach to remark that we had not merely lost, but had been ___.
(A) triumphant (B) congratulated (C) conquered (D) marvelous (E) victorious

A 14. In spite of widespread unemployment, there were ___ shortages of skilled workers such as chefs, bakers, and cabinetmakers.
(A) numerous (B) few (C) obvious (D) additional (E) extreme

C 15. A person learns to write well only through long and ___ practice.
(A) casual (B) enjoyable (C) diligent (D) unaided (E) occasional

A 16. Once a year we check our ___ by taking everything off the shelves and counting each item one by one.
(A) inventory (B) profit (C) ordering (D) proceeds (E) salesmanship

Sentence Completion

E 17. Linda writes fascinating stories and poems as well as straightforward, convincing ____.
(A) equations (B) music (C) games (D) ambiguity
(E) persuasion

C 18. Because gas fumes ____ the human presence, visitors to African game preserves must stay in their cars to be safe.
(A) camouflage (B) annoy (C) reveal
(D) convince (E) encourage

B 19. All the visible colors of the ____ can be seen through a prism.
(A) sky (B) spectrum (C) universe (D) facet
(E) palette

B 20. First-aid instruction for children under 16 is optional, but for all others it is ____.
(A) pointless (B) desirable (C) stimulating
(D) certain (E) fatiguing

EXERCISE 6 Sentence Completion with Two Blanks
Write the letter of the pair of words that best completes each of the following sentences.

C 1. There is nothing quite so ____ as to assemble a complicated model airplane and have two or three parts ____ left over.
(A) humorous . . . vaguely
(B) gruesome . . . simply
(C) frustrating . . . unaccountably
(D) neat . . . cleverly (E) burdensome . . . dismally

E 2. Across the road stood a ____ house, its frame sagging, its shingles loose, its chimney crumbling, and its windows ____.
(A) cheerful . . . sparkling
(B) new . . . cobwebbed (C) rambling . . . intact
(D) Victorian . . . insulated (E) deserted . . . broken

A 3. Tom is a ____ actor, whose every word, every ____, and every movement is correct.
(A) superb . . . expression
(B) professional . . . error
(C) handsome . . . thought (D) failed . . . line
(E) disdainful . . . blush

589

Standardized Tests

D 4. The ____ town of Odessa, Delaware, now has a population of only about 500, but it once was a ____ seaport.
(A) inland . . . fascinating (B) growing . . . tiny
(C) unusual . . . Pacific (D) little . . . bustling
(E) mining . . . sleepy

B 5. Although ____ listeners to the radio broadcast recognized it as a fictional drama, some listeners thought the events were ____.
(A) few . . . outrageous (B) careful . . . authentic
(C) cynical . . . hilarious (D) naive . . . tragic
(E) local . . . dubious

C 6. The last rays of the sun ____, and darkness ____ the land.
(A) glared . . . swallowed (B) disappeared . . . lit
(C) faded . . . enveloped
(D) sparkled . . . abandoned
(E) disengaged . . . pacified

A 7. Most of the ____ cities in the United States are not state capitals, but Phoenix — among the most populous — is an ____.
(A) largest . . . exception (B) oldest . . . original
(C) growing . . . example
(D) commonplace . . . oddity (E) urban . . . ideal

C 8. Just as the typewriter ____ office practices in the late nineteenth century, the ____ has transformed them in modern times.
(A) improved . . . boss (B) upset . . . calculator
(C) revolutionized . . . computer
(D) restricted . . . union (E) enlivened . . . software

E 9. During the dark days of World War II, Winston Churchill ____ his countrymen to the ____ of England.
(A) cautioned . . . harm (B) scolded . . . plight
(C) offered . . . transfer
(D) reassured . . . betterment
(E) rallied . . . defense

D 10. Many of the most ____ architects since the 1930s have ____ buildings for the city of Columbus, Indiana.
(A) eager . . . built (B) moody . . . criticized
(C) imaginative . . . razed
(D) renowned . . . designed
(E) argumentative . . . defended

Standardized Tests

A pebble begins as part of a larger rock and often ends up as part of a larger rock. As rocks erode, break away, become fragmented, and are transported by water, they become pebbles. Pebbles are generally rounded and smooth, some more so than others. If the rounding and smoothing proceed far enough, the pebbles become gravel or sand. Although large pebbles, small pebbles, gravel, and sand all exist independently, they can also form the basis of new rocks. Pebbles of any size, or of varying sizes, can be bonded together to form either a breccia or a conglomerate.

Some rock fragments travel only a short distance by stream or river, and thus retain the sharp, angular features of the fragments produced by the original fracturing. If consolidation occurs at this point—perhaps by iron oxide's or mud's cementing the fragments together—the result is a *breccia*. A breccia is a rock formed by the natural cementing together of sharp, unrounded fragments into a fine-grained matrix.

As the traveling distance of the original eroded rock increases, rounding continues. The bonded rock that comes from these pebbles is called a *conglomerate*. Many of the pebbles in a conglomerate, unlike those in a breccia, will not have derived from rocks in the immediate vicinity. Some will have been transported long distances, perhaps moved along a seacoast by the action of tides. One famous deposit is at Budleigh Salterton in Devon, England. The pebbles in this conglomerate, most of them quartzite cemented by silica, are thought to have come from the rock of ancient mountains in Brittany, France, and to have been washed to England by waves and tides.

D 1. The best title for this passage is
   (A) Rocks, Wind, and Waves
   (B) What Is a Conglomerate?
   (C) A Brief Look at Geology
   (D) The Life Cycle of Pebbles
   (E) Pebbles at Budleigh Salterton

C 2. Breccia contains sharp, angular pebbles
   (A) there was no water to transport t'
   (B) water molded the pebbles into
   (C) the pebbles did not go far in
   (D) some pebbles are too hard
   (E) cementing made the pebble

READING COMPREHENSION TESTS

Reading-comprehension tests measure your ability to understand and analyze written passages. The information you need to answer the test questions may be either directly stated or implied in the passage. You must study, analyze, and interpret a passage in order to answer the questions that follow it. The strategies below will help you answer the questions.

> **Strategies for Answering Reading-Comprehension Questions**
> 1. Begin by skimming the questions that follow the passage.
> 2. Read the passage carefully and closely. Notice the main ideas, organization, style, and key words.
> 3. Study all possible answers. Avoid choosing an answer the moment you think it is a reasonable choice.
> 4. Use only the information in the passage when you answer the questions. Do not rely on your own knowledge or ideas on this kind of test.

Most reading-comprehension questions will ask you to interpret or evaluate one or more of the following characteristics of a written passage.

• *Main idea.* At least one question will focus on the central idea of the passage. Remember that the main idea of a passage covers all sections of that passage—not just one section or paragraph.

• *Supporting details.* Questions about supporting details test your ability to identify the statements in the passage that back up the main idea.

• *Implied meanings.* In some passages not all information is directly stated. Some questions ask you to interpret information that the author has merely implied.

• *Tone.* Questions on tone require that you interpret or analyze the author's attitude toward his or her subject.

The following passage is an example of the kind you will find reading-comprehension tests. Study it, use the strategies recommended in this chapter, and then answer the questions follow the passage.

A 3. A conglomerate contains pebbles that
   (A) are rounded and smooth
   (B) probably came from another country
   (C) did not originate with eroded rock
   (D) are exceptionally large
   (E) could not have been in rivers or streams
E 4. The writer's attitude toward the subject of pebbles is
   (A) impassioned (B) skeptical (C) friendly
   (D) pessimistic (E) objective

If you used the test-taking strategies on page 591, you should have chosen the following answers.

1. *(D) The Life Cycle of Pebbles.* This title expresses the main idea of the passage. The other choices are either too limited (*B* and *E*) or too broad (*A* and *C*).

2. *(C) the pebbles did not go far in a stream or river.* This supporting detail is stated directly, in slightly different words, in the first sentence of the second paragraph.

3. *(A) are rounded and smooth.* Although this fact is not directly stated, it is well supported by the passage as a whole. The other choices are not supported by the information in the passage.

4. *(E) objective.* The tone of the passage is entirely without emotion. The writing is clear and direct, with no hint of passion, skepticism, friendliness, or pessimism.

EXERCISE 7   Reading Comprehension
Read the following passage and write the letter of each correct answer.

   Although a floppy disk looks like a 45-rpm record in a protective jacket, you have to treat a floppy a lot more carefully. Floppy disks are thin, flexible—and fragile. You must never touch the surface of a floppy. There are many additional *"never*'s." Never take the disk out of its sealed jacket. Never fold, bend, or crease a disk. Never write on its surface. Never leave a disk in direct sunlight or near any source of heat. Never stack disks—store them upright. Never place a disk near a magnet. Never attach paper clips or rubber bands to a disk. Never use any kind of cleaning solution on a disk. After all those *never*'s, how about one *"always"*? All right. Since disks are so delicate, *always* make a backup disk (a duplicate copy) for each floppy disk that contains important material.

593

Standardized Tests

B 1. The main purpose of this passage is to
(A) entertain (B) inform (C) argue (D) describe
(E) amuse

D 2. The writer does *not* warn the reader against
(A) using cleaning fluid on a disk (B) bending a disk
(C) placing a disk close to a magnet
(D) putting one label over another on a disk
(E) stacking disks

C 3. The writer regards floppy disks as
(A) irreplaceable (B) poorly made
(C) easily damaged (D) too costly (E) dangerous

D 4. If you were to damage a disk, the likely result would be
(A) loss of the backup disk
(B) damage to the computer
(C) replacement by the manufacturer
(D) loss of the information on the disk
(E) no particular problem

A 5. The tone of the passage is
(A) imperative (B) despairing (C) cheerful
(D) indifferent (E) hysterical

TESTS OF WRITING ABILITY

There are two kinds of standardized tests that measure writing ability. One is an objective test of standard written English. This multiple-choice test asks you to identify sentence errors or to choose the best wording from a number of choices. The second is a writing sample. This essay test requires you to write one or more original paragraphs on an assigned topic.

Tests of Standard Written English

Objective tests of Standard written English contain sentences with underlined words, phrases, and punctuation. The underlined parts will contain errors in grammar, usage, mechanics, vocabulary, and spelling. You are asked to find the error in each sentence or, on some tests, to identify the best way to correct or change a sentence.

Error Recognition. The most familiar way to test grammar, usage, capitalization, punctuation, word choice, and spelling

594

Tests of Writing Ability

is through an error-recognition sentence. A typical test item of this kind is a sentence with five underlined choices. Four of the choices suggest possible errors in the sentence. The fifth states that there is no error. Study the following sentence and try to identify the error, if there is one.

Thomas <u>Jeffersons'</u> design <u>for</u> Monticello included the first
          A   **B**
dome to be <u>built</u> on an <u>American</u> house.   <u>No error</u>.
          C   **D**   **E**

The answer is *A*. The possessive form is *Jefferson's*, not *Jeffersons'*. Sometimes you will find a sentence that contains no error. Be careful, however, before you choose *E* as the answer. It is easy to overlook a mistake, since common errors are the kind generally included on this kind of test.

Remember that the parts of a sentence that are not underlined are correct. You can use this knowledge to help you search for errors in the underlined parts.

EXERCISE 8   Recognizing Errors in Writing

Write the letter of the underlined word or punctuation mark that is incorrect. If the sentence contains no error, write *E*.

Popular Prints

C 1. In the year 1835<u>,</u> Nathaniel Currier<u>,</u> a lithographer,
                  A   **B**
<u>begun</u> producing <u>black-and-white</u> and colored
  C   **D**
prints. <u>No error</u>
         E

D 2. These prints<u>,</u> which often had sentimental, sports<u>,</u> or
          A   **B**
<u>humorous</u> subjects, were popular in <u>alot</u> of homes.
    C   **D**
<u>No error</u>
   E

B 3. James M. Ives joined the company in 1857<u>,</u> and the firm
                                        A
Currier and Ives <u>acheived</u> fame <u>throughout</u> <u>America</u>.
                     B   **C**   **D**
<u>No error</u>
   E

A 4. Selling a large <u>amount</u> of prints from pushcarts and
                  A
from <u>their</u> office in Manhattan<u>,</u> the partners <u>became</u>
    B   **C**   **D**
wealthy. <u>No error</u>
            E

Standardized Tests

A 5. They offered customers more <u>then</u> 7,000 pictures<u>;</u>
                                    A   B
     <u>several</u> of the pictures <u>were</u> hand-colored. <u>No error</u>
       C   D   E

A 6. <u>Irregardless</u> of the hand-coloring and <u>unusual</u> quality,
        A   B   C
     small prints sold for the <u>incredible</u> price of fifteen cents
                                   D
     each. <u>No error</u>
                E

E 7. The cost of the more <u>sizable</u> prints, which later <u>became</u>
                                A   B
     widely <u>recognized</u>, rarely <u>exceeded</u> three dollars.
               C   D
     <u>No error</u>
        E

D 8. By the time Ives died in 1895, photographs <u>had</u> caused
                                      A   B
     Currier and Ives prints to <u>become</u> a <u>rareity</u>. <u>No error</u>
                                  C   D   E

E 9. Within a few years, in fact, the prints had become
                          A
     collectors' items, and prices of the <u>unique</u> prints <u>rose</u>
                   B   C   D
     rapidly. <u>No error</u>
                    E

E 10. As early as the 1920s, one rare print, "The Life <u>of</u> a
                      A   B
     Hunter—A Tight Fix," <u>brought</u> three thousand dollars.
                           C   D
     <u>No error</u>
        E

Sentence Correction. Sentence-correction questions test your ability to recognize appropriate phrasing. Instead of locating an error in a sentence, you select the most appropriate and effective way to write the sentence.

In this kind of question, a part of the sentence is underlined. The sentence is followed by five different ways of writing the underlined part. The first way shown, *A*, simply repeats the original underlined portion. The other four ways, *B* through *E*, give alternative ways of writing the underlined part. The choices may involve grammar, usage, capitalization, punctuation, or word choice. Be sure that the answer you choose does not change the meaning of the original sentence. Look at the following example.

Tests of Writing Ability

Tiny St. John's College in Annapolis, Maryland, is the third oldest college in the United States <u>it was founded in 1696.</u>
- (A) it was founded in 1696.
- (B) that was founded in 1696.
- (C) ; it was founded in 1696.
- (D) , once founded in 1696.
- (E) , it was founded in 1696.

The answer is *C*. As written, the sentence is a run-on. Choices *B* and *D* change the meaning of the sentence in illogical ways. Choice *E* does not correct the run-on sentence.

EXERCISE 9 Correcting Sentences

Write the letter of the correct way or the best way of phrasing the underlined part of each sentence.

E 1. Is it true that Abraham Lincoln wrote the Gettysburg Address <u>while riding to Gettysburg on a scrap of paper?</u>
- (A) while riding to Gettysburg on a scrap of paper?
- (B) , as he rode to Gettysburg on a scrap of paper?
- (C) , riding to Gettysburg on a train?
- (D) on a scrap of paper and he rode to Gettysburg?
- (E) on a scrap of paper while riding to Gettysburg?

B 2. "Fair is <u>foul, wrote Shakespeare, and</u> foul is fair."
- (A) foul, wrote Shakespeare, and
- (B) foul," wrote Shakespeare, "and
- (C) foul", wrote Shakespeare, "and
- (D) foul," wrote Shakespeare, "And
- (E) foul," wrote Shakespeare, and

D 3. If a person wishes to leave the room<u>, they should obtain</u> a permission slip.
- (A) , they should obtain
- (B) he should obtain
- (C) , you should obtain
- (D) , he or she should obtain
- (E) they would obtain

C 4. As the miner <u>descended down into the pit,</u> he whistled.
- (A) descended down into the pit,
- (B) ascended down into the pit,
- (C) descended into the pit,
- (D) descended down in the pit,
- (E) , descended into the pit,

597

Standardized Tests

A 5. The report that thousands of unexpected voters <u>had cast ballots was confirmed.</u>
   (A) had cast ballots was confirmed.
   (B) has cast ballots was confirmed.
   (C) had cast ballots were confirmed.
   (D) , having cast ballots, was confirmed.
   (E) had cast ballots, was confirmed.

C 6. Our coach said that Tim was a fine fielder, an excellent base runner, <u>and that he could hit good.</u>
   (A) and that he could hit good.
   (B) and that he could hit well.
   (C) and a good hitter.
   (D) and he could hit well.
   (E) and he could hit good.

B 7. Valerie stated her intent to study computer science, <u>pointed out its being a growing field.</u>
   (A) pointed out its being a growing field.
   (B) pointing out that it is a growing field.
   (C) pointed out its being a growing field.
   (D) since she pointed out that it is growing field.
   (E) pointed out that it is a growing field.

E 8. <u>Neither Terry nor him was</u> at the meeting.
   (A) Neither Terry nor him was
   (B) Neither him nor Terry was
   (C) Neither Terry or him was
   (D) Neither Terry nor he were
   (E) Neither Terry nor he was

A 9. The sale was limited to <u>women's and boys'</u> clothing.
   (A) women's and boys'
   (B) womens and boys
   (C) womens' and boys'
   (D) women's and boy's
   (E) womens and boys'

E 10. Our star <u>center convinced of her ability to make the winning shot waited</u> until the final seconds of the game.
   (A) center convinced of her ability to make the winning shot waited
   (B) center, convinced of her ability to make the winning shot waited
   (C) center was convinced of her ability to make the winning shot, she waited

598

(D) center—convinced of her ability to make the winning shot, waited

(E) center, convinced of her ability to make the winning shot, waited

Sentence Rephrasing. A question that calls for sentence rephrasing tests your ability not only to reword a sentence but also to retain its original meaning. First you are given a correct sentence. Then you are asked to revise the sentence, using a given phrase in a certain position. The addition of this phrase will require that you change other parts of the sentence as well. Finally, from a list of choices, you must find the word or phrase, based on your revised sentence, that is likely to appear somewhere in the rephrased sentence. Note the following: an example sentence, instructions for rephrasing the sentence, and five choices of phrasing that could appear in the revised sentence.

ORIGINAL SENTENCE *Moby Dick* by Herman Melville is a powerful illustration of the author's observation that "to produce a mighty book, you must choose a mighty theme."

REPHRASING INSTRUCTIONS Begin your rephrased sentence with *Herman Melville's observation*.

The following sentence shows one way you might rephrase the sentence.

Herman Melville's observation that "to produce a mighty book you must choose a mighty theme" is powerfully illustrated in his book *Moby Dick*.

Now find the phrase that is likely to appear in the correctly rephrased sentence.

(A) illustrative of power
(B) by Herman Melville
(C) powerfully illustrated
(D) without *Moby Dick*
(E) illustrates powerfully

The correct choice—the one that appears in the rephrased sentence—is *(C) powerfully illustrated*. The four other choices would make the rephrased sentence awkward, if not ungrammatical.

Standardized Tests

Now try to work out the following example.

Opossums are about the size of cats, belong to the marsupial order, usually have prehensile tails, and look a bit like large rats.

Rephrase the sentence, inserting the clause *which look a bit like large rats* after *opossums*. Then choose the phrase that should appear as part of the revised sentence.

(A) and belong to the marsupial order.
(B) cats, which look a bit
(C) tails, which look a bit
(D) rats, usually have
(E) and usually have prehensile tails.

The answer is *(E) and usually have prehensile tails.* When the *which* clause is placed in its logical position after *opossums*, the sentence will end with the phrase about prehensile tails. Since that is the last in the series of three parallel phrases, the sentence requires the insertion of the conjunction *and* after the last comma.

EXERCISE 10   Rephrasing Sentences

Write the letter of the word or phrase that would most likely be included in each rephrased sentence.

B   1. In *Old Jules,* Mari Sandoz wrote movingly of life on the sod-house frontier.

   Begin with *Few authors have.*

   (A) in Mari Sandoz's *Old Jules*
   (B) written more movingly
   (C) while in a sod house
   (D) from *Old Jules*
   (E) except for Mari Sandoz

D   2. Patrick Henry spoke before the Virginia House of Burgesses and demanded, "Give me liberty or give me death!"

   Begin with *Speaking before.*

   (A) he demanded
   (B) and spoke, "Give
   (C) demanded as he spoke
   (D) Patrick Henry demanded
   (E) he could demand

600

B 3. Bob insisted that he knew where Mo had hidden the bat.

Change the sentence into a direct quotation.

(A) "He knew where Mo had hidden the bat."
(B) "I know where Mo has hidden the bat."
(C) "Bob knows where Mo had hidden the bat."
(D) "I insist that Mo has hidden the bat."
(E) "He knows where Mo had hidden the bat."

A 4. There were nearly 200 dogs entered in the show, many of them previous prizewinners.

Begin with *Nearly*.

(A) dogs were entered
(B) show, and many dogs
(C) many of them was
(D) dogs entered the show
(E) of which there were many

C 5. The ancient Egyptians built large, seagoing reed vessels, which were perhaps the first true ships.

End with *by the ancient Egyptians*.

(A) were perhaps built
(B) Perhaps the Egyptians
(C) were built
(D) ships, were first
(E) vessels of reed

E 6. We climbed most of the day and reached the summit just before sunset.

Begin with *We reached*.

(A) before climbing
(B) once climbing
(C) without climbing
(D) trying to climb
(E) having climbed

A 7. No one knows to this day if there is a Loch Ness monster, despite the numerous attempts to discover the truth.

End with *Loch Ness monster*.

(A) the truth, no one
(B) really is there
(C) Despite the truth
(D) to discover the monster
(E) attempts, to this day

601

Standardized Tests

B 8. The bus leaves at 5:30 A.M. and arrives at the Milwaukee terminal at noon.

   Begin with *Departure time*.

   (A) leaves the bus
   (B) and arrival time
   (C) but arrives at
   (D) or it will arrive
   (E) although arrival

C 9. The first-class postage rate for a letter was three cents for many years.

   Begin with *It used to cost*.

   (A) three-cent rate
   (B) postage for many years
   (C) three cents to mail
   (D) many letters
   (E) still three cents

D 10. Mindy said, "The implied theme of the poem 'Ozymandias' is that fame is temporary."

   Change the sentence to an indirect quotation.

   (A) that 'Ozymandias' states
   (B) the poem "Ozymandias" was
   (C) "Mindy said, 'That
   (D) said that the implied theme
   (E) theme of the poem was

The 20-Minute Essay

   The essay section of a standardized test measures your ability to write clearly and logically on an assigned topic. You will be given guidelines to follow when you write the essay of approximately 175 to 200 words.

   Writing the essay on a standardized test is basically the same as writing a short composition or an essay for a classroom test. Tests vary, however, and you may be asked to observe certain rules that would not apply to a classroom test. The essays on most standardized tests call for fairly general responses, rather than for answers containing specific subject matter. Following are some points to remember when you write an essay on a standardized test.

The 20-Minute Essay

Guidelines for Writing Essay Answers

1. **Preview the test.** Plan the amount of time you will spend on each part of the test. Allot more time to questions worth the most points. If you have a choice of questions, select carefully the ones you can answer best.
2. **Read and interpret directions.** Find key words, such as those that follow, that tell what task is required and how you should construct your answer.

Analyze	Separate into parts and examine each part.
Compare	Point out similarities and differences.
Contrast	Point out differences.
Define	Clarify meaning.
Discuss	Examine in detail.
Evaluate	Give your opinion.
Explain	Tell how, what, or why.
Illustrate	Give examples.
Summarize	Briefly review main points.
Trace	Show development or progress.

3. **Organize your answer.** List the main points you will need to cover, numbering them in logical order. This simple but useful outline will give structure to your essay and will help you avoid omitting important points.
4. **Write your essay,** keeping the following points in mind.
   - Write an introductory paragraph that states the main idea of your essay.
   - Follow the order of your outline. Write one paragraph for each main point and include a topic sentence in each paragraph.
   - Be specific. Provide adequate support for each main point, using facts, examples, and supporting details.
   - Proofread your essay, correcting any errors you find in grammar, usage, spelling, and punctuation.
5. **Pay close attention to all special test requirements,** such as the following.
   - You will have a definite time limit. Before you write, plan what you want to say in each paragraph or section of the essay.
   - You will be graded only on your essay, not on your outline or notes. Therefore, apportion your time efficiently between the planning and the writing stages.

Standardized Tests

EXERCISE 11 Writing a 20-Minute Essay
Choose one of the following essay topics. Allow yourself exactly 20 minutes to outline and write the essay.
Answers will vary.

1. If you were to live for one year in any country other than the United States, what country would you choose? Explain your choice.
2. Over the past several years, the salaries paid to professional athletes have risen dramatically. What do you think of this trend? Discuss whether you consider it a positive or a negative trend in professional sports.
3. Since the invention of photography, there has been a continuing debate about whether photography is a true art. Evaluate the issue.

CHAPTER REVIEW

A. Write the letter of the word or group of words most nearly the same *or* most nearly the opposite in meaning to the word in capital letters.

D 1. RIVALRY   (A) royalty (B) possession (C) protection (D) teamwork (E) lecture
B 2. TOLERABLE   (A) hostile (B) unbearable (C) knowledgeable (D) predictable (E) unimaginative
D 3. AFFIRMATIVE   (A) changeable (B) noisy (C) nearby (D) positive (E) outgoing
A 4. FIDELITY   (A) loyalty (B) variety (C) significance (D) work (E) management
B 5. SUPERFLUOUS   (A) minute (B) unnecessary (C) logical (D) careless (E) elegant
C 6. POTENT   (A) loud (B) hasty (C) powerful (D) sour (E) crooked
B 7. FICKLE   (A) domineering (B) constant (C) far (D) humorous (E) courageous
E 8. STEADFAST   (A) structured (B) timid (C) watchful (D) ashamed (E) loyal
D 9. FRAUDULENT   (A) secure (B) detailed (C) final (D) honest (E) convincing
A 10. DEMURE   (A) reserved (B) informative (C) useful (D) unimportant (E) brief

604

Chapter Review

B. Write the letter of the word pair that has the same relationship as the word pair in capital letters.

C 1. STUCCO : WALL :: (A) house : home (B) bridge : water
   (C) slate : roof (D) paint : brush (E) wood : brick

D 2. ELUDE : ESCAPE :: (A) hostile : amiable (B) wise : owl
   (C) run : march (D) fret : fuss (E) manager : worker

A 3. NUTRITIOUS : NOURISHING :: (A) inverse : opposite
   (B) milk : delicious (C) unfriendly : personable
   (D) obscure : obvious (E) tortilla : food

E 4. PAUPER : MILLIONAIRE :: (A) invisible : hidden
   (B) broker : stock (C) music : chorus (D) rule : game
   (E) dissimilar : alike

C 5. LIMESTONE : ROCK :: (A) ore : copper (B) fish : shark
   (C) lettuce : vegetable (D) astronomer : telescope
   (E) modern : antiquated

E 6. PEDIGREE : DOG :: (A) auction : art (B) herb : spice
   (C) island : ocean (D) repel : attract
   (E) genealogy : family

A 7. COURT : JUDGE :: (A) state : governor
   (B) quarterback : team (C) license : drive
   (D) whale : mammal (E) dashboard : automobile

B 8. REALISTIC : IMPRACTICAL :: (A) politician : statesman
   (B) factual : fictional (C) microscope : lens
   (D) playwright : actor (E) iron : steel

B 9. TORSO : BODY :: (A) yarn : wool
   (B) tentacle : octopus (C) prism : color
   (D) church : steeple (E) trowel : bricklayer

D 10. REASON : PHILOSOPHER :: (A) pilot : navigate
   (B) think : imagine (C) library : student
   (D) experiment : scientist (E) photographer : shutter

C. Write the letter that is below the underlined word, phrase, or punctuation mark that is incorrect. If the sentence contains no error, write *E*.

Notable Structures

A 1. The <u>prominant</u> architect Frank Lloyd Wright designed
         A
   the house "Fallingwater<u>,</u>" <u>which</u> was <u>actually</u> built over a
                            B   **C**   **D**
   waterfall. <u>No error</u>
              E

605

Standardized Tests

E 2. Highways <u>developed</u> by the <u>Incas</u> show a <u>noticeable</u>
       　　　　　A　　　　　　　B　　　　　　　　C
   <u>similarity</u> to modern roads in length and engineering
   　　D
   skill.　<u>No error</u>
   　　　　　　E

D 3. The <u>famous</u> Gateway <u>Arch</u> in St. Louis, Missouri<u>,</u> is one
   　　　　A　　　　　　　B　　　　　　　　　　　　　C
   of the <u>worlds'</u> tallest monuments.　<u>No error</u>
   　　　　　D　　　　　　　　　　　　　　　　　E

C 4. In <u>comparison</u> with St. Peter's in Rome, other cathedrals
   　　　A
   are <u>small ;</u> most could fit <u>inside of</u> <u>its</u> main section.
   　　　　B　　　　　　　　　　　C　　　　D
   <u>No error</u>
   　E

B 5. One Kentucky church can hold only three people at
   once<u>;</u> it is <u>representitive</u> of the <u>smallest</u> <u>churches</u> in the
   　　A　　　　　B　　　　　　　　　　C　　　　　D
   country.　<u>No error</u>
   　　　　　　　E

B 6. The Great Wall <u>of</u> China was <u>formally</u> the <u>longest</u>
   　　　　　　　　　　A　　　　　　　　B　　　　　　C
   structure in the <u>world</u>.　<u>No error</u>
   　　　　　　　　　　D　　　　　E

C 7. One Indian raja <u>advised</u> that gold bricks should support
   　　　　　　　　　　　A
   the gateway of a fortress<u>,</u> <u>being that</u> the structure was
   　　　　　　　　　　　　　　B　　　　C
   <u>set</u> on a marsh.　<u>No error</u>
   　D　　　　　　　　　　　E

E 8. <u>Seventeen</u> miles of corridors make up the <u>immense</u>
   　　A　　　　　　　　　　　　　　　　　　　　　　B
   Pentagon<u>,</u> located in the <u>United</u> States capital.
   　　　　C　　　　　　　　　D
   <u>No error</u>
   　E

C 9. Some visitors <u>to</u> the Winchester Mansion<u>,</u> a little <u>ways</u>
   　　　　　　　　　　A　　　　　　　　　　　　　　B　　　　　　C
   from San Jose, California, try <u>to</u> count the 10,000
   　　　　　　　　　　　　　　　　　　D
   windows.　<u>No error</u>
   　　　　　　　　E

E 10. A beam of light passes <u>through</u> a <u>hole</u> in the dome of a
   　　　　　　　　　　　　　　　A　　　　　B
   cathedral in Florence, <u>Italy</u> <u>;</u> and every June 21, the
   　　　　　　　　　　　　　　C　　D
   beam strikes a metal plate.　<u>No error</u>
   　　　　　　　　　　　　　　　　　　　E

Appendix

Study Skills
  Taking Notes
  Studying for a Test
  Using Standard Manuscript Form
  Using Proofreading Symbols
  Using Correct Footnote Form

Communication Skills
  Speaking to an Audience
  Participating in Group Discussions
  Listening for Information
  Glossary of Computer Terms

Career Skills
  Writing a Résumé
  Writing Letters about Employment
  Writing Letters to Schools and Colleges
  Interviewing for a Job

TAKING NOTES

For additional practice for this chapter, see the Teacher's Resource Book.

Note-taking is an important skill for helping you remember what you have read in a textbook or heard during a lecture. Notes are also a valuable study aid in preparing for a test.

Two methods for taking notes are the modified outline and the summary. In a *modified outline,* words and phrases are used to record main ideas and important details. A modified outline is especially useful in studying for a multiple-choice test because it allows you to see the most important details and facts.

In a *summary* sentences are used to express important ideas in your own words. Summaries are especially useful in preparing for an essay test. Writing a summary requires you to think about the information, to see relationships between ideas, and to draw conclusions. It is also good practice in stating information briefly and clearly.

Whether taking notes in modified-outline form or in summary form, you should include only main ideas and important details. In the following passage from a textbook on word processing, the essential information is underlined. Following the passage are examples of notes in both modified-outline form and summary form.

> There are two basic kinds of computer printers: letter quality and dot matrix. The choice between them depends on the kind of output needed.
>
> Letter-quality printers produce type when the print element strikes the paper through a ribbon. Thus, they are termed "impact printers." Some of these printers have an element shaped like a daisy and are thus called daisy-wheel printers. Some, however, use a thimble-shaped element rather than a daisy wheel. Although letter-quality printers produce type more slowly than other printers, they produce printing equal in quality to that of an expensive electric typewriter.
>
> Dot-matrix printers form characters with closely spaced dots of ink. Many of them can print up to ten times faster than letter-quality printers. Unlike letter-quality printers, they can also produce graphics — that is, charts and graphs. The quality of dot-matrix printing is generally lower than that of letter-quality printing, but improvements continue to be made.

MODIFIED
OUTLINE

Computer Printers
1. Letter-quality printers—"impact"
   a. Slower than other printers
   b. Like costly typewriters in print quality
2. Dot-matrix printers—ink dots
   a. Faster than letter-quality; do graphics
   b. Lower in print quality

SUMMARY

Computer Printers

    Letter-quality printers, or "impact printers," produce type more slowly than other printers. Their print quality, however, equals that of costly typewriters.

    Dot-matrix printers, which use ink dots, print much faster than letter-quality printers and can produce graphics. Their print quality is usually less than that of letter-quality printers.

The guidelines below will help you take well-organized notes.

Taking Notes

- Record only the main ideas and important details.
- Use the titles, subtitles, and words in special type or color to help you select the most important information.
- Use your own words; do not copy word for word.
- Use as few words as possible.

Modified Outline
- Use words and phrases.
- Use main ideas for headings.
- List any supporting details under each heading.

Summary
- Write complete sentences, using your own words.
- Show the relationship between ideas, being careful to use only the facts stated in the textbook or lecture.
- Include only essential information.
- Organize ideas logically.

STUDYING FOR A TEST

You should begin to study for a test long before test day. To do well on a test, you must keep up with your daily reading assignments, take clear and complete notes, and review the material in each subject regularly.

Developing Effective Study Habits. If you develop good study habits, you will find them useful for test-taking as well as for daily classroom assignments. Use the following procedures to help you study more effectively and improve your test grades.

How to Study Effectively

- Choose an area that is well lighted and free from noise and other distractions.
- Equip your study area with everything you need for reading and writing, including a dictionary, a thesaurus, and other reference books.
- Keep an assignment book for recording assignments and due dates.
- Allow plenty of time for studying. Begin your reading and writing assignments early.

Preparing for Tests. If you keep up with your assignments and take good notes, you should have no difficulty preparing for tests. The following guidelines will help you do your best.

How to Prepare for a Test

1. Study the notes you took in class and those you took on assigned reading.
2. Focus on topics that were discussed in class or stressed by the teacher.
3. Review the questions at the end of main sections in your textbook. Write the answer to each question to help you organize your thoughts and recall important details.
4. Review any prior tests or quizzes you have taken that cover the material on which you will be tested.

USING STANDARD MANUSCRIPT FORM

The appearance of your composition can be almost as important as its content. A paper with jagged margins and words crossed out or crowded together is difficult to read. A neat, legible paper, however, makes a positive impression on your reader. Use the following guidelines for standard manuscript form to help you prepare the final copy of a composition or report.

Standard Manuscript Form

1. Use standard-size 8½- by 11-inch white paper. Use one side of the paper only.
2. If handwriting, use black or blue ink. If typing, use a black typewriter ribbon and double-space the lines.
3. Leave a 1¼-inch margin at the left and a 1-inch margin at the right. The left margin must be even. The right margin should be as even as possible, without too many hyphenated words.
4. Put your name, the course title, the name of your teacher, and the date in the upper right-hand corner of the first page.
5. Center the title about 2 inches from the top of the first page. Do not underline or put quotation marks around your title.
6. If handwriting, skip 2 lines between the title and the first paragraph. If typing, skip 4 lines.
7. If handwriting, indent the first line of each paragraph 1 inch. If typing, indent 5 spaces.
8. Leave a 1-inch margin at the bottom of all pages.
9. Starting on page 2, number each page in the upper right-hand corner. Begin the first line 1 inch from the top of the page.

The following sample illustrates the first page of a typewritten composition. Note the placement of the name, class, teacher, date, and composition title. Notice that the margins are consistent. When writing or typing your compositions, be sure your paper is double-spaced, clear, and easy to read. Also remember to number each page of your composition.

Standard Manuscript Form

Sample of Standard Manuscript Form

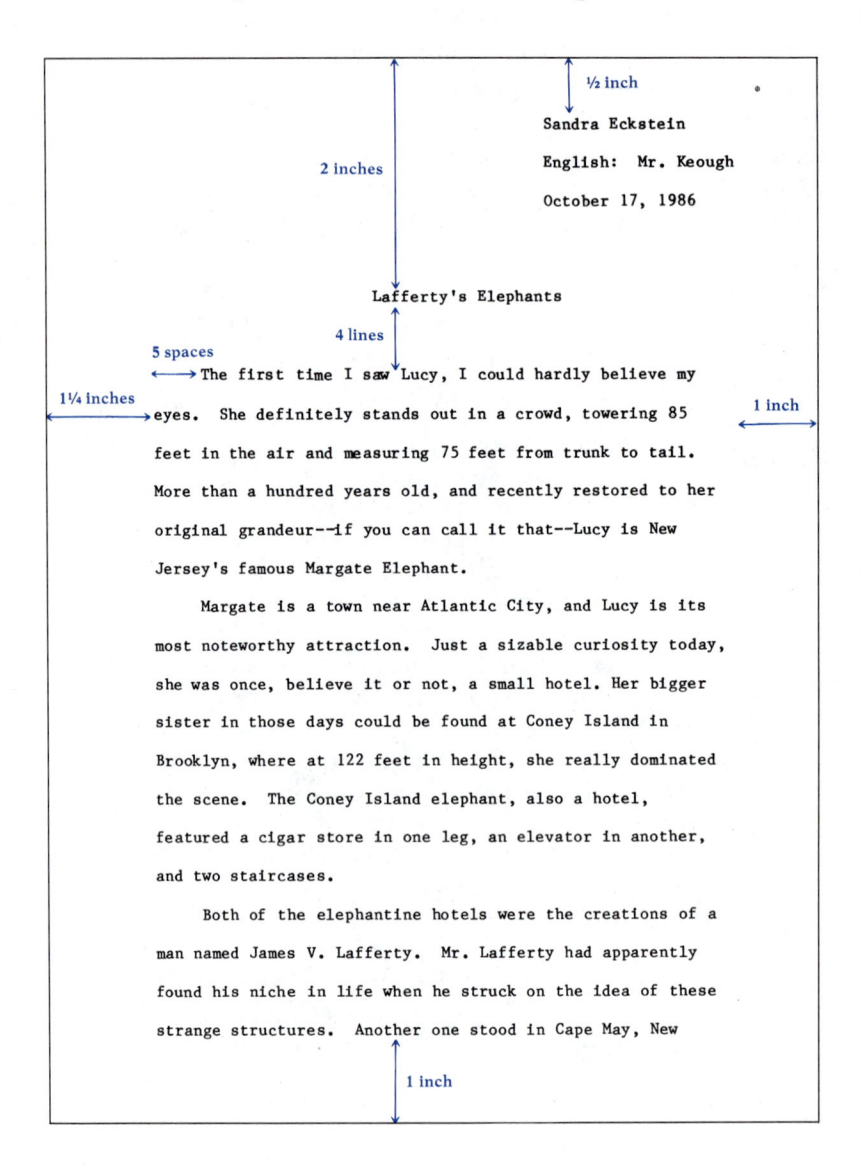

(½ inch from top)

Sandra Eckstein
English: Mr. Keough
October 17, 1986

(2 inches from top)

Lafferty's Elephants

(4 lines)

(5 spaces) The first time I saw Lucy, I could hardly believe my eyes. She definitely stands out in a crowd, towering 85 feet in the air and measuring 75 feet from trunk to tail. More than a hundred years old, and recently restored to her original grandeur--if you can call it that--Lucy is New Jersey's famous Margate Elephant.

Margate is a town near Atlantic City, and Lucy is its most noteworthy attraction. Just a sizable curiosity today, she was once, believe it or not, a small hotel. Her bigger sister in those days could be found at Coney Island in Brooklyn, where at 122 feet in height, she really dominated the scene. The Coney Island elephant, also a hotel, featured a cigar store in one leg, an elevator in another, and two staircases.

Both of the elephantine hotels were the creations of a man named James V. Lafferty. Mr. Lafferty had apparently found his niche in life when he struck on the idea of these strange structures. Another one stood in Cape May, New

(margins: 1¼ inches left, 1 inch right, 1 inch bottom)

In addition to using standard form, you should always proofread your completed work carefully. Also, keep in mind the following guidelines as well as the usage, mechanics, and spelling chapters in this book.

612

Dividing Words. Although you should avoid dividing words whenever possible, sometimes doing so is necessary to keep the right-hand margin of your paper fairly even. For dividing words, follow the rules for dividing words on page 295.

Writing Numbers. In general, spell out the numbers one through ten. Use numerals for numbers above ten.

   one   ten   11   83   416   2,198   1,450,421

To avoid six or more zeros, use a combination of numerals and words.

   four million   37 million   195 billion   2.8 billion

Always spell out a number at the beginning of a sentence, or revise the sentence.

> Four thousand six hundred two people bought tickets.
> Ticket purchases totaled 4,602.
> Thirty-two people were invited to our party.
> We invited 32 people to our party.

Use numerals for dates, street and room numbers, page numbers, percents, decimals, and times with A.M. or P.M.

   April 9, 1912   182 Concord Street   room 4   page 7
              3 percent   8.5   8:20 P.M.

Using Abbreviations. Most abbreviations should be avoided in formal writing. Do not abbreviate names of states, countries, days of the week, months, weights, or measurements. See page 251 for examples of abbreviations that are acceptable in formal writing.

Quoting Long Passages. When you write a research paper and want to quote a passage of five or more lines from a source, skip two lines and indent ten spaces along the left margin. Quotation marks are not necessary for a quotation of this length. Whenever you use someone else's words, always remember to give credit to the author for the quoted material. Failure to give credit for borrowed material is called plagiarism. *(See pages 554–559.)*

Proofreading Symbols

USING PROOFREADING SYMBOLS

Proofreading symbols make revising and editing easier. The most commonly used symbols are shown below. Use these symbols when you revise and edit your writing.

Proofreading Symbols

Symbol	Meaning	Example
∧	insert	Gary took ∧the bus to Atlanta.
✐	delete	Refer ~~back~~ to your notes.
...	let it stand	President ~~Jimmy~~ Carter spoke.
#	add space	She will be all#right in a moment.
⌒	close up	An airplane waited on the run⌒way.
∽	transpose	T⁀h⁀ey only⁀have⁀two dollars left.
no ¶	no paragraph	no # The dachshund trotted away.
¶	new paragraph	¶ Finally Balboa saw the Pacific.
≡	capital letter	The ≡south voted solidly for Jones.
/	lowercase	Drive S̸outh on Monroe Street.

Sample Student Paper with Proofreading Symbols

¶ Electrical current consists of the flow ∧of electrons between two points of a wire. The three common measurements of electricity are based on this stream of electrons. An ampere measures rate of flow, a volt measures force of flow, and a ̸watt measures power to do work.

Electrical current flows very fast, coursing through a copper wire at about 20,000 miles per ~~each~~ second. Separate electrons do not go that fast, how⌒ever. They move at a fairly slow pace. the lig⁀h⁀tning speed of the current is caused by electrons nudging each other for the entire length of travel.

There are a#lot of electrons at work in electricity. no ¶ An ordinary 50-watt bulb requires about three billion ~~billion~~ electrons flowing through it each second. A typical

614

USING CORRECT FOOTNOTE FORM

Footnotes or endnotes are used to identify the sources of borrowed material in research papers. The following guidelines describe how to place notes so that they are neat and easy to read.

Placement of Footnotes

1. Skip three lines after the last line of your main text before typing the first footnote.
2. Indent the first line of the footnote five spaces.
3. Type the number of the note slightly above the line. Leave one space between the number and the first word of the note.
4. Single space each footnote, but leave a double space between footnotes.
5. Number your footnotes consecutively throughout the research paper.

Placement of Endnotes

1. Endnotes appear on a separate sheet of paper at the end of the research paper before the bibliography.
2. Write the title *Notes* two inches from the top of the page. Center it.
3. Skip three lines below the title, indent five spaces, and write the first note (in the same manner as for footnotes).
4. Double space within and between notes.
5. Number the notes consecutively.

All footnotes and endnotes present information in the same order. Not all of the information, however, will apply to each source you use. Omit whatever information does not apply, but present the remaining information in the following order: (1) author's name (in normal order); (2) title of article (in quotation marks); (3) title of book or magazine (underlined); (4) translator's name; (5) editor's name; (6) edition; (7) location and name of book publisher; (8) date of publication (in

Footnote Form

parentheses, after book publisher's location and name); (9) volume number; (10) issue number; (11) page number.

You need not memorize this order of information, but use the following sample footnotes as models when you write a research paper. The models show the correct order and punctuation of notes for a variety of sources.

Books

1. A book with a single author

    [1] Richard Attenborough, In Search of Gandhi (Piscataway: New Century, 1982), p. 14.

2. A book with two authors (Give the names in the order they appear on the title page.)

    [2] Katherine E. Wilkie and Elizabeth R. Mosely, Atlantis (New York: Messner, 1979), p. 31.

3. A book with four or more authors

    [3] Helen C. White and others, Seventeeth-Century Verse and Prose, 4th ed. (New York: Macmillan, 1971), p. 17.

4. A book that contains a collection of works by different authors

    [4] Dorothy B. Vitaliano, "Atlantis from a Geological Point of View," in Atlantis: Fact or Fiction? ed. Edwin S. Ramage (Bloomington: Indiana University Press, 1978), p. 139.

5. A book that has been translated

    [5] Otto Muck, The Secret of Atlantis, trans. Fred Bradley (New York: Times Books, 1978), p. 131.

6. An edition other than the first

    [6] John Kenneth Galbraith, The Affluent Society, 3rd rev. ed. (Boston: Houghton Mifflin, 1976), p. 201.

7. A book that is part of a series

    [7] Clarence L. Ver Steeg, The Formative Years: 1607-1763, The Making of America, Vol. 1 (London: Macmillan, 1965), p. 125.

8. A work in several volumes, each with a separate title

    [8] Dumas Malone, The Sage of Monticello, Vol. VI of Jefferson and His Time (Boston: Little, Brown, 1981), pp. 20-28.

9. A work in several volumes without individual titles

    [9] David Daiches, A Critical History of English Literature, 2nd ed. (New York: Ronald, 1970), II, pp. 690-93.

Footnote Form

Articles and Other Sources

10. A magazine article with author's name given

[10] Sharon Bealey, "Giving Sharks a Good Name," <u>Newsweek</u>, 2 Aug. 1982, p. 64.

11. A magazine article with no author's name given

[11] "Mysterious Island," <u>National Geographic World</u>, Oct. 1983, p. 8.

12. A newspaper article

[12] "Green Backs Plato Theory on Where to Find Atlantis," <u>New York Times</u>, 29 Aug. 1979, Sec. A, p. 4, col. 3.

13. An article in an encyclopedia

[13] Chester G. Starr, "Julius Caesar," <u>World Book Encyclopedia</u>, 1983 ed., p. 13.

14. An editorial

[14] "Framed—in Poland," Editorial, <u>New York Times</u>, 31 May 1984, Sec. A, p. 22, cols. 1–2.

15. An article from a journal with volume and issue numbers

[15] Kenneth G. Johnson, "Hemingway and Cézanne: Doing the Country," <u>American Literature</u>, 56, No. 1 (1984), 31–32.

16. An interview

[16] Personal interview with Dr. Stan Harrison, Professor of Classics, Harperstown College, 23 April 1984.

Notice that abbreviations are used in notes in order to keep the notes as short as possible. Following are some abbreviations commonly used in citing sources.

Abbreviations Used in Citing Sources

Abbreviation	Meaning
ed.	editor, edited, edition
rev. ed.	revised edition
trans.	translator, translated
p., pp.	page, pages
col.	column
sec.	section

SPEAKING TO AN AUDIENCE

A speech may be formal or informal, long or short. Whatever its nature, you will find the following guidelines helpful when you prepare and deliver a speech.

Choosing and Limiting a Subject

The first step you should take when you prepare a speech is to choose the subject of your speech carefully. Then limit your subject and determine the purpose of your speech.

How to Choose and Limit a Subject

1. Choose a subject that interests you and is likely to interest your audience.
2. Choose a subject that you know well or can research thoroughly.
3. Limit the subject to one that can be covered in the time allowed.
4. Determine the purpose of your speech—to explain or inform, to persuade, or to entertain.

Gathering Information

After you have chosen and limited your topic, begin to gather information. One source of information is your own experience. You may know more about your subject than you realize. Start by brainstorming. *(See pages 460–461.)* Jot down your ideas freely without stopping to evaluate each one.

You may want to interview people who are knowledgeable about your subject. Make a list of the questions you want to ask during the interview. The usefulness of the information you gather will depend in large part on how well you have prepared your questions.

Another excellent source of information is the library. Look for useful encyclopedia articles, books, and magazines. *(See pages 356–361.)*

Taking Notes

Be sure to take notes throughout your research. If you take notes based on personal experience, group your ideas into categories. *(See pages 538–541.)* If you interview someone, take notes in modified outline form or use a tape recorder. If you plan to use quotations, write down accurately the words you intend to quote and use quotation marks.

Note cards are the best way to record information from encyclopedias, magazines, and books. Note cards make it easy to organize the information later. The following sample note card was written by a student preparing for a speech on the construction of the Statue of Liberty.

Sample Note Card

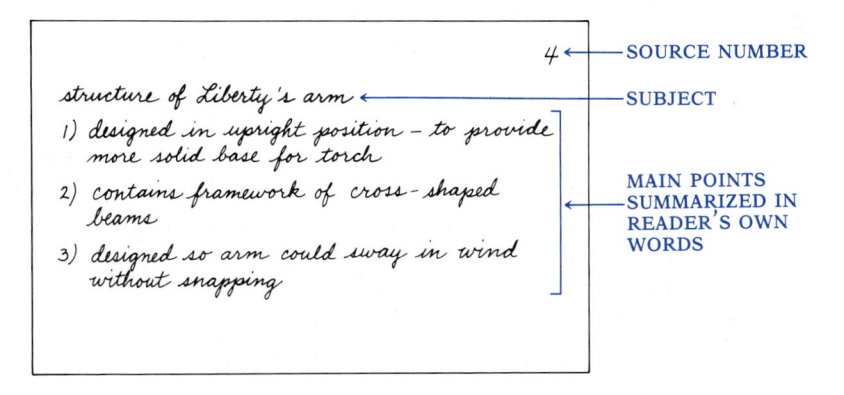

```
                                              4  ←── SOURCE NUMBER
structure of Liberty's arm ←─────────────────── SUBJECT
1) designed in upright position — to provide
   more solid base for torch                     MAIN POINTS
2) contains framework of cross-shaped       ←── SUMMARIZED IN
   beams                                         READER'S OWN
3) designed so arm could sway in wind           WORDS
   without snapping
```

Organizing Information

Begin to organize your information by writing a working thesis statement. *(See page 541.)* Your working thesis statement should indicate the main idea and the purpose of your speech. Next prepare an outline for the body of your speech. *(See pages 542–544.)* The body of the speech should support your thesis statement and should logically develop the main points of your outline with facts, details, examples, and illustrations. Use a Roman numeral for each main topic and a capital letter for each subtopic. Use Arabic numerals for supporting details. Remember to write headings in the same grammatical form (either phrases or sentences). Also, if you subdivide a topic, always have at least two subdivisions. Use the following form for outlining the body of your speech.

Speaking to an Audience

> **Form for Outlining a Speech**
> Limited Subject:_____
> Thesis Statement:_____
>   Body: I. (Main Topic)
>   A. (Subtopic 1)
>   1. (Supporting Detail)
>   2. (Supporting Detail)
>   3. (Supporting Detail)
>   B. (Subtopic 2)
>   1. (Supporting Detail)
>   2. (Supporting Detail)
>   C. (Subtopic 3)
>   II. (Main Topic)
>   A. (Subtopic 1)
>   B. (Subtopic 2)
>   C. (Subtopic 3)

After you have completed the outline, you will be ready to write your introduction and conclusion. To catch the interest of your audience, begin the introduction with an anecdote, an unusual fact, a question, or an attention-getting quotation. Include your thesis statement at the end of the introduction, revising it as necessary. *(See pages 546–547.)*

The conclusion of the speech is your final opportunity to reinforce the ideas you want your listeners to remember. Restate your thesis statement in your conclusion. The last few sentences of your speech should signal the audience that you have finished.

Preparing to Deliver the Speech

Although you should rehearse your speech, you should not memorize it. Instead, use either your outline or your cue cards to remind you of the important points of your speech. Cue cards contain key words and phrases or key topics listed in the order you want to follow in your speech. The kind of cue card you make will depend on the type of information in your speech and on your style of presentation. Following is an example of a cue card for a speech entitled "What Is Word Processing?"

Sample Cue Card

> 7
>
> Similarities to typewriting
> — character keys and space bar the same
> — printed page often identical
>
> Differences from typewriting
> — corrections made on display screen
> — function keys permit text editing
> — text stored on magnetic media

Number your cue cards to simplify keeping them in order. A good set of cue cards will help you speak with confidence.

Rehearsing the Speech

Practice your speech until you know it well. If possible, record your speech on a tape recorder. Listen to your delivery and note where you should use more emphasis, show greater enthusiasm, or speak more slowly and distinctly.

Delivering the Speech

If you have researched your subject well, planned the content carefully, and rehearsed, you will deliver a good speech. Be confident! You are now an expert on your subject. Following are five tips for delivering a speech.

Tips for Delivering a Speech

1. Relax and breathe deeply before you speak.
2. Glance at your outline or cue cards to refresh your memory. Avoid reading your speech.
3. Look at your audience. Either make eye contact or focus on points just behind the audience.
4. Speak slowly, clearly, and loudly enough to be heard.
5. Use gestures and facial expressions to help you emphasize your main points.

PARTICIPATING IN GROUP DISCUSSIONS

Group discussion is a method of communicating ideas, exchanging opinions, solving problems, and reaching conclusions. Group discussions may be as informal as a small-group discussion or as formal as a symposium or a forum. Learning group-discussion skills will help you to present your own ideas effectively and to listen thoughtfully to the ideas of others.

Types of Group Discussions

There are five common kinds of group discussions, each with its own format and rules.

Classroom Discussion. All members of the class participate in the discussion. First, students prepare information for the topic of discussion, which is often based on a homework or classroom assignment. Then they exchange information or discuss the problem or topic. The teacher or a student leads the discussion.

Small-Group Discussion. Sometimes the leader of a large group breaks it up into small groups to discuss a specific question or topic. After the discussion one member of each small group reports its results to the large group.

Panel Discussion. The panel consists of four to eight members. Each panelist is knowledgeable about a particular aspect of the topic. Panelists express opinions and may disagree with and challenge each other. A leader directs the discussion and summarizes it at the end. Members of the audience may ask questions of the panelists.

Symposium. Speakers in a symposium present prepared talks on the subject being discussed. After these talks the speakers question one another. Finally the discussion leader invites the audience to question or challenge the speakers.

Forum. A forum differs from a symposium in that it has only one speaker. Following the talk or lecture, the discussion leader asks for questions and comments from the audience.

Duties of Discussion Leaders

When you act as a group-discussion leader—also called a moderator or a chairperson—you have responsibility for guiding and directing the discussion.

Responsibilities of Discussion Leaders

1. Introduce the topic, question, or problem.
2. Control the discussion so that everyone has a chance to contribute.
3. Act as timekeeper, allowing an appropriate amount of time to each speaker and each subtopic.
4. Make sure the discussion stays on target.
5. Keep the discussion well paced, asking questions or shifting the direction of the discussion if necessary.
6. Help participants settle differences and arrive at a general agreement.
7. Summarize the main points of the discussion and note any conclusions or decisions the group has reached.

Duties of Discussion Participants

No matter how effective a discussion leader is, the ultimate success of any group discussion depends on the participants. When you act as a participant in a group discussion, you will have an important role to play in making it work.

Responsibilities of Discussion Participants

1. Prepare for the discussion by reading about the topic.
2. Take part in the discussion by expressing ideas and asking questions.
3. Listen carefully to the ideas expressed by others.
4. When recognized by the chairperson, speak clearly and distinctly, supporting main points with reasons, facts, and other evidence.
5. Be objective and tactful when responding to other participants, making an effort to understand opposing points of view.

LISTENING FOR INFORMATION

Listening to a speech or lecture requires that you pay close attention in order to gain information and to evaluate what you hear.

Concentrate on the speaker's words. Sit comfortably but stay alert. Focus on what the speaker is saying, without being distracted by noise or by the speaker's appearance, gestures, or mannerisms. Determine the speaker's purpose. As the speaker begins, determine the purpose of the speech—to inform, to explain, or to persuade.

Listen for verbal clues. Identify the speaker's main ideas. A speaker may use key words or phrases to show you connections between ideas, to alert you to important information, or to signal you that the speech is about to end. Often a speaker will use verbal signals such as the following to emphasize important points.

Let me begin	Also consider	Most important
Remember that	Finally	In summation

Notice nonverbal clues. A speaker may use gestures that will help you understand a key point. The movement of an arm or a change in pace of speaking, for example, can signal that the speaker is saying something important.

Evaluate the information. Listen critically and evaluate what you hear. Try to separate fact from opinion. Watch out for propaganda devices that try to persuade you to believe as the speaker does. One such device is the slogan. A slogan is a simple word or phrase that oversimplifies a complex issue by reducing it to a word or a phrase.

Take notes. Writing notes can help you organize your thoughts and remember details. Use a modified outline when you take notes on a speech. You may also find it helpful to write a summary of the speech. *(See pages 608–609.)*

GLOSSARY OF COMPUTER TERMS

Computers have introduced a large number of new words into the English language. The following glossary will help you become familiar with some common computer terms.

algorithm: a set of rules providing a step-by-step procedure for solving a problem

assembly language: a computer language that makes it possible to write machine-language instructions in a simplified form, using specified abbreviations

backup: files and programs copied onto a second disk or tape; used to prevent loss of data

bit: a binary digit; that is, a 0 or a 1

bug: an error in a computer program or system

byte: a group of adjacent binary digits that the computer processes as a unit

card: a printed electronic circuit board that is added to a microcomputer to extend its capabilities

central processing unit (CPU): the part of a computer system that interprets and executes instructions

chip: a tiny integrated circuit, often made with silicon

code: a set of symbols and rules for writing programs

debugging: correcting mistakes in a computer program

disk drive: a device for recording and retrieving information on floppy disks

flowchart: a diagram showing the logic and sequence between various parts of a program

FORTRAN: *for*mula *tran*slation, a computer language designed mainly for programming in the sciences

input: introduce information into a computer

magnetic disk: a flat circular plate with a magnetic surface, for storing data

microprocessor: typically, a chip containing the CPU for a microcomputer, and thus the "brains" of the system

software: programs, usually on magnetic disks or tapes, created for use with hardware

time-sharing: a means by which a CPU is shared by users on several terminals at the same time

WRITING A RÉSUMÉ

A résumé is a summary of your work experience, education, and interests. The purpose of a résumé is to give a potential employer a brief but positive overview of your qualifications for a job. The following guidelines will help you write your own résumé.

How to Write a Résumé

Form
1. Use one sheet of white 8½- by 11-inch paper.
2. Use even margins and leave space between sections.
3. Center your name, address, and telephone number at the top of the page.

Work Experience
1. List your most recent job first.
2. Include part-time, summer, and volunteer jobs.
3. For each job, list the dates you worked, your employer's name, your title, and your primary responsibilities.

Education
1. List the name and address of each school and the years you attended.
2. List any special courses you have taken that would help make you a valuable employee.

Skills, Activities, Awards, Interests
1. List skills, such as typing, computer programming, or fluency in a foreign language, that relate to the position for which you are applying.
2. List school or community activities in which you have participated, such as music lessons or volunteer work.
3. List awards or certificates of merit you have earned.
4. Include your hobbies and special interests.

References
1. Give the names and addresses of people who have agreed to give you a recommendation, or state that references are available on request.
2. As references, list one previous employer, one teacher or school administrator, and one family friend. Be sure you obtain permission in advance from the people you list as references.

Writing a Résumé

Sample of a Résumé

Use the following sample as a model when you prepare your own résumé.

```
                      David Gilbert
                 1782 La Habra Boulevard
               Los Angeles, California  91283
                    Telephone:  426-7135



WORK EXPERIENCE

1985 - present          Apogee Computer Center, Inc.,
                        South Turnbull Mall, Los Angeles,
                        California  91296
                        Position:  Clerk
                        Responsibilities:  Wait on customers,
                        stock shelves, clean

1983 - 1985             Burger Chef, Olinda Road at Brea,
                        Rio Oro, California  91148
                        Position:  Cook
                        Responsibilities:  Prepared food
                        for serving


EDUCATION

1984 - present          Alvarado High School, 3777 Las
                        Altas Way, Los Angeles,
                        California  91283
                        Special courses:  introduction to
                        computers, BASIC programming

1982 - 1984             Box Canyon Middle School, Route
                        71, Sierra, California  90368


SPECIAL SKILLS          Program in BASIC and Pascal,
                        type 60 words per minute,
                        speak Spanish and German


ACTIVITIES              Computer Club president, Math
                        Club treasurer, varsity tennis player


AWARDS                  National Honor Society, Kasner
                        Achievement Award for 10th grade
                        math


SPECIAL INTERESTS       Computer science and programming


REFERENCES              Available on request
```

627

WRITING LETTERS ABOUT EMPLOYMENT

When you apply for a job, you may write a letter to your potential employer. First and foremost, your letter must be specific. State whether you are looking for part-time employment (a few hours a week), temporary employment (a vacation or summer job), or full-time employment (35 or more hours a week for the whole year). As a student you are likely to be looking for part-time or temporary work.

In addition, your job application should make a strong, favorable impression. Remember that the purpose of an employment letter is to get you an interview. If there are many applicants for a particular job, some of them will be rejected on the basis of the letter. Your letter should be grammatically correct, informative, and neat. Make sure it contains the following information.

Position Sought. The first paragraph should state the job you are seeking and should tell where you learned about the opening.

Education. Include both your age and your grade in school. Emphasize courses you have taken that apply directly to the job you are seeking.

Experience. As a student you may not have much work experience that relates to the position open. However, any positions of responsibility you have held, whether paid or unpaid, are valuable work experiences. State the kinds of work you have done and emphasize your belief that you can meet the requirements of the job if it is offered to you.

References. Include at least two references, with either an address or a telephone number for each. You will need to obtain permission in advance from the people you name as references. These people should be able to testify to your character and abilities. A teacher, a member of the clergy, a community leader, and a former employer are all good choices.

Letters About Employment

Request for Interview. The last paragraph should ask for an interview. Indicate where and when you can be reached to make an appointment.

Sample of an Employment Letter

The following sample illustrates an employment letter. Note that the letter is typed neatly and that it includes all the important information listed.

```
                                      4173 Hartford Road
                                      Hull, Tennessee  37300
                                      May 4, 1986

Ms. Florence Campbell
Jeans for Teens
772 Route 45
Hull, Tennessee  37300

Dear Ms. Campbell:

     I would like to apply for the summer position advertised
in this morning's Courier-Advocate.  I am a high school student
with a strong interest in retail sales.  My electives at Nimitz
High School have included courses in retailing and business
procedures.

     A 17-year-old junior, I have worked part-time for the
past two years as a stock clerk at Renfrew's Pharmacy.  I
have also done baby-sitting for Mr. and Mrs. Fred Schofield,
390 Winona Road, West Hull, for several years.

     Mr. Renfrew and Mrs. Schofield have agreed to supply
references.  The business number of Renfrew's Pharmacy is
337-8902.  Mrs. Schofield can be reached at 337-2216.

     I believe that my background and interests qualify me
for the position you have advertised.  I would be pleased
to come in for a personal interview at your convenience.
My home telephone number is 337-3884.  I am usually home
after 3:00 p.m. on weekdays.

                                      Sincerely yours,

                                      Janice Connelly

                                      Janice Connelly
```

Letters to Schools and Colleges

WRITING LETTERS TO SCHOOLS AND COLLEGES

If you plan to continue your education after high school, there are two kinds of letters you will probably write. The first kind is a request for information from a professional school or college. This should be a short letter, usually asking for a catalog. If you want specific material—such as information on costs or on particular courses—be sure to ask for it. The following letter is a brief, general request for information.

```
                                    255 Chestnut Street
                                    Sedgwick, New York  14600
                                    October 22, 1986

Admissions Office
Bucknell University
Lewisburg, Pennsylvania  17837

Dear Sir or Madam:

        Please send me your catalog and an application for
admission to Bucknell University.  I am a junior at
Sedgwick High School.  My college major will be business
administration.

                                    Very truly yours,

                                    Bernard Schwartz
                                    Bernard Schwartz
```

Letters to Schools and Colleges

The second kind of letter you will write is one requesting an interview. Your letter should express your interest in the college and should suggest a convenient time for your visit to the campus or your meeting with the interviewer. Like the request for information, your letter should be as brief and specific as possible. From the response to your first letter, you may know the name of the director of admissions. If not, you can obtain it from a book such as *Barron's Profiles of American Colleges*. The following letter is one requesting an interview.

```
                                        76 Harrison Avenue
                                        Tarkington, Indiana  46300
                                        March 4, 1986

Ms. June A. Yoder
Director of Admissions
Goshen College
Goshen, Indiana  46526

Dear Ms. Yoder:

     Having gone over the materials that you sent me, I
have decided that I would like to find out more about
Goshen College.  If it can be arranged, I would like to
visit your campus and talk with someone from the admissions
office.

     I will be on vacation during the week of April 7-11.
Since your college classes will be in session that week, I
believe it would be an ideal time to visit.  Would this be
convenient for you?  I can come on any day and at any time
you suggest.

     Please let me know if this interview can be arranged.
I look forward to seeing Goshen College and learning more
about it.

                              Sincerely,

                              Marie Aiello

                              Marie Aiello
```

INTERVIEWING FOR A JOB

When you apply for a job, the employer may ask you to come in for an interview. The more preparation you do prior to your interview, the more confident you will be during your appointment. The way you present yourself during the interview may also determine whether or not you get the job.

An excellent way to prepare for an interview is to learn as much as possible about the employer's business. The more you know about what the employer does and how the business operates, the better you will be able to discuss the job for which you are interviewing. The following suggestions will help you increase your chances of success in an interview.

Hints on Interviewing for a Job

1. Before your interview, try to get printed information about the company or consult with people you know who are employed there.
2. Prepare a list of questions about the job that you would like to ask the person who interviews you.
3. Be on time for the interview.
4. Present a neat, clean appearance.
5. Be polite to the interviewer.
6. Look at the interviewer when you speak.
7. Speak clearly and distinctly.
8. Answer all questions carefully and honestly.
9. Ask questions about the job that show your interest in the work and in the place of employment.
10. Thank the interviewer when the interview is over.
11. Follow up the interview with a letter thanking the interviewer and expressing your interest in the position. Include in your letter reasons why you think you are a good candidate for the job.

Index
Tab Index

Index

A

a, an, 202
Abbreviations
  capitalization of, 232
  in formal writing, 251, 613
  period after, 251–252
Abstract nouns, 4
Accent marks in dictionary, 342
accept, except, 203
Action verbs, 8–9
Active voice, 133–134, 388
adapt, adopt, 203
Addresses, commas with, 258
Adjective clause, 82–85
  commas with, 85, 262–263
  defined, 83
  as misplaced modifier, 86
  relative pronoun in, 83, 153–154
  in sentence combining, 93, 378
Adjective phrase, 53–54
Adjectives, 14–16, 23
  articles *(a, an, the),* 15
  comma with, 253–254
  comparison of, 187–190
  compound, 14, 293–294
  defined, 14
  nouns used as, 15
  position of, 14–15
  predicate, 41
  pronouns used as, 15–16
  proper, 14
adopt, adapt, 203
Adverb clause, 79–80
  commas with, 80, 257
  defined, 79
  in sentence combining, 93, 378
  subordinating conjunction in, 80, 378
Adverb phrase, 54–55
  commas with, 55, 257
Adverbs, 16–17, 24
  comparison of, 187–190
  defined, 16
  distinguished from adjectives, 195
  distinguished from prepositions, 20
  nouns used as, 17

advice, advise, 203
affect, effect, 203
Agreement of pronoun and antecedent, 158–161
Agreement of subject and verb, 167–181
  a number of, the number of, 178
  collective-noun subject, 177
  compound subject, 171–172
  doesn't and *don't,* 180
  I as subject, 167
  indefinite pronoun subject, 174–175
  interrupting words and, 169–170
  inverted order, 176
  linking verbs, 180–181
  problems with, 174–181
  singular nouns plural in form, 178–179
  title as subject, 181
  verb phrase, 168
  words expressing amount, 177–178
  you as subject, 167
ain't, 203
all ready, already, 203
all together, altogether, 203
allusion, illusion, 204
Almanac, 357–358
a lot, 204
among, between, 204
amount, number, 204
an, a, 202
Analogies, 582–583
Antecedent
  agreement of pronoun with, 158–161
  defined, 5, 158
  indefinite pronoun as, 160–161
Antonyms, 317, 345, 579–580
anymore, 204
anywhere, 204
Apostrophe, 271–275
  in contractions, 273
  to form plurals, 275, 327
  to form possessive nouns, 271–272
  with indefinite pronouns, 273
  misuse of, with personal pronouns, 273
  to show joint or separate ownership, 274

635

Index

Application, letter of
  for employment, 628–629
  to a school, 571, 630–631
Appositive, 56–57
  commas with, 57, 261–262
  dash with, 296
  defined, 56
  pronoun as, 143–144, 148–149
Appositive phrase, 57
  commas with, 57, 261–262
  dashes with, 296
  defined, 57
  in sentence combining, 72, 375
Articles *(a, an, the)*, 15, 202
as, like, 214
as far as, 205
at, 205
Atlas, 357
Auxiliary verbs. *See* Helping verbs.
a while, awhile, 205

B

bad, badly, 205
be
  conjugation, 126–127
  forms of, 10, 168
because, 206
being as, being that, 207
beside, besides, 206
between, among, 204
Bias, 497, 500
Bibliography for report, 558–559
Biographical reference works, 357, 361
Body
  of a business letter, 564–565, 566
  of an essay, 448–449, 453–454, 472–474, 485–487, 491–494, 501–504
  of a paragraph, 410, 413, 416, 420, 430, 439–440
  of a research paper, 548–554
both, each, 207
Brackets, 297
Brainstorming, 435–436, 460–461
bring, take, 207

C

Call number, 350
can, may, 207

can't help but, 208
capital, capitol, 208
Capitalization, 230–247
  abbreviations, 232
  awards, 236
  brand names, 236
  buildings, 236
  closing of letter, 242
  course names, 236
  direct quotations, 287
  documents, 235
  events or time periods, 235
  first word in line of poetry, 231
  first word in sentence, 231
  geographical names, 232
  government bodies, 234
  historical events, 235
  holidays, 235
  I and *O*, 231–232
  languages, 235
  letters, 242
  monuments and memorials, 236
  name of groups or businesses, 234
  name of persons or animals, 232
  nationalities, 235
  periods of time, 235
  political parties, 234
  proper adjectives, 14, 238–239
  proper nouns, 232–236
  races, 235
  religious references, 235
  salutation of a letter, 242
  seasons, 235
  special events, 235
  stars, planets, and constellations, 233
  titles of people, 232, 240–241
  titles of written works and other works of art, 241
  titles showing family relationships, 241
  vehicles, 236
Card catalog, 352–355
Case
  defined, 141
  nominative, 141, 142–144
  objective, 141, 145–148
  possessive, 141, 150–151
Choosing a subject, 434–435, 458, 532–533, 618
Chronological order, 416–417, 426, 463, 472, 489, 498, 506, 542
Citing sources, 554–559
Clause, 76–97
  adjective, 82–85, 378
  adverb, 79–80, 378, 381

Index

defined, 77
elliptical, 82, 156
essential (restrictive), 85
faulty subordination, 382–384
independent (main), 77–78
nonessential (nonrestrictive), 85, 262–263
noun, 87
semicolon with, 277–278
in sentence combining, 93–94, 378
subordinate (dependent), 78–90
Cliché, 369
Clincher sentence, 476
Closing of letter
  capitalization, 242
  punctuation, 258
coarse, course, 208
Coherence
  of essay, 472–474, 478
  of paragraph, 441–442
Collective noun, 4
  agreement with verb, 177
Colon, 280–281
Combining sentences. *See* Sentence combining.
Comma, 252–263
  with addresses, 258
  with adjective clauses, 85, 262–263
  with adjectives before noun, 253–254
  with adverb clauses, 80, 257
  with adverb phrases, 55, 257
  with appositives, 57, 261–262
  with closing of letter, 258, 566
  in compound sentences, 93, 255–256
  with dates, 258
  with degrees, 261–262
  with direct address, 260
  with direct quotations, 288
  with essential (restrictive) elements, 57, 60, 85, 263
  with interjections, 21
  after introductory elements, 55, 60, 80, 256–257
  with nonessential (nonrestrictive) elements, 57, 60, 85, 262–263
  with parenthetical expressions, 260–261
  with participial phrases, 60, 257, 262–263
  with prepositional phrases, 55, 257
  with quotation marks, 288
  with salutation of letter, 258
  in a series, 253
  with titles, 261–262
Common noun, 3

Comparative degree, 187–190
Comparison
  of adjectives, 187–190
  of adverbs, 187–190
  degrees of, 187–190
  double, 191
  with *else* and *other,* 191
  in figurative language, 368, 420
  illogical, 193
  irregular, 189–190
  regular, 188–189
Complaint letter, 569
Complement, 36–41
  direct object, 36–37
  indirect object, 38
  objective complement, 39
  predicate adjective, 40
  predicate nominative, 41, 180–181
  in sentence combining, 377
  subject, 40–41
Complete predicate, 30
Complete subject, 30
Complex sentence
  defined, 89–90
  faulty subordination, 382–384
  in sentence combining, 93–94, 378
  subordination, 93–94, 378
Compositions. *See* Essay; Paragraph; Research paper.
Compound adjective, 14
  hyphen with, 293–294
Compound-complex sentence, 90
Compound noun, 4
  hyphen and, 4, 293–294
  plural of, 271
Compound preposition, 19
Compound sentence
  comma in, 255–256
  coordination, 376–377
  defined, 89
  faulty coordination, 382–384
  semicolon in, 276–278
  in sentence combining, 93–94, 376–377
Compound subject, 33
  agreement with verb, 171–172
  pronouns in, 142
  in sentence combining, 35, 376
Compound verb, 34
  in sentence combining, 35, 376
Computer terms, 625
Concise sentences, 370–373, 391
Concluding sentence of a paragraph, 410, 414–415, 440–441
  in descriptive paragraph, 420

637

Index

in expository paragraph, 410, 414–415, 440–441
in narrative paragraph, 416
in persuasive paragraph, 430, 432
Conclusion
  of critical essay, 501–504
  of descriptive essay, 485–487
  of expository essay, 448–449, 455–456, 475–476
  of persuasive essay, 491–494
  of report, 548–553
Concrete noun, 4
Condensing, 521–526
Conjugation of verb, 123–127
Conjunctions, 20–21, 24
  coordinating, 20–21
  correlative, 20–21
  defined, 20
  subordinating, 80, 378
Connectives. *See* Transitional words.
Connotation, 364–365
Context clues, 305–306, 364
continual, continuous, 208
Contractions
  agreement with subject, 180
  apostrophe with, 274
  distinguished from possessive pronouns, 273
Coordinating conjunctions, 20–21
Coordination, 89, 376–377
  faulty, 382–385
Correlative conjunctions, 20–21
course, coarse, 208
Critical essay, 500–506, 511
Critical thinking. *See* Thinking skills.

D

Dangling modifier, 67–68
Dash, 296–297
Date, comma with, 258
Declarative sentence, 249
Definition in dictionary, 337, 339–345
Definition paragraph, 467
Degrees of comparison, 187–190
Demonstrative pronouns, 7, 15
Dependent clause. *See* Subordinate clause.
Derived words in dictionary, 343–344
Descriptive essay, 484–489, 511
Descriptive paragraph, 419–422, 447
Development, methods of, 437, 460
  analogy, 424

analysis, 424
cause and effect, 424
classification, 424
comparison and contrast, 424, 436, 460
definition, 423, 436
descriptive details, 420, 436, 485–489
facts and examples, 423, 429–431, 436, 491–494
incident, 423, 491
reasons, 429–430, 436, 491–494
steps in a process, 423
Developmental order, 426–427, 463–466, 472, 506, 543
Dewey decimal system, 348–350
Diagram, sentence
  adjective and adverb, 44–45
  adjective clause, 91–92
  adjective phrase, 69
  adverb clause, 91
  adverb phrase, 69
  appositive and appositive phrase, 70
  complement, 45–47
  complex sentence, 91
  compound complement, 45–47
  compound-complex sentence, 92
  compound object, 45
  compound sentence, 91
  compound subject, 43
  compound verb, 43
  conjunction, 43, 45, 91
  direct and indirect object, 45–46
  gerund phrase, 70–71
  infinitive phrase, 71
  inverted order, 44
  noun clause, 92
  objective complement, 46
  participial phrase, 70
  prepositional phrase, 69
  simple sentence, 43–47
  subject and verb, 43
  subject complement, 46–47
  understood subject, 44
  verb phrase, 43
Dialogue, 291–292
Dictionary, 336–345
  abridged, 336–337
  accent marks, 342
  alternate spellings, 340
  arrangement, 338
  biographical entries, 338
  definitions, 337, 345
  derived words, 343–344
  diacritical marks, 342
  etymologies, 344

Index

geographical entries, 338
inflected forms, 343–344
kinds, 336–337, 358, 360
multiple meanings, 345
part of speech labels, 343
preferred and variant spellings, 340
pronunciation guide, 341–342
schwa, 342
specialized, 358, 360
special sections, 338
spelling reference, 340, 343–344
stress, 342
subject labels, 345
syllable division, 341
synonyms and antonyms, 345
unabridged, 336
usage labels, 345
word origins, 344
different from, 208
Direct address, 260
Direct object, 36–37
   pronoun as, 146
Direct quotation. *See* Quotation, direct.
discover, invent, 209
Discussion group, 622–623
Dividing words, 295, 613
do, forms, of, 168
doesn't, don't, 108, 209
done, 209
Double comparison, 191
Double negative, 193–194

E

each, both, 207
Editing, 443, 479, 527, 561
   checklist, 444, 480, 510, 527, 562
   proofreading symbols, 614
   standard manuscript form, 611–613
effect, affect, 203
Ellipsis, 292
Elliptical clause, 82, 156
else in comparisons, 191–192
emigrate, immigrate, 209
Emphasis in essay, 478
Emphatic form of verb, 125–126
Employment letter, 628–629
Empty expressions, 371
Encyclopedia, 356, 360
End mark. *See* Exclamation point; Period; Question mark.

Endnotes in research paper, 557–558, 615–617
Entry word, 340
Envelope, 565
Essay, 448–511
   audience, 462
   body, 448–449, 453–454, 472–474, 485–487, 491–494, 501–504
   brainstorming, 460
   choosing a subject, 457–458
   clincher sentence, 476
   coherence, 472–473, 478
   conclusion, 448–449, 455–456, 475–476, 485–487, 491–494, 501–504
   connecting paragraphs, 472–474
   critical essay, 500–506, 511
   defined, 448
   descriptive essay, 484–489, 511
   development, methods of, 460, 485–489, 491–494
   editing, 479–480, 510, 527
   emphasis in, 478
   expository essay, 448–483
   grouping ideas, 462–463
   introduction, 449–450, 469–470, 485, 491, 502
   limiting a subject, 458–459
   literary essay, 500–506, 511
   manuscript form, 611–613
   model, 449, 453–454, 470–476, 485–487, 491–494, 502–504
   organization, methods of, 462–466, 472, 488–489, 497–498, 504–506
   outlining, 462–465
   paragraphing, 453–454, 472
   persuasive essay, 490–498, 511
   prewriting, 456–465, 483, 510
   proofreading symbols, 614
   purpose, 448, 484, 490
   revising, 477–479, 483, 510–511
   structure, 448–465, 485, 491, 501
   supporting details, 460
   supporting paragraphs, 448–449, 453–454, 472–474, 485–487, 491–494, 501–504
   thesis statement, 448–450, 468–470, 485, 491–492, 501–502
   title, 476
   tone, 449
   transitions, 472–474, 498
   unity in, 477
   writing, steps for, 456–480, 483, 510
   writing the first draft, 468–476

Index

Essential (restrictive) elements, 57, 60, 85, 263
etc., 210
Etymology, 318–320, 344
everywhere, 204
except, accept, 203
Exclamation point, 21, 250, 252, 289–290
Exclamatory sentence, 250
Expository essay, 448–483. *See also* Essay.
Expository paragraph, 423–426, 447, 467

F

farther, further, 210
Faulty sentences, 99–103, 382–388, 391
fewer, less, 211
Fiction, analyzing, 505
Figurative language, 367–368, 420
First person point of view, 418
Footnotes in research paper, 557–558, 615–617
Formal English, 201
former, latter, 211
Fraction, hyphen with, 293
Fragment, 29, 99–101
further, farther, 210

G

Gender, 158
Gerund, 62
Gerund phrase, 62–63, 73
Glossary of Usage, 200–224
good, well, 195, 211
Group discussion, 622–623

H

had, 212
have, forms of, 168
have, of, 212
hear, here, 212
Helping verbs, 11–12
  agreement with subject, 168
  list of, 12
here, 212
  beginning sentence with, 32, 176
Historical present, 128

hole, whole, 212
Hyphen, 4, 293–295

I

I, agreement of verb with, 167
illusion, allusion, 204
immigrate, emigrate, 209
Imperative mood, 135
Imperative sentence, 33, 250
imply, infer, 212
in, into, 212
Indefinite pronouns, 7
  as antecedent, 160–161
  list of, 7, 161, 174
  possessive form of, 273
  as subject, 160–161, 174–175
Independent (main) clause, 77–78, 89–90
Indicative mood, 135
Indirect object, 38
  pronoun as, 146
Indirect quotation, 285
infer, imply, 212
Infinitive, 64–65
Infinitive phrase, 65, 73
Inflected forms in dictionary, 343
Informal English, 201
Interjections, 21, 24, 250
Intensive pronoun, 6
Interrogative pronoun, 7
Interrogative sentence, 250
  subject in, 32
  subject-verb agreement in, 176
Interrupting words, agreement and, 169–170
Interview, job, 632
into, in, 212
Intransitive verb, 8–9
Introduction
  of essay, 449–450, 467–470, 485, 491, 502
  of research paper, 548–549
invent, discover, 209
Inverted order, 32
  agreement and, 176
irregardless, 212
Irregular comparison, 189–190
Irregular verbs
  defined, 112
  list of, 113, 115, 118
Italics (underlining), 282–283
its, it's, 213

640

Index

J
Job
  interview, 632
  letter of application, 628–629
  résumé, 626–627

K
kind, 213
kind of, 213
knew, new, 213

L
latter, former, 211
lay, lie, 214
learn, teach, 213
leave, let, 213
less, fewer, 211
Letter, business, 564–574
  application, 571, 628–629
  closing, 242, 258, 565–566
  of complaint, 569
  for employment, 628–629
  envelope, 565
  form, 564–566
  opinion letter, 570
  order letter, 568
  parts, 566
  of request, 567
  salutation, 242, 258, 565–566
  to a school, 571, 630–631
Library, 348–361
  arrangement, 348–355
  call numbers, 350
  card catalog, 352–355, 532
  Dewey decimal system, 348–350
  fiction and nonfiction, 348–349
  finding books, 348–355
  Library of Congress system, 352
  reference material, 356–361
lie, lay, 214
like, as, 214
Limiting a subject, 435, 459, 533, 618
Linking verbs, 9–10, 23
  agreement with subject, 180
  complement with, 40–41
  defined, 9
  list of, 10
Listening skills, 624. *See also* Thinking skills.
Literary essay, 500–506, 511
Loaded words, 496–497
loose, lose, 216

M
Main clause. *See* Independent clause.
Manuscript form, 611–613
may, can, 207
Metaphor, 368, 420
Misplaced modifier, 67–68, 86
Modified outline, 608, 609
Modifier. *See also* Adjectives; Adverbs.
  dangling, 67–68
  misplaced, 67–68, 86
Mood, 135–136

N
Narrative paragraph, 415–418, 447
Negative, double, 193–194, 209
new, knew, 213
Nominative case, 141, 142–144
Nonessential (nonrestrictive) elements, 57, 60, 85, 262–263
Nonstandard English, 202
nor, or, 217
Note card, 539, 619
Note-taking, 538–539, 608–609, 619
Noun clause, 87
  in sentence combining, 94
Nouns, 3–4, 23
  abstract, 4
  collective, 4, 177
  common, 3
  compound, 4, 271, 293–294
  concrete, 4
  defined, 3
  number of, 167–168, 178
  plural, formation of, 167, 275, 327
  possessive form of, 271–272
  proper, 3, 232–236
  singular, plural in form, 178–179
  used as adjectives, 15
  used as adverbs, 17
nowhere, 204
Number
  of noun or pronoun, 167–168
  of verb, 167–168
number, amount, 204

641

Index

Numbers
hyphen with, 293
rules for writing, 613

O
Object
  direct, 36–37, 146
  indirect, 38, 146
  of preposition, 19, 53, 147
  of verbal, 148
Objective case, 141, 145–149
Objective complement, 39–40
of, 217
of, have, 212
Onomatopoeia, 368
Opinion
  distinguishing fact from, 392–393
  letter expressing, 570
or, nor, 217
Order, 437, 463
  chronological, 416–417, 426, 463, 472, 489, 498, 506, 542
  developmental, 426–427, 463–466, 472, 506, 543
  of importance, 426–427, 429–430, 437–438, 463, 472, 497, 506, 543
  spatial, 421–422, 426, 463, 472, 488–489, 498, 543
Order letter, 568
Organizing ideas. *See also* Order.
  in an essay, 462–466, 472, 488–489, 497–498, 504–506
  in a paragraph, 416–417, 421–422, 426–427, 429–430, 437
  in a research paper, 541
  in a speech, 619–620
other, in comparisons, 191–192
ought, 217
Outlining, 462–465, 542–543, 620
  modified outline, 608, 609

P
Paragraph
  audience, 433
  body, 410, 413, 416, 420, 430, 439–440
  brainstorming, 435–436
  choosing a subject, 434–435
  coherence, 441–442
  concluding, of essay, 448–449, 455–456, 475–476, 485–487, 491–494, 501–504
  concluding sentence, 410, 414–415, 440–441
  defined, 410
  as definition, 467
  descriptive, 419–422, 447
  development, methods of. *See* Development, methods of.
  editing, 443–444
  expository, 423–426, 447
  indenting, 611–612
  introductory, of essay. *See* Essay.
  limiting a subject for, 435
  narrative, 415–418, 447
  organization, methods of. *See* Organizing ideas.
  persuasive, 429–431, 447
  prewriting, 433–437, 446
  purpose, 415, 423, 429, 433–434
  revising, 441–443, 446–447
  structure, 410–415, 448
  supporting sentences, 410–411, 413, 416–417, 420–422, 423–427, 429–432, 439–440
  topic sentence, 410–411, 416, 419–420, 423–424, 429–431, 438–439
  transitional expressions, 416–417, 421–422, 426–427, 429–430, 439–440, 498
  unity, 441
  writing, steps for, 433–444, 446
  writing the first draft, 438–440, 446
Paragraphing, 453–454, 472
Parallelism, 386–387
Paraphrasing, 524, 555
Parentheses, 297
Parenthetical citation, 557
Parenthetical expression, 260–261, 296
Participial phrase, 59–60
  comma with, 60
  dangling, 67–68
  misplaced, 67–68
  nonessential (nonrestrictive), 60, 262–263
  in sentence combining, 72, 375
Participle, 59
Parts of speech, 2–24
  adjective, 14–16, 23
  adverb, 16–17, 20, 24
  conjunction, 20–21, 24
  interjection, 21, 24
  noun, 3–4, 15, 17, 23

642

Index

preposition, 18–20, 24
pronoun, 5–7, 15, 23
verb, 8–12, 23
passed, past, 217
Passive voice, 133–135, 388
Past participle, 59, 111
Patterns, sentence, 48–49
Period
　with abbreviation, 251–252
　with declarative sentence, 249, 297
　with direct quotation, 289
　with imperative sentence, 250
Personal pronouns, 5
　list of, 5, 273
　nominative form, 142–144
　objective form, 145–148
　possessive form, 150–151, 273
Personification, 367
Persuasive essay, 490–498, 511
Persuasive paragraph, 429–431, 447
Phrase, 53–65
　adjective, 53–54
　adverb, 54–55
　appositive, 56–57
　defined, 53
　gerund, 62–63
　infinitive, 64–65
　participial, 59–60
　prepositional, 19, 53
　verb, 12
　verbal, 59–65
Plagiarism, 554
Plural, formation of, 325–328
　compound nouns, 328
　letters, 275, 327
　nouns, 167, 325–328
　numbers, 275, 327
　symbols, 275, 327
　verbs, 167–168
　words as words, 327
Poetry, analyzing, 505
Point of view, 418
Positive degree of comparison, 187
Possessive case, 141, 150–151
Possessive form
　with gerunds, 63, 151
　of nouns, 271–272, 274–275
　of pronouns, 141, 150–151, 273
precede, proceed, 217
Précis, 512–529
Predicate, 29–34
　complete, 30
　compound, 33–34
　simple, 30–33

Predicate adjective, 41
　compound, 377
Predicate nominative, 40–41, 143, 180–181
　compound, 40–41, 143, 377
　pronoun as, 143
Prefixes, 308–311
　hyphen with, 294
　list of, 310–311
　spelling with, 328
Prepositional phrase, 19–20, 53–55
　as adjective, 53–54
　as adverb, 54–55
　comma with, 55, 257
　in sentence combining, 72, 375
Prepositions, 18–19, 24
　compound, 19
　compound objects of, 19, 147, 376
　defined, 19
　distinguished from adverbs, 20
　list of, 19
　objects of, 19, 53, 147, 161
Present participle, 59, 111
Prewriting
　essay, 456–465, 483, 510
　paragraph, 433–437, 446
　research paper, 531–543, 563
　summary, 517–519, 529
principal, principle, 218
Principal parts of verbs, 111–118
　in conjugation, 124, 126
　defined, 111
　of irregular verbs, 112–118
　of regular verbs, 111–112
proceed, precede, 217
Progressive forms of verbs, 125
Pronouns, 5–7, 23
　agreement with antecedent, 158–161
　as appositive, 143, 148
　case of, 141
　defined, 5
　demonstrative, 7, 15
　as direct object, 146, 154
　in elliptical clause, 156
　gender, 158
　indefinite, 7, 160–161, 174–175, 273
　as indirect object, 146
　intensive, 6
　interrogative, 7
　nominative case, 142–144
　number of, 167
　as object of preposition, 147, 154
　as object of verbal, 148
　objective case, 145–148

643

Index

personal, 5, 142–151, 273
possessive case, 141, 150–151
as predicate nominative, 143
problems, 153–156
reflexive, 6
relative, 83–84, 153–154, 378
as subject, 142
used as adjective, 15
who, whom, whose, 153–154
Proofreading symbols, 614
Propaganda, 624
Proper adjective, 14, 238–239
Proper noun, 3–4, 232–236
Public speaking, 618–621
Punctuation marks
  apostrophe, 271–275
  brackets, 297
  colon, 280–281
  comma, 21, 55, 57, 60, 80, 85, 252–263, 288
  dash, 296–297
  ellipsis, 292
  exclamation point, 21, 250, 252, 289–290
  hyphen, 4, 293–295
  parentheses, 297
  period, 249–252, 289, 297
  question mark, 250, 252, 289–290
  quotation marks, 284–292
  semicolon, 276–278
  underlining (italics), 282–283

Q

Question. *See* Interrogative sentence.
Question mark
  with direct quotation, 289–290
  with interrogative sentence, 250, 252
Quotation, direct, 285–292
  brackets in, 297
  capital letter with, 287
  commas with, 288
  end mark with, 289–290
  of long passage, 292, 613
  within quotation, 292
  of research source, 613
Quotation, indirect, 285
Quotation marks, 284–292
  in dialogue, 291–292
  with direct quotation, 285–286
  with long passage, 292, 613
  single, 292
  with title, 284
Quotations, book of, 361

R

raise, rise, 218
Rambling sentence, 384–385
Readers' Guide to Periodical Literature, 358–359, 532
Reading comprehension test, 591–593
Redundancy, 370
Reference materials, 352–361
  almanac, 357
  atlas, 357–358
  biographical reference, 357, 361
  book of quotations, 361
  encyclopedia, 356
  handbook, 361
  index, 361
  literary references, 360–361
  Readers' Guide, 358–359, 532
  specialized dictionary, 358, 360
  specialized encyclopedia, 356, 360
  specialized references, 360–361
  thesaurus, 317, 358
  vertical file, 360
  yearbook, 357–358
Reflexive pronoun, 6
Regular comparison, 188–189
Regular verbs, 111–112
Relative pronouns, 83–84, 153–154, 378
  case, 153–154
  defined, 83
  list of, 83, 378
  uses of, 84, 153–154
Report. *See* Research paper.
Request, letter of, 567
Research paper, 530–563
  bibliography, 548, 553, 558–559
  body, 548–552
  choosing a subject, 531–533
  conclusion, 548, 552–553
  defined, 530
  editing, 561–562
  endnotes, 557–558
  footnotes, 548–552, 557–558
  gathering information, 534–539
  introduction, 548–550
  limiting a subject, 532–533
  model, 549–553
  organizing information, 541–544

Index

outlining, 542–544
paragraphing, 549–553
paraphrasing, 524, 555
parenthetical citations, 557
plagiarism, 554
prewriting, 531–544, 563
purpose, 530
revising, 560–561
sources, evaluating, 535–537
sources, using and citing, 550–551, 554–559
structure, 548–553
taking notes, 538–539
thesis statement, 541, 546–547, 548, 550
title, 548–549
transitions, 554
writing, steps for, 531–562, 563
writing the first draft, 546–559, 563
respectively, respectfully, 218
Restrictive clause. *See* Essential clause.
Résumé, 626–627
Revising, 441–443, 447, 477–479, 560–561
checklists, 443, 447, 479, 510–511, 526, 561
rise, raise, 218
Roots, 308–315
defined, 308
list of, 315
Run-on sentence, 102–103

S

Salutation
of business letter, 566
capitalization in, 242
punctuation with, 258, 281
says, 218
Schwa, 342
-self, -selves, 218
Semicolon, 276–278
Sensory detail, 420, 488
Sentence
base, 29–49
beginning, 380–381
combining. *See* Sentence combining.
complex, 89
compound, 89
compound, punctuation of, 255–256, 276–278
compound-complex, 90
concise, 370–373, 391

coordination, 89, 376–377
coordination, faulty, 382–385
declarative, 249
defined, 29
empty expressions in, 371
end marks, 249–250
errors, 99–103, 382–388, 391
exclamatory, 250
faulty, 99–103, 382–388, 391
fragment, 29, 99–101
imperative, 250
incomplete, 29
interrogative, 32, 250
inverted and natural order, 32, 176
parallelism, faulty, 386–387
predicate, 29–34
rambling, 384–385
recognizing a, 29–30, 99–103
redundancy, 370
run-on, 102–103
simple, 89
subject, 29–34. *See* Subject of sentence.
subordination, 79–90, 378
subordination, faulty, 382–385
variety, 374–381, 391
wordy, 372–373
Sentence combining, 35, 72–73, 93–94, 374–378
with adjective clause, 93–94, 378
with adverb clause, 93, 378
with appositive phrase, 72, 375
with compound complement, 377
with compound object of preposition, 376
into compound sentence, 93, 376
with compound subject, 35, 376
with compound verb, 35, 376
with gerund phrase, 73
with infinitive phrase, 73
with noun clause, 94
with participial phrase, 72, 375
with prepositional phrase, 72, 375
Sentence diagram. *See* Diagram, sentence.
Sentence patterns, 48–49
set, sit, 219
shall, will, 218
Shift in tense, 131–132
Simile, 368, 420
Simple predicate, 30
Simple sentence, 89
Simple subject, 30
sit, set, 219
Slang, 202
Slogan as propaganda, 624

645

Index

so, 219
some, somewhat, 219
somewhere, 204
sort, kind, type, 213
sort of, 213
Sources
   citing, 548–552, 557–559
   evaluating, 535–537
   using, 550–551, 554–555
Spatial order, 421–422, 426, 463, 472, 488–489, 498, 543
Speaking skills, 618–623
Specific words, 25, 365
Spelling, 324–331
   commonly misspelled words, 331
   ei, ie, 324–325
   plurals, 325–328
   preferred and variant, 340
   prefixes, 328
   suffixes, 329–330
Standard English, 200–201
Standardized tests, 578–606
Standard written English, tests of, 594–602
Stress marks, 342
Study skills, 610
Subject and verb agreement. *See* Agreement of subject and verb.
Subject complement, 40–41
Subject of composition
   choosing, 434–435, 458, 532–533, 618
   limiting, 435, 459, 533, 618
Subject of sentence, 29–34
   complete, 30
   compound, 33–35, 142, 171–172, 376
   defined, 30
   indefinite pronoun as, 174–175
   in inverted order, 32, 176
   position of, 32–33
   pronoun as, 142, 174–175
   simple, 30
   understood, 33
Subjunctive mood, 136
Subordinate (dependent) clause, 78–90
   as adjective, 82–85
   as adverb, 79–80
   commas with, 80, 85, 257, 262–263
   in complex sentence, 89–90
   defined, 78
   as noun, 87
   relative pronoun in, 83–84, 153–154
   in sentence combining, 93–94, 378
Subordinating conjunction, 80, 378
Subordination, 78–90, 93–94, 378
   faulty, 382–385

Suffixes, 308–309, 312–314
   list of, 313–314
   spelling with, 328–330
Summary, 512–529, 538–539, 608–609
   editing, 527
   features, 512–514
   model, 513–514
   prewriting, 517–519, 529
   revising, 526
   steps for writing, 517–527, 529
   writing, 521–524, 529
Superlative degree, 187
Supporting paragraphs
   in critical essay, 501–504
   in descriptive essay, 485–487
   in expository essay, 448–449, 453–454, 472–474
   in persuasive essay, 491–494
   in research paper, 548–554
Supporting sentences, 410–411, 413, 439–440
   in descriptive paragraph, 420–422
   in expository paragraph, 410–411, 413, 423–427
   in narrative paragraph, 416–417
   in persuasive paragraph, 429–432
Syllables, 295, 341
Symbols, proofreading, 614
Synonyms, 317, 345, 579–580

T

take, bring, 207
Taking notes, 538–539, 608–609, 619
teach, learn, 213
Tense, 123–132
   consistency of, 131–132
   future, 124, 129
   future perfect, 125, 130
   past, 124, 129
   past perfect, 125, 130
   present, 124, 128
   present perfect, 124, 129
   shift in, 131–132
Tests, standardized, 578–606
   analogies, 582–586
   essay, 602–604
   reading comprehension, 591–594
   sentence completion, 586–590
   of standard written English, 594–602
   strategies for taking, 578, 591, 603, 610
   studying for, 610

Index

nonessential (nonrestrictive), 60, 262–263
  in sentence combining, 72–73, 375
Verbals, 59–65
  gerund, 62
  infinitive, 65
  participle, 59
Verb phrase, 11–12
  agreement with subject, 168
  defined, 12
Verbs
  action, 8–9
  active voice, 133–134
  agreement with subject. *See* Agreement of subject and verb.
  be, conjugation of, 126–127
  be, forms of, 10, 168
  compound, 34–35, 376
  conjugation of, 123–127
  defined, 30
  do, forms of, 168
  emphatic forms of, 125–126
  have, forms of, 168
  helping, 11–12
  indicative mood, 135
  intransitive, 8–9
  irregular, 112–118
  linking, 9–10, 180
  number, 167–168
  passive voice, 133–135, 388
  principal parts, 111–118
  progressive forms of, 125
  regular, 111–112
  subjunctive mood, 136
  tense, 123–132
  tense, shift in, 131–132
  transitive, 8–9
  voice, 133–135, 388
Vertical file, 360
Vocabulary, 304–322
  analogies, 582–583
  antonyms, 317, 345, 579–580
  context clues, 305–306, 586
  etymologies, 318–320, 344
  list of, 322
  prefixes, roots, suffixes, 308–315
  synonyms, 317, 345, 579–580
  word meaning, 304–317, 345
Vocabulary tests, 579–590
  analogies, 582–586
  antonyms and synonyms, 579–582
  sentence completion, 586–590
Voice, active and passive, 133–135, 388

W

way, ways, 223
weak, week, 223
well, good, 211
what, that, 223
when, where, 223
where, that, 224
which, that, who, 221
who, whom, 224
who, whom, whose, 153–154
  in clauses, 153–154
  in questions, 153
whole, hole, 212
whose, who's, 224
will, shall, 218
Word choice, 364–369, 391
  connotation and denotation, 364–365
  inflated language, 366
  loaded words, 496–497
  sensory words, 420, 488
  specific words, 25, 365
Word division, 295, 613
Word origin, 318–320, 344
Wordiness, 372–373
Words with multiple meanings, 345
Writing, steps for
  essay, 456–480, 483, 510
  paragraph, 433–444, 446
  research paper, 531–562, 563
  summary, 517–527, 529
Writing ability, tests of, 594–603
Writing a first draft
  essay, 468–476, 483, 510
  paragraph, 438–441, 446
  research paper, 546–559, 563
  summary, 521–524

Y

you
  agreement of verb with, 167
  understood, 33
your, you're, 224

Index

synonyms and antonyms, 579–582
vocabulary, 579–590
of writing ability, 594–604
Test taking, 610–611
than, then, 219
that, 222
that, what, 223
that, where, 224
that, which, who, 221
that there, 222
their, there, they're, 222
theirs, there's, 222
them, those, 222
then, than, 219
the number of, 178
there, 222
there's, theirs, 222
Thesaurus, 317, 358
Thesis statement
of essay, 448–450, 468–470, 485, 491–492, 501–502
of research paper, 541, 546–547
of speech, 619–620
Thinking skills, 392–409
ad hominem fallacy, 400
analyzing fiction and poetry, 505
begging the question, 406–407, 428
bias, 497, 500
cause-effect fallacy, 403–404
circular reasoning, 406–407, 428
classifying and condensing, 525–526
critical analysis, 500–506
deduction, 397–398
distinguishing between fact and opinion, 392–393
either-or fallacy, 401
empty rhetoric, 398–399
evaluating sources, 535–538
false analogy, 405, 428
hasty generalizations, 395–396
induction, 397
inflated language, 366
loaded words, 496–497
non sequiturs, 402–403, 428
platitudes, 398–399
propaganda, 624
summarizing, 512–529
unproved assumptions, 406–407
Third person point of view, 418
this, that, these, those, 222
this here, 222
those, 222
threw, through, 222
Time order. *See* Chronological order.
Title
agreement with verb, 181
capitalizing a, 240–241
commas with, 261–262
of essay, 476
position of, in manuscript, 611–612
quotation marks with, 284
of research paper, 548–549
underlining (italics), 283
to, omission of, in infinitive, 65
to, too, two, 222
Tone, 449
Tools of persuasion, 431, 624
Topic. *See* Subject of composition.
Topic sentence, 410–411, 438–439
of descriptive paragraph, 419–420
of expository paragraph, 410–411, 423–424
of narrative paragraph, 416
of persuasive paragraph, 429, 431
steps for writing, 438–439
Transitional words
list of, 277, 416, 422, 426, 472, 498
within a paragraph, 416–417, 421–422, 426–427, 429–430, 439–440, 498
between paragraphs, 472–474, 498
punctuation with, 277
within a sentence, 277
Transitive verb, 8–9
try to, 223
two, 222
type, kind, sort, 213

U

Underlining, 282–283
Understood subject, 33
unique, 223
Unity
of essay, 477
of paragraph, 441
Usage, Glossary of, 200–224
Usage label in dictionary entry, 345

V

Variety in sentences, 374–381, 391
Verbal phrase, 59–65
as dangling modifier, 67–68
as misplaced modifier, 67–68

647

Tab Index

Grammar

Chapter 1 The Parts of Speech

1a	noun 3	1f	adjective 14
1b	pronoun 5	1g	adverb 16
1c	action verb 8	1h	preposition 19
1d	linking verb 9	1i	conjunction 20
1e	verb phrase 12	1j	interjection 21

Chapter 2 The Sentence Base

2a	sentence defined 29		
2b	sentence parts 30	2g	direct object 37
2c	simple subject 30	2h	indirect object 38
2d	simple predicate 30	2i	objective complement 39
2e	compound subject 33	2j	predicate nominative 40
2f	compound verb 34	2k	predicate adjective 41

Chapter 3 Phrases

3a	phrase defined 53	3f	participial phrase 60
3b	adjective phrase 53	3g	gerund 62
3c	adverb phrase 54	3h	gerund phrase 62
3d	appositive defined 56	3i	infinitive 65
3e	participle 59	3j	infinitive phrase 65

Chapter 4 Clauses

4a	clause defined 77	4f	noun clause 87
4b	independent clause 77	4g	simple sentence 89
4c	subordinate clause 78	4h	compound sentence 89
4d	adverb clause 79	4i	complex sentence 89
4e	adjective clause 83	4j	compound-complex sentence 90

Chapter 5 Sound Sentences

5a	sentence fragment 99	5b	run-on sentence 102

649

Tab Index

Usage

Chapter 6 Using Verbs

6a	principal parts 111	6e	active voice 133
6b	regular verb 111	6f	passive voice 133
6c	irregular verb 112	6g	subjunctive mood 136
6d	avoid shifting tenses 131		

Chapter 7 Using Pronouns

7a	case 141	7e	*who* and *whom* 153
7b	nominative case 142	7f	elliptical clauses 156
7c	objective case 145	7g–i	pronoun and antecedent
7d	possessive case 151		agreement 158–159

Chapter 8 Subject and Verb Agreement

8a	agreement in number 167	8j	collective noun subject 177
8b–c	singular and plural subjects 168	8k	words expressing an amount 178
8d	helping verb 168	8l	*a number of, the number of* 178
8e	interrupting words 169	8m	singular nouns plural in form 178
8f–g	compound subjects 171	8n	contractions 180
8h	indefinite pronoun subject 174	8o	subjects with linking verbs 180
8i	inverted sentence 176	8p	titles as subjects 181

Chapter 9 Using Adjectives and Adverbs

9a	comparison 187	9f	*other* and *else* 191
9b–d	forming comparative and superlative degrees 188–189	9g	logical comparisons 193
		9h	double negative 194
9e	double comparison 191		

Mechanics

Chapter 10 Capital Letters

10a	first word in a sentence 231	10d	proper adjectives 239
10b	*I* and *O* 231	10e	titles 240
10c	proper nouns 232	10f	letters 242

650

Tab Index

Chapter 11 End Marks and Commas

11a–d	end punctuation 249–250		11k	commas in letters 258
11e	periods after abbreviations 251		11l	commas with direct address 260
11f–g	commas in series 253–254		11m	commas with parenthetical expressions 260
11h	commas in compound sentences 255		11n	commas with appositives 261
11i	commas after introductory elements 256		11o	commas with nonessential elements 262
11j	commas with dates and addresses 258			

Chapter 12 Other Punctuation

12a–b	apostrophes to show possession 271–272		12q	hyphens with numbers and fractions 293
12c	apostrophes in contractions 274		12r	hyphens with compound nouns and adjectives 294
12d	apostrophes with joint or separate ownership 274		12s	hyphens with prefixes 294
12e	apostrophes to form plurals 275		12t	hyphens to divide words 295
12f–h	semicolons in compound sentences 277–278		12u	dashes to set off changes in thought 296
12i	semicolons in series 280		12v	dashes with appositives 296
12j–k	underlining 282–283		12w	dashes with parenthetical expressions 296
12l	quotation marks with titles 284		12x	dashes with phrases and clauses 296
12m	quotation marks with exact words 285		12y	parentheses with additional information 297
12n	capital letters in direct quotations 287		12z	brackets in quotations 297
12o	commas with direct quotations 288			
12p	end marks with direct quotations 289			

Composition

Chapter 17 Words and Sentences

17a	word choice 365		17e	faulty sentences 382
17b	figurative language 367		17f	coordination and subordination 384
17c	concise sentences 370			
17d	sentence variety 374		17g	passive voice 388

Chapter 18 Clear Thinking

18a	facts and opinions 392		18d	hasty generalizations 396
18b	verifying facts 393		18e	platitudes and empty rhetoric 399
18c	supporting opinions 393		18f	fallacies 400

651

Tab Index

Chapter 19 Paragraphs

19a	paragraph defined 410			
19b	topic sentence 411			PREWRITING
19c	supporting sentences 413		19q	choosing a subject 434
19d	concluding sentence 414		19r	limiting a subject 435
19e	narrative paragraph defined 415		19s	types of supporting details 436
19f–g	chronological order and transitions 416			WRITING
			19t	writing a topic sentence 438
19h	point of view 418		19u	writing the body 439
19i	descriptive paragraph defined 419		19v	writing a concluding sentence 440
19j	sensory details and figurative language 420			REVISING
			19w	unity 441
19k	spatial order and transitions 422		19x	coherence 442
19l	expository paragraph defined 423		19y	revision checklist 443
19m–n	order of importance, developmental order and transitions 426			EDITING
			19z	editing checklist 444
19o	persuasive paragraph defined 429			
19p	tools of persuasion 431			

Chapter 20 Expository Essays

20a	expository essay defined 448			
20b	essay structure 448		20n	writing a thesis statement 468
20c	tone 449		20o	writing the introduction 470
20d	thesis statement 450		20p	transitions 472
20e	introduction 450		20q	achieving coherence 473
20f	supporting paragraphs 453		20r	writing the conclusion 476
20g	conclusion 455		20s	writing the title 476
	PREWRITING			REVISING
20h	choosing a subject 458		20t–w	unity, coherence, and emphasis 477–478
20i	limiting a subject 459			
20j	types of supporting details 460		20x	revision checklist 479
20k	outlining 462			EDITING
20l	methods of organization 463		20y	editing checklist 480
20m	checking outline form 465			

Chapter 21 Other Kinds of Essays

21a	descriptive essay defined 484		21g	developing an argument 497
21b	structure of a descriptive essay 485		21h	transitions showing contrast or concession 498
21c	descriptive details 488		21i	critical essay defined 501
21d	spatial order and transitions 489		21j	structure of a critical essay 501
21e	persuasive essay defined 491		21k	features of a critical essay 502
21f	structure of a persuasive essay 491		21l	analyzing fiction 505
			21m	analyzing poetry 505

Tab Index

Chapter 22 The Summary

22a	summary defined 512		REVISING	
22b	features of a summary 514	22g	revision checklist 526
	PREWRITING		EDITING	
22c	understanding vocabulary 517	22h	editing checklist 527
22d	finding main ideas 519			
	WRITING			
22e	condensing 522			
22f	paraphrasing 524			

Chapter 23 Research Papers

23a	research paper defined 530	23m	connecting ideas 554
	PREWRITING	23n	using sources 555
23b	choosing a subject 532	23o–p	citing sources 557
23c	limiting a subject 533	23q	bibliography 558
23d	gathering information 535		REVISING
23e–f	evaluating sources 536	23r	revision checklist 561
23g	note-taking and summarizing 538		EDITING
23h	organizing notes 541	23s	editing checklist 562
23i–j	outlining 543		
	WRITING		
23k	writing a thesis statement 546		
23l	structuring the research paper 548		

Chapter 24 Business Letters

24a	parts of a business letter 566	24b	types of business letters 567

653

Acknowledgments

The authors and editors have made every effort to trace the ownership of all copyrighted selections found in this book and to make full acknowledgment of their use. Grateful acknowledgment is made to the following authors, publishers, agents, and individuals for their permission to reprint copyrighted materials.

Pages 18 and 183–184. "No Relief," from "The Year without a Summer" and "Outer Space Litter," from "Littering Outer Space," from SIGNIFICA, by Irving Wallace, Amy Wallace, and David Wallechinsky, copyright © 1983, E. P. Dutton, Inc., Publishers. Reprinted by permission of Ed Victor Ltd.

Page 357. "Gifford, Frank Newton." Copyright © 1982, *Who's Who in America,* 42nd Edition, by Marquis Who's Who, Incorporated. Reprinted by permission.

Page 416. "A Long Shot," from *The Reader's Digest Treasury of American Humor,* copyright © 1972 by the Reader's Digest Association, Inc. Reprinted by permission of the Reader's Digest Press.

Page 451. "How to Name a Dog," copyright © 1948 James Thurber. Copyright © 1976 Helen W. Thurber and Rosemary J. Sauers. From *The Beast in Me and Other Animals.*

Page 454. From *Science in the World around Us,* by William C. Vergara, copyright © 1973. Reprinted by permission of Harper & Row, Publishers.

Page 475. "What It's Like to Fly into Space," by Warren R. Young, April 13, 1959. From *Great Reading from Life,* copyright © 1938. Reprinted by permission of Time, Inc.

Pages 480–481. "Only He Can Prevent Forest Fires," by Larry Doolittle, from *Psychology Today,* May 1984. Reprinted by permission of *Psychology Today.*

Pages 485–487. "Watching the Dolphins," from *Mind in the Waters,* assembled by Joan McIntyre, copyright © 1974 Project Jonah. Reprinted by permission of Charles Scribner's Sons.

Page 506. "The Pasture," from *The Poetry of Robert Frost,* edited by Edward Connery Lathem. Copyright © 1939, © 1967, © 1969 by Holt, Rinehart, and Winston. Reprinted by permission of Holt, Rinehart, and Winston, Publishers.

Page 513. From *Windows in Space,* by Ann Elwood and Linda C. Wood, copyright © 1982 by Ann Elwood and Linda C. Wood. Reprinted by permission of Walker and Company.

Pages 514–516. Excerpt from *Great Animals of the Movies,* by Edward Edelson, copyright © 1980 by Edward Edelson. Reprinted by permission of Doubleday & Company, Inc.

Page 521. "Why Tadpoles Love Fast Food," by Richard Wassersug, with permission from *Natural History,* Vol. 93, No. 4; Copyright © the American Museum of Natural History, 1984.

Pages 522–523. From *Ways to Improve Your Personality,* by Virginia Bailard and Ruth Strang. Published by McGraw-Hill Book Company, copyright © 1965. Reprinted by permission of the publisher.

Pages 524–525. "Clearing the Air," from *Fueling the Future: An Environment and Energy Primer,* by Richard T. Sheahan, copyright © 1976 by Richard T. Sheahan. Reprinted by permission of St. Martin's Press.

Page 527. "Robots at Home," from *Robotics, Past, Present, & Future,* by David C. Knight, copyright © 1983 by David C. Knight. By permission of William Morrow & Company.